CENSUS OF INDIA 1911

Census of India 1871-1951, 9 Sets In 384 Bindings (9788121258876) Rs. 700000

Census of India 1911, 23 Vols. In 41 Bindings (9788121271271) Rs. 69000

1. India - Report (9788121275071) Rs. 2475 (Vol. I, Pt. 1)
2. India - Tables (9788121275057) Rs. 2225 (Vol. I, Pt. 2)
3. Andaman and Nicobar Islands - Report & Tables (9788121275033) Rs. 900 (Vol. II, Pt. 1 & 2)
4. Assam - Report (9788121275019) Rs. 1000 (Vol. III, Pt. 1)
5. Assam - Tables (9788121274999) Rs. 1300 (Vol. III, Pt. 2)
6. Baluchistan - Report & Tables (9788121274975) Rs. 950 (Vol. IV, Pt. 1 & 2)
7. Bengal, Bihar And Orissa And Sikkim - Report (9788121274951) Rs. 3100 (Vol. V, Pt. 1)
8. Bengal - Tables (9788121274937) Rs. 2250 (Vol. V, Pt. 2)
9. Bihar And Orissa - Tables and Bengal And Sikkim - Chapter I of Administrative Volume (9788121274913) Rs. 1800 (Vol. V, Pt. 3 & 4)
10. City of Calcutta - Report and Tables and Administrative (9788121274876) Rs. 1300 (Vol. VI, Pt. 1 & 2 & 3)
11. Bombay - Report (9788121274814) Rs. 1950 (Vol. VII, Pt. 1)
12. Bombay - Imperial Tables and Administrative Report (9788121274791) Rs. 3300 (Vol. VII, Pt. 2 & 3)
13. Bombay (Town And Island) - Report And Tables (9788121274753) Rs. 1250 (Vol. VIII, Pt. 1 & 2)
14. Burma - Report (9788121274739) Rs. 2250 (Vol. IX, Pt. 1)
15. Burma - Tables (9788121274715) Rs. 1480 (Vol. IX, Pt. 2)
16. Central Provinces And Berar - Report (9788121274692) Rs. 1475 (Vol. X, Pt. 1)
17. Central Provinces And Berar - Tables (9788121274678) Rs. 1900 (Vol. X, Pt. 2)
18. Coorg - Report And Tables Madras - Report (9788121274630) Rs. 1740 (Vol. XI & Vol. XII, Pt. 1)
19. Madras - Imperial And Provincial Tables (9788121274616) Rs. 1500 (Vol. XII, Pt. 2)
20. Madras - Administrative Report and city of Madras (9788121274593) Rs. 630 (Vol. XII, Pt. 3 & 4)
21. North - West Frontier Province - Report & Tables (9788121274579) Rs. 2150 (Vol. XIII, Pt. 1 & 2)
22. Punjab - Report (9788121274555) Rs. 3000 (Vol. XIV, Pt. 1)
23. Punjab - Tables (9788121274531) Rs. 2200 (Vol. XIV, Pt. 2)
24. Punjab - Appendices To The - Imperial Tables (9788121274517) Rs. 950 (Vol. XIV, Pt. 3)
25. United Provinces of Agra And Oudh - Report (9788121274494) Rs. 2225 (Vol. XV, Pt. 1)
26. United Provinces of Agra And Oudh - Tables (9788121274470) Rs. 4000 (Vol. XV, Pt. 2)
27. United Provinces of Agra And Oudh - Provincial Tables And Appendices (9788121274456) Rs. 570 (Vol. XV, Pt. 3)
28. Baroda - Report (9788121274432) Rs. 2000 (Vol. XVI, Pt. 1)
29. Baroda State - The Imperial Tables (9788121274418) Rs. 850 (Vol. XVI, Pt. 2)
30. Central India Agency - Report And Tables (9788121274395) Rs. 1470 (Vol. XVII)
31. Cochin - Report And Imperial Tables (9788121274371) Rs. 1150 (Vol. XVIII, Pt. 1 & 2)
32. Hyderabad State - Report (9788121274357) Rs. 890 (Vol. XIX, Pt. 1)
33. Hyderabad State - Imperial And Provincial Tables (9788121274333) Rs. 1750 (Vol. XIX, Pt. 2)
34. Kashmir - Report (9788121274319) Rs. 950 (Vol. XX, Pt. 1)
35. Kashmir - Tables (9788121274296) Rs. 1170 (Vol. XX, Pt. 2)
36. Mysore - Report (9788121274272) Rs. 1200 (Vol. XXI, Pt. 1)
37. Mysore - Tables (9788121274258) Rs. 1500 (Vol. XXI, Pt. 2)
38. Rajputana And Ajmer-Merwara - Report (9788121274234) Rs. 1470 (Vol. XXII, Pt. 1)
39. Rajputana And Ajmer-Merwara - Tables (9788121274210) Rs. 1700 (Vol. XXII, Pt. 2)
40. Travancore - Report (9788121274197) Rs. 1870 (Vol. XXIII, Pt. 1)
41. Travancore - Imperial Tables (9788121274173) Rs. 870 (Vol. XXIII, Pt. 2)

Owing to the antiquity and rarity of this book, certain pages are regrettably absent, and readability is compromised due to the blurring of the original text. If you possess any insights regarding the availability of these missing sections, kindly inform us. Your assistance is crucial in ensuring the completion of this significant work for the benefit of future generations.

CENSUS OF INDIA, 1911

VOLUME - XIII

NORTH - WEST FRONTIER PROVINCE

PART I - REPORT

PART II - TABLES

C. LATIMER

GYAN

Published by

Gyan Publishing House
5, Ansari Road
Daryaganj, New Delhi-110002
Phone: 011-47034999, 9811692060
E-mail: books@gyanbooks.com

Distribution Network
gyanbooks.com
India, USA, Canada, UK, Australia

ISBN: 978-81-212-7127-1 (Set) 23 Vols. In 41 Bindings

ISBN: 978-81-212-7457-9 (PB) Vol. XIII, Pt. I, II

First Published, 1912

2nd Impression 2024

Printed at: Gyan Press, Delhi.

CENSUS OF INDIA 1911

CENSUS OF INDIA, 1911.

VOLUME XIII.

NORTH-WEST FRONTIER PROVINCE.

PART I.—REPORT.

PART II.—TABLES.

Agents for the Sale of Government Publications.

IN EUROPE.

Messrs. Constable & Co., 10, Orange Street, Leicester Square, W. C., London.

Messrs. Grindlay & Co., 54, Parliament Street, London, S. W.

Messrs. Henry S. King & Co., 65, Cornhill, London, E. C.

Messrs. Kegan Paul, Trench, Trubner & Co., 68—74, Carter Lane, London, E. C.

Mr. Bernard Quaritch, 11, Grafton Street, New Bond Street, W. London.

Messrs. P. S. King & Son, 2 & 4, Great Smith Street, Westminster, London, S. W.

Mr. T. Fisher Unwin, 1, Adelphi Terrace, London, W. C.

Messrs. W. Thacker & Co., 2, Creed Lane, London, E. C.

Mr. Otto Harrassowitz, } Leipzig.
Mr. Karl Hiersemann, }

Messrs. R. Friedlander & Sohn, Berlin, W. N. Carlstrasse, 11.

Mr. Ernest Leroux, 28. Rue Bonaparte, Paris.

Mr. Martinus Nijhoff, Hague, Holland.

Mr. B. H. Blackwell, 50 & 51, Broad Street, Oxford.

Messrs. Deighton Bell & Co., Cambridge.

Messrs. Lusac & Co., 46, Great Russell Street, London, W. C.

IN INDIA.

Messrs. Thacker, Spink & Co., Calcutta & Simla.

Messrs. Newman & Co., Calcutta.

Messrs. R. Cambray & Co., Calcutta.

Messrs. S. K. Lahiri & Co., Calcutta.

Messrs. Higganbotham & Co., Madras.

Messrs. V. Kalyanarama Iyer & Co., Madras.

Messrs. Thacker & Co., Ltd., Bombay.

Messrs. G. A. Natesan & Co., Madras.

Messrs. Combridge & Co., Madras.

Messrs. A. J. Combridge & Co., Bombay.

Messrs. D. B. Taraporewala, Sons & Co., Bombay.

Mrs. Radhabai Atmaram Sagoon, Bombay.

Superintendent, American Baptist Mission Press, Rangoon.

Rai Sahib Munshi Gulab Singh & Sons, Mufid-i-'Am Press, Lahore and Calcutta.

Mr. N. B. Mathur, Superintendent, Nazair Kanun Hind Press, Allahabad.

Mr. Sunder Pandurang, Bombay.

Messrs. Thompson & Co., Madras.

Messrs. S. Murthy & Co., Madras.

Messrs. Temple & Co., Madras.

Messrs. Gopal Narayen & Co., Bombay.

Messrs. P. R. Rama Iyar & Co., Madras.

Messrs. A. Chand & Co., Punjab.

Messrs. B. Banerjee & Co., Calcutta.

Babu S. C. Talukdar, Proprietor, Students and Company, Cooch Behar.

Messrs. Ramchandra Govind & Son, Booksellers and Publishers, Kalbadevi, Bombay.

The Calcutta School Book and useful Literature Society, 1, Wellington Square, Calcutta.

Messrs. P. Varadachary & Co., Madras.

Messrs. T. Fisher Univen, Calcutta.

Messrs. Butterworth & Co., Limited, Calcutta.

The Weldon Library, 18/5 Chowringhee Road, Calcutta.

IN CEYLON.

Messrs. A. M. and J. Ferguson.

CENSUS OF INDIA, 1911.

VOLUME XIII.

NORTH-WEST FRONTIER PROVINCE.

PART I.—REPORT.

PART II.—TABLES.

BY

C. LATIMER, I. C. S.,
Superintendent of Census Operations.

Peshawar:
PRINTED AT THE COMMERCIAL PRESS, BY D. C. ANAND & SONS, GOVT. PRINTERS, N.-W. F. PROVINCE.
1912.

CONTENTS.

PART I.—REPORT.

INTRODUCTION.

	PAGE.
Notices of previous Censuses	1
Scope of present Census compared with earlier ones	*ib.*
Outline of Census procedure	*ib.*
Cost of the Census	4
Acknowledgements	*ib.*

CHAPTER I.—DISTRIBUTION OF POPULATION.

Administrative divisions of the N.-W. F. Province	5
Natural divisions	*ib.*
Density	8
Culturable, cultivated and irrigated area	9
Rainfall and soils	*ib.*
Towns	13
Villages	18
Houses and house-room	20
Subsidiary Tables	23

CHAPTER II.—MOVEMENT OF POPULATION.

Notices regarding the condition of the Province prior to British rule ...	27
Condition of the Province at annexation	28
Movement of population 1855—1911	30
Conditions during decade 1901—1911	31
The vital statistics—their degree of accuracy	33
Growth of population since 1901 in individual districts	34
Variation in natural population since 1901	38
Future growth of population	40
Subsidiary Tables	42

CHAPTER III.—BIRTH-PLACE.

Reference to statistics	44
Types of migration	*ib.*
Extent of migration to and from N.-W. F. Province	45
Immigration to the N.-W. F. Province and its sources	*ib.*
Immigration by religion	48
Variation in immigration 1901—1911	49
Immigration from Afghanistan and tribal territory since 1881	52
Emigration	56
Subsidiary Tables	58

CHAPTER IV.—RELIGION.

Religious distribution of the population	61
The figures for Hindus	*ib.*
Distinction between Hindus and Sikhs	62
Local distribution of population by religion	64
Variations of population by religion	65

	PAGE.
SECT	71
Mohammadan sects	ib.
Hindu sects	75
Sikh sects	85
POPULAR RELIGION	86
Islam in the Province	ib.
Superstitions	88
The evil eye	89
Charms and spells	90
Lucky and unlucky days	91
Belief in evil spirits	92
Other superstitions	ib.
Hinduism in the North-West Frontier Province	93
Subsidiary Tables	95

CHAPTER V.—AGE.

Inaccuracy of the age returns	101
Variations in the age distribution since 1881	103
Age distribution of population by religion	106
Age distribution by caste	108
Mean age	110
Birth and death rates calculated from the age statistics	111
Subsidiary Tables	113

CHAPTER VI.—SEX.

Disproportion of the sexes in the North-West Frontier Province ...	119
Causes held responsible in other parts of India	120
Reticence regarding females	122
Sex proportions in the North-West Frontier Province at different Censuses	123
Sex proportions at different age periods	124
Mis-statement of age and its effect on the sex proportions at different ages	126
Omissions of females from the Census record	127
Influence of migration	ib.
Variations in the sex proportions in different natural divisions ...	128
Sex proportions and the vital statistics	130
Causes of an excess of males	132
Summary	133
Subsidiary Tables	134

CHAPTER VII.—CIVIL CONDITION.

PART I.—DESCRIPTIVE	139
Mohammadan marriage customs	ib.
Bride price	ib.
Betrothal	140
Field of choice of a wife	ib.
Marriage ceremonies	141
Marriage customs of Hindus	143
Mohammadan influences	144
Rules regarding inter-marriage	145
The age of marriage and bride price	ib.
Terms of relationship	146
Rights and obligations of certain kin	ib.
Birth customs	ib.

	Page.
Part II.—Statistical	... 151
Accuracy of the return	.. *ib.*
Universality of marriage	... *ib.*
I.—At all ages	... *ib.*
II.—Among adults	... 153
Statistics of marriage by religion	... 154
Child marriage	... 155
Marriage during adolescence	... 156
Re-marriage among both sexes	... 157
Polygamy	... 158
Variations in distribution of population by civil condition at different Censuses	... 159
Subsidiary Tables	... 161

CHAPTER VIII.—EDUCATION.

Reference to statistics	... 169
Scope of the return	... *ib.*
Extent of literacy in the Province	... *ib.*
Variations in different districts	... 170
Literacy by age	... 172
Literacy by religion	... 175
Literacy by caste	... 177
English education	... 178
Education statistics of 1911 compared with those of 1901 ...	... 179
Comparison with Censuses previous to 1901	... 184
The departmental statistics	... 185
Subsidiary Tables	... 187

CHAPTER IX.—LANGUAGE.

Reference to statistics	... 194
The accuracy of the return	... *ib.*
General distribution of population by language	... 195
Local distribution of speakers of each language	... 196
Pashto	... 197
Persian	... 199
Baluchi and Kashmiri	... *ib.*
Chitiari, Kohistani and Pashai	... 200
Punjabi and Hindko	... 201
Punjabi	... *ib.*
Lahnda	... 203
Hindostani	... 204
Gujari	... *ib.*
Naipali	... 205
English and other European languages	... *ib.*
Other Indian Vernaculars	... *ib.*
Subsidiary Tables	... 206

CHAPTER X.—INFIRMITIES.

Introductory	... 208
Accuracy of the statistics	... *ib.*
Insanity	... *ib.*
Deaf-mutism	... 209
Blindness	... 210
Leprosy	... 211

	PAGE.
Variation in prevalence of infirmities since 1881	... 211
Insanity	... 212
Deaf-mutism	... 214
Blindness	... 215
Leprosy	... 216
Subsidiary Tables	... 220

CHAPTER XI.—CASTE.

Reference to statistics	... 222
Method of caste classification	... *ib.*
Accuracy of the statistics	... 223
Caste units and community of occupation	... 224
Tribal groups	... 226
Occupational groups	... 227
Hindu and Sikh castes	... 229
(*a*) the indigenous castes	... *ib.*
(*b*) the foreign castes	... 230
System of caste Government	... *ib.*
(*a*) among Hindus	... *ib.*
(*b*) among Mohammadans	... 231
Caste Government among the occupational groups	... 232
Variations in the numbers of the various tribes and castes at different Censuses	... *ib.*
(*a*) since 1901	... 233
(*b*) since 1881	... 234
Notes regarding some menial and professional groups ...	... 236
Subsidiary Tables	... 239

CHAPTER XII —OCCUPATION.

Reference to statistics	... 243
Scheme of classification of occupations	... *ib.*
Principles followed in classification	... *ib.*
Instructions in regard to record of occupation	... 244
Accuracy of the statistics	... 245
Subsidiary occupations	... 247
Distinction between actual workers and dependants ...	... *ib.*
Influence on the statistics of the season at which the Census was taken	... 248
General distribution of population by occupation	... 249
Agriculture combined with other occupations	... 250
Occupations of females	... *ib.*
Occupation statistics of 1911 compared with those of 1901 ...	... 251
Subsidiary Tables	... 254

MAPS ACCOMPANYING THE REPORT.

Showing density of population by tahsils and in the trans frontier area	... 10
Showing variation of population by districts since 1901 ...	... 34
Showing increase of density since 1901 by districts ...	... 35
Showing variation of population since 1901 by tahsils ..	... *ib.*

PART II.—TABLES.

IMPERIAL TABLES.

No. of table.		Page.
I.—Area, Houses and Population	... ...	i
II.—Variation in population since 1881	... ...	iv
III.—Towns and villages classified by population	... ...	ix
IV.—Towns classified by population with variation since 1881	...	xi
V.—Towns arranged territorially with population by religion	...	xv
VI.—Religion	... ...	xix
VII.—Age, Sex and Civil Condition :—		
Part I.—Provincial Totals	... ...	xxiii
Part II.—District Tables ...	... ...	xxvii
VIII.—Education by Religion and Age :—		
Part I.—General Table ...	... ...	xxxiii
Part II.—District Tables ...	... ...	xxxv
IX.—Education by selected Tribes, Castes or Races	... ...	xli
X.—Language	... ...	xliii
XI.—Birth-place	... ...	xlvii
XII.—Infirmities :—		
Part I.—Distribution by Age	... ...	liii
Part II.—Distribution by Districts	... ...	liii
XII-A.—Infirmities by selected Tribes, Castes or Races	... ...	lv
XIII.—Caste, Tribe, Race or Nationality	... ...	lvii
XIV.—Civil condition by Age for selected castes	... ...	lxvii
XV.—Occupation or means of livelihood :—		
Part A.—General Table ...	... ...	lxxiii
Part B.—Subsidiary Occupations of Agriculturists	...	cvii
Part E.—Statistics of Industries	... ...	cxi
XVI.—Occupations of Europeans, Anglo-Indians and Armenians	...	cxiii
XVII.—Christians by Sect and Race ...	... ...	cxv
XVIII.—Europeans, Armenians and Anglo-Indians by race and age	...	cxix

PROVINCIAL TABLES.

I.—Area and Population of Tahsils	... .	cxxiii
II.—Population of Tahsils by religion and education	... ...	cxxvii

PART I.

CORRIGENDA.

PART I.

Page 14.	Last line, *for* 15,353 *read* 15,356					
,, 18.	Line 38,	,,	99	,,	100	
,, ,,	,, 39,	,,	549	,,	550	
,, ,,	,, 40,	,,	979	,,	980	
,, 19.	,, 55,	,,	V	,,	III	
,, 38.	Marginal statement, against Hazara,					*for* 898·7 *read* 855·7
			,,	D. I. Khan,		,, 297·4 ,, 302·4
,, 40.	Line 23, *for* Khushalgarh *read* Kalabagh.					

REPORT ON THE CENSUS

OF THE

NORTH-WEST FRONTIER PROVINCE, 1911.

INTRODUCTION.

Previous Censuses.

THE enumeration to which this report relates is the sixth which the districts included in the North-West Frontier Province have undergone. Previous enumerations, carried out respectively on the 31st December 1854 and January 1st, 1855, on the 10th January 1868, on the 17th February 1881, on the 26th February 1891, and on the 1st March 1901, were conducted under the orders of the Government of the Punjab, of which the districts we are now concerned with then formed a part. Of previous Censuses that of 1881 was the first to be carried out with the care and thoroughness which distinguish Census Operations in India to-day; and from it date the variations of population shown in Table II in Part II of this volume. Under the Proclamation of October 25th, 1901, the districts now administered by the Chief Commissioner were separated from the Punjab, and formed, with certain areas across the administrative border, into a separate charge under the name of the North-West Frontier Province.

The present Census.

The present enumeration, which took place on the night of March 10th, 1911, was accordingly the first to be carried out since the Province possessed a separate existence. In the Punjab Census Report, 1901, figures were, however, given separately throughout the tables for the Punjab and for the North-West Frontier Province.

Areas comprised within the Province, and scope of the present Census, as compared with previous ones.

The latter Province consists of (*a*) the five settled districts of Hazara, Peshawar, Kohat, Bannu and Dera Ismail Khan, and (*b*) a tract stretching, from the mountains of the Hindu Kush to Baluchistan, between Afghanistan on the west and the borders of British India on the east. The boundaries of the five settled districts as now constituted were determined in October 1901, and the only change made since that time has been in the transference of the village of Naranji from the Dera Ghazi Khan District in the Punjab to Dera Ismail Khan. The trans-border tract contains five Political Agencies, known respectively as the Malakand, Khyber, Kurram, Tochi and Wano Agencies, together with areas under the political control of the Deputy Commissioners of the five settled districts. The figures given in Tables I and II of the present volume (Part II), contain for the first time an estimate of the population of the whole area trans-border which is included in the Province; in this area, however, only the population of British posts has been enumerated on the regular Schedule. In 1901 the population of British posts across the border was similarly enumerated (the figures for the Khyber, Tochi and Wano Agencies being included, in the Punjab Census Report, 1901, in the figures for the Peshawar, Bannu and Dera Ismail Districts respectively); and the scope of the present (regular) Census has been smaller than that of 1901 in so far as the Sherani country, under the political control of the Deputy Commissioner of Dera Ismail Khan, and a portion of the Kurram Agency, which were included in the operations of that year, have been omitted on the present occasion.

Outline of Census procedure. Census divisions and Agency and the Preliminary Enumeration

The detailed instructions for the taking of a Census are lengthy, and the Provincial Census Code, based on an Imperial Code issued by the Census Commissioner, presented a formidable appearance to district officers, whose work is already sufficiently heavy, without the extra burden which a Census places upon them. The Census methods adopted in India can, however, be explained in outline in a few words. The bulk of the population being illiterate, the Census record has to be prepared by a special staff, known as Enumerators. For purposes of supervision a group of 10 or 12 Enumerators is placed under a Supervisor, groups of Supervisors again are controlled by Charge Superintendents ; the Tahsildar exercises a general superintendence over Census operations in his Tahsil, and a District Census Officer or Sub-Divisional Census Officer superintends the operations in the district or sub-division. In nearly all cases the whole Census staff is unpaid, officials being employed as far as possible. Each Enumerator is responsible for recording the necessary details for the persons living in a group of about 40 houses or other structures, known as a Block; Blocks are grouped into Circles, and Circles into Charges, under the supervision of the Supervisor and Charge Superintendent, respectively. The necessary registers having been prepared, showing Census divisions and officers, numbers are affixed to every house or other structure in which persons are likely to be found. The object of house numbering is to insure that no house is overlooked ; a house list, showing all the houses in the Circle, is prepared at the same time, and against each house in the list is shown the number affixed to it. In towns house numbering was carried out under the supervision of the Supervisor ; in villages it was done in all cases by the Patwari, though he had not necessarily been appointed as a Supervisor. The instructions laid down that house numbering should be completed by November 15th, 1910 ; within a fortnight of that time it was concluded everywhere. The Census staff having been trained in its duties, the next important step is the Preliminary Enumeration. This portion of the work, which the rules laid down to be completed in 20 days, began on February 1st in villages, and a fortnight later in towns. In villages, like house numbering, it was carried out by the Patwari ; in towns by the Enumerator. The procedure is as follows :—The Patwari or Enumerator, having copied into a list, called the Block List, a list of the houses contained in the Block to be dealt with, visited each house in turn and wrote on a form called the General Schedule particulars regarding all the persons found residing there.

The Final Enumeration, and the Provisional Totals.

The period between the close of the Preliminary Enumeration, and the Final Enumeration, or the Census, on the night of March 10th, 1911, was spent by Supervisors, Charge Superintendents and other inspecting officers in checking the entries made during the Preliminary Enumeration. On the night of March 10th from 7 to 12 p. m. each Enumerator again went round his Block, and corrected the entries in the General Schedules made at the time of the Preliminary Enumeration, by scratching out the names of persons who had died or gone away, and adding the names of new comers and newly born children. Europeans, and Eurasians (styled in the tables appended to this report Anglo-Indians) of the better class were provided with schedules in which they themselves filled up the necessary particulars for themselves and their households. The schedules were collected by the Enumerator on the morning of March 11th. On the same morning all the Enumerators of a Circle met their Supervisor, and the total number of houses, males and females in the Circle was compiled. The Circle totals were compiled into Charge totals and the Charge into District totals in the same way. The District totals were telegraphed as soon as ready to the Census Commissioner and to the Provincial Superintendent, the last District total being received on March 17th. The figures obtained at this stage are known as the Provisional totals. In rural areas in general cases the Patwaris met their Charge Superintendents at the head-quarters of the Tahsil, where the Tahsil total was prepared under the supervision of the Tahsildar. When distances were too great to permit of this, the Charge totals were despatched by sowar to Tahsil head-quarters. Tahsil totals were telegraphed to District head-quarters. In towns the preparation of the Provisional totals was an easy matter, as all the Census Officers concerned could meet the officer in charge of Census arrangements in the town on March 11th. The total number of Enumerators employed in the Province, exclusive of Agencies,* was 12,932, of Supervisors 1,095 and of Charge Superintendents 133. We were fortunate in having no big gathering to deal with. Heavy rain on the night of the Census kept most people within doors, which was matter for

* To enumerate the population of posts in Agencies there were employed 7 Charge Superintendents, 20 Supervisors, and 126 Enumerators.

congratulation, except in so far as it probably induced a certain number of Enumerators to stay indoors also.

Estimate of population in the trans-frontier area.

In the trans-frontier area, as I have noted above, no regular enumeration was attempted of the bulk of the population. An estimate was prepared, from returns maintained by the various Political Agents and Deputy Commissioners of the fighting strength of the tribes under their political control, on the assumption that there are 4 women and children to each fighting man. It was assumed that the distribution by sex in the various Agencies, etc., is the same as for the Mohammadan population in contiguous areas in British Territory. It is of course impossible to say how great a degree of accuracy has been attained. British Officers do not commonly visit those portions of the area which are not, like the Kurram and Tochi Valleys, under Government control, or traverse roads other than those which, like the Khyber Pass, the road up the Gomal Valley, or that through tribal territory which links Peshawar with Kohat, are kept open by British authority ; and from native sources we possess nothing on which to base trustworthy figures.

The tabulation of the results.
Slip copying & sorting.

The actual Census over and the Provisional Totals reported, it remained to tabulate the results. All the enumeration books were sent as soon as possible to Peshawar, where a copying and supervising staff had been collected. The slip system, introduced in 1901, was used again. Under this system the entries relating to each person were copied on to a slip two inches broad by four and a half long In order to save copying, religion was indicated by the colour of the slip; and sex and civil condition by a symbol printed on it. When the entries in the schedules had been copied, the slips were sorted, first by religion and sex, and later by civil condition, age, caste, and the various other items of information shown in the Census Tables. (For infirmities, which are found among a small proportion of the population only, special slips were copied, and these were afterwards sorted by age and sex, caste and infirmity). Each sorter entered the results of his sorting on a form called a sorter's ticket ; the totals borne on the sorter's tickets were then entered in compilation registers, on which the totals for the district were obtained.

Staff employed and time spent on slip copying and sorting. Compilation.

The copyists, who were subsequently employed as sorters, were all Patwaris and Patwari candidates, sent in to Peshawar for the purpose from all the districts of the Province, except Dera Ismail Khan, from which the absence of a considerable number of Patwaris was rendered impossible by the existence of a system of fluctuating assessments. I had arranged that 150 Patwaris and Patwari candidates should join the Tabulation Office. It was, however, some time before all joined, and, as some were always absent from sickness or other causes, the number present on any one day never exceeded 140, whom I grouped into 14 gangs of 10 men each. Each gang was under the charge of a Supervisor, assisted by a Naib. Slip copying began on March 16th, and was concluded on April 22nd, except for a portion of the English entries, which were copied by a special English knowing copyist, and not completed till later. Patwaris, as had been found on previous occasions, proved excellent copyists. For the first few days the slips copied by each only averaged a little over 300 per diem, but this was soon improved upon, and in one week, towards the close of the time spent on copying, an average as high as 778 slips per day per man was arrived at. On the conclusion of slip copying the services of the Naib Supervisors were dispensed with. The slips were arranged for sorting in 298 boxes, each containing on an average 7,500 slips. Each copyist, now become a sorter, was given two boxes of slips ; a few of the fastest workers were given a third box, and sorting began. When he had completed the sorting of the slips in a box for one table, a sorter informed his supervisor, who proceeded to check his sorting, while the sorter went on with the sorting of his second box. Sorting, except in the case of Christian slips, which had begun later, was completed for all tables by May 27th. During the period spent in sorting and copying, besides the staff already mentioned, there were also 3 Inspectors, one in charge of four, and the other two each in charge of five, supervisors and their gangs. The Inspectors were Field Kanungos deputed respectively from the Hazara, Peshawar and Kohat Districts. There were also a Record-keeper, with an assistant, an Accountant, and a Deputy Superintendent in charge of the whole office. The bulk of this staff was dispensed with on the conclusion of the work of sorting, when the Patwaris returned to their villages. The work of compilation, however, still remained. For this a staff of five compilers was entertained ; they had begun their labours on the earlier tables before the sorting for the later ones was completed. A Supervisor was placed in charge of them ; and the best of the Inspectors with a gang of five men selected from among the Supervisors, was retained to tabulate and compile the entries shown on the sorters' tickets for Table XV—Occupation. A small staff of four men which was retained to finish the sorting of Christian slips after the bulk of the sorters had left, remained to check the copying and sorting of slips for literacy which had given rise to doubts as to their accuracy in my mind, but with the exception of the five compilers and their Supervisor, the Deputy Superintendent, and the six men retained to classify the entries of occupations, the whole staff had left the office by June 6th, 1911. The classification of occupations, and the preparation of a return showing the actual entries which had been included in each of the castes and tribes shown in Table XIII (Part II of this Volume) was not, however, completed till the end of August ; and it was not until the following month that I was able to dispense with the bungalow which I had had to hire in Peshawar as a Tabulation office. The remainder of the work of compilation was completed in a set of rooms I rented outside the Edwardes Gate of Peshawar city. The work of compilation was finally completed on October 27th, 1911.

The cost of the Census.

The Census taken in 1901 of the districts of the North-West Frontier Province was carried out as part of the Census of the Punjab. No separate accounts therefore could be kept of the expenditure in the two Provinces ; and it is impossible to compare that incurred on the present occasion with that of 1901. It will suffice if I note here that the cost of our operations was approximately Rs. 33,400, of which Rs. 12,302 were spent in 1910-11, Rs. 15,045 in 1911-12, and an allotment of Rs. 6,000* was provided to meet bills remaining over to be paid in the ensuing year.

Acknowledgments.

I have to thank all the private persons who gave their services without pay in the cause of the Census. My acknowledgments are also due to all Deputy Commissioners and Sub-Divisional Officers and their staffs, but for whose co-operation I need hardly say the Census could not have been taken at all. The burden laid upon Political Agents was not a heavy one, as only the inhabitants of posts were enumerated, but in the Kurram and Tochi Valleys, where a Census of portions of the Agencies was originally intended, a good deal of labour in house numbering and the preparation of Census registers was imposed upon the local staff. My Deputy Superintendent M. Agha Jan worked throughout with the greatest zeal, and to him, and to Field Kanungos Ghulam Jilani, Autar Singh and Narain Das, is due much of the credit for the prompt way in which the laborious processes of slip copying and sorting were completed.

---

* This report was completed before the bills for printing could be adjusted.

CHAPTER I.

DISTRIBUTION OF POPULATION.

The North-West Frontier Province and its administrative divisions.

The North-West Frontier Province, "as its name denotes, is situated on the North-West Frontier of the Indian Empire. It is in form" (I quote from the first Administration Report of the Province) "an irregular strip of country lying north by east and south by west. Although the Hazara District and part of Kohistan are cis-Indus, and the trans-Indus tahsil of Isa Khel is included in the Punjab, the Province may generally be defined as the tract of country north of Baluchistan lying between the Indus and the Durand Boundary Line with Afghanistan." To the north it extends to the mountains of the Hindu Kush. Its greatest length is 408, its greatest breadth 279 miles; and its total area is about 39,000 square miles. The Province includes within its limits the five regularly administered districts of Hazara, Peshawar, Kohat, Bannu, and Dera Ismail Khan, the total area of which is 13,418 square miles; while to the north and west of these, and outside the boundaries of British India, is a tract occupied by tribes subject only to the political control of the Chief Commissioner in his capacity as Agent to the Governor-General. In this tract, the area of which is roughly 25,500 square miles, are situated, from north to south, the Political Agencies known respectively as the Malakand, Khyber, Kurram, Tochi and Wana Agencies, and each of the Deputy Commissioners of the five administered districts is responsible for the management of political relations with certain tribes or sections of tribes across the border. A few hundred miles of this trans-border territory are internally administered by the Political Agents to whom their control is entrusted; but the bulk of the trans-border population is free from any interference with internal affairs, so long as offences are not committed in British districts or protectorates and in Afghanistan, and so long as the tribes observe the conditions on which allowances are paid to many of them. The North-West Frontier Province, as at present constituted, came into existence in October 1901. The districts of Hazara, Peshawar and Kohat, together with the trans-Indus portions of Bannu and Dera Ismail Khan and the Political Agencies in the Khyber, the Kurram, Tochi and Wana, were in that year removed from the control of the Government of the Punjab. To them was added the political charge of Dir, Swat and Chitral (Malakand Agency), and the whole was placed under a Chief Commissioner and Agent to the Governor-General in direct subordination to the Government of India in the Foreign Department.

Natural divisions.
I.—The Hazara District.

2. Geographically the districts of the Province fall into two main divisions. The first of these is the district of Hazara, which stretches in a north eastern direction from the north of the Attock District of the Punjab far into the outer Himalayan range. The most northerly portion of British India, it is marked off from the other districts of the Province as being the only one which lies to the east of the river Indus. The Mansehra Tahsil, which, with the area known as Feudal Tanawal, forms the northern half of the district, is bounded and intersected by well wooded mountain chains which, with the spurs thrown out by them, divide up the country into numerous isolated valleys. The general elevation of the tahsil is considerable, and rises, at the crest of the peak known as Mali-ka-Parbat, to over 17,000 feet. The southern portion of the district is divided roughly into two halves, of which the eastern forms the Abbottabad and the western the Haripur Tahsil. The Abbottabad Tahsil is also mountainous and well-wooded. Abbottabad, the head-quarters of the district, is situated in a valley some 4,000 feet above sea level, and the Dunga Gali range, which forms the eastern boundary between the tahsil and the territories of the Maharaja of Kashmir, has a general altitude of between 10,000 and 7,000 feet. The Haripur Tahsil, which occupies the south-western portion of the district, consists for the most part of an open plain which slopes gradually from 3,000 to 1,600 feet above sea level.

II.—The trans-Indus districts.

The second of the two divisions into which the administered portion of the Province is divided geographically is occupied from north to south by the four districts of Peshawar, Kohat, Bannu and Dera Ismail Khan. For the whole of its length, except where the Punjab district of Mianwali extends across the river to form the eastern boundary of portions of Bannu and Kohat, this tract is bounded on the east by the river Indus. On the west it stretches to the hills which bound the trans-border portion of the Province referred to above. Peshawar "a lacustrine basin encircled by hills" is separated from "the rugged tableland" of Kohat by the Jowaki range. Bannu forms a broad basin irrigated by the Kurram river and completely surrounded by low ranges. The district of Dera Ismail Khan, to the south of Bannu, consists of "a broad expanse of barren plain enclosed between the Suleiman range on the west and the Indus on the east, and tapering to a blunt point at its southern extremity." The hills, which form so noticeable a feature of the scenery at almost every point within these districts, are rugged and barren and of no great height, and the whole area is in the main plain country, distinguished, especially towards its southern portion, by the heat and other climatic conditions characteristic of the plains. In Hazara, we have an entirely mountainous or sub-montane tract; in the four southern districts a tract, which though intersected by low ranges, is essentially a portion of the plains and the riverain.

III.—The trans-border area.

There remains the trans-border portion of the Province, situated between the boundaries of British India on the one hand, and those of Afghanistan on the other. Extending in the north of Chitral as far as the mountains of the Hindu Kush, in the south it is bounded by Baluchistan, and within these extremes the greatest variations of scenery and temperature are met with. Chitral, the most northerly portion of this area, "is a region of deep valleys and lofty ranges, for the most part bare and treeless. Further south lie the thickly wooded hills of Dir and Bajaur and the fertile valleys of the Panjkora and Swat rivers. South-west of this are the Mohmand hills, a rough and rocky tract with little cultivation. Further south comes the narrow gorge of the Khyber Pass, leading westward from Jamrud on the Peshawar border with Afghanistan. South of the Pass lies Tirah, the maze of mountains and valleys held by the Afridi and Orakzai tribes, and bordered on the western extremity of its northern border by the Safed Koh. Further west this range (the Safed Koh) still forms the border of the Province, and flanks the Kurram Valley....... This fertile valley stretches south-eastwards from the great peak of Sikaram, in which the Safed Koh culminates, and the Peiwar Kotal Pass to the western extremity of the Miranzai Valley in Kohat. South of Kurram lies Waziristan, a confused mass of hills, intersected on the north by the Tochi Valley, and on the south by the gorges that descend to the Wana plain. The hills are for the most part barren and treeless, but on some of the higher ranges, such as Shawal and Pir Ghal, fine forests are found. The valleys also broaden out into plains and form fertile and well irrigated dales." From a census point of view, our information regarding the whole area is scanty, no regular enumeration being attempted except of the inhabitants of British posts; and in spite of the diversity of climate and scenery which it presents, it is convenient to treat it, as indeed in essentials it is, as a single natural division.

The three natural divisions contrasted.
(a) Climatically.

3. If the Hazara District is distinguished in its physical aspects from the trans-Indus districts of the Province, it is no less clearly contrasted in its climatic conditions and in the character of its inhabitants. The Hazara District has an annual rainfall of about 45 inches; in the other four districts the fall is lighter, varying from 11 inches in the Dera Ismail Khan District to one of from 10 to 25 inches in the districts to the north of it. The climate of the greater part of the Hazara District is marked by extreme cold in winter, when large parts of the country are under snow; in the summer, as might be expected from its altitude, the climate is temperate, though in the plain country round Haripur it resembles that of the Northern Punjab. In the trans-Indus districts the weather is cold in winter, and frost is experienced almost every year; the summers however bring great heat, the thermometer rising to between 114° and 120° at Peshawar, and to between 115° and 122° at Dera Ismail Khan. The trans-frontier area of the Province possesses within its borders diversities of temperature and climate too great to permit of any succinct account of its climatic conditions, even if we possessed the data for more than a quite inconsiderable number of places within it. Of this tract generally, however, it may be said that its characteristics are a temperate climate in summer, with extreme cold in winter, and a winter rainfall considerably exceeding that of the summer.

(b) Ethnologically.

4. Ethnologically the three divisions are no less distinct. In Hazara is to be found a mixed population, mainly of Indian origin, the most numerous tribes being Awans, Gujars and Tanaolis, while large numbers are contributed by the Dhunds, Saiads and Kashmiris. Pathans, though found in large numbers, still do not form the most numerous race of the district, and are not marked by the characteristics of violence and vindictiveness which distinguish them elsewhere. It has been noted that the Hazara peasant is somewhat lacking in robust qualities. Organised crime does not exist in the district; murders are rare, and dacoities hardly ever occur, though the people are much addicted to litigation. Hazara has not in fact the characteristics of a frontier district. On the west it possesses for some portion of its length a natural boundary in the Indus such as does not exist in the southern districts, where the hills, if they present an obstacle against the pursuit of offenders into the trans-frontier area behind them, are no bar to the incursion of armed bands into British territory. In the four southern districts, and especially in Peshawar, Kohat and Bannu, conditions are different. Jats and Baluches form the majority of the agricultural population in Dera Ismail Khan, but in the three districts directly north of it, Pathans contribute nearly one-half of the total population. This is not the place in which to discuss the origin of the Pathan; it is sufficient to note that his characteristics mark him off clearly from the bulk of the other inhabitants of the Province. In the trans-Indus districts murders and crimes of violence are of frequent occurrence, the blood-feud flourishes, and the inhabitants cannot be accused of a want of manliness or robustness of character, however much one may reprobate their methods of prosecuting their quarrels. Even if criminals within the district be few, there are generally raiders from *Yaghistan* to be reckoned with, while the presence of a safe asylum across the border removes a powerful deterrent to crime in British territory itself. We have then in the four southern districts of the Province an area in which Pathans roughly equal in numbers the members of all other sections of the population put together, and in which they possess to the full those qualities of courage and vindictiveness which are generally associated with the name. In the third or trans-border tract the population consists almost entirely of Pathans. The area is marked off politically from the rest of the Province as being, with the exception of small isolated tracts, a sort of no man's land, subject to no government, and torn continually, except in the face of a common enemy from without, by internecine feuds. The Pathan in the trans-border area possesses the same characteristics as his fellows in British territory. They are, however, exaggerated by the absence of those restraints which the existence of civilized government imposes.

Summary.

5. In these three areas we have then three natural divisions clearly distinguished from one another by one or the other, or by all, of the considerations referred to in the foregoing paragraphs. If the inhabitants of the trans-border tract are of the same race as a large proportion of those of the British districts which lie to the west of the river Indus, the conditions under which they live are from every point of view wholly diverse. In the same way, though in some respects the climate and physical aspects of the tribal territory, or at least of the northern portion of it, resemble those of Hazara, the populations of the two areas are separated by ethnological as well as by political considerations. There is no need to insist further on points of resemblance or of difference. In spite of the mixed character of the population of one, and of the considerable variations of climate and scenery which are to be found in all, it will be well to consider the results of the Census in relation to these three more or less homogeneous areas.

Population of natural divisions.

6. In table I at the beginning of Part II of this volume will be found a statement of the area and population of each of the administrative divisions (districts, agencies, etc.), of the Province, while Provincial Table I at the end of the volume gives similar statistics for tahsils. In the margin is shown the population, according to the recent Census, of each of the three natural divisions referred to above.

	Population.
Hazara	603,028
Districts trans-Indus	1,593,905
Trans-border area ...	*1,622,094
N.-W. F. Province...	3,819,027

Population compared with that of other provinces, etc.

7. The newest, if we except the administrative units lately formed in Bengal, the North-West Frontier Province possesses almost the fewest

* Estimated population.

inhabitants of all the provinces of India. Those which fall below it are Baluchistan (811,011*), Ajmir Merwara (501,436) and Coorg (175,004). The population we have to deal with is only one-twelfth of that of the United Provinces, which is now the largest in this respect of the Indian provinces: it amounts to nearly one quarter of that of Bombay (excluding Sind and Aden) and rather exceeds that of Sind. Taking the districts of the North-West Frontier Province alone, some idea will be formed of the number of their inhabitants if we say that it only exceeds by about 7,000 souls the combined population of the cities of Calcutta and Bombay with their suburbs, and that it is approached to within about 160,000 persons by that of Baroda State.

Area.

8. The area of the Province is a little more than half that of Bombay (excluding Sind and Aden), and rather less than half that of Kashmir. It amounts to something more than three-fifths the size of England without Wales. If we omit the trans-frontier tracts, the area of the remainder is just over half that of Gwalior, and nearly double that of Baroda, or, to compare it with a more familiar example, scarcely more than twice the size of Yorkshire.

Density of population. (a) in the trans-border area.

9. Taking the Province as a whole, the pressure of the population on the soil is light, amounting to only 98 persons per square mile. This figure has, however, no great significance. Nearly two-thirds of the area are taken up by the trans-border tract, for which we have only an estimate of population, while a large proportion of the 25,500 square miles which are included in it consist of uninhabited and unculturable waste. We have no figures for the inhabited and cultivated area of this portion of the Province; and the real density of the population can hardly therefore be calculated. The actual figure arrived at by dividing the area by the estimated population is 63 persons per square mile, but in the more favoured portions the pressure of the population is much greater. We can hardly therefore profitably discuss statistics of density for this portion of the Province.

(b) in British territory.

Turning to the British Districts which are included in the Province, the density of population for the total area of British territory is 164 persons per square mile. In the cis-Indus portion of the Province, the Hazara District, however, it is considerably greater, amounting to 207 persons per square mile; while for the plains tract which comprises the trans-Indus area it is only 152.

Comparison with other provinces, etc.

The significance of these figures will be rendered clearer by the statement in the margin, in which the density of population in the Province and in its various natural divisions is compared with that in some other provinces and states in India. The figures for other provinces are for British territory only. It will be seen that the Hazara District has a comparatively dense population, denser than the districts of the Punjab, though much less dense than Madras, and not quite half as dense as the United Provinces. The pressure of the population on the soil in the trans-Indus districts is considerably lighter, being less than that of the Central Provinces with its large areas of jungle. To find a parallel to the density in the trans-frontier portion of the Province we have to look at the figures for Sind and Burma, the former with its great waterless tracts, and the latter with its enormous areas not yet opened up to cultivation. Still, as remarked above, when we consider the great areas, especially in the Malakand Agency, where human habitations are impossible, the population can hardly be considered scanty, especially when we compare it with the figures for the districts and administered territories of Baluchistan. In the agency tracts of that province the figure is even less than 9 persons per square mile.

Provinces, etc.	*Density per square mile.*
United Provinces ...	440
Madras ...	292
Hazara ...	*207*
Punjab ...	205
Districts N.-W. F. P. ...	*164*
Hyderabad ...	161
Central Provinces ...	160
Trans-Indus Districts N.-W. F. P.	*152*
N.-W. F. P. total area ...	*98*
Rajputana ...	82
Sind ...	74
Trans-frontier Area N.-W. F. P.	*63*
Burma ...	50
Baluchistan (districts and administered territories)	9

Variations of density between districts and their causes.

10. It has been seen that there are considerable variations of density between the three natural divisions into which the Province has been divided

*The populations of other provinces quoted on this page, and on which density is calculated, are those according to the Provisional Totals, Census 1911.

above. But the figures for individual districts bring out even more clearly the differences that exist. In a province where so large a proportion of the population is supported by agriculture, the conditions affecting the cultivation of the soil naturally have the greatest influence on the growth of population ; and it will be suitable to discuss these first. In subsidiary Table I appended to this Chapter will be found a statement showing the mean density per square mile for each of the districts separately, together with figures for the percentage of culturable, cultivated and irrigated area, and for rainfall. The table shows the percentage of the cultivated area under each of the crops most widely sown, but I have not succeeded in tracing any clear connection between density and crops, except in so far as the choice of crops depends on the question which is itself the ultimate factor in determining population, *i.e.* the presence or absence of water for purposes of cultivation. It is to be noticed that the population is least dense in the districts in which the largest proportion of the cultivated area is under *jowar, bajra* and other cereals ; but this only means that in areas where cultivation, from scarcity of water, is precarious, an autumn crop is more successful than a spring one. The high proportion, as compared with other districts, of the cultivated area in Hazara which is under maize is also noticeable, but this fact has, so far as I am aware, no direct relation to the relative density of Hazara and other districts, except in so far as maize is a crop which needs much water. On the whole as might be expected in so small an area as that of the North-West Frontier Province, the crops sown show little variation in different districts.

Culturable area in different districts.

In the previous paragraph I have referred to the presence or absence of water as being the ultimate factor which determines density in the North-West Frontier Province. This statement needs some qualification, but, broadly speaking, it is true. The configuration of the soil is of course of very great importance, for no one can plough, nor will water remain on a hill side of more than a certain degree of steepness. In this connection the figures given in column 3 of subsidiary Table I at the end of this Chapter are not without interest. Hazara, with its vast areas of mountain and forest, and the rugged and stony district of Kohat naturally stand low in order of area available for cultivation. It will be seen that the district with the largest proportion of culturable land, Peshawar, has, as might be expected, the greatest density of population, and that Kohat, of which only 30 per cent. of the total area is culturable, stands low in the order of density. But the figures show of how little importance comparatively is the area which is classed as culturable. This amounts to only one per cent. less in Dera Ismail Khan than in Peshawar, and yet Dera Ismail Khan has a lower density than any other district of the Province, lower than Kohat, where the proportion of the total area classed as culturable is less than half that in Dera Ismail Khan. A better indication is given by the cultivated area (column 4 of subsidiary Table I.) Speaking broadly, it may be said that the average cultivated area over a period of years (the figures in subsidiary Table I are worked out for the average of the last ten years) represents the area which, under existing conditions of water supply, it is possible to cultivate. But to explain the causes of variations of density, in so far as they depend on agricultural conditions, we must look further. Leaving on one side Hazara, where there are special sources of livelihood apart from the cultivation of the soil, which will be mentioned in their place, it will be seen that the districts in order of density stand in the same order as they do in the matter of irrigation facilities, (column 5 of subsidiary Table I) except that Kohat though it has a smaller proportion of irrigated area, has a higher density than Dera Ismail Khan. But the supply of water for purposes of cultivation does not depend on irrigation alone : it also depends on rainfall ; and it is when we look at the figures of columns 5 and 6 of the table referred to taken together, that we find the main indication of the causes of density in so far as it depends on agriculture. The rainfall of Kohat is nearly double that of Dera Ismail Khan, and it is not surprising therefore that the population is more dense, in spite of the fact that there is less irrigation. The rainfall of Bannu is small, little less than that of Dera Ismail Khan, but the irrigated area is proportionately far greater ; and in the heavy rainfall of Hazara we have a partial explanation of the high density of population, in spite of the fact that the irrigated area is so small, and that the area available for cultivation amounts to so small a proportion of the whole.

Cultivated area.

Irrigated area.

Rainfall.

Between the Peshawar and Bannu Districts there is proportionately no great variation in cultivated area. The large difference in density is partly due to the comparatively large urban population of the former; in so far as it depends on agricultural conditions, it must be referred to the difference in the irrigated area and in the rainfall.

Soils.

It will be noticed that in the preceding discussion I have not referred to variations in the quality of the soil as having any influence on density. The reason for this is that though variations of course exist, their influence, like that of all other factors in the matter, is small when compared with the grand and all important one of the presence or absence of water. In several of the districts soil has been classified for settlement purposes according to its capacity for irrigation alone, and if the clay soil, *e. g.* of the Bannu Tahsil, is superior to the sandy soil of Marwat, the difference is mainly due to the silt brought down by the Kurram and Tochi rivers in their course through the former. For the purposes of this discussion it may be assumed that the culturable soil in the districts of the Province is all profitable alike, if only the presence of water renders cultivation possible at all.

Variations of density by tahsils.

11. A discussion of the causes relating to density cannot however be complete unless areas smaller than districts are taken into consideration. A reference to Provincial Table I at the end of this volume will show that even within a single district there are found considerable variations, *e. g.* in the Bannu District, while the Bannu Tahsil has a density as high as 307 persons per square mile, the figure for the Marwat Tahsil is only 89. In the following paragraphs therefore the figures for the tahsils of the Province will be considered.

Greater density of head-quarters tahsils.

Provincial Table I shows the density per square mile, according to the present Census, in each tahsil of the Province; while the map on this page is shaded to show variations of density throughout the Province, the trans-border area, for which we have no accurate demarcation of boundaries between the different agencies and tribal areas, being treated as one, while in the five British Districts each tahsil is shown. Looking at Provincial Table I, it will be noticed, as might be expected, that, except in the Kohat District, the density is in each case higher in the tahsil containing the head-quarters of the district than in others. Each of the district head-quarters contains a cantonment in which is located a considerable force, the cantonments of Abbott-abad, Kohat, Bannu and Dera Ismail Khan being each the head-quarters of a brigade, while Peshawar is the head-quarters of the First Division. The

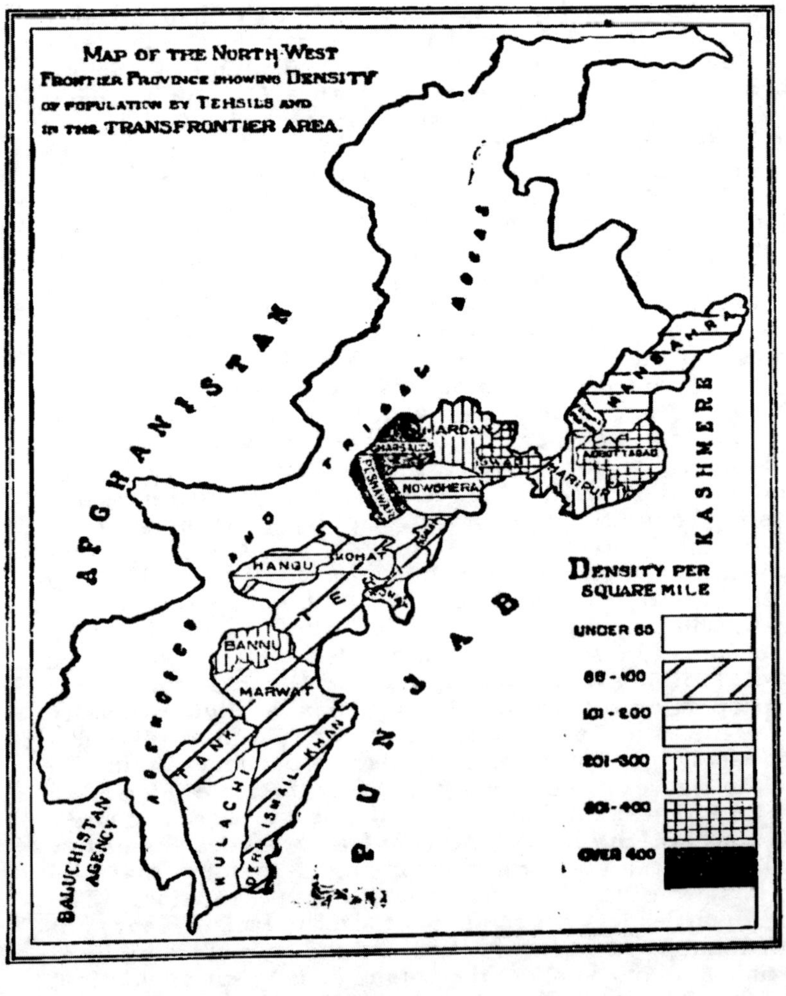

NOTE.—In the reference to the hatchings in the accompanying map *for* 201—300 *read* 201—309 and *for* 301—400 *read* 310—400.

presence of the cantonment in each case has led to the growth of a considerable bazaar to supply the needs of the troops located in it; and the district head-quarters have, in each case except that of Abbottabad, themselves been chosen as being centres of trade before annexation. In the case of Abbottabad the presence of the cantonment has led to the formation of a town, outside the cantonment limits, of 4,000 inhabitants.

The presence of a town naturally increases density directly; indirectly it increases it still further. To supply its needs there is bound to be a growth of population even outside its limits, as the marginally noted figures will show. Except in Hazara, where the village unit in Feudal Tanawal, which has never been brought under the British revenue system, evidently has a different meaning than it has where that system is in force, the average area in square miles of each village is considerably less in the head-quarters tahsil than elsewhere in the district. Even in Kohat the average size of the village is smaller in the head-quarters tahsil than in Hangu, though the density is higher in the latter, and the comparatively high density in Hangu is probably to be explained by the presence there in March of large numbers of immigrants from Afghanistan and *Yagistan*, who visit the Province every winter to find pasture for their flocks and herds, and for purposes of trade. The population of the Hangu Tahsil is also increased by the detachments of troops stationed within it.

Tahsil, etc.		*Average area of each village in square miles.*
Mansehra	...	5·8
Haripur	...	2·1
Abbottabad	...	1·8
Feudal Tanawal	...	·8
Mardan	...	4·6
Swabi	...	4·7
Charsadda	...	2·2
Nowshera	...	4·9
Peshawar	...	1·7
Teri	...	9·8
Hangu	...	9·6
Kohat	...	8·7
Marwat	...	8·2
Bannu	...	2·0
Tank	...	8·1
Kulachi	...	14·5
Dera Ismail Khan	...	6·4

We have seen partially the influence of the presence of towns as affecting density of population in tahsils. To see it fully, however, it is necessary to consider the figures for the rural population only. If we place by these figures for the rainfall and for the cultivated and irrigated area of each tahsil separately, the fact that the chief factor in determining density is the presence or absence of water for purposes of cultivation will be even clearer than it appeared on a consideration of the figures for districts. In this connection a reference should be made to subsidiary Table I-A* appended to this Chapter. In the figures there shown we see the reason of the great difference between density in the Bannu and Marwat Tahsils of the Bannu District (difference in irrigated area), and in the Nowshera and Charsadda tahsils of the Peshawar District (difference in cultivated and irrigated area). The influence of rainfall also, in different tracts of which the cultivated area is proportionately equal or nearly so, is shown by a comparison of the figures for the Swabi and Mardan Tahsils of the Peshawar District. Subsidiary Table II at the end of this Chapter is of interest as showing the proportions borne to the total area and population of the Province (including the trans-frontier tract) by the areas and populations of tahsils classified according to density. Rainfall and irrigation in tahsils.

12. An examination of subsidiary Tables I and I-A appended to this Chapter will, as I have attempted to show, throw considerable light on the reasons for variations of density in the various parts of the Province. I have also indicated the effect of the district head-quarters with their concentration of population in cantonments and trade centres. These are not however the only causes. I shall attempt in the following chapter to show what has been the effect caused by the recent history of the tract comprised in the Province. But others may be indicated here. The foregoing paragraphs deal with the causes which affect almost entirely the population dependent on agriculture as a source of livelihood. In the margin is shown the density of population per square mile of cultivated area. The figures have been worked out on the total population of each district, except in Hazara, where the population of Feudal Tanawal has been left out of account, as no figures are available for the cultivated area of that tract. The figures illustrate the tendency for the pressure of the population on the area under cultivation to be heaviest where means of livelihood other than agriculture exist in greatest abundance.† In Hazara, as the figures Density as affected by sources of livelihood other than agriculture.

District.		*Density per square mile of cultivated area.*
Hazara	...	856
Peshawar	...	607
Kohat	...	498
Bannu	...	305
Dera Ismail Khan		302

* It should be noticed that in Subsidiary Table I-A the density of the rural population only is shown, while Provincial Table I and the map on page 10 refer to the density of the total population of tahsils.

† In Dera Ismail Khan however not even the high proportion dependent on trade can render the density per square mile of cultivation other than low.

indicate, the cultivation of the soil alone affords livelihood to a comparatively small proportion of the population. The people of Hazara are largely graziers. The profits from livestock in the district are estimated at about eleven lakhs of rupees annually. "Most of the grain being required for home consumption" (I quote from the recent Settlement Report of the Hazara District) "it is chiefly to milk, butter and *ghee* that the ordinary *zamindar* in the hills looks for the payment of revenue or for the means whereby he may borrow money. The Government forests and other waste lands of the district are a very valuable asset. From them are obtained grass and wood for sale or for home consumption" (though there are of course restrictions on grazing and wood cutting in them) "and they enable the *zamindars* to maintain a great number of livestock from which they can supplement their other income and also obtain manure for the benefit of their fields." The sale of walnuts, honey, pears and other fruits, and the hiring out of transport for the Kashmir trade also afford considerable profits; and Government service alone, for the Hazarawal shows a considerable spirit of adventure in pushing his fortunes, affords the district an annual income of over eight lakhs of rupees. In Peshawar also, with its large urban population, due mainly to its commanding position as an entrepôt for Central Asia trade, there is a large population dependent on sources of livelihood other than agriculture. In the Mardan and Swabi Tahsils the income from pay and pensions from Government service was estimated in 1897 to amount to over Rs. 3,60,000 annually, and" the Khattaks of Nowshera are more dependent for a livelihood on their pack animals than upon the produce of their lands." In Bannu, outside the district head-quarters, any source of livelihood other than agriculture hardly exists. In Kohat on the other hand sources of livelihood independent of agriculture are numerous. The Khattaks and Bangashes especially among the tribes of the district enlist freely in the army, and the income of the district from Government service in pay and pensions is estimated at over 6½ lakhs of rupees per annum. In bad seasons the people travel far afield in search of employment as labourers and the like; and from their camels, cattle and flocks, as well as from the products of their wastes, such as wood, and the *mazri* or dwarf palm, they have considerable sources of income. The salt mines in the Teri Tahsil also provide a source of income to the neighbouring villagers.*

Influence of health on density.

13. Health and the conditions of life generally have much weight in determining the distribution of the population. In this connection it is interesting to see what proportion of the total population enumerated at the recent Census had reached the age of 60 years and over. In Hazara the percentage is 6·1 in Peshawar 5·7, in Kohat 4·8, and in Bannu and Dera Ismail Khan 3·9 and 4·7, respectively. The figures are on the whole what might be expected from a consideration of the conditions of the various tracts. The climate of Hazara is very healthy:" Scarcity and plague have scarcely touched it and the poverty of even the least prosperous tracts is not sufficient to affect the birth rate." The climate of Peshawar is trying in the autumn, from the great daily range of temperature, but the conditions of life on the whole are easy. In Kohat too the climate may be called a good one, bracing in winter, if fiercely hot in summer. Of that of Bannu all that the writer of the report on the recent settlement can say is that it is trying. As regards the conditions of life in Dera Ismail Khan, in the Kulachi Tahsil of which the density of population is as low as 50 persons per square mile, I cannot resist the temptation to quote a description, by the late Captain Crosthwaite, of the Daman, or the high ground above the Indus bed which stretches to the Suleiman range on the west. "There is no tract" says Captain Crosthwaite "in the Punjab or North-West Frontier Province in which the conditions of life are so arduous. The extremely precarious cultivation depends on the hill torrents. These often fail. On the other hand heavy floods may sweep away every dam, scour out the channels, make the rebuilding of the dams impossible and finally run to waste in the Indus. Years of scarcity follow brief periods of prosperity. The harvest in good years is so plentiful that the people make shift to tide over the cycles of bad years. There is always a scarcity of drinking water. A few villages near the passes get their drinking water from the Kalapani *zams* (perennial streams from the hills). A few near the river get it from wells. But in the Daman proper wells are most expensive to sink and their water brackish and undrinkable.

* The sources of income, other than agriculture, which are here referred to are not duly reflected in our returns. These latter are naturally not affected by supplies of money sent home by men living at a distance; and graziers and carriers generally possess some land, and have returned their principal occupation as agriculture.

Most villages are dependent on kachcha tanks, which breed guinea-worm in profusion. Some villages derive a supply from water holes sunk in the beds of the large torrents. Both these supplies fail at the beginning of the hot weather. Men and cattle then migrate to the Indus. Those who remain have to go long distances for water. Men drink once a day and the cattle every second day. Washing is an impossible luxury. . . . . It is possible in the hot weather to ride thirty miles and neither hear a dog bark nor see the smoke of a single fire. . . . . The climate of the Daman is very trying and alternates between excessive heat and cold. The virulent Daman fever and pneumonia cause an excessive mortality at intervals of a few years."

14. This attempt to indicate the causes on which is dependent the distribution of population in the districts of the Province may well be closed with some account of the degree to which they have been subjected in the past to the vicissitudes to which the cultivation of the soil in India is so generally subject. "Since the terrible drought of the year 1783, when popular accounts describe the district as almost depopulated, Hazara has been almost untouched by famine, and enjoying as it does so ample and constant a rainfall, may be considered practically secure from such a calamity. At various periods in the last twenty years there have been failures of crops in the unirrigated portions of the district, but no widespread distress has been occasioned, and only small suspensions of revenue have been necessary." In Peshawar (I quote from the latest Settlement Report) "there has been no difficulty in collecting revenue since annexation except in the Charsadda and Peshawar Tahsils, where the difficulty was due rather to the ingrained habit, which grew up in the Doaba and Peshawar since the days of the Sikhs, of paying nothing except under compulsion, than to an excess in the revenue demanded; and in Hashtnagar to the turbulent character of many of the leading men." The Kohat District similarly is not liable to famine, but the greater portion of it depends wholly on the rainfall, and a good deal of hardship results in the event of its failure or unseasonable distribution. In Bannu the head-quarters tahsil is well protected by irrigation, and cultivation may be considered secure. In Marwat however, where cultivation depends almost wholly on the rainfall, occasional remissions of revenue have been necessary. The Dera Ismail Khan District is the only one in the Province where anything like famine conditions have prevailed since annexation. Cultivation here is uncertain in the extreme. "In the 18 years preceding the last settlement* the amount of revenue suspended amounted to almost double the realisations, which were again only in the ratio of 4 to 3 to the remissions."

Scarcity.

TOWNS AND VILLAGES.

Definition of town.

15. The word town, as defined for Census purposes, includes every Municipality, all Civil Lines not included in municipal limits, every cantonment, and every other continuous collection of houses inhabited by not less than 5000 persons which it may be decided to treat as a town for Census purposes. It was pointed out in the Imperial Census Code, on which the local rules were based, that it is undesirable to treat as towns places which have no urban characteristics; and in determining the classification of places other than Municipalities, Civil Lines, and Cantonments, regard was paid not only to the number, but also to the character of their inhabitants.

Difficulty of distinguishing urban and rural areas.

16. But although every attempt was made to class as towns only those areas which possess true urban characteristics, it is not to be supposed that it is possible to draw the line of distinction with any certainty. In the Punjab Census Report, 1881, the late Sir Denzil Ibbetson pointed out how strong is the contrast, especially between the smaller towns in the Punjab, and urban areas as the term is understood in Europe. The passage in which Sir Denzil Ibbetson discusses the point is worth quoting in full. After indicating briefly the main characteristics of towns in England, he observes: "In the Punjab the distribution of the population presents the strongest possible contrast with that which I have sketched above. In the case of the larger towns indeed the contrast is not so apparent. There are no vast local industries, prosecuted by large bodies of men working for hire at the bidding of a capitalist whose money and machinery they make use of, and attended by the commerce which they call into existence. But where the presence of a court, facilities of communication, or other local

* Concluded in 1906.

circumstances have created a political, religious, or commercial centre, the skill and capital of the neighbourhood have collected round it, and the result is a city like Delhi, Amritsar or Lahore"—or, it might have been added, Peshawar.

"It is in the smaller towns that the contrast is most striking; and especially in the fact that gradation from the city just described to the purely agricultural village is so imperceptible, and the series of intermediate forms so unbroken that it is impossible to lay down any hard-and-fast line of demarcation. And this may, I think, be attributed to several causes. In the first place the local manufactures are so insignificant that the commerce of the country is largely independent of them, and, being concerned rather with the collection and exportation of the raw produce of the rural tracts than with supplying the needs of industrial activity, tends to be widely scattered over the country which yields its staples, rather than to be concentrated in a few great urban centres. Again such industries as are necessary to supply the simple needs of the villager are prosecuted in the village itself. The Punjab village" (for this might be substituted the village of North-West Frontier Province) "is eminently self-sustaining. It grows its own food, it weaves its own clothes, it tans its own leather, it builds its own houses, it makes its own implements, it moulds its own domestic vessels, its priests live within its walls, it does without a doctor, and looks to the outside world for little more than its salt, its spices, its fine cloth for its holiday clothes, and the coin in which to pay its revenue. Nor are the wants of the higher classes much less simple than those of the peasant. The rich man dresses a little better, his wife wears more expensive ornaments, and his family live in a larger and more expensive house. But his food and furniture are only a degree in advance of those of his rustic neighbours, and he marks his superior position chiefly by profuse hospitality" (this trait is very marked in the North-West Frontier Province) "and by supporting a bevy of useless retainers. Thus, both the distributing agency and the professional element which give its characteristic features to the population of an English country town are in India far less complex in their nature, far less important in point of number, and far less localised in their habitation than in England. Almost all the smaller Punjab towns have extensive arable lands attached to them, and include considerable cultivating communities; and they often have little to distinguish them from the true village beyond their larger size, the greater extent, activity, and importance of their trade, and the superior skill of their workmen. The difference, in short, is one of degree rather than of kind."

Places treated as towns in the N.-W. F. P.

17. In this passage we have an accurate description of the state of affairs in the North-West Frontier Province to-day. In towns like the five district head-quarters, and in large cantonments like Nowshera we have areas which undoubtedly possess the true urban characteristics; but in the case of many among the remainder of the nineteen places shown as towns in Tables IV and V in Part II of this volume, doubt must always arise as to their true classification. Kulachi and Haripur, which possess Municipal Committees, are necessarily included among the towns under the orders issued for the taking of the Census; and Notified Areas also have in most cases been classed as towns. Tangi, Prang and Charsadda have been so classed on account of their importance as centres for the distribution of the produce of the neighbourhood; but it is perhaps an open question whether they, and other places, such as Baffa, should be so treated or not. They have all however been regarded as towns since the Census of 1881, and in cases of doubt it seemed best to follow past practice in cases where there has been some increase of population. It is worth noticing that the Hangu Tahsil of the Kohat District is shown as possessing no town, though detachments of troops are stationed both at Hangu and at Thall within its limits. Troops can in no circumstances be regarded as constituting part of the rural population, but in this case they do not reside within cantonment limits, and necessarily form part in our tables of the rural population.

Average size of towns.

18. Table IV in Part II of this volume shows the towns of the Province classified by population, and in subsidiary Table III appended to this Chapter will be found the ratio of the urban population residing in towns arranged according to size. It will be seen that considerably more than half the total urban population resides in towns of 20,000 inhabitants or over, and that the average population per town for the Province is 15,353 persons. Only 49 per

mille of the urban population live in towns possessing less than 5,000 inhabitants. This is natural; for the difference between towns and villages being one of degree rather than of kind, the size of the population becomes one of the chief criteria in determining how any particular area shall be classed. The figures therefore can hardly be said to indicate any tendency among the inhabitants of the Province to gather into large urban centres.

Distribution of population between towns and villages.

19. Of the total population of the Province, only 7 per cent. at the present Census were recorded as residing in towns, as compared with 12 per cent. in 1901. It is not however to be supposed that there has been the general exodus from the towns which those figures would imply, or that the number of places treated as towns has been fewer on the present occasion than in 1901. The reason for the decrease lies in the fact that the total population of the Province as shown in this Report includes for the first time an estimate of the population of the trans-frontier area, the population of the whole of which has been treated as rural. The only fair comparison between conditions now and in 1901 will be obtained by a consideration of the ratio of the urban to the total population of that portion of the Province which is included in British India Taking the districts of the Province alone, we find that the urban population amounts now to 13 per cent. of the whole, as compared with a percentage of 12 in 1901, the urban population having risen by 12 per cent. from 258,930 ten years ago to 291,714 on March 10th, 1911.

Increase of urban population since 1901.

20. The ratio borne by the urban to the total population was high in 1901, when compared with that in other provinces of India; being only exceeded in Berar (15 per cent.) and Bombay (19 per cent.), and being only equalled in a province which, like the North-West Frontier Province, would not naturally occur to one as having a large urban population, *viz.*, British Baluchistan. On the present occasion the ratio is even higher. The increase is not however so great as would at first sight appear. Out of the increase of 32,784 shown in Table IV between the years 1901 and 1911, the considerable figure of 20,256 is due to the fact that the Nowshera and Mardan Notified Areas have now for the first time been treated as towns, and to the creation since 1901 of the cantonment at Risalpur in the Peshawar District. While therefore the urban population as shown in Table IV has increased since 1901 by 12 per cent., in reality, if we neglect the increase due to the inclusion of new urban areas, it has grown only by just under 5 per cent., as compared with an increase of 6 per cent. in the same period in the rural population.

Cantonments and other urban areas, and their relative rates of growth.

21. Of the total urban population, no less than 70,254 persons, or between one-fourth and one-fifth of the whole, reside in cantonments. In other words nearly one-quarter of the population concentrated in towns does not represent any spontaneous desire for town life on the part of inhabitants of the Province, but merely the fact that strategical considerations have led to the massing of large bodies of troops along the Frontier. Taking the figures as they stand in Table IV we find that the cantonment population has increased in the last decade from 61,828 persons to 70,254, or by 13 per cent., while the population of towns other than cantonments has grown by 12 per cent, *viz.*, from 197,102 in 1901 to 221,460 at the present Census. But if we examine the figures further, it will be seen that the growth of cantonment population has outpaced that of other towns more than these figures would suggest. In the first place the figure given for Kohat Cantonment in 1901 includes some 5,000 persons who were not present in the cantonment at all, being troops, Pioneer Regiments and others, employed in constructing or guarding the construction of the railway line from Khushalgarh to Kohat. As they were located in comparatively small scattered bodies, the troops were included in the population of Kohat Cantonment, as it was thought that their inclusion in the population of the rural area of the tahsil would have the effect of causing confusion in the village Census tables. If we deduct 5,000 persons from the population of the Kohat cantonment in 1901, (as we may fairly do, for this population was not present in the cantonment at the time of the Census, nor was it a part of its ordinary population) the cantonment population of the Province has risen from 56,828 in 1901 to 70,254 at the present Census, or by 23 per cent. On the other hand in calculating the increase of population in towns other than cantonments, it is only fair to make allowance for places treated for the first time as towns on the present occasion. If we compare the population of all places treated as towns in 1901, other than canton-

ments, with the population of the same towns in 1911, we find that the increase has been from 197,102 persons in 1901 to 204,371 in 1911, an increase of only 3 per cent., or half the rate of increase in the rural population of the Province.

In 1901, 12 per cent. of the population of the districts of the Province resided in towns, 3 per cent. in cantonments and 9 per cent. in other towns. 13 per cent. of the population now live in towns, of whom 3 per cent. are found in cantonments, and 10 per cent. in other towns. As I have pointed out above however, these figures do not accurately represent the relative rate of growth in cantonments and other towns respectively. It should be noted that in the case of cantonments, I have included, in the calculation of increase, the new cantonment of Risalpur, because this does represent a real increase of cantonment population. In the case of towns other than cantonments I have disregarded new areas, because the places now treated as towns for the first time were in existence in 1901, and it is impossible to say at what precise moment their population ceased to be rural, and definitely began to assume urban characteristics. Of the Province generally then we may say that there has been no tendency during the last decade towards concentration of population in towns. This indeed should afford no cause for surprise.

The towns as centres of trade.

22. The Province is practically without manufactures. A reference to Table XV-E will show that on March 10th, 1911, there were only 8 factories in which more than 20 persons were employed, and that the total number of persons employed in them was only 265. All except one, which is in the Peshawar tahsil, are situated in Peshawar city or cantonment. There is no considerable surplus of commercial products for export. Any commercial importance which the Province possesses, it owes, (I quote from the Provincial Gazetteer, 1908) "to the fact that it lies across the great trade routes which connect the trans-border tribal territories and the marts of Afghanistan and Central Asia with India." But the influx of population and of trade from this cause is not so great as might be expected. The influence of the railways has been in the direction of taking trade farther afield.* The travelling traders (or Powindahs) from Afghanistan and from the trans-frontier area of the Province (the Yaghistan of the last Census) have always pursued their wanderings far into India; but the tendency to use the lines of rail has naturally increased year after year. The railway now extends to Jamrud at the foot of the Khyber Pass, and the extension of the line from Khushalgarh on the Indus to Thall at the entrance of the Kurram valley; and from Nowshera in the Peshawar District to Dargai at the foot of the Malakand Pass (both extensions carried out in the decade since last Census) have done much to increase this tendency, and to shorten the time during which immigrants from the west are to be found within the Province.

Movement of population in individual towns.

23. With these general remarks we can proceed to discuss the movement of population in individual towns. To take first the five head-quarter stations of districts, the most surprising figures are those for Kohat, where the population of the cantonment area has decreased by 53 and of the municipal area by 7 per cent. Mention has been made above of the reason for the decrease in the population of the Kohat Cantonment. The figures for 1901 were swollen by the inclusion of a large body of troops, who were not actually present in the cantonment at all; in addition a portion of the garrison was absent from the district at manœuvres at the date of the present Census. The decrease in the population of the municipal area is also apparently to be attributed to the fact that in 1901 the railway line from Khushalgarh was under construction. This fact must have brought a large body of engineering employés and of skilled and unskilled labourers to the town, and the completion of the railway line to Thall has probably decreased the length of stay in the town of temporary immigrants from the west. It is to be noted too that the rate of increase in the population of the district generally has been slow, amounting to only 3 per cent, and that the male population has actually decreased from 122,174 in 1901 to 119,001 in 1911. This latter decrease is no doubt to be attributed principally to the presence of a large body of temporary male immigrants in 1901 in connection with the building of the railway, but even if we deduct from the 1901 population 6,000 males on this account, we still have a

* It is interesting to note that the writer of the Dera Ismail Khan Settlement Report 1906, remarks, "The old trading centres of the District, Dera, Kulachi and Tank, have decreased in importance since the opening of the Railway. The Powindahs, who formerly did much of their trading there, now go by train to large towns in India."

rate of increase in the male population of only 2 per cent. The next town the figures for which invite comment is the head-quarters of the Province, Peshawar. While the population of the cantonment has increased in the last decade by 9, that of the municipal area has increased only by ·9 per cent., in spite of the fact that the rate of increase of population in the district generally has also been 9 per cent. Here again the small rate of increase can be mainly attributed to a specific cause. Just a year before the taking of the Census, the date of the Hindu festival of the Holi coincided with the Mohammedan day of mourning, the Barawafat. The result was an explosion of religious animosity, which resulted in affrays between Hindus and Mohammedans, in which there was considerable loss of life. As a result many Hindus left the city for a time; and though they had returned by the following spring, a similar coincidence of dates early in March 1911 naturally gave rise to much apprehension, and there was again among Hindus a considerable exodus. Every precaution was taken by the authorities to preserve the peace; the city was picketted with troops; trans-border men and bad characters were warned not to enter it, and those who were already inside it were expelled. But for this cause an increase similar to that in the cantonment and in the district generally might have been expected also in the municipal area. The other district head-quarter towns call for little remark. There has been a large increase in the cantonment population in each case, varying from one of 21 per cent. in Bannu to one of 71 per cent. in Abbottabad, and the increase in the municipal areas has been proportionate to that in the adjoining cantonment and the district generally. At Abbottabad where the municipal area derives its importance as a place of trade principally from the presence of the cantonment, the considerable increase of the number of troops, leading to a growth of cantonment population of 71 per cent., has resulted in an increase in the population of the municipal area of 18 per cent., a rate considerably in increase of that (10 per cent.) for the district as a whole. The importance of Edwardesabad (Bannu) and of Dera Ismail Khan as centres of trade is independent of the existence of cantonments beside them, and the rate of increase in the population of the municipal area of the former (6 per cent.) and of the latter (4 per cent.) is roughly analogous to the rate of increase in the general population of the district in each case. The variations in the population of cantonments are due to other than economic causes, and there is no need to discuss them here, except in so far as they affect the population of areas outside their own limits. The other towns of the Province are hardly of sufficient importance to deserve separate remark. Taken as a whole, the small towns of the Province, exclusive of cantonments, and exclusive of areas now for the first time treated as urban, show an increase of population of 7 per cent., or exactly the same as that for the total population of the districts of the Province.

Relatively slow growth of larger towns.

24. As I have observed above, there is no object to be gained by subjecting to a minute scrutiny the figures for cantonments, depending as they do on the scheme which happens to be in force for the distribution of troops. Taking other urban areas however it is interesting to note that the tendency to expansion is far stronger in the towns with a population of from 5,000 to 20,000 than in larger towns, (*vide* subsidiary Table V, at the close of this Chapter.) If we exclude cantonments and the four most populous municipal areas of the Province, *viz.* Peshawar, Dera Ismail Khan, Kohat and Edwardesabad (Bannu), we find the rate of increase in the population of the remainder to be 7 per cent. between 1901 and 1911, whereas for the four large towns mentioned (municipal area only) it is under 2 per cent. How far the figures are affected by the considerations mentioned above, as bearing on the variations in the populations of Peshawar and Kohat municipal areas since last Census, it is of course impossible to say, but the evidence which is available certainly seems to point to the prospect of no large centres of population growing up in the Province under existing conditions. With the growth of industries, and should the extension or adoption of improved methods in agriculture lead to the production of grain in quantities sufficient to permit of extensive export beyond the Province, the people may be expected to turn in time to an urban life. At present there are no signs of any such tendency.

Proportion of the sexes in towns and rural areas.

25. It might be expected that the proportion of females to males would be smaller in towns than in rural areas. It is in towns that immigrants largely

congregate, and it is common for persons in India, who leave their homes, even for long periods, not to be accompanied by their families. If we compare the sex proportion in the total urban areas of the Province with that in the rural areas, the difference is found to be very marked, there being only 625·6 females per 1,000 males in towns as against 900 in rural areas. If we exclude the figures for cantonments however, the difference is not so great; for in all other towns females are to males in the proportion of 802·8 to 1,000. In ordinary cases of course the Indian sepoy or sowar is not accompanied by his family, and the figures for cantonments vary from 99 females per 1000 males in Bannu to 314 females per 1,000 males in Nowshera. The highest proportion of females to males in the rural areas of the Province is also, curiously enough, in the Nowshera Tahsil, where females are as numerous as 963 per 1,000 males. Of towns other than cantonments the highest proportionate number of females is found in Kulachi in the Dera Ismail Khan District, where there are 1,007 females per 1,000 males, and the lowest in Abbottabad where females only amount to 528 per 1000 males. The high figure in Kulachi appears to be due to immigration, for the Powindah traders in the Dera Ismail Khan District come accompanied by their families, and leave their women and children near the border, while the men proceed with their wares far into India. The figures for Abbottabad suggest that the population of the municipal area, which has grown up purely as a *bazaar* to supply the needs of the cantonment, is largely composed of temporary visitors who come in from the surrounding countries to sell their wares. In the Mardan Notified Area also the proportion of females is very small, amounting to only 599 for each 1,000 males. The low figure here is probably due to the presence of the Mohmand labourers and other temporary visitors from the west, who come into the district unaccompanied by their wives.

Proportion of followers of each main religion found in towns.

26. Since the first annexation of the districts of the Province the tendency of Hindus to concentrate in towns has been noticed; and considering the low estimation in which they were held in a country of which the predominant religion has been Mohammedan since the days of Mahmud of Ghazni, and considering also the danger to which they were subjected in outlying tracts, a tendency to gather together in strong places for protection need cause us no surprise. Moreover they are essentially a trading community. The same reasons have led to the congregation in towns of Sikhs also. In subsidiary Table IV, appended to this Chapter, will be found a statement showing the number per thousand of the total population and of the population of each main religion who live in towns. While of Mohammdans only 99 per 1,000 are inhabitants of urban areas, in the case of Hindus the figure is 540; in the case of Sikhs it is as high as 549, while of every 1,000 Christians in the Province no less than 979 reside in towns. The same fact with regard to Christians will probably be noticed in every province of India in which there is no large population of native Christians. In the North-West Frontier Province the Christians are nearly all Europeans employed as troops or in civil employ, whose duties attach them to the headquarters of districts, or to cantonments elsewhere.

Definition of village.

27. For the purposes of this Census, as on the last occasion, village means an estate as defined in the Punjab Land Revenue Act, *i.e.*, any area which has been separately assessed to land revenue, or for which a separate record-of-rights has been made. The Census village is therefore the same as the revenue village; and, as is to be expected from that fact, there has been no variation between 1901 and 1911 in the number of places treated as villages in the Peshawar District, the last settlement of which was completed before the Census of 1901. In the case of the other four districts on the other hand, all of which were resettled between the enumerations of 1901 and 1911, the number of villages shown in Tables I and III printed in the second part of this volume differs from that shown in the Punjab Census Report, 1901. But as the village is merely a revenue unit, the variations call for no discussion here.

The Census village not necessarily the residential village.

28. The Census village has no necessary connection with the residential village. This is particularly the case in Hazara, where, from the large area and mountainous nature of the district, many families live in isolated homesteads built on their own lands. In many cases (I quote from the Hazara Gazetteer, 1907) "one so called village is made up of several hamlets" and

occasionally "the site to which the name of the village is applied is but a tiny cluster of huts with a mosque attached." Throughout the other districts of the Province also are to be found hamlets, known as *bandas*, which have been thrown out from the main village, in some cases to provide a place of residence for immigrants of a different tribe from the original land-holders, or in others to enable the proprietors to live near lands situated at a distance from the main village site. I have no statistics from which to calculate the ratio which such *bandas* bear to the number of revenue villages, but we shall not, I think, be above the mark if we assume that the number of residential villages in the Province is at least 10 per cent. in excess of the number of villages shown in Table I.

29. The character of the villages varies considerably in the different divisions of the Province. As I have noted above, in Hazara, in the more hilly tracts, scattered homesteads are very common, instead of groups of houses collected together. In Peshawar the rural population live for the most part in large villages, divided up into quarters or *kandis*, in each of which resides a separate clan, and each of which possesses its own mosque and *hujra* (a general meeting place and guest house). 'The villages,' says the writer of the Peshawar Gazetteer "have for the most part an air of great comfort, the court-yards being large, with, in most instances, a patch of vegetables or a clump of mulberries in the enclosure; the mosques and *hujras* are chiefly in the outskirts with wells and groves in the vicinity. In most villages there is a good supply of running water, which not only encourages plantations of this kind, but saves the female portion of the community the labour of grinding, as water mills are universal, and hand mills unknown." The typical Kohat village, as might be expected from the barren and rugged nature of the country, is smaller, less comfortable in appearance, and divided by greater distances from its nearest neighbours. In Bannu the villages are of widely differing types. In the rich and densely populated lands of the Bannu Tahsil the residential villages or hamlets are small, and at short distances from one another, the houses being crowded together on the valuable space withdrawn from agriculture. Water-courses are commonly carried through the middle of the village, as in Peshawar; and the smallest village has its *chauk* and its mosque shaded by *shisham* or *pipal*. On the other hand in the Marwat Tahsil, where irrigation is rare and cultivation difficult, the villages are generally large and far apart. Near the border outlying hamlets are rare, though they are commonly met with towards the Indus. Unlike the villagers of the Bannu Tahsil, those of Marwat are compelled to dig tanks to store their water; but these contain no water for nine months of the year, during which it has to be brought from a distance on the backs of donkeys. In Dera Ismail Khan the villages are usually small, nearly three quarters of them having fewer than 500 inhabitants. The conditions of life in the district are perhaps harder than those to be found elsewhere in the Province, and the villages have none of the look of comfort and solidity which they present, for instance, in the Peshawar District. The reason is not far to seek. In the riverain cultivation depends almost entirely on floods, but the river's action is uncertain, and it is no unusual thing for the people to be driven by it away from their homes. "As soon as the wheat is garnered, the inhabitants move off with their cattle to the higher villages, till the floods subside. During the floods a few miserable families may be found perched on platforms or the roof beams of their houses." Many of the inhabitants of the high land known as the 'Daman' between the Indus and the hills are also driven away from their homes annually by want of water, as the people of the riverain by excess of it.

Villages described in the different districts of the Province.

30. As there is no necessary connection between the Census and the residential village, the statistics given in subsidiary Table V (at the end of this Chapter) have no great significance as bearing on the mode of life of the people in different parts of the Province. The figures do not accurately reflect the size of the communities in which people live, but they are probably correct in suggesting that the district which has proportionately the largest number of very large villages (5,000 inhabitants and over) is Kohat, and that Hazara, Bannu and Dera Ismail Khan all possess relatively large numbers of small ones (under 500 inhabitants).

Size of villages

HOUSES.

Variety in character of houses.

31. As might be expected, the character of the houses occupied by the people varies largely in different portions of the Province. The villager of the Mansehra Tahsil of Abbottabad, whose dwelling is burried in snow for several months in the year, naturally adopts a style of building differing widely from that of the dweller in the torrid riverain of Derā Ismail Khan, whose chief consideration in choice of building materials is not so much strength and permanence as portability and cheapness.

Description of the houses of the Province.

32. In Dera Ismail Khan, both in towns and villages, mud huts with flat roofs are those generally used. Each hut consists of one room only, which is occupied by the whole family. The cow is sometimes put up in the same room with the family, but there is more often a shed outside for cattle. Near the river houses are commonly built with mud or grass sides, and covered over with a moveable roof of *moonj* grass or matting; and in those parts which are more particularly exposed to floods, the people often live in a hut which consists merely of a piece of grass matting put up in the form of an arch, with the two ends touching the ground. In the level portions of the Hazara District the houses are of the mud-walled, flat-roofed type common in the Punjab plains. In the hills they are often constructed of wood, with a lower story occupied by the cattle, and an upper one by the owner and his family. In Peshawar, except in the hills of the Nowshera tahsil, where stone can easily be procured for building, the houses are as a rule built of mud, and in nearly all cases the house proper stands inside a walled enclosure, in which the cattle are tethered. The houses of the richer villagers occasionally have a small garden attached to them. In Kohat the building material most commonly used consists of the loose stones and boulders which are everywhere to be found. These are roughly cemented together with mud. If stone is not to be procured, the houses are built of clay sods dried in the sun. The ordinary cultivator's house consists of a single room, in one end of which the cattle are stabled, while the grain safes are in another corner, and the family occupy the rest of the place. In some cases there is a shed for the cattle outside. Windows are not provided, but there is a hole in the roof which serves as chimney In the Bannu District the houses are all built of sundried mud, and in the poorer tracts are often roofed with reeds. The use of mud instead of brick is not the result of poverty, but of the fact that houses of the former material are cooler in the hot weather. The Wazirs of Bannu commonly live, men, women, children, cattle and fowls in one room, while other Pathans keep their animals in a separate building. Finally must be mentioned the habitations of the *Kirri* folk, nomad graziers from Afghanistan and tribal territory, who are found in the winter throughout the trans-Indus districts of the Province, and whose homes consist merely of stout woollen blankets stretched over curved sticks.

Definition of house for purposes of the Census.

33. On the present occasion house was defined for the purposes of the Census as meaning the dwelling place of a commensal family, with its resident dependants, such as widows and servants. With the object of insuring that no one should escape enumeration, it was laid down that numbers should be affixed, as if they were houses, to shops, schools and any detached structures which have no hearth, but in which people might be found sleeping on the Census night. The instructions provided however that such places should not be included in the return of occupied houses.

It will be seen that under the instructions the return of houses would be in effect a return of *chulhas*, or hearths, with certain reservations. This is a conception easily understood by the ordinary enumerator; but it was necessary to elaborate it somewhat further to prevent misconception. In the instructions to supervisors it was explained that "when people are living in one house, and are either paid by one of the inhabitants, such as servants, or are supported by him, as wife, mother, children, and eat food cooked at one hearth, they comprise one family" *i.e.*, their common dwelling place is a house in the Census meaning of the term. "If one of these conditions is absent," the instructions proceeded "it makes no difference, *i.e.*, if the servants, though living in the same house, have a separate hearth at which to cook their food, they are still included in the family. But if two conditions of these are absent, if for instance two men, with their wives and children, live under the same roof, but eat separately, and live each on their own earnings, they are the heads of two separate families."

Difficulties of definition.

34. I have indicated that the object aimed at in the definition of house was to obtain a return of families, including in the family servants when they resided under the same roof with their master. The instructions, if accurately followed, would have given us a return of families in the English sense of the word. A married son, living with his father, commonly has a separate hearth, whether supported by his father or not. But if so supported, he and his wife and children would be shown under the instructions as occupants of one and the same 'house' as his father. If on the other hand he earned his own living, he and his father would be regarded as living in different houses. I am aware that this distinction is a rather subtle one to be grasped by the ordinary enumerator; but it seemed necessary to qualify the bare statement that the return of houses was to be a return of *chulhas*, or, in the very common case of servants cooking their food at a different hearth from their masters, we should have had one house represented as two. It is true that the instructions issued may have led in some cases to two houses being counted as one; but to treat a married son, living with his parents, as part of his parents' family is less repugnant to European conceptions than to treat a servant as constituting a distinct family because, as is usually the case, he cooks at a separate hearth from his master.

The value of the return of occupied houses as indicating the normal size of the family.

35. It would, I think, be over-sanguine to suppose that in the return of occupied houses we have any very accurate indication of the normal size of the family in the Province. There are various considerations which no doubt had the effect of throwing out the calculation. The instructions laid down that large enclosures, such as *serais* and the residences of wealthy *khans*, would be best treated as blocks, the houses within their enclosing walls being separately numbered. But there was a tendency to number such buildings, unless their size rendered such a course obviously out of the question, once only; and in the case of police posts, small forts occupied by Border Military Police, etc., it is unlikely that a separate number was attached to the *kothi* occupied by each sepoy. It may also be mentioned, though it will have had little effect on the figures, that in the case of servants' quarters attached to houses occupied by Europeans, each block of servants' quarters was treated as one house. But perhaps the most potent influence tending to qualify the value of the statistics as representing a return of families is to be found in the fact that the instructions issued on the present occasion were a new departure; for the tendency of the local Census staff to follow instructions with which they had grown familiar at a previous Census, in spite of the issue of entirely different ones during the one which is being taken, has often been remarked. During the Census of 1901, house was defined to mean any *makan*, *ahata* or *ghar* used for human habitation. As at the previous Census, the word used to translate house was *ahata* or enclosure; and in the instructions to supervisors issued in 1901 it was laid down that if doubt arose as to whether a building should be numbered as one house or more, the test was to be the number of main entrances (*dahlij* or *deohri*). Thus a house containing several families, but only one *deohri* was to be numbered as one house. I found in several instances during my inspections that a house containing several families had been treated as one, and though I directed the addition of fresh numbers in each case which I came across, and did my best to see that the orders were generally understood, I have no doubt that many such instances remained undetected.

It is obvious that the main object to be aimed at during a Census is a correct enumeration of population, and that the obtaining of a correct return of occupied houses must be made subservient to this end. Mr. Maclagan, who supervised the Census of the Province as part of the Punjab in 1891, considered *ahata* (enclosure) the most comprehensive and easily intelligible term to be used in this connection. It would seem, however, that to require that a number should be affixed for each *chulha*, with the corollary that the name of the head of each family is entered in the Block List, certainly does not militate against the obtaining of a correct return of population, while it brings us nearer a correct estimate of the normal size of the family than can be obtained by defining the house as the enclosure.

Average size of households at present and at previous Censuses.

36. A reference to subsidiary Table VI at the end of this Chapter will show the effect which the difference in the instructions issued on the present occasion has had on the number of persons per house. For the period 1881 to 1901 there had been little difference in the number of occupants of each house.

In the trans-Indus districts the number had varied between 6 and 6·2 persons per house in the years 1881-1901. It is now 5·1. In Hazara the number had dropped from 6·3 in 1891 to 5·5 in 1901. The decrease was accounted for (Punjab Census Report, 1901, page 25) by the increasing tendency of the people to build homesteads on their own lands away from the village sites. At the present Census the number has dropped again to 4·7, which may be in part attributable to the tendency noticed in 1901, but is due, I believe, in a greater degree to the change made in the definition of house. Of the Province generally it may be said that the decrease since 1901 in the number of persons per house is due to the change in the instructions issued, and not to any tend ncy for the size of the family to decrease.

Size of households in rural and urban areas.

37. Our statistics showing the average number of persons per house throw no clear light on the conditions which determine the size of the family. But it is interesting to notice that in the trans-Indus districts of the Province the average number of persons per house is higher in rural than in urban areas, and that in Hazara the figure is but little higher in towns than in villages. It is in towns that we should expect to find the larger households. The Hindus who, except in the case of men in military employ, mainly belong to the commercial classes, live here, as elsewhere, in joint families; and it is in towns that more than half of them are to be found (while contributing only 2·8 per cent. to the total rural population, they contribute as much as 22 per cent. to the total urban population of the Province). It is moreover in towns chiefly that there exist those circumstances which I have mentioned above as tending to diminish the value of our returns as indicating the average size of families, *i.e.*, the existence of *serais*, etc., and of houses inhabited by more than one family. The inference which can be drawn therefore from the figures is that the family unit tends to be considerably larger in rural than in urban areas, especially in view of the fact that among Pathans, whose customs naturally dominate social observances outside the towns of the Province, the very antithesis of the joint family system is in vogue. Probably as a result of the interior arrangement of the houses, which allows of no privacy to the women, the male unmarried members of the family, from about the age of fourteen years, do not sleep at home, but at the *hujra*, (the guest house and general meeting place) which each quarter of the village possesses, or at the family threshing floor, irrigation well or water mill. At the age of about 20, a son "receives a portion of his father's land as his share of the patrimony, and seeks a wife, if about to settle at home; otherwise he leaves his home and seeks a livelihood by military service in foreign countries." The inference as to the normal size of the family which is herein suggested is supported by the figures which show that in the last ten years the rural population has increased faster than the urban, and that the growth of the Mohammedan population has far outstripped that of the Hindu. There has been in fact an actual decrease since 1901 in the Hindu population of the Province; but this does not imply that Hindus are dying out. The proportion of Hindus, as of Sikhs, (who have increased from 28,091 persons in 1901 to 31,459 in 1911) depends largely on the composition of the regiments which happen to be stationed here from time to time; and an attempt to indicate the other causes to which the decrease is due will be found in Chapter IV of this report.

Average number of persons per house—

District etc.	*In towns.*	*In rural areas.*
Total Districts N.-W. F. P.—	5·07	5·04
Hazara ...	4·9	4·7
Trans-Indus Dists.	5·09	5·3
Peshawar ...	5·2	5·2
Kohat ...	5·9	5·2
Bannu ...	4·8	5·5
D. I. Khan ...	4·6	4·7

SUBSIDIARY TABLE I.—*Density, Water Supply and Crops.*

District and Natural Division.	Mean density per square mile in 1911.	Percentage of total area.		Percentage of cultivated area which is irrigated.	Normal rainfall.	Percentage of cultivated area under			
		Culturable.	Cultivated.			Wheat.	Barley.	Maize.	Jowar, Bajra and other cereals.
1	2	3	4	5	6	7	8	9	10
N.-W. F. P. Total Districts.	**164**	**55**	**31**	**22·8**	**21·19**	**34·8**	**9·2**	**13·5**	**14·0**
Hazara	207	30	24	9	40·83	24	12	40	9
Total Districts Trans-Indus.	**152**	**62**	**33**	**25·7**	**16·28**	**37**	**9**	**8**	**14**
Peshawar	332	75	53	35	19·1	27·8	17·9	13·4	7·8
Kohat	82	30	16	12	21·9	39·9	2·8	8·1	35·4
Bannu	149	69	49	26	12·56	48	4	9	5
Dera Ismail Khan ...	74	74	24	17	11·56	40·5	2·3	...	26·8
Trans-frontier area ...	63	...	...	...	...	...	...	...	...

NOTE.—The figures in columns 3, 4, 5 and 6 are worked out on the average of the last 10 years. The figures for Hazara are exclusive of Feudal Tanawal for which the cultivated area is not available.

SUBSIDIARY TABLE I-A.—*Statistics of Density and Rainfall, Irrigated and Cultivated Area for Tahsils.*

Tahsil.	District.	Area in square miles.	Percentage of total area.		Rainfall in inches.	Rural population.	Density of rural population.
			Cultivated.	Irrigated.			
1	2	3	4	5	6	7	8
Mansehra	Hazara ...	1,427	16	1	37·78	189,328	133
Abbottabad	Hazara ...	689	29	1	36·20	204,885	297
Haripur	Hazara ...	664	35	5	48·51	151,512	228
Tanawal	Hazara ...	204	...	...	...	27,559	135
Peshawar	Peshawar ...	450	46	34	13·76	162,254	360
Charsadda	Peshawar ...	379	68	46	13·63	129,038	340
Swabi	Peshawar ...	465	69	9	28·09	153,723	330
Mardan	Peshawar ...	609	67	19	22·13	144,404	237
Nowshera	Peshawar ...	702	26	6	17·93	108,422	154
Kohat	Kohat ...	751	16	5	20·13	51,508	68
Teri	Kohat ...	1,528	18	·19	19·54	104,462	68
Hangu	Kohat ...	416	11	3	25·95	44,066	106
Bannu	Bannu ...	464	58	32	12·44	125,446	270
Marwat	Bannu ...	1,210	45	5	12·78	102,852	85
Dera Ismail Khan ...	Dera Ismail Khan	1,733	26	*1	10·96	118,285	68
Tank	Dera Ismail Khan	638	28	*16	10·73	42,450	67
Kulachi	Dera Ismail Khan	1,089	20	*2	10·61	45,045	41

*Only shows irrigation by canals and not by wells or Kalapani.

SUBSIDIARY TABLE II.—*Population classified according to density.*

District, etc.	Tahsils with a population per square mile of—													
	Under 100		100—150		150—200		200—300		300—350		350—450		450—600	
	Area.	Population.	Area.	Population.	Area.	Population.	Area.	Population.	Area.	Population.	Area.	Population.	Area.	Population.
1	2	3	4	5	6	7	8	9	10	11	12	13	14	15
N.-W. F. P. Total Districts and Trans-Frontier area.	**32,449** *83·4*	**2,165** *56·7*	**2,047** *5·3*	**268** *7·0*	**702** *1·8*	**137** *3·6*	**1,273** *3·3*	**311** *8·1*	**1,618** *4·1*	**517** *13·5*	**379** *·9*	**159** *4·2*	**450** *1·2*	**262** *6·9*
Hazara	...	...	1,631 *4·2*	224 *5·9*	...	...	664 *1·7*	158 *4·1*	689 *1·7*	221 *5·8*	...	...	...	...
Peshawar	...	...	...	...	702 *1·8*	137 *3·6*	609 *1·6*	153 *4·0*	465 *1·2*	154 *4·0*	379 *·9*	159 *4·2*	450 *1·2*	262 *6·9*
Kohat	2,279 *5·8*	179 *4·7*	416 *1·1*	44 *1·1*	...	...	...	...	...	...	...	...	...	...
Bannu	1,210 *3·1*	108 *2·8*	...	...	...	...	...	...	464 *1·2*	142 *3·7*	...	...	...	...
Dera Ismail Khan ...	3,460 *8·9*	256 *6·7*	...	...	...	...	...	...	...	...	...	...	...	...
*Agencies and tribal areas ...	25,500 *65·6*	1,622 *42·5*	...	...	...	...	...	...	...	...	...	...	...	...

NOTE.—In the figures given in columns 3, 5, etc., 000s. are omitted.

NOTE.—The figures in *italics* show the percentage of the area and population in each case to the total area and population of the Province.

*The boundaries of agencies and tribal areas have not been exactly defined, and the density has been calculated therefore on the whole area.

SUBSIDIARY TABLE III —*Distribution of the population between towns and villages.*

District.	Average population per		Number per mille residing in		Number per mille of urban population residing in towns with a population of—				Number per mille of rural population residing in villages with a population of—			
	Town.	Village.	Towns.	Villages.	20,000 and over.	10,000 to 20,000	5,000 to 10,000	Under 5,000	5,000 and over.	2,000 to 5,000.	500 to 2,000	Under 500
1	2	3	4	5	6	7	8	9	10	11	12	13
N.-W. F. P. Total Districts	**15,356**	**628**	**133**	**867**	**621**	**170**	**160**	**49**	**45**	**278**	**465**	**211**
Hazara	7,436	496	49	951	...	387	456	157	21	216	499	264
Peshawar	18,574	881	193	807	738	66	168	28	56	380	426	138
Kohat	22,654	689	102	898	1,000	...	...	...	121	247	436	196
Bannu	10,894	605	87	913	...	774	...	226	25	191	535	249
Dera Ismail Khan ...	16,787	492	197	803	698	202	100	...	27	255	433	285

SUBSIDIARY TABLE IV.—*Number per mille of the total population and of each main religion who live in towns.*

District.	NUMBER PER MILLE WHO LIVE IN TOWNS :—				
	Total population.	Mohammadan.	Hindu.	Sikh.	Christian.
1	2	3	4	5	6
N.-W. F. P. Total Districts ...	**133**	**100**	**540**	**550**	**980**
Hazara	49	29	432	623	958
Peshawar	193	157	709	556	981
Kohat	102	76	447	618	756
Bannu	87	43	426	792	922
Dera Ismail Khan	197	148	525	716	991

SUBSIDIARY TABLE V.—*Towns classified by population.*

Class of town.	Number of towns of each class in 1911.	Proportion to total urban population.	Number of females per 1,000 males.	VARIATION PER CENT. IN TOWNS AS CLASSED AT PREVIOUS CENSUSES.			VARIATION PER CENT. IN URBAN POPULATION OF EACH CLASS FROM 1881 to 1911.	
				1901 to 1911	1891 to 1901	1881 to 1891	(a) In towns as classed in 1881.	(b) In the total of each class in 1911 as compared with the corresponding total in 1881.
1	2	3	4	5	6	7	8	9
Total	**19**	**100**	**626**	**+4·8**	**+9**	**+19·5**	**+36·1**	**+31·5**
II.—50,000 to 100,000...	1	34	641	+2·9	+13	+5·2	+22·4	+22·4
III.—20,000 to 50,000 ...	3	28	568	—7·5	+16·0	+21·3	+58·5	+275·8
IV.—10,000 to 20,000 ...	4	17	598	+13·5	—18·1	+48·5	+24·6	+59·1
V.—5,000 to 10,000 ...	6	16	750	+18·2	+10·4	+21·3	+46·4	—17·7
VI.—Under 5,000 ...	5	5	588	—1·6	+21·2	+42·9	+48·7	—55

NOTE.—The percentage in column 5 represents the variation shown by the Census of 1911 in the population of the towns included in each class in the Census of 1901. The figures in columns 7 and 8 similarly represent the variation in the periods 1881—1891, 1891—1901 and 1881—1911. In none of these columns are the variations due to the classing of additional areas as urban taken into account. Column 9 shows the increase in the population of towns as classed in 1911 over the population of towns as classed in 1881, *i.e.*, it shows the gross increase including new areas classed as urban and including the population of towns which have come up from a lower class during the period under comparison.

SUBSIDIARY TABLE VI.—*Persons per house and houses per square mile.*

District and Natural Division.	AVERAGE NUMBER OF PERSONS PER HOUSE.				AVERAGE NUMBER OF HOUSES PER SQUARE MILE.			
	1911	1901	1891	1881	1911	1901	1891	1881
1	2	3	4	5	6	7	8	9
N.-W. F. P. Total Districts ...	**5·0**	**6·0**	**6·1**	**6·0**	**32·4**	**21·3**	**17·9**	**15·0**
Hazara	4·7	5·5	6·3	6	42	33	27	25
Trans-Indus Districts—Total ...	**5·1**	**6·2**	**6**	**6·1**	**29**	**22**	**16**	**13**
Peshawar	5·2	6·4	6·6	6·7	63	46	44	42
Kohat	5·2	7·3	8·9	8·1	15	10	8	9
Bannu	5·5	6·2	5·6	5·8	27	22	18	18
Dera Ismail Khan	4·7	5·1	4·9	4·9	16	14	10	12

NOTE.—The figures in columns 4, 5, 8 and 9 are calculated on the statistics of the districts of Bannu and Dera Ismail Khan as constituted before the year 1901, when they included a large tract cis-Indus which now forms the Mianwali District of the Punjab.

CHAPTER II.

MOVEMENT OF POPULATION.

38. In a report such as the present there is no need for me to attempt to write a history, however brief, and however limited its point of view, of the North-West Frontier Province. In the various District Gazetteers, and in the Provincial Gazetteer, 1908, will be found more or less detailed accounts of the subject. At the same time it is necessary that I should try to indicate in a few words the conditions affecting variations of population in the past so far as, from the scanty records available, they are known to us. Alexander of Macedon, when he invaded the Province in 327 B. C, found its northern portion held by a dense population of Indian races, Hindu by religion, living under a more or less settled government, and enjoying a considerable degree of civilization. On the collapse of the Macedonian Satrapy set up by him, the country passed under the sway of Chandragupta, whose grandson, Asoka, made Buddhism the dominant religion in the modern districts of Hazara and Peshawar. After the extinction of the Buddhist dynasty about 165 B. C., the Province was ruled for 200 years by Greek princes of Bactria. The latter were expelled by the Sakas, or Scythians, who were followed in succession by the Kushans, known to the Chinese annalists as the Yueh-Chi, and the Epthalites, or, as they were styled by the Byzantines, the White Huns, who established a vast empire which stretched from Persia to Chinese Turkestan. In the year 986 A. D. the first Mohammadan invasion took place.

Rulers of the Province prior to first appearance of the Mohammadan invaders.

39. From the time of Alexander to the first appearance of the Mohammadans the Province, although it passed under a succession of conquerors, seems to have enjoyed a considerable degree of prosperity. The civilization which they found neither Alexander nor his Buddhist and Bactrian successors did anything to destroy. In fact it is evident from the archæological remains, which have been from time to time discovered, that the reverse was the case. As regards the Huns, Kushans and Scythians, Mr. Merk, C. S. I., in a paper read recently at a meeting of the Royal Society of Arts in London, remarks:—"Whoever they were, they were civilized themselves, or else rapidly assimilated the civilization existing on the spot, for it is evident that their assumptions of power were not associated with cataclysms" Mr. Merks adds, "The mass of still extant ruins of monuments and villages, the roads that were cut by the Buddhists over the Kohat and Malakand passes, and exist to this day . . . . . the rock engraven edicts of Asoka, which can still be read in Hazara and Peshawar, all proclaim that the country from Chitral to Bannu and from the Jhelum to Cabul must have enjoyed protracted peace and order."

Archæological remains, and early references to the condition of the Province.

The Chinese pilgrims, Fa-Hien and Hiuen Tsang, who visited the Province at the beginning of the 5th and 7th centuries of our era respectively, going, among other places, to Chitral, Swat, Peshawar, Tirah, Kurram and Bannu, have left their testimony of the state of the country in their time. They found it inhabited by a dense and settled population. Peshawar had already become a large city. Buddhism was the dominant religion at the time of the earlier Chinese visit; but in the 7th century was already in its decline, its place being taken by Hinduism.

40. What Mr. Merk calls the halcyon time of the Province passed away with the first appearance of the Mohammadans. In 986 A.D. occurred the first raid of Sabuktagin of the slave dynasty of Ghazni. From about 1000 to 1100 A.D. what is now the Peshawar District formed a province of Ghazni under the successors of Sabuktagin, the most famous of whom was Mahmud. Neither Mahmud nor his immediate successors were settlers, but robbers who took all they could from the country, and passed on to plunder elsewhere. Bellew, writing of Yusafzai, now one of the most densely populated areas of the Province, remarks that "the invasions of Mahmud had left it a deserted wilderness, the haunt of the tiger and the rhinoceros, and only occasionally visited for the sake of pasture by the shepherd tribes accustomed to roam about the neighbouring countries.........The country has never recovered its former condition

Effect of the invasions of Mahmud of Ghazni and his successors.

of prosperity." These words were written in 1864, before the country had had time to recover from the effects of the Sikh domination and the confusion to which it succeeded, but, as illustrating the condition of the country long before the first appearance of the Sikhs, it is interesting to note that the Emperor Babar, writing in the 16th century, records in his Memoirs that his followers hunted the rhinoceros in the swamps of what is now the Peshawar District. There is no need to follow the history of the Province from the date of the first Mohammadan invasion. It will suffice to mention that the Indian races which had inhabited it were largely replaced by invaders from the west, the bulk of the Pathan tribes in British territory, with the exception of those of Hazara, whose appearance dates from some two centuries later, having settled in their present homes during the 15th and 16th centuries. Up till 1818, when all except the transborder portion fell under the sway of the Sikhs, the Province, more or less nominally, formed part of the territories of successive Mohammadan dynasties, Ghorids, Afghans, Moghals and Durranis, ruling either from Kabul or from Delhi. It was continually the scene of conflicts between rival claimants to rule it. No interference seems to have been attemped with the local chiefs in internal affairs, and rebellions and insurrections were frequent. Even the strongest rulers were able to obtain revenue only from the more accessible plain portions of the country; and the more common arrangement was the assignment to tribal chiefs of the bulk of the revenue as a method of securing peace. Meanwhile tribal feuds between the people themselves were prosecuted without intermission.

The Province in the 16th Century.

Its condition up to the beginning of the 19th Century.

Appearance of the Sikhs. State of the Province under Sikh rule.

41. With the decay of the Durrani power the Sikhs stepped in. Their invasions began in 1818, and from that date to annexation by the British which followed the second Sikh war, they steadily strengthened their hold on the districts of the Province. As illustrating the condition of the country at the time of annexation I cannot do better than quote in full the remarks of the late Sir Denzil Ibbetson in the Punjab Census Report, 1881 (now for many years out of print). After describing the miserable condition of the Punjab when first it passed under British rule, Sir Denzil remarks :—

" If such was the state of affairs among the comparatively peaceable population of the east and north of the Province, it may be imagined what was the state of the frontier, where wild hill tribes, still many of them semi-savage, accustomed to assert their independence even of the Kabul kingdom, and habitually fighting one with another for sheer love of the game, were brought under the rule of the hated Sikh. Even Ahmad Shah :—

" Collected tribute by an army sent periodically to extort it at the sword's point," and as the Durrani power over the frontier grew weak " his quondam vassals in the Indus provinces grew stronger, till one by one each declared himself independent, and began to make war on his neighbour, only to fall an easy prey a few years later to the devouring Sikh. The present century opened with a general scramble for territory. Each group of villages was a little independent state, now warring with its neighbours, now at peace, now gaining and now losing territory. Might was right, and the general law of the land was Islam corrected by assassination. Between 1823 and 1845 the country was every second or third year invaded by a large Sikh army, which harried their fields, trod down their harvests, burnt their houses, and inflicted injuries which it took the intervals of peace to repair." (Thorburn.)

Condition of Bannu before annexation.

42. " Sir Herbert Edwardes thus describes the state of the country in 1847 :—

" The Bannuchis are bad specimens of Afghans. Could worse be said of any human race? They have all the vices of Pathans rankly luxuriant, the virtues stunted. Except in Sindh I have never seen such a degraded people. They are not of pure descent from any common stock, but represent the ebb and flow of might, right, possession and spoliation in a corner of the Kabul Empire, whose remoteness and fertility offered to outlaws and vagabonds a secure asylum against both law and labour. Let the reader take these people and arm them to the teeth; then, throwing them down in the beautiful country I have described, bid them scramble for its fat meads and fertilizing waters, its fruits and flowers; and he will have a good idea of the state of landed property and laws of tenure as I found them in 1847. Owing no external allegiance, let us see what internal government this impatient race submitted to: in truth none. Freed from a king, they could not agree upon a chief, but every village threw a mud wall around its limits, chose its own *malik* (master), and went to war with all its neighbours."

" And Mr. Thorburn says of the same parts :—

" At that time most of the bed of the Indus (now a sheet of splendid cultivation) was a jungle of trees and tiger grass, in which the sportsmen of both banks used to drive pig, hog-deer, and other game. To contrast the difference between 1850 and 1877 in a few words, I may say that since the former year cultivation has more than doubled, population has increased 20 per cent., 7,000 nomadic and mostly pastoral Waziri have grown into 14,000 holding 60,000 acres of cultivated land, and crime has fallen to the level of an orderly district like Shahpur. Instead of one high road 60 miles in length and destitute of bridges, there are now 300 miles of high road with scores of masonry bridges; and finally, instead of a restless suspicious population, there is now a quiet law abiding trustful people, the great mass of which is, I honestly believe, thoroughly loyal."

43. "In Peshawar the state of things was even worse :— *Peshawar, 1800—1849.*

"From 1800 to 1820 Peshawar remained in a state of constant excitement and confusion, passing from one ruler to another, none of whom could exercise much real control over its wild occupants, and the hill tribes transferring their allegiance to the highest bidder."

"The Sikh occupation brought no alleviation :—

"The periodical visits of the Sikhs were calamitous to the people: their approach was the signal for the removal of property and valuables and even of the window and door-frames from the houses; crowds of women and children fled frightened from their houses, and the country presented the appearance of an emigrating colony. As the hated host advanced, they overran the neighbourhood, pillaging and destroying whatever came within their reach, and laying waste the fields. There is scarce a village from the head of the valley to the Indus, which has not been burnt and plundered by the Sikh Commander; his visitations were held in such awe that his name was used by mothers as a term of affright to hush their unruly children; and at the present day, in travelling through the country, old grey beards with many scars point out the hills over which they were chased like sheep by the Singh, and young men show where their fathers fought and fell. Destruction was so certain that the few villages which, from the extreme difficulty of their positions, were either passed by the enemy or, resisting attack, were but partially destroyed, claimed a triumph, and came to be looked upon as invincible.

"But the people of this unhappy country did not enjoy peace, even during the respites which the withdrawal of the Sikhs allowed them; and it is hard to say whether they suffered most from those terrible but passing invasions, or from the bitter feuds which followed them, arising out of hostile acts committed towards each other, either to find favour with the invaders, or to gratify personal feelings of hatred and revenge; for, as is common with people in such a depraved condition, they had no scruple in betraying each other for such purposes, and as spies and informers in bringing the Sikh scourge upon their neighbours with a baseness from which their ancestors would have revolted." One of the terms on which the Chamkanni chief held his tenure of the Sikhs was "the annual production of twenty Afridi heads; and the old man relates without a blush the treacherous methods he was sometimes compelled to adopt to fulfill the conditions of his tenure." (James' Peshawar Report)."

44. At annexation then the country was in a parlous condition. Cultivation, in all but the most inaccessible and least fertile areas, was insecure in the highest degree, not from the vicissitudes of the seasons, but from the cultivator's uncertainty of ever being able to enjoy the proceeds of the crops which he had sown and tended to maturity. The population was thinned by massacre; and that part of it which had not been destroyed was largely a semi-nomadic one, which took refuge periodically in the hills when danger threatened. At the same time the climate is good, the soil fertile, and famine almost unknown. It was only to be expected therefore that the establishment of an organised government and the growth of public security would be followed in no long period by a large increase of population, and the recent political history of the Province is clearly reflected in the results of the various enumerations undertaken up to the year 1891. *Summary.*

45. The notices which I have been able to collect in the foregoing paragraphs as to the conditions affecting the movement of population in the past relate almost exclusively to the British Districts included in the Province. Moreover it was not until the year 1901 that any enumeration was carried out beyond the administrative border; and the trans-frontier census in that year was too partial to afford any ground for a comparison with the population as estimated in connection with the present operations. I will merely glance therefore at the figures for the trans-border area. *No materials available to discuss movement of population in trans-frontier area.*

46. In table II in Part II of this volume will be found a statement of variation of population in the Province since 1881. It will at once be noticed that out of the increase of 267,977 souls shown as having occurred between the years 1891 and 1901, the addition of 83,962 is due to the inclusion of new *Figures for variation from 1881 to 1911.*

areas in the scope of the enumeration of the latter year. Similarly of the enormous increase (1,693,551 persons) exhibited in the results of the present Census, over a million and a half have been added as a result of the inclusion in the figures of an estimate of the population of the whole trans-border area of the Province. More instructive than the figures given in the first line of Table II are those given in line 2, which show variation in British Districts since 1881. No enlargement of the Census area has here to be taken into account; and allowance has been made for differences due merely to changes effected since that year in district boundaries.

Movement of population since 1855.

47. A reference to the opening of the introduction of this Report will show that the emumeration of 1881, though it may be described as the first regular Census of the Province, was not the first to be taken. There were earlier enumerations in 1855 and in 1868. It is impossible to ascertain with absolute accuracy the population in those years of the areas now included in the districts of the Province, for there were changes of boundaries previous to 1881 of which no exact record seems to have been preserved, but allowance has been made for those which can be traced, and the figures printed in the margin may be taken as stating the facts with sufficient accuracy for all practical purposes.

Population of the districts of the Province.

Year.	Population.	Percentage of increase.	
1855	1,144,047	...	...
1868	1,339,566	17	Period 1855-68
1881	1,575,943	17	„ 1868-81
1891	1,857,519	17	„ 1881-91
1901	2,041,534	9	„ 1891-01
1911	2,196,933	7	„ 1901-11
		92	„ 1855-11

Rates of increase at different periods.

48. The enumeration of 1855 is so near in time to annexation that we may accept the figures for that year as representing no large increase over the population when first the districts were taken over from the Sikhs As we have seen, at that period it must have been at a low ebb; and a large increase was only to be expected, as soon as the tranquillity which accompanied a civilized government had had time to show its effects. How large a one occurred between 1855 and 1881 is shown by the fact that, whereas for the whole of the old Punjab, including the districts of the North-West Frontier Province, the increase during this period was one of 24 per cent., for the districts with which we are concerned taken by themselves, it amounted to 37 per cent. The difference in the rates of increase found in the two areas is particularly marked in the latter half of this period, for between the years 1868—1881, the increase in the case of the latter was 17 per cent., as against only 6 per cent. in the case of the former. Still more striking is the fact that the same high rate of increase (17 per cent.) was maintained for the period 1881—1891. Thereafter as the land capable of cultivation was taken up, and the effects of the anarchy of the earlier period subsided, the rate of increase naturally declined, to 9 per cent. for the period 1891—1901, and to 7 per cent. for the period 1901—1911.

Effect of increased accuracy of enumeration.

49. The increase in the population of any given administrative division as brought out by one Census when compared with the one preceding it does not necessarily represent a real increase only. Besides the factor introduced by the inclusion of new areas, which has been allowed for in the figures on which the present discussion is based, we have to consider how far the variation shown is due to more accurate enumeration at each successive Census. In the present case of course the increases are too large to be wholly explicable on any such supposition; but those shown by the earlier enumerations are probably in part to be attributed to this cause. The Censuses of 1855 and 1868 were not carried out with the thoroughness which marked the later operations; in one particular the difference of method was so striking as to deserve special mention here. Instead of recording, as at present, the name of each member of the population separately, the enumerators in those years merely wrote down the number of persons present in each house. It is obvious that the latter method involves far greater chances of error than the former; and, though in one instance at least a district officer writing in 1881 could only explain the figures on the assumption that those of 1868 were exaggerated, the conclusion arrived at by Sir Denzil Ibbetson when he discussed the subject in the Punjab Census Report 1881, was that part of the increase

shown by his figures was due to those for the Census of 1868 being under the mark. Sir Denzil went into the matter in some detail, and in particular it is interesting to notice that he guaged the accuracy of successive Censuses in part by the ratio of females to males which they disclosed, (a topic which will be adverted to in the appropriate portion of this Report); but he was unable to make any calculation to show how much of the growth of population recorded in 1881 was fictitious, and how much was real. At the present day we are perhaps in a somewhat better position to consider the question. It will be noticed that, as they stand, the figures printed in the marginal statement on page 30 show the rate of increase to have been the same for the three periods 1856-68, 1868-81 and 1881-91. The first two are however periods of 13 years each, while the third is a decade only, and the increase is therefore greater in the last period than in the preceding two. This is hardly what would be expected Even assuming that up to the year 1868 the era of anarchy which had preceded annexation was too near to allow of confidence having been fully restored, after that year its memory can hardly have operated to prevent the return of natives who had fled from their homes, or the settlement of immigrants from elsewhere. There was no large extension of irrigation, or any other special cause, in the decade 1881-1891 such as to explain a rate of growth in excess of that for the two intercensual periods which preceded it. Mr. Maclagan, in discussing the question in 1891, remarked that a recognisable part of the increase in Peshawar might be due to more careful enumeration "but not so much probably as in Hazara, where the increase shown by our figures is quite startling." Since the year 1891 there has probably been little improvement in the accuracy of succeeding Censuses. It is true that in the outlying areas of Kohat, for instance, I am assured that even up to the year 1901 it can have been impossible to prepare a correct record. But taking the districts of the Province as a whole, it may be said with confidence that no appreciable portion of the increase shown since 1891 is due to improved enumeration. For the period up to 1891 however it is at least a plausible hypothesis to say that the figures for the earlier Censuses should be increased to show a gradually descending ratio of increase from the year 1868 to that of the present operations.

Conditions during the decade 1901—1911.

State of the Public Health.

50. The causes of the growth of population between the years 1901 and 1911 need to be examined in more detail, and in this connection we must consider the conditions of the decade which elapsed between the two enumerations. In the first place the Province has suffered from no serious outbreak of plague, such as has caused so heavy a mortality elsewhere. In the year 1907-08 there were indeed 2,110 deaths from plague in the Province, but for the remainder of the period the number was trifling. Cholera and small-pox have from time to time caused considerable mortality, (there were 2,845 deaths from cholera in the year 1908); and malaria is always prevalent in the autumn and winter in the trans-Indus districts. But taking the Province as a whole the public health has been good. Some notion of the relative healthiness of the various districts will be afforded by the figures given in columns 4—6 of Subsidiary Table III appended to this Chapter. If we work out the ratio borne to the population at the Census of 1901 by the natural increase of population *i. e.* the excess of births over deaths recorded since that date, we get the figures shown in the margin, (right hand column), which show the inference we may draw from the vital statistics to be that Dera Ismail Khan has been the least, and Hazara and Kohat the most, healthy districts in the Province since 1901; that Bannu falls not far behind the two latter, while Peshawar stands in a little better position than Dera Ismail Khan. It is however perhaps worth noticing here that, except in Hazara and Dera Ismail Khan, the ratio borne by the natural increase to the population of 1901 is by no means the same as the percentage of increase in the actual population as recorded at the two Censuses of 1901 and 1911 (*vide* left hand column of the marginal statement). The conclusion to be drawn from this discrepancy will be found discussed in in paragraphs 54 and 55 below.

District.	*Percentage of increase of population 1901.*	*Ratio borne by natural increase to population of 1901.*
Hazara ...	7	7 per cent.
Peshawar ...	9	4 "
Kohat ...	2	7 "
Bannu ...	10	6 "
Dera Ismail Khan	3	3 "

Agricultural conditions.

51. No conditions resembling those of famine have prevailed in the Province during the decade prior to the present Census, or indeed for a very much longer period. The Province is exceptionally well furnished with irrigation facilities, and where the proportion of irrigated land is small, as in the Hazara and Kohat Districts, the rainfall is comparatively heavy and constant. In this connection a reference should be made to paragraph 10 of Chapter I, and to Subsidiary Table I appended to that chapter. There has been some extension of irrigation during the decade, principally in the Peshawar and Dera Ismail Khan Districts, and the proportion of irrigated land, which represented 25 per cent. of the total cropped area in 1901, was 30 per cent. of the area under crops in 1911.* On the other hand the cultivated area has only increased by 3 per cent. between the years 1901 and 1911.

Extension of irrigation.

Means of communication.

52. Since 1901 means of communication have been improved to a considerable degree, notably in the case of railways. On January 1st, 1901, a line was opened from Nowshera in the Peshawar District to Dargai at the foot of the Malakand Pass, and April 1903 saw the first trains running from Khushalgarh on the Indus to Thall at the entrance to the Kurram Valley. In the same period the trade with Afghanistan has nearly doubled; and this is no doubt in part due to the extension of railway facilities. It is doubtful however how far the increase of trade from Afghanistan and the countries to the west has led to any corresponding growth of prosperity or population in the Province itself. It was observed many years ago that the advent of the railway on the left bank of the Indus had lessened the importance as trade centres of the towns of the Dera Ismail Khan District; and similar causes appear to have had the same effects elsewhere in the Province. The railways have facilitated the carriage of merchandise far into India. It has always been the custom of the Powindah traders from the west to carry their goods to long distances beyond the Indus; the railways have given a greater impetus to this tendency, and while the amount of trade as registered at the frontier stations has largely increased, there has been no corresponding rise in the importance of the markets of the Province; for goods, instead of being sold in them, are carried further and further afield to be disposed of.

Prices of food grains.

53. The prices of agricultural produce have in general been high, but agriculturists, owing to the poverty of means of communication, have been to some extent deprived of access to the Indian markets, and have been unable to profit by the rates prevailing. On the other hand high prices are a hardship to the ordinary labouring classes, who do not themselves own land, and to Government employés dependent on their pay. Indeed the fact that there has been no general distress among the population must be attributed mainly to the wide field for employment offered in the Province. In the previous chapter (paragraph 12) some account will be found of the degree to which the inhabitants of the different districts depend on sources of livelihood other than agriculture. Besides the field found everywhere in the Police, the people have open to them employment in the Frontier Militia Corps, and in the Border Military Police Battalions, of which there is one in each district. Pathans and others are enlisted freely in the army, and the separation of the Province from the Punjab, involving as it has a large increase in the Government establishments maintained at the provincial head-quarters, has widened the field of permanent employment both clerical and menial. Peshawar is the head-quarters of the 1st Division of the army in India, and each of the district head-quarters is also the head-quarters of a Brigade. Besides the opportunities of permanent employment above glanced at, the past decade has offered still wider ones to unskilled labour. The expenditure on Public Works (Roads and Buildings) has been large, averaging 20 lakhs of rupees per annum, and the work done on the Upper Swat River Canal (of which the results in an extension of irrigation have yet to be awaited) has required large numbers of earth workers and others during the last 3 years. The construction of the Paharpur Canal, begun in the year 1904-05, provided employment to many in the southern portion of the Province, and the building of the Kalabagh-Bannu Railway line, which is now proceeding, has also demanded considerable supplies of labour. The same

Employment.

* It should be observed that the figures here given are worked out on the cropped areas of the two years in question, while those given in Subsidiary Table I appended to Chapter I show the ratio borne by the average irrigated area to the average cultivated area for the ten years 1901—1911.

may be said of the Railway construction mentioned in paragraph 52 of this chapter. In fact, speaking of the decade generally, it may be said that the demand for labour has always exceeded the supply. In favourable years it has been necessary to draw on the Punjab for agricultural labourers at harvest time; and if the prices of food grains have been commonly high, the rate of wages has been high also.

54. If the registration of births and deaths were accurate, it is obvious that in order to ascertain the population of a tract at any given time, except in so far as it has been affected by subsequent migration, it would only be necessary to add to or subtract from the results of the previous Census the net gain or loss of population registered in the vital statistics. Unfortunately however the returns can not yet be relied upon to any full extent. In Kagan, in the Konsh and Bhogarmang valleys and in Feudal Tanawal in the Hazara District, registration is not carried out Elsewhere births and deaths are recorded by the village chaukidars, and reported periodically at the local thana. Most of the chaukidars are illiterate, and get their registers writt n up by the patwari, or by a literate lambardar. In these circumstances, even if the people themselves could be trusted to report births and deaths in all cases, there would always be much room for error; but it is notorious that they show no desire to do so. In themselves the vital statistics give rise to doubts as to their accuracy when compared with those of other provinces in India. Both the birth and the death rates are abnormally low. In the year 1910 the death rate for the Province was only 26·9 per thousand; while of other provinces in India the Central Provinces headed the list with 44·9 per thousand, and the lowest death rate was returned by the Bombay Presidency with 30·3 per thousand. Similarly the birth rate was only 38·1 per mille, the only province which fell below it being the Bombay Presidency, with a ratio per thousand of 37·32. The figures for a province in any particular year may of course be due to special circumstances which are not in existence elsewhere; but taken over a series of years the figures for the death rates, and particularly the lowness of the birth rates in the area we are concerned with cannot fail to give rise to suspicion, when compared with those for other provinces in India. If the rate of increase of population in the North-West Frontier Province were low, the fact of the birth rate being low would be easily intelligible, but it will be seen from a reference to Subsidiary Table III printed at the end of this Chapter that the excess of births over deaths is far from accounting for the increase in the population actually enumerated. The increase is not due to a large influx of immigrants, the number of persons born outside the Province having decreased since 1901; nor to any diminution in the number of emigrants. It is true that the population in 1901 of the areas in which registration is carried out amounted to 1,908,184 only, out of 2,041,534 inhabitants of the districts of the Province in that year. But the population of the areas excluded is not sufficient to account for the discrepancy.

Comparison of the result of the census with those shown in the vital statistics. The accuracy of the latter.

55. Considerable attention at various times during the last decade has been given to the question of improving the registration of vital statistics; and the fact that the birth and death rates have steadily risen would suggest that the attempts devoted to this end have met with some measure of success. The annual birth rate recorded has mounted from 29·5 per mille in 1901 to 38·1 per mille in 1910, and the death rate has risen similarly from 19·2 to 26·9. But when it is remembered that the rates are calculated on a fixed figure, that of the population of 1901, whereas in point of fact the population dealt with has been year by year increasing, it will be seen that the improvement is not so rapid as might at first sight appear. And the results of the checking, which has been carried out from time to time, prove clearly how large a proportion of vital occurrences escape record. In the year 1901, following on inspections in various parts of the Province, 17 per cent. of the births and 11 per cent. of the deaths were found not to have been reported. In the year 1909 a similar examination showed that 7·73 per cent. of the births and 4·73 per cent. of the deaths had been left out of the registers; and inquiry made in 1907 in the Peshawar District, with a view to discovering how far the abnormally high ratio of male births recorded corresponded to the actual facts, led to the conclusion that the ratio between male and female births is actually normal, and that the preponderance of male births hitherto observed is attributable to defective registration. In commenting on the registration of births

Results of checking the registration of births and deaths.

for a period as recent as the year 1910 the Chief Medical Officer of the Province could only explain the low ratio shown, as compared with that of other provinces, on the assumption that births are not so accurately recorded here as elsewhere. It will have been noticed, from the remarks made above, that the register of deaths appears to be more complete than that of births, and that female births are left out more often than the birth of boys. No doubt the police are more interested to know the number of persons who leave the world than of those who enter it, and the Pathan, for whatever reason, regards the birth of a daughter as a misfortune, the less said about which the better. Whatever be the cause, births seem to be returned with less regularity than deaths, and it will be at any rate in general conformity with the results arrived at by checking the registers, if we assume that during the decade preceding the Census 10 per cent. of the births and 5 per cent. of the deaths have gone unrecorded, and increase the total accordingly. If we do so, we shall arrive at a figure which agrees closely with the actual increase of population as shown by the enumerations of 1901 and 1911. It will be noticed, from a reference to Subsidiary Table III printed at the end of this Chapter, that it is in Peshawar that the greatest discrepancy is to be found between the excess of births over deaths on the one hand, and the increase of the population as arrived at by enumeration on the other. After commenting on the great difference between the figures, the Deputy Commissioner remarks, "I think there is little doubt however that these figures do not correctly represent the facts. If they were accepted as conclusive, it would be necessary to ascribe the remainder of the increase . . . . . entirely to immigration, and perhaps to more correct enumeration." (No part of the difference, as has been noticed, proves to be due to immigration). "It seems more likely that the fallacy is the result of incorrect registration of births and deaths It is certain that many deaths and a still larger number of births pass unregistered every year."

Growth of population since last Census in individual districts.

56. It remains to consider the variations since 1901 in the populations of individual districts. These are in no degree artificial. We deal with no areas not included in the scope of the operations of 1901, and more accurate enumeration is probably responsible for nothing beyond a trifling part of the increase shown. Subsidiary Table I appended to this chapter gives figures (*vide* column 2) for the percentage of variation in districts and natural divisions during the period with which we are concerned, and the same information is given in pictorial form in the map printed in the margin. It will be noticed that the increase of population has been most rapid in Bannu, and little less so in Peshawar, that in Hazara it has proceeded almost as quickly, while in Kohat and Dera Ismail Khan it has been

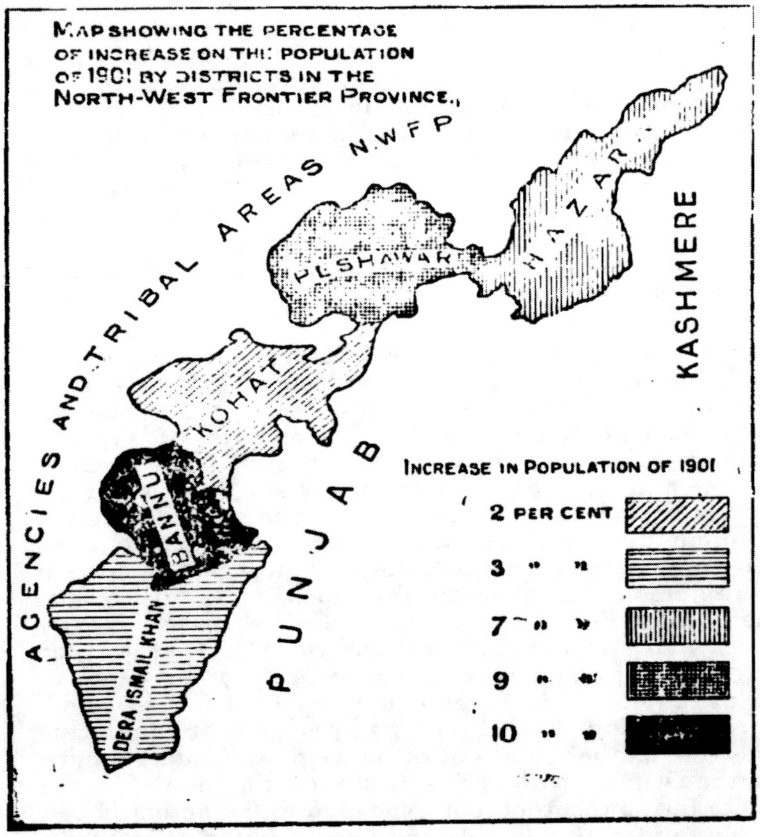

comparatively slow. The first map printed on this page is shaded to show the increase of density since 1901 in each of the districts of the Province. We are here dealing with actual, not proportional increase, and accordingly we do not find the districts falling into the same order as in the former map. Columns 6 to 9 of Subsidiary Table I appended to this chapter show the density for each district and natural division at each of the last four Censuses. It will be seen that Peshawar in this respect stands far above any other district of the Province, and it is no matter for surprise therefore that, while the actual rise in density here is highest, the proportionate increase of population falls below that of Bannu.

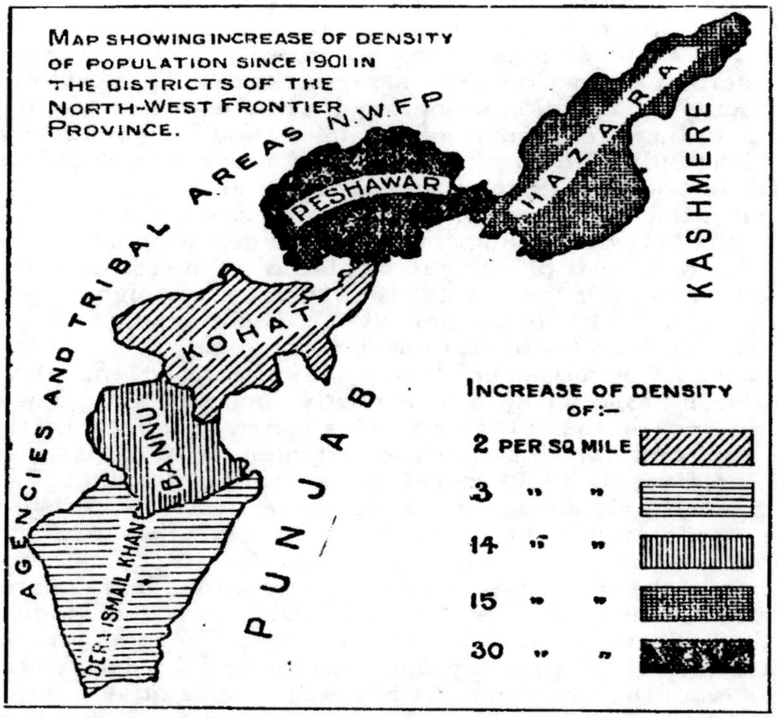

NOTE.—In the reference to the hatchings shown in the above map *for* 2 *read* 1, *for* 3 *read* 2, *for* 15 *read* 19, and *for* 30 *read* 29.

Similar considerations explain the variations between the order of other districts also as shown on the two maps The districts in order of actual increase (for the figures in each case a reference should be made to Table II in Part II of this volume) stand in the same position as when arranged in order of density, except that, though this latter is higher in Kohat than in Dera Ismail Khan, the actual increase of population is less.

Necessity of considering figures for tahsils.

57. In discussing the distribution of population we saw (*vide* Chapter I paragraph 11) that conditions may be widely different in differents parts of one and the same district, and that, in order to consider the question adequately, areas smaller than districts have to be taken into account. In the same way the causes of variation in districts will be clearest, if we deal separately with the figures for the individual tahsils which are included in each. A reference to Provincial Table I at the end of this volume will show the percentage of variation in each of these smaller units; and the map printed in the margin of this paragraph is shaded to give the same information in a form in which it is perhaps more readily intelligible.

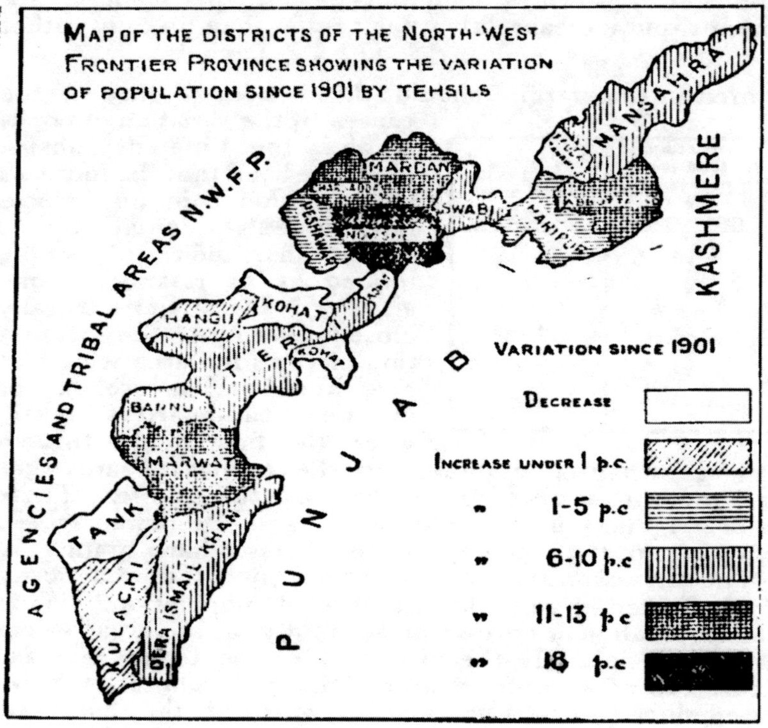

Hazara.

58. I will deal with the districts in their geographical order from north to south. The population of Hazara has increased by 7·6 per cent. since 1901. There is a good deal of variation between different portions of the area. In Feudal Tanawal our figures show a considerable decrease. This is ascribed locally to emigration; but the Deputy Commissioner remarks that "it is probably due still more to the faulty enumeration which was inevitable in a non-settled tract exempt from the ordinary machinery of administration." The revenue establishment, by which the bulk of the work of enumeration was done elsewhere, does not exist in Feudal Tanawal; in these circumstances, and considering the hilly nature of the country, the sparseness of the habitations, and the fact that the time of the present, as of previous, enumerations coincided with that of considerable snowfall, no great reliance is probably to be placed on the result of any Census that has yet been taken. Of the tahsils of the district, the highest proportionate increase is found in the head-quarters tahsil, Abbottabad, (13·6 per cent). Mansehra shows one of 7.8 and Haripur one of 4 per cent. "It is remarkable," says the Deputy Commissioner, "that the increase in the three tahsils . . . . has been proportional to their relative healthiness." There has been a decrease since 1901 in the cultivated and irrigated area both of the Abbottabad and of the Mansehra tahsil, and in the irrigated area of Haripur, where cultivation has however been extended by a trifling amount. The decreases are in part apparent only, being due to the more accurate measurements taken during the recent settlement operations. In part they are due to the stoppage of cultivation within the limits of village forests. The point I would wish to make here is that the increase of population is due in no degree to an increase of cultivation or of protection against drought, from which indeed the district is guarded by its ample rainfall. The difference in the rate of growth between Mansehra and Haripur appears to be mainly due to the difference in the healthiness of the two tracts; while the comparatively rapid growth in the head-quarters tahsil is due, partly to the same cause, and partly to the abnormally rapid growth of the urban population within it. This is to be accounted for mainly by the accidental circumstance that the garrison of Abbottabad has been largely augmented, the population of the Cantonment area having grown, as a reference to Table IV in Part II of this volume will show, from 4,369 in 1901 to 7,503 in 1911, or by 71 per cent.

Peshawar.

59. In Peshawar also the high percentage of increase shown (9·6) is by no means uniform throughout the district. The head-quarters tahsil shows a much lower one (5·5 per cent); Swabi (6·4) stands but little above this latter figure; Charsadda and Mardan have both grown by something over 11 per cent., while in Nowshera we find a more rapid increase (18·1 per cent) than in any other tahsil in the Province.

The statement printed in the margin should throw some light on the causes of the variation of population in the different tahsils. It will be seen that the increase of population is in an inverse ratio to density for all tahsils except Charsadda and Swabi, looked at in relation to one another. Density is naturally closely related to the proportion of the total area which is cultivated in each case, except in the head-quarters tahsil, where the figures are thrown out by the presence of a large urban population; and the cultivated area has increased most, where it forms the smallest proportion of the whole. There has been some extension of irrigation in the Nowshera and Peshawar tahsils during the last ten years, owing to the opening of the Hazar Khani branch of the Kabul River Canal; but the extension is too recent, and the area newly irrigated too small, to have affected largely the growth of population. What our figures do show is that population has grown most rapidly in the areas where there is most room for expansion. In the case of Nowshera the increase is the more marked, because the new Cantonment of Risalpur within it (population 3,167) has been created since last Census, and because of the additions made to the garrison of the Nowshera Cantonment itself, the inhabitants of

Tahsil.	Density 1911.	Increase of population per cent. 1901-11.	Percentage of total area cultivated (average 1901—1911.)	Variation per cent. of cultivated area 1901—1911.
Nowshera ...	193	18·1	26	+ 13
Mardan ...	251	11·7	67	— ·2
Charsadda ...	420	11·5	68	+ ·9
Swabi ...	331	6·4	69	+ 1·1
Peshawar ...	581	5·5	46	+ 5

which have increased from 9,518 in 1901 to 14,543 in 1911. In the head-quarters tahsil I believe that a greater increase might have been looked for, had there not been, for the reasons mentioned in paragraph 23 above, a trifling increase only in Peshawar city; but the population is already too dense to have allowed in any case of an increase similar to that found in Nowshera.

60. The Kohat District as a whole shows a low rate of increase only (2·2 per cent). In the Teri tahsil however it is higher (10·7 per cent.) than we find in the total area comprising the Peshawar or the Hazara District; and our low figure for the district is due to the very small increase in Hangu (·4 per cent.) and the actual decrease of 6·8 per cent. in the head-quarters tahsil. I have not dealt with the influence of migration in the case of other districts, though I have referred, in paragraph 54 above, to its effect on the movement of population in the British territory of the Province taken as a whole; and I do not propose to make more than a passing reference here to a subject which will be discussed in Chapter III. But it is necessary to mention that the variation of population in the Kohat and Hangu tahsils is due, I believe entirely, to the decrease of immigration on the present occasion as compared with 1901. The total immigrants enumerated in the Kohat District have decreased by 45* per cent. since 1901; and the fall has been principally in these two tahsils. In the former the difference is largely due to the absence on the present occasion of the immigrants from the Punjab who were engaged in 1901 on the construction of the Khushalgarh—Kohat railway; and in the latter to the smaller number of nomad graziers from Afghanistan and tribal territory who were enumerated in the tahsil. The land available for graziers from outside the district naturally grows smaller in extent year by year; (for a general statement of the causes which have led to a shrinkage of immigration from the west along the whole length of the Province a reference should be made to the following Chapter) and the decrease need cause no surprise. It has been suggested that the fact that there has been no larger increase of population in the Hangu tahsil is due to emigration, "the large number of men who now leave the valley to work at the docks and in steamships at Bombay, and who enlist in the army." This may be a contributing cause; but, seeing that it is in Hangu that nomad graziers from the west are most numerous, it is clear that the variation in the figures for immigration is the factor chiefly responsible, when it is considered that, if we add to our present population the difference between immigrants enumerated in the district in 1901 and 1911, we get a rate of increase of population of 12 per cent. Extension of cultivation or of irrigation is in no way responsible for differences in the various parts of the district, and neither here, nor elsewhere in the Province have there been within the last 20 years any visitations of disease or famine such as to have left their effects still unexhausted up to the date of the present enumeration. Kohat.

61. We find in Bannu the greatest proportionate increase of population recorded in the Province. Between the two tahsils which make up the district no great variation is to be found. In the head-quarters tahsil, where the density is as high as 307 persons per square mile, we naturally have a smaller proportionate increase (9·1 per cent) than in Marwat (11·9 per cent), where the figure is only 89. At first sight it may appear surprising that the difference between the two tahsils in rate of growth is not larger than it proves to be. The density of Bannu approaches that of the densest areas of the Province, excluding Peshawar and Charsadda, while Marwat is little more thickly inhabited than Dera Ismail Khan; and one might expect that the surplus population of the densely inhabited tahsil would move to vacant areas in the thinly inhabited one. But the larger area (Marwat), owing to the small proportion of it which is protected by irrigation, is not capable of supporting a population proportionate to its size; and accordingly we find a rate of increase but little in advance of that of the smaller and more densely inhabited tract (Bannu). The actual facts are moreover obscured if we regard the total population of each tahsil. The increase in the Bannu tahsil is partly due to the rapid growth (18 per cent.) of the municipal and cantonment areas of Edwardesabad; and if we compare the growth of rural population only in Bannu and Marwat respectively, it will be found that, while the former has grown by 8, the latter has increased by as much as 13 per cent. Bannu.

* The actual figures for immigrants are :—1901, 46,960; 1911, 25,593.

Some attempt must also be made to explain the rapid growth of population in the district as a whole The cultivated area* is larger proportionately than is to be found elsewhere in the Province, except in Peshawar ; and the density being comparatively *low, there is naturally much room for expansion The statement printed in the margin, which shows the density per square mile of cultivated area in the different districts of the Province is not without interest in this connexion. Except Dera Ismail Khan, where cultivation is so much more precarious, and the conditions of life generally are so much harder, no other district in the Province possesses anything like the possibilities of expansion within the present limits of cultivation which are to be found in Bannu. And when it is remembered that in this district the figures of 1901 were increased by, and those of 1911 were decreased by no, accidental causes ; that the climate is on the whole good, and that a considerable proportion of the population consists of sturdy immigrants (Wazirs) recently reclaimed from a nomadic existence, the comparatively rapid growth recorded need be cause for no surprise.

District.		*Density per square mile of cultivated area.*
Hazara	...	898·7
Peshawar	...	607·4
Kohat	...	498·1
Bannu	...	305·3
Dera Ismail Khan	...	297·4

Dera Ismail Khan.

62. In Dera Ismail Khan on the other hand the rate of increase (3·3 per cent.) is but little in advance of that of Kohat. This is accounted for by several reasons. In the first place, as a reference to paragraph 13 above will show, the district is the least healthy of those included in the Province, and the cultivated and irrigated areas (*vide* Subsidiary Table I appended to Chapter I) are low, though both are in excess of the proportion for Kohat. In Kohat however the variation in migration is chiefly responsible for the small rate of increase, whereas the decrease in the number of immigrants to Dera Ismail Khan since 1901 has been trifling (it has been one of 1 per cent. as against 45 per cent. in Kohat). It is to the hardness of the conditions of life generally in the district that we must attribute the fact that in the Dera Ismail Khan tahsil, where the increase of population has been most rapid, it has only amounted to one of 6·3 per cent. or something below the rate for the Province as a whole. In Kulachi it has only been ·3 per cent., and in Tank there has been an actual decrease of 2 per cent. In the latter tahsil the irrigated area has fallen in the last ten years, and the cultivated area has only increased by an inconsiderable amount. In Kulachi, though cultivation has contracted, irrigation has been extended. It is only in the head-quarters tahsil that there has been any substantial increase in cultivation, while, as a result of the construction of the Paharpur Canal, the land which is irrigated has more than doubled. It was not indeed till the year 1907 that the opening of the canal had any marked effect in the extension of irrigation ; but the Deputy Comissioner notes that it "has brought more residents into the tahsil" and that "the people are undoubtedly more prosperous." The comparatively rapid rate of increase which the tahsil shows must be attributed in part also to the fact that it contains within it a cantonment and a municipal area which are responsible between them for 3,394 out of the total of 9,059 persons by which the population of the tahsil as a whole has been increased. The decrease in the population of Tank, it should be noted, is more apparent than real "for the figures of 1901 were inflated by the addition of the troops which were encamped there for the Mahsud Blockade then in progress."

Variation in the natural population.

63. In discussing variations of population up to this point, except for occasional references to migration, I have dealt entirely with the figures for the persons enumerated in the area dealt with, wherever they may have been born. It is perhaps more interesting to compare the natural population, *viz.* that born in the Province or in either of its districts, wherever enumerated, in the years 1901 and 1911, respectively. The effect of doing so will be, of course, to discount the influence of migration. The figures will be found in Subsidiary Table II appended to this chapter. Those for 1901 require a few words of explanation. At the time of the Census of 1901 a large area now forming the Mianwali District of the Punjab was included, partly in Bannu, and partly

* *Vide* Subsidiary Table I, appended to Chapter I.

in Dera Ismail Khan. Persons born in that tract recorded their birth place as being Bannu or Dera Ismail Khan as the case might be, and it was impossible afterwards to distinguish them from persons born within the limits of the two districts as at present constituted.* The result is that the persons shown as emigrants from them are more numerous than in fact was the case, and we have here the explanation of the large apparent decrease in emigration recorded at the present Census which the two districts display. Their natural population, which is obtained by subtracting the immigrants from, and adding the emigrants to, the actual population, was actually therefore smaller in 1901 that it is shown as having been in column 9 of Subsidiary Table II, and the growth of natural population in the last ten years has been more rapid than is suggested in column 10 of the same table. If we assume that emigrants from the districts as at present constituted were no more numerous in 1901 than in 1911 (and in point of fact they were probably fewer), we get a percentage of increase of 11·6 in Bannu and one of 4·1 in Dera Ismail Khan. This probably corresponds fairly nearly with the actual facts. The statistics for the trans-Indus districts as a whole, and for the total area of British territory included in the Province, are of course also affected, though to a far less degree, by the changes of area which I here refer to.

64. The figures in Subsidiary Table II, read in the light of these remarks, bring out the fact that in the Province as a whole (British territory), and in each of the districts within it, the growth of the natural population has been considerably greater than the increase in the number of persons actually enumerated therein. Regarded from this point of view Kohat, instead of the smallest, shows the largest proportionate increase. The relative positions of Peshawar and Hazara remain the same. Bannu, which stands above them in growth of actual, falls below them when the variation in the natural, population is regarded; while in Dera Ismail Khan the expansion recorded is much the same whichever set of figures be taken as the basis of comparison. The figures render still more marked the discrepancy between the natural increase of population as recorded by the vital statistics on the one hand and by the Census on the other. In Peshawar, where the divergence is most marked, the excess of recorded births over deaths amounts to little more than one-third of the increase of natural population as elicited from the census results. In Bannu and Dera Ismail Khan on the other hand the registration figures are in excess of those obtained by enumeration; but those latter, as I explained in the previous paragraph, must be increased before it is likely that they will correspond with the actual facts. The two sets of statistics are in fact irreconcilable for any area included in the Province.

65. The increase of population throughout the Province is to be attributed entirely to natural expansion, *i.e.* to the excess of births over deaths. General conclusions.
No areas have been affected by famine or plague since 1901, and none show the later effects of abnormal circumstances of a similar nature. The increase of natural population† (*i.e.* the population born in the North-West Frontier Province, wherever enumerated) has been greater than the increase of the actual population enumerated in the Province, immigration having decreased in the various districts as shown in the margin, while there has been no corresponding fall in the number of emigrants. Subsidiary Table IV, appended to this Chapter shows that except for the most sparsely inhabited areas in the trans-Indus districts, where the small population already in existence is due to the same causes as prevent its rapid expansion, the increase of population has been in an inverse ratio to the density of the area concerned. The effects of an extension of irrigation are seen in the growth of population in the Dera Ismail Khan and Nowshera tahsils, in both of which it is far in advance of other tahsils of the same district. The small proportionate increase is due, in the Dera Ismail Khan District, to the unhealthiness of the climate and the hard conditions of life prevailing there, and in Kohat to the notable decrease in immigration which our figures show. It should be noted that in Dera Ismail Khan

District.	*Variation per cent. in immigration* 1901—1911. *Increase* (+), *Decrease* (—).
Hazara ...	—13
Peshawar ...	—13
Kohat ...	—45
Bannu ...	—7
Dera Ismail Khan ...	—1

* Where allowance can be, it has been, made, *i.e.* persons enumerated in Mianwali who showed their birth district as Bannu or Dera Ismail Khan have been shown as native to Mianwali and not as immigrants.

† *Vide* Subsidiary Table III appended to this Chapter.

also (*vide* paragraph 62 above), the population has actually grown faster than our figures suggest, those of 1901 in this district also having contained a number of troops camped at Tank in connexion with the Mahsud Blockade. The comparatively slow growth of Hazara, as compared with both Peshawar and Bannu, in spite of the fact that it is a healthier district than either, is due to extensive emigration, and to the fact that the district contains no large centres of trade to attract immigrants in large numbers from elsewhere.

Future growth of population.

66. Although the density in the Peshawar and Charsadda Tahsils of the Peshawar District is high (581 and 420 persons respectively per square mile), nowhere in the Province can there be said to be overcrowding, such as seriously to restrict the growth of population in the next 20 years. On the other hand increasing density means a decreasing rate of growth; and a reference to Subsidiary Table I, appended to this Chapter, shows that in every district of the Province the percentage of increase has been lower at the end of each decennium than at the end of the one preceding it. Other things being equal then we may expect in 1921 to find that the population has increased at a rate lower, but not much lower than that for the decennium 1901—1911. This would certainly seem to be the case in regard to Hazara and Bannu. In these two districts there has not been in the immediate past, nor is there to be expected in the immediate future, any alteration of circumstances such as materially to affect the movement of population.

(*a*) in Hazara and Bannu.

A reference should perhaps be made here to the railway now under construction from Khushalgarh on the Indus to Bannu, with an eventual extension to Pezu and Tank. Whatever strategic and educational value such a railway may possess, and it may be expected to be considerable, railway construction has not in the past been found to lead to that immediate expansion of population in the Province, which might at first sight be expected from it. I have already noticed (*vide* footnote to paragraph 22 above), the effect on the towns of Dera Ismail Khan of the bringing of the railway to points not far distant from them. The building of a railway to Kohat has not resulted in any increase in the population of the Kohat municipal area or cantonment, and the line built ten years ago to connect Dargai and Nowshera in the Peshawar district, a line which passes through Mardan, has brought no access of population to the cantonment* at the last mentioned place. The Province possesses no great purchasing power; and the trade which is to be found within it is largely a transport one. The chief result of improved communications' from this point of view, is to transfer the marts further to the east; and past experience therefore does not suggest tnat any great access of population is to be looked for in the near future in the Bannu District as a result of railway construction within it.

(*b*) in Dera Ismail Khan.

67. In Dera Ismail Khan on the other hand we may expect a larger proportional increase of population at next Census than we have found at the present one. The increase of irrigation in the head-quarters tahsil should by then be beginning to show its full effects, and as the population of the other tahsils enumerated on the present occasion has been swollen by none other than the usual periodic immigrants, the figures for variation should not be affected as they have been on the present occasion by this cause. In Kohat similarly the percentage of increase may be expected to be larger on the next than on the present occasion, seeing that no extraordinary immigration has added to our present figures. It may be noted however that the periodic immigration from Afghanistan and tribal territory shows in all districts a tendency to diminish, and it is of course impossible to say how much this will influence the results of future Censuses.

(*c*) in Kohat.

(*d*) in Peshawar.

68. The population born outside the Peshawar District fell from 106,854 persons in 1901 to 92,601 on the present occasion. The decrease in the numbers of immigrants from the west, which was noticed in 1901 also, may be expected to continue; and the density in the Peshawar and Charsadda tahsils is already high enough to seem to preclude the expectation of any rapid rise in the future. Nevertheless in the district as a whole I believe we may expect a larger growth to be recorded at the end of the present decennium than has

* The Notified Area of Mardan was not classed as a town in 1901 and we have no figures with which to compare its population in 1911.

been witnessed by that which is just over. The construction of the Hazar Khani branch of the Kabul River Canal has already considerably increased the area of irrigated land in the Peshawar and Nowshera tahsils; and its effects on population, when ten years have passed, should be far more noticeable than they are at present. A far more important undertaking however is the construction of the Upper Swat River Canal, which will result within the next few years in the bringing under irrigation of a large additional tract of land in the Mardan and Swabi tahsils, and may be expected to lead to a corresponding expansion in the Census figures. The full effects of the work will no doubt not be felt by the time of the next Census, for the new irrigation can then only have been in operation at the most for a short time; but eventually they must be striking. The population of the Peshawar municipal area was indeed found to be almost stationary on a comparison of the enumerations of 1901 and 1911, but this was due to unusual circumstances, for on account of which a reference should be made to paragraph 23 (Chapter I). The urban areas, other than cantonments, of the Peshawar district taken as a whole also show no sign of rapid increase, but the growth which may be expected in the rural population should be sufficient to make up for a comparatively slow increase among the dwellers in towns.

SUBSIDIARY TABLE I.—*Variation in relation to density since 1881.*

District and Natural Division.	Percentage of variation Increase (+), Decrease (—).			Percentage of net variation 1881 to 1911.	Mean density per square mile.			
	1901 to 1911.	1891 to 1901.	1881 to 1891.		1911.	1901.	1891.	1881.
1	2	3	4	5	6	7	8	9
N.-W. F. P. Total Districts ...	**+7·6**	**+9·9**	**+17·9**	**+39·4**	**164**	**152**	**138**	**117**
Hazara	+7·6	+8·5	+26·8	+48·1	207	188	173	136
Trans-Indus Districts ...	**+7·6**	**+10·4**	**+14·7**	**+36·4**	**152**	**142**	**129**	**112**
Peshawar	+9·6	+10·8	+17·1	+42·4	332	303	273	233
Kohat	+2·2	+11·6	+11·6	+27·4	82	81	72	65
Bannu	+10·3	+10·9	+11·8	+36·9	149	135	122	109
Dera Ismail Khan	+3·3	+7·8	+12·8	+25·7	74	72	66	59

SUBSIDIARY TABLE II.—*Variation in natural population.*

District and Natural Division.	Population in 1911.				Population in 1901.				Variation per cent (1901-1911) in natural population. Increase (+) Decrease (—).
	Actual population.	Immigrants.	Emigrants.	Natural population.	Actual population.	Immigrants.	Emigrants.	Natural population	
1	2	3	4	5	6	7	8	9	10
N.-W. F. P. Total Districts ...	**2,196,933**	**184,504**	**64,591**	**2,077,020**	**2,041,534**	**215,860**	**56,838**	**1,882,512**	**+10·3**
Hazara	603,028	18,009	27,844	612,863	560,288	20,820	22,007	561,475	+9·2
Trans-Indus Districts ...	**1,593,905**	**170,073**	**38,224**	**1,462,056**	**1,481,246**	**200,377**	**40,465**	**1,321,334**	**+10·6**
Peshawar	865,009	92,601	24,144	796,552	788,707	106,854	20,293	702,146	+13·4
Kohat	222,690	25,593	8,109	205,206	217,865	46,960	9,494	180,399	+13·8
Bannu	250,086	18,627	5,510	236,969	226,801	20,061	13,895	220,635	+7·4
Dera Ismail Khan	256,120	42,068	9,277	223,329	247,873	42,608	14,664	219,929	+1·5

NOTE 1.—The term "actual population" means the population actually present at the time of the Census irrespective of birthplace. "Natural population" means the population born in the district, irrespective of the place of enumeration.

2.—Owing to changes of area since the Census of 1901 the figures shown in column 8 **are only approximately correct.**

SUBSIDIARY TABLE III.—*Comparison with vital statistics.*

District and Natural Division.	In 1901—1910, total number of Births.	Deaths.	Number per cent. of population of 1901 of Births.	Deaths.	Excess (+) or deficiency (—) of births over deaths.	Increase (+) or decrease (—) of population of 1911 compared with 1901 Natural population.	Actual population.
1	2	3	4	5	6	7	8
N.-W. F. P. Total Districts ...	**679.069**	**559,016**	**35·6**	**29·3**	**+120,053**	**+194.508**	**+155,399**
Hazara	184,721	141,958	39·1	30·1	+42,763	+51,388	+42,740
Trans-Indus Districts ...	**494.348**	**417,058**	**34·6**	**29·1**	**+77.290**	**+140,722**	**+112,659**
Peshawar	243,150	208,515	32·3	27·7	+34,635	+94,406	+76,302
Kohat	79,175	63,123	38·6	30·8	+16,052	+24,807	+4,825
Bannu	85,157	66,079	37·5	29·1	+19,078	+16,334	+23,285
Dera Ismail Khan	86,866	79,341	34·9	31·9	+7,525	+3,400	+8,247

NOTE.—The percentage of births and deaths in columns 4 and 5 respectively has been worked out on the population of 1901 shown in the Sanitary Administration Report 1910, as being under registration of births and deaths.

SUBSIDIARY TABLE IV.—*Variation by tahsils classified according to density.—(a) actual variation.*

Natural Division.	Decade.	Variation in tahsils* with a population per square mile at beginning of decade of Under 150.	150—300	300—450	450—600
1	2	3	4	5	6
Total Districts N.-W. F. P. ...	1881—1891	+146,445	+95,121	+48,183	...
	1891—1901	+70,042	+82,187	+31,786	...
	1901—1911	+38,831	+77,428	+25,559	+13,581
Hazara	1881—1891	+50,640	+58,573	...	...
	1891—1901	+17,084	+26,916	...	...
	1901—1911	+14,316	+28,424	...	...
Trans-Indus Districts	1881—1891	+95,805	+36,548	+48,183	...
	1891—1901	+52,958	+55,271	+31,786	...
	1901—1911	+24,515	+49,004	+25,559	+13,581

(b).—Proportionate variation.

Natural Division.	Decade.	Variation per cent. in tahsils* with a population per square mile at beginning of decade of Under 150.	150—300	300—450	450—600
1	2	3	4	5	6
Total Districts N.-W. F. P. ...	1881—1891	+18·7	+20·1	+15·6	...
	1891—1901	+10·4	+9·9	+8·9	...
	1901—1911	+5·2	+10·2	+8·9	+5·5
Hazara	1881—1891	+34·6	+22·5	...	...
	1891—1901	+10·3	+7·7	...	...
	1901—1911	+7·8	+7·5	...	...
Trans-Indus Districts	1881—1891	+15·1	+17·1	+15·6	...
	1891—1901	+10·1	+11·7	+8·9	...
	1901—1911	+4·4	+12·8	+8·9	+5·5

* For the purposes of this Table Feudal Tanawal in the Hazara District has been treated as a tahsil.

CHAPTER III.

BIRTH-PLACE.

Scope of the chapter and reference to statistics.

69. The degree to which the variation of population in different parts of the Province has been affected by migration has been indicated in the previous chapter. In the present one I propose to consider the second point of view from which the statistics of birth-place are of interest, *viz.* as showing the extent to which the people move from one part of the country to another. The figures on which the discussion is based will be found in Table XI in the second part of this volume, and in the subsidiary tables appended to this chapter. These are as follows :—

(*i*) Showing the actual numbers of immigrants (in hundreds) under a few main groups of birth-places.

(*ii*) Showing similar details for emigrants.

(*iii*) Showing proportionate migration to and from each district and natural division of the Province.

(*iv*) Showing migration, as compared with 1901, between districts and natural divisions.

(*v*) Showing migration between the Province and other parts of India in 1911 and 1901.

Figures for British districts only to be discussed.

70. In discussing the subject I will confine my remarks to the figures for the migrants to and from the British districts ; for, with regard to the areas outside them, the information I possess is so scanty that any conclusions based upon it would be misleading. The distribution by birth-place of the occupants of British posts, who alone were enumerated of the population beyond the administrative frontier, is not typical either of that of the trans-frontier area as a whole, or of the British territory included in the Province. In the first three subsidiary tables appended to this chapter the figures will be found therefore to refer to the British districts only. There is a good deal of periodic migration from Afghanistan into tribal territory, (notably into the Kurram Valley) but from British districts, with the exception of a certain number of persons who are to be found in trans-frontier posts, there can be into this area practically none at all.

Five types of migration—(*a*) Casual.

71. Five different types of migration have been recognised in India. In the first place there is that of the casual type, or the minor movements between adjacent villages, which only affect the birth-place statistics when the villages in question happen to lie on different sides of a district or provincial boundary.

(*b*) Temporary.

Secondly we have temporary migration, such as journeys on business, visits to places of pilgrimage, movements in response to passing demands for labour, and the like.

(*c*) Periodic.

The third type may be described as periodic, and includes the annual migration which takes place in different tracts at harvest time, and the seasonal movements of pastoral nomads.

(*d*) Semi-permanent.

Finally we have two varieties which have been distinguished as semi-permanent and permanent respectively. The former is exemplified by the natives of one place, who live and earn their living in another, retaining all the time their connection with their own homes, where they leave their families, and to which they return in their old age and at more or less regular intervals in the meantime.

(*e*) Permanent.

Permanent migration occurs where overcrowding drives people away, or the superior attractions of some area outside that of their birth induces persons to settle there.

72. It has been usual in Indian Census literature to base conclusions on the question as to which of the types mentioned above any particular stream of migration represents largely on the proportion of females to males which the figures exhibit, females being usually in excess in movements of the casual, and males in those of the temporary, periodic and semi-permanent type, while permanent migrants are generally found to contain fairly equal proportions of the two sexes The sex proportions undoubtedly furnish a valuable guide as to the character of the migrants to or from any particular area; but they can not always be relied upon. Immigrants from Asiatic countries beyond India contain very different sex proportions in Hazara and in Dera Ismail Khan; for whereas among those in the former district females are only one-fifth of the males, among those in the latter they amount to four-fifths. Yet the one stream of migration is no more permanent than the other; in fact, seeing that among the Hazara immigrants shown under this head the bulk are Gurkha sepoys belonging to regiments permanently located in Abbottabad, while the Dera Ismail Khan figures refer to Powindahs, who visit the Province for a few months only, the immigration to the former district approaches more nearly to the permanent type than does that to the latter.

Proportion of the sexes as an indication of the character of migration.

73. As a reference to Subsidiary Table III will show, numerically the immigrants are of far greater importance than the emigrants in the case of the North-West Frontier Province. The former amount to 8·4 per cent. of the total population of the districts as a whole; but this comparatively low figure is due to the fact that the volume of immigration into Hazara is small. In the trans-Indus districts 10·6 per cent. of the total population were born outside the area dealt with; and in Dera Ismail Khan the foreign born amounted to as much as 16·4 per cent. of the inhabitants.

Extent of migration.

74. In Subsidiary Table I, the birth-places of immigrants to British territory are shown under a few main heads. The largest stream *(54,400 persons) comes from the trans-frontier area of the Province. From countries outside India (mainly Afghanistan) comes a slightly smaller volume, (52,000 persons), though larger from that proceeding from other provinces and states of India, excluding areas contiguous to the North-West Frontier Province, (44,100); and lastly are shown the 33,900 souls enumerated in the districts of the Province, and born in areas (Kashmir and portions of the Punjab) contiguous to them.

Directions from which immigrants come.

75. It will be seen therefore that immigrants from the west (*i. e.* from Afghanistan and the tribal territory immediately to the east of it) amount to more than all the others put together; and it will be suitable to consider these first. The stream of migration with which we are here concerned belongs almost entirely to the periodic type; and the results of a Census taken in the summer would be widely different from that of enumerations undertaken, as the last four have been, before the close of the cold weather, and the return of the migratory population to their summer homes. There have occurred permanent or semi-permanent settlements of immigrants from the tribal (trans-frontier) area, of which the most recent on a large scale has been that of the Wazirs in Bannu. In fact all up and down the frontier the establishment of settled government has been followed by a considerable degree of permanent immigration from the west. But as the land available has been taken up, and the population within the Province itself has increased, this stream of migration has gradually slackened; and it is probable that it accounts for but few of those who have recorded their birth-place as *Yaghistan* at the present Census. Such settlers, the numbers of whom must always have been trifling when compared with the periodic immigrants who will presently be described, must by now nearly all have died, and their places have been taken by descendants born in British territory. The very causes which have led to a decrease in the number of the permanent settlers, if not to their actual disappearance, have also caused a shrinkage in the numbers of certain classes among the periodic immigrants.

Immigration from Afghanistan and the trans-frontier territory of the Province.

These latter may be divided roughly into four main groups. The first consists of the carriers between Peshawar and Kabul. Of these are made up the *Kafilas* (caravans) which pass through the Khyber in both directions twice

Immigrants from the west fall into four groups. (*a*) Carriers between Kabul and Peshawar.

* In this paragraph, as in Subsidiary Table I, the figures given are in round hundreds.

a week. Seeing however that they do not, like the other groups which will be mentioned, pass the winter in British territory, but spend it in journeys to and fro, they do not affect to any great extent the population of the Province.

(b) Winter labourers.

The second group consists of labourers who come down to the districts of the Province for the winter, mainly by the Khyber, Kurram (Peiwar Kotal) and Gomal routes. Well known types of these are the Hazara coolies from the mountainous country west of Kabul, and Mohmands from the hills which flank the Peshawar Valley. Though they are to be found all along the frontier, they have been enumerated in the greatest numbers in Peshawar. The next group we have to consider is that which includes the Powindah traders, who enter the Province principally by the Gomal route. They are met with in greatest numbers in the Dera Ismail Khan District. The following account of them is derived from G. Oliver's '*Across the the border, or Pathan and Biloch,' 1890.

(c) The Powindahs.

76. "Every cold weather strings of camels laden with merchandise from Bokhara and Afghanistan find their way through this pass" (the Gomal); "and scatter through the length and breadth of India; and, as summer approaches, return to the cooler highlands, carrying back in exchange either cash or goods for distribution as far as the Persian and the Russian borders; their owners a border people of considerable importance. Not so much by his fruits, is the Afghan merchant known in every Indian bazaar, as by his strange appearance, his great stature, physical strength, and rude independence of manner. It is not necessary to see him to be fully conscious of his presence. The "rankest compound of villanous smells" pervades the atmosphere through which he passes. "His loose untidy dress," as Bellew describes him, "generally in a state of dirt beyond the washerman's cure, and often covered with a shaggy sheepskin coat, travel-stained and sweat-begrimed to an extent that proclaims the presence of the wearer to the nostrils though he be out of sight in the crowd; his long unkempt and frayed locks, loosely held together by some careless twists of a coarse cotton turban, soiled to the last degree, if not tattered, also add to the wildness of his unwashed and weather-worn features, whilst his loud voice and rough manners complete the barbarian he is proud to pass for. Such is the common Powindah as seen in the bazaar." The term *powindah*, possiblly from *parwindah*, the Persian for a bale of goods, is the collective name of all the migratory Pathans who engage in the carrying trade, in fact monoplise all the trade between Central Asia, Afghanistan, and India. ....Assembling every year in the plains of Zermut or Katawaz, east of Ghazni, with their families, flocks, herds, and droves rather than herds of camels, the clans combine and march in enormous caravans, often numbering several thousands of fighting men, disposed in military order against the attacks of the Waziris, Kakars, and other Border tribes through whose territory they have very often to literally fight their way: the mass of them by the Gomal pass."

(d) Graziers.

77. The Powindahs no longer fight their way into India. In their passage through the difficulties of the Gomal route they are now protected by escorts furnished by the Southern Waziristan Militia, just as the caravans going up and down the Khyber are protected; and beyond the limits of the Wana Agency to the east the country is open and free from opportunities for attack. It is to be noticed that the Powindahs are partly merchants and partly graziers, and, in so far as they enter the Province in the latter capacity, are hardly to be distinguished from the fourth group into which the periodic immigrants from the west are to be divided. These last, the majority of whom dwell during the summer in the hilly country which makes up the trans-frontier area of the Province, consist exclusively of graziers, who wander to the lowlands in the cold weather in search of pasture. They are to be found in all the trans-Indus districts, but principally in Peshawar and Kohat.

Immigrants from Afghanistan in districts separately.

78. The proportions in which members of the various groups described are to be found in the districts of the Province will be clearest if we consider separately the figures for each district. 42,480 persons in the Province returned their birth-place as Afghanistan. Just under one-half, or 21,060, of these were enumerated in Dera Ismail Khan, 15,973 were enumerated in Peshawar, Bannu returned just over three, and Kohat just under two, thousand, while the figures for Hazara and for trans-frontier posts are inconsiderable.

* pp. 78 following.

Dera Ismail Khan.

79. Our figures for Dera Ismail Khan refer almost entirely to the Powindahs described above, who commonly enter the Province accompanied by their families, as is shown by the fact that among them the females amount to as much as 80 per cent. of the males. This figure hardly represents, however, the proportion of the sexes among them at their first entry into British territory. Many of the men commonly travel far into India to trade, leaving women and children, with their flocks and herds, encamped for the cold weather in Dera Ismail Khan.

In other districts.

In the other districts the population we are dealing with consists principally of winter labourers, reapers, earth workers, and the like. These, as our figures show, are especially numerous in Peshawar; they are in the majority of cases unaccompanied by their women, and the proportion of females to males is accordingly much lower, being 49 per cent. in Peshawar and 41 and 51 per cent., respectively in Kohat and Bannu. It is to be noted that in every district the numbers who returned their birth-place as Afghanistan are probably considerably less than the numbers who live for a portion of the year at least under the jurisdiction of the Amir. As long ago as the year 1881 the number of persons in Dera Ismail Khan who returned their birth-place as Afghanistan was found to be far less than the number of Powindahs, who, as a result of a special check kept at the passes, were known to have entered the district in the Census year. The discrepancy was accounted for by the fact that, as the annual migration was no new thing, the caravans contained many persons who were born in British territory during their parents' sojourn there; and for the same reason a return of persons who live for part of the year in Afghanistan or tribal territory would be considerably larger than the statistics, obtained at the recent Census, of immigration from the two areas.

Immigration from the trans-frontier area of the Province.

80. The immigrants from the trans-frontier area of the Province, the Yaghistan of the last Census, are considerably more numerous than those from Afghanistan. The total number enumerated was 60,166, but of these no less than 5,732 were found in trans-frontier posts, and the number of true immigrants is therefore 54,434. They consist in the main of graziers, who come down annually to the plains in the cold weather, when their upland homes are covered in snow; though some are labourers, carriers and the like, who bring down wood from the hills, and engage in the transport trade of the Province. The greatest number (29,393) was enumerated in Peshawar, just over 12,000 were found in Kohat, and something over 4,000 in each of the other three districts. In many cases they are accompanied by their families, as the sex proportion shows, there being 65 females to every 100 males among the total number enumerated in British territory. The highest proportion of females is found in Kohat, where there are 80 to every 100 males, the proportions of the sexes no doubt being rendered more equal by the fact that it is not unusual for men in the district to take wives from the tribal area. The bulk of the immigration with which we are dealing under this head is, however, purely seasonal.

Immigration from Nepal.

81. In Table XI Afghanistan appears under head (c) Countries in Asia beyond India. The immigration from most of the countries there shown, other than Afghanistan, is trifling in amount, but a passing reference should be made here to that from Nepal. It will be seen that 5,653 persons have returned their birth-place as Nepal, of whom 4,663 were enumerated in Hazara, and 742 in trans-frontier posts. These consist nearly all of males, being sepoys employed in Gurkha regiments stationed at Abbottabad in the Hazara District, and in the Malakand Agency. The figures for Hazara show that a small proportion of these have their wives and families with them.

Immigration from other places.

82. Following the arrangement in Table XI, immigration into the Province may be classified as in the marginal statement. That from the first and third groups of birth-places shown we have already considered. That from other provinces and states in India, and from countries beyond Asia, will be dealt with in the following paragraphs.

Enumerated in the North-West Frontier Province.

Birth-place.	Number.
Agencies and tribal areas, N.-W. F. P.	60,166
Other provinces and states in India ...	82,139
Countries in Asia beyond India ...	48,234
Countries beyond Asia	4,972

(a) Beyond Asia.

The immigration from countries beyond Asia can be dismissed in a few words. It is nearly all from the United Kingdom, and only reaches so high a figure from the fact that British regiments are stationed at Nowshera, and at the head-quarters of the Peshawar District. The immigration from other provinces and states in India needs more careful notice. More than four-fifths of it is from the Punjab, which is natural enough, considering the contiguity of the two provinces, and the fact that the Indian Army is recruited so largely from the Land of the Five Rivers. In a larger province, where cantonments are fewer and further between than is the case in the North-West Frontier Province, this last consideration would hardly be expected to affect to any great extent the statistics of birth-place. But when it is remembered that military service is between fifteen and sixteen times as common proportionately in the North-West Frontier Province as it was in 1901 for India as a whole, it will be seen how much more important from this point of view is the recruiting area in the case of the former than it is in the case of the latter. The immigrants from the Punjab contain a very high proportion of males, the females being only 35 per 100 of the other sex; and even in the case of those districts which are contiguous to the North-West Frontier Province, and from which permanent immigrants, if they came at all, might be expected to find their way, the figure is only 2 per cent. higher. Periodic immigration from the Punjab can be left out of account; and the sex proportions, whether among persons born in contiguous, or among those born in non-contiguous areas, show clearly that the migration we are here concerned with is temporary, or semi-permanent in type. Military service, with its accompanying trains of followers, service of Government in other departments, such as the Post Office and the telegraphs, the service of railways, trade and domestic service are responsible for the presence in the Province of most of the immigrants from the Punjab.

(b) Other provinces and states in India. The Punjab.

Number per mille of total population supported by military service.

India ...	... 1901— 1·2.
N.-W. F. Province ...	1911—18·3.

Other provinces and states in India.

Those from other provinces and states come in insignificant numbers. Domestic service probably brings most of the 4,923 persons returned as born in the United Provinces, and the 4,655 persons, nearly five-sixth of whom are males, shown in Table XI against Kashmir, are for the most part winter immigrants, who find employment annually as agricultural labourers in the Hazara and Peshawar Districts.

Immigration by religion.

83. Column 2 of Subsidiary Table III appended to this chapter shows the ratio per mille borne by the total immigrants to the total population, of the districts of the Province taken separately, and of the natural divisions into which they have been arranged in paragraph 2 of this Report. It is of interest to compare the proportions for all religions with those for Hindus and Sikhs separately (*vide* marginal statement); and, in view of the large proportion of foreign born found among the followers of the two latter religions, I have shown separately in their case the figures for each sex. The statement shows clearly how large a proportion of the Hindus and Sikhs in the Province are birds of passage only; and emphasis is laid on the temporary nature of their sojourn by the fact that female immigrants not only fall below the males in actual numbers, but also bear a lower proportion to the total female population of their religion, small as this is when compared with the male population. Of the total number (184,504) of immigrants enumerated in the districts of the Province, 30,558 are Hindus, and 11,288 are Sikhs. That is to say that the followers of these two religions are jointly responsible for between one-fourth and one-fifth of the total immigration into our area, a high figure when it is remembered that more than half of our immigrants come from the west, where the population is almost exclusively Mohammadan.

Number per 1,000 of actual population of group dealt with who were born outside area shown.

Districts, etc.	All religions both sexes.	Hindus.		Sikhs.	
		M.	F.	M.	F.
Total Districts ...	84	320	159	477	169
Hazara ...	29	361	174	251	97
Trans-Indus Districts	106	313	157	528	191
Peshawar ...	107	481	337	494	181
Kohat ...	114	439	190	857	252
Bannu ...	74	193	63	415	198
D. I. Khan ...	164	141	62	708	344

84. Subsidiary Table V appended to this chapter shows migration between the North-West Frontier Province and other parts of India in 1901 and 1911 respectively. The information thus given needs, however, to be supplemented by the statement (printed in the margin), which compares immigration in the two years from other places, the stream flowing from which is more copious, as we have seen, than that flowing from the areas shown in the Subsidiary Table referred to. The geographical position and political history of the North-West Frontier Province entitle the question of variation in immigration to more consideration than it deserves in other parts of India, and I propose therefore to go into it in considerable detail. Looking at the marginal statement printed against this paragraph and at that given in Subsidiary Table V taken together, it will be seen that immigrants as a whole have decreased from 229,737 persons in 1901 to 195,511 in 1911, or by 15 per cent. Variation in immigration between 1901 & 1911.

Immigration in 1901 and 1911 from Afghanistan, tribal territory, Nepal, etc.

Birth-place.	PERSONS ENUMERATED IN N.-W. F. P.		
	1901.	1911.	Variation.
Afghanistan ...	63,035*	42,480	—20,555
Trans-frontier area, N.-W. F. P.	48,372*	60,166	+11,794
Nepal ...	3,288	5,653	+2,365
Other Asiatic countries ...	5,227	101	—5,126
Countries outside Asia ...	3,952	4,972	+1,020

*These figures are approximate only. It is to be noted that the persons enumerated in the Kurram, which was brought within the scope of the regular enumeration in 1901, but was omitted on the present occasion, have not been included.

85. As the areas from which immigration has increased are few, and the numbers concerned of comparatively small importance, it will be best to deal with these first, thus leaving the remainder, which determine the variation of immigration as a whole, to be considered together. The figures for Nepal and for countries outside Asia can be dismissed summarily. Both depend mainly on the troops stationed within the Province, the Gurkha regiments in the Hazara District, and the British troops in Peshawar having been augmented since 1901. Areas from which immigration has increased.

A more detailed explanation is required regarding the figures for immigrants from the trans-frontier area of the Province. It will be seen from the note printed below the marginal statement against paragraph 84 that the figures for 1901 are approximate only. In the Punjab Census Report of that year, immigrants from Afghanistan and Yaghistan are shown together, and we have no guide as to their distribution between these two areas beyond the information contained in a footnote to Table XI, which is to the effect that, out of the total persons shown under this head, 3·3 per cent. only (the actual figures are given) were born in Yaghistan. All that can be done therefore is to assume that the same proportion holds good for the North-West Frontier Province taken by itself; and the proof that the figures obtained on such an assumption are not likely to be below the true numbers for Yaghistan is furnished by the fact that, even if we attribute to the North-West Frontier Province the whole of the immigrants from tribal territory, who are shown as having been enumerated in that province plus the Punjab, the figure only amounts to 3·9 per cent. of the immigrants from Afghanistan plus Yaghistan who are shown as enumerated in our Province. But the immigrants from tribal territory in 1901, as shown in the marginal statement printed against paragraph 84, amount to very much more than 3·3 per cent. of the immigrants from Afghanistan plus Yaghistan in that year. The balance is made up of persons who are classified in Table XI, Punjab Census Report, 1901, as born in 'Asia part unspecified.' From a reference to the text of the Report it appears that the persons who returned their birthplace as *mulk-i-ghair, ghair ilaqa* or some similar entry, were thus exhibited. There can be little reasonable doubt that entries of the nature quoted referred to tribal territory, and I have accordingly shown them under that head. At the same time it is conceivable that some of them were Afghan subjects, and, in any case, we can not discriminate with certainty, as to the distribution of the population credited to 'Afghanistan and Yaghistan.' Still the figures, though frankly an approximation, are accurate enough for our purpose. Uncertainty of figures for 1901 for tribal area.

86. We have then to explain an increase of 11,794 persons (24 per cent.) since 1901 in the number of immigrants from the tribal territory to the west. At first sight this looks startling, when accompanied by so marked a shrinkage in Variation in immigration from tribal territory.

immigration from elsewhere, and in particular when accompanied by a decrease in the number of persons who returned their birth-place as Afghanistan. When we look, however, at the figures for individual districts, the apparent anomaly disappears. It is only in the three southern districts of the Province that the figures are larger now than ten years ago.* In Bannu and Dera Ismail Khan the number of immigrants from tribal territory was negligiable in 1901, whereas it is now 8,651 ; and in Kohat the figures have risen in the same period from under 5,000 to 12,071. Here we have an obvious result of the Mahsud Blockade operations which were being undertaken at the time of the Census of 1901. They were directed against the very tribes who furnish a large proportion of the winter immigrants from tribal terriory to these districts. Bannu and Dera Ismail Khan they found it impossible to enter, and, though the line of the blockade did not extend along the Kohat border also, the district is close enough to the scene of the operations for the figures for immigration to be largely affected by it. On the other hand the Powindah caravans from Afghan territory were not apparently interfered with (there was indeed no reason why they should be) ; and, as we shall see when the place comes to discuss immigration from Afghanistan, there is no great difference in the figures for the two years we are now considering. But coming to the Hazara and the Peshawar Districts, which were far enough from the scene of the blockade to be uninfluenced by it, we find a very different state of things. In the former district the figures have sunk from 5,368 in 1901 to 4,319 on the present occasion, and in the latter to 29,393 from over 36,000. The cause of the decrease will be considered in the course of the discussion of the figures for Afghanistan.

Variation in immigration from Afghanistan.

87. Immigration to the Province from Afghanistan has decreased since 1901 by 33 per cent. Here too, as is evident from the remarks above on the subject of immigration from tribal territory in 1901, we can not be quite certain of our figures for the earlier year; but they are correct enough for all practical purposes. The decrease is not found equally in the various districts of the Province. The figures for Dera Ismail Khan will be reverted to presently, but, taking them as they stand, we get an increase of some 1,000 souls there returned as born in Afghanistan. In Bannu the figures have fallen from over 7,000 to 3,077, in Kohat from about 16,000 to 1,954, in Peshawar from something over 19,000 to 15,903, and in Hazara from about 700 to 99.

The figures for Kohat in the year 1901, I confess, I can not understand. Immigration from Afghanistan into Kohat in 1891 amounted to 3,714 souls ; and I know of no reason why it should suddenly have increased by some 400† per cent. ten years later. The decreases since 1901 elsewhere are smaller, and not, I think, incapable of explanation. It should in the first place be premised that the figures for Afghan immigrants depend very largely on the Powindah migration, and that this is governed to a great extent by the quality of the pasture available in Afghanistan in any particular year. I have made enquiries regarding agricultural conditions in Afghanistan in the months preceding the enumerations of 1901 and 1911, respectively. For the most part no comparison is possible, as no record seems to have been kept regarding the earlier period. The Political Agent, Malakand, however, writing of his Agency and the part of Afghanistan which adjoins it, remarks that the harvests in those tracts were bad in 1900-1901, and good in 1910-11. We have here one reason for a decreased immigration into the Peshawar District ; and, if the area of which the Political Agent, Malakand, is writing may be taken as typical of the conditions in Afghanistan generally in the two years, one reason for decreased immigration from that country all along the frontier ; for a poor harvest, and in particular a poor quality of grazing, drives the trans-frontier tribesmen in large numbers into British territory.

88. But though variations in the agricultural conditions prevailing in any two years naturally affect largely the immigration from the area we are considering, in comparing the figures for ten years ago with those of the present enumeration, we have to take into account other considerations also. Quite apart from the quality of the grazing in the areas from which they come, the number of winter immigrants to the Province from Afghanistan has shown during the last few years a tendency to decrease.‡

---

* The figures will be found in Subsidiary Table IV printed at the end of this chapter.

† Immigrants in connection with the building of the Khushalgarh—Kohat Railway could not have accounted for so large an increase.

‡ For the greater part of the information contained in the following paragraphs on the subject of immigration from Afghanistan and tribal territory I am indebted to K. B. Sahibzada Abdul Qaiyum, C. I. E., Assistant Political Agent, Khyber.

In the first place it is generally believed that Afghans are happier and more prosperous at home under the present Amir than under the regime of Amir Abdur Rahman. The rule of the former is milder than was that of his father, and exile for political offences or for non-payment of revenue is now comparatively rare. One result of the succession of the present ruler in 1901 has been therefore that, since that date, no Afghan subjects, or comparatively few, have sought a refuge in British territory; so far is this from being the case that many who were already here have returned to their homes. About a year after his accession the present Amir issued a proclamation recalling exiles to their homes. Copies of it came into the hands of the British authorities in the Khyber; and many persons availed themselves of the permission to return. They were seen in large numbers going westward through the Khyber. Not only this; but emigration from Afghanistan is now definitely discouraged. Passports have to be taken out by all but the migratory classes (Powindahs and Kuchis), and these, since they are not easy to obtain, furnish a deterrent to the settlement, whether temporary or permanent, of Afghans in British territory.

Tendency of immigrants from the west to travel beyond the Province.

89. Another factor which has to be taken into account in connection with this matter of migration is the extension of the railways since last Census, and the increased use of those which existed prior to that date. As regards the extensions made the reader should refer to paragraph 22 above. Both labouring and trading immigrants now go farther afield in search of employment, or of a market for their goods. The number of Afghans to be found in Karachi and other seaports, as lascars on steamers and the like, is believed to have largely increased (*vide* figures for emigration to Bombay in Subsidiary Table V). They have been seen as far east as Singapore. Coming to the traders, some of these pursue their wanderings even to Australia; and, as an example of the effect of the railways in decreasing the importance as trade centres of towns within the Province, it may be mentioned that the Afghan Agency (a large trading firm), which used to do all its business in Peshawar, now sends the produce in which it deals (fruits, furs, rugs, etc.,) direct down country. The labouring classes (such as the Hazara coolies), naturally go where work is to be found; and at the date of the present Census there were being undertaken no large public works* in the Province, such as to attract immigrants in large numbers. Before leaving the subject of the influence of the railways, it is necessary that I should revert to the subject of the figures for immigration from Afghanistan into the Dera Ismail Khan District. It is stated in paragraph 87 above that our figures show an increase of about 1,000 persons. The actual figures (those for 1901 being approximate only) are as stated in the margin; but Table XI for 1901 contains also an entry (reproduced in the margin) of a large number of immigrants to the district from Persia. These latter make up the majority of the persons, shown in the statement printed in the margin of paragraph 84 above, as born in 'Other Asiatic countries' and enumerated in Dera Ismail Khan; and, incidentally, the variation under this head will be disposed of in this place. No immigratation from Persia is known to have taken place in recent times into Dera Ismail Khan, and it seems most likely that the persons shown as born in that country were those who returned their birth-place as Khorasan, which is now of course the name of a province of Persia. More than 3,000 persons returned the same birth-place on the present occasion, regarding whom the Deputy Commissioner writes, "the term Khorasan† is used by the Powindah immigrants into this district to describe the tract of Afghan territory from which they come. I doubt whether there are many people in this district whose birth-place is Persia." Accordingly I have included such returns among the population born in Afghanistan; and I believe that the figures in 1901 should have been shown under the same head. If we proceed on this assumption, we find that immigrants from Afghanistan to Dera Ismail Khan have decreased from 25,011 in 1901 to 21,060 in 1911, or by 16 per cent., which is in general agreement with the tendency shown by the figures for other districts of the Province. The decrease here also is to be attributed to the wider field which is now covered by trade from the west, and not to any

Immigrants to Dera Ismail Khan.

Birth-place.	1901	1911
Afghanistan ...	19,939	21,060
Persia ...	5,072	...
Total ...	25,011	21,060

* With the exception of the Upper Swat River Canal, most of the work on which has been done in tribal territory.

†Afghanistan was formerly known as Khorasan.

fall in the volume which enters British territory. So far is this from being the case that the returns maintained at the passes show the value of the goods entering the Province from Afghanistan and tribal territory to have increased in the last ten years by about 63 per cent.

Graziers.

90. The third class of immigrants with which we have to deal consists of graziers. It has been noted in the description of the Powindah caravans quoted in paragraph 76 above that the persons included in them come into the country in a dual capacity, in search of pasture, as well as for purposes of trade. The Province provides a grazing ground also for a certain number of Afghan subjects who do not engage in trade at all, and in this connection, as promised in the passage dealing with variation of immigration from tribal territory into the Peshawar and Kohat Districts, the graziers from tribal territory also may be considered. The natural result of the extension of cultivation and the growth of population in British territory has been the limitation of the area available for graziers from outside. In the Kohat and Dera Ismail Khan Districts, where alone they are levied, the *tirni*, or grazing dues have been enhanced, and, in the former district at any rate, they are now collected with far greater rigour than formerly. In consequence of the rise in the rates the actual sums collected under this head were considerably larger in the cold weather of 1910-11 than they were ten years previously ; but, had the rates remained the same for both years, the figures would have been as given in the margin, and indicate a decrease in the actual numbers of animals brought to graze of 29 and 10 per cent., respectively, for the two areas concerned. Moreover, apart from the reasons for a restriction of grazing from outside, which exist in British districts themselves, the difficulty of reaching British territory has been enhanced of recent years. The tribes of the trans-frontier area of the Province smile less and less on visitors from the west of them, who would seek to pass through their territory, in order to get a share of grazing grounds which are becoming insufficient for themselves; and the diffusion of weapons of precision, which has followed the large importation of rifles from the Persian Gulf, has rendered their objection an even more serious obstacle to intending visitors than it must always have been. The result is that Afghans look for their grazing grounds rather to Turkistan and Central Asia than to the East. The effect of present conditions on graziers from the trans-frontier area of the Province we have already seen. The immigation from Afghanistan to Hazara was never large, but the decrease (from about 700 to 99 persons) is so striking that some comment should perhaps be made on it here. "The decrease" writes the Deputy Commissioner, "can be explained by an obvious cause. At the end of January 1911 two serious dacoities were committed by Afghan immigrants, and a wholesale arrest of all Afghan aliens was ordered during the enquiry. As a consequence practically every Afghan subject, (with the exception of a few of assured position) left the district before the middle of February."

Tirni levied in 1901 and 1911.

District.	1901.	1911.	Variation per cent.
	Rs.	Rs.	
Kohat ...	7,915	5,550	—29
Dera Ismail Khan	62,032	55,591	—10

Immigration from Afghanistan and tribal territory since 1881.

91. The discussion of immigration from the west may be concluded with some consideration of the variations found in the figures from 1881 onwards. As we have seen, it is impossible to say with certainty what was the number of immigrants found in the Province as a whole in 1901 from each of the two areas (Afghanistan and tribal territory). Still less can we do so for the districts separately. In 1881 also Afghanistan and tribal territory were not distinguished for the purposes of the birth-place table. The results will be most satisfactory therefore if we consider the figures from Afghanistan and tribal territory taken together, and this procedure is the more appropriate, because the two sets of immigrants are hardly to be distinguished from one another in race, are brought into the Province largely by the same set of circumstances, and, once arrived, pursue very much the same callings. I have so shown them in the statement printed in the margin. It will be seen that the falling off in immigration from the west, which forms

Immigrants from Afghanistan and tribal territory enumerated in the districts of the N.-W. F. Province at last 4 Censuses.

District.	1881.	1891.	1901.	1911.
Hazara ...	7,231	7,259	6,087	4,418
Peshawar ...	35,892	56 089	55,537	45,366
Kohat ...	18,405	19,653	20,827	14,025
Bannu ...	11,416	11,781	7,578	7 436
D. I. Khan ...	28,954	28,843	25,876*	25,352
Total Districts ...	101,898	123,625	115,905	96,597

* Includes persons shown in Punjab Census Report, 1901, as born in Persia.

so marked a feature of the statistics of birth-place for the present Census, had begun to show itself at the end of the decade 1891—1901. The figures for the years 1881 and 1891 are of course thrown out by the fact that, previous to 1901, the Bannu and Dera Ismail Khan Districts included a large area, part of which lies to the east of the river Indus, which now forms the Mianwali District of the Punjab; and it is impossible at this distance of time to discover how many of the immigrants attributed to those two districts were enumerated in the areas now included in them. It is certain, however, that the number who were found in the tract which forms the present Mianwali District must have been comparatively small; and it will be best to subject our figures to no process of manipulation, remembering merely that the figures for the two southern districts in 1881 and 1891 are a little larger than would have been the case had they referred only to the districts as at present constituted. That the alteration of boundaries is not, however, the sole cause for the decrease, which the figures of 1901 exhibit as compared with those of 1891, is proved by the fact that the total of the figures for the three northern districts was lower in the year 1901 than ten years previously. This fact is seen to be of particular importance when it is remembered that there is an undoubted reason for the smaller number of immigrants from the west, which the figures for the Bannu and Dera Ismail Khan Districts in 1901 exhibit, in the Mahsud Blockade which was in force in that year. It is indeed this fact, rather than any change of boundaries, which is responsible for the decrease. Had it not been for the Blockade, I have no doubt that the figures for Bannu and Dera Ismail Khan would have been as little smaller in 1901 than those of ten years before, as the figures of the northern districts in the same year are smaller than the corresponding ones for 1891. The inference to be drawn from the marginal statement printed at the beginning of this paragraph is that it was not until 1901 that the factors tending to restrict immigration from the west began to show their effects. The more important of the reasons which I have adduced, such as the extended use of the railways, the spread of cultivation, and the growth of population within the North-West Frontier Province, are ones which naturally have greater force with every year that passes, and it is matter therefore for no surprise that the rate of decrease should be very much more rapid in the decade 1901—11 than in the one preceding it. Up to the year 1891 the circumstances which had led to extensive immigration from across the border, *viz.* the establishment of civilised Government in an area capable of supporting a very much larger population than was to be found living in it, had not yet exhausted their effects. Thereafter the space which the immigrants in question were able to fill became smaller and smaller, and to this, since the year 1901, must be added the changes referred to above, which were incident on the succession to his father of the present Amir of Afghanistan.

Variation in immigration from other parts of India.

92. It remains to consider variations between the immigration from other parts of India in 1901 and 1911 respectively, the details for which will be found in Subsidiary Table V appended to this chapter. The figures for the Punjab demand our attention first. From the total province (States as well as British territory) immigrants have decreased, from *89,378 persons in 1901, to 68,893 in 1911, or by 23 per cent.

From the Punjab.

As some of the reasons of the decrease are of local application only, it will be best to consider the figures for each district separately, (*vide* statement printed in the margin). In the three southern districts there were special circumstances in existence in 1901 for the presence of a larger number of immigrants from the Punjab than on the present occasion. In considering the movement of population in the Kohat municipal area and cantonment (*vide* paragraph 23) it was pointed out how largely the 1901 figures were influenced by the special immigration in that year due to the building of the Khushalgarh—Thall Railway. The persons employed on the work came largely from the Punjab, and their absence on

Population born in the Punjab and enumerated in the districts of the N.-W. F. Province.

District of enumeration.	Born in Punjab.		Variation.
	1901	1911	per cent.
Hazara ...	8,815	6,083	—31
Peshawar ...	34,787	32,963	—5
Kohat ...	16,162	7,823	—52
Bannu ...	10,383	6,687	—35
D. I. Khan ...	11,234	11,664	+4

*From this figure there are omitted the total population of the Sheranni country (12,171) who are shown in the Punjab Census Report, 1901, as born in "Punjab part unspecified". The majority at any rate must have been natives of this tribal area, which the enumerators, not knowing how to describe more precisely, returned merely as 'Punjab.'

the present occasion undoubtedly has something to do with the extraordinary decrease which our figures show. Similarly in 1901 the populations of the Bannu and Dera Ismail Khan Districts included a population, of 4,684 in the one case, and of 4,522 in the other, who were actually outside the district boundaries, and consisted of troops and followers stationed in the Tochi and Wano Agencies in connexion with the Mahsud Blockade. It is of course impossible to estimate how many of these persons were born in the Punjab, but it will not be unreasonable to suppose that a large proportion of them were natives of that province, and, but for this circumstance, our Dera Ismail Khan figures would no doubt have shown a much larger rate of increase than actually proves to be the case. In the other districts the falling off in immigration from this direction would appear to be due to a combination of causes. Probably the small number of natives of Jhelum, Shahpur, Gujrat, Sialkot, Hoshiarpur, Gurdaspur and other districts enumerated in the Province on the present occasion is in part due to their surplus population having been diverted to the Jhelum and Chenab Canal Colonies. In the first place the opening up to cultivation of the large areas brought under irrigation has provided a field which formerly did not exist for the employment of casual immigrants, such as agricultural labourers and the like, and in the second the increase of population within the North-West Frontier Province itself has led to smaller supplies of labour from outside being required in order to harvest the crops. It is also conceivable that the effects of plague and scarcity in the Punjab during the last decade have been manifested not only in a decreased population in the Punjab itself, but also in a decreased capacity for sending out emigrants elsewhere. Then the influence of the separation of the North-West Frontier Province from the Punjab has also to be taken into account. The severing of the connexion of our districts with the larger province of which they originally formed a part would naturally be to diminish migration between the two areas. Politically the Punjab is now no more to the North-West Frontier Province than Burma. To take one example, in all departments of Government service, if natives of the Province are available, persons born outside it are not employed. The effect of such a change is not to be measured by the actual number of natives of the Punjab formerly employed in the North-West Frontier Province, and now employed no longer. They are but a small proportion of the whole decrease likely to result. "The territorial separation of the North-West Frontier Province from the Punjab", writes the Deputy Commissioner of Bannu, "has also affected the private relations of the people of the two provinces". He adds that the disturbed state of the border was also responsible for materially reducing the influx of Punjabis into the district.

93. On reflection, a decrease in immigration to the Province from the Punjab is intelligible enough. Annexation was naturally followed by a large influx of persons into the area then first opened up. The land was rich, water was plentiful, and large areas of ground remained to be brought under cultivation. More important than this, from the point of view of immigration from the east, was the great demand for all sorts of supplies and services which was not felt under Sikh rule. For instance, the Dhobi appears first as a caste in the Province subsequent to annexation. The Pathan washed his own clothes, or employed a general servant to wash them, and other similar examples could be quoted. But from 1849 onwards, as traders, domestic servants and the like, Punjabis (and Purbias too) flocked into the Province. But the places of the original settlers have been taken either by their descendants, who were born within the Province, or by persons forming part of the earlier population, among whom caste restrictions hardly exist, and a man will turn his hand to any occupation from which a livelihood is to be obtained. A large part of the washing, for instance, is now done by Mohammadan Dhobis, who are such by occupation only. In talking with members of the trading and menial classess in Peshawar I have been surprised to find how many of my interlocutors, though born within the Province themselves, stated that their fathers or grandfathers were born in the Punjab.

94. In the foregoing paragraphs I have been considering mainly what may be called permanent causes of a decrease of immigration, that is, causes which may be expected to affect the figures for future Censuses also, when compared with those of 1901. Other causes, leading to a transient decrease only, may also be mentioned. It is clear from the sex proportions that

immigration from the Punjab is now seldom permanent in its character. It is partly periodic (agricultural labourers) and partly semi-permanent (employés in the various branches of Government service, notably the army). Migration of this character is particularly sensitive to variation from causes which are only of short-lived operation. Among these may be mentioned the temporary exodus of Hindus from Peshawar just before the recent Census (*vide* paragraph 23) which, considering the high proportion of Hindus among immigrants from the Punjab, may be expected to have materially affected the figures for that district. Throughout the districts of the Province the holidays which coincided with the time of the Census (from *March 10th to 14th inclusive) may also be expected to have taken a large number of semi-permanent immigrants to their homes, especially as they culminated in the Holi and the Bara-wafat, when Hindus and Mohammadans alike return, if possible, to be among their friends.

Immigration from the United Provinces.

95. Immigration from the United Provinces has also decreased largely (by 44 per cent.) since 1901. The decrease is no new feature in the Census statistics, and was noticed as long ago as 1891, when Mr. Maclagan attributed it to the fact that immigrants from this area consisted mainly of domestic servants, camp followers and others, who had followed our troops when first they took up their station in the newly annexed territories. As the original settlers have died off, they have been replaced either by children born within the North-West Frontier Province, or by other natives of the Province. In these circumstances it is natural that the decrease should proceed more rapidly with every succeeding Census. The only other area the immigrants from which are numerous enough to entitle it to special mention is Kashmir. Here too the proportion of the sexes indicates the temporary character of the immigrants (the females are only 22 per 100 males). The persons who returned their birth-place as Kashmir are mainly either agricultural labourers, who enter the Province for the cold weather, or persons earning a livelihood in menial occupations, such as dyeing. The causes which have led to a reduction in the volume of immigration of agricultural labourers from the Punjab and from the tribal territory have also had their effect on the figures for Kashmir. These last have indeed been fewer at every succesive Census since 1881, in which year they reached an abnormally high figure in consequence of the scarcity which prevailed in that country in the years 1878—1880. Of the original immigrants, some of whom appear to have been permanent, some have returned to their homes and more have died, while the need for temporary immigrants has decreased year by year.

Variation of migration within the districts of the Province.

96. Immigration from the tribal territory included in the Province has already been discussed. It remains to consider inter-district migration. The actual figures for 1901 and 1911 will be found in Subsidiary Table IV appended to this chapter. With a few trifling exceptions we are faced here too by a notable decrease. Obviously, if the proportions of the sexes are any guide, in this case too the migration is temporary in its character. Columns 6 and 7 of Subsidiary Table I at the end of this chapter show how low is the proportion of females, the female migrants in the case of every district being less than half of the males. There is bound to be a certain amount of inter-marriage across district boundaries, but it is swamped by the movement of males unaccompanied by their families. The whole volume is, however, exceedingly small. The temporary male immigrants are probably composed almost entirely of men employed in the army and in other branches of Government service. The extension, to Hazara, Bannu, and Dera Ismail Khan of the Punjab Alienation of Land Act in 1904, and of the Punjab Pre-emption Act in 1906 to all the districts have no doubt had some effect in restricting movement within the Province. Both have had the effect of limiting the power of outsiders to acquire an interest in land, and consequently one inducement to migrate is lacking. It is to be noticed, however, that Pathans are very jealous of allowing men of other castes or tribes to get possession of land (the bulk of which is owned by them), and this fact tends rather to restrict immigration altogether than the particular branch of it which we are now discussing. The low figure reached by inter-provincial migration is probably due in a greater degree to holidays which fell on and after the date of the final enumeration, and which are referred to in paragraph 94.

*The first two days on account of the Census; the 12th fell on a Sunday, and the 13th and 14th were gazetted as holidays for the Holi and Bara-wafat.

Emigration from the North-West Frontier Province.

97. Up to this point I have been concerned only with those persons who enter the Province from without. Their actual and proportional numbers have been noted, and attention has been drawn to their sex proportion, to the character of their occupations, the homes from which they come, and the smaller number enumerated on the present occasion as compared with ten years ago. It remains to consider the degree in which natives of the Province leave it to seek a livelihood elsewhere, together with the other points which have been discussed in connexion with immigration.

Reference to Subsidiary Table V.

The actual numbers of emigrants enumerated in 1911 are shown in Subsidiary Table V. In that table, unlike the others appended to this chapter, I have shown emigrants from the total area of the Province, and not from British territory only, partly because, owing to the small scope of Census operations outside British territory, the statistics for emigration from the trans-frontier area have more significance than those for immigration to it, and partly owing to the necessity of including in the table the 2,000 odd persons who are shown in the tables of other provinces and states as born in the "North-West Frontier Province unspecified." A native of one of the districts would never refer to his birth-place as the "North-West Frontier Province" (if he can not give the name of his birth district, he will probably say he was born in the Punjab), and it seems likely that the entries mainly refer, especially in Bombay where they were most numerous, to the trans-frontier area.

Areas to which emigrants go.

98. As is only natural, the greatest body of emigrants has been enumerated in the Punjab, where they amount to 34,713 persons (British territory) plus 558 (Punjab States). The next largest body has been enumerated in Kashmir (11,488 persons), most of whom were born in the neighbouring district of Hazara. In the Bombay Presidency were found 6,870 natives of the Province, and in Baluchistan 4,080. The figures for other provinces and states are not sufficiently large to possess great importance. The United Provinces show 1,896 persons born in our area, and Bengal 1,217. For no other part of India or Ceylon do the figures amount to as much as 800 souls. The total volume of emigration is not very large (*vide* Subsidiary Table III), representing 29 per mille only of the total population of British territory. Taking the Province as a whole (districts only) first, over one-half of the emigrants leave their homes for contiguous areas in the Punjab or Kashmir, but this result is chiefly due to the large numbers of natives of Hazara who were enumerated in the neighbouring State; for, if the figures for the trans-Indus districts be looked at. it will be seen that emigrants to areas which do not march with them are three times as numerous relatively as those going to areas which do. It is to be noticed (*vide* note to Subsidiary Table III) that, among emigrants to contiguous areas in the case of individual districts, are included persons migrating not only to areas, outside the Province, but also those going to another district within it. It is from Peshawar that emigrants to distant places are relatively most numerous. They amount here to six times the number migrating to contiguous areas.

Proportion of the sexes among emigrants.
Occupation of emigrants.

99. Looking at columns 10 and 11 of Subsidiary Table III it will be seen that females are everywhere more numerous among emigrants to neighbouring districts than among those going further afield. The relatively large numbers of females leaving Hazara and Dera Ismail Khan for adjacent tracts indicates the existence of a good deal of migration of the reciprocal and permanent type. In those districts close marriages are not so common as in the other three included in the Province, and probably a good many women leave their birth district on marriage. But on the whole the sexes are in great disproportion among emigrants wherever they go, and this is noticeably the case in regard to those taking their way from Peshawar. Our emigrants, like our immigrants, are in fact largely periodic or semi-permanent in character. A large number of them consist of men employed in the army, Pathans being recruited freely in many regiments throughout the service. Many more are traders, or labourers employed in dockyards and on earth works, and the like. Of the 6,484 persons enumerated in the Bombay Presidency, of whom about four-fifths were males, large numbers were enumerated in Bombay itself, or in Karachi, and probably consisted mainly of dock hands, lascars, etc. Male emigrants to Baluchistan are

nearly five times as numerous as female, and our figures point to men in military employ. Those for emigrants to Bengal, among whom males are to females in the ratio of six to one, probably refer chiefly to traders, who, if they have left their homes for good, evidently have not taken their women with them. Even among emigrants to the Punjab males are nearly twice as numerous as females. Just as in the case of immigrants to the Province the presence of troops disturbs the normal proportion of the sexes, in the case of the emigrants from it we are met with precisely the same phenomenon. The only group of migrants of whom this statement is not true is that leaving the Province for Kashmir. Among these there are as many as 81 females per 100 males. This is almost the solitary example which our statistics display of migration of the permanent type. I do not mean that there is no permanent migration from the Province to other areas. It no doubt takes place, but it is lost sight of in the greater volume of a periodic or semi-permanent character.

Variation in emigration since 1901.

100. I have said that emigrants only amount to 29 per mille of the actual population of the Province (British districts). Immigrants on the other hand amount to as much as 84 per mille. The Province therefore gains by migration far more than it loses. At the same time, while immigration is contracting, emigration is becoming yearly more common. This is indeed intelligible enough. The same causes, *viz.* the extension of cultivation, and the growth of population within the Province, which have operated to check the streams of migration towards it, have been effective to induce the native population to tend to look for outlets elsewhere. There is not yet of course any such pressure of population as to drive any large numbers to look beyond the Province for a livelihood. At the same time, whatever the causes (and they are presumably not unconnected with growing density at home and increasing opportunities of getting away), those who turn their eyes to areas outside it are increasing. Subsidiary Table V shows emigrants from the Province to other areas in India to have increased by 10,618 persons, or by 19 per cent., since 1901. Almost every province and state in India now shows a greater number of persons born in the North-West Frontier Province than it did ten years ago. The only instance of the reverse where the figures are of importance is the Punjab. Even here, for the reasons given in paragraph 63, I believe the decrease to be apparent only. If our figures for emigration in 1901 from the Bannu and Dera Ismail Khan Distiricts were not vitiated by the inaccuracies necessarily arising from any serious re-arrangement of district boundaries, I believe that the figures for these two districts, like those of the districts north of them, would have indicated a larger flow of population, than those of ten years ago, from the smaller to the larger province, from the poorer to the wealthier area, from an out of the way corner of India towards the centres of civilization in the continent.

SUBSIDIARY TABLE I.—*Immigration (actual figures.)*

District and natural division where enumerated.	Born in (00s omitted.)																	
	District or natural division.			*Other districts in Province.*			*Trans-Frontier area of Province.*			*Contiguous parts of other provinces, etc.*			*Non-contiguous parts of other Provinces, etc.*			*Outside India.*		
	Total.	Males.	Females.	Total.	Males.	Females.	Total.	Males.	Females.	Total.	Males.	Females.	Total.	Males.	Females.	Total.	Males.	Females.
1	2	3	4	5	6	7	8	9	10	11	12	13	14	15	16	17	18	19
Total Districts N.-W. F. P.	**20.124**	**10.560**	**9.564**	...	...	...	**544**	**330**	**214**	**339**	**249**	**90**	**441**	**337**	**104**	**520**	**345**	**175**
Hazara ...	5,850	3,081	2,769	4	3	1	43	27	16	55	32	23	29	21	8	48	40	8
Trans-Indus Districts	**14.238**	**7.450**	**6.788**	**31**	**25**	**6**	**501**	**303**	**198**	**181**	**134**	**47**	**515**	**399**	**116**	**472**	**305**	**167**
Peshawar ...	7,724	4,050	3,674	33	26	7	293	179	114	76	60	16	316	238	78	208	151	57
Kohat ...	1,971	1,018	953	20	15	5	121	67	54	20	14	6	75	63	12	21	15	6
Bannu ...	2,315	1,202	1,113	32	22	10	44	29	15	16	12	4	63	52	11	31	21	10
Dera Ismail Khan ...	2,140	1,118	1,022	34	24	10	43	28	15	53	34	19	78	62	16	212	118	94

The figures in columns 2—7 and 11—16 for Total Districts North-West Frontier Province, and for Trans-Indus Districts, are not the totals of the figures for the districts contained in these two areas. Those in columns 2—4, for instance, include not only the persons enumerated in each of the said districts who were born there, but also those who were born in any other district in the group concerned. The area referred to as contiguous parts of other provinces is different in the case of each district or group of districts dealt with, and, as a natural consequence, the figures in columns 14—16 refer to different areas in the case of different entries in column 1. In the case of North-West Frontier Province (Total Districts) the contiguous districts of other provinces, etc., are the Rawalpindi, Attock, Mianwali and Dera Ghazi Khan Districts of the Punjab and Kashmir State. In the case of Hazara the Rawalpindi and Attock Districts and Kashmir; in the case of Trans-Indus Districts the Attock, Mianwali and Dera Ghazi Khan Districts; in the case of Peshawar the Attock District; in the case of Kohat the Attock and Mianwali Districts; in the case of Bannu the Mianwali District; and in the case of Dera Ismail Khan the Mianwali and Dera Ghazi Khan Districts.

SUBSIDIARY TABLE II.—*Emigration (actual figures.)*

District and natural division where born.	Enumerated in (00s omitted).														
	District or natural division.			*Other districts of province.*			*Trans-Frontier Posts, N.-W. F. P.*			*Contiguous parts of other provinces, etc.*			*Non-contiguous parts of other provinces.*		
	Total.	Males.	Females.	Total.	Males.	Females.	Total.	Males	Females.	Total.	Males.	Females.	Total.	Males.	Females
1	2	3	4	5	6	7	8	9	10	11	12	13	14	15	16
Total Districts N.-W.F.P.	**20.124**	**10.560**	**9.564**	...	...	...	**25**	**24**	**1**	**298**	**173**	**125**	**323**	**251**	**72**
Hazara	5,850	3,081	2,769	31	25	6	2	2	...	190	107	83	55	47	8
Trans-Indus Districts ...	**14.238**	**7.450**	**6.788**	**4**	**3**	**1**	**23**	**22**	**1**	**70**	**39**	**31**	**286**	**214**	**72**
Peshawar	7,724	4,050	3.674	28	24	4	10	9	1	14	9	5	190	148	42
Kohat	1,971	1,018	953	23	15	8	9	9	...	16	9	7	33	26	7
Bannu	2.315	1,202	1,113	29	18	11	2	2	...	5	3	2	19	13	6
Dera Ismail Khan ...	2,140	1,118	1,022	13	8	5	2	2	...	27	14	13	51	31	20

For areas treated as contiguous parts of other provinces, etc. see the footnote to Subsidiary Table I.

SUBSIDIARY TABLE III.—*Proportional migration to and from each district.*

DISTRICT AND NATURAL DIVISION.	NUMBER PER MILLE OF ACTUAL POPULATION OF—						NUMBER OF FEMALES TO 100 MALES AMONG			
	Immigrants.			*Emigrants.*			*Immigrants.*		*Emigrants.*	
	Total.	From contiguous areas.	From other places.	Total.	To contiguous areas.	To other places.	From contiguous areas.	From other places.	To contiguous areas.	To other places.
1	2	3	4	5	6	7	8	9	10	11
Total Districts N.-W. F. P. ...	**84**	**40**	**44**	**29**	**15**	**14**	**52**	**41**	**64**	**29**
Hazara	30	17	13	46	35	11	66	26	68	19
Trans-Indus Districts ...	**107**	**45**	**62**	**24**	**6**	**18**	**54**	**40**	**52**	**34**
Peshawar	107	46	61	28	4	24	52	35	28	27
Kohat	115	69	46	36	21	15	70	24	49	27
Bannu	74	33	41	22	14	8	48	30	63	44
Dera Ismail Khan ...	164	46	118	36	15	21	57	59	77	64

NOTE.—The areas treated as contiguous are as follows :—

In the case of Total districts—
The Attock, Rawalpindi, Mianwali, and Dera Ghazi Khan Districts of the Punjab, Kashmir and Agencies and Tribal Areas, North-West Frontier Province.

In the case of Hazara—
The Attock and Rawalpindi Districts of the Punjab, Peshawar, Kashmir and Agencies and Tribal Areas, North-West Frontier Province

In the case of Peshawar—
The Attock District of the Punjab, Hazara, and Kohat, and Agencies and Tribal areas North-West Frontier Province.

In the case of Kohat—
The Attock and Mianwali Districts of the Punjab, the Peshawar and Bannu Districts and Agencies and Tribal Areas, North-West Frontier Province.

In the case of Bannu—
The Mianwali District of the Punjab, with Kohat, and Dera Ismail Khan, and Agencies and Tribal Areas, North-West Frontier Province.

In the cases of Dera Ismail Khan—
The Mianwali and Dera Ghazi Khan Districts of the Punjab, Bannu, and Agencies and Tribal Areas, North-West Frontier Province.

In the case of Trans-Indus Districts—
The Attock, Mianwali, and Dera Ghazi Khan Districts of the Punjab, Hazara, and Agencies and Tribal Areas, North-West Frontier Province.

SUBSIDIARY TABLE IV.—*Migration between districts, etc., (actual figures) compared with* 1901.

DISTRICTS OF BIRTH.		NUMBER ENUMERATED IN DISTRICTS.				
		Hazara.	Peshawar.	Kohat.	Bannu.	D. I. Khan.
1		2	3	4	5	6
Hazara	1911 ...	585,019	2,167	473	339	109
	1901 ...	539,468	3,275	823	154	120
Peshawar	1911 ...	392	772,408	889	619	893
	1901 ...	864	681,853	2,169	751	325
Kohat	1911 ...	28	595	197,097	1,486	153
	1901 ...	39	721	170,905	2,995	340
Bannu	1911 ...	16	192	465	231,459	2,257
	1901 ...	15	329	1,439	206,740	5,122
Dera Ismail Khan	1911 ...	42	327	125	815	214,052
	1901 ...	47	150	312	1,453	205,265
Trans-Frontier area N.-W. F. P.	1911 ...	4,319	29,393	12,071	4,359	4,292
	1901 ...	5,369	36,325	4,915	225	803

The figures for immigrants to the districts from the Trans-Frontier area of the Province in 1901 can not be accurately determined. In the Punjab Census, Report, 1901, the figures for persons born in Yaghistan and Afghanistan are lumped together, the only indication of their respective number being given by a footnote which shows that, out of total immigrants into the Punjab and North-West Frontier Province from these two countries, only 3 per cent. were born in Yaghistan. For want of a better guide the same percentage has been assumed to hold good for the districts with which we are concerned above. I have also included in the table under the head of persons born in the Trans-Frontier area those persons who are shown in the Punjab Census Report, 1901, as having been born in 'Asia part unspecified,' as a reference to the report shows that persons who returned their birth-place as Mulk-i-Ghair were so tabulated.

SUBSIDIARY TABLE V.—*Migration between the North-West Frontier Province and other parts of India.*

Province or State.	Immigrants to North-West Frontier Province.			Emigrants from North-West Frontier Province.			Excess (+) or deficiency (—) of immigration over emigration.	
	1911.	1901.	Variation.	1911.	1901.	Variation.	1911.	1901.
1	2	3	4	5	6	7	8	9
Total ...	**82,139**	**105,863**	**—23,724**	**65,476**	**54,858**	**+10,618**	**+16,663**	**+51,005**
Total Provinces ...	**73,415**	**94,955**	**—21,540**	**51,000**	**41,277**	**+9,723**	**+22,405**	**+53,678**
Ajmer Merwara	16	...	+16	106	79	+27	—90	—79
Andamans and Nicobars... ...	11	13	—2	459	...	+459	—448	+13
Baluchistan	269	263	+6	4,080	2,483	+1,597	—3,811	—2,220
Bengal	209	564	—355	1,217	1,351	—134	—1,008	—787
Bombay	558	1,158	—600	6,870	386	+6,484	—6,312	+772
Burma	29	22	+7	743	...	+743	—714	+22
Central Provinces and Berar ...	86	117	—31	618	178	+440	—532	—61
Eastern Bengal and Assam ...	110	...	+110	219	...	+219	—109	...
Madras	72	352	—280	79	19	+60	—7	+333
Punjab	67,132	83,690	—16,558	34,713	35,400	—687	+32,419	+48,290
United Provinces	4,923	8,776	—3,853	1,896	1,381	+515	+3,027	+7,395
Total States ...	**8,411**	**10,211**	**—1,800**	**14,476**	**13,581**	**+895**	**—6,065**	**—3,370**
Baluchistan States	...	...	...	20	...	+20	—20	...
Baroda	11	16	—5	39	130	—91	—28	—114
Bengal States	...	...	...	53	...	+53	—53	...
Bombay States	108	...	+108	271	...	+271	—163	...
Central India Agency	91	163	—72	791	...	+791	—700	+163
Central Provinces States ...	1	...	+1	80	...	+80	—79	...
Cochin	...	...	...	1	...	+1	—1	...
Eastern Bengal and Assam States ...	10	...	+10	5	...	+5	+5	...
Hyderabad	94	105	—11	364	...	+364	—270	+105
Kashmir	4,655	5,938	—1,283	11,488	10,813	+675	—6,833	—4,875
Madras States	...	...	...	3	...	+3	—3	...
Mysore	45	134	—89	288	...	+288	—243	+134
Punjab States	1,761	2,688	—927	558	2,018	—1,460	+1,203	+670
Rajputana Agency	1,492	1,167	+325	507	620	—113	+985	+547
Travancore	2	...	+2	8	...	+8	—6	...
United Provinces States ...	141	...	+141	...	...	...	+141	...
India unspecified ...	**211**	**686**	**—475**	...	...	...	**+211**	**+686**
Portuguese Settlements	**102**	**11**	**+91**	...	...	...	**+102**	**+11**

The figures in column 3 for Provinces, except in the case of the Punjab, include also the figures for Native States in relation with the Local Governments concerned. The figures for Bengal in the same column include those for Eastern Bengal and Assam.

In addition to the emigrants from the Province shown in this table 13 males were enumerated at sea, and 418 persons (283 males and 135 females) in Ceylon, besides 42 males and 8 females in Hong Kong.

This table, unlike Subsidiary Tables I, II and III appended to Chapter III includes migrants to and from trans-frontier posts as well as British territory.

CHAPTER IV.

RELIGION.

Religious distribution of (a) the enumerated population.

101. The figures for the religious distribution of the people of the Province will be found in Table VI, in Part II of this Volume. Of the enumerated population, 93 per cent. are Mohammadan, and only 7 per cent. are followers of other religions, being mainly Hindus. Hindus are to Sikhs in the proportion of 4, and to Christians in the proportion of 18, to 1. Other religions are represented only by 67 persons, of whom 49 are Zoroastrians, 14 are Jews, and 4 are Jains. By the side of Islam therefore other religions are numerically of very minor importance.

(b) Of the estimated population

102. In Table VI, as in other tables, except Tables I and II, no figures are given for the estimated population of the trans-border tract of the Province. Islam is here also the predominant religion, the proportion of non-Mussalmans probably being even smaller than it is in British territory. Of the population of the Kurram Agency which was enumerated in 1901, Hindus formed 4, and Sikhs ·9 per cent. and at the Census of a portion of the Tochi Agency, which was undertaken in 1903 in connection with settlement operations, 9.4 per cent. of the population were found to be Hindus. There are a certain number of Sikhs scattered over Tirah. I am indebted to the Hon'ble the Chief Commissioner, North-West Frontier Province, for the following information about them: "Banias live in big villages under the protection of Khans. I should say their number is under 500 men" (say 2,500 souls including women and children). "They profess the Sikh religion, idolatry being unpopular locally, but hardly practise any religion at all. They shave and smoke as a rule." While, however, the presence of a few non-Muslims across the border is beyond doubt, we have not the material to estimate their total number. They probably do not exceed 5 per cent. of the whole; and it is likely that, like the Sikhs in Tirah, they are lax in their observance of the customs of their religion.

The Hindu figures Chuhras.

103 In the case of Mohammadans no question as to the correct classifications of the returns made can arise. The followers of the Prophet, in every case, returned their religion as Mussalman. In the case of Hindus, however, some doubt not uncommonly exists. There is, first, the case of the scavenger class, who in some cases returned their religion as Mehtar, Chuhra, Balmiki and the like. If these names indicate a religion, it is one that we know little about; but the persons in question, in reply to enquiries, state that they are Hindus. They are not generally recognized as Hindus by the more respectable castes; and their social observances, though influenced largely by Hinduism, are not those of Hindus in all particulars, for, to take a striking instance, some of them at any rate do not burn their dead, but bury them. At the same time, in view of their small numbers, and of the fact that they possess no religious literature, it seemed best to include them on the present, as on former occasions, among Hindus. At the Census of 1891 Mr. Maclagan explained (page 89, Punjab Census Report, 1891) that persons who could not be definitely assigned to any one of the other well-known religions were classed as Hindus, and he tells us that 90 per cent. of the persons tabulated "by main force, as it were" under the head Hindu belonged to the sweeper or scavenger class. "One of the questions raised," continues Mr. Maclagan, "in respect of a religious Census in India is whether we are justified in ignoring the fact that the scavengers, who do not profess Sikhism or Islam are followers of a form of religion which is in many ways distinct from Hinduism proper, and which is looked on by most high-caste Hindus as a degraded form of worship quite outside the pale of their own faith." On a consideration mainly of various practical difficulties which would arise in tabulating the followers of the Chuhra religion separately Mr.

Maclagan came to the conclusion that it would be best to adhere to the system adopted in 1881 of including all as Hindus. On the present occasion the numbers included in the Hindu figures, who returned their religion as other than Hindu, are as follows:—Mehtar 2,046, Chamar 15 and Purbia 6.

This does not, however, exhaust the number of sweepers who find a place among the Hindus. The number of Hindu Chuhras shown in Table XIII is 4,884, and out of the total Hindu population, including the persons mentioned above as having entered their religion as Mehtar, etc., 3,775 returned in the column of sect the name of one of the sweeper sub-divisions.

Distinction between Hindus and Sikhs.
Definition issued in 1891 and 1901.

104. The second case in which question may arise as to the correctness of classification is that of the distinction between Sikhs and Hindus. The difficulty has long been recognised. In 1891 Mr. Maclagan (page 91, Punjab Census Report, 1891) remarked "in the case of the Sikhs there is a just this ....difficulty that the line between them and the Hindus is vague in the extreme.* Not only is a true Sikh commonly called Hindu in common parlance, but many of those who are spoken of as Sikhs are not true Sikhs, but Hindus. By a true Sikh is meant a member of the Khalsa, a follower of the ordinances of Guru Govind Singh." Mr Maclagan went on to observe that the best practical test of a Sikh for Census purposes was to ascertain, whether, calling himself a Sikh, a man wore uncut hair and abstained from smoking; and the instructions issued to the Census staff in 1891 were to enter as Sikh by religion only those who answered this test, and to class others as Hindus by religion, and Sikh, or Nanakpanthi, or whatever they liked to return, by sect. Virtually the same instructions were issued also in 1901.

Confusion between followers of the two religions.

105. With a definition as plain as that issued in 1891, it might be supposed that no question could arise as to whether any particular person is a Sikh or not. But this is not the case. The Sikh religion was born out of Hinduism, and fears have been expressed of its being reabsorbed into it.† "Truly wonderful is the strength and vitality of Hinduism. It is like the boa constrictor of the Indian forests; when a petty enemy appears to worry it, it winds round its opponent, crushes it in its folds, and finally causes it to disappear in its capacious interior In this way, many centuries ago, Hinduism on its own ground disposed of Buddhism which was largely a Hindu reformation; in this way in a prehistoric period it absorbed the religion of the Scythian invaders of Northern India; in this way it has converted educated Islam in India into a semi-paganism; and in this way it is disposing of the reformed and once hopeful religion of Baba Nanak. Hinduism has embraced Sikhism in its folds; the still comparatively young religion is making a vigorous struggle for life, but its ultimate destruction is, it is apprehended, inevitable without State support. Notwithstanding the Sikh Guru's powerful denunciation of Brahmans, secular Sikhs now rarely do anything without their assistance. Brahmans help them to be born, help them to wed, help them to die and help their souls after death to obtain a state of bliss. And Brahmans, with all the deftness of Roman Catholic missionaries in Protestant countries have partially succeeded in persuading the Sikhs to restore to their niches the images of Devi, the Queen of Heaven, and the Saints and gods of the ancient faith." The following remarks may serve to illustrate the confusion which arises. In the first place no clear line of cleavage is drawn between the two religions by prohibition of intermarriage; and it is not unusual to find a Kesdhari Sikh (*i. e.* wearing the long hair or *Kes*) in a family of which the other members are Hindus, and a Hindu in one mainly composed of Kesdhari Sikhs. As an example of the current Hindu view of Sikhs, I may quote the opinions expressed to me by a well educated Hindu of Peshawar City. The Sahij dhari Sikh (who cuts his hair) he would not admit to be a Sikh at all, and considered that he should be entered in the schedule as a Hindu by religion, and a Nanakpanthi (or follower of the first Guru Nanak) by sect. Kesdhari Sikhs he would divide into (*i*) the *Tat-Khalsa*, (*ii*) Sanatanist Sikhs. The Tat-Khalsa Sikh has no reverence

* See also Punjab Census Report, 1881, para 265 (end) "So again on the frontier the saying runs, 'the origin of a Sikh is in his hair', implying that there is no other distinction."

† Macauliffe.—The Sikh religion, Volume I, pages lvi, lvii.

for the Vedas and Shastras, and regards his religion as entirely distinct from Hinduism. The Sanatanist Sikh on the other hand, even though he wears the *Kes*, reverences the Vedas and Shastras, as well as the Granth Sahib. But in reverencing the Granth Sahib as an inspired writing, he is not to be distinguished, my informant added, from the ordinary Hindu of the Province. He explained that he himself was an (orthodox) Sanatanist Hindu, that he had his own Brahman and worshipped daily according to the forms of the Hindu ritual; but that he also regarded the Granth Sahib as a sacred book and attended worship in a Sikh Dharamsala every week. According to the Hindu view therefore, which seemed inspired by the spirit of absorption which has always characterised Hinduism, and which, in the passage above quoted, Mr. Macauliffe compares to a boa constrictor, not even all of those who wear the *Kes* and abstain from smoking are to be regarded as Sikhs. The Sikhs on the other hand are not prepared to admit that persons recorded as Sikhs should be limited to those who wear the *Kes*. Shortly before the Census I was visited by a deputation from the Singh Sabha at Peshawar, who came to protest against the inclusion in the specimen schedule of certain entries showing religion as Hindu with sect as Nanakpanthi. Their contention was that all followers of Guru Nanak, the first Guru, should be recorded as Sikhs by religion, and that Hindu Nanakpanthi was a contradiction in terms. (A reference to the later portion of this Chapter which deals with the sect return will show nevertheless how common this entry proved to be). It was, they contended, perfectly true that it was not until the time of the tenth and last Guru that Sikhism became a militant faith, and that the various observances, such as the wearing of the *Kes*, were prescribed; but that to argue that the followers of earlier Gurus, notably Guru Nanak, should be regarded as Hindus, was tantamount to maintaining that Guru Nanak regarded himself as a Hindu This they were able to show conclusively that he did not; and their argument would have possessed considerable force, were it not that Hinduism connotes rather a social system than the holding of any particular beliefs, and that it is by that system that the lives of perhaps the majority of the persons calling themselves Sikhs are regulated.

No definition of Sikh issued at the present Census.

106. If only the definition is acted upon, it is obviously desirable to define the persons who should be entered as Sikhs in the Census schedules, and Mr. Maclagan's definition is so clear that it should have presented no difficulties to enumerators. But it was not carefully observed. Mr. Maclagan estimated that the Sikh figures for 1891 exceeded by 30 per cent. the numbers which should have been returned as those of the true Sikhs. In 1901 Mr. Rose observed that he had little doubt that the definition of Sikh, again issued in that year, was almost universally ignored. His remarks on the subject are worth quoting: "These results" he says, (page 124, Census Report, Punjab, 1901) "are the reverse of satisfactory. If a rule is laid down and only partially followed, the returns obtained must be of uncertain value. We cannot say with accuracy in how many cases the rule was followed, and in how many disobeyed. The question then arises whether such a rule can be enforced, as if not, it should be amended or revoked. I am inclined to think that at a future Census this attempt at definition should be abandoned."

The instructions issued to the Census staff are necessarily lengthy; and, especially in the case of persons of the educational standard of the bulk of the enumerators in this Province, there is always a danger that over-elaboration may lead to a neglect of essentials. On the present occasion therefore, reverting to the course followed in 1881, I attempted no definition of the persons who should be classed as Sikhs, merely explaining that, if a person said he was a Sikh, he should be entered as such, and not as Hindu, even though he also said he was a Hindu. This was in accordance with the standard form of instructions issued by the Census Commissioner, which laid down that the answer which each person gave about his religion must be accepted. On the present occasion then the Sikh figures include all who chose to return themselves as such.

Local distribution of the population by religion.

107. Subsidiary Table II appended to this Chapter shows the proportion of Muhammadans, Hindus and Sikhs to the total population of each district, and

of the districts of the Province taken as a whole. Of the total population ·93 per cent. are Mohammadans, 5 per cent. are Hindus and 1 per cent only are Sikhs. The proportion of Hindus is highest in Dera Ismail Khan, where it amounts to 11 per cent. In Bannu it is 8 per cent. while in the three northern districts it is only 4 per cent., respectively. Proportionately the largest numbers of Sikhs are found in Peshawar, where they amount to 1·8 per cent. of the whole population. In Bannu they amount to 1·4, and in Kohat to 1·2 per cent.; in Hazara they are only ·9 and in Dera Ismail Khan ·8 per cent. of the whole. More than five sixths of the Christians enumerated in the Province are found in Peshawar, where they consist almost entirely of European troops stationed at Nowshera and at the head-quarters of the Province.

Distribution of Hindus & Sikhs by tahsils.

108. Hindus and Sikhs are largely soldiers and followers, and, wherever there is a Cantonment, a comparatively large proportion of them is to be found. Their presence in these areas, however, has little interest; for it depends merely on the 'Reliefs' ordered. The statement in the margin, which shows their distribution by tahsils, cantonment population being left out of account, perhaps deserves more attention. In the first place it will be noticed that both communities are present in comparatively large numbers in the head-quarters tahsils. The reason is that as they are almost entirely dependent on trade or service for a livelihood, they naturally congregate in the markets of the Province. The Abbottabad tahsil has indeed a smaller proportion of Hindus than Haripur, owing to the small importance of Abbottabad town as a trade centre. Kohat also has but a slightly larger ratio of Hindus than Hangu, and a smaller number of Sikhs, proportionately to its total population; but this is due to the presence of troops in the latter tahsil, who, as they do not live in Cantonment, have not been eliminated from our figures. The second point which will be noticed is that the Sikhs are most numerous proportionately in Peshawar, and the Hindus in the south of the Province; while the total non-Muslim element (*i.e.* Hindus plus Sikhs) is considerably more common in the two southern districts, Bannu and Dera Ismail Khan, than elsewhere.

Number of the Hindus and Sikhs per 1,000 of the total population in each taksil excluding those of Cantonment.

District.	Tahsil.	Hindus.	Sikhs.
Hazara ...	Mansehra ...	21	4
Do. ...	Abbottabad ...	32	15
Do. ...	Haripur ...	45	7
Do. ...	Amb ...	20	...
Do. ...	Phulra ...	11	...
Peshawar ...	Peshawar ...	46	18
Do. ...	Charsadda ...	14	9
Do. ...	Mardan ...	27	20
Do. ...	Swabi ...	15	15
Do. ...	Nowshera ...	18	6
Kohat ...	Kohat ...	54	12
Do. ...	Teri ...	24	3
Do. ...	Hangu ...	53	15
Bannu ...	Bannu ...	85	17
Do. ...	Marwat ...	68	7
Dera Ismail Khan ...	D. I. Khan ...	129	5
Do. ...	Tank ...	73	4
Do. ...	Kulachi ...	91	6

The history of the Province as bearing on the local distribution of the population by religion.

109. The reason for the local distribution of the population by religion is to be found in the past history of the Province. The high road, along which the Mohammadan conquerors and rulers of India passed and repassed, lay through the north (the Khyber, Kurram and other routes); and it is probable that Islam never took so firm a hold of the inhabitants of the southern districts as of the people to the north of them. In this connection it is interesting to notice that the Mussalman of the Derajat is less strict in his observance of the duties of his religion, such as fasts, prayers and the like, than his northern neighbours. Through Hazara lay the road by which the Emperors of Delhi went to and fro between the capital and their summer retreat in Kashmir, and it was natural that Islam should thoroughly permeate the district. Similarly Kohat, from its situation with regard to the Kurram Valley, which at no very distant period was, nominally at least, a portion of the Afghan kingdom, has been more influenced in the past by its Mohammadan neighbours to the west than have the districts to the south of it. There is no need to consider here the probable date at which the bulk of the Pathans living in the Province, or rather their ancestors, were converted to Islam. It is enough to notice that they had long been Mohammadan when they settled in their present homes, and that their fanaticism and intolerance, especially in the districts where they are strongest, rendered the Province no very inviting place of residence for settlers of a different creed. If no fanaticism in

its inhabitants acted as a bar to the settlement of Hindus in Hazara, the absence of any large trade centres was at least equally efficatious. The only other district in which there is a non-Pathan element in the population in any way commensurate to that of Hazara is Dera Ismail Khan. The population here is mainly composed of tribes of Indian origin. Its conversion to Islam is of much later date ; fanaticism does not exist, and no particular dislike to the Hindu seems ever to have existed. In the greater part of the area included in the Province Hindus are never found in the possession of land. In Dera Ismail Khan on the other hand, Hindu agriculturists, though rare, are not unknown. The history of the district at the beginning of the nineteenth century also throws some light on the comparatively high proportion of non-Muslims found there. The Saddozai Nawabs, who ruled it, as well as part of Bannu, until overthrown by the Sikhs, commonly employed Hindus as generals and governors, and it was in the hands of a Hindu, Diwan Daulat Rai, that it was left by the Sikhs. This is in strong contrast with their action, for instance, in Kohat where the Khattak chiefship of Teri, we are told, "was but little affected by the Sikh conquest" and the Teri chief "at annexation was continued in the management of the whole Teri tahsil". The Sikhs form but a trifling element of the population anywhere in the Province ; and their comparatively high numbers in Peshawar are no doubt to be explained by the fact that the attractions of the district are greater than those of others from the greater importance of the markets contained in it. I have no figures to show the distribution by religion of the population of tahsils previous to the year of the present Census, and it is impossible therefore to say how far the existing one (the persons enumerated in the cantonments being left out of account) is normal. I think it worth record here, however, for purposes of comparison with the results of future Censuses.

Variation of population by religion.

110. Subsidiary Tables I and II appended to this Chapter are of interest as showing variations in the ratio borne to the total by the population of each main religion. To deal first with the variation since 1901, it will be seen that while the proportion both of Mohammadans and Sikhs has increased, that of Hindus has gone down.

The statement printed in the margin shows the percentage of

Variation of population of each main religion 1901—1911.

District.	Percentage of variation. Increase (+). Decrease (—)			
	All religions.	Muhmds.	Hindus.	Sikhs.
Hazara ...	+7·6	+7	+6	+36
Pesha war ...	+9·6	+10	—11·9	+43
Kohat ...	+2·2	+4·5	—25	—18
Bannu ...	+10·2	+9	—6·5	+40
Dera Ismail Khan	+3·3	+3·9	—2·7	—50
Total districts ...	+7	+8	—7	+18

NOTE.—The percentages of variation (all religions) in the Bannu and Dera Ismail Khan, as in other districts, in the statement above are worked out from the figures given in Table II, which exclude (*vide* footnotes to table) the troops enumerated in the Tochi and Wano agencies. No details are, however, available to show the distribution by religion of these persons taken by themselves, and the figures for each religion separately are based therefore on the population of the districts as shown in the Punjab Census Report, 1901. The result is that the rate of increase for all religions is higher than it should be on a consideration of the figures for each individual religion.

variation for each religion separately as compared with that for the total population of the area dealt with. The figures for Mohammadans require no discussion here. Amounting as they do to so large a proportion of the whole, they naturally determine almost entirely the rate of growth of the total population. The variation in the case of Sikhs appears at first sight very extraordinary. But in the first place it must be remembered that the Sikhs form so small a community in the Province (their total numbers are only 31,459 souls according to the present Census) that the addition to or removal from the garrison of a single Sikh regiment has an appreciable effect. If this is seen when the whole population of the Province is looked at, it is still more striking when we regard the figures for a single district. In the second place

(*a*) Mohammadans.

(*b*) Sikhs.

we have the dislocation of the figures caused by the difference in the instructions issued in 1901 and on the present occasion. It has been explained in paragraph 106 above that our tables show as Sikhs all those persons who chose so to record themselves, whereas in 1901 an attempt was made, though Mr. Rose believed it met with little success, to limit the returns so that they should include only true Khalsa Sikhs. Of more importance, however, than the difference in the instructions given to the enumerators was, I believe, the great effort made by Sikhs to ensure that a full return of their community was obtained. Whether they are beginning to share the apprehensions expressed by Mr. Macauliffe in the passage quoted in paragraph 105 above I do not know; their anxiety that no one should be omitted who could possibly be called a Sikh was obvious. As I have indicated in a foregoing paragraph, they wished me to tabulate as Sikhs all persons who recorded a sect which takes its name from one of the Sikh Gurus or teachers, whatever the entry of religion might be. The Sabha professed itself ready to send out a band of volunteers to accompany enumerators on their rounds, in order to ensure that entries of religion were correctly made. I discouraged this plan as likely to lead to quarrels; but recommended that instead they should instruct the members of their community how to reply to the questions as to religion and sect which would be put to them. I also saw copies of circulars issued by various Singh Sabhas in the Punjab, in which the followers of Guru Nanak and the other Gurus were enjoined to record themselves as Sikhs and not as Hindus. It is, I believe, largely as the result of the action taken by the Singh Sabha at Peshawar and elsewhere that so large an increase has been recorded in the numbers of Sikhs in the Province. The growth of the Sikh population has indeed outpaced that of the Mohammadan, the ratio borne by the former to the total being higher now than it was in 1901. The growth is, however, if my conclusions are correct, largely apparent rather than real.

Variation since 1901 in number of Sikhs by sex.

111. Further light is thrown on the question by a consideration of the figures for each sex separately. It will be seen that the increase is confined to the females, the figures for males being now slightly smaller than was the case ten years ago. The figures at first sight certainly do not suggest that to any difference in the instructions issued is due the variation appearing in the case of the male population. The enormous rise (by 58 per cent.) in the number of females is probably to be attributed principally to this cause. At the same time I believe my figures are nearer the truth than those of 1901. In that year supervisors were directed to enter as Sikhs those only who wore uncut hair and abstained from smoking; but seeing that the majority of females answer this test, there would have been a tendency to enter them as Hindus from the obvious absurdity of classing all as Sikhs if they did not smoke, and if they wore their hair long. It is true that the instructions contained a qualifying clause to the effect that the religion of women should be entered as stated; but my experience of Census enumerators leads me to believe that, if it is possible to loose sight of an important qualification, they will do so, finding it quite as much as they can manage to grasp and give effect to the instructions qualified. Apart from this point, which is largely a matter of opinion, it is in the case of females that variations due to a change in the instructions at various Censuses might be expected chiefly to appear. In the case of men, provided the enumerators were drilled sufficiently well, it should always be possible to discriminate between the true Khalsa Sikhs and others. We can either apply the simple formula designed by Mr. Maclagan, *viz.* that no one is to be returned as a Sikh unless he wears long hair and abstains from tobacco from religious motives; or we might lay down that only those persons were to be returned as Sikhs who had been initiated into the community by the ***Khande ki pahul*** prescribed by Guru Govind Singh. But in the case of the women one test will aid us as little as the other. A Sikh female is not alone in the wearing of long tresses and in the avoidance of tobacco; and women are seldom initiated

Sikhs enumerated in 1901 and 1911.

Sex.	1911.	1901.
Males ...	21,017	21,467
Females ...	10,442	6,624

(though their initiation is not unknown). "As for the women," observed Sir Denzil Ibbetson (*vide* Punjab Census Report, 1881, paragraph 264), "Hindus and Sikhs intermarry freely, and all that the bride does on changing her religion with her home is to alter the arrangement of her hair."

The large increase in the number of Sikh females since 1901 probably apparent only.

112. The position may be summed up as follows:—The relaxation of the definition of Sikh males, which has been given effect to at the present Census, has resulted in no increase in the number returned. We have on the contrary a slight decrease, which might have been greater if a stricter definition had been issued, though we have no strong grounds for believing so. (At any rate the proportion of Sikhs who returned their sect as Guru Govind Singhi, or as Khalsa, is considerably higher now than it was in 1901.) In the case of the women the instructions issued on the present occasion have been the same as those circulated in 1901, the only difference being that while on the present occasion the direction to enter the religion of the women as stated formed the main clause, in 1901 it qualified a different one, which was to be followed in the case of the males. It is unlikely that the proportion of females in Sikh households has actually changed from 31 per 100 males in 1901 to ·50 per 100 males in 1911. Among Hindus the number of females per 100 males was 62 in 1901 and 66 in 1911, and it will be seen therefore that the proportion of females among Sikhs was peculiarly low in both years.

Local variations in Sikh male population since 1901.

113. To explain the variation since 1901 in the number of Sikhs males, it is necessary to look separately at the figures for the different districts, and for the trans-frontier area. The figures for the trans-frontier area are not properly comparable, and can be left out of account. Those shown against it in 1901 refer to the Kurram, and to posts in the Malakand Agency only, whereas those of 1911 include Sikhs enumerated in posts in all five agencies of the Province. But the troops stationed in the Malakand Agency were twice as numerous in 1901 as in 1911, and evidently included one or two Sikh Regiments, the numbers of which alone were more than those of the scattered Sikhs enumerated in trans-frontier posts on the present occasion. In British territory it will be seen that Sikh males have increased by 4 per cent. While the numbers in Kohat and Dera Ismail Khan have decreased by 36 and 33 per cent., respectively, those in Hazara and Peshawar have increased by slightly larger percentages. The variations are obviously due in part to alterations in the composition of the garrisons in the various places. But the decreases in the three southern districts are also referable to abnormal (temporary) immigration in 1901. In that year the building of the Khushalgarh-Thall Railway (*vide* paragraphs 21 and 23 *supra*), which was partly carried out by Pioneer Regiments, no doubt accounted for the presence of an unusually large number of Sikhs in the district. In the population of Bannu and Dera Ismail Khan in 1901 were included over 9,000 troops and followers stationed in the Tochi and Wano Agencies in connection with the Mahsud Blockade (*vide* footnotes to Table II). As we do not know their distribution by religion, it has been impossible to deduct from the 1901 figures those who should be eliminated as not having been actually present in either of the two districts. We can not say how many of these were Sikhs, but it is likely that a considerable number were of that religion, and that the actual decrease among the Sikh males is not so large as our figures would suggest.

Sikh males enumerated in the N.-W. F. P. in 1901 and 1911.

District, etc.	1911.	1901.	Variation per cent. 1901-1911.
Hazara ...	3,339	2,416	+38
Peshawar ...	10,630	7,675	+39
Kohat ...	2,069	2,813	—36
Bannu ...	2,362	2,449	—4
D. I. Khan ...	1,567	3,807	—33
TOTAL DISTRICTS ...	19,967	19,160	+4
TRANS-FRONTIER AREA ...	1,050	2,307	—54

Variations in numbers of Hindus by sex since 1901.

114. Among Hindus we find a decrease in the numbers of both sexes, one of 11 per cent. in the case of males, and one of 5 per cent only in the case of females. If the large increase which has been recorded in the number of Sikh females were due in any marked degree to differences of

Hindus in 1911 and 1901.

Sex.	1911.	1901.
Males ...	73,732	82,812
Females ...	48,896	51,440

classification now and in 1901, we should expect to see it accompanied by a corresponding fall in the number of Hindus of the same sex, and the figures at any rate support the theory. Our Sikh females have increased by 3,818 souls. Our Hindu females have decreased by 2,544. It looks therefore as if a large part of the difference were due to difference of classification. If we assume that, say, 3,618 females returned as Sikhs on the present occasion, were of the class which was shown as being Hindu in 1901, and treat them as Hindus for the purpose of the present comparison, we then get an increase among Hindu females of 1,074, or by 2 per cent and among Sikh females of 200 or by 3 per cent.

Hindu males in 1911 and 1901.

115. The figures for Hindu males by districts are given in the margin. For the reasons mentioned above in discussing the statistics for Sikhs the number shown against the trans-frontier area can be neglected But we still have a large decrease to account for, the only district in which the figures show a rise being Hazara. The increase since 1901 recorded in the number of Sikh males in British territory is far from counterbalancing the decrease among Hindus; and it appears unlikely that differences of classification have anything to do with the variation, which must be explained on other considerations The Hazara figures need no comment. Those for Peshawar are probably to be explained in part, if not wholly, by the abnormal temporary emigration of Hindus in March 1911. In paragraph 23 above, I have referred to the effect which this emigration had on the population of Peshawar city. The apprehension which induced Hindus to leave the head-quarters of the Province was not, however, confined to one area only. Hindus left also the other towns scattered about the district, and possibly even those further afield. One cause for the fall which our statistics for the other districts of the Province exhibit is probably to be found in the same circumstances as I have referred to above in discussing the figures for Sikhs.

Hindu males enumerated in N.-W. F. P.

District, etc.		1911.	1901.
Hazara	... ...	14,882	13,504
Peshawar	... ...	22,599	25,253
Kohat	.. ...	6,758	10,317
Bannu	... ...	11,648	13,077
Dera Ismail Khan	...	15,510	16,677
TOTAL DISTRICTS	...	71,397	78,828
TRANS-FRONTIER AREA	...	2,335	3,984

Decrease in Hindu *cum* Sikh population since 1901.

116. In view of the small numbers included in the non-Muslim community, and of the doubt which arises as to the classification of Hindus and Sikhs respectively in 1901 and 1911, it will be interesting to consider the variation since 1901 in the number of Hindus *cum* Sikhs. It is obvious that the tendency during the last ten years has been in the direction of making the Province an exclusively Mohammadan one. The influence of migration has been considered in the foregoing paragraphs. Differences in the rate of natural increase should also be taken into account. But to discuss the question in its relation to the Hindu and Sikh figures is hardly possible The influence of migration is too great. Of the Hindus, 32 per cent. of the males and 16 per cent. of the females are immigrants, and in the case of the Sikhs the figures are as high as 48 and 17 per cent., respectively. They are, moreover, temporary immigrants only, and the proportion of females to males is abnormally low. In the circumstances the only figures on which conclusions of any value could be based would be those showing the rate of increase in the natural population, *i e.* the population born in the Province wherever enumerated. Unfortunately I have no figures for the religion of immigrants in 1901, or in any earlier year; and there are none therefore with which I can compare those arrived at during the present operations.

District.		*Variation per cent.* 1901-1911.	
		All religions.	Hindu *cum* Sikhs.
Hazara	...	+7·6	+10·3
Peshawar	...	+9·6	—·1
Kohat	...	+2·2	—23·7
Bannu	...	+10·2	—1·5
Dera Ismail Khan	...	+3·3	—3·1
Total Districts	...	+7	—1·7

Causes of the decrease. Indications of a rise in the native born population.

117. The marginal statement printed against the foregoing paragraph appears at first sight to show that the conditions of life in the various districts on which the movement of population as a whole so largely depends, have

considerable influence on the Hindu and Sikh element. It will be noticed that, leaving Hazara on one side, the decrease in the Hindus *cum* Sikhs has been greatest where the rate of increase in the population as a whole has been least. But I am not sure that this correspondence proves anything, when it is remembered that the very circumstance (*viz.* immigration in 1901), which has been adduced to explain the large decrease in the non-Mohammadan population in Kohat, is that to which, I believe, must be attributed the small rise in the total population of the district (*vide* paragraph 60 *supra*). I do not mean that, *e. g.* a healthy climate, if associated with a rapid increase of the Mohammadan population, will not produce the same effect among a Hindu one, but only that our figures do not show it There can be no natural increase except among persons who reside with their wives and families more or less permanently in any area. There is of course such an element among the Hindus and Sikhs of the Province, but the movement of population among them is lost sight of in the greater variations due merely to migration. At the same time the variation in the number of the Hindu *cum* Sikh population by sex since 1901 shows that, in spite of the temporary set back due to migration which the non-Muslim community as a whole has suffered during the last ten years, the process of growth in the permanently settled population, though possibly slow, has not been arrested. The sex least affected by migration is the female, and it is significant that, while males (Hindus with Sikhs) have decreased since 1901 from 104,279 to 94,749, or by 9 per cent., the number of females has increased by 2 per cent., from 58,064 in 1901 to 59,338 in 1911. The contrast in the conditions prevailing in the two years is even more marked when it is stated that while in 1901 there were only 557 females per 1,000 males among these two communities taken together, the number per 1,000 males is now 626. Were it not for the striking decrease in the male population which I can only attribute to migration, it might be argued that the rise in the proportion of females is due to the fact, that the confidence of non-Muslims in the security afforded by a settled Government is growing stronger year by year, with the consequence that new settlers have less and less hesitation in bringing their women with them to spare their lives on what is still regarded as a dangerous frontier. But seeing that, ex-hypothesi, immigrants are now less numerous than was the case ten years ago, this explanation will not fit in with the facts. The growth of the female population can therefore only point to natural growth among the Hindu *cum* Sikh community living permanently within the Province. Indeed the natural growth must have been larger than the figures for females suggest, for a decrease in the number of male immigrants must have been accompanied by a fall, though a smaller one, in the number of female immigrants also.

Variations in the numbers for each religion 1881—1911.

118. Before leaving the subject of movement of population among the followers of the various religions, it will be interesting to consider the figures for a longer period than that which has been dealt with above. Subsidiary Table I appended to this Chapter shows the variation per cent. disclosed, at the various Censuses since 1881, for each religion in the two natural divisions into which the districts of the Province have been divided. No continued tendency is to be observed in the movement of the Hindu population. While the Mussalmans show a gradually descending ratio of increase since 1881, the Hindu population grew more rapidly in the second of the decades dealt with than in the first, which in the third it has actually fallen off. The Sikhs also show a descending ratio of increase at the end of each decade. It is interesting to notice that, although an effort was made both in 1891 and in 1901 to limit the population shown to true Khalsa Sikhs, while in 1881 and on the present occasion the figures include all who chose to return themselves as Sikhs, the increase shown in this community in 1891 was startlingly high, and that recorded in 1901 was nearly twice as large as that shown in 1911. The result is in agreement with the tendency noticed* by Mr. Maclagan in 1891, *viz.* that, whereas in areas where the community is strong, an attempt to define accurately the persons who shall be recorded as belonging to it results in a decrease in the numbers returned, in areas where it is weak, the reverse is the case.

* Paragraph 36, Punjab Census Report, 1891.

Causes of the increasing preponderance of the Mohammadan population.

119. It will be noticed that, with the exception of the period 1891 to 1901, the preponderance of the Mohammadan population has grown steadily greater. In 1881 it amounted to 92·1 per cent. of the whole. Ten years later it was 92·3 per cent. In 1901 it dropped to 92·2, and it has now risen to 92·9. The proportion of Hindus has decreased from 7 per cent in 1881 to 6·4 per cent. in 1891; in 1901 it fell again to 6·3, and it now stands at 5·5 per cent. The Sikhs on the other hand, who in 1881 contributed a percentage of ·5 only to the total population, are responsible now for one of 1·4. The drop in the proportion of Mohammadans between the years 1891 and 1901 is due, I believe to the abnormal immigration of non-Muslims in the later year, which I have referred to above. The rise at the close of each of the other decades on the other hand would seem to indicate something more than an accidental variation. The figures for Hindus are too large to be seriously affected by the composition of the regiments who happen to be stationed in the Province from time to time; and in any case this is a cause which could hardly be expected to result at three successive Censuses in precisely the same effect. For the cause of the increasing preponderance of Mohammadans we must look elsewhere than to migration. It lies probably in the spread of education. At the first annexation of the districts of the Province, the native Mohammadan population was almost entirely illiterate; and it must have been necessary, for the purposes of administration, to import a large number of educated persons from outside. The Hindus have hitherto shown more eagerness for education than the Mohammadans, and at first of necessity the bulk of the educated immigrants must have been Hindus. The advent of British rule, however, meant the advent of education, and though, as will be seen from a reference to Chapter VIII of this Report, the rate of progress, in the last ten years at all events, has not been rapid, education began to spread among the Mohammadans of the Province. Thus the bringing in of outsiders to fill posts for which literate men are required has become less and less necessary. The various openings for educated men, whether in private enterprise or in Government service, have been more and more filled up by natives of the Province (among whom, as we have seen, Mohammadans amount to 93 per cent.); indeed in many branches of the public service it is now the rule to employ strangers only if qualified natives are not obtainable. The separation of the Province from the Punjab has naturally had a great effect in this connection. There was no reason why a local Government ruling at Lahore over a population of which Mohammadans amounted to little more than one half* should prefer to employ them rather than the followers of any other religion. The position is far different in the case of a local administration situated at Peshawar and entrusted with the control of a population among which Mohammadans are in an overwhelming majority; and in this "Partition" we have, I believe, one reason why the proportion borne by the Mussalman element has shown so rapid a rise during the last decade. It is to be noticed too that, apart from Government employés, the formation of the new Province has no doubt tended to sever connexions between the districts on either side of the Indus, witness the drop, from 86,378 in 1901 to 68,893 in 1911, in the number of natives of the Punjab enumerated in our area.

Christians.

120. The total number of Christians enumerated in this Province was 6,718 on the present occasion as compared with 5,273 in 1901. Of these 5,741 are Europeans, 100 Anglo-Indians, and 877 Native Christians, against 4,698 Europeans, 42 Anglo-Indians and 533 Native Christians ten years ago. The numbers therefore are too small to be of great interest. The increase in the number of Europeans and Anglo-Indians is only what might be expected, and the figures for Native Christians show that conversions are not being made with any great rapidity. The Christian Missions at work in the Province all belong to the Anglican Communion, and devote their attention largely to educational and medical work. The mission schools and colleges, like the mission hospitals, are among the most efficient in the Province. Advantage is taken of them freely by the people, but a Mohammadan population do not offer a likely field for conversions. Table XVII in Part II of this volume shows the distribution by sect and race of the Christian population, and in Subsidiary Tables III—V

*Punjab 1891:—Total population 25,130,127, Mohammadans, 12,915,643.

appended to this Chapter will be found figures for the numbers and variations of Christians since 1881, and for the actual and proportional distribution of Christian sects by races and races by sects. Members of the Anglican Communion are preponderant among Christians of all races, and among each of the races represented. Roman Catholics have nearly trebled their numbers since last Census as a result of the presence of an Irish regiment in the Peshawar district. Among Native Christians 264 per mille returned no sect. For the rest the figures call for little remark.

SECT.

Mussalman sects.

121. A list of the Mussalman sects which were entered in our schedules will be found in Subsidiary Table VII appended to this Chapter. Of the total population, 987 per mille showed their sect as Sunni, 11 per mille recorded it as Shia, and only 2 per mille returned other denominations, among whom the greater number were people of the sweeper or scavenger class, who appeared in the column of sect as Mehtar, Chuhra, Balmik, Lalbegi and the like.

Nearly all Mohammadans either Sunnis or Shias.

122. In discussing sect in 1891, Mr. Maclagan (Punjab Census Report, 1891, page 186) remarked that the Mussalman figures had proved somewhat disappointing from the small number of the sects shown in the schedules. Among Mohammadans, he points out, almost every one is either a Sunni or a Shia, and the sects which are not comprised in either are exceedingly few and unimportant. In 1901 the only sects for which figures were separately shown for the districts of the North-West Frontier Province were Sunni, Shia and Ahl-i-Hadis. On the present occasion also few sects have been returned, and the number of persons concerned is trifling for all except Sunni and Shia.

Main points of difference between Sunnis and Shias.

123. The main points of difference between Sunnis and Shias are well summarised in the following passage which I quote from the Punjab Census Report, 1891, (page 187).

" "The Mussalman world is mainly divided into the two comprehensive classes of Sunnis and Shias. And of these the Sunnis may be looked upon as representing the orthodox faith, while the Shias are sectarian. The Shias and Sunnis in the Punjab differ from each other in much the same points as elsewhere. "The Sunnis," writes Mr. Ibbetson, "are those who believe in the Sunnat or customs and traditions of the faith, but the other sects are bound by the traditions, differing only on the question of what traditions should be accepted. The Shia or Imamia school declares that the Mussalman religion consists in a knowledge of the true Imam, a point which the Sunnis consider as unimportant, and consists of the followers of Ali, the husband of Fatimah, the daughter of Mahomed, and the fourth Caliph. They maintain that on the death of the Prophet the office of Imam vested by divine right in Ali, and after him in his two sons Hassan and Hussain, and add to the Mohammadan formula of belief the words "Ali is the Caliph of God," while some of them even regard him as an incarnation of the Deity. They necessarily reject as usurpers the first three Imams, Abu Bakar, Umar and Usman, whom the Sunnis accept, and detest the memory of the Ummeyid Caliphs, who wrested the Caliphate from its rightful holder, and in particular that of Yazid, who slew the martyr Hussain. They observe the first ten days of the month of Muharram as a fast in commemoration of the martyrdom of Ali and his two sons, and carry about Tazias, meant to represent the tombs of the two latter, with loud lamentation and mourning. The Sunnis observe only the tenth day of Muharram, and abhor the Tazias. The Shia is allowed by his creed to conceal his belief whenever it may seem advisable to do so, either in order to obtain converts, or to escape persecution, and to this end he may pass himself off as a Sunni, or even curse his twelve Imams." "

" "The chief difference between the Shias and the Sunnis," says Mr. Wilson writing from Shahpur, "seems to be that they consider Karbala a sacred place as well as Mecca and Medina, add to the Kalima a clause 'Ali Wali Ullah' (Ali is the vicegerant of God), keep their hands at their sides during prayer instead of crossing them in front like the Sunnis, say 'God is Great' five times, instead of four, at funerals, and carry out Tazias with lamentations during the first ten days of the Muharram." "

Variations in numbers of Shias since 1881.

124. In the statement in the margin is shown the total number of Shias recorded in the districts of the Province at the last four enumerations. The figures as they stand are not very instructive. The areas of Bannu and Dera Ismail Khan were much larger previous to 1901 than they are now, and the figures for 1901, showing males over 15 years of age only, can hardly be compared with those of the other years. In the second marginal statement I show the percentage of Shias to total Mussalmans, that for 1901 being calculated on the male population of over 15 years of age. The figures call for little remark. In Peshawar and Dera Ismail Khan the proportion of Shias has risen slightly since 1901, and in Kohat, where followers of this sect are most numerous, it has fallen by just over a half per cent. The proportion for Hazara has fallen to the figure of 1891; while in Bannu Shias seem to be dying out, though the absence of figures for 1901 makes it difficult to say whether the drop from the year 1891 has been continuous. Across the border Shias are to be found in Tirah; and in Kurram they are numerous, as the Turis, who are the dominant tribe of the valley, belong to this sect. In 1901, when a regular Census was taken of the administered portion of the Kurram Agency, 4,980 males of over 15 years of age, or 30 per cent. of the male Mohammadan population of that age period, were recorded as Shias by sect. On the present occasion we have no figures to compare to these. In trans-frontier posts, however, there were enumerated 1,436 Shias, nearly all of whom were in the Kurram.

Variations in numbers of Shias since 1881.

District.	1881.	1891.	1901.*	1911.
Hazara ...	17	221	303	330
Peshawar ...	2,954	2,557	744	3,577
Kohat ...	10,591	10,350	3,601	10,576
Bannu ...	2,861	4,550	...	415
D. I. Khan...	11,273	21,723	2,376	7,927

* Males over 15 only.

Percentage of Shias to total Mussalmans.

District.	1881.	1891.	1901.	1911.
Hazara ...	...	·05	·19	·05
Peshawar ...	·54	39	·32	·44
Kohat ...	6 27	5·52	5·61	5·06
Bannu ...	·95	1·35	...	·18
D. I. Khan...	2·93	5·17	3·51	3·52

The Shia tribes.

125. Sect among the Mohammadans seems to be largely a matter of race. At any rate the Shias mainly belong to a few tribes only, *e. g.*, Kashmiri and Kizzalbash (the latter a small community only) in Hazara and Peshawar, Bangash in Kohat, and Jats, Saiads, Ghilzais or Rangrez in Dera Ismail Khan. In view of the fact that Shias are allowed by their religious tenets to deny their sect in order to avoid persecution, it is interesting to notice that I am informed by one of the senior members of the community that the Shias recorded in Peshawar are largely in excess of the actual numbers. It is suggested to me (I give the explanation for what it is worth) that the exaggeration is due to the enmity of Sunni enumerators, who, if they had a grudge against any one residing in the block with which they had to deal, would be likely to record him as Shia by sect. Sunnis call Shias Kafirs, or infidels, and are fond of abusing their cattle and asses as 'Kafir Shia' or 'Rafizia'.*

Shias of Tirah and Kohat.

126. In paragraph 284 of the Punjab Census Report, 1881, Sir Denzil Ibbetson gives some sayings indicating the abomination in which the Sunnis of the North-West Frontier Province hold Shias. He observes that the Saiads and Orakzais Pathans of Tirah, and their neighbours, the Bangash in the Samilzai country in Kohat, are for the most part known as Shias, "though they are really followers of a sect called Roshania, which arose among the Pathans about the middle of the 16th century. It was founded by one Baz'd, who proclaimed himself a prophet, and styled himself Pir Roshan or the saint of Light .... He laid aside the Koran, and taught that nothing existed but God, who required no set forms of worship, but an implicit obedience to his Prophet. His doctrine.................met with many supporters.............. he preached a sort of social communism, and authorised his followers to seize the land and property of all who would not accept his creed. At one time this sect embraced nearly half the Pathan nation, including all the Afridis of

**Vide* Punjab Census Report. 1881, page 146. "Rafizi is a term commonly applied to Shias on the Frontier either from *rifz*, abuse, because they curse the first three Imams and their supporters, or meaning deserters, because, a section of the Shias is said once to have deserted the standard of Zaid, a grandson of Hussain, because he refused to curse the first two Imams".

Tirah and many of the Yusafzais............................ But meddling with politics led to their fall: they were crushed by Akbar, and finally dispersed by Jehangir, and their tenets are now professed only by the people of Tirah, by many, but not all, of the Bangash of Kohat, and by a few adherents scattered along the trans-Indus Salt Range from the Kohat to the Dera Ismail Khan District. They are called Shia more because they are rejected by the Sunnis than because they follow the Shia doctrines." The Shias of Kohat seem to be slowly dying out; at any rate their numbers are not increasing as rapidly as those of other Mohammadans, the percentage which they bear to the Mohammadan population having fallen from 6·27 in 1881 to 5·06 on the present occasion. I am informed that they are now accepted as true Shias by members of the community elsewhere.

127. The Wahabis and the Ahl-i-Hadis are identical. For an account of the sect the reader is referred to paragraph 134 of the Punjab Census Report, 1891. "The whole sect as found in the Punjab" wrote the late Sir Denzil Ibbetson in 1881, "reject the name of Wahabi as a term of reproach, and as now having a political stigma attached to it, and prefer to call themselves Ahl-i-Hadis, 'people of the traditions,' or Muwahidin, 'Unitarians', while in the eastern districts (though not apparently on the Frontier) they commonly style themselves Mohammadi, substituting the personal name of their founder Mohammad-ibn-Abdul Wahab for his patronymic". All three names have been returned on the present occasion, but in insignificant numbers. In 1901 under the head 'Ahl-i-Hadis sects' only 4 males of 15 years of age and over were returned in Peshawar and Kohat, and none in the other districts trans-Indus. 126 were returned in parts in the Malakand Agency, and in Kurram (none have been returned in agencies on the present occasion), and 2,580 in Hazara. The Hazara Wahabis were said in 1907 (*vide* Hazara Gazetteer of that year, paragraph 39) to be Karals, descendants of the converts of one Maulvi Mohammad Kasim, who visited the Karal country in 1845; and it was remarked that most of the leading families who were gained over by him had now abjured his doctrines. The trifling figures on the present occasion (only 25 persons) suggest that the sect has now almost died out in the district; and information supplied to me by the Deputy Commissioner confirms this view. "Owing to the death", he writes, "of the late K. Mir Alam, Extra Assistant Commissioner, and Maulvi Hayat Gul, who were the leaders of the Ahl-i-Hadis in the district, their followers have ceased to record themselves as such, and have merged into Mohammadanism". Our return for Peshawar (83 persons) is larger than that recorded in 1901, but I am told that it is certainly defective, as the Wahabis have four or five mosques of their own in Peshawar city; and the suggestion is that they have shrunk from recording the name of their true sect. The Wahabis.

128. One hundred and forty eight persons have recorded their sect as Ahamadiya, of whom 21 were found in Hazara, 199 in Peshawar and 8 in Kohat. I am told that these figures are considerably below the actual numbers. The sect is of recent growth, but had excited notice in 1901, when 1,113 males over 15 years of age returned it in the Punjab and North-West Frontier Province. I have no figures however to show their local distribution. There is a reference to the sect in paragraph 653 of the last India Census Report as consisting of the followers of "a religious teacher of the name of Ghulam Ahmad who claims to be the Mahdi or Messiah expected by Mohammadans and Christians alike........ he repudiates the doctrine of Jehad with the sword, and regards as absolutely unlawful wars undertaken for the propogation of religion." As regards the founder of the sect Mr. Rose wrote in 1901: "The leader of the sect is a Barlas Mughal, whose family came from Persia in the time of Babar, and obtained a Jagir in the present district of Gurdaspur. Beginning as a Maulvi with a special mission to the† sweepers, the Mirza eventually advanced claims to be the Mahdi or Messiah expected by Mohammadans and Christians alike". Some further information about the sect is contained in a paper on Islam, read before a gathering described as the Convention of Religions, at Allahabad in January 1911 by Khwaja Kamal-ud-Din of Lahore, who opened his lecture by remarking, "I belong to the Ahmadiyia sect of Islam, a sect founded by Hazrat Mirza Ghulam Ahmad* of Qadian" (in the Gurdaspur District of the Punjab), "in the Ahmadiyas.

* Born in 1835, died in May 1908.

† The correctness of this statement is challenged by the Secretary, Anjuman-i-Ahmadia, Peshawar.

last decade of the 19th century. The sect does not differ from other Islamic sects in any cardinal principle of Mohammadanism but in one thing. Our holy Prophet Mohammad promised us a Messiah who will come to revive religion in days to come, and we accept the fulfilment of these prophetic words in the person of our master, the founder of Ahmadiya movement". The main characteristic of the sect appears to be a spirit of toleration. Its adherents lay stress on the passages in the Qoran which remind the Faithful that God has given his sun and his moon to all mankind, and argue that the revelation of his truth has been granted with a like impartiality. "This generous teaching of Al-Qoran," proceeds the reader of the paper referred to above, "if it prompts me to cherish feelings of love and reverence for Moses and Jesus, enjoins upon me also to pay my respect and allegiance to Rama Chandra, Krishna and Lord Budha. If with al-Qoran I accept authenticated portion of the Bible as the word of God, I regard the Gita and the other holy scriptures of India as my joint property with other Hindu brethren." This standpoint is of course one diametrically opposed to the position of the Muslim as generally conceived, and the acceptance of Mirza Ghulam Ahmad as a prophet is distasteful to the orthodox. The name of the sect is well-known, but its tenets are not apparently so familiar among Mohammadans, for I was informed by a Shia of some education that its adherents revile Christ and the Virgin with unspeakable abuse. The followers of the sect are perhaps equally well known as Mirzais, after the title used before Ghulam Ahmad's name, and Qadianis from his place of residence. Mr. Rose notes that the designation Ahmadiya was adopted in October 1900 in view of the approaching Census. All the Ahmadiyas have been enumerated in towns.

Other sects Hanifis & Shafis.

129. The other sect entries refer to trifling numbers only. The Hanifis and the Shafis are the names of two out of the four great Sunni schools of doctrine, the other two being the Malakias and the Hanbalis. The Jafri and the Ismail are from among the 32 sects assigned to the Shias, many of which, * wrote Mr. Maclagan, "relate to the rights of succession to the Imamate. One of the most notable schisms of this kind........................originated on the death of the Imam Jafir, called As-Sadiq, or the truth-teller (A D. 702—764), one of the most learned and distinguished characters in Mohammadan history. The Imam, having found his eldest son Ismail drunk, excluded him from the Imamate, and appointed his second son Musa as his successor The greater number of Shiahs follow the wishes of Jafir-us-Sadiq and acknowledge Musa as the Imam, and these are often called Imamiah, but a certain section, preferring the claims of the family of Ismail, are called Ismailiah". The entries of Shamsi, Shamsi Shia and Pir Mir Agha Khan (only 9 persons in all) are apparently to be grouped together. Mr. Maclagan (*vide* Punjab Census Report, 1891, paragraph 77) writes as follows regarding this sect: "A sect more curious in some ways than any yet mentioned is that of the Shamsis, or followers of Pir Shams Tabrez, the great Saint of Mooltan. This saint has a reputation in all parts of the Punjab and among persons of all creeds, more especially from having been flayed alive and being able to walk with his skin in his hand. But there is in the north of the Province a sect which is in some special way devoted to the cult of this saint. It gives alms in the name of its Pir, it worships no idols, but reverences the Bhagwat Gita, and is usually held in abhorrence by orthodox Hindus.................There is reason to believe that the sect is closely connected with the Khojas of Bombay, of whom the Agha Khan is spiritual head" Mr. Maclagan deals with the Shamsis as a Hindu sect, and 289 Hindus have shown themselves as belonging to it on the present occasion; the reference here however is to Mussalman followers of the Mooltan saint. Sufi and Rabbani have been recorded as the sect of 6 and 5 males, respectively. For a brief account of Sufism I would refer the reader to paragraph 136 of the Punjab Census Report, 1891. The Rabbanis (the followers of Imam Rabbani, called the Sirhind Sahib from his greatest shrine), are one of the divisions of the Naqshbandis, who with the Chishtis, the Qadiris and the Saharwardis, form the four regular orders among the Sunnis, all of whom agree in upholding Sufism. Leaving on one side Arab, which has been returned as a sect by one female, and regarding which I have no information, the only other sect recorded

The Jafri and Ismail.

Shamsis.

Sufi.

Rabbani.

* Punjab Census Report, 1891, pragraph 132.

is Ahl-i-Qoran, which has been shown by 16 persons (5 males and 11 females.) I am informed that this is a new sect, the centre of which is at Chakriana in the Punjab, founded by one Maulvi Sheikh Abdullah of Lahore. His followers regard the Qoran only, and not the Hadis, and leave out all the forms of prayer prescribed in the latter, They differ from other Mohammadans in not giving the call to prayers (*azan*). Ahl-i-Qoran.

130. In the margin are shown the numbers of Mohammadans who returned sweeper sects, or instead of a sect, the name of a sweeper caste. Below these figures are shown the numbers of Mohammadan Chuhras as printed in Table XIII. It will be seen that the figures correspond closely in the case of males. Of the females many no doubt returned their sect as Sunni, especially if they were not themselves employed as scavengers. Sweeper sects.

Sweeper sects.

	Males.	Females.
Mohammadans who returned sweeper sects.	520	281
Mohammadan Chuhras ...	533	346

131. The majority of the names shown as those of Hindu sects also appear in the sect table of the Sikhs, and I will mention together the persons who have returned them, irrespective of the creed which they profess. The fact that there is hardly a name appearing in the Sikh list, including even Guru Govind Singh, which does not also find a place in that of the Hindus, illustrates very clearly the absence of any distinct line of cleavage between the two communities. At the close of this section of the present chapter, I will devote a few remarks to the names which have been returned as those of Sikh sects alone, and some further consideration to the numbers of Sikhs who have shown themselves as Nanakpanthis and followers of Guru Gobind Singh, respectively. In the following paragraphs, except where it is distinctly stated to the contrary, the entries mentioned are to be understood as referring exclusively to the Hindus. Sects of the Hindus & Sikhs.

132. The names returned as those of Hindu sects are very numerous, amounting in all to 359 different entries. Many are those of castes and tribes such as Agarwal, Arora, Brahman, Bhat, Bhatiara, Chamar, Chuhra, Dhobi, Dogra, Gorkha, Jat, Meo and the like. Some indicate occupations or occupational castes as for instance, Zamindar, Mahajan, Bhishti, Mallah, Nai and Hajjam. A good many more are clan or family names like Kapur, Sarsut, Muhial, Utradi and Janjua. Religions such as Hindu,* Sikh and Jaini, and local names such as Bengali, Hindustani and Purbi have also been shown as sects ; and the meaning of the some of the entries (the numbers concerned are however trifling) I have not succeeded in tracing. There would have been no object to be gained in printing the list as it stood ; and the one which forms Subsidiary Table VIII to this chapter accordingly reproduces two-fifths only of the names contained in the Census Schedules. It refers, however, to 92 per cent. of the total Hindu population of the Province. Hindu sects.

In Chapter IV of the Punjab Census Report, 1891, Mr. Maclagan has given a very full account of the religious sects of the Punjab and North-West Frontier Province, and to that place I would refer the reader for details. In the following paragraphs I have merely attempted to arrange our returns under the various heads shown by Mr. Maclagan, such information only being included as is necessary to throw my account into the form of an intelligible narrative.

133. Mr. Maclagan opens his account† of the sects of the Hindus and Sikhs by dealing with some names in his returns 'relating to the more primitive forms of worship, the adoration of the earth, the heavenly bodies, of snakes and rivers.' These are but meagrely represented in the North-West Frontier Province. In Peshawar one male showed his sect as Budh, or Budh worshipper. "Those returned as Budh worshippers", remarks Mr. Maclagan, "may be men with a reverence for Budha, but more probably they refer to the planet Mercury, from whom Budhwar, or Wednesday is named." Two males in Peshawar and two females in Kohat have returned their sect as Suraj Bansi, which I take to refer to the worship of the sun. This form of worship was never apparently Veneration of the heavenly bodies, rivers and the minor deities.

* Five persons returned religion as Sikh and sect as Hindu.

† Punjab Census Report, 1891, Chapter IV, Part I.

common in our Frontier districts, and is of merely accidental occurrence now, our sun worshippers being probably emigrants from the south-east. Owing to its position with regard to the Indus, the veneration of rivers is naturally more common in the Province. Sanatan Darya and Darya Panthi have been returned by 25 and 56 persons respectively in the Dera Ismail Khan District, the reference being undoubtedly to the Indus. "The Hindus of the Indus also very generally worship the river itself under the name of Khwaja Khizr or Zinda Pir." (Ibbetson Census Report, paragraph 240.) One Sikh in our returns has shown his sect as Khwaja Khizr. Veneration of the Ganges is represented only by 3 females in Peshawar, in which district, from its superior attractions to immigrants, settlers from the east are naturally most numerous. The entry of Itwar I do not understand, unless it be regarded as a shortened form of Itward Upashak, or Sunday worshipper. "The common method of worshipping the river." (*i. e.*, the Indus) "of an evening is to make a small raft of reeds, and to place on it a lamp, which is then lit, and set afloat in the river or in some canal. In the morning some flowers and scent and sweetmeats are placed upon a plate, hymns are sung, and the offerings then thrown into the river. These forms of worship are commonly gone through on a Sunday, and the entry of Sunday worshippers (Itwar Upashak) in the Census returns means merely one who worships the Indus on a Sunday." The form of worship here described is that practised in the Derajat, whereas the 4 males and 1 female in our returns who showed their sect as Itwar were enumerated in the Hazara District. Unless therefore it be assumed that they are immigrants from the Derajat, the identification of 'Itwar' with 'Itwar Upashak' would appear to be unlikely. Of worshippers of minor deities among the orthodox gods our returns show only 2 (males) in Peshawar, who have recorded their sect as Hanuman, *i. e.*, persons whose reverence is devoted in particular to the monkey god.

Veneration of Rivers.

Sects.		Males.	Females.
Sanatan Darya	...	...	25
Darya Panthi	...	37	19
Pamnar Ganga	...	...	3
Itwar ...	...	4	1

Vaishnavas and Saivas.

134. It was suggested by Dr. G. A. Grierson some time before the Census that it might be possible to classify the majority of Hindus as either Vaishnavas or Saivas. "Putting a few dissenting sects, insignificant in number, to one side" he wrote, "every Hindu may be classed as either a Vaishnava or a Saiva, though he may not know it himself;" and he went on to explain wherein in his view lay the importance of the distinction : "I am now satisfied that the religion of every Vaishnava is, though he may not know it, based upon monotheism, while the religion of many Saivas is based upon the pantheism which thousands of people think to be the only book religion of India. Vaishnavism is the daughter of the old Bhagavarta religion, which laid stress upon the existence of a kindly personal god, and strongly denied the absorption theory of the soul's salvation. To them the soul is eternal, and, when it is saved, it lives for ever near God...................... Every one who is at all a Vaishnava loathes the idea of Sankarâs '*Maya*', and all the theory of loss of identity in salvation which is connected with it".

135. The record of sect was a matter left to the discretion of the Local Governments of the various Provinces, and no standard instructions were issued on the subject by the Census Commissioner. Some time after the actual enumeration, however, he noted that it would be interesting to consider certain questions arising out of the position taken up by Dr. Grierson with regard to the sects of Hindus. The first of these was whether it could be said that all Hindus, whatever their sect, could be classified either as Vaishnavas or Saivas, and whether there are any standards which could be taken for the purpose of such a classification ; and secondly whether they could be applied by persons of the stamp of the Census enumerators. Other points the consideration of which is suggested by Dr. Grierson's remarks are, whether it is correct to say that all Vaishanavas are at heart monotheistic, and that they believe in the continued separate existence of the soul after *Mukti* has been obtained, (*i. e.*, that they reject the doctrine of *Maya*). What again is the common conception of *Mukti*, or salvation ? Does it, in the mind of the ordinary uneducated

person, mean anything but an advantageous re-incarnation? And, finally, is it true to say that the effect of ***Karma*** is merely to obtain an advantageous re-birth, and that emancipation from the cycle of births and deaths is obtained only by ***Bhagti.***?

136. Previous experience in India could give no very hopeful answer to the question as to whether it is possible to classify Hindus under the two main heads suggested. One and the same person comes under the head of the Vaishnavas, if one part of this practise be regarded, and under that of the Saivas if another be taken into account, while it was stated* of the United Provinces in 1901 that "the sectarian divisions of Saivism and Vaishnavism are recognised by a very small portion of the Hindu population." The reports I have received on the subject from the different districts of the North-West Frontier Province are unanimous in expressing the view that no standard exists, which could have been applied, or even understood, by the ordinary enumerator who, it will be remembered, is nearly always a Mohammadan. In most districts it is recognised that all Hindus are either Saivas or Vaishnavas, but no line can be drawn between them from the point of view of belief alone. It would indeed be possible to class all meat-eaters as Saivas and all vegetarians as Vaishnavas, but the distinction would be largely an arbitrary one; and the belief of the communities thus forcibly differentiated would not support Dr. Grierson's view that "the religion of every Vaishnava is, though he may not know it, based upon monotheism, while the religion of many Saivas is based upon the pantheism which thousands of people think to be the only book religion of India." From most of the districts of the Province I am informed that the Vaishnavas are monotheistic at heart and "though they worship images, yet they worship that image as god,"; but one gentleman, himself an orthodox Hindu, writes that "there are no monotheists among the Hindus except the Arya Samaj." Moreover the statement, made with regard to Dera Ismail Khan, that the Saivas are Nanakpanthis, certainly does not suggest that it is among Saivas that pantheism is to be found.

137. Dr. Grierson's view that "everyone who is at all a Vaishnava loathes the idea of Sankarás '*Maya*' and all the theory of loss of identity in salvation which is connected with it" is not supported by any form of Hinduism which is to be found in the North-West Frontier Province. The replies I have received from all districts state distinctly that Vaishnavas do not believe in the separate existence of the soul after ***Mukti*** (salvation), but profess that "the soul merges in the soul of the Supreme Being, and becomes one with it." That is to say they accept the doctrine of '***Maya***' or absorption in the Supreme Being as the ultimate goal of all human effort. ***Mukti***, or salvation, to the Hindus of the Province generally, means, if my informants are correct, the cessation from the cycle of births and deaths which is involved in the merging of personal identity in that of the Creator. The effect of ***Karma*** is merely to obtain an advantageous re-birth; and emancipation from the cycle of re-births is obtained only by ***Bhagti***.

138. The isolated position of the Hindus in the Province perhaps gives an interest to their views, which, in view of the small numbers of the community, they could not otherwise possess. It is for this reason that I have included the remarks contained in the foregoing paragraphs. After what has been said, it need cause no surprise that few persons only have returned themselves as Vaishnavas (the numbers are given in the margin); especially when it is remembered that no instructions were given to enumerators as to showing Hindus either as Saiva or Vaishnava. Our Vaishnavas are returned from every district of the Province, but they are most numerous proportionately in Bannu and Dera Ismail Khan. We have also a few miscellaneous entries which should be included under this head, such as Sri Ram Chand, Ram Chandarji and Krishn. Vaishnavas.

Sect.	Males.	Females
Vaishnava	934	324
Vaishno Kohistani ...	1	...
Puranic Vaishno ...	15	...

* *Vide* United Provinces Census Report, 1901, page 72.

The actual entries are shown in the margin; they do not add any large number to those who should be attributed to Vaishnavism. Among other names Vishnu is reverenced as Narain and Thakur, or Thakurji, while "of the minor Avartars of this deity, the only noticeable ones are those of Narsingh the man-lion, who tore into pieces the tyrant Harnakas (Hiranaya-Kasipa) to save the pious Prahlad; and Parasram, the axe-hero, who fell with such fury on the Khatri caste.* The most popular incarnations are however, of course those of Ram Chandr and Krishna". "The Jai Kishnis" (*ibid paragraph* 120) "worship none but Krishn and are remarkable for the combination they present of the extreme Shaiva and Vaishnava practices." Krishn is also known as Gopal, and it is to this name of the God that our entry of Sevak Gopal would seem to refer. Sewak Gopal has also been given as their sect by 2 Sikhs (males), and Ram Chand by 1 male and 2 females of the same religion.

Sect.		Males.	Females.
Baba Narsingh	...	6	...
Chah Narain...	...	...	2
Jai Kishni ...	...	26	8
Jeo Narain Panthi	...	1	...
Krishn ...	...	5	...
Meo Narain Panthi	...	1	...
Narain Panthi	...	6	...
Parasrami ...	...	20	12
Ram Chandji	...	152	21
Ramdaji ...	...	4	...
Sewak Gopal	...	...	3
Sri Ram Chand	...	2	...
Thakurji ...	...	1	...
Thakur Pujari	...	71	83
Total	...	295	129

Radha Swamis.

139. One hundred and sixty nine persons, who returned their sect as Radha Swami, and 11 who showed it as Salig Ram may perhaps be included under the head of Vaishnavas, in view of the fact that abstinence from animal food forms one of the conditions necessarily observed by them. They appear to be mystics who profess that the spirit can at the will of the devotee leave the body and reach the highest spiritual sphere. R. B. Salig Ram, a retired Government official, who died about 1895, succeeded, on the death of the founder, to the spiritual leadership of the sect. For an account of its tenets the reader is referred to pages 131 and 132 of Mr. Rose's Census Report, Punjab, 1901. In addition to the Hindus already noted 10 Sikhs have shown their sect as Radha Swami.

		Male.	Female.
Radha Swami	...	91	78
Salig Ram ...	...	11	...

The Bairagis and their followers.

140. "The various orders who attach themselves more especially to the worship of Ram and Krishn are known generally as Bairagi," says Mr. Maclagan,† to whom (*loc cit*) I would refer the reader for an account of them; and accordingly I will mention here the Bairagis and their followers, (*vide* list printed in the margin) who find a place in our returns. It is doubtful whether the phrases "Bairagi Fakir" and 'Sadhu Bairagi' possess any very definite connotation, but it seems best to include them here, though they suggest little more than the word ascetic. The greater number of the persons shown in the marginal list are followers of the Gosains. After noting on the vagueness with which the words Sanniasi and Bairagi are used, Mr. Maclagan (page 125 Panjab Census Report, 1891), remarks: "a word more vaguely used still, and very difficult to define is Gosain. The term may, roughly speaking, be said to denote an ascetic of any order, but with a slight implication that the ascetic is a man of some standing and influence.................On the whole the commonest meaning of the term appears to be that which refers to Bairagis who are of high caste, such as the Brahmans. The word is also applied in the south-west

Bairagis and their followers.

Sect.		Male.	Female.
Bairagi Faqir ...	...	12	3
Gosain ...	...	70	43
Gosain Khandwala	...	...	2
Guru Gosain ...	..	...	4
Khemdasi ...	...	3	19
Nagarpanthi ...	...	56	14
Sadhu Bairagi ...	...	39	...
Sewak ...	...	2,736	2,088
Sewak Gosain ...	...	14	3
Sewak Lalji ...	...	3,478	1,550
Sewak Mahajan	...	11	...
Sewak Panthi ...	...	...	30
Shamji Panthi ...	...	29	...
Tulsi Das ..	...	29	35
Total	...	6,477	3,791

* *Vide* Punjab Census Report, 1901, page 119.

† *Vide* Punjab Census Report, 1891, page 122.

of the Province in a special sense to the followers of the saints Lalji and Shamji," with whose names is connected "the most celebrated of all the Bairagi movements in the Punjab." Mr. Maclagan adds that "these two men were the leaders of a great revivalist movement among the Kirars, or Hindu traders, of the south-west some three or four hundred years ago." Their influence "in favour of the Hindu religion has been enormous, and they have in all probability reclaimed the whole of the trading community of the south-west from a virtual conversion to Sikhism or Mohammadanism. To be Hindu by religion is in those parts almost synonymous with being a follower of these Gosains. The Khatris and Aroras of the south-west are divided into Sikhs and Sewak, the followers of Nanak and the disciples of the Gosains; and it is due to Shamji and Lalji that the latter are as numerous as they are." It is interesting, however, to notice that Lalji Panthi (5 males and 7 females), Sewak (14 males and 2 females), Sewak Panthi (1 male), Tulsi Dass (2 males and 1 female), in addition to the numbers given in the foregoing marginal statement, were returned as the name of their sects by Sikhs. It is no doubt as a result of the contrast locally observed between Sikhs and Sewaks, and of the fact that the latter are Vaishnavas, that the Saivas of Dera Ismail Khan (*vide* paragraph 136 *supra*) are said to be Nanak Panthis, all who are not Vaishnavas being regarded locally as Saivas, in spite of the fact that the disciples of Nanak would hardly be expected to be referable to one of the two main denominational sections into which Hindus proper may be divided. We have here an example of the fact noticed by Mr. Maclagan (*vide* Punjab Census Report, 1891, page 111) that in the Punjab "the distinction is less one of religion or of the god worshipped than of practice and ceremony and the manner of food eaten,' the Saivas having in general no objection to the eating of meat while the Vaishnavas have. It is to be observed that of the total number (9,852 persons) who have returned their sect as Sewak Lalji, or as Sewak alone, no less than 5,841 were enumerated in Dera Ismail Khan, while 2,876 come from the neighbouring district of Bannu. It will be noticed also that, while I have shown the whole under the general heading of Bairagis, all but a trifling minority are not ascetics, but secular Hindus, most of whom are engaged in trade. Other Bairagi teachers whose names appear in our returns are Tulsi Das probably "a recent reformer from Ajniawala in Hafizabad Tahsil" of the Gujranwala District, and Khemdas, a Gosain of the family of Lalji. Nagar Panthi appears to refer to the followers of some celebate Bairagi, (Nagar Bairagi), those who marry being styled Gharbasi.

Minor Hindu sects.

141. Baba Lala Jasrai (1 female in Peshawar) indicates apparently a follower of one Lala Jasrai, "a Khatri whose shrine is in Depalpur in Montgomery. A large number of Khatris put their faith in him, and take their children to his shrine to have their heads shaved" * while the entry of Jinda Kaliana (Dera Ismail Khan District) indicates devotees of the Jhang saints, Jinda and Kaliana, some account of whom will be found in paragraph 68 of Maclagan's Census Report.

Jinda Kaliana ...	11 males...	24 females.

Saivas.

142. So far we have been considering the sects which may be referred to Vaishnavism. The Saivas, under which general head I include also the Sanniasis and the Jogis, are less numerous, though the names returned are many and various. I will mention first those persons who have given as their sect the name of Shiv himself, Shivnarain or Sheonarain, and Mahadeo, or the Great God, being among the commonest of the alternative names for this deity. Returns referring to the worship of his consort Devi are more frequent, (see marginal list on the following page). Kalka, Bhagvati and Bhavani are three among the many names by which goddess is

Name returned.	Males.	Females.
Shivji ...	55	21
Shiv Narain ...	163	88
Shiv Panthi ...	33	17
Shiv Ramdass ...	...	1
Shiv Ramji ...	3	...
Mahadev ...	12	...
Total ...	266	127

* *Vide* Punjab Census Report, 1891, page 129.

Devi Worshippers.

Sects returned.		Males.	Females.
Bhagat ...	...	9	2
Bhagat Rani ...	...	1	2
Bhagwati ...	...	27	31
Bhavani ...	...	6	...
Calcutta Devi	...	1	...
Devi ...	...	190	1
Devi ke Mannewala	...	41	...
Devi ka Pujari	...	120	98
Devi Panthi ...	...	6	1
Devi Parat ...	...	7	4
Devi Pum ...	...	21	...
Devi Sanatan	...	...	7
Devna Pujari	...	35	54
Kali Devi ...	...	6	3
Kalka Mai ...	...	1	...
Sewak Devi ...	...	41	47
Upashak Devi	...	9	16
Total	...	521	266

worshipped, while Bhagat has a special meaning as indicating her devotees. Our Devi worshippers have nearly all been enumerated in Hazara or Peshawar, and in so far as a line can be drawn, it may be said that the influence of Saivism is strongest in the north of the Province and that of Vaishnavism in the south. In addition to the persons shown in the margin, all of whom are Hindus, one Sikh male also has returned his sect as Devi.

Sanniasis and Jogis.

143. "The Shaivas," says *Mr Maclagan "have generally been defenders of the faith against innovation. The final struggles against Buddhism in the south and centre of the peninsula gave rise to one sect of Shaivas, known henceforth as Sanniasis, and the contest against the innovating Bhagats of Northern India in the 15th century gave rise to another sect, now known as Jogis. Properly speaking the term Sanniasi is applied to any person undergoing the last or meditative stage (Ashram) of existence prescribed by Manu ; but the term is applied more especially to the followers of Shankar Acharaj, the well-known commentator, a very vigorous defender of orthodoxy, who is supposed to have lived in the ninth or tenth, or according to Professor Monier Williams, in the eighth century, and to have helped in the final extinction of Buddhism in India." Acharaj is the name by which one of the groups of Sanniasi is known. In all we have few entries (*vide* marginal list) which indicate the Sanniasis or their followers. Sanniasi has been returned as her sect by one Sikh female also. Amar Nathi I include here, as probably referring to the fact that Amar Nath is one of the chief places of pilgrimage of the sect.

Names returned.		Males.	Females.
Sanniasi ...	...	2	2
Acharaj ...	...	9	15
Dev Acharaj...	...	1	...
Bhat Acharaj	...	1	...
Guru Saniasi...	...	...	3
Amar Nathi...	...	...	5

Jogis.

144. The Jogis † are more frequently referred to in our sect returns. "The Jogi or Yogi, properly so called" says‡ Mr. Maclagan "is a follower of the Joga system of philosophy founded by Patanjali, the main characteristics of which are a belief in the power of man over nature by means of austerities and the occult influence of the will. The purer forms of this teaching pass, as may be easily imagined, into a theosophic creed which is independent of religion. .... The general tendency, however, is not towards speculative developments of this kind, but rather in the direction of confusing the Jogi with the wonder worker or charlatan of every day life, and the name is often adopted by wandering beggars who have no claim whatever to religious merit." The most common account is that the founder of the sect was one Gorakhnath, who is represented in fiction as a contemporary of King Vikramaditya, and his name is given by **86** persons in our returns. Another Jogi saint mentioned is Ratan Nath. "The prevalence of the Jogis on and beyond the Frontier," says Mr. Maclagan " is a matter worthy of notice, more especially in connection with the supposed relation of the Jogis to ancient

Sects returned.			Males.	Females.
Gorakhnath	...	...	49	30
Gorakhpanthi	...	..	4	2
Jogi Gorakhnathi	...	...	1	...

* *Vide* Punjab Census Report 1891, paragraph 55.

† The actual entries are Bawa Jogi, Digar Jogi, Jog, Jogi, Jograni, Jogi Panthi, Guru Jogi, Sewak Jogi, Sewak Jogiani, Sewak Gopichand, Pujari Jogi, Gorakh Nath, Gorakh Panthi, Jogi Gorakh Nath, Tirath Nath, Pir Ratan Nath, Sewak Pir Ratan Nath Sahib, Ratan Nathi, Ratan Panthi and Sewak Baba Ratan Nath.

‡ *Vide* Punjab Census Report, 1891, paragraph 54.

Buddhism. The Gorkhatri at Peshawar, which Sir A. Cunningham identifies with an old Buddhist monastery, is connected by legend with the name of Gorakh Nath, and was in former times a haunt of Jogis. "I had heard" says Baber, "the fame of the Gorkhatri, which is one of the holy places of the Jogis of the Hindus, who come from great distances to cut off their hair and shave their beard at this Gorkhatri ;" and Abul Fazl writes : "here is a temple called Gorkhatri, a place of religious resort especially for Jogis" At present the chief Jogi saint of this part of country is Pir Ratan Nath. There are shrines connected with his name at Peshawar, Jelalabad and Kabul". Nearly all our returns of the name of Pir Ratan Nath come from Peshawar. Two males in the same district have shown themselves as followers of Raja Gopi Chand, the nephew of King Vikramaditya, who adopted the life of a Jogi ; and in Tirath Nath, whose name is returned by 27 persons also in Peshawar, we have apparently the name of another Jogi Saint. In addition to the entries already referred to one Sikh male has returned his sect as Jog.

Sects returned.	Males.	Females.
Pir Ratan Nathi	73	73
Sewak Pir Ratan Nath Sahib ...	6	..
Ratan Nathi	109	52
Ratan Panthi	4	2
Sewak Baba Ratan Nath ...	15	...

Tirath Nath ... 15 Males—12 Females.

Sanatan Dharam.

145. The attempt to class the Hindus of the Province as either Vaishnavas or Saivas can be pursued no further, for the remainder of our entries indicate either orthodox Hinduism, Sikh influences, sweeper religions, modern developments, such as the Arya Samaj or a few minor sects which can not be referred to either of the two main divisions of Hindus. By far the commonest entry in our returns is Sanatan Dharam. I show in the margin the numbers of those who have returned this or other names, the meaning of which appears to be the same. Of Sanatan Dharam Mr. Maclagan wrote that it merely implies that the persons returning it belong to the old school ; and "it is generally used in contradistinction to the followers of the Arya Samaj." Most of the entries in my marginal list explain themselves. Sam Hindu appears to mean merely orthodox Hindu (Sam in Pashtu means straight). Bram Chari (correctly spelt Brahmchari) describes a student going through the orthodox course of instruction, and Karam Kandi implies "followers of the Hindu body of ceremonial which is known as Karm Kand."

Sects returned.	Males.	Females.
Sanatan Dharam (Hindu)	34,025	18,876
" " (Sikh)	225	104
Sewak Sanatan ...	85	...
Sewak Sanatan Dharam ...	78	...
Karam Kandi ...	13	5
Sam Hindu	5	...
Bram Chari	4	1
Sikh Bram Chari ...	...	1
Pandit Sanatan ...	1	...
Gurkha Sanatan Dharam ...	1	...

Sikh influences.

146. The extent to which the Hindus of the Province have been influenced by Sikhism is indicated by the figures in the margin, in which I have collected together those entries which refer to persons belonging to the class commonly described as Sahijdhari Sikhs, or Sikhs who do not observe the ordinances of Guru Govind Singh, notably the prohibition of shaving and smoking. They have commonly given as that of their sect the name of the founder of Sikhism, Guru Nanak. Still more striking as indicating the absence of any distinct line of cleavage between Hindus and Sikhs is the fact that as many as 1,738 of the former appear in the sect column as followers of Guru Govind Singh, Kesdhari and the like *. These would appear to be persons who have taken the *Pahul*, or have gone

Sects returned.	Males.	Females.
HINDUS		
Nanak Panthi ...	14,837	13,651
Nanak Sanatani ...	5	...
Sahij Dhari ...	7	...
Guru Nanak ...	3,247	3,457
Sikh ...	80	91
Sanatan Nanak Panthi ...	226	186
Sikh Sabha ...	...	8
Hindu Singh ...	48	...
Granthi ...	1	2
SIKHS		
Nanak Panthi ...	7,464	5,347
Sahij Dhari ...	174	110
Guru Nanak ...	588	51
Sikh Sabha ...	47	7

*The entries here referred to are :—Guru Govind Singh, Khalsa, Khalsa Panthi, Kes Dhari, Singh Sabha, Guru Govindji, Mahajan Singh and Gada Govind ke.

through the form of initiation or baptism ordained by the tenth Guru ; and the correctness of the entry of Hindu in the column of religion is at any rate open to question. To other Sikh influences may be attributed the few miscellaneous entries shown in the margin. The Udasi are an ascetic order founded by Sri Chand, one of the sons of Guru Nanak. Mula Panthi indicates followers of a Baba Mula, apparently the founder of a Nanak Panthi sect, but whose identification is uncertain (*vide* Maclagan's Census Report, paragraph 93). The Nirankaris are followers, either of Guru Nanak who, from his use of the word "Nirankar" or "the Formless," with reference to the deity, was known as 'Nanak Nirankari,' or more probably of one "Bhai Dial Das, a Dhaigar Khatri of Peshawar, who settled in Rawalpindi as a shop-keeper some fifty* years ago, and established the sect some five years after. He died about 1870." The sect, which is recruited from all castes, pays particular respect to the Adi-Granth of Guru Nanak. For an account of the Nirmalas the reader is referred to paragraph 108 Maclagan's Census Report. Though originating in the time of Guru Govind Singh, the "order has by degrees rid itself of the main distinguishing marks of the Khalsa faith, and is gradually returning to a pure form of orthodox Hinduism." Habiasi is one of the names by which were known the followers of Balak Singh, the founder of the Kuka sect, almost the only one in which, since the annexation of the Punjab, Sikhism has taken a militant form (see paragraphs 109-111 Maclagan's Census Report). The Kukas also describe themselves as Namdharis, a name which has been returned on the present occasion by 3 Sikhs. The sect consists of Sikhs of Guru Govind Singh, and their record as Hindu can hardly be correct. The one male who has returned his sect as Baba Kartar Singh Sanatani appears to be an adherent of the Sodhi family of Kartarpur founded by Guru Arjan who, with all the Gurus from Ram Das onwards, was of the Sodhi clan of the Khatris. Baba Khem Singh is the name of a member of the Bedi family, to which Guru Nanak belonged, while Baba Kalu was a Kahar, the most celebrated of the followers of Guru Arjan. The adherents of neither are Sikhs of the Khalsa, and their occurrence among the Hindus need cause no surprise.

Sects returned.	Males.	Females.
Udasi	7	...
Mula Panthi... ...	2	...
Nirankari	9	1
" Sikh ...	4	1
Nirmala	7	3
Habiasi	1	1
Baba Kartar Singh Sanatani.	1	...
Baba Khem Singh ...	1	...
" " " (Sikh)...	2	...
Baba Kalu	5	...

Some miscellaneous entries.

147. A few adherents of the reformers within the circle of Hinduism and prior to the appearance of Guru Nanak also find a place in our returns. The numbers are small and I will content myself by reproducing them in the margin, referring the curious to paragraphs 81 and 86 of Maclagan's Census Report. 289 persons have also shown themselves as Shamsi, or as Agha Khani, by sect, regarding which entries a reference should be made to paragraph 129 above.

Sects returned.	Males.	Females.
Udho Dass	...	5
Guru Kabir Singhi ...	...	4
Kabir Panthi... ...	5	...

Sects returned.	Males.	Females.
Shamsi	179	109
Agha Khani... ...	3	...

The Arya Samaj.

148. Of greater interest than any of the foregoing are perhaps our figures for Aryas. It is to be noticed that Arya or Arya Samaj has not in any case been returned as a religion. The entry when made, has in every instance appeared in the column of sect, and it is perhaps largely due to the isolated position of the Hindus in the Province that they appear to show no tendency to regard Aryas as standing outside their own community ; nor the Aryas to insist on a position distinct from the Hindus. Intermarriages commonly take place between Aryas and Sanatanists (orthodox Hindus), according to the caste system of the latter, and they eat together. On the other hand, I am informed

* Written in 1891.

that there is no tendency for members of the Samaj to be re-absorbed into orthodox Hinduism. 4,130* Hindus (2,550 males and 1,580 females) and 18 Sikhs (12 males and 6 females) have recorded themselves as Arya, Vedak, or similar entries. In 1901, 496 males of 15 years or over appeared under this head. We can hardly compare our crude figures with those of 1901 which do not include females or males aged under 15. It is worth noting, however, that male Aryas now amount to 3 per cent. of the total male Hindu population, whereas those returned in 1901 only amounted to 1 per cent. of the population concerned (*i.e.*, Hindu males aged 15 and over) When it is remembered that Aryas are not likely to have been returned in any large number under the age of 15, it will be seen that the movement has made even more progress in the Province than the above figures would suggest. We can not of course assume that all our Aryas were aged 15 or over, but there must have been a disproportionate number who had passed that age. With reference to the use of the term Vedak it is interesting to observe that 622 Gurkha sepoys stationed, some at Chitral and some at Drosh, in the Malakand Agency, returned their sect as Vedak. It seemed improbable in the extreme that the entries here referred to the Arya Samaj, and I enquired from the Adjutant of the men's regiment as to what it meant From his reply I gather that the men intended only to convey their reverence for the Vedas, *i.e.*, that they are orthodox Hindus; and they are not therefore included in the figures quoted above. The circumstance is, however, bound to throw some degree of doubt as to the correctness of a classification which includes together entries of. Vedak and Arya Samaj. I have also therefore eliminated from my figures for Vedak shown in this paragraph 302 males and 238 females, residing in rural areas, who returned this name in the column of sect. All the Vedaks shown having been enumerated in towns, it can probably be assumed that they are actually members of the Arya Samaj.

149. The large number of persons recorded on the present occassion as Aryas, added to the fact that many are to be found in the rural areas of an intellectually backward Province, suggests that the movement here is becoming a popular one, and that its adherents are by no means confined to those who are capable of an intelligent appreciation of its tenets. I am inclined to suspect that the views inculcated on social questions, such as widow re-marriage, are particularly attractive to the Hindu of the Province Those of them who profess orthodoxy have not succeeded, in spite of the defect of females and of the influence of a Mussalman environment, in breaking away from the rule forbidding the re-marriage of widows. On the other hand the orthodox Hindu (witness a case recently reported to me from Dera Ismail Khan) has no objection to taking in marriage an Arya Samajist widow, and no one of his caste fellows apparently thinks the worse of him for doing so.

150. The kindred movement, *viz*, the Brahmo Samaj has no adherents in the Province, unless we are to suppose that they are referred to in the 67 males and 44 females in Peshawar who appear as Brahman Panthis.† The Dev Samaj or followers of Dev Dharm, are represented by 45 males and 34 females in the same district. Mr. Maclagan (Punjab Census Report, 1891, paragraph 120) refers to the "little sect" of the Dev Dharm as founded in 1887 in Lahore by a Brahman, Pandit Satyanand Agnihotri, where, as a master of the Government College, he became a missionary of the Sadharan Brahmo Samaj. Mr. Maclagan continues "he subsequently gave up his public posts, and finding himself unable to continue with the Brahmos started a religion of his own." He treats the Dev Dharam as a community distinct from the Brahmo Samaj; but notes that two persons at the Census of 1891 returned their religion as Brahmo and their sect as Dev Dharam. This indicates, however, the fact that the Dev Dharam arose out of the Brahmo Samaj, and does not imply that it is now in any sense a branch The Dev Dharam.

	Males.	*Females.*
Dev Dharm ...	41	...
Dharm Samaj ...	4	34

* The entries making up the total are as follows :—Aryas 96 males, 126 females, Arya Samaj 1,400 males, 783 females, Vedak Sanatan 7 males, Ved Dharam 1 female, Swami, (followers of the Swami, *i.e.*, Daya Nand) 2 males, Vedak 1,045 males and 70 females.

† From enquiries I have made I gather that the Brahmo Samaj is not represented in the district.

of it. By the Secretary of the Dev Samaj Council at Lahore I am informed that the followers of the Dev Dharam should not be classed under Hindu (Brahmanic), Hindu (Brahmo) or Hindu (Arya) as they neither subscribe to the Brahmincal writings "nor to a faith in the Theo like the Aryas and Brahmos." He considers that they should be classed as a separate group under the general heading of the Hindus. The following information is derived from pamphlets forwarded to me by the same gentleman. The founder of the sect, who is still alive, was born in 1850 in the Cawnpore district. It was in 1882 that he gave up his post in Lahore and took up his mission. The next five years, however, he devoted to a study of the problems of religion, of life and of morality, and the Dev Samaj was founded on 1887. Starting with a few followers only, the movement is believed to have made considerable progress in the Punjab and in Sindh. The Samaj now maintains a boys' and a girls' boarding school in the Ferozepur District, free day and night primary schools for the depressed classes of the Hindu community at Raipur in the Ambala District, married women's and widow's homes at Bhatinda, Ferozepur and Rawalpindi, where moral and domestic training are given, and free primary schools both for boys and girls in various places in the Punjab and Sindh The views of Pandit Satyanand Agnihotri, styled by his followers Shri Dev Guru Bhagwan are set forth in a work called the Dev Shastra. His attitude appears closely to resemble that of various agnostic ethical societies existing in Europe and America. The science grounded religion, as it is called, teaches that "there is no being called God and, therefore, there can not be, nor ever was, any revelation or inspiration from him" ; that man, like every other organism, is a product of the natural course of evolution, and consequently "all teachings based on his supernatural origin and assigning him immunity from the operations of the natural laws of evolution and dissolution, are fundamentally wrong." Happiness is not the only, or the true, end of man's existence, which is to be found in the 'preservation, development and completion' of his inner organism. The Samaj prides itself therefore on freedom from all superstitious beliefs, and though it prescribes "a regular course of religious exercise such as worship, communion, prayer, service, reading, etc.," greater stress is laid upon conduct. The members are required to take a vow to abstain from the ten great sins, among which 'flesh eating' and 'leading an indolent life' appear side by side with adultery and theft. The society sets its face against early marriages, the prohibition of widow re-marriage, extravagent expenditure on the occasion of births, marriages or deaths, and the payment of a bride or bridegroom price. It encourages commensality and intermarriage between the different castes, female education and a loosening, if not the abolition, of the rules of *pardah*. It appears to be doing useful work. and to have induced among its members some practical recognition of the high moral code which it inculcates.

Sweepers.

151. Our return of sect enable us in some degree to eliminate those persons who are not recognised as Hindus by the bulk of the followers of Hinduism. I give in the margin the number of those who showed as their sect the name of one of the divisions of sweepers. It will be noticed that the greater number of the names returned are such as cannot by any stretch of the word be regarded as referring to sects. Except for Lalbegi and Balmiki, all are the names of caste or occupational groups It is of interest to notice that even with the aid of the sect column we can not separate from true Hindus the total number of those who, while possessing no real claim to the title, for want of any distinctive name have shown themselves, or have been included in tabulation, among them ; for the caste table (Table XIII) shows the number of Hindu Chuhras, with Mehtars, by caste to be 2,978 males and 1,906 females.

Sweepers appearing in the Sect Table.

Entry in column of sect.	Males.	Females.
Balmiki	972	743
" (Sikh)	10	...
Bhangi	104	59
Chuhra	62	50
Hindu Mehtar	...	15
Khakrob	30	12
Kutana	...	2
Lalbegi	490	526
Mehtar	424	192
Balashahi	59	35
Total ...	2,151	1,634

152. Of the total number of Sikhs enumerated in the Province 15,969, or just over one half, have recorded their sect as Guru Govind Singhi or other names which clearly indicate the true Sikhs of the Khalsa (*vide* marginal list). The corresponding figures shown in the Punjab Census Report, 1901, (Subsidiary Table V of Chapter III) only amount to 3,027 males and 413 females; and if the sect returns of last Census can be in any degree relied upon, it would appear that the increase we have noticed in the number of Sikhs in the Province is in the main a real one, and not due, as seemed likely to be the case, to the inclusion among Sikhs on the present occasion of many persons who appeared among the Hindus on the last. The increase here, (between three and four hunderd per cent.) is far larger than we find among the Nanak Panthi Sikhs, the figures for whom now, and in 1901 are as shown in the margin. Sikh sects.

Sikhs of the Khalsa.	Males.	Females.
Guru Govind Singh	10,519	4,054
Khalsa	611	35
Kes Dhari	199	135
Singh	...	26
Singh Sabia	...	12
Tat Khalsa	221	157
Total ...	11,550	4,419

Nanak Panthis.

	Males.	*Females.*
1911	8,226	5,508
1901	5,316	3,965

153. In Hazara the Sikhs of Guru Govind Singh amount to 3,152 persons, or 57 per cent. of all those shown as Sikhs in the district in Table VI, in Peshawar to 6,968, or 43 per cent. of the whole, in Kohat to 1,922, or as much as 70 per cent. of the whole; in Bannu to 1,925, or 51 per cent., in Dera Ismail Khan to 1,242 or 57 per cent. In a marginal statement I show the numbers in each district who returned themselves as followers of Guru Govind Singh in 1901 and at the recent Census, respectively. Distribution by districts of Sikhs of Guru Govind Singh.

Sikhs of Guru Govind Singh.

District.	Males.		Females.	
	1901.	1911.	1901.	1911.
Hazara ...	...	1,895	...	1,257
Peshawar ...	2,607	5,100	403	1,868
Kohat ...	10	1,671	6	251
Bannu ..	270	1,221	...	704
D. I. Khan ...	28	959	1	283

154. The figures for Nanak Panthis by districts now and in 1901 are as shown in the margin. It will be seen that in Hazara the number of Nanak Panthi Sikhs has decreased on the present occasion, while the followers of Guru Govind Singh have grown from nothing to a considerable figure. In Peshawar, though the number of Nanak Panthis has increased, the rise is in no way comparable to the rise in the number of the followers of the 10th Guru. In Kohat also the astonishing rise is in the number of Khalsa Sikhs. In Bannu the rise has been more marked among the followers of Guru Nanak than among those of Guru Govind Singh. In Dera Ismail Khan the reverse is the case. Taking the districts of the Province as a whole, while the Nanak Panthis have increased by 30, the Sikhs of Guru Govind Singh have increased by over 300 per cent. Of the Sikhs enumerated in the North-West Frontier Province and in the Panjab in 1901, 40 per cent. (*vide* page 124, Census Report, Punjab, 1901) returned no sect. The variations noticed above are no doubt principally due to the fact that the sect return of 1901 was incomplete; but in so far as any inference can be drawn from the figures, we cannot argue from them that the variations noticed in the numbers of the Hindu and Sikh populations respectively, are due to the word Sikh having been less strictly interpreted on the present occasion than in 1901. Local distribution of Nanak Panthis.

Nanak Panthi Sikhs.

District.	Males.		Females.	
	1901.	1911.	1901.	1911.
Hazara ...	1,508	1,266	995	873
Peshawar ...	4,396	4,845	2,852	3,441
Kohat ...	57	351	33	245
Bannu ...	216	1,117	105	677
D. I. Khan ...	139	419	80	266

155. Sodh Bans and Sodh Bans Khalsa have been returned as their sect by 6 and 3 Sikhs, respectively. This is one of the few sect names which Other Sikh sects.

have not also been returned by Hindus. Mr. Rose writing in 1901 remarks* "the Khalsa Sodhi Bans is a new reforming movement among the Sikhs, which has only just been started, and it aims at a return to the pure religion of Guru Nanak................The term Sodhi Bans, or, as it is also spelt, Sodh Bansi or Sohdi Bans, is however not new, as it has long been used for one belonging to the Sodhi class, for every Sikh, when taking the *Pahul*, must leave the caste in which he was born, and enter that of Guru Govind Singh, who was a Khatri of the Sodhi section." The persons referred to may be understood, I am informed by the Secretary of the Singh Sabha at Peshawar, to be true Sikhs of Guru Govind Singh. Other names which have not appeared in our Hindu sect returns are, Bedi (1 male), Gurmukh Singhi (1 female), Mazhabi (14 males and 4 females), Sadhu Singh (2 males), and Sanwal Shahi (3 males and 2 females). Bedi refers to the veneration felt by Sikhs for the Bedi sub-section of the Khatris to which Guru Nanak belonged. "It must not be supposed" says Mr. Maclagan† "that the Bedis are entirely, or even generally Nanak Panthis in the narrower sense of the term, for the most famous of them are true Sikhs of the school of Govind Singh." Gurmukh Singhi indicates, I am informed, an adherent of one Gurmukh Singh, who was born in the Amritsar District and died some 20 years ago. Like Khem Singh, who is referred to in paragraph 146, Gurmukh Singh was a Bedi: and there is a Dharmsala called after him in Peshawar city. His adherents are found among both Nanak Panthis and the followers of the tenth Guru. The entries of Mazhabi refer to sweepers who have adopted the Sikh faith. Sadhu Singh was a member of the Sodhi family of Kartarpur, adherents of whom (Hindus) appear in the sect column under the name Baba Kartar Singh Sanatani (*vide* paragraph 146 above), while Sanwal Shahi (returned from the Dera Ismail Khan District) refers to the followers of one Sanwal Shah, as to whose identity some doubt appears to exist. "According to one version" (*vide* Maclagan's Census Report, paragraph 94) "Baba Nanak, when travelling in Sambat 1545 (A. D. 1489), into the Sindh country, found the Kirars very ignorant of religion (Shamji and Lalji not having yet put in an appearance) and appointed his servant, Sanwal Shah, to be their Guru, and to teach them the way of salvation. The descendants of the Guru are known as Sanwal Shah Potras, and their disciples as Nanak Shahis. Another story tells us that Sanwal Shah was the grandson, or great grandson of Some Shah, a Chawala Arora of Dera Ismail Khan, who was money-lender (or Shah) to Guru Arjan, and who in consequence of the patronage of the Guru collected a considerable religious following...........A third story connects Sanwal Shah more closely with the teaching of Govind Singh. He is said to have been an Arora of Amritsar, whose father had been treasurer to Guru Ram Das and had supplied the Guru with funds for building the Golden Temple. In the time of Guru Govind Singh, Sanwal Shah, or more properly Sanwal Shah Singh preached Sikhism on the frontier, and Some Shah by this account is said to have been a brother of Sanwal Shah Singh."

POPULAR RELIGION

Islam in the Province.

156. The religion of the ordinary villager in the North-West Frontier Province is of course Islam, and I propose to make some attempt here to picture what this means. The religion of the Mussalman is to this extent more definite than that of the Hindu, in that he knows that its precepts are contained in the Qoran. The Mohammadan, the Christian and the Jew he classes together as Ahl-i-Kitab, or the peoples who possess a sacred book, in contradistinction to Hindus and other idol worshippers who in his view have none. But with the teaching of his own scripture he has no personal acquaintance; and the bulk of his religious ideas are composed of what Europeans would style superstitions merely. It was with reference to superstitions that Sir Denzil Ibbetson wrote ‡ "Indeed there is little to chose in this respect between the Mussalman of the west and the Hindu of the east; the only practical difference being that the former worships saints only and the latter godlings as well, and that while the latter holds in small reverence the Brahman on whom he squanders his substance, the former trembles before the priest whom he sustains in idleness."

---

* *Vide* page 125, Census Report, Punjab, 1901.
† Punjab Census Report, 1891, page 151.
‡ *Vide* paragraph 277, Punjab Census Report, 1881.

157. Bellew in his 'General Report on the Yusafzais,' has the following account of the religion of this, the most numerous of the Pathan tribes of the Peshawar District. The report in question was published in 1864, but the essential features of the picture have not changed since that time. Bellew on the Yusafzais.

"In religious tenets they are Sunni Mohammadans, and distinguish themselves as Chariaris. In common with other Mussalmans they hold the observance of prayer, alms, fasts and pilgrimages to be the binding and fundamental duties of their religion. To omit any of these is considered a great sin, and if persevered in exposes the offender to ex-communication as an infidel. The observation of prayer especially, with the appointed ceremonies and at fixed periods, is deemed the most important duty, and is less neglected than any of the others. The prayer consists of two parts, termed *Farz* and *Sunnat*. The former must be repeated, the latter may be omitted in cases of pressing hurry. Before any payer can be repeated, the ablution by *Audas*, or, in the absence of water, the purification by *taiamum* "(purification with sand or earth)" must be performed; the place of prayer as well as the body and clothes of the person must be *pak* or pure. A multitude of trifles are always conspiring to render either impure or *palit*. The religious man is consequently always on the look out and dodging about to avoid contact with imaginary impurities. The fixed praying times are "*Sahr*, at day-light; *Mazpakhin*, at noon; *Mazdigar*, after noon *Mazkham* at sun-set and *Mazkhotan* at evening" (or rather night.)

158. The insistence on the duty of prayer, which Bellew mentions as characteristic of the Yusafzais, marks the Pathans generally, and indeed the whole Mohammadan population, at any rate in the northern districts of the Province. In Dera Ismail Khan far greater laxity is found. Everywhere are to be seen by the roadside little platforms of earth on which the Faithful make their devotions at the appointed times. As my own experience shows, it is not unusual, if visiting the house of a *Khan* about sunset, to be deserted by one's host and his whole family, when the sinking sun shows that the hour of evening prayer has arrived; and on a shooting expedition, when waiting for the duck to come over at evening, I remember my companion, an Afridi, excusing himself and retiring a few paces away to say his prayers. Every Kandi, (as the different quarters of a village are called) has its mosque or *jumaat*, and five times in the twenty four hours the air is filled with the *azan*, the call to prayer. Prayer.

159. Next after prayer comes the duty of distributing alms: "the distribution of alms", says Bellew, "is very generally observed by all classes according to their means. The priesthood, widows, orphans, the maimed, blind, aged, etc., are the recipients. They are of two kinds named *zakat* and *khairat*. The former are appointed by the Qoran, the latter are according to the inclination of the donor. Alms are sometimes given in money, but more generally they are gifts from the produce of the fields or flock, etc." Alms giving.

160. "The fast is the Mohammadan Ramzan. It is very strictly kept from sunrise to sunset every day during the month, and is considered a meritorious pennance, ensuring abundant future reward. Only travellers and invalids are allowed to eat during the fast; children are classed with the latter. Keeping the fast is termed *roza*, and not keeping it *koza*," (correctly spelt Khoja). "Those who can not keep the fast, in whole or in part, during the month of Ramzan, must make up the difference afterwards before the arrival of the next Ramzan." Although the keeping of the fast is not obligatory in the case of travellers, it is commonly observed by the more devout portion of the population, even when on a journey. Fasts.

161. As among Mohmmadans elsewhere, the pilgrimage to Mecca is regarded as the most efficacious, but few have the power to make the journey. In default visits are made to the Jhanda Mela, held annually at Peshawar in honour of Sakhi Sarwar, and to the fair which is held every year at the Ziarat Kaka Sahib in the Khattak country. The shrine of Pir Baba in Buner is also Pilgrimages.

a favourite place of pilgrimage. These for the Peshawar District. The Kohat Gazetteer contains a list of 20 shrines which are frequented by the Mohammadans of the district. A pilgrimage to a Ziarat is generally prompted by some wish which it is hoped may be attained by this means. Some shrines have a reputation for the gaining of particular objects. Thus the Nasak Baba Ziarat in the Teri tahsil is "resorted to by bad riders who gallop their horses in the plain in front of the shrine, invoking the aid of the saint to improve their horsemanship." The Ziarat Shekh Nikai Sahib, near Bahadur Khel, is visited by persons suffering from erysipelas, and the Ziarat Mianji Sahib and the Ziarat Haji Bahadur Sahib by barren women. In the Ziarat Pir Fatteh Shah in Kohat the Shias have a popular place of pilgrimage. The Bannu District possesses many shrines, "but none are of more than local repute, so that, in addition to visits to local shrines, pilgrimages to Swat, Peshawar and Mooltan are fairly common. The Wazirs hold in high repute the shrine of their reputed progenitor Musa Nika in Waziristan, and it is said that a Wazir, who will perjure himself on the Qoran will never take a false oath on the name of Musa Nika." The Mohammadans of Dera Ismail Khan also have the strongest belief in saints and shrines, "and in the efficacy of pilgrimages to groves and high places There is scarcely an old mound in the country on which the flag of some faqir is not flying." In Hazara local shrines are hardly less numerous; and the tank and shrine at Mangal, and the Ziarat of Jamal Ghazi in the Abbottabad tahsil are visited by Hindus as well as by Mohammadans. The people of Dir and Bajaur in the Malakand Agency, visit the shrine at Ajmere, in the hope of becoming rich, and the Ziarat of Pir Baba in Buner, if the birth of a son is the object of their desires.

Superstitions.

162. The popularity of pilgrimages to shrines throughout the Province is explained by the superstitious character of the people. Writing of the Yusafzais, Bellew says, "their superstition is incredible and has no limits. Miracles, charms and omens are believed in as a matter of course. An inordinate reverence for saints and the religious classes generally is universal, and their absurdly impossible and contradictory dicta are received and acted on with eager credulity. The *ziarat* or sacred shrine is habitually resorted to by all classes and by both sexes. At these the devotees confess their sins, and implore forgiveness, unburden their hearts of all manner of secret desires, and beseech favours, all in the full belief of a sure hearing and answer. The wayfarer never passes one without checking his steps to render obeisance or invoke a blessing. The people pride themselves on these outward signs of a holy life, and boast of their love and reverence for their "pure prophet" and his "blessed religion", and congratulate themselves on their resigned obedience to his commands as conveyed to them through their holy men and priests. In all this they act sincerely from the heart, for they certainly do cherish and pamper a very numerous priesthood at considerable self-denial." In the last sentence Bellew is referring to the custom by which the descendants of "buzurgs" or saints, whose graves form the shrines (*Ziarats*) referred to, are supported by the offerings of the laity, as well as to the reverence which is paid to Saiads, to Pirs, Mians, et hoc genus omne. The women, Bellew notes, are even more superstitious and religiously disposed than the men.

Sir Herbert Edwardes on the Bannochis.

163. In this connection I can hardly omit the forcible, though perhaps somewhat unkind, passage* in which Sir Herbert Edwardes describes the character of the people of Bannu at the time of annexation: "A more utterly ignorant and superstitious people than the Bannochis, I never saw. The vilest jargon was to them pure Arabic from the blessed Qoran, the clumsiest imposture a miracle, and the fattest *fakeer* a saint. The myriads of holy vagabonds, who are the spawn of the prophet, found in the Bannochis an easy prey, and in their fertile fields are easy livelihood. "Where the carcase is, there are the eagles gathered together." Far and near from the barren and ungrateful fields around the Mulla and the Kazee, the Pir and the Syad descended to the smiling vale, armed with a panoply of spectacles and owl-like looks, miraculous rosaries, infallible amulets, and tables of descent from Mohammad. Each new comer, like St. Peter, held the key of Heaven; and the whole, like Irish beggars, were equally prepared to bless or curse to all eternity him who

* *Vide* Edwardes' Year on the Punjab Frontier, Volume I, page 82.

gave or who withheld. These were 'air-drawn daggers' against which the Bannochi peasant had no defence. For him the whistle of the far-thrown bullet or the nearer sheen of his enemy's 'Shumsher' had no terrors; blood was simply a red fluid; and to remove a neighbour's head at the shoulders as easy as cutting cucumbers. But to be cursed in Arabic or anything that sounded like it; to be told that the blessed prophet had put a black mark against his soul for not giving his best field to one of the prophet's own posterity, to have the saliva of a disappointed saint left in anger on his door-post; or behold a Hajee, who had gone three times to Mecca, deliberately sit down and enchant his camels with the itch and his sheep with the rot; these were things which made the dagger drop out of the hand of the awe-stricken savage, his knees to knock together, his liver to turn to water, and his parched tongue to be scarce able to articulate a full and complete concession of the blasphemous demand." As illustrating the credulity of the people Sir Herbert Edwardes quotes the account of an intelligent native traveller (Agha Abbas) who found it easy to practise impostures to sustain his assumed character of a saint. Among these was the giving of a charm to a women who wished to attract the attention of her husband, who neglected her in favour of his other wives. He gave her a piece of paper on which some Persian writing was inscribed, after charming it by wetting it with saliva and repeating supposed incantations over it. This she was to give her husband to eat She went away, and did as she had been directed. "Whether he was pleased," says Agha Abbas in telling the story, "with the perhaps unusual attention and fondness of manner of his wife, or how it was, I know not; but she returned to me next morning with the present of a sheep, much pleased with the effect of my charm."

Superstitions show small signs of dying out.

164. The influence of superstition may be supposed to have decreased in the sixty odd years which have elapsed since annexation, at any rate in that part of the Province which is included in British India. From all the districts the reports from which refer to the subject, I am informed that with the advance of education the people grow less credulous. Yet even in British territory superstition is very far from dead. An account of the powers of healing popularly supposed to be possessed by members of certain tribes in the Dera Ismail Khan District will be found on page 161 of the last Punjab Census Report, and some equally illogical beliefs I will mention here. Moreover in the trans-frontier area there seems no reason to suppose that any marked change in this respect has taken place in the last few years. On the great trade routes such as the Khyber and, in a less degree, the Gumal, the influeuce of civilization is no doubt slowly having its natural effect. Referring to superstitions the Political Agent, Wana, writes "beliefs of this nature are gradually dying out since the British Government came in," and of the Khyber Sahibzada Abdul Qaiyum says that "these notions are more or less on the wane with the advance of comparative civilization." But off the beaten track of commerce men's ideas move slowly. "These beliefs" writes the Political Agent, Malakand, "show little tendency to die out," and the view taken by the Assistant Political Agent, Chitral, is much the same. After hazarding the opinion that they are possibly less strong than they were, among the upper classes at any rate, he adds "it may be that there is only a reticence in relating them to people whom they know do not believe in them, and who they think only look on them as silly tales."

The evil eye.

165. Among superstitions* which gain ready credence to-day, none is more common or more deeply seated than a belief in the evil eye. It derives a religious sanction from the fact that the Prophet Mohammad shared it, and is reported to have authorised the use of spells against this influence, remarking that "if there were anything in the world which would overcome fate, it would be an evil eye."† In Bannu women after child birth, a man who is naked, and people out after dark are held to be especially susceptible, but animals and inanimate objects, especially crops, are also considered to be subject to it. Even

*.—If the beliefs here referred to seem to be somewhat remote from the title of this chapter it should be remembered that what to the reader appears the most illogical superstition is a serious matter, part and parcel of their religion in fact, to the people of whom I write.

† *Vide* Hughes' Dictionary of Islam, page 112.

a stone (Wana) can be broken in pieces by the evil eye. The common view appears to be that any person or thing that may excite jealousy is subject to it, whether it be a stalwart man, a pretty child, a handsome animal, a fine building, or a rich crop. It is enough for either to attract the attention of a man who has the evil eye and disaster will follow. The man or child will fall sick and may die, the building will fall, the crop wither. Food will disagree with the eater if bewitched in this way. I am told that nearly every large village possess one or more persons who can exercise the harmful influence, and are universally recognised and detested. From Chitral, I have received a particularly interesting report prepared by the Assistant Political Agent. He remarks that "the evil eye (*glechari*) is universally believed in. There are three men in Chitral village who have been pointed out to me as having this power........................The evil eye has no effect apparently unless the person who has it remarks on the good qualities of a person or a thing while looking at it. A man with a twisted face, a stone in the middle of the field split in two, and a lame pony have all been pointed to me at different times as the result of it."

Means taken to avert or neutralise its influence.

166 The means of averting the baneful influence are many and various; in most of them the process of reasoning from cause to effect is equally difficult to follow. "A pious Mohammadan," noted the author of the Bannu Gazetteer, 1907, "guards himself against it by wearing an amulet obtained from a Mulla, but among the more superstitious there are various ways of averting this misfortune, all more or less mysterious, *e. g.* waving three red chillies in succession round the afflicted person's head, and dropping them one by one with an incantation into the fire," or prayer may be resorted to and sacrifices offered. Throughout the Province amulets (*tawiz*), such as green stones or pieces of paper on which a Mulla has written a text from the Qoran, or more commonly a meaningless hieroglyphic, and the like, are thought to have strong protective influence; or it is considered enough to add some superficial blemish to the person or object to be protected. If the aim be to protect a crop, the bare skull of a dead ox or buffalo, or an old earthenware pot, may be stuck up on a rod in the midst In the case of a building an old earthen pot mounted on the doorway will confer immunity (in the Malakand Agency a black pot is always hung up on a new house to avert the evil eye); and with this end in view a child's face may be smeared with lamp soot From Kohat I have received the following prescription for removing the disastrous effects of the evil eye. The body of the unfortunate sufferer "is measured seven times with a piece of thread, which is then attached to the hasp of the door, soaked in oil and ignited from the bottom. The subject is instructed to gaze on the burning thread till it is completely consumed. This ceremony is repeated for three successive days, when a cure is believed to result." From Bannu comes another specific "a lead bullet is melted in an iron spoon, which is thrice turned round the head of the affected person. The molten lead is then poured into oil. This practice is performed for three days." I have received notes of other similar methods in addition, but it seems hardly worth while to reproduce them here. One however, which seems to be widely known, should perhaps be mentioned. To remove the curse, a piece of the foot-gear (Chitral), or dust from the feet, (Dera Ismail Khan) of the man who has caused it should be burnt

Charms and spells.

167. Charms and spells are employed for other purposes besides guarding against, or neutralising the results of, being 'over-looked.' For the cure of infantile diseases they are everywhere in request. "They also ensure protection from injury, and victory in games, sports and fighting. A well-known charm, '*Tegh-bandi*,' is supposed to make the wearer or possessor invulnerable against weapons of destruction They are also resorted to in love affairs to melt the heart of the wayward" (Khyber). They are nearly always obtained from Mullas. "The illiterate classes of both communities," writes the Deputy Commissioner of Kohat, "usually consult Faqirs and learned Mullas before engaging on any important business; and the latter profess to give the prospective result of the intended undertaking as the result of the incantations and jugglery which they go through." "Charms," says the Assistant Political Agent, Chitral, "consist of '*tawiz*,' texts of the Qoran sewn up in a piece of

cloth. They are largely used in case of sickness to cure the individual, and are hung about his body and clothes. I have also seen them hung about a pony's neck to keep him from falling. Charms are also used by lovers, and by subordinates who have incurred the displeasure of their superiors in order to appease them. In Resham a small village some 40 miles north of Chitral, there is a large rock, in shape something like a horse. Chitralis who are about to give any girl away in marriage, ride on this, and beat it, and pull at it, etc. as if it really was a pony. This is supposed to obtain the rider a good pony (a pony is always given by the bridegroom to the girl's father or guardian). Stones for this and other similar purposes are to be found in many places in Chitral. There is a large rock in the middle of the Lutkoh river, and it is considered to be an auspicious thing to throw a pebble on the flat top of it. Also two or three stones balanced on the top of each other are frequently found along the road side. Some of these are put up opposite a *Ziarat* as a sign, others are simply done to bring the man who makes them good luck."

Lucky and unlucky days.

168. A belief in the good or ill-omen of certain days and numbers is by no means confined to the East, witness the dislike of sailors to starting on a voyage on a Friday, and the very common superstition connected with the number thirteen. It is curious in this connection to notice that the 13th of the lunar month is considered unlucky by Mohammadans; and they have a strong objection to entering upon any new undertaking on a Friday. The latter objection is intelligible enough. Friday is the Mohammadan Sabbath; and just as a devout Christian refuses to engage in secular occupations on Sunday, so a pious Mussalman prefers not to undertake them on a Friday. The objection is particularly strong before the hour of the mid-day prayer, after which, duty to God having been performed, the affairs of the world may be considered. But there are certain things which it is good to do on Friday. Superstition in the Province in regard to lucky and unlucky days is a good deal concerned with the selection of the day on which to be shaved and the like. On Friday the Mussalman thinks it lucky to be shaved and to put on new clothes; and, considering his views on the subject of ceremonial cleanliness, this need cause us no suprise. It is, I imagine, with reference to such undertakings that the Mohammadans of Kohat and Bannu, as I am informed, hold Friday to be an auspicious day. It is also presumably due solely to religious considerations that Friday is thought lucky for laying the foundations of a mosque or a school; and the preference of the Chitrali to bring home his wife or to get his son circumcised on this day can also be referred to the same origin

The regard in which Friday is held can therefore hardly be referred to superstition. But every other day of the week has its own particular character in some area or another. Mondays and Thursdays are indeed considered to be lucky by Mohammadans throughout the Province especially for getting shaved and for starting on a journey. In Chitral, however, the latter is only a good day if the journey be to the south; while the Chitrali shows an especial solicitude about the happiness of his married life by selecting one of these two days on which to bring his newly wedded wife to her home. The other objects, for which Thursday is especially fortunate, are visits to shrines (Khyber), starting a child's education (Bannu) and circumcision (Chitral). Tuesday is an unlucky day in popular belief everywhere. Wednesday is in most areas considered ill-omened; but in the Khyber it argues well for a journey or a new work which is begun on this day. The other days of the week have no universal reputation as being of good omen or the reverse. The Khyberi will not put on new clothes or set about any undertaking, particularly a journey to the east, on a Saturday, but he seems to be alone in his objection. Sunday, reported to be considered an auspicious day in Bannu and in the Malakand Agency, is held to be the reverse in Kohat and the Khyber. In other areas there seems to be no particular feeling about it. It has been suggested to me that, where Sunday is regarded as a lucky day, this is due to the fact that officials, who are engaged on the other days of the week, naturally defer their private engagements till Sunday. I am not sure that the explanation has any value, and in regard to the reputation of the other days of the week, except Friday, I have preferred not to hazard any. Even in the case of Friday religious feelings do not always influence men in the same direction. A lawyer, writing of Peshawar, remarks "that in the case of serious works like litigation" a Mohammadan would try to begin on Friday, "if he is very religiously disposed." Certain families consider particular days of the month or week to be lucky for them or the reverse; but we have here an example of individual superstition such as not unknown in Europe.

A belief in *jinns* and evil spirits.

169. It is generally known that a belief in *jinns* and evil spirits is common in the Province, (*vide* the account in Thorburn's 'Bannu or our Afghan Frontier' of an interview between a peasant and a witch who professed to be in the service of a *jinn*.) I have attempted to obtain some details, but with little success. "Belief in *jinns* and evil spirits" writes Sahibzada Abdul Qaiyum, C.I.E., Assistant Political Officer, Khyber, "is very common, and a holy terror is felt of them. The only antagonistic influence to ward them off is the invocation of holy men and their enchantments". The Political Agent, Wana, writes to the same effect. The Bannu villager, I am informed, thinks that *jinns* can torture human beings, and in order to avert their influence, visits shrines, offers sacrifices, purchases charms, etc. In the Malakand Agency fits are attributed to *jinns*, and even in Hazara, where I am told that the Mohammadan population has risen superior to a belief in lucky and unlucky days, the illiterate of all religions credit the existence of evil spirits, "which have power to cause harm and are dangerous". Of Chitral the Assistant Political Agent writes "Fairies are supposed to inhabit Tirich Mir, which is their stronghold. It is commonly believed that there is a tree there laden with precious stones. This tree is protected by the fairies, and, if any body tries to approach it, he is seized and carried off. The stories about fairies, *jinns* and devils are very numerous.........and they are universally believed in. Numerous people have been carried off or seized by them at different times." In Chitral *jinns* are also thought to hang on to a pony's tail, and to ride it by night; and a method of preventing this is to tie a knot in the tail. Should the tail be knotted at night, and be found untied in the morning, *jinns* or fairies are held responsible. Throughout the Province *jinns* (Pashtu *parian*) are commonly supposed to take possession of human beings, much in the same way as we read in the New Testament of men being "possessed of a devil," and Mullas are called in to cast them out. Graveyards often have the reputation of being haunted by these evil spirits, and visits to them after nightfall are avoided. As an instance of beliefs of this nature I may mention a story which was told me of a burying ground in the Mardan Sub-Division of Peshawar. My informant said that a friend of his youth was in love with a girl, and wished to marry her. There were difficulties in the way, which the lover was informed would be removed if he went by night to a certain grave, situated some three miles from his village, and drove a peg into the ground by it. The daring nature of the act is explained by the fact that the graveyard possessed an evil reputation for being haunted by *jinns*. The lover, however, mastered his fears, and proceeded to the spot; and, too frightened to see what he was doing, drove the peg into the ground. Having done so, he attempted to rise, but fouud he was caught fast. With a struggle he freed himself, and rushed from the spot, mad with terror. He returned home ill, and soon afterwards died. No doubt in his agitation he failed to notice that he was driving the peg through the loose folds of his wide Pathan trousers, and it was not until these were torn in his endeavours to escape that they were released from the peg. His death may be attributed to fright, chill, a weak heart or to other natural causes. The supernatural explanation, however, as might be expected, was the one which was accepted, and the occurrence established more firmly than ever in the minds of the neighbouring villagers the graveyard's evil reputation.

Observances at the occupation of a new house.

170. Another set of superstitions is that connected with the means taken to render lucky the building or occupation of a new house. In Hazara I am told that these are confined to the uneducated among the Hindu community, who, "before occupying the new house, take an earthen vessel full of water over the threshold, and at the same time pour oil outside the door, to prevent calamity entering." In Chitral "the foundations of the building are laid on a Friday. If any one dies or any thing unlucky happens on that day,

then the heir of the man who is building takes the site. Before the house is occupied, food and entertainment are given to neighbours, relatives, and the poor. After this the *azan* is called by a Mulla from each corner of the house." In other parts of the Malakand Agency a feast is given before a new house is occupied, but no other ceremonies are observed. The giving of a feast and the distribution of alms are common throughout the Province on such occasions. The religious attempt to obtain divine sanction to the occupation by other means also. A *fakir*, or holy man, may be called in to lay the foundations (Wana), or its "occupation may be signalised by first introducing the holy Qoran into it" (Khyber). The burning of *spelenai* (a sort of incense) is held to be efficacious to counteract unfavourable influences, and as a disinfectant (Khyber), while in Kohat "Mohammadan women usually send a vessel of water covered with flowers to a new house which it is intended to occupy."

Miscellaneous superstitions in Chitral.

171. I will conclude this account with a note of a few curious beliefs which have reached me from Chitral. Little seems to be known of the origin of the inhabitants of this tract, though some are certainly of Aryan descent. It may be assumed, however, that their stock is distinct from that of the bulk of the inhabitants of the Province; some of their superstitions find no counterpart elsewhere within it. I have already made some reference to beliefs common in the state in paragraph 169. There is, however, to be found among them a wide field of superstitions as yet unexplored, one or two of which are mentioned here. "The owl, the fox, the monkey and the bear are considered to be unlucky and to contain the spirits of dead men. This is believed more especially of the monkey." A howling dog foretells failure while a horse will not readily find a purchaser "if the star on its forehead can be covered by the hand, or if the roof of its mouth is black." Fowls are taboo among the Bashgali Kafirs, and formerly they would not allow them, or even eggs, to be brought into their villages. On the other hand it is considered auspicious to see an eagle; and in spite of a superstitious fear of meeting a fox, to hear it bark, is by some considered a happy augury for any undertaking to be entered upon on the morrow. Another curious belief is held as to the cause of an earthquake. "It is supposed that on account of excessive sins on the part of the people, a scorpion comes to sting the bull on whose horns the earth rests. The bull shakes itself, and comes the earthquake," a presage of calamity according to the Mullas. Another version is that an earthquake is due to an army of fairies passing through the earth. An eclipse of the moon is accounted for by somewhat similar explanations. A snake comes to eat the moon, and so obscures it, or the same effect is caused by an army of fairies flying between it and the earth.

Hinduism in the North-West Frontier Province

172. Hinduism, as it exists in the North-West Frontier Province, is but a pale reflection of the system which flourishes in the United Provinces and other areas to the east. Even of the Derajat, where, as we have seen, the Hindu population is proportionately most numerous, the writer of the Dera Ismail Khan Gazetteer notes, "the Hindus of this district are less particular in the matter of caste prejudices and observances than down country Hindus. Most of them will drink water that has been carried in *Mussaks* (skins for carrying water) or out of *lotas* detached from a working well. They habitually ride on donkeys, and do a multitude of other things which an orthodox Hindu would shrink from. All idolatrous observances are kept very much in the background. Except a few small images (*thakurs*) kept in their *mandars* they have no idols at all. Nor is it their habit to take their gods about in procession. No one, in fact, sees anything of their worship. They burn their dead, and throw the ashes into the Indus. They always keep a few of the bones, and take them, when opportunity offers, to the Ganges. Often, instead of taking the bones themselves, they send them by the hand of a friend, who may be going on his own account. There are a good many *dharamsalas*, *mandars* and *dawaras*, at Dera Ismail Khan and in the cis-Indus tahsils" (the passage was written when the Bhakkar and Leiah tahsils, mainly cis-Indus, were included in the district); "there are not many in the rest of the trans-Indus tract." In Chapter VII will be found some account of the degree to which the marriage customs of the

Hindus have been influenced by Islam, notably in regard to the age of marriage ; and in Chaper XI I will endeavour to show how Hindu rules regarding commensality between different castes have been relaxed, and how any distinct caste organisation is virtually non-existent in rural areas. Outside the towns Hindus still live in a condition of dependence on their Mohammadan overlords. The Arora, the Khatri or the Bhatia shop-keeper in a village is a *hamsaya* of the proprietors of the land ; that is to say he lives rent free in a house which does not belong to him, and in return for this, and for being allowed to reside unmolested in the village, has to render certain services to his protectors. The whole subject belongs more properly to the discussion of caste which will be found in Chapter XI ; but this chapter would be more incomplete than it need be without some reference to the position locally accorded to Hindus, and the degree to which the characteristic customs of their religion are observed by them.

SUBSIDIARY TABLE I.—*General distribution of population by religion.*

Religion and locality.	Actual number in 1911.	Proportion per 10,000 of population in				Variation per cent. Increase (+) Decrease (—).			Variation per cent.
		1911.	1901.	1891.	1881.	1901—1911.	1891—1901.	1881—1891.	1881—1911.
1	2	3	4	5	6	7	8	9	10
Mohammadan.									
N.-W. F. P. Districts	**2,039,994**	**9,286**	**9,221**	**9,230**	**9,212**	**+8**	**+10**	**+18**	**+41**
Hazara	572,972	9,502	9,515	9,461	9,477	+7	+9	+27	+49
Trans-Indus Districts	1,467,022	9,204	9,109	9,141	9,120	+9	+10	+15	+38
Hindu.									
N.-W. F. P. Districts	**119,942**	**546**	**629**	**638**	**708**	**—7**	**+8**	**+6**	**+8**
Hazara	24,389	404	411	464	487	+6	—4	+21	+23
Trans-Indus Districts	95,553	599	711	705	784	—9	+11	+3	+4
Sikh.									
N.-W. F. P. Districts	**30,345**	**138**	**125**	**103**	**50**	**+19**	**+34**	**+139**	**+280**
Hazara	5,489	91	72	70	34	+36	+12	+161	+297
Trans-Indus Districts	24,856	156	146	116	56	+15	+39	+134	+277
Christian.									
N.-W. F. P. Districts	**6,585**	**30**	**25**	**29**	**30**	**+29**	**—5**	**+15**	**+39**
Hazara	178	3	2	5	2	+76	—57	+162	+98
Trans-Indus Districts	6,407	41	34	38	39	+28	—3	+12	+38

NOTE.—No figures are available to show the distribution of population by religion in 1881 and 1891 in the districts of the Province as now constituted, their boundaries having been changed since 1891. The figures in columns 5 and 6 and 8—10 have been obtained by assuming that the proportion of the adherents of each religion to the total population was the same in the present districts as it was in the old ones.

SUBSIDIARY TABLE II.—*Distribution by districts of the main religions.*

District and natural division.	Number per 10,000 of the population who are :—											
	Hindu.				*Mohammadan.*				*Sikh.*			
	1911.	1901.	1891.	1881.	1911.	1901.	1891.	1881.	1911.	1901.	1891.	1881.
1	2	3	4	5	6	7	8	9	10	11	12	13
N.-W. F. P. Districts ...	**546**	**629**	**638**	**708**	**9,286**	**9,221**	**9,230**	**9,212**	**138**	**125**	**103**	**50**
Hazara	404	411	464	487	9,502	9,515	9,461	9,477	91	72	70	34
Trans-Indus Districts ...	**599**	**711**	**705**	**784**	**9,204**	**9,109**	**9,141**	**9,120**	**156**	**146**	**116**	**56**
Peshawar	409	509	503	663	9,339	9,292	9,299	9,215	187	144	129	53
Kohat	487	666	531	541	9,379	9,167	9,237	9,321	123	153	220	124
Bannu	829	958	909	921	9,012	8,918	9,060	9,051	149	115	28	24
Dera Ismail Khan ...	1,117	1,166	1,296	1,233	8,785	8,651	8,642	8,723	85	173	58	38

SUBSIDIARY TABLE III.—*Christians; number and variation.*

District and natural division.	Actual number.				Variation per cent.			
	1911.	1901.	1891.	1881.	1901—1911	1891—1901	1881—1891	1881—1911
1	2	3	4	5	6	7	8	9
Total N.-W. F. P. Districts ...	**6,585**	**5,119**	**5,437**	**4,725**	**—29**	**—6**	**—15**	**—39**
Hazara	178	101	236	90	—76	—57	—162	—98
Trans-Indus Districts	**6,407**	**5,018**	**5,201**	**4,635**	**—28**	**—4**	**—12**	**—38**
Peshawar	5,604	4,288	4,742	4,088	—31	—10	—16	—37
Kohat	222	317	197	212	—30	—61	—7	—5
Bannu	245	183	58	82	—34	—216	—29	—199
Dera Ismail Khan	336	230	204	253	—46	—13	—19	—33

SUBSIDIARY TABLE IV.—*Races and sects of Christians. (Actual numbers.)*

Sect.	European.		Anglo-Indian.		Native.		Total.		Variation + or —
	Male.	Female.	Male.	Female.	Male.	Female.	1911.	1901.	
1	2	3	4	5	6	7	8	9	10
Anglican Communion	3,346 *280*	590 *58*	28 *2*	36 *4*	254 *21*	208 *20*	4,462 *202*	4,018 *189*	—444
Methodist	212 *18*	17 *2*	2 ...	... ...	6 ...	6 *1*	243 *11*	304 *14*	—61
Presbyterian	130 *11*	50 *5*	4 ...	4 ...	1 ...	4 ...	193 *9*	86 *4*	—107
Baptist	27 *2*	5 *1*	... ...	... ...	... ...	... ...	32 *1*	19 *1*	—13
Syrian	... ...	1 ...	... ...	... ...	... ...	... ...	1 ...	... ...	—1
Quaker	1 ...	1 ...	... ...	... ...	... ...	... ...	2 ..	... ...	—2
Roman Catholic	1,148 *96*	132 *13*	11 *1*	7 *1*	118 *10*	28 *3*	1,444 *65*	542 *26*	—902
Greek	1 ...	1 ...	... ...	... ...	7 *1*	5 *1*	14 *1*	... ...	—14
Lutheran	3 ...	4 ...	... ...	... ...	... ...	... ...	7 ...	1 ...	—6
Congregationalist	6 *1*	6 *1*	... ...	... ...	... ...	... ...	12 *1*	... ...	—12
Indefinite Belief	3 ...	2 ...	... ...	... ...	.. ...	... ...	5 ...	3 ...	—2
Minor Protestant denomination	.. ...	... ...	... ...	... ...	3 ...	5 ...	8 *1*	4 ...	—4
Armenian	... ...	... ...	... ...	... ...	... ...	... ...	... ...	4 ...	—4
Sect not returned	45 *4*	10 *1*	5 *1*	3 ...	163 *14*	69 *7*	295 *13*	292 *14*	—3

NOTE.—The figures in *italics* show the proportion per 100,000 of the total population of the Province of the sex concerned.

SUBSIDIARY TABLE V.—*Distribution of Christians per mille (a) Races by sect, (b) Sects by race.*

Sect.	Races distributed by sect.				Sects distributed by race.			
	European.	Anglo-Indian.	Native.	Total.	European.	Anglo-Indian.	Native.	Total.
1	2	3	4	5	6	7	8	9
Anglican Communion	686	640	527	664	882	14	104	1,000
Methodist	40	20	14	36	943	8	49	1,000
Presbyterian	32	80	6	29	933	41	26	1,000
Baptist	6	...	...	5	1,000	...	...	1,000
Syrian	...	...	...	...	1,000	...	...	1,000
Quaker	...	...	...	...	1,000	...	...	1,000
Roman Catholic	223	180	166	215	887	12	101	1,000
Greek	...	...	14	2	143	...	857	1,000
Lutheran	1	...	...	1	1,000	...	...	1,000
Congregationalist	2	...	...	2	1,000	...	...	1,000
Indefinite Belief	1	...	...	1	1,000	...	...	1,000
Minor Protestant denominations ...	...	...	9	1	...	...	1,000	1,000
Armenian	...	...	...	...	...	...	...	...
Sect not returned	9	80	264	44	186	27	787	1,000
Total Sects ...	1,000	1,000	1,000	1,000	855	15	130	1,000

SUBSIDIARY TABLE VI.—*Religions of urban and rural population.*

Natural Division.	Number per 10,000 of urban population who are :—					Number per 10,000 of rural population who are :—				
	Hindus.	Mohammadans.	Sikhs.	Christians.	Others.	Hindus.	Mohammadans.	Sikhs.	Christians.	Others.
1	2	3	4	5	6	7	8	9	10	11
Total Districts N.-W. F. P. ...	**2,220**	**6,984**	**572**	**221**	**2**	**289**	**9,638**	**72**	**1**	...
Hazara	3,681	5,775	487	57	...	234	9,695	71	...	...
Trans-Indus Districts	2,054	7,122	582	240	2	313	9,614	72	1	...

SUBSIDIARY TABLE VII.—*Mohammadan Sects.*

Sect.	Males.	Females.	Sect.	Males.	Females.
1	2	3	1	2	3
Ahl-i-Hadis	73	25	Shamsi Shiah	...	4
Ahl-i-Qoran	5	11	Shiah	14,120	10,141
Ahmadi	112	36	Sufi	6	...
Arab	...	1	Sunni	1,079,558	944,644
Hanifi	6	7	Wahabi	9	22
Ismail	1	...	**Sweeper Sects :—**		
Jafri	1	...	Bhangi	...	6
Mohammadia	...	5	Mehtar	17	4
Pir Mir Agha Khan ...	1	...	Chuhra	70	12
Rabbani	5	...	Balmiki	251	137
Shafi	1	...	Lalbegi	96	61
Shamsi	4	...	Balashahi	86	61
			Total Sects ...	1,094,422	955,177

SUBSIDIARY TABLE VIII.—*Hindu Sects.*

SECT.	Males.	Females.
1	2	3
Acharji	9	15
Agha Khani	3	...
Aitwar	4	1
Amar Nathi	...	5
Arya	96	126
Arya Samaj	1,400	703
Baba Kalu	5	...
Baba Kirtar Smgh Sanatani	1	...
Baba Khem Singh	1	...
Baba Lala Jasrae	...	1
Baba Narsingh	6	...
Bairagi Faqir	12	3
Bawa Jogi	4	2
Bhagat	9	2
Bhagat Rani	1	2
Bhagwati	27	31
Bhat Acharji	1	...
Bhavani	6	...
Bramchari	4	1
Budh	1	...
Calcutta Devi	1	...
Chah Narain	...	2
Darya Panthi	37	19
Deb Acharaj	1	...
Dev Dharam	41	...
Devi	190	1
Devi ke mannewala	41	...
Devi ke Pujari	120	98
Devi Panthi	6	1
Devi Parat	7	4
Devi Pum	21	...
Dev Samaj	4	34
Devi Sanatan	...	7
Devna Pujari	35	54
Digar Jogi	2	...
Gada Govind ke	1	...
Gorakhnath	49	30
Gorakh Panthi	4	2
Gosain	70	43
Gosain Khandwala	...	2
Granthi	1	2
Gurkha Sanatan Dharam	1	...
Guru Gosain	...	4
Guru Govind Ji	2	1
Guru Govind Singhi	750	964
Guru Jogi	3	...
Guru Kabir Singhi	...	4
Guru Nanak	3,247	3,457
Guru Sanniasi	...	3
Habiasi	1	1
Hanuman	2	...
Hindu Singh	48	...
Jai Kishni	26	8
Jeo Narain Panthi	1	...
Jinda Kaliana	11	24
Jog	2	2
Jogi	110	58
Jogi Gorakhnathi	1	...
Jogi Panthi	6	14
Jog Rani	...	1
Kabir Panthi	5	...
Kali Devi	6	3
Kalka Mai	1	...
Karam Kandi	13	5
Kesdhàri	1	...
Khalsa	2	...
Khalsa Panthi	1	...
Khem Dasi	3	19
Krishan	5	...
Mahadev	12	...
Mahajan Singh	1	1
Meo Narain Panthi	1	...
Mula Panthi	2	...
Nagar Panthi	56	14
Nanak Panthi	14,837	13,651
Nanak Sanatan	5	...
Narain Panthi	6	...
Nirankari	9	1
Nirmala	7	3
Pamnar Ganga	...	3
Pandit Sanatan	1	...
Parasrami	20	12
Pir Ratan Nathi	73	73
Pujari Jogi	9	8

SUBSIDIARY TABLE VIII.—*Hindu Sects*—concluded.

Sect.	Males.	Females.
1	2	3
Puranic Vaishnav	15	...
Radha Swami	91	78
Ram Chandarji	152	21
Ramdaji	4	...
Rattan Nath	109	52
Ratan Panthi	4	2
Sadhu Bairagi	39	...
Sahij Dhari	7	...
Salig Ram	11	...
Sam Hindu	5	...
Sanatan Dharam	34,025	18,876
Sanatan Darya	...	25
Sanatan Nanak Panthi ...	226	186
Sanniasi	2	2
Sewak	2,736	2.088
Sewak Baba Ratan Nath ...	15	...
Sewak Devi	41	47
Sawak Gopal	...	3
Sewak Gopi Chand	2	...
Sewak Gosain	14	3
Sewak Jogi	20	40
Sewak Jogiani	89	37
Sewak Lalji	3,478	1,550
Sewak Mahajan	11	...
Sewak Panthi	...	30
Sewak Pir Ratan Nath Sahib ...	6	...
Sewak Sanatan	85	...
Sewak Sanatan Dharam ...	78	...
Shamji Panthi	29	...
Shamsi	179	109
Shiv Ji	55	21
Shiv Narain	163	88
Shiv Panthi	33	17
Shiv Ram Das	...	1
Shiv Ramji	3	...
Sikh	80	91
Sikh Sabha	...	8
Singh Sabha	14	...
Sri Ram Chand	2	...
Suraj Bansi	2	2
Swami	2	...
Thakur Ji	1	...

Sect.	Males.	Females.
1	2	3
Thakur Pujari ...	71	83
Tirath Nath ...	15	12
Tulsi Das	29	35
Udasi	7	...
Udhu Das	...	5
Upashak Devi	9	16
Vedak	1,045	750
Vedak Sanatan	7	...
Ved Dharam	...	1
Vaishnav	934	324
Vaishnav Kohistani ...	1	...
Sweeper Sects—		
Bala Shahi	59	35
Balmiki	972	743
Bhangi	104	59
Chuhra	62	50
Hindu Mehtar	...	15
Khakrob	30	12
Kutana	...	2
Lalbegi	490	526
Mehtar	424	192
Sect not returned or unintelligible	6,137	3,134
TOTAL SECTS ...	73,732	48,896

SUBSIDIARY TABLE IX.—*Sikh Sects.*

SECT.	Males.	Females.	SECT.	Males.	Females.
1	2	3	1	2	3
* Arya Samaj	12	6	Sadhu Singh	2	...
Bawa Khem Singh... ...	2	...	Sanatan Dharam	225	104
Balmiki	10	3	Sanniasi	...	1
Bedi	1	...	Sanwal Shahi	3	2
Devi	1	...	Sewak	14	7
Gurmukh Singhi	...	1	Sewak Gopal	2	...
† Guru Govind Singhi ...	11,550	4,419	Sewak Panthi	1	...
Hindu	4	1	Sikh Bramchari	...	1
Jog	1	...	Sikh Sabha	47	7
Khwaja Khizr	1	...	Sodh Bans	2	4
Lalji Panthi	5	7	Sodh Bans Khalsa	3	...
Mazhabi	14	4	Tulsi Dass	2	1
Namdhari	3	...	§ Sect not returned	871	363
‡ Nanak Panthi ...	8,226	5,508			
Narankari	4	1			
Radha Swami	10	...			
Ram Chand	1	2	TOTAL SIKHS ...	21,017	10,442

		Males.	Females.
* *Includes*—	Arya Samaj	3	4
	Arya	6	1
	Vedak	3	1
† *Includes*—	Guru Govind Singhi	10,519	4,054
	Khalsa	611	35
	Kes Dhari	199	135
	Singh	...	26
	Singh Sabia	...	12
	Tat Khalsa	221	157
‡ *Includes*—	Nanak Panthi	7,464	5,347
	Sahij Dhari	174	110
	Guru Nanak	588	51

§ Under this head are included, besides those persons for whom no sect was recorded, a certain number who returned caste or occupational names, as well as 731 (431 males and 300 females) who returned it simply as Sikh, and 73 (28 males and 45 females) whose sect was returned as Bhai Khel, namely the class of Bhais (Bhai being the characteristic title of Sikhs).

CHAPTER V.

AGE.

Causes which have been noticed in the past as impairing the value of the age returns in India.

173. The statistics of age are known to be perhaps the least trustworthy of those which are compiled in connection with Census operations. Even in England, as Mr. Gait pointed out in 1901, the greater number of adults can only state their age approximately ; and a preference for giving it as some exact multiple of ten, the vagueness which characterises the returns for children, and wilful mis-statement on the part of women, together with the tendency for old people to exaggerate their ages, were also indicated as fruitful sources of error. Mr. Gait went on to remark that the age return is naturally vastly more inaccurate in India than in England, and that at the Indian Census of 1901 the entries made in the schedules were often little better than very wild guesses. The causes which have been noticed in India as leading to a mis-statement of age in the past have been as follows : First there is the tendency to select certain round numbers, notably multiples of five, and to a still greater extent, of ten. Secondly there is the inaccuracy of the entries for children of under 5 years of age. Thirdly the propensity is to return the current, and not the completed year of age. Then there is *" at certain ages a general bias in favour of minimising or exaggerating age, quite apart from the fondness for certain round numbers already alluded to. Among men approaching middle age, and especially among widowers, there is frequently a desire to be considered young, and it is not at all uncommon for persons of 35 or even 40 to describe themselves as being 25 years of age............With females the proneness to mis-statement comes earlier. It is considered disgraceful for a woman to attain puberty while still unmarried, and when this happens her true age will not be reported......................Once a woman is married, her age in often exaggerated while she is still very young, but the estimate then remains unchanged so long as she is capable of child-bearing, and, until this period of life has passed, she is often shown as much younger than she really is. Amongst old people of both sexes, but especially in the case of females, exaggeration in the matter of age is very common."

Their illustration in the tables of the present Census.

174. Table VII, printed in the second Part of this volume, in which is shown the distribution by age of the population of the Province, together with the Subsidiary Tables appended to this Chapter, afford ample exemplification of most of the causes of error noted above. Indeed from the small population dealt with, the vagaries of the statistics are naturally more pronounced than in larger areas, where the law of large numbers has fuller effect. A statement showing the age distribution by annual age periods of any portion of the population has not been prepared for the North-West Frontier Province, but even in Table VII, in which the population, after the first five years of life, is grouped in quinquennial age periods, the tendency to plump for multiples of ten is clearly marked. The age group "5 to 10" consists of persons who returned their age as being 5, 6, 7, 8 or 9 years, similarly the group "10 to 15" consists of those who returned it as 10, 11, 12, 13, and 14, and so on through the series of age groups. It is therefore those groups, in which 10 or a multiple of 10 forms the first of the two ages which form the limits of the age period, in which the persons who recorded their age as being 10 or a multiple of 10 are included. For the first 19 years of life, the tendency in question has no effect on the figures, for the total population aged "5 to 10" is largely in excess of that aged "10 to 15," but for the remaining age periods the group containing a multiple of 10 is largely in excess of the one it immediately follows. Thus the population aged "20 to 25" is much more numerous than that aged "15 to 20," that aged "30 to 35" is largely in excess of that aged "25 to 35" and so on. Particularly striking are the figures for the age groups "65 to 70" and "70 and over" respectively, for those for the former are only just over one-third of those for the latter. When it is

Tendency to return age as a multiple of ten.

* India Census Report, 1901, paragraph 749.

remembered that in a stationary or progressive population the greatest number should be at the age group "under one year", and that the population of each age group should steadily decrease from year to year, it will be realized how greatly the correctness of the statistics is impaired by the tendency referred to.

Inaccuracy of age return for young children.

175. The figures give ample evidence of the inaccuracy of the age returns for children of under five years of age. A reference to Subsidiary Table IX, appended to this chapter, will show how high is the mortality of children during the first year of life, though it may be mentioned in passing that the record of the age at which death occurs, as prepared for the vital statistics, is no more accurate than the age statistics prepared in connection with Census operations. But even the high death-rate among children aged under one year can hardly explain the fact that the population recorded as under one year of age should be two and two-third times as large as that aged from 1 to 2 years. With the object of avoiding the confusion likely to arise in tabulation, if age were recorded in months for children of under one year, the instructions to enumerators on the present, as on previous occasions, explained that children who had not completed one year of life should be recorded as 'infants.' The term used to translate infant means literally a child at the breast, and as children in the Province are often, and indeed perhaps commonly, suckled by their mothers for a longer period than one year, many children would naturally be recorded as still at the breast, in spite of the fact that they had completed one year of life. I am not aware of any word commonly in use in the Province for infant except *shir khwar baccha* or *dud pita baccha*, both of which have the meaning indicated above. It would perhaps be less likely to lead to confusion if the enumerators were instructed to enter the age of children of under one year of age as nil.

But whatever be the degree of inaccuracy which our figures present in the first two annual age periods, the successive increases in the number of children aged 2, 3, and 4 years respectively cannot be in accordance with the actual facts; nor is it likely, seeing that migration has little influence at so early an age, that the population for the age period "5 to 10" should exceed, as it will be found to do in our Table VII, that living at the age period "0 to 5." The tendency to return the current instead of the completed * year of age is no doubt partly responsible for the vagaries of the figures, but to explain them fully one can only assume that it is almost a matter of chance what age is returned for children between the ages of one and ten years. It is perhaps worth noting however that, if it appears to be common to return boys of four as being five years old (male population all religions aged "0 to 5," 167,927; aged "5 to 10," 185,116), in the case of females there seems to be no such bias, for the figures show, as would naturally be the case, a decrease in the second as compared with the first quinquennium of life.

Understatement of age by the middle aged.

176. As throwing light on the period of life at which age is commonly understated, it may be noticed that both for males and females, if we take the quinquenniums which contain the ages returned as a multiple of ten, *viz.* "10 to 15," "20 to 25," "30 to 35" and so on, each successive group contains a smaller population than the one preceding it, except in the case of the group "30 to 35," the population of which is largely in excess of that for the group "20 to 25." This is no doubt partly due to the tendency referred to above, which leads men of middle age and married women capable of child-bearing to state their age as less than it really is In the case of the widowed the disparity between both males and females aged "30 to 35" and the population for the quinquenniums immediately preceding and following that age period is particularly marked. The population shown for the age periods "20 to 25" and "25 to 30" is also in excess of that for the period "15 to 20," and, though in comparing the figures for each of the quinquenniums between the ages of 20 and 45 with those for the period "15 to 20," the fact that immigrants are mainly persons of over 20 years of age has to be taken into account, the excess of population at each of the age periods from 20 to 35 years is partially due to the understatement of age by persons of middle age.

* The instructions to supervisors specially mentioned that the completed and not the current year of life was to be entered. The instructions to enumerators, though they should have been plain enough, did not specifically draw attention to the fact that the current year of life was not to be entered.

Misstatement of age of young females.

177. As regards females, there is in the North-West Frontier Province less inducement than elsewhere in India to misstate the ages of those who have not completed the age of 20 or 25 years. Among the Mohammadans of the Province there is no feeling of disgrace associated with the possession of an unmarried adult daughter, and, as is pointed out in paragraph 263 (Chapter VII), even Hindu females marry considerably later than in those areas where Hindu sentiment and tradition are stronger. The strength of the feeling which imposes the pardah on females, especially on those of marriageable age, is however reflected in our statistics, which represent females of the period "15 to 20" as being less numerous than those aged "20 to 25."* That they are in reality less numerous is hardly conceivable, and the figures for males, whose existence at the age period "15 to 20" there is no desire to conceal, no doubt represent the actual facts, when they show the numbers aged "15 to 20" as being in excess of those living in the following quinquennium.

Exaggeration of age of males.

178. Last must be mentioned the tendency of the old to exaggerate their age. In Pathan communities, where a voice in the tribal counsels is ordinarily possessed only by the *spin-giri* or grey beard, the desire might be expected to be strong. Taking India as a whole in 1901 the number per 10,000 of the population whose age was recorded as "60 years and over" was 466, as compared with 522 in the North-West Frontier Province in the same year. This number was only exceeded in the Punjab, where the proportion was 599 per 10,000 males of all ages. How far the variations are due to local circumstances, such as famine and plague, from which the North-West Frontier Province has up to now been exempt, I find it impossible to say, but it is perhaps worth remarking how high in 1901 was the proportion of aged males in the Province. The proportion recorded at the present Census is even higher, being 575 per 10,000 males. On the other hand, whereas in India generally exaggeration of age is believed to be more common among old women than among old men, in the North-West Frontier Province, this does not seem to be the case; for the proportion of those aged "60 and over" per 10,000 of all ages of the sex concerned, is considerably lower in the case of females than in that of males. In 1901 in India as a whole the figure for females was 555, but in the Province in the same year it was only 479. No doubt the comparatively small proportion of females aged "60 and over" as compared with the corresponding figure for males, in the Province corresponds largely with the actual facts, for a reference to Subsidiary Table IX, appended to this chapter, will show that, taking the average of the decade 1901—1910, the death-rate for females is higher than that of males in every age period after the first two quinquenniums of life. On the other hand in the majority of the other Provinces of India during the same period the reverse has been the case, and the relative position of the figures is not likely to have been largely different in previous decades. The point, however, which is perhaps worth making here is that there is not in the North-West Frontier Province the same inducement for a woman to exaggerate her age as there is for a man.

Variations in the age distribution since 1881.

Difference in the instructions issued as to record of age in 1891 and at the other Censuses respectively.

179. Subsidiary Table II, appended to this chapter, shows the age distribution of 10,000 of each sex at the last four enumerations for the Province (total British Districts) and for Natural Divisions, while in Subsidiary Table VI is shown the variation in population at certain age periods. But before discussing the figures, it is necessary to consider how they have been arrived at. At the present Census enumerators were directed to enter the completed year of life, and supervisors were warned that the age should be entered as it would be on the night of the final enumeration. This warning was rendered necessary by the fact that the preliminary enumeration was begun in villages six weeks, and in towns four weeks, before the final Census; and without such a warning a man's age, in completed years of life, as it stood on February 1st, would be different from the age of the same person on March 10th, should his birth-day fall in the interval. The difference in time is so small that it made little practical difference if the instructions as to entering the age of the person

* That the low proportion of females returned as aged 15—20 is due to the pardah system is suggested by the figures contained in Subsidiary Table III at the end of this chapter, from which it will be seen that the proportion of females living at this age is considerably higher in the case of Hindus and Sikhs than in that of Mohammadans.

enumerated as it would stand on March 10th, 1911, were neglected, as I fancy they were in the majority of cases. This is, however, beside the point which it is now desired to make. The instructions issued in 1881 and in 1901 were precisely similar to those given on the present occassion. At the Census of 1891, however, enumerators were directed to enter the current, and not the completed year of life, as it was thought that, whatever orders were given, the age returned would be the current year since birth. But in order to make the statistics for the Punjab uniform with those for the rest of India, where the completed year of life was, under the instructions issued, to be recorded, the Punjab returns were, in all cases, except of those for Europeans, who recorded, as is their custom, their completed age, thrown back by one year. That is to say a man who recorded his age as 30 was treated as being in reality 29 years of age, and was included in the age group "25 to 29," or, as it is printed in the tables of the present Census, "25 to 30."

Effect on the statistics of the difference in the instructions issued.

180. The result of this manipulation appears, if we look at Subsidiary Table II, appended to this chapter, to show clearly that, whatever be the instructions issued, the age returned will be the same, for no one, except perhaps a few Hindus, knows his age with sufficient exactness to distinguish between the current and completed year. The proportionate figures for the years 1881, 1901 and 1911 (*vide* Subsidiary Table II at the end of this chapter) all profess to show the completed year of life of the population, and it will be observed that the variations in the proportion recorded as being of the separate age periods selected vary comparatively little from year to year. On the other hand the figures for 1891 professed, in the form in which they were recorded, to show the current year of life of each member of the population, and the effect of throwing back each person's age by one year should have been, had the figures for the various Censuses fulfilled their pretensions, to bring the proportions of the population at each age period into something approaching agreement with the proportions arrived at from the figures of the Censuses of 1881, 1901 and 1911. In point of fact no such result was reached. Whereas in the proportionate population for the years 1881, 1901 and 1911 (*vide* Subsidiary Table II, appended to this chapter), the figures for the age groups including the ages returned as a multiple of 10, from the age group "30 to 35" onwards ("30 to 35," "40 to 45" and so on), are in each case larger than those for the following quinquennium ("35 to 40," "45 to 50," and so on), in the figures for the year 1891 the proportion of persons aged "35 to 40" exceeds that of those aged "30 to 35," the proportion of persons aged "45 to 50" exceeds that for those aged "40 to 45" and the like. And the reason for this is plain. Whether the age recorded profess to be the completed or the current year of life, people will more frequently return their age as 30, 40, 50, or some other multiple of ten, than as any other age near to those numbers. The large aggregation of persons who show their age as a multiple of 10 has always been noticed in connection with Census operations in India, and whereas in the years 1881, 1901 and 1911 the numbers whose ages have been so returned have gone to swell the population of the age groups "30 to 35," "40 to 45" and so on, in the year 1891, by throwing back the age of each by one year, such persons have been included in the previous age period, "25 to 29" (or, as it is shown in our tables, "25 to 30"), and the like. The effect of the adjustment of the ages actually returned in 1891 is seen in other parts also of Subsidiary Table II appended to this chapter. For instance, the number of children whose age was recorded as five, is naturally, from the preference for round numbers, larger than of those whose age was given as four, years. But in 1891 the children whose ages were returned as five years were tabulated as being aged four, and the result is that, while males aged "0 to 5" (*i. e.* children who were returned as either infants, or as aged one, two, three or four years) amounted in 1881 to 1,363 per 10,000 of the total male population, in 1901 to 1,402, and in 1911 to 1,420 per 10,000, in the year 1891 they amounted to the high figure of 1,792 per 10,000. The conclusion to which one is forced is, incidentally, that it makes little difference whether the enumerators are directed to record the current or the completed year of age (for the people do not know their ages with sufficient accuracy to distinguish between them), and that nothing is to be gained by comparing the proportion at each age period in 1891 with those living at the same age period in the other years.

181. The dislocation which has been occasioned in the figures by the manipulation to which they were subjected in 1891 is also shown in a glaring form by a reference to Subsidiary Table VI appended to this chapter, in which is shown the variation of the population at certain age periods between the years 1881—1891 and 1891—1901. At the end of the former decade it resulted in the appearance of an abnormal increase in the population aged under ten years, and an abnormal decrease in the population aged "60 and over," while at the end of the latter decade the appearance was given of a precisely opposite development. In the figures for the years 1901 and 1911, however, we have statistics in which the sources of error, however large, are at any rate constant. It will be seen that while the total population of the districts of the Province has increased between the years 1901 and 1911 by 7 per cent, the increase has occurred principally among persons aged 40 and over, persons between the ages of 40 and 60 having increased by 11 and persons aged "60 and over" by 16 per cent. Children of under the age of 10 have also increased at a quicker rate than the population as a whole, while the increase in the population between the age of puberty and middle age has been only half of that of the total population. The population aged "10 to 15" has also failed to keep pace in its rate of increase with the population as a whole. The comparatively slow rate of growth of the population between the ages of 10 and 40 years is no doubt largely due to the decrease as compared with the figures for 1901 in the number of immigrants enumerated in the Province on the present occasion, for it is of persons between these ages that the immigrants mainly consist.

Increase and decrease of population at the different age periods since 1881.

The influence of immigration naturally affects the figures for persons aged between 15 and 40 more than those for the age period "10 to 15." We have no figures to show the age distribution of immigrants, and in their absence it is only possible to theorise on the subject. It is clear, however, that to immigration is due much of the contrast presented by the relative rates of increase in the population aged 0—10 and in the population aged 15—40. The comparatively large increase in the population aged 40 years and over would appear to be due entirely to improving conditions of public health, with a consequent increase of longevity among the population.

182. It follows from what has been said above that the proportionate distribution of the population by age periods in the year 1891 cannot usefully be compared with that in other years for which statistics are shown in Subsidiary Table II. A comparison between the three years 1881, 1901 and 1911 is not, however, without interest. Some of the figures for the last two years have already been discussed, in connection with the rate of increase of the population at the various age periods in the last decade. It may, however, be added that the fact that immigration has little effect up to the age of 15 is shown by Subsidiary Table II, for there is only a difference of 1 per ,000 in the proportion of the total male population aged "10 to 15" in the years 1901 and 1911, respectively. But from the age 15 to 45, each decennium of life shows a smaller proportionate population now than in 1901, while it is only to be expected from the remarks in the last paragraph that the reverse is the case for every quinquennium of age beyond the age of 45. Coming to the figures for 1881, we find in both sexes a higher proportionate population at the prime of life (20—45) than in either of the two later years. As the figures in the margin show, there has been a continuous decrease in the proportion of the population living at this period of life since 1881. The proportion of children under 5 years old has on the contrary steadily increased from 13·6 per cent. in 1881 to 14·0 in 1901, and 14·2 per cent. in 1911 in the case of males, and in the case of females from 15·9 per cent. in 1881 to 16·5 in 1901, though there has been a slight drop to 16·4 per cent. on the present occasion. The proportion living at the age period 5—20 has varied but slightly in the three years, the percentage for each sex at each year being as given in the margin on the following page. The proportionate figures for persons alive at each of the three

Proportionate distribution of population at the different age periods since 1881.

Percentage living at the age 20—45.

Year.	Males.	Females.
1881	37·8	38·8
1901	37·3	37·8
1911	35·7	37·3

Censuses in question at the age period 45 and over similarly show no persistent tendency in either direction since 1881, for while the proportion of middle aged and aged persons (age period 45 and over) of both sexes was smaller in 1901 than it was in 1881, at the present Census it shows a rise to a figure higher than that arrived at in 1881.

Percentage living at age 5—20.

Year.	Males.	Females.
1881	34·6	32·0
1901	33·1	33·2
1911	35·1	32·8

Large proportionate increase in the number of young children and aged persons.

183. In the case of the North-West Frontier Province we are able to point to no periods of famine, and to no widespread outbreaks of disease such as in other parts of India have largely affected the growth of the population as a whole, or its proportionate age distribution. It is natural, therefore, that the figures of any two successive Censuses should exhibit no great fluctuation. The figures, however, are of interest as showing a persistent decline since 1881 in the proportion of the population aged from 20 to 45 years, a drop which is to be attributed to a decrease of immigration to, and an increase of emigration from, the Province. In this connection a reference should be made to paragraph 100 (Chapter III—Birth-place). The persistent rise in 1911 and 1901 in the proportion of children aged under 5 years as compared with 1881 is of course in part merely a reflection of the result on the age statistics of the shrinkage of immigration, but in part it would seem to represent an increased fertility of the population, (*Vide* Subsidiary Table V, appended to this chapter) If we regard the figures for the present Census and for that of 1901, we find that, though the proportion of married women of child-bearing age has not increased, and indeed in the trans-Indus districts of the Province has actually decreased since 1901, there has been a rise in every district alike in the proportion of children under 10 to married women of the age for child-bearing, and in every district except Hazara, when the drop has been trifling, in the proportion of children under 10 to persons aged from 15 to 40 years. The figures in column 8—11 inclusive of Subsidiary Table V support the conclusion come to in paragraph 181 above as to the greater longevity of the population now than in 1901.

Age distribution by religion.
(a) persons aged under 15.

184. Subsidiary Table III at the end of this chapter shows clearly how different is the age distribution of the population of Mohammadans, Hindus and Sikhs respectively. At the present Census, whereas, out of 100 Mohammadan males of all ages, 42·8 are under the age of 15, the corresponding figure for Hindus is 30·9 and for Sikhs only 26. In the case of females of the same age period the contrast is not so marked, and it is noticeable that for the age group "10 to 15" the percentage is higher in the case of Hindus and Sikhs than in that of Mohammadans. The fact that Hindu and Sikh girls of under 15 should bulk larger in the total figures for their sex than boys of the same age do in theirs* is curious at first sight, for seeing that the abnormal age distribution of Hindus and Sikhs is due to immigration, it might be supposed that fewer girl than boy children would accompany parents living for a time only in the Province. The explanation, however, apparently lies in the fact that since, as is shown by the low proportion of females to males among Hindus and Sikhs (*vide* paragraph 208) immigrants of those religions are comparatively seldom accompanied by their wives, in those cases in which a woman accompanies her husband, she more often brings her female than her male children along with her. The fact that the proportion of Hindu and Sikh females aged 10—15 should not only exceed that of males of the same religion, but also exceed the corresponding figure for Mohammadan females, is perhaps to be attributed to the absence of pardah among the two first mentioned communities.

(b) Persons aged 15 and over.

185. In the proportions living at the other age periods for the three religions respectively, the influence of immigration is clearly apparent. The bulk of the immigrants to any area, especially if they be largely temporary immigrants, such as men employed in the army, consist of persons in the prime of life. In this fact we have the explanation of the large proportion of the Hindu

* *Vide* Subsidiary Table III appended to this Chapter.

and Sikh population which is included in the age period 20—40. It is naturally in the case of males that the difference between the age distribution of the followers of the three religions is most clearly marked. Whereas of the total Mohammadan males 28 per cent. are between the ages of 20 and 40, in the case of Hindu males the figure is 40, and in the case of Sikh males 47 per cent. The figures for females of the same age period are 33 and 34 per cent. respectively in the case of Hindus and Sikhs, and 31 per cent. in the case of Mohammedans. The age period 40—60 on the other hand includes few immigrants, and in this period of life accordingly Mohammadans, both males and females, are proportionately more numerous than either Hindus or Sikhs. The same is true, in a more marked degree, of the age period '60 and over,' with the curious exception that Sikh females of this age group are proportionately more numerous than Mohammadan. In view of the fact that the figures for Sikh show more clearly than those for Hindu males the influence of migration (*viz.* low proportion of population in youth and age and high proportion of those in the prime of life) one would expect old women among Sikhs to be proportionately few. The variation can, I think, only be explained by the fact that the figures for Sikh females in the Province (the female Sikh population of British territory is only 10,378) are so small that accidental abberrations naturally occur. It remains to consider the relative proportion of the population of each religion contributed by Mohammadans, Hindus and Sikhs between the ages of 15 and 20 years. Among males the proportion of Hindus, and still more noticeably the proportion of Sikhs, of this age exceeds that of Mohammadans. I believe that here also the difference is due to immigration, for, especially towards the close of the quinquennium, persons of this age period are considerably represented among immigrants. In the case of females, where the disparity between the figures for the three religions is less, the influence of immigration (which causes a real difference in the age distribution) and the existence of the pardah among Mohammadans (which exaggerates in our statistics a difference which is in part based on actual facts) are probably both responsible.

Variation of age distribution by religion in different years.

186. Among Mohammadans, the statistics of the enumerations of 1881, 1901 and 1911 show (*vide* marginal statement) a small but steady rise in the percentage, both male and female, living at the age period 0—15. But whereas the figures for this period of life indicate a population among whom the tendency to expansion by natural increase is based, as it were, upon a broad and secure foundation, the figures for the other age periods show no persistent tendency in either direction. The proportion of Hindus of both sexes living at the same age period (0—15) present the same general features as those for Mohammadans (except that there was a slight drop between the years 1881 and 1901 in the proportion of males of this age) and the proportion living at the following age period (15—20) also shows a persistent rise in the case of each sex. It must be remembered, however, that in the case of the Hindus we are dealing with a population which, instead of increasing steadily since 1881 like that of Mohammadans, has fallen considerably in the last decade. I have attempted in Chapter IV to show (*vide* paragraph 115) that the decrease is mainly due to accidental causes, and notably, to an extraordinary influx of Hindu immigrants into the three southern districts of the Province in 1901. I show in the margin the actual figures for

Percentage of population of each sex living at age period 0—15 (Mohammadans).

Year.	Males.	Females.
1881	41·7	40·6
1901	42·2	42·84
1911	42·8	42·29

Percentage of population of each sex living at age period 0—15 (Hindus).

Year.	Males.	Females.
1881	30·3	37·8
1901	29·5	38·9
1911	30·9	39·2

Hindus by main age periods in 1901 and 1911 respectively, together with the percentage of decrease at each. Alone of the districts of the Province, the Hindu population of Hazara * has increased. The Punjab Census Report, 1901, only gives the age distribution of Hindus for the Peshawar and Kohat Districts taken together, and for the Bannu and Dera Ismail Khan Districts similarly in one set of figures. The figures for the Peshawar and Kohat Districts are as given in the margin, and those for Bannu and Dera Ismail Khan are given below them. It will be seen that in all the trans-Indus districts the largest decrease of population is at the age periods "15 to 20" and "20 to 40," *viz.* the age groups to which purely temporary immigrants, such as the troops included in the population of Bannu and Dera Ismail Khan and the men employed on railway construction in Kohat, in 1901, principally belonged. In Bannu and Dera Ismail Khan the influence of migration is very noticeable. The decrease in the population aged "0 to 5" appears indeed to be due to a smaller birth-rate among Hindus during the latter half of the decade 1901—1911; for the temporary immigrants in 1901, whose absence in 1911 accounts of the decrease in the population of the age groups from 15 to 60 years, were not accompanied by children, consisting as they did of troops on service. In the other age periods our figures show a small increase. In the case of the Peshawar and Kohat Districts the figures do not in the same way bear upon the face of them the influence of migration. The decrease at the age period "15 to 20," and the marked fall in the number of persons between the ages of 20 and 40 years point indeed clearly enough to such an explanation, but the high rates of decrease at the other age periods are more difficult to understand. It is likely, however, that the engineering staff employed on railway construction in Kohat in 1901 were in many cases accompanied by their families, and the Hindus who left Peshawar just before the Census were certainly accompanied by theirs. In the discussion of the whole subject, however, we are not on very sure ground. The numbers dealt with are so small as to be affected largely by accidental circumstances, especially when the large proportion of immigrants among them is considered. For this reason I do not discuss the figures for the age distribution of Sikhs, for here we are dealing with even smaller numbers, and with a population of which an even larger proportion was born outside the Province than in the case of Hindus.

Population of Hindus (both sexes) in the districts of the Province by age periods in 1901 and 1911, with percentage of decrease for each age period.

Age period.	1911.	1901.	Decrease per cent. 1901-1911.
0—5	14.304	15,377	6·9
5—10	14,680	15,133	2·9
10—15	12,136	12,431	2·4
15—20	11,001	11,874	7·3
20—40	44,574	49,821	10·5
40—60	18,002	19,129	5·8
60 and over	5,245	5,541	5·3
All ages ...	119,942	129,306	7·2

Actual number of Hindus in Peshawar and Kohat in 1911 and 1901 with percentage of decrease in former year.

Age period.	1901.	1911.	Decrease per cent, 1901-1911.
0—5	5,831	4,945	15·2
5—10	5,624	5,076	9·7
10—15	4,817	4,285	11·0
15—20	5,201	4,388	15·6
20—40	22,984	18,520	19·4
40—60	7,872	6,971	11·4
60 and over	2,334	2,030	13·0
All ages ...	54,663	46,215	15·5

Actual number of Hindus in Bannu and Dera Ismail Khan in 1901 and 1911 respectively with percentage of variation in the period 1901-1911.

Age period.	1901.	1911.	Variation per cent 1901-1911.
0—5	6,762	6,508	— 3·7
5—10	6,700	6,945	+ 3·6
10—15	5,224	5,499	+ 5·2
15—20	4,620	4,082	—11·6
20—40	18,488	16,652	— 9·9
40—60	7,837	7,628	— 2·6
60 and over	1,981	2,024	+ 2·2
All ages ...	51,612	49,338	— 4·4

Age distribution by caste.

187. Subsidiary Table IV shows the proportionate age distribution of those castes and tribes the actual figures for which are shown in Table XIV in the second Part of this volume. The influence of migration is here too perhaps the most potent one affecting the figures. Those tribes and castes which are not native to the Province, but are largely composed of temporary sojourners

* Though even in Hazara there has been a slight decrease of population at the age periods 5—10, 10—15 and 60 and over.

within it, such as Rajput, *Khatri, Brahman, Chuhra, will be found to have a low proportion of children and a high proportion of persons at the prime of life (*vide* marginal statement.) The disparity is naturally greater in the case of males than in that of females, for it is among males that the figures are dominated by the ages of the actual workers. Among tribes native to the Province the variations will be found to be less. In the margin I have placed the proportions living at the age periods 0 to 15 and 15 to 40 for the more numerous of the local tribes below the figures for the total population of the Province. It will be seen that among agricultural tribes the proportions vary little, except that Jat males show a low proportion of children under 5 and a high one of males aged 15 to 40 years. A reference to Table XIII will show that there were enumerated in the Province over 7,000 Sikh and Hindu Jats (males). These are mainly immigrants employed in the army, and the preponderance among them of men between the ages of 15 and 40 naturally throws out the proportion for the total number of males returned as Jats. For menial tribes from among the population native to the Province the proportions will be seen to be roughly the same as for the land owing and cultivating classes.

Number per 100 of each sex aged under 5 and between ages of 15—40 years.

Caste.	0—5		15—40.	
	Males.	Females.	Males.	Females.
Total population	14	16	37	38
Rajput ...	8	14	62	41
Brahman ...	10	15	45	39
Khatri ...	9	14	48	41
Chuhra ...	10	12	50	48

No. per cent. of each sex aged 0-5 and between the ages of 15 and 40 years.

Tribe.	0—5.		—40.	
	Males.	Females.	Males.	Females.
All tribes, etc. ...	14	16	37	38
AGRICULTURAL TRIBES :—				
Awan ...	14	18	36	38
Baghban ...	14	18	35	37
Dhund ...	17	17	34	36
Gujar ...	14	17	35	39
Pathan ...	15	16	36	37
Baluch ...	14	16	37	39
Jat ...	12	15	47	39
Maliar ...	13	17	37	37
Qureshi ...	14	17	37	39
Saiad ...	13	16	36	37
Swathi ...	15	16	33	38
Tanaoli ...	14	17	34	39
ARTISAN AND MENIAL TRIBES :—				
Jolaha ...	13	17	36	38
Kumhar ...	16	17	36	38
Mochi ...	15	17	37	39
Nai ...	15	17	36	40
Tarkhan ...	15	17	37	39

Of the caste or tribal groups shown in Subsidiary Table IV the Jolahas possess the largest, and the Sararas the lowest proportion of males aged 40 and over. The Sarara males only number 4,616 in all, and the low proportion in their case is probably accidental. The next lowest proportion of males of over 40 years is among Rajputs. In their case the low figure is intelligible enough, being due to the fact that many of them are present in the Province as temporary immigrants only; but the low proportion of males of this age period for Karals and Dhunds (like the Sararas both are agricultural tribes of the Hazara District), I am not able to explain, especially in view of the fact that, as a reference to Subsidiary Table II appended to this chapter will show, the proportion of males aged 40 and over is higher in Hazara than in the trans-Indus districts of the Province. The life of the Jolaha involves little exposure or hardship, and that a high proportion should live beyond the age of 40 is not surprising. Among females the highest proportion aged 40 and over is found among Mallahs (299 per mille), and the lowest among Chuhras and Lohars (163 per mille). The figures for Mallahs are perhaps too small (only 2,109 females were enumerated at the recent Census) to allow any valid deduction to be drawn from their age distribution. I note in the margin (on the next page) the other tribes and castes showing a high proportion of females aged 40 and over. Probably none of the figures are much affected by migration. Agriculturists (Baghban

* The bulk of the Khatris and Brahmans are permanent residents, but immigrants of these castes are also numerous.

and Maliar), traders (Paracha and Khatri), and artisan and menial castes, (Chamar, Machhi and Teli) are all represented, while the Kashmiris partake of the character both of the agriculturist and the menial. In the Chuhras and Lohars, who possess the lowest proportion of females aged 40 and over, we also have menial castes, and I find it impossible from the evidence before me to give any general explanation of the causes on which the variations depend.

Caste.	Number per 1,000 females aged 40 and over.
Baghban ...	213
Chamar ...	232
Kashmiri ...	214
Khatri ...	215
Machhi ...	219
Maliar ...	211
Paracha ...	225
Teli ...	214

Mean age.

188. The mean age of the population, of the Province and its natural divisions, and of the main religions taken separately, as shown in Subsidiary Tables II and III, refers to the average age of the persons of each of the groups indicated, and not to the mean duration of life or the expectation of life at birth.* It will be seen that a rise in the mean age, thus understood, does not necessarily imply an increase of longevity among the population, or a fall in the mean age the reverse. The figures depend, not only on the death-rate at the several age periods, but also on the birth-rate, for in a growing population, with a large proportion of young children, the mean age will be lower than in a stationary or declining one with a high proportion of persons in the prime of life. An examination of the figures by religion (*vide* Subsidiary Table III) affords ample illustration of the working of the principle referred to. The mean age of males among both Hindus and Sikhs is higher than that among Mohammadans of the same sex, but this does not mean that the lives of the last are shorter than those of the two first mentioned communities. Males aged 60 and over, who amount to 59 per mille of the total male population in the case of Mohammadans, contribute only 42 and 41 per mille respectively in the case of Hindus and Sikhs. The difference is not indeed here due to differences in the birth and death-rates in the various communities but to migration. The effect, however, is the same, for children, who are relatively so rare among Hindus and Sikhs, do not contribute to the same degree, as in the case of Mussalmans, to reducing the mean age of the community of the religion concerned as a whole.

Variations in the mean age recorded at different enumerations.

189. Taking the population of the Province as a whole (all religions) a reference to Subsidiary Table II will show that the mean age is now higher in the case of males than at any previous enumeration from 1881 onwards; while in the case of females it is higher than in 1901 or 1891, and only a trifle lower than that recorded in 1881 In Hazara the mean age is now greater than at any period dealt with in our tables for both the sexes alike, while in the trans-border districts it is now the same for males as it was in 1881 (the figures for the two intermediate Censuses were lower), and lower than it was in 1881 in the case of females. But for the influence of migration, the tendency seems to be for the mean age to rise. It is in Hazara that the influence of this factor is least, while in the trans-border districts it possesses considerable importance. The figures for the main religions taken separately also support this view. The Mohammadan is the only element in the population the figures for which are not appreciably affected by migration, and the mean age of Mussalmans, both male and female, is higher now than it has been from the year 1881 onwards. On the other hand in the case of Hindus and Sikhs, among whom immigrants bulk so large, the figures show rather a downward than an upward trend. But neither among the community whose mean age has decreased, nor

*NOTE.—The method followed in obtaining the mean age of the population is that described in the French Census Report for 1891. The following account of it is quoted from page 390 of the India Census Report (Administrative Volume) 1901. " It is easy to calculate the mean age of the population by sex and civil condition. In order to ascertain the number of years lived by the aggregate population we must first determine the total number of persons living at the close of each age period " (*i. e.* the number of persons living at the close of the age period 0—5 means the population aged 5 and over, at the close of the age period 5—10 the population aged 10 and over, and so on). " The sum of these totals multiplied by 5, the difference of the age divisions, and raised by two and a half times the number of persons of that sex and civil condition, gives the number of years lived. The mean age is obtained by dividing this last number by the number of persons living". An example of the working of the method is given in the India Administrative Volume, 1901. (Loc. Cit.)

among those where it has risen, since 1901 do our figures point to a stationary or declining (natural) population. Among Mohammadans the rise is not due to any decrease in the relative number of children of under ten years, but to an increase in the population of the aged (age group "60 and over"), and it indicates consequently greater longevity. In the case of the Hindus and Sikhs it is doubtful how far any inference can be drawn. At the same time the fact that the fall since 1901 in the proportion of the whole who are aged 20—40 among both communities has been accompanied, not only by a rise in the ratio of children of under ten years of age, but also by an increase in the ratio aged "60 and over," suggests that here too the longer lives of the people have to be taken into account.

True birth and death-rates as calculated from the age statistics.

190. In paragraph 761 of the last India Census Report Mr. Gait attempted to calculate the true death and birth rates from the age statistics for India as a whole. The mean age of the living of both sexes he found to be 24·9 years. "If the population," he observed, "had been stationary for a generation...........this would correspond fairly closely to the mean duration of life. The population, however, is growing.........and the mean duration of life is therefore greater than the mean age of the living. We have seen, moreover, that the ages at the Census are, on the whole, somewhat understated, and a further increase must be allowed on this account. The true mean duration of life is probably not less than 26 years." If we apply Mr. Gait's conclusions to this Province (and the factors which he adduced in respect of India are equally applicable here), we may put the mean duration of life at 26 years in the case of males (the figure is of course a rough approximation only) and 25 years in the case of females. It will be observed that in making this calculation, I have neglected the effect of migration on the figures, though it would seem that, so far as this is effective at all, it must be in the direction of raising the mean age ; for the bulk of immigrants are aged between 20 and 40, and their mean age must be somewhat higher than that of the native population. But taking the figures suggested above, and following on the lines of Mr. Gait's calculation, we may say that they give us an annual death-rate of $\frac{1000}{26}$ or 38 4 per mille in the case of males, and one of $\frac{1000}{29}$ or 40 per mille in that of females. In showing a higher death-rate for females than for the other sex we are at least in agreement with the vital statistics for every year of the last decade except 1910 (*vide* Subsidiary Table VIII), but there the correspondence stops; for in no year since 1900 has the actual death-rate recorded reached nearly so high a figure. If we proceed to apply Mr. Gait's argument to the calculation of the true birth-rate per mille, we get results which are even farther from supporting the vital statistics. In the districts of the Province the male population has increased since 1901 by 7 and the female by 8 per cent., *i. e.* by 7 and 8 respectively per mille annually. The annual birth rate which would be required to account for this figure by excess of births over deaths would be one of 45·4 in the case of males, and of 48 per mille in the case of females. In actual fact the excess of births over deaths must be something larger than the actual increase of population, for the number of immigrants has decreased since 1901, while emigrants are more numerous than was the case ten years ago. But the birth-rates actually recorded have varied in the last decade between 17 and 20 per mille annually in the case of males, and between 13 and 17 only per mille in the case of female births. These figures, however, it will be observed, are calculated on the total population (both sexes), while those arrived at above represent the ratios borne by the births of each sex to the population of that sex. It seems hardly worth while to calculate the birth-rates anew on the basis of the male and female populations separately. It will be sufficient, although the figures will admittedly be not correct owing to the excess of males in the population, to double, for the purposes of the comparison here suggested, the birth-rates shown in Subsidiary Table VII.* Even after doubling them, however, it will be clear that the age statistics give a higher birth, as they give a higher death-rate, than

---

*The effect of the inequality in the numbers of the two sexes will be that the true male birth-rate, calculated on the total number of males living, will be something less than double the figure shown in Subsidiary Table VII, while the female birth-rate, similarly calculated, will be something more than double the figure shown.

that obtained by registration, and further that they suggest the figure (birth-rate) for females to be higher than that for males, whereas the vital statistics give an opposite conclusion. The calculations, however little claims to accuracy their results may profess, have probably some value as indicating, if such further indication were needed, the small value, for statistical purposes, which is possessed by the registers of births and deaths. They agree with the conclusions, elsewhere arrived at, that deaths are reported with more regularity than births, and that omissions to record female are more numerous than those to record male births. But in view of the character of the material available, little profit can be expected to attach to a further discussion.

SUBSIDIARY TABLE II.*—*Age distribution of* 10,000 *of each sex in the Province and each natural division.*

Age.	1911.		1901.		1891.		1881.	
	Male.	Female.	Male.	Female.	Male.	Female.	Male.	Female.
1	2	3	4	5	6	7	8	9
N.-W. F. P. (TOTAL DISTRICTS).								
0 and under 1	363	411	335	390	412	478	258	292
1 " 2	133	154	156	183	314	372	187	222
2 " 3	278	335	289	345	354	413	253	316
3 " 4	317	375	303	366	362	400	318	377
4 " 5	329	366	319	369	350	375	347	389
Total 0 and under 5 ...	**1420**	**1.641**	**1.402**	**1.653**	**1,792**	**2.038**	**1.363**	**1.596**
5 and under 10	1.564	1,592	1,503	1,548	1,575	1,530	1,584	1,552
10 " 15	1,180	975	1,170	1,002	949	792	1,093	896
15 " 20	774	715	839	770	992	1,082	788	760
20 " 25	755	833	788	831	863	841	839	907
25 " 30	821	858	855	852	1,022	1,051	834	824
30 " 35	875	931	941	968	640	550	991	1,010
35 " 40	522	470	526	471	664	705	442	395
40 " 45	600	644	621	661	299	267	680	749
45 " 50	325	292	296	256	435	436	251	225
50 " 55	437	414	411	403	155	131	462	449
55 " 60	152	126	126	106	331	324	116	100
60 " 65	301	276	522	479	283	253	557	537
65 " 70	68	59	..	...	...	...	...	...
70 and over	206	174	...	...	...	...	...	...
Mean age	24·2	23·5	23·8	23·0	21·7	21·1	23·9	23·6
HAZARA.								
0 and under 5	1,463	1,664	1,428	1,622	1,963	2,249	1,367	1,585
5 " 10	1,560	1,606	1,630	1,667	1,619	1,598	1,693	1,654
10 " 15	1,275	1,062	1,361	1,147	966	791	1,260	1,010
15 " 20	795	792	834	809	1,017	1,147	848	875
20 " 40	2,759	3,051	2,737	2,984	3,063	3,016	2,976	3,184
40 " 60	1,469	1,293	1,418	1,284	1,058	943	1,308	1,218
60 and over	679	532	592	487	314	256	548	474
Mean age	24·2	22·9	23·4	22·3	21·0	19·9	22·9	22·2
TRANS-INDUS DISTRICTS.								
0 and under 5	1,403	1,633	1,392	1,666	1,743	1,977	1,361	1,599
5 " 10	1,566	1,587	1,456	1,502	1,562	1,510	1,566	1,524
10 " 15	1,145	942	1,100	944	944	792	1,051	866
15 " 20	767	686	840	756	986	1,063	773	729
20 " 40	3,052	3,107	3.248	3,176	3,225	3,185	3,140	3,124
40 " 60	1,531	1,546	1,467	1,479	1,267	1,221	1,560	1,605
60 and over	536	499	497	477	273	252	559	553
Mean age	24·3	23·7	23·9	23·3	21·9	21·4	24·2	23·9

*Subsidiary Table I was not prepared for the North-West Frontier Province.

SUBSIDIARY TABLE III.—*Age distribution of* 10,000 *of each sex in each main religion.* (*For British districts only*).

Age.	1911.		1901.		1891.		1881.	
	Male.	Female.	Male.	Female.	Male.	Female.	Male.	Female.
1	2	3	4	5	6	7	8	9
MOHAMMADANS (TOTAL DISTRICTS).								
9 and under 5 ...	1,462	1,653	1,455	1,661	1,850	2,053	1,409	1,607
5 " 10 ...	1,616	1,603	1,563	1,560	1,629	1,541	1,646	1,563
10 " 15 ...	1,203	973	1,203	1,003	966	790	1,118	895
15 " 20 ...	759	708	829	763	983	1,080	783	760
20 " 40 ...	2,847	3,075	2,951	3,110	3,065	3,136	2,978	3,125
40 " 60 ...	1,523	1,477	1,461	1,423	1,217	1,148	1,495	1,515
60 and over ...	590	511	538	480	290	252	571	535
Mean age ...	24·1	23·5	23·5	23·0	21·5	21·0	23·7	23·4
HINDUS (TOTAL DISTICTS).								
0 and under 5 ...	1,013	1,457	979	1,517	1,386	1,840	1,015	1,457
5 " 10 ...	1,079	1,437	1,027	1,394	1,188	1,403	1,096	1,400
10 " 15 ...	1,002	1,026	950	980	867	818	923	927
15 " 20 ...	974	834	932	896	1,107	1,106	848	762
20 " 40 ...	3,994	3,308	4,214	3,289	3,860	3,272	3,965	3,257
40 " 60 ...	1,514	1,481	1,496	1,454	1,357	1,297	1,707	1,643
60 and over ...	424	457	402	470	235	264	446	554
Mean age ...	25·5	23·8	25·7	23·6	23·4	22·0	26·1	24·5
SIKHS (TOTAL DISTRICTS).								
0 and under 5 ...	814	1,443	531	1,501	716	1,891	429	1,358
5 " 10 ...	896	1,405	563	1,187	587	1,291	469	1,402
10 " 15 ...	890	995	606	980	500	808	488	833
15 " 20 ...	1,035	855	1,101	935	1,116	1,325	967	878
20 " 40 ...	4,698	3,381	5,735	3,370	6,030	3,275	6,050	3,485
40 " 60 ...	1,261	1,361	1,164	1,514	880	1,164	1,314	1,466
60 and over ...	406	560	300	513	171	246	283	578
Mean age ...	25·8	24·0	26·8	24·1	25·1	21·4	27·5	24·3

SUBSIDIARY TABLE IV.—*Age distribution of 1000 of each sex in certain castes.*

CASTE.	MALES—NUMBER PER MILLE AGED:—					FEMALES—NUMBER PER MILLE AGED:—				
	0—5	5—12	12—15	15—40	40 and over.	0—5	5—12	12—15	15—40	40 and over.
1	2	3	4	5	6	7	8	9	10	11
Arora	122	174	78	420	206	146	181	73	407	193
Awan	142	191	92	365	210	179	186	68	383	184
Baghban	143	202	80	354	221	176	187	57	367	213
Baluch	142	199	78	372	209	163	188	59	392	198
Bhatiara	134	212	72	351	231	163	180	82	380	195
Brahman	101	152	78	451	218	153	184	73	392	198
Chamar	173	158	83	366	220	159	159	75	375	232
Chuhra	104	124	69	500	203	123	165	72	477	163
Dhobi	133	177	73	377	240	166	169	68	391	206
Dhund	166	212	84	340	198	168	217	73	361	181
Gakkhar	117	184	69	427	203	169	183	64	400	184
Gujar	145	195	84	349	227	167	195	64	384	190
Jat	122	184	59	468	167	155	208	55	388	194
Jhinwar	76	127	55	530	212	157	176	103	375	189
Jolaha	130	189	77	359	245	168	181	65	384	202
Karal	163	229	85	325	198	186	211	68	359	176
Kashmiri	129	176	82	369	244	153	183	75	375	214
Khatri	94	132	72	483	219	137	165	69	414	215
Kumhar	156	194	83	357	210	172	185	61	384	198
Lohar	149	210	81	351	209	187	201	62	387	163
Machhi	132	202	86	366	214	157	184	62	378	219
Maliar	131	178	80	369	242	172	175	68	374	211
Mallah	115	129	125	396	235	144	115	89	353	299
Mirasi	132	186	76	365	241	160	167	69	396	208
Mochi	148	199	73	372	208	169	199	66	392	174
Moghal	123	186	70	386	235	158	196	62	394	190
Musalli (with Kutana)	139	181	73	384	223	147	202	76	385	190
Nai	149	187	77	360	227	171	190	70	398	171
Paracha	134	209	89	328	240	152	184	60	379	225
Pathan	151	187	96	364	202	162	182	77	371	208
Qassab	150	207	74	358	211	154	189	72	384	201
Qureshi	138	202	70	366	224	166	195	68	393	179
Rajput	78	98	60	616	148	144	192	78	407	179
Saiad	126	197	99	364	214	162	178	86	370	204
Sarara	161	235	82	399	123	170	212	57	384	177
Sheikh	118	149	66	446	221	143	170	73	422	192
Sonar	136	206	76	367	215	167	186	69	378	200
Swathi	148	219	80	332	221	161	213	63	385	178
Tanaoli	144	208	82	341	225	166	184	66	395	189
Tarkhan	148	191	82	371	208	171	190	67	387	185
Teli	130	197	85	362	226	145	169	70	402	214

SUBSIDIARY TABLE V.—*Proportion of children under 10 and of persons over 50 to those aged 15—40; also of married females aged 15—40 per 100 females.*

District and Natural Division.	Proportion of children both sexes per 100.						Proportion of persons over 50 per 100 aged 15—40.						Number of married females aged 15—40 per 100 females of all ages.		
	Persons aged 15—40.			*Married females aged 15—40.*			1911.		1901.		1891.				
	1911	1901	1891	1911	1901	1891	M.	F.	M.	F.	M.	F.	1911	1901	1891
1	2	3	4	5	6	7	8	9	10	11	12	13	14	15	16
N.-W. F. P. Districts ...	**82**	**77**	**82**	**212**	**205**	**213**	**31**	**28**	**27**	**25**	**18**	**17**	**32**	**32**	**35**
Hazara	85	86	90	203	206	220	35	26	31	25	18	16	33	33	36
Trans-Indus Districts ...	**81**	**74**	**80**	**215**	**205**	**210**	**30**	**28**	**25**	**26**	**18**	**17**	**31**	**32**	**35**
Peshawar	78	74	75	208	201	203	33	29	29	27	18	15	31	32	36
Kohat	92	75	81	243	224	238	27	28	21	25	14	17	30	32	33
Bannu	88	78	89	234	216	223	25	24	21	23	20	19	31	32	34
Dera Ismail Khan ...	76	72	81	198	190	201	26	28	23	24	20	19	33	34	36

SUBSIDIARY TABLE VI.—*Variation in population at certain age periods.*

Natural Division.	Period.	Variation per cent. in population (increase + decrease —).					
		All ages.	0—10	10—15	15—40	40—60	60 and over.
1	2	3	4	5	6	7	8
N. W. F. P. Districts ...	1901—1911 ...	+7	+9	+6	+3	+11	+16
	1891—1901 ...	+10	—3	+38	+3	+33	+106
	1881—1891 ..	+17	+33	+2	+26	—8	—43
Hazara	1901—1911 ..	+8	+7	+2	+8	+10	+21
	1891—1901 ...	+9	—7	+55	—3	+46	+105
	1881—1891 ..	+27	+49	—2	+33	+0·7	—29
Trans-Indus Districts ...	1901—1911 ...	+7	+10	+9	+1	+12	+14
	1891—1901 ..	+11	—2	+31	+6	+31	+106
	1881—1891 ...	+14	+28	+3	+24	—10	—46

SUBSIDIARY TABLE VII.—*Reported birth-rate by sex and natural division.*

Year.	Number of births per 1,000 of total population (Census of 1901).					
	Province (total districts).		*Hazara.*		*Trans-Indus districts.*	
	Male.	Female.	Male.	Female.	Male.	Female.
1	2	3	4	5	6	7
1901 ...	16·3	13·2	16·9	15·2	16·1	12·4
1902 ...	18·5	15·2	16·6	15·2	19·2	15·1
1903 ...	17·4	14·2	15·7	14·3	18·0	14·1
1904 ...	19·2	15·8	16·8	15·5	20·1	15·9
1905 ...	19·5	15·9	17·7	14·7	20·4	16·3
1906 ...	21·0	17·6	19·3	17·8	21·5	17·5
1907 ...	17·8	14·8	19·3	17·4	17·2	13·7
1908 ...	20·6	16·7	20·2	18·0	20·0	16·2
1909 ...	19·0	15·7	22·0	20·0	18·0	14·2
1910 ...	21·1	17·0	23·1	21·0	20·5	15·6

SUBSIDIARY TABLE VIII.—*Reported death-rate by sex and natural division.*

Year.	Number of deaths per 1,000 of each sex (Census of 1901).					
	Province (total districts).		*Hazara.*		*Trans-Indus districts.*	
	Male.	Female.	Male.	Female.	Male.	Female.
1	2	3	4	5	6	7
1901 ...	18·8	19·7	16·0	17·2	19·7	20·5
1902 ...	24·0	24·9	19·3	22·4	25·8	25·9
1903 ...	27·6	29·4	21·7	24·4	29·8	31·3
1904 ...	27·7	29·6	26·9	32·0	27·9	28·7
1905 ...	26·2	27·5	25·1	28·5	26·6	27·0
1906 ...	31·7	36·0	29·7	34·4	32·5	36·6
1907 ...	34·4	36·0	34·4	36·0	34·6	35·4
1908 ...	35·2	36·5	36·7	38·9	34·7	35·9
1909 ...	26·5	26·7	24·2	24·9	27·2	27·2
1910 ...	26·9	26·8	27·6	29·3	26·6	25·9

SUBSIDIARY TABLE IX.—*Reported death-rate by sex and age in decade 1901—1910 and in selected years per mille living at same age according to the Census of 1901.*

Age.	Average of decade.		1903.		1905.		1907.		1909.	
	Male.	Female.	Male.	Female.	Male.	Female.	Male.	Female.	Male.	Female.
1	2	3	4	5	6	7	8	9	10	11
All ages ...	27·8	29·3	27·57	29·35	26·21	27·45	34·37	35·98	26·5	26·7
0 and under 1 ...	202·2	165·0	188·54	153·66	211·28	167·09	209·64	173·72	194·7	156·2
1 " 5 ...	46·7	46·2	56·60	58·05	41·33	39·20	52·13	51·63	34·4	33·2
5 " 10 ...	11·5	12·4	12·09	13·56	8·76	9·77	13·23	13·94	10·1	10·5
10 " 15 ...	7·7	9·9	7·99	9·98	6·75	8·68	8·70	11·75	7·0	9·1
15 " 20 ...	8·1	10·4	8·49	11·23	7·08	9·73	11·75	9·38	8·5	10·3
20 " 30 ...	10·3	13·9	9·24	13·24	10·48	14·47	12·69	16·64	10·2	12·0
30 " 40 ...	14·1	18·8	13·58	17·73	13·63	19·43	18·29	25·14	13·8	17·2
40 " 50 ...	21·8	24·9	21·04	23·73	21·01	24·72	30·43	33·08	22·3	24·6
50 " 60 ...	34·6	35·4	31·70	31·56	33·63	33·43	47·44	48·93	35·9	36·5
60 and over ...	67·7	70·4	65·66	65·98	65·94	69·57	95·07	99·05	63·6	65·1

SUBSIDIARY TABLE X.—*Reported deaths from certain diseases per mille of each sex.*

Year.	Fever.					Cholera.					Small-pox.				
	Actual number of deaths.			*Ratio per mille of each sex.*		*Actual number of deaths.*			*Ratio per mille of each sex.*		*Actual number of deaths.*			*Ratio per mille of each sex.*	
	Total.	Male.	Female.	Male.	Female.	Total.	Male.	Female.	Male.	Female.	Total.	Male.	Female.	Male.	Female.
1	2	3	4	5	6	7	8	9	10	11	12	13	14	15	16
1901 ...	29,108	15,066	14,042	13·56	15·01	117	68	49	0·06	0·05	955	503	452	0·45	0·48
1902 ...	37,663	19,494	18,169	18·29	19·65	...	...	...	...	...	1,081	536	545	0·50	0·59
1903 ...	42,549	21,699	20,850	20·36	22·55	1,354	771	583	0·72	0·63	2,694	1,356	1,338	1·27	1·45
1904 ...	44,387	22,706	21,681	21·30	23·44	1	1	...	0·001	...	1,561	787	774	0·74	0·84
1905 ...	41,190	21,212	19,978	19·90	21·60	300	173	127	0·16	0·14	571	268	303	0·25	0·33
1906 ...	52,039	25,756	26,283	24·16	28·42	...	...	...	...	...	1,127	547	580	0·51	0·63
1907 ...	52,361	27,066	25,295	26·56	28·45	266	134	132	0·13	0·15	769	415	354	0·41	0·40
1908 ...	50,795	26,099	24,696	25·61	27·77	2,845	1,667	1,178	1·64	1·32	734	387	347	0·38	0·39
1909 ...	39,403	20,683	18,720	20·30	21·05	134	74	60	0·07	0·07	611	327	284	0·32	0·32
1910 ...	37,268	19,526	17,742	19·16	19·96	1,605	970	635	0·95	0·71	830	449	381	0·44	0·43

CHAPTER VI.

SEX.

Comparison of sex proportions in the Province and in other countries and provinces.

191. The distribution of the population by sex is of interest throughout India from the contrast which it presents to the proportions found in Europe, where females are generally in excess. In the North-West Frontier Province the deficiency of females is particularly striking. I give in the margin the figures for some other areas for purposes of comparison with those of this Province, which, it will be seen, comes very near the bottom of a list of those tracts for which the proportion of the sexes is known to me. Before proceeding further one word of explanation is necessary as to the entry opposite the North-West Frontier Province (Total area). Our figures, as the reader is aware, are based, as far as the trans-frontier portion is concerned, on an estimate, and not on actual enumeration. The proportion of the sexes has been assumed to be the same as for the Mohammadans in contiguous areas. As we shall see when the place comes to consider the statistics for the different religions, the numbers of the sexes are more nearly equal among this than among other communities, and the ratio of females to males is therefore higher in the Province as a whole (including the non-administered area) than in the administered area taken alone The proportion of females to males for the trans-frontier area is, however, somewhat reduced by the inclusion in the figures of the small population which was enumerated in trans-frontier posts (13,538 persons), among whom there are only 71 women for each 1,000 men. If this portion of the population be left out of account, the proportion for the trans-frontier area is 887 females per 1,000 males.

Census of	Country, Province, etc.	Number of females per 1,000 males.
1911	England and Wales	1,068
1911	Madras	1,031
1910	German Empire	1,026
1911	Central Provinces and Berar ...	1,008
1911	Ireland	1,004
1911	Bengal	1,004
1907	Egypt	992
1911	Burma	975
1897	Siberia	955
1911	India	954
1911	Eastern Bengal and Assam ...	953
1900	Servia	946
1911	United Provinces	915
1897	Caucasus	897
1911	Kashmere	886
1911	North-West Frontier Province (total area).	866
1911	North-West Frontier Province (British territory).	859
1911	Punjab	817
1911	Sind	812
1911	Coorg	799
1911	Baluchistan	733

*NOTE.—The figures for Indian Provinces (except the North-West Frontier Province) shown above are for British territory only.

Proportion of the sexes in British territory. (a) In the actual population.

192. Subsidiary Table I, appended to this chapter, shows the proportion of the sexes by districts, and by the two natural divisions into which these have been grouped. The table gives the proportion not only in the actual population enumerated in each area shown, but also in the natural population, *i. e.* the population born in the area, irrespective of the place of enumeration. In India as a whole the influence of migration in this respect is small. In the North-West Frontier Province, where immigrants are relatively numerous, and where they contain a majority of males, it possesses considerable importance.

(b) In the natural population.

While there are only 858 females per 1,000 males in the actual, in the natural, population (British territory) the figure rises to 887 per 1,000.

The greatest variation between the two sets of statistics is found in Dera Ismail Khan, where it amounts to 54 per 1,000. In all the trans-Indus districts migration reduces the ratio borne by the females to the males actually enumerated within them. This is only to be expected in view of the fact that immigrants to them largely exceed in number emigrants from them. In Hazara on the other hand, which loses by migration more than it gains, the reverse is the case.

Proportion of the sexes among the followers of the different religions.
(a) in the actual population.

193. Subsidiary Table II shows the ratio borne by females to males among the followers of different religions. The contrast between the Mohammadans on the one hand, and Hindus and Sikhs on the other (actual population), is very striking. Whereas among Mohammadans there are 880 females to every 1,000 males, among Hindus the number is 680, and among Sikhs 520 only. The difference is due to the circumstance that Hindus and Sikhs are largely immigrants to the Province, who are not accompanied by their women folk. This is shown by the fact that in the natural population the proportions are far more equal.

(b) in the natural population.

The variation, where it is greatest, between Mohammadans on the one hand and Sikhs on the other, which amounts to 360 per 1,000 in the actual, is only 90 per mille in the natural, population. Some explanation is required in regard to the manner in which the figures for the natural population have been arrived at. From four areas only, *viz.* the Punjab, Kashmir, the United Provinces and the Andamans and Nicobars, have I received statements showing the distribution by religion of emigrants from the North-West Frontier Province. In the case of the two last mentioned the statistics supplied only deal with emigrants from the Province as a whole, and the districts of birth are not shown. In the case of the emigrants to them from our two natural divisions, therefore, I have been compelled to adopt the plan I have followed in the case of emigrants to all areas other than the four mentioned above, that is to assume that they were all Mohammadans. The assumption is not of course entirely justified, for a certain number of non-Muslims must have been included among them. There is, however, in view of the large preponderance of Mussalmans which the Province contains, every reason to believe that the numbers of such must have been trifling, and the persons of whose religions distribution I have received information amount to 74 per cent. of the total number of emigrants. It is to be noticed that the effect of the error, so far as it exists, in my statistics is to depress the proportion of females among Mohammadans (natural population), and to raise it among the members of the other two communities. Females are proportionately less numerous among emigrants than among persons enumerated at their homes in the Province, and their inclusion among the figures on which the calculation is based is, naturally, to depress the proportion of females to males in the whole. The figures, however, correspond as nearly with the actual facts as can as expected from the nature of our material.

Circumstances adduced in the past to support the relatively small number of females recorded at Indian Censuses.

194. Even after making allowance, however, for the element introduced by migration, it will be seen that the number of females is relatively very low; and it is of special importance to consider whether the Census statistics correctly represent the actual facts. Various reasons, applicable to India as a whole, have been adduced in support of the belief that in India the males in reality outnumber the females, the chief of which are :—

(*i*) The prevalence of female infanticide, though it is admitted that this is comparatively rare at the present day.

(*ii*) A neglect of female infant life, found among those communities which pay for bridegrooms, and which are therefore involved in considerable expense by possessing daughters, who sooner or later have to be married.

(*iii*) Infant marriage, accompanied by premature sexual intercourse and child-bearing.

(*iv*) A very high birth-rate, which is associated in the natural course of events with a high female death-rate.

(*v*) Unskillful midwifery.

(*vi*) The causing of abortions, with consequent danger to life, as for instance in the case of pregnant widows.

(*vii*) Confinement and bad feeding of women at puberty, during their menstrual periods, and after child birth.

(*viii*) The hard life of widows.

(*ix*) The severe labour which women of the lower classes have to perform.

195. The conditions summarised in the preceding paragraph are for the most part not prevalent in the North-West Frontier Province, but, before passing on to consider other reasons which may account for the phenomena with which we are confronted, it will be as well to consider each separately. The first two, *viz.*, female infanticide and neglect of infant female life, may be taken together. It is to be noticed that the motive both of neglect and of the actual causing of death is to be found in the embarassment to which fathers are subjected in certain areas by the possession of daughters. In tracts where Hindu sentiment is strong, there is in the first place an obligation to marry a daughter before she has attained puberty, and, in the second, to pay a considerable sum in order to do so. In the North-West Frontier Province on the other hand neither obligation is in existence. There appears to be no social or religious penalty attached, not only to failing to marry one's daughter before the age of puberty, but even to omitting to arrange a marriage for her at all. And so far from the marriage of a daughter being a cause of expense to her father, it results in most cases in the placing in his pocket of a substantial sum in cash. The reason for the payment of a bride price, and the inference to be drawn from it as to the actual proportion of the sexes, will be discussed later. It will be sufficient to mention here that in the Province there is no strong motive to neglect the lives of girl children, still less any inducement to put them out of the world; and no suspicion of the prevalence of female infanticide has ever been entertained. It is an undoubted fact that the birth of a girl is not welcomed ; and it seems likely that she is not looked after with as much care as a boy. But there seems no ground for supposing that neglect in infancy has any appreciable effect on the sex proportions. The desire for sons appears to be in part a feeling entertained in common by all societies, even highly civilized ones, and in part to be a survival from the conditions of anarchy in which, for almost the whole period of which we possess any knowledge, the ancestors of the present inhabitants of the Province have lived.

How far prevalent in the North-West Frontier Province.

Female infanticide and neglect of girl children.

196. Infant marriage, with its accompaniments of premature sexual intercourse and child-bearing, has also little to say to the sex proportions in the Province. A reference to the following chapter will show that only just over 10 per cent. of the females of that age are married between the ages of 10 and 15, and it is not till after the latter age that marriage becomes in any degree universal among them. Even in the prime of life marriage is less common here than in most of the other areas in India, and the birth-rate is correspondingly low. Marriage is of course much more common than in Europe, and the birth-rate is higher; but we can hardly quote as reasons for a low female population causes which have far greater strength in India as a whole, where, however, they are accompanied by something far nearer to equality between the sexes that is to be found in the North-West Frontier Province.

Infant marriage.

197. Unskillful midwifery is undoubtedly a factor which has to be taken into account. There is little knowledge of the most elementary principles of sanitation and hygiene, and surgical remedies are barbarous in the extreme. That females suffer from ignorance in this respect more than men is shown by the fact that, unlike the conditions in India generally, the death-rate is considerably higher among females than among males (*vide* Subsidiary Table VIII, appended to Chapter V), though, (see Subsidiary Table IX at the end of the same chapter) it can not be said that the variation between the death-rates of the two sexes is conspicuously greater at the age at which birth is given to most children than at others. The confinement of women after child birth no doubt also has some influence in reducing the proportion of females (in this connection a reference should be made to paragraph 247 in the following chapter). The causing of abortions, for instance in cases where a widow has become pregnant, can however be put on one side at once. It has been suggested that a Pathan widow would welcome pregnancy as an inducement to her paramour to marry her. It must be remembered, however, that it might provoke her death at the hands of the enraged relatives of her deceased husband. But though the Pathan has extravagant notions of honour where his females relatives and connections are concerned, they can in nearly

Unskillful midwifery.

Confinement of women after child birth.

Causing of abortions.

every case be assuaged by a handsome payment in cash, and unless there were previous bad blood between the parties, the payment of the price which the widow had cost her deceased husband's family, plus something added as *sharmana*, would probably settle the question.

Hard life of women.

198 The hard life of widows, and the severe labour which women of the lower classes have to perform may be considered together. In the first place it must be premised that the lot of widows in the North-West Frontier Province is no harder than that of females generally. A virgin is a chattel of her father, a widow is a chattel of her husband's heirs. Both the one and the other are probably treated with a degree of consideration which is in a direct ratio to their youth and good looks, and the consequent likelihood of their bringing in a round sum of money by attracting an eligible suitor. No doubt the lives of women are hard ; in rural areas they certainly earn their keep, and one of the reasons quoted for the frequency of agriculturists in Kohat taking a bride from across the border is that such a woman is hardy and capable of unlimited work. No doubt the life of women has something to say to the death-rate among them being higher than among men, though it is worth noticing that, in so far as our figures are any guide, it may be inferred that Mohammadan females live longer than Hindu, in spite of the fact that the lives of the latter are no doubt easier than those of the former.*

A priori probability of omissions of females.

199. The reason of the inclusion of a discussion of conditions which, however fully they may explain a low proportion of females in India as a whole, can hardly account for a still lower figure in our area, in which for the most part they do not exist, is mainly to be found in the fact that this volume forms one of the series in which the results of the Census of the whole of India are to be published. We have here moreover to consider, not only the reasons which have been adduced in support of the Indian Census statistics in the past, but also the grounds on which several German critics, notably von Mayr and Kirchhoff, have argued that they point to considerable omissions from the Census record. One of these is the a priori probability of omissions in view of the reticence of certain classes regarding their females, and the absence of any explanation which these critics regard as sufficient to explain the difference in the sex proportions as shown in Census statistics in Europe on the one hand and in India on the other. Now it must at once be admitted that, if reticence regarding their females is to be found among any classes in India, it might be expected among the Pathans of the North-West Frontier Province. The purdah, among the rural population, is observed with as much, or as little, strictness as among the rural Mohammadan population in the north of India generally ; and no greater probability of omissions on this account exists here than elsewhere. But at first sight it may appear that the estimation in which women are held is very low, witness the way in which they are disposed of like any other article which can be bought and sold ; and omissions due to their not being considered worth counting may therefore be suspected. In the second place the Pathan is exceedingly jealous of his women ; or at any rate his jealousy manifests itself in acts of violence which bring the subject continually and forcibly before the notice of the courts. The amount of crime which is due to quarrels over women can certainly amount to no small proportion of the whole. But it is doubtful whether they are held in lower estimation among Pathans than among natives of India elsewhere. The fact that they are bought and sold proves nothing ; it is due merely to the peculiar circumstances of the case ; and women elsewhere in India are certainly disposed of with as little reference to their own inclination as they are in the North-West Frontier Province. The quarrels and acts of violence also of which they are the cause hardly prove that Pathans are more jealous where their female connections are concerned that natives of other provinces of India. They only prove that the Pathan temper is peculiarly vindictive, and that the circumstances of his life for many generations

(a) due to reticence regarding them.

(b) due to their not being considered worth counting.

* NOTE.—See Subsidiary Table III appended to Chapter V. Of 10,000 females among Mohammadans 2,113 are aged 40 and over. The corresponding figure is 1,938 in the case of Hindus, and 1,667 in the case of Sikhs. The figures are not however conclusive, for the proportions living at each age period depend primarily on the ratio to the whole found at the age period 20 to 40, and the variations here between the different religions are no doubt due to immigration.

have naturally impelled him to revenge any injury by violent methods. We are of course here discussing a subject which can not be measured by quantitative standards. It is impossible to say with certainty of a Peshawar Pathan and Delhi Shekh that the one is more jealous about his women, or holds them in lower estimation than the other. It is certain that neither will talk about them And even if we admit that the jealousy of the Pathan is greater than that of the other, it may well be argued that this fact points not to the likelihood of omissions so much as to a real shortage of women such as to render the omission theory unnecessary. The high bride price paid in the North-West Frontier Province (see paragraph 222, Chapter VII), the distinct traces of marriage by capture which survive (see paragraph 227 in the same chapter), the very jealousy of women, which would seem to be the most likely cause of reticence about them, all point to women being always in a distinct minority. Among the Mohammadans of the North-West Frontier Province caste and tribal restrictions on intermarriage hardly exist, and if there were enough women to provide every one with a wife without difficulty, the working of the law of supply and demand would prevent the bride price ever reaching its present figure. It would never have been necessary to capture brides by force, as certain elements of the marriage ceremony prove they must not so long ago have been captured, if the tribes had possessed enough women of their own. Lastly men are most jealous of what possesses most value ; and value again is determined by the relation which the supply of any given article bears to the demand. The very disregard of the wishes of women, which is implied in the manner in which their hands are disposed of in marriage, points again to their smaller numbers. A man naturally keeps under his own power of disposal a sex of which the high value depends on its rarity, and that women are regarded as having a definite money value is proved (if the proposition be thought to require proof) by the fact that in parts of tribal territory there is a regular tariff, in which the price of injuries is reckoned indifferently in women or rupees.

Variation in sex proportions at different Censuses

200. The fact that at each of the last three Censuses there has been a rise in the proportion of females may be regarded as an argument in favour of believing that the low figure hitherto observed is due to imperfect enumeration. As long ago as 1881 the late Sir Denzil Ibbetson wrote : * "It is notorious that the prejudices of the Indian people disincline them to state the number of their women folk, or even to admit their existence; and no better proof can be adduced of the greater care with which one enumeration has been effected in comparison with another, or of the greater success with which it has approximated to the actual facts than its showing a smaller ratio of males to total population." In the Punjab taken as a whole the proportion of females to males rose between the years 1868 (the date of the previous Census) and 1881, but for the districts now included in the North-West Frontier Province the reverse was the case. I show in the margin the number of females per 1,000 males at each successive Census since 1855. As regards the proportion for the two first Censuses a few words of explanation are necessary. I have no figures for the population by sex before 1881 of the areas which now form the districts of Bannu and Dera Ismail Khan, and I have been compelled to make the calculation, on which the marginal statement is based, on the populations of the old districts, which contained a large tract of country to the east of the river Indus, now the Mianwali district of the Punjab. In the

Number of females per 1,000 males in the districts of the North-West Frontier Province.

Year.	Females per 1,000 males.
1855 ...	820
1868 ...	859
1881 ...	819
1891 ...	843
1901 ...	846
1911 ...	858

NOTE.—The proportions in the above statement, like those in Subsidiary Table I, are calculated on the population for the years 1881, 1891 and 1911 as given in Table II of the present Census, from which persons enumerated outside the districts of the Province as at present constituted have been excluded. On the other hand the figures shown in Subsidiary Table II have been calculated on the population in 1891 and 1901 as shown in the Punjab Census Reports for those years, the distribution by age of the persons excluded from Table II of the present Census not being available.

* Punjab Census Report 1881, paragraph 179.

Mianwali District in 1901 there were as many as 895 females per 1,000 males, or a very much higher figure than that for the North-West Frontier Province (British territory) in the same year; and the effect of the inclusion of the population of this area before 1881 in the figures on which my statistics are based would naturally be to raise considerably the proportion of females. It is not worth while to attempt to calculate the relative numbers of females and males in the area with which we are concerned for the years 1855 and 1868, because it is clear, from the figures given in the Punjab Census Report, 1881, that the proportion of females fell between the years 1868 and 1881, in the three northern districts of the Province, the boundaries of which have not been modified to any considerable extent up to the present day. It is sufficient to notice here that the proportion of females undoubtedly showed a decrease between the years 1868 and 1881, and that we have therefore no continuous increase relatively in the number of females shown in our statistics from 1855 to the present day. Now if more accurate enumeration were always marked by a rise in the relative number of females, we should not expect to find a decrease between the years 1868 and 1881. It is beyond doubt that the latter year saw a great improvement in enumeration over the former. Again, though the proportion for the Province as a whole (British territory) has shown a continuous rise since 1881, the same can not be said of separate districts within it. A glance at Subsidiary Table I, appended to this chapter, will show several instances of the reverse. In Dera Ismail Khan females have decreased, as compared with males, by 1 per cent. since 1901. "There can, I think," writes the Deputy Commissioner, "be no doubt that this Census has been conducted with more approach to accuracy than the preceding one. Consequently the omission of females from enumeration in previous years will not explain adequately the considerable disproportion of females." And if it is replied that a district is too small a unit on which to base any conclusions on such a subject, and that the variations found are due to accidental causes only, it is sufficient to point to the figures for the Punjab (British territory) for the years 1901 and 1911. The proportion of females, which was 858 in 1901, has fallen to 817, per 1,000 males at the present Census, which shows conclusively that variations do actually occur from time to time in the distribution of the population by sex.

Argument based on disproportion of the sexes at certain age periods.

201. It must be admitted nevertheless that none of the arguments which have been adduced are sufficient to prove that omissions do not occur. They prove indeed that considerable variations from time to time take place in the sex proportions, a proposition which probably no one would venture to dispute, but they are not inconsistent with the belief that at every Census hitherto undertaken in India there has been a certain amount of leakage from the returns of females, though probably a decreasing one. Another argument, which has been advanced in favour of the belief that the low proportion of females found in so many areas in India is due principally to defective enumertion, is based on the very low proportion of females to males which is found at certain age periods, at which omissions would a priori be expected to occur, notably at the age group '10 to 15'. Before considering this, however, it will make for clearness if I devote some attention to the sex proportions as disclosed at the Census for each of the age groups shown in our tables.

Sex proportions at the different age periods.

202. The figures required in this connection will be found in Subsidiary Table II appended to this chapter. Those for the population of all religions can hardly be taken as typical of the Province, for they are too much disturbed by the Hindu and Sikh element in which females are abnormally few. It will be better therefore to look first at the sex distribution for Mohammadans only. It will be seen (Subsidiary Table II*) that up to the age of 5 (Census of 1911) there are 995 females to every 1,000 males, an excess of males, that is, of only one-half per cent. For all ages up to 30 the figure drops to 894 per 1,000, and for persons aged 30 and over it is only 854 For the various quinquennial periods between the ages of 5 and 30 years there is considerable fluctuation. The figures for the period '10 to 15' are 161 per 1,000 lower than

(a) Mohammadans.

* The sex proportions among the population of British posts trans-border are abnormal. The figures in Subsidiary Tables II and III are calculated therefore on those for the districts of the Province only.

those for the period '5 to 10.' Up to the age of 25 there is a rise at each of the two intervening age periods, and from that age onwards there is a continuous decrease till the end of life. The steady decrease in the proportion of females in the three main groups, *i. e.* from 0 to 5 years, from 0 to 30, and for persons aged 30 and over, is the natural result of the fact that for each year in the last decade the death-rate of females has been higher than that of males (*vide* Subsidiary Table VIII, appended to the previous chapter), and that, taking the average of the decade, the only age period for which the female death-rate has fallen below the male is that from the age of one to that of five years (*vide* Subsidiary Table IX to Chapter V). In the light of the same facts the continuous decrease at each successive quinquennial period from the age of 25 onwards is also easily intelligible; indeed any other result would be surprising, and so far the vital statistics and the results of the Census confirm one another. The same may be said of the proportion at the age period '5 to 10' falling below that at the period '0 to 5.' The figures for the three following quinquennial periods, however, require some discussion. Between the ages of 20 and 25 the females are in excess of the males. This result would seem in part to be due to the influence of migration. Emigrants from the Province consist mainly of military sepoys, temporary labourers and the like, the bulk of whom are naturally composed of males who have not long reached maturity; and the consequence of the absence of a large number of males at the age period we are now concerned with is a rise in the proportion of females. In the case of immigrants also the male element is a largely preponderating one; and it may seem curious at first sight that figures for immigration should be called in to support a high proportion of females. The ages of persons born outside the Province have not been tabulated, and to speak with certainty is therefore impossible, but there seems every likelihood that a large proportion of the female immigrants consist of persons in the prime of life, or between the ages of 20 and 25. Our immigrants (males) are largely graziers, Powindahs, winter labourers from the west, and sepoys and others from the east, and the women they bring with them would naturally consist in the bulk of those who are at an age best calculated to resist the hardships which their sojourn in the Province involves, and of those who possess children too young to be left behind. The same circumstance would also help to explain the high proportion of females to males (963 per 1,000) found at the next age period ('25 to 30').

At age periods '10 to 15' and '15 to 20.'

203. But what are we to say of the very low proportion of females found at the age period '10 to 15', and of the higher but still low one found at the following age group? The figures given in the margin will show how relatively few are the females returned as living at both age groups, notably at the former. It will be noticed that this age period ('10 to 15') is precisely the one the figures at which in India as a whole have been pointed to by various critics as indicating the existence of omissions of females from the Census record. In India generally, or at any rate in those areas where very early marriages are the rule, even if reticence regarding the presence of females of this age group is not to be expected, at least a mis-statement of age is believed to be common, from a desire to represent unmarried girls as younger, and married ones as older, than they really are. In addition the actual numbers are no doubt much reduced by premature child-bearing and the consequent danger to life. But in the North-West Frontier Province, as a reference to Subsidiary Table I, appended to the next chapter, will show, 88 per cent. of the females of this group are unmarried, and even at the following one spinsters are relatively numerous (35 per cent). Mortality consequent on child-birth must be very rare, and the female death-rate at the ages we are concerned with is low (*vide* Subsidiary Table IX at the end of Chapter V). Migration can not much affect the figures for the population aged between 10 and 15 years; and I know of no other reason why the proportion of females to males should be actually low. It is in fact incredible that our figures correspond with the facts. On the other hand at first sight there would

Age group.	Number of Mohammadan females per 1,000 males.
10—15 ...	712
15—20 ...	821
20—30 ...	894
30 and over ...	854
60 and over ...	760

not appear to be any particular reason why the existence of girls at this time of life should be concealed, or their ages mis-stated. They have not yet arrived at an age when sex is of peculiar interest; and if they are unmarried, no disgrace is attached to the fact. Moreover if their ages are mis-stated, we should expect one or other of the age periods near to the one in question to show signs of an abnormal accretion of females; but indications of this are not perhaps at first sight very plain. In the North-West Frontier Province therefore not only are the causes absent on which depends an actual deficiency of females at this age; but any strong temptation to mis-state their ages, or to omit females altogether, appears to be wanting.

Mis-statement of age.

204. In paragraph 202 I have suggested that it is to migration that we must attribute the fact that females aged 20 to 25 outnumber males of the same age period, and in the following paragraph signs of any abnormal accretion of females in any age period near to '15 to 20' have been denied. The explanation suggested would be plausible enough if we had only the figures for our area to go upon. In the North-West Frontier Province the immigrants are relatively very numerous, and Mohammadan females among them amount to 61 per cent. of the persons of that religion and sex enumerated in the Province as falling within the age period '20 to 25.' If, as seems likely to be the case, a large proportion of immigrant females are comprised in this age-group, their presence would have a very striking effect on the sex proportion at this particular time of life, for the ages of male immigrants cover a far wider range. It is obvious also that the effect of emigration is to raise the proportion of females to males at this age. But the interesting thing to notice is that the features presented by our statistics are to be observed in the case of other areas also. The marginal statement shows that in India as a whole in 1901, as in the North-West Frontier Province in 1911, Mohammadan females were found to be relatively least numerous at the age period '10 to 15,' while they were actually in excess of the males, after the age of 5, only at the period '20 to 25.' Over the total area of India the influence of migration may be left out of account, and the question is at once raised as to how far we are justified in appealing to it in this instance in regard to the North-West Frontier Province. The explanation commonly offered is that mis-statement of age is responsible. As Mr. Maclagan* remarked "the tendency appears to be to overstate the age of marriageable girls almost as much as to under-state it. The head of the house fancies that he will escape worry if he conceals the presence of a marriageable girl in his house. He does not go so far as to deny the existence of his girls, but as long as he avoids the marriageable ages he is indifferent whether he goes above or below the limit."

Proportion of the sexes among Mohammadans at certain age periods.

Age period.	Number of females per 1,000 males.	
	India 1901.	N.-W. F. P. 1911.
0—5 ...	1,016 ...	995
5—10 ...	938 ...	873
10—15 ...	794 ...	712
15—20 ...	970 ...	821
20—25 ...	1,115 ...	1,047
25—30 ...	974 ...	963
30—35 ...	928 ...	894
35—40 ...	809 ...	
40—45 ...	926 ...	887
45—50 ...	813 ...	
50—55 ...	939 ...	801
55—60 ...	845 ...	
60 & over ...	991 ...	760

Untrustworthy character of the return of age in the case of males.

205. The sex proportions are affected of course not only by untrustworthy returns in the case of females. Any errors in the age statistics for males will also have the effect of throwing out the correspondence which might be expected at the various age periods. Looking at the figures given in Subsidiary Table III, appended to Chapter V, it will be seen that Mohammadan females aged 10 to 15 are more than 2 per cent. less of the total female population than males of the same age are of the total male figures, and that whereas males aged 10 to 15 form 12 per cent. of the whole, those aged 15 to 20 form 7·6 per cent. only. This would suggest than 10 is a favourite age to be returned for boys, but not for girls, and to some such preference may be due in part the abnormality which our sex proportions present at this age period.

*Vide Punjab Census Report, 1891, paragraph 164.

Among persons aged 5 to 20, and in particular at age period '10 to 15' sex disproportion probably due in part to omission of females.

206. The point we have then to decide is how far the low proportion of females at the age group '10 to 15' is explained by the comparatively high one found at the following one, and by the actual excess of females over males (Mohammadans) at the period '20 to 25.' I think there can be no doubt that the figures are inter-related, and that mis-statement of age is largely responsible for them. At the same time my own view is that it is in part to omissions from the record that we must refer the statistics with which the enumeration has provided us. As a report sent to me from Hazara naively expresses it: "Men of high social status consider it beneath their dignity to disclose the names of female members of their family" (it is to be noted that the instructions to enumerators laid special stress upon the point that no one was to be pressed to give the names of females, if he had any objection to doing so) "specially of unmarried young girls, and consequently the Census record remains incomplete and not thoroughly reliable." A report received from Peshawar is to much the same effect. "Some of the Afghans consider it a flagrant insult to let the names or even the numbers, of their wives, sisters, etc., be known to the public. Consequently they are always on the look-out to omit them from the Census record." The Deputy Commissioner of Kohat also writes that "probably the enumeration of females at the Census is not so complete as that of males." It is not contended that omissions are the only cause of a low proportion of females. I have already mentioned the indications which seem to me to point to a genuine deficiency. But I think it is in part due to omissions, in particular at the age period '10 to 15' which we are now discussing. Even after making every allowance for the influence of migration and misstatement of age, it is difficult to understand why the proportion of females living at ages from 5 to 20 years, should be so much lower than we find at the age groups '0 to 5' and '20 to 25.' One can only infer that among the inhabitants of the Province reluctance to mention the existence of girls begins to be effective for some time before it is possible to arrange for their marriage

Proportions at other age periods.

207. At the other age periods (*i. e.* excepting those from the age of 5 to 20 years), our figures have a stronger appearance of corresponding with the actual facts. I will deal presently with the inference to be drawn from a comparison between the proportion of the sexes at birth, as disclosed in the vital statistics, and the sex proportion disclosed by the Census. I may mention here, however, that the fact that females, relatively to males, are more numerous at the age period '0 to 5' than at that from birth to 30, and at ages from 0 to 30 than from 30 to the end of life, is in agreement with the probabilities arising from the death statistics (which show a relatively high death-rate for females) to a degree which has not always been found as a result of Census operations in India.

Proportions of the sexes by age. (*b*) Among Hindus & Sikhs.

208. So far we have been considering the proportion of the sexes by age among the Mohammadans, for, as I have said, the figures for the followers of this religion are more typical of the conditions of the Province than those for the total population. It remains to look at the statistics for Hindus and Sikhs. In the case of these two religious also we find females proportionately most numerous under the age of 5 years, the figures being 978 and 921, respectively, per 1,000 males as compared with 995 in the case of Mohammadans. For females up to the age of 30 the proportion shows a much larger drop. There are only 703 Hindu and 525 Sikh females per 1,000 males of the same age period, whereas in the case of Mohammadans the proportion is 894 per 1,000. And very much the same difference is found in the case of the three religions when the proportion of females aged 30 and over is regarded.

Influence of migration.

209 Now it is clear that it is only among children of less than 5 years that there is anything approaching equality between the sexes among Hindus and Sikhs, and even at this early age, to take round numbers, the females only amount to nine-tenths* of the males. For the first 30 years of life Hindu females only amount to seven-tenths and Sikh females to little over one-half of the males, and for persons over 30 the proportion is nearly the same. The great variation between the Mussalman on the one hand, and the Hindu and

*For the lower proportion of females to males under 5 years among Hindus and Sikhs than among Mohammadans I can suggest no explanation, unless it be that immigrants to the Province, when accompanied by children, more commonly bring with them little boys than little girls.

Sikh, figures on the other is not to be referred, or to any beyond a trifling degree, to differences in the social usages of the different communities. In part it is no doubt due to the later age at which Mohammadan females are married, to the frequency of widow remarriage, and the like, but the variation due to this cause is merged and lost in that dependent on the one all important element in the matter, *viz.*, migration. Emigration in the case of these communities may be left out of account. Immigration on the other hand has an enormous influence. A reference to the marginal statement printed against paragraph 83 (Chapter III) will show that 32 of the Hindu, and no less than 49 per cent. of Sikh males were born outside the districts of the Province ; in the case of females the percentages are 16·1 and 16·9 respectively. It is not only the proportion of immigrant males to the total males of the religion concerned which is higher than the corresponding proportion in the case of females. The actual number of males greatly exceeds that of females ; and the natural result of this great influx of male immigrants is to reduce the proportion of total females to the total male population. At both extremes of life, *viz*. at the ages 0 to 10, and 60 and over, the figures are disturbed comparatively little by migration, for the immigrants consist almost entirely of persons between these ages. From the age of 20 to that of 60 on the other hand the proportion of females is strikingly lower among Hindus and Sikhs than among Mohammadans. It is interesting to notice that at the age period '10 to 15,' Mohammadan females are little more numerous when compared with males than are Hindu. Among the latter also the age of marriage in the Province is later than among the same community elsewhere in India ; and it need cause little surprise that the proportions for the two religions at this age period are so nearly equal. What is more difficult to explain is the fact of both being so low.

210. We have seen that among Mohammadans the proportion borne by females to males descends at each successive age period from 25 years onwards, and that the figures are supported by the vital statistics. Among Hindus on the other hand, after dropping at each quinquennial age period between birth and the age of 30, thereafter it rises, and for the age group '60 and over' is little lower than for Mohammadans. The same general tendency is to be observed also in the case of Sikhs. The question as to whether widow re-marriage is prohibited or the reverse might seem to have something to say to these variations. In point of fact they are due, I believe, to the fact that, after the age of 30, the influence of migration has less and less effect on the figures, so that, by the time the age of 60 is reached, we are dealing with little beyond the native-born population. Seeing, however, that the bulk of the Mohammadans are agriculturists living in rural tracts, while Hindus and Sikhs, especially at the end of life, are composed in the main of traders living in towns, it is not perhaps surprising that the women should be more long-lived among the former than among the latter, from the superior healthiness of the life of women in rural areas over that lived by them in towns.

In different natural divisions. All religions.

211. The foregoing discussion has dealt with the sex proportions for the total area of British territory included in the Province. It will be interesting to see how far they vary in different natural divisions. In this connection Subsidiary Table III, appended to this chapter, should be referred to. Females are proportionately more numerous in Hazara than in the trans-Indus districts both among Mohammadans and among Sikhs. Among Hindus, of whom immigrants from Nepal employed in Gurkha Battalions at Abbottabad form a not inconsiderable part, the reverse is the case. I doubt whether much profit is to be obtained from examining in any minuteness the figures for Hindus and Sikhs in the small numbers to be found in these limited areas. Even if the number were not too small to show the working of general tendencies, the figures are too much influenced by migration. The figures shown in the margin have some interest here. In the trans-Indus districts more than half the Sikh males and nearly one-fifth of the Sikh females are immigrants, and what is

Number per 1,000 of group dealt with who were born outside the area shown.

Natural division.	All religions both sexes.	Hindus.		Sikhs.	
		Males.	Females.	Males.	Females.
Hazara ...	29	361	174	251	97
Trans-Indus Districts	106	313	157	528	191

perhaps of even more importance in this connection, temporary immigrants. In Hazara the proportion of Hindus, both males and females, who were born outside the district is very high; and the same is true of Sikhs in that district, and of Hindus in British territory to the west of the Indus. The statement also shows how much less importance immigration possesses in Hazara than in the trans-Indus districts, among the population of all religions. This fact, seeing that immigrants in both areas consist chiefly of males, added to the circumstance that there is a large emigration of males from Hazara, is no doubt chiefly responsible for the high proportion of females to males found there among the population (all religions) which has not reached the age of 30. Among persons aged 30 and over on the other hand females are, in proportion to males, more numerous in the latter area than in the former. The variation here appears to point to the lives of women tending to be shorter in Hazara than elsewhere. This indeed seems to be the case. A reference to Subsidiary Table II, appended to the last chapter, shows that, while in the trans-Indus districts females aged 20 and over amount to 51·5 per cent. of the whole, in Hazara they only amount to 48·7, and the mean age of the living is higher in the former area than in the latter. The superior climate of Hazara seems to benefit men more than women. If we look at the death-rate by sex for the natural divisions separately (Subsidiary Table VIII at the end of the previous chapter), it will be seen that, while the death-rate for both sexes has been generally higher during the last decade in the other districts than in Hazara, the lowness of the Hazara rate is chiefly noticeable among the male population The mean age of the females living is, as has been said, actually lower in Hazara than elsewhere, but it is not this which so much affects the proportion of the sexes for the latter half of life as the smaller relative mortality of males in the district It looks in fact as if men were more susceptible than women to climatic influences, so that they benefit more by a good climate than do women. Coming to the quinquennial age periods given in the third Subsidiary Table appended to this chapter, we may begin by considering the first five years of life. Whereas in Hazara girls under 5 actually outnumber boys of the same age, in the trans-Indus districts they only amount to 989 per 1,000 of the other sex. The difference here appears to be mainly due to the female birth-rate more nearly approaching the male in Hazara than in the other districts. If Subsidiary Table VII, appended to Chapter V, is looked at, it will be seen that the difference between the male and female birth-rate has been smaller for almost every year during the last decade in the former area than in the latter. Why more girls should be born in Hazara it is hard to say The problem is an example of the truth of the saying that statistical enquiries are more valuable for the questions they suggest than for the answers furnished in the course of them. One is in a realm of pure conjecture when one hazards a reply at all; but the explanation perhaps lies in the fact that in the population of Hazara we have mainly one of Indian, as opposed to what we may here assume to be largely one of Iranian extraction in the trans-Indus districts of the Province. In most Indian Provinces the sex proportions are more equal than we find them in the North-West Frontier Province, and the difference may be explained by saying that we are dealing in the two sets of areas with different racial stocks. Even so however one has only answered one question by asking another; for the reason why the race of Iranian origin should produce fewer daughters than that of an origin which, for convenience, I may here refer to as Indian* is still obscure. One theory might be that it is part of a provision made by nature to meet the different conditions of different areas. The discussion, however, does not properly belong here, and the reader is referred to the earlier portion of the chapter in which an attempt is made to explain the low proportion of females which our figures present.

212. The comparatively high proportion of females found in Hazara for each successive quinquennium of age from 5 to 30 years follows naturally from the larger proportion of that sex who are born into the world. The very small number of females, relatively to males at the age period '10 to 15,' which

Figures for Mohammadans aged 10 to 15.

*I do not of course mean that India is inhabited by races of one and the same stock only I only mean to contrast these races as a whole with the Pathan element in the population of the North-West Frontier Province.

we have noticed above is found however in both our natural divisions. If we look at the figures for the Mohammadans alone, it will be seen that in Hazara the figure is 736, in the trans-Indus districts 700, per 1,000 males. It is perhaps worth noticing that the proportion of females at this age period who are married is higher in Hazara than in the other districts ; and the proportion of females to males does not therefore vary with the degree to which marriage is common among them. This is indeed is accordance with the conclusion already arrived at, *viz.* that the small number of females returned as being aged 10 to 15 years has nothing to do with marriage. The variation between the proportions for the natural divisions is more likely to be dependent on the race of their inhabitants; for the tribes of Hazara are less jealous of, and probably less reticent about, their women than are Pathans. At the following age period (*viz.* 15 to 20) the contrast between conditions in Hazara and in the trans-Indus districts is more marked. In Hazara there are as many as 906 (Mohammadan) females per 1,000 males, whereas in the districts west of the Indus there are only 787. The variation here is more easy to understand. In Hazara perhaps the most marked influence on the statistics of age and sex is exercised by the large emigration of males. In the trans-Indus districts it is exercised by a large immigration of males. From the age of 15 to that of 20 years, migration begins to affect our figures, for a good many persons who leave their homes are aged between these two limits. From Hazara they go away to carve out their fortunes elsewhere, leaving the proportion of females comparatively high. To the trans-Indus districts of the Province they come for the winter months, including the date of the Census, bringing down with them the proportion of females to males.

Figures for Mohammadans aged 15 to 20.

Light thrown on the proportions of the sexes by the vital statistics.

(*a*) as pointing to a rise or fall in the proportion of females in last two decades.

213. It remains to consider the light thrown on the proportion of the sexes as disclosed at the Census by the vital statistics. The two sets of data may be compared in different ways. We can first see how far they point respectively to a rise or a drop in the proportion of females to males in the intervals between different Censuses. To take first the decade 1891 to 1900, Subsidiary Table V at the end of this chapter shows that, during this period, male births exceeded male deaths by 5,368 only, while female births exceeded females deaths by 12,052. It may be mentioned incidentally that the natural increase of population, as thus shown by the vital statistics, amounted to only 17,420 persons, whereas, as a reference to Table II of the present Census will show, the actual increase in British territory between the years 1891 and 1901, amounted to as much as 184,015. This points to exceedingly defective registration of births, for we have no traces in the records of the two Censuses of such an increase of immigration in the latter year as to make up the difference. But leaving this point on one side, it is to be noticed that the vital statistics point to a rise in the proportion of females to males. This is in agreement with the results of the Census if the actual population be looked at. But we are concerned in this instance with the natural population, *i. e.*, the population born in the Province, wherever enumerated, and here (*vide* Subsidiary Table I) the proportion of females to males showed a decrease. The contradiction is however probably not so great as it appears. The figures given in column 7 of Subsidiary Table I (*vide* footnotes) take no account of emigrants to places beyond the Punjab as then constituted, for none are shown in the Punjab Census Report for 1891. On the other hand the figures for the year 1901 are based on statistics which include emigrants from the Province to all other Indian areas. When it is remembered that emigrants from the Province, especially those who go far afield, consist very largely of males only, it becomes plain that the effect of their inclusion in the natural population of 1901 would have been slightly to depress the proportion borne by females to males. But it seems hardly possible to argue that the results of the Census and of registration show here any very close correspondence.

214. In the following decade (1901—1910) the vital statistics show a tendency in the opposite direction. The male births recorded exceeded the male deaths by as much as 80,861, whereas female births exceeded deaths among the same sex by only 39,192. On the other hand, according to the Census, there are now 12 more females per 1,000 males than there were in

1901, in the actual population enumerated in the Province. There has also been a rise, though a smaller one, in the proportion of females to males found in the natural population, in which there are now 887 females per 1,000 males, as against 885 ten years age. The rise has occurred, however, in one natural division only, *viz.* Hazara. In the trans-Indus districts the natural population shows proportionately fewer females than were to be found in 1901. But the fall here is a small one only (2 per 1,000), whereas that suggested by the vital statistics is considerable.

(*b*) Proportion of the sexes at birth.

215. Another point of view from which we can compare the results given by the two sets of statistics is to be found in a comparison between the relative number, of male and female births registered, and of persons of the two sexes recorded in the Census as living. The proportion of female to male births in the Province is strikingly low, far lower than in any other area for which I possess statistics. If the registration of births could be accepted as being substantially accurate, we should have here an ample justification of the Census figures; for the proportion of females to males as ascertained by actual enumeration (858 per 1,000) is considerably higher than the ratio in existence at birth. We could proceed to discuss the causes for the births of males so far outnumbering those of females, and might leave the subject with a glow of satisfaction at the thought of the frankness of the population enumerated and the diligence of the Census officials who did the work.

Area.	Number of females per 1,000 male births.	Year or years of registration.
England	963	1900
Madras	960	1891—00
Germany	950	1900
Ireland	944	1900
Bengal	940	1891—00
India	930	1891—00
United Provinces ...	920	1891—00
Punjab	900	1891—00
N.-W. F. Province (districts)	819	1901—11
N.-W. F. Province (districts)	816	1891—00

216. Unfortunately, however, if our Census statistics of sex are open to suspicion, at least as strong a one falls on the birth registers. In fact a stronger, for, after discussing the question with one or two districts officers, I decided that any checking of the Census enumeration of females would be out of the question, whereas the registers of births have been scrutinised, and have been found to fail. If paragraph 55 (Chapter II) be referred to, some account will be found of the results of checking the birth-register. The record of births is not complete in the case of either sex; and it is in the case of females that omissions most largely occur. As a result of special enquiries made in Peshawar in 1901 the opinion was formed that the proportions of the sexes at birth are actually normal, and that the preponderance of male births hitherto observed is due to defective registration. Certainly it will be only in accordance with a priori probabilities, if female births are at all commonly left unregistered. In this connection paragraph 246 (Chapter VII) should be referred to. The birth of a son is an occasion for rejoicing; every one is informed and relatives and friends are feasted. The birth of a daughter on the other hand is in no way noticed except as a misfortune; no unnecessary references are made to it, and, at any rate in the larger villages, there appears to be no reason why it should ever come to the ears of the Chaukidar responsible for reporting it. There is therefore a strong probability, which has been confirmed by special enquiries devoted to the subject, that female births should be omitted. More than this, the actual Census records tend to cast doubt upon the vital statistics. Immigration, as we have seen, tends to lower the proportion of females to males, not to raise it; and emigration of which there is any trace in the information which is available to me, is insufficient to repair the balance. The Census shows more females alive than the vital statistics record as being born. We can only invoke the vital statistics to support the results of the Census, if the former are more trustworthy than the latter; but so far is this from being the case that the latter are enough to convince us of the inaccuracy of the former.

217. It may, however, be argued that the large mortality of infant boys is responsible for the fact that the females living are more numerous relatively

to males than the females to males at birth. No doubt this factor has some influence, but, on examination, it will be found to be insufficient. In the last decade the births of 819 girls were registered per 1,000 boys For children aged under one year the average death-rate for the same period was 165 per 1,000 in the case of girls, and 202·2 per mille in the case of boys. 165 per 1,000 amounts to 135 out of 819, and according to the death statistics we can therefore infer that at the end of the first year after birth there are 684 girls to every 798 boys, or 857 females per 1,000 males. But this is a far lower proportion than our Census figures indicate Among children of all religions aged between 1 and 2 years there are (*vide* Subsidiary Table II) 995 females per 1,000 males. The Census figures are hardly likely to exaggerate the number of females, and, considering that the death-rate for males and females from the age of one year to that of 5 (*vide* Subsidiary Table IX appended to Chapter V) has been in the last decade so nearly equal, the result of this examination also can only be to throw doubt on the figures as worked out from the vital statistics.

Indications, other than statistical, of the proportions of the sexes at birth.

218. In default of the statistics afforded us by registration and by the Census, we have little to guide us as to the actual proportions of the sexes at birth, for any theories which have been propounded on the subject are based on these very materials. It is, however, perhaps worth while to consider what are the probabilities of the case. In this connection I quote the following remarks which were furnished to me by the Chief Medical Officer of the Province: "Personally," he writes, "I regard the excess of males in the North-West Frontier Province as exemplifying a provision of nature, to prevent over population in a country unfitted by nature to support many inhabitants. It is obvious that the greater the number of females in a given population, the more rapid the increase of that population will tend to be, and *vice versa*........................Probably also there is, owing to blood feuds and the poverty of the country, a good deal of in-breeding. This also, I think, tends to produce more males." The Chief Medical Officer, that is to say, assumes the Census and the vital statistics, in so far as they suggest the existence of a small female population, to be accurate, but he goes on to observe: "This is a very large and interesting question, and, much as I should like to discuss it, it is useless my writing more. I have not been here long enough, nor have I had the opportunity of verifying personally the facts connected with the North-West Frontier Province." The suggestion that in-breeding tends to produce more males is, however, an interesting one in this connection, for it will be shown (*vide* paragraph 225 in the following chapter) that close marriages among Pathans, and indeed among the Mohammadans of the Province generally are very common. And further, whatever be the capacities of their present homes to support a large population, it is certain that no very long period has elapsed since the Pathans of the Province lived in areas (tribal territory and eastern Afghanistan) which can certainly only provide the means of subsistence for a limited one. If nature redresses the balance in such matters, a greater tendency for the production of males than of females might certainly be expected to be found among the inhabitants of the wild and rugged country on our frontier; and such a tendency it would no doubt take more than a few generations of life in a richer and more settled area to remove. Besides the nature of the country we have also to consider the nature of its inhabitants. The ancestors of our Pathans, and no very distant ancestors either, whether living in the hills beyond what is now the administrative frontier, or in the plains which are now included in the districts of the Province, lived in a state of society in which the birth of sons was ardently to be desired. If women were lacking they could always be seized from others (*vide* paragraph 227 on traces of marriage by capture); but if men were wanting, the tribe went to the wall. The greater desire for sons is intelligible in these circumstances; neglect of female infant life would also cause no surprise. The result of such an environment for many generations might well be to turn out a race in which males predominate; and, once the type were fixed, it would take more than a few generations of altered circumstances to change it.

219. The conclusions which have been arrived at may be summarised as follows:—The past history of the bulk of the inhabitants of the Province, as well as their present customs, point to a genuine deficiency of females. Indications given by other sources of information (the vital statistics) also suggest that the males considerably outnumber the females, in showing, (1) that the proportion of females is very low at birth, and (2) that they die in greater numbers than males. On the other hand the vital statistics, particularly the record of births, are not themselves beyond suspicion. Special attention devoted to the subject has elicited the fact that female births not uncommonly go unrecorded; and the Census figures themselves point to the same conclusion. The circumstances, which have been adduced to explain an actual deficiency of women in India generally, are hardly in existence in the North-West Frontier Province, and can not explain an even greater disproportion of the sexes. Further when we look at the sex proportions at the different age periods the Census statistics do not justify themselves. From the age of 5 to that of 20 years females are more rare than might be expected from their numbers at other periods of life. The defect is particularly marked at the age group '10 to 15.' There appears to be no reason to explain a genuine deficiency, so much more marked than at others, at this age period; and though it is undoubtedly due in part to mis-statement of age, I am inclined also to refer it to omissions from the record. The temptation to conceal the existence of girls of this age does not at first sight seem to be strong; but sensitiveness regarding mention of them appears to begin considerably before the time at which they are usually married. At the other age groups, *viz* from 0 to 5 years and among persons aged 20 and over the figures, judging by internal evidence, have a stronger appearance of correctness (though the fact that Mohammadan women aged 20 to 25 outnumber males of the same religion and age group points to over-statement of the ages of young girls); and it may be surmised that omissions, if they do occur, are, at any rate, not numerous. Finally, in spite of the admitted fact that variations in the sex proportions do take place from time to time, the gradual aud steady rise in the proportion of females enumerated at successive Censuses points to more accurate enumeration, and a decrease of tne sentiment which leads to the existence of females being concealed. Summary.

SUBSIDIARY TABLE I.—*Proportion of the sexes.*

DISTRICT AND NATURAL DIVISION.	NUMBER OF FEMALES PER 1,000 MALES :—							
	1911.		1901.		1891.		1881.	
	Actual population.	Natural population.	Actual population.	Natural population.	Actual population.	Natural population.	Actual population.	Natural population.
1	2	3	4	5	6	7	8	9
Total Districts N.-W. F. P. ...	**858**	**887**	**846**	**885**	**843**	**892**	**819**	**879**
Hazara	881	878	869	866	855	878	862	869
Trans-Indus Districts ...	**849**	**892**	**837**	**894**	**838**	**897**	**814**	**882**
Peshawar	838	878	840	893	838	897	781	880
Kohat	870	906	783	915	796	910	788	900
Bannu	870	915	859	863	859	908	838	906
Dera Ismail Khan	850	904	860	911	860	883	862	860

NOTE :—The figures in column 9 are based on the population of the districts of Peshawar, Kohat, Bannu and Dera Ismail Khan as constituted in 1881, when the two latter districts comprised a large area now forming the Mianwali District of the Punjab, and when the Kohat District contained 24 villages now forming part of the Peshawar District. See pages 85 and 86 of Volume I, Punjab Census Report, 1881.

The figures in column 7 do not take into account emigrants to places beyond the Punjab and the North-West Frontier Province.

SUBSIDIARY TABLE II.—(British Districts only).

Number of females per 1,000 males at different age periods by religions at each of the last three Censuses.

AGES.	ALL RELIGIONS.			HINDUS.			MUSSALMANS.			SIKHS.		
	1891	1901	1911	1891	1901	1911	1891	1901	1911	1891	1901	1911
1	2	3	4	5	6	7	8	9	10	11	12	13
0 and under 1 ...	992	979	972	949	1,011	940	989	978	975	920	865	872
1 " 2 ...	1,009	987	995	978	947	857	1,012	990	1,003	833	1,000	1,069
2 " 3 ...	995	1,002	1,036	989	986	1,044	996	1,003	1,037	949	1,108	936
3 " 4 ...	941	1,017	1,018	989	1,015	972	939	1,018	1,020	876	964	945
4 " 5 ...	912	972	955	902	991	1,036	912	1,000	953	990	979	892
Total 0 and under 5	**968**	**927**	**993**	**961**	**992**	**978**	**969**	**991**	**995**	**913**	**969**	**921**
5 and under 10 ...	827	866	874	855	869	905	826	866	873	760	724	815
10 " 15 ...	710	719	709	683	661	697	713	724	712	558	555	581
15 " 20 ...	929	773	793	724	615	583	958	799	821	410	292	429
20 " 25 ...	830	886	947	571	532	561	979	984	1,047	146	185	323
25 " 30 ...	876	837	898	615	451	537	932	927	963	199	202	385
Total 0 & under 30	**868**	**853**	**872**	**744**	**672**	**703**	**890**	**880**	**894**	**355**	**355**	**525**
30 and under 40 ...	819	824	861	649	514	584	849	873	894	235	217	417
40 " 50 ...	816	840	868	664	586	670	837	866	887	433	431	579
50 " 60 ...	778	795	788	742	643	657	803	811	801	504	479	527
60 and over ...	761	770	759	820	748	732	760	774	760	493	587	716
Total 30 and over	**809**	**816**	**833**	**681**	**577**	**637**	**829**	**846**	**854**	**321**	**323**	**507**
Total all ages—actual population.	**851**	**830**	**858**	**724**	**640**	**680**	**873**	**868**	**880**	**345**	**343**	**520**
Total all ages—natural population.	...	...	**887**	...	...	**834**	...	...	**891**	...	...	**801**

SUBSIDIARY TABLE III.—*Number of females per 1,000 males at different age periods by religions and natural divisions (Census of 1911.)*

Ages.	Hazara.				Trans-Indus Districts.			
	All religions.	Hindus.	Mussalmans.	Sikhs.	All religions.	Hindus.	Mussalmans.	Sikhs.
1	2	3	4	5	6	7	8	9
0 and under 1	1,001	1,021	1,001	990	965	680	963	841
1 " 2	948	771	957	647	1,019	885	1,027	1,219
2 " 3	1,090	984	1,095	913	1,013	1,061	1,012	943
3 " 4	1,006	907	1,010	940	1,022	989	1,024	946
4 " 5	942	880	944	900	961	1,073	957	890
Total 0 and under 5 ...	**1,003**	**930**	**1,006**	**911**	**989**	**896**	**990**	**924**
5 and under 10	907	909	908	764	861	809	860	830
10 " 15	734	707	736	613	699	695	700	571
15 " 20	878	516	906	704	760	603	787	386
20 " 25	1,123	463	1,217	510	888	510	987	293
25 " 30	1,022	516	1,073	513	859	551	927	359
Total 0 and under 30 ...	**887**	**645**	**945**	**664**	**851**	**707**	**874**	**497**
30 and under 40	874	577	892	583	856	586	894	393
40 " 50	799	709	852	615	892	681	962	570
50 " 60	742	643	769	618	806	586	822	515
60 and over	692	612	695	631	790	771	810	744
Total 30 and over ...	**796**	**626**	**807**	**605**	**847**	**603**	**866**	**490**
Total all ages—actual population ...	**882**	**639**	**896**	**644**	**850**	**691**	**873**	**494**
Total all ages—natural population	**878**	**820**	**882**	**732**	**892**	**842**	**896**	**825**

SUBSIDIARY TABLE IV.—(For N.-W. F. Province including Trans-frontier Posts).

Number of females per 1,000 males for certain selected castes.

Caste.	Number of females per 1,000 males.						
	All ages.	0—5	5—12	12—15	15—20	20—40	40 and over.
1	2	3	4	5	6	7	8
Arora	824	989	858	767	731	815	774
Awan	843	1,058	819	629	824	905	739
Baghban	881	1,084	814	634	779	949	848
Baluch	833	962	788	622	908	867	792
Bhatiara	961	1,165	814	1,108	1,054	1,035	810
Brahman	681	1,038	820	642	572	597	620
Chamar	758	697	763	686	571	840	800
Chuhra	629	742	838	656	758	571	504
Dhobi	836	1,038	799	783	921	853	719
Dhund	931	944	951	802	1,000	987	856
Gakkhar	852	1,227	848	787	984	752	771
Gujar	845	973	847	637	755	985	708
Jat	762	970	861	706	525	654	885
Jhinwar	530	1,102	733	986	479	358	473
Jolaha	870	1,121	834	739	757	981	718
Karal	953	1,090	877	765	1,042	1,056	847
Kashmiri	884	1,047	916	810	887	901	777
Khatri	649	946	809	625	619	540	639
Kumhar	936	1,033	895	688	944	1,023	882
Lohar	865	1,080	828	669	842	987	673
Machhi	858	1,021	783	613	882	886	879
Maliar	917	1,201	902	784	917	930	799
Mallah	782	984	693	556	685	702	997
Mirasi	870	1,052	781	784	893	958	751
Mochi	861	983	862	775	882	911	722
Moghal	798	1,029	841	706	867	800	645
Musalli (with Kutana)	819	863	914	853	801	828	698
Nai	895	1,028	911	817	926	1,008	672
Paracha	841	947	744	565	837	1,010	788
Pathan	880	945	855	705	746	938	905
Qassab	913	934	834	893	768	1,048	871
Qureshi	894	1,078	863	870	901	972	712
Rajput	425	783	832	558	444	250	513
Saiad	915	1,180	824	794	881	944	872
Sarara	843	891	761	584	925	782	1,217
Shekh	787	955	896	872	794	732	685
Sonar	930	1,138	837	853	909	972	868
Swathi	899	980	876	710	943	1,071	723
Tanaoli	919	1,056	813	741	813	1,142	771
Tarkhan	872	1,007	870	706	860	926	774
Teli	885	987	759	729	990	982	836

SUBSIDIARY TABLE V.—*Actual number of births and deaths reported for each sex during the decades* 1891—1900 *and* 1901—1910.

Year.	Number of births.			Number of deaths.			Difference between columns 2 and 3. Excess of latter over former + Defect —.	Difference between columns 5 and 6. Excess of latter over former + Defect —.	Difference between columns 4 and 7. Excess of former over latter + Defect —.	Number of female births per 1,000 male births.	Number of female deaths per 1,000 male deaths.
	Males.	Females.	Total.	Males.	Females.	Total.					
1	2	3	4	5	6	7	8	9	10	11	12
1891 ...	31,735	24,438	56,173	31,165	26,440	57,605	—7,297	—4,725	—1,432	770·06	848·39
1892 ...	36,945	28,499	65,444	57,705	51,082	10,887	—8,446	—6,623	—43,343	771·39	885·23
1893 ...	16,416	12,255	28,671	27,424	23,234	50,658	—4,161	—4,190	—21,987	746·53	847·21
1894 ...	42,978	34,873	77,851	28,878	25,377	54,255	—8,105	—3,501	+23,596	811·42	878·77
1895 ...	44,702	37,007	81,709	28,907	24,751	53,658	—7,695	—4,156	+28,051	827·86	856·23
1896 ...	42,947	35,728	78,675	35,317	30,493	65,810	—7,219	—4,824	+12,865	831·91	863·41
1897 ...	43,788	35,866	79,654	73,381	35,570	108,951	—7,922	—37,811	—35,570	819·08	484·73
1898 ...	38,501	32,649	17,150	33,830	29,486	63,316	—5,852	—4,344	+7,834	848·00	871·59
1899 ...	44,895	38,497	83,392	30,098	26,640	56,738	—6,398	—3,458	+26,654	857·49	885·11
1900 ...	43,845	35,907	79,752	34,679	30,594	65,273	—7,938	—4,085	+14,479	818·95	882·21
1891—1900	**386,752**	**315,719**	**702,471**	**381,384**	**303,667**	**685,051**	**—71,033**	**—77,717**	**+17,420**	**816·33**	**796·42**
1901 ...	33,345	27,068	60,413	20,826	18,382	39,208	—6,277	—2,444	+21,205	811·76	882·65
1902 ...	36,751	30,153	66,904	25,574	23,050	48,624	—6,598	—2,524	+18,280	820·47	901·31
1903 ...	34,655	28,211	62,866	29,393	27,146	56,539	—6,444	—2,247	+6,327	814·05	923·55
1904 ...	38,140	31,404	69,544	29,480	27,379	56,859	—6,736	—2,101	+12,685	823·39	928·73
1905 ...	38,761	31,608	70,369	27,941	25,386	53,327	—7,153	—2,555	+17,042	815·46	908·56
1906 ...	41,722	35,112	76,834	33,834	33,315	67,149	—6,610	—519	+9,685	841·57	984·66
1907 ...	33,899	28,163	62,062	35,031	31,986	67,017	—5,736	—3,045	—4,955	830·79	913·07
1908 ...	39,344	31,837	71,181	35,888	32,473	68,361	—7,507	—3,415	+2,820	809·20	904·08
1909 ...	36,247	29,864	66,111	26,979	23,712	50,691	—6,383	—3,267	+15,420	823·90	878·91
1910 ...	40,355	32,430	72,785	27,412	23,829	51,241	—7,925	—3,583	+21,544	803·62	869·29
1901—1910	**373,219**	**305,850**	**679,069**	**292,358**	**266,658**	**559,016**	**—67,369**	**—25,700**	**+125,053**	**819·49**	**912·09**

SUBSIDIARY TABLE VI.—*Number of deaths of each sex at different ages.*

AGE.	1905.		1906.		1907.		1908.		1909.		TOTAL.		Average number of female deaths per 1,000 male deaths.
	Males.	Females.	Males.	Females.	Males.	Females.	Males.	Females.	Males.	Females.	Males.	Females.	
1	2	3	4	5	6	7	8	9	10	11	12	13	14
0 and under 1	7,878	6,097	9,367	7,889	7,817	6,339	8,654	6,949	7,259	5,701	40,975	32,975	804·76
1 „ 5	4,909	4,633	7,960	8,606	6,191	6,102	6,601	6,407	4,079	3,923	29,740	29,671	997·68
5 „ 10	1,466	1,415	2,669	2,686	2,215	2,019	2,643	2,450	1,686	1,516	10,679	10,086	944·47
10 „ 15	888	814	1,158	1,136	1,144	1,101	1,386	1,218	917	855	5,493	5,124	932·82
15 „ 20	661	702	689	853	876	813	886	798	793	746	3,905	3,912	1,001·79
20 „ 30	1,919	2,279	1,740	2,408	2,323	2,621	2,490	2,734	1,865	1,888	10,337	11,930	1,154·11
30 „ 40	2,227	2,617	2,134	2,570	2,989	3,387	2,899	3,146	2,256	2,318	12,505	14,038	1,122·59
40 „ 50	2,147	2,122	2,065	2,055	3,110	2,839	2,816	2,793	2,276	2,113	12,414	11,922	960·37
50 „ 60	2,009	1,588	1,992	1,714	2,834	2,324	2,589	2,067	2,145	1,733	11,569	9,426	814·76
60 and over ...	3,887	3,119	4,060	3,398	5,532	4,441	4,924	3,911	3,703	2,919	22,056	17,788	806·49
Total ...	**27,941**	**25,386**	**33,834**	**33,315**	**35,031**	**31,986**	**35,888**	**32,473**	**26,979**	**33,712**	**159,673**	**146,872**	**919·83**

CHAPTER VII.

CIVIL CONDITION.

220. Under the orders in accordance with which this report has been prepared this chapter contains descriptive as well as statistical matter. Of the subjects dealt with under the former head, some, such as the account of birth-customs, and of the words used in the vernaculars of the Province to describe degrees of affinity, are related indirectly only to that indicated in the title of the chapter. Others, such as the remarks on bride price, and on the form of the marriage ceremony, can hardly be introduced with propriety into the middle of a discussion of the figures. I have thought it best therefore to divide the chapter into two parts, beginning, since this is the order in which it can most usefully be read, with the purely descriptive portion. At the same time I have found it impossible to keep the two portions absolutely distinct, and there will be found a certain amount of overlapping.

Chapter divided into two parts.

PART I.—DESCRIPTIVE.

221. In India generally the most potent influence which has moulded marriage customs has been that of Hinduism; and it is an influence which has had its effect, not only on Hindus, but also, and perhaps to an almost equal degree, on Mussalmans. On the other hand we have here to deal with a Mohammadan population, which has not only escaped falling under the yoke of the Hindu social system, but has been able in some degree to impose its own on the small Hindu community which is to be found in its midst. The degree to which this is the case will be discussed later. It is sufficient here to notice that for nine hundred years the dominant religion of the Province has been Islam, and that, among Mohammadans, traces of Hindu influence, whatever strength it may have possessed till then, have not survived the succeeding waves of migration which planted the Pathan tribes in their present homes.

Marriage customs of the North-West Frontier Province uninfluenced by Hinduism.

222. The marriage customs of Mohammadans naturally call for first attention. Among them, while there are certain groups, such as the Khojas, Parachas, and, in so far as the name indicates a caste as distinct from an occupation, the Telis, who are essentially foreigners, and have retained, with but slight modifications, the customs of their original homes in the Punjab and elsewhere, the influence of the Pathan social code is predominant. In the realm of marriage the first point to be noticed is that it is brides who are paid for, and not bridegrooms. The bride price varies largely in different parts of the Province, and, in the same area, with the status of the parties and the attractions of the girl. To begin at the bottom of the social scale, I am informed that among the Hindkis (or non-Pathans) of the Peshawar District it varies from Rs. 80 to Rs. 150, though among the poorer classes it is no doubt less. A no higher figure is quoted for the Teri Tahsil of Kohat, where the people are poor, but among Pathans elsewhere it is generally considerably larger. In Dera Ismail Khan it is said to range from Rs. 100 to Rs. 300; and in most areas of the Province the price paid probably falls between these two figures. In the Hangu Tahsil of Kohat, however, it is reported to rise to Rs. 500, and never to fall below Rs. 200 The prices given are of course rough averages only; and much larger sums are paid if the parties are well-to-do. In Kohat a man who wants a useful helpmate often buys a wife from tribal territory. Such women, though they may have little beauty to commend them, are hardy and will work like beasts of burden; and they can be got for about Rs. 150. Among the Gujars of Hazara, and among the poorer members of other tribes also, it is not unusual for the prospective bridegroom, like Jacob in the house of Laban, to serve the father of his bride in lieu of payment in cash.

Mohammadan marriage customs. Bride price.

Ceremonies of betrothal.

223. The bride price is handed over at, or soon after, the betrothal which is always effected at the house of the father of the girl, to which the boy's father goes accompanied by friends. In the trans-frontier area, where the population is almost entirely Pathan, it is frankly the arrangement and ratification of a monetary bargain. The boy's father states the price he is prepared to pay, and, if the father of the girl accepts it, both sides publicly announce that the betrothal has been made, clasp hands *(lasniwai)* or go through the ceremony (Kurram) of *las porta kawal i. e.*, raising the hands in token of clinching the bargain. In British territory the monetary element of the transaction is kept out of sight. The parties publicly announce their consent to the engagement, and in Hazara among some of the tribes added solemnity is given to the declaration by the presence of a Mullah, in reply to whose questions it is made. This public announcement (*shara jawab* or *ijab qabul*) makes the engagement to all intents and purposes as binding as a marriage; and in Hazara, when made in reply to questions from a Mullah, is called the *ibtidai nikah*, or preliminary marriage. In most cases sweets are distributed or a feast is given, but this forms no essential part of the betrothal. It is to be observed, however, that all the expenses are borne by the father of the boy.

I have said that in the British districts the monetary part of the transaction is kept out of sight. Frankly to sell a daughter is considered hardly in good taste. In Bannu a small sum out of the bride price is often returned by the girl's father, and Bannuchis sometimes absent themselves from their homes at the time of payment, and allow a menial to act for them. Yet a Pathan father in Bannu would never forego the price of his daughter; and throughout the Province, in spite of the dislike expressed by educated men to the sale of a daughter's hand in marriage, I believe it to be almost universal in the rural tracts. In nearly every case connected with the breaking of a contract of betrothal that comes before the courts it is found that the betrothal, if it actually took place, has been broken, either because the money agreed upon has not been paid, or because a higher bidder has appeared. Betrothal commonly precedes marriage, which, as will be seen later, is usually deferred to a comparatively advanced age, by a short period only. Children are, however, sometimes betrothed, and in Peshawar it is said that a promise of marriage may be made even before birth, but such an engagement is not binding.

Binding nature of a contract of betrothal.

224. The District Codes of Customary Law give various grounds as valid for the annulling of a contract of betrothal. In Hazara and Dera Ismail Khan the view most widely held is that the promise of marriage can be revoked in the event of either party being found to be a leper or of the boy being discovered to be impotent. Other grounds are also held to be valid by some tribes, such as epilepsy, insanity, the apostasy of the boy or the immorality of the girl. On the other hand, in the Pathan districts, (except in Kurram, where similar grounds to those in Dera Ismail Khan and Hazara are admitted) the view commonly held is that the betrothal can not in any case be broken off by the girl or her parents, except possibly in the event of the apostasy of the boy; but that, on the boy's side, it can be relinquished at any time. Since, however, a refusal to carry out a marriage contract is considered equivalent to a divorce, it can only be effected by the intended bridegroom himself after he comes of age. Should a betrothal be broken off for any cause, the party which has incurred expenditure must be refunded the amount by the other Throughout the Province the breaking of an engagement is a serious matter, and a fertile source of feuds. This is easy to understand. The boy's family naturally do not wish to be off with an engagement on which considerable sums have been spent, and, if the girl's family break it, they have the other party to the contract to reckon with. The betrothal is therefore regarded as tanatamount to a marriage, and it is probable that some of the 68,407 Mohammadans of under 20 years of age, who are shown in Table VII as married, are in reality only betrothed.

Absence of restrictions on intermarriage among Mohammadans.

225. In India Mohammadans are generally little less affected by caste restrictions in regard to intermarriage than are the Hindus themselves. In the North-West Frontier Province on the other hand we find a state of affairs

which far more nearly resembles that of Europe. Any marriage which is not prohibited by the *Shariat* is valid. The Mohammadan Law imposes few restrictions. A Mussalman may not marry with an infidel or within the prohibited degrees of blood relationship, but that is all. In Swat it is noted that if a bride is available in the family, no search is made for one outside, " as it is always considered advisable to cement the bonds of possible union in each family. The Mohammadan Law provides a wide field for selection among relations, and close marriages are very common". Throughout the Province marriages are usually determined by considerations of family convenience. For instance, a man wanting to marry his son arranges to take for him the daughter of his brother or his cousin, agreeing to give his own daughter in exchange after a year or two; and the widow of a Pathan's brother is by custom his right, should he be unmarried, and wish to take her for his wife. Coming to marriages outside the family circle, Sunnis do not commonly marry with Shias, or either with Wahabis; but such marriages are not unknown, and are placed under no ban. There is everywhere a tendency to marry within the tribe, and Pathans will not give their daughters in marriage to non-Pathans, though they will take Hindki wives. Saiads similarly will not give their daughters to men who are not Saiads. In the Kurram it is noticed that the Turis, Bangashes and Saiads do not ordinarily give their daughters to poor people; but if they can find a bridegroom of position and wealth they care little what his tribe may be. This proposition is, I think, true of the Province as a whole, and of most of the (Mohammadan) castes and tribes to be found within it, if it be remembered that any marriage outside the circle of the blood relations is regarded as a *pis aller*. *Taqdir ka muamala* (it can't be helped) is the comment which finds expression in such a case. Generally speaking it may be said that girls of a superior tribe are not married into an inferior one; and the same tendency exists, though it possesses far less weight, in the case of boys also. In the main the restrictions on marriage are hardly more stringent than they are in Europe, where people are careful to avoid their daughters making mêsalliances. The preference which we find in the Province for marriage within the family, or at any rate within the tribe, in part represents a survival from a time of lawlessness, when a strengthening of tribal and family ties was naturally to be desired; in part it proceeds from pride of race. The tribes which, like the Bannuchi, are of very mixed descent, are looked down upon as mongrels by Pathans of purer race.

Description of marriage ceremony. Its essential elements.

226. The ceremonies performed at marriage differ in different parts of the Province, but in all the essential element is the *ijab qabul* (*ijab*-assent, *qabul*-consent) pronounced by each of the parties or their guardians, in the presence of witnesses, and followed by the reading of the *Nikah* by a Mullah.* In the trans-Indus districts the bride, if an adult, names a representative (called in Dera Ismail Khan, *vakil*; in Peshawar *nikah plar*, marriage father, or, in Yusafzai, *nikah wror*, marriage brother) who announces her consent for her. In Hazara there is no representative of the bride other than her father or guardian, and it is considered suitable for him to act for her, even if she be an adult. In the trans-frontier area also her father or guardian always gives consent on the part of the bride, whatever her age. The ceremonies at the marriage of a widow are precisely the same as for that of a virgin, except that in the case of the former, the *janj* which is described in the following paragraph, is omitted.

Other ceremonies. Traces of marriage by capture.

227. There are other ceremonies varying in different areas, but none of them are essential. The most interesting of these is the *janj*, or marriage procession†, in which clear traces of marriage by capture survive. The *janj* consists of a party of the bridegroom's friends, who accompany him to the bride's house, and later escort both bride and bridegroom to their home. The party, which proceeds with an appearance of warlike pomp, often accompanied by the discharge of fire-arms into the air, represents the armed force

*In Peshawar if a Mulla can not be present, a layman is allowed to act for him.

† The *janj* appears to be a Pathan custom, but it is practised by Mohammadans generally, and, in outlying areas at any rate, by Hindus also.

which in a ruder age carried off the bride from the resistence of her friends. In Northern Waziristan the *janj*, on reaching the bride's house, is met by a party of the bride's friends who turn out to oppose it. A sham fight then takes place in which clods of earth and stones are used as missiles by both sides, and swords are drawn. Though rare, cases are not unknown in which there has been loss of life in these encounters. This sham fight is called *warro.* Much the same thing is found in other portions of the Province also. Both in Swat and in the Kurram the local codes of customary law make provision for death and injury inflicted at the ceremony of stone throwing at a marriage procession; and casualties occurring at such times are attributed to *kismet*, and the delinquent is absolved from the consequences of his act. The Wazirs of Bannu, who are comparatively recent settlers from the tribal territory across the border, have preserved the custom of the *warro* in their new homes. In Marwat, the writer of the Bannu Gazetteer, 1907 (page 49) notes that the *janj* 'may expect to be pelted with clods and rotten eggs' and he adds that 'among Wazirs serious injuries are often inflicted in the course of the pretended defence of the bride from the invading strangers.' The usual custom in the Province is for the marriage to be celebrated at the bride's home, but that which, at any rate until recently, was in force in Yusafzai in the Peshawar district, whereby the bride is taken to the bridegroom's house and married there, her relatives not being present, is another survival of a time when wives were taken possession of by force. In Bannu to the present day it is the rule for the marriage to be solemnised at the bridegroom's house.

Power of making a contract of betrothal.

228. Whereas in Northern Europe betrothals are arranged by adults acting on their own behalf, in the North-West Frontier Province, as in the East generally, the right to effect such contracts rests, in the case of minors and adult females always, and among some communities even in the case of adult males, with the father or other guardian. In the British districts an adult male usually has the right to arrange his own betrothal, but in practice it is nearly always arranged for him by his father, if he should be alive. On the other hand in Swat, and among the Wazirs of Northern Waziristan the betrothal can only be valid if effected by the father or the guardian. Even an adult male must do as he is told and marry the girl, and, if he objects to her, he can divorce her afterwards.

If the father be dead, in most of the areas included in the Province the right rests in practice with the nearest male of the father's family, *i. e.*, the boy or girl's elder brother, paternal grandfather, paternal uncle and the like. In theory the mother also often has certain rights in the matter. Thus in Hazara and Dera Ismail Khan her right to contract comes next after the father's, and in Peshawar after that of the elder brother, paternal grandfather and paternal uncle. But it is rarely unfettered. In Hazara she can only arrange a betrothal within her husband's tribe, and in Dera Ismail Khan only with the consent of her deceased husband's agnates. In Peshawar her right, coming after that of the brother, paternal grandfather and paternal uncle, is little likely to be exercised, and the Halimzai Mohmands never allow it to her at all. In the trans-frontier area of the Province, where the patriarchal idea is strongest, the facts may be simply stated by saying that the right rests, in the absence of the father, with the next of kin among the male agnates who inherit the estate.

A woman is regarded as a chattel. If she be unmarried, she belongs to her father's estate. As such she has a realisable value, and any one who entices her away without paying her price commits a particularly heinous form of theft. At marriage she becomes part of the property of her husband, and, after his death, of that of his heirs. Her position *qua* her husband and his heirs is precisely the same, after marriage, as it was *qua* her father, before it. It follows that at no time in her life has she any power to dispose of her hand in marriage. And this is not only the theory of the case, for practice follows it with an exactness of correspondence which the two do not always display. I do not mean that marriages are never made without the consent of the woman's kin. They are not uncommon, but the price is always exacted. And it is not only the sale price of the woman which is demanded, but something over and beyond it by way of ***sharmana***, or compensation for wounded honour. Pathans, whose customs dominate the social practice of Mohammadans in the Province, are abnormally sensitive on the subject of their female relatives. Abductions of women, whether married, unmarried or widowed, are perhaps a more fertile source of feuds than any other. If the seducer is prepared to pay the price demanded, the matter can generally be settled on this basis. But if not, he must fly beyond the reach of the woman's injured relatives, or he will run great risk of being murdered. Tribal customs on the subject of women are supported by the legal system in force in the Province, by which disputes of this nature are commonly referred to a *jirga*, or committee of tribesman, for settlement, under the Frontier Crimes Regulation. The *jirga* state what in their opinion are the facts of the case, and the degree of compensation which will meet it; and to their finding, should it appear to be a just one, effect is given by the authorities. The compensation generally takes the form of a sum of money, but in some cases a girl may be given in exchange for her .who has been abducted On the whole, however, in spite of the authority to which women are subject, and the degree to which they are compelled to bow to it, the element of personal choice enters more freely into the marriages arranged than is common among the less independent population which occupies so much of the area of India.

Intermediaries employed.

229. The arrangements are commonly settled direct between the parents of the parties who are to be betrothed ; and this is the easier because, as has been seen, betrothals are often arranged between near relations. If, however, an intermediary is employed, the negotiations take place through a *dum* (drummer); in Dera Ismail Khan, the *nai* (barber) also plays the part of go-between. The following account of the part played by the *dum* is taken from some notes published in 1904, in the Journal of the Royal Asiatic Society of Bengal, Volume LXXIII, Part III, on tribal customs in Swat : "When recourse has to be had to the outer world, enquiries are undertaken by agents and go-betweens before the scheme can be seriously started by either side. The jealous care with which women are generally kept concealed renders the selection of a bride a matter of extreme interest and difficulty. This mission is undertaken by professional negotiators in the persons of *dums*, who are a privileged class. They are entrusted with the secret counsels of a family, and their wives act as servants to the ladies Through their agency they know both the character and the personal appearance of every eligible young woman in the countryside. They are a prominent factor in all matrimonial engagements, and, being critics of experience, their advice is followed to a considerable extent "

Marriage customs of Hindus.

230. The Hindus in the Province, (and in speaking of Hindus, I refer also to Sikhs), form a small community, isolated, though to a less degree than in the past, from the great body of their co-religionists to the East and South. It is their isolation which renders some consideration due to their marriage customs; for no one would go to the North-West Frontier Province for an account of the distinctive traits of Hinduism, nor are the numbers we have to deal with sufficient to entitle the subject otherwise to more than the most cursory notice. It may be mentioned here that the difficulty of drawing correct inferences from our statistics for these religions is enhanced by the fact that both Hindus and Sikhs are present in the Province largely as purely temporary immigrants, notably as military sepoys and sowars. The age distribution of the population, particularly in the case of males, is therefore abnormal, the persons living at both extremes of life being comparatively few in number; and the proportions of the sexes are also unusual. But some of the Hindus and Sikhs consist of permanent residents. In order to get a clear notion how far the figures are affected by immigration it would be necessary to tabulate separately the age and civil condition of immigrants on the one hand and of permanent residents on the other ; and we could not do this on a return of birthplace alone, for age and occupation would have to be taken into account. It is doubtful how far the importance of the subject deserves the detailed examination I have suggested, and certainly the time at my disposal does not allow of it. In the circumstances it will suffice if I point out here the limitations to which my conclusions are subject.

Hindus comprise two distinct groups :—
(i) Native born.
(ii) Immigrant.

Possibility of distinguishing between them.

231. At the same time it is possible, by the aid of the statistics of caste, in some degree to distinguish between permanent and temporary residents. In the former class may be included the majority of our Aroras, Bhatias, Khatris, Brahmans and Hindu Sonars, while all other Hindus and Sikhs are comprised in the other. The members of the five castes mentioned have been in many cases so long resident in the Province that they have lost any memory of their place of origin, and for all practical purposes they may be regarded as natives. The distinction is important because of the great differences in the social customs of the two groups. In Chapter XI will be found some account of the caste organisation in each case, and of the great relaxation among Hindus native to the Province of the Hindu rules regarding commensality. We are here concerned with marriage customs only. Of those of the immigrant castes I need say little. They have brought with them those of the areas from which they come. The Hindu Dhobis for instance (they are only to be found in Cantonments, where they wash for the European community) have only resided in the Province for one or two generations. Their marriage customs are those of the United Provinces, and the Census Reports of those Provinces contain full accounts of them. Similarly my syce (a Jaiswara) goes to Jaunpur when he wants to get married. But of the Hindus native to the Province more must be said.

Dependence of the native born Hindus under Mohammadan rule.

232. At the present day the spread of means of communication and the freedom accorded to all religions under British rule have done much to free Sikhs and Hindus from subjection to the social system of the dominant Mohammadan population. But this freedom is of comparatively recent date. In his 'Year on the Punjab Frontier' Sir Herbert Edwardes relates how, at his first visit in 1848 to Bannu, the Hindus went to their Mohammadan overlords for permission to marry as regularly as an English gentleman for a license to Doctor's Commons; and it is not to be supposed that they escaped from the influence of example, even in matters in which they were left to follow their own choice. Small communities, living in scattered groups among an alien population, and the members of which, as Sir Herbert Edwardes tells us, could not even visit friends in an adjoining village, except when provided with an escort by the *Malik* under whose protection they lived,* might have been expected to find it impossible to practise fully the rules of exogamy and endogamy which limit and define the sphere of possible marriages among Hindus elsewhere. Marriages with Mohammadans were obviously out of the question. The Musalman would not allow his daughters to intermarry with a community he despised, even if his religion had sanctioned a union with a worshipper of idols; and the objections on the side of the Hindus were just as strong.

Comparatively slight influence of their Mohammadan environment on Hindu rules of inter-marriage.

233. In other spheres than that concerned with the groups with which intermarriage is allowed, the influence on our Hindus of their Mohammadan environment is clearly apparent. I have already referred to the weakness of caste organisation among them, and its bearing on the age of marriage will be discussed later. But we find no clear signs, in the present practice of the groups native to the Province, to show that the rules of Hinduism regulating intermarriage were ever seriously relaxed. Minor modifications have no doubt taken place. A Hindu must in theory marry within his caste, but should not marry one of his own or his mother's *gotra*.† But actually the prohibition of marriage within the mother's *gotra* does not extend beyond the descendants of the great grandmother, and the Mohial Brahmans and Khukrain Khatris of Hazara do not observe it at all. Hypergamy also does not appear to be found, and the various exogamous sub-sections of a caste intermarry freely, with reference to nothing beyond the means of the parties. Mr. Lorimer, in his notes on the Customary Law of the Peshawar District written in 1899, remarked that the rule that different castes may not intermarry was not absolute in practice and that disregard of it was increasingly common. My enquiries, however, lead me to believe that the statement is only true if caste be understood to mean,

* One of my informants tells me that he has heard from his grandfather of the same state of affairs existing in Peshawar.

† The word *gotra* appears not to be understood among Hindus in Peshawar. I tried to explain it to an educated Hindu, who said the right word, in the case of mother's *gotra*, would be *tabar* (the Pashto word for family); on the father's side no word existed.

not the main groups such as the Khatris, which are usually understood by the term, but the chief sub-divisions under them, such as Dhaigar, Bonjai, and Khukrain, which have in the past been strictly endogamous. There is indeed in Peshawar a slight tendency to allow intermarriage between these groups, but far less strong, I am informed, than, for instance, in Lahore. There seems to be considerable indifference, or at least carelessness, as to the caste of the bride. I remember a case which came into my own court, in which a Khatri of Peshawar accused of cheating a man who appeared to be a dealer in women. The latter brought to Peshawar a female from Kashmir, and handed her over to the complainant, who married her on the strength of the other's assertion that she was a Khatri by caste. It was discovered later that she was not even a Hindu, and that she had a previous husband living. However much the complainant was deceived by the other's statement, it is incredible that he should have accepted an entirely unsupported assertion, had he been really interested in the caste of the bride; and his action, in bringing the case to court, was prompted by fear of loss of respect, as the matter had become public property, in the eyes of his caste fellows.

Restrictions on intermarriage among Hindus.

234. But in the main, restrictions on marriage have persisted to a striking degree. The Khatris, for instance, are divided into four main endogamous sub-divisions, the Dhaigars, the Chargarhi Khatris, the Bonjais and the Khukrains. These again are divided into exogamous groups. Those of the Dhaigars are four, the Khanna, the Kapur, the Mehra and the Seth. The exogamous groups of the Chargrahi Khatris are twelve, four bearing the same names as those of the Dhaigars, and eight more. Bonjai is said to be derived from *Bawanja* (fifty-two), for there are no less than fifty-two exogamous divisions of the Bonjais, of which only about 20 are represented in the Province. The Khukrains, divided into 8 sub-divisions in the Punjab, possess 10 in the North-West Frontier Province; two fresh ones from Kabul, the Chadda and the Chandiok, having been recently admitted. Others are the Kohli, the Anand, the Sethi, the Sahni and the Basin. A Khukrain must marry a Khukarain, a Bonjai must marry a Bonjai, and so on. But among Khukrains a Kohli may not marry a Kohli, but must seek for a wife among the other exogamous groups of the Khukrains. In the same way the Aroras have two main (endogamous) groups, the Dakhna and the Utradhi. Beneath these again are exogamous sub-divisions, such as the Taneja, the Jhano, the Chanda, the Mata, and many more, of the Dakhna, the Chokra, the Gorawara and others, of the Utradhi. One might have supposed that, along with other caste restrictions, the rules regarding intermarriage would have been relaxed, especially when it is remembered that women are often in defect. But this is not the case. It may be necessary to go far afield to find a wife. A man may never be able to find one at all. But rather than marry with a group interdicted by caste rules he becomes a Musalman and marries a Musalmani, as I am informed that two Utradhi Aroras of Tank recently did. Whatever the men's actual motives may have been, it is commonly believed that their conversion to Islam was solely due to a deficiency of females among the groups with which they could marry.

That these restrictions on marriage have continued to be effective, in spite of the influence of a Muhammadan environment, and of the great practical difficulties which they give rise to (difficulties which, it may be noted, were far greater 60 years ago than at present) is probably due to the small numbers of Hindus to be found in the Province. Except in a large city like Peshawar, each of the exogamous groups must be so small in any given area that what is elsewhere a fiction of common descent becomes here a reality. But even when the matter is regarded in this light, with the Hindus the objection to close marriages seems to be particularly strong. Among Mohammadans such marriages, as we have seen, are very common; but the Hindu speaks with the greatest contempt of their practice in this respect. One may conjecture therefore that the objection is something racial, something too deep-seated to be affected by accidents of environment.

The age of marriage and bride price.

235. A reference to the discussion of the statistics of marriage by age contained in the second part of this chapter will show that child marriage is

virtually unknown among both Hindus and Sikhs in the Province.* Temporary immigrants, if they possess child wives themselves, or have married their girl children to others, naturally do not bring them with them. In the case of the permanent residents the late age at which marriage takes place is largely due to the force of example. In Kabul, for instance, I am told that Hindu girls are often not married till they have passed the age of 20 years. It is partly also due to the cost of obtaining a wife. Whatever be the cause, and it is presumably not unconnected with the sex distribution, as among Mohammadans, so among Hindus, the expenditure on the marriage of a daughter is low, while that on the marriage of a son is considerable. Among the poorer classes the sale of daughters in marriage is not unknown, and marriage by exchange is common. A man does not therefore seek for a wife for his son till the latter is prepared to support her, and a wife of an age to be of use to her husband is naturally looked for in return for more or less heavy outlay. In such cases the first overtures are made by the bridegroom's family, and not, as among Hindus elsewhere, by the bride's. In the various accounts of Hindu marriage customs I find no mention of the *mukhlawa*, which marks the beginning of married life where child marriage is the rule; and the reason no doubt lies in the fact that, as marriage commonly takes place between adults, it is followed at once by cohabitation.

No mention of *mukhlawa*.

Terms of relationship.

236. The words used by any people to indicate degrees of relationship to the speaker are capable of throwing much light on their social observances, and it is for this reason that some account is given of them here. The language used by the bulk of the population of the Province is either Pashto, which is spoken by all Pathans, or some form of Lahnda or Western Punjabi, which is that used by the non-Pathan tribes, such as the Awans, Gujars, Jats and others, who in the Hazara and Dera Ismail Khan Districts form such a large proportion of the inhabitants. In the remarks which follow therefore I will confine myself to these two languages. In the case of Hazara and Dera Ismail Khan the language referred to should be understood as being Lahnda, while in the case of the other three districts the reference is to Pashto.

Terms expressing nearest degrees of relationship.

237. The words for father and mother, son and daughter call for no remark. The same may be said of those used to describe brother and sister, the elder and younger of whom are distinguished in Pashto, as in English, by the use of a prefix (*mashar*-elder, *kishar*-younger). It is, however, worth noting that in addressing one another, while the elder brother designates the younger by name, the younger addresses his elder as *Lala* (as in Hazara, and Dera Ismail Khan), or as *Dada* (Bannu and Kohat). The respect thus indicated for an elder male agnate is characteristic of a state of society in which, as among the Mohammadans of the Province generally, succession is through the male only and a voice in the tribal councils is possessed by men of ripe age and experience alone, while the females of the family are regarded as part of the family estate.

Maternal and paternal uncle.

238. These facts, *viz*. exclusively male succession and the regarding of women as chattels, lie at the root of most of those points in which the nomenclature of the people to describe relationship differs from that of other languages and states of society; and it is well therefore to draw attention to them at once. The distinction between the words for a maternal and a paternal uncle illustrate my point. In English we call both an uncle merely, for the importance of an uncle's position in regard to his nephews and nieces rests in England on purely adventitious circumstances, such as whether he be a poor uncle or a rich uncle, a bachelor uncle or an uncle with a family of his own to provide for. Among the Pathans of the North-West Frontier Province the position is far different. A maternal uncle is of no importance to his nephews and nieces. Their mother, (*i.e.*, his sister) on her marriage lost the only claim, the claim to maintenance, which she ever possessed on her father's estate. Should she be left a widow, it is her husband's family, and not her father's, which have the privilege of providing for her and the right of disposing of her, should

* In Peshawar the marriage of a child of either sex of less than 7 years of age is supposed to be prohibited by the Shastras.

they wish, in marriage to another. Her brother is no more to her than any other male, and no more to her children. They call him *mama* throughout the the Province both in Pashto and in Lahnda. He must be clearly distinguished from the relative known as *tra, trah, tre* or *tara* in Pashto, and as *chacha, kaka* or *baba* in Lahnda, which means a father's brother. The paternal uncle will inherit equally with the father the family estate. He will have a voice with the father in disposing of the hands of his unmarried nieces, and will be acting generally in accordance with precedent if he takes his brother's widow as his own wife. The relationship is something very different from that indicated by the word *mama*, and it is only fitting it should have another name. On the other hand, the sister of a Pathan's father, and the sister of his mother are much in the same position. Ties of affection may unite these to their nephews and nieces, but nothing more; and both are known in Pashto as *tror*, which is a derivative of the word used for a paternal uncle. In Lahnda on the other hand, which is a language spoken largely, in the Punjab, if not in the North-West Frontier Province, by Hindus, a maternal is distinguished from a paternal aunt, the former being *phuphi* and the later *masi*.

Uncle by marriage.

239. Of the words for an uncle by marriage, *i.e.*, the husband of a maternal or of a paternal aunt there is little to be said. In Pashto both are indicated merely by the equivalent of the word 'aunt' followed by the equivalent of the word 'husband' (*tror mera*); or, as in Peshawar, the same word (*mama*) is used for a paternal aunt's husband as for a maternal uncle. The one is of as little importance as the other, and it is not surprising that both are described by a single comprehensive word. In Peshawar a maternal aunt's husband is called *nasakka mama* (*sakka* true, own, *nasakka* being the opposite).

Cousin.

240. The words "first cousin" comprehend a relationship which can be resolved into four separate ones, each of which in the Lahnda of Dera Ismail Khan possesses a distinct name. There is first a father's brother's child (*bhai* or *petrer*), secondly a father's sister's child (*phupher*), thirdly a mother's brother's child (*malver*) and lastly a mother's sister's child (*masat*). In the Lahnda of Hazara we have an exact antithesis to this copious vocabulary, all four senses being conveyed by the word *bhra*, which is also used for brother. The position of Pashto in this matter is intermediate between these two extremes. Throughout the Province wherever Pushto is spoken, the child of a mother's brother or sister and the child of a father's sister can only be described as uncle's child or aunt's child as the case may be. Thus father's sister is *tror*, son is *zoi*, father's sister's child is *tror zoi*. Similarly we have *mamazoi* These relationships are all through females, and therefore do not count or deserve a separate name. But the relationship of a man, or of an unmarried woman, to a paternal uncle's son is different. Such a cousin is, as I have indicated, potentially a co-heir, and this nearer relationship is marked in most forms of Pashto by a distinct name. In Bannu it is true that the equivalent given for this meaning is *tarazoi* (*tara* being the Bannu form of *tra* or father's brother), but elsewhere, although the form *trazoi* is also in use in Peshawar, the child of a father's brother is indicated by *tarbur*. The closeness of the tie between *tarburs* lies in the fact that they are co-heirs to the family estate, and the result is much jeolousy, so that the popular saying * represents a *tarbur* and an enemy as identical.

Brother-and sister-in-law.

241. Coming to the terms for a brother-in-law we find a precisely similar distinction. Among Pathans a man speaking of his wife's brother, or a woman speaking of a sister's husband, refers to a relative who is united to him or to her possibly by bonds of affection, but by nothing else. Both relationships therefore are described by the same word, *viz. auge, aukhe* or (Bannu) *woksha*. When, however, a woman speaks of her husband's brother, she speaks of one of the persons (her husband's agnates) into whose control she passes on the death of her husband, and he has therefore a distinct name, *lewar*.† In this respect the Pashto words are distinguished from those used in Lahnda, in which tongue a man calls his wife's brother *sala*, a woman calls her husband's brother

*In Peshawar there is a saying which runs :—Tarbur da aspane ambur che nizde kegi, no chichi laka zambur *i.e.*, a tarbur and iron pincers are alike; coming near, either bites like a wasp. In paragraph 391 of the Punjab Census Report, 1881, the late Sir Denzil Ibbetson quotes the following Pashto proverbs :—A cousin's tooth breaks upon a cousin'. 'Keep a cousin poor, but use him'; and 'when he is little, play with him; when he is grown up he is a cousin, fight him.'

† In Peshawar *lewar* is said to refer to a husband's elder brother.

deor or *der*, while a sister's husband to either sex is *bhanwiya*. I do not find equally intelligible the distinctions in Pashto between the words used to describe a sister-in-law. Speaking of his wife's sister a Pathan male uses the word *augina* (the feminine of *auge* a wife's brother) or *khina*, or *kashina*, whereas a male or a female refers to a brother's wife as *wandiar* or *wrandar*, while a woman speaks of her husband's sister as *andror*, *indror*, *nandrer* or, in the Kohat trans-frontier area, simply as *de mire khor*, or the sister of the husband.

Nephew and niece.

The words for nephew and niece call for no remark either in Pashto or Lahnda. They are the same whether a man or a woman be the speaker, and are derivatives, in the case of a brother's children, of the word for brother, and in the case of a sister's children, of the word for sister. Similarly for a nephew or niece by marriage the word used, though it varies in different localities, is made up in Pashto generally by affixing the word for a son to that which indicates a brother- or sister-in-law, as the case may be, while in Lahnda the same words as are used for a nephew or niece by blood are employed.

Other terms of relationship

242. Other terms of relationship may be referred to briefly. It is curious to note, and I do not understand the reason, that whereas in Lahnda a paternal and maternal grandfather are distinguished, the one being *dada* and the other *nana*, in Pashto the same word *nika* is used for both, and the same is the case with the words for a paternal and maternal grandmother, Lahnda *dadi* and *nani* respectively, and Pashto *nia* for both. Lahnda similarly distinguishes between a son's son and a daughter's son (*potra* and *dhotra*); in Pashto, both are *nawasai* or a cognate form. Father-in-law is the same (Pashto *skhar*, Lahnda *sohra*) for a wife's and for a husband's father, though in Dera Ismail Khan Lahnda has an alternative form (*susar*) for the former. For mother-in-law (Pashto *khwakhe* or *khoshai*, Lahnda *sas*) the same word is used throughout the Province, whether it be the wife's or the husband's mother that is referred to. It is matter for surprise that Pashto makes no distinction between the words for paternal and maternal grand parents, and between those for parents-in-law on the husband's and on the wife's side. There is obviously a marked difference in the relative position with regard to the speaker of those persons according as their connection is on the male or the female side, and I can only suppose the reason to be found in the fact that parents usually predecease their children, and do not therefore exercise the rights which, as surviving male agnates, the males among them would possess. Of other relationships, a wife's sister's husband is described in Kohat by *augina mera* the former word meaning the wife's sister and the latter meaning husband, but the Pashto of Peshawar and of Bannu has adopted the word, *viz.*, *Sandhu*, used in Lahnda, which is spoken generally in the neighbouring districts of Hazara and Dera Ismail Khan respectively. The wives of brothers both belong to one family estate, and there is therefore a special term in Pashto by which one describes the other, *viz.*, *yore*, (spelt also in different localities *yonr*, *yor* and *yer*) and also in Lahnda *darani* or *dirrani*. Son's wife's parents have a special term in Lahnda *sainr* (Dera Ismail Khan) or *kurm* (Hazara). In Pashto they are described merely by a combination of words as in English, *viz.*, *de zöe khwakhe skhar*, *i. e.*, son's parents-in-law or *de ingor mor plar*, *i.e.*, daughter-in-law's parents. Son-in-law and daughter-in-law, it may be mentioned, each have a separate word, daughter's husband being *zum* or *zeem* in Pashto and *jawai* or *jamai* in Lahnda, while daughter-in-law is expressed variously in Pashto as *andror*, *ingor* or *nazir*, and as *nooh* or *nuhn* in Lahnda.

Relationships distinguished in English but not in the Provincial vernaculars.

243. So far we have been dealing with the cases in which the languages of the Province distinguish between relationships which are not distinguished in English, and in most cases it has been possible to assign a cause for the difference. It remains to consider the converse, *i.e.* relationships which are distinguished in English but not in the provincial vernaculars. Examples of these are more rare. But in Bannu a woman speaking of her husband's brother's child calls him *yer*, which also means a husband's brother's wife, or *lewar* which also means a husband's brother. In Hangu (Kohat) a woman speaking of her husband's sister's child refers to him as *andror*, which also means her husband's sister, and can mean as well her son's wife. Both these examples refer to Pashto. In the Lahnda of Hazara a first cousin, whether on the mother's or

the father's side, and whether the child of an aunt or of an uncle, is *bhra*, which also means an own brother, and a woman refers to her husband's brother's child as *jeth*, or *deor*, both of which terms also indicate her husband's brother. In all these cases the confusion is easily referable to a state of society in which women are regarded as chattels, and succession is only through agnates.

Words used in a classificatory sense.

244. Both in Pashto and in Lahnda a father is commonly addressed by his son as *baba*; another word used in Pashto is *dada*. Both terms are also used, especially by non-Pathan tribes, to address any old man, as also is the term *kaka*, used in both languages in addressing a paternal uncle. *Lala*, (Pashto and Lahnda) used when addressing an elder brother, is also applied to any one, much as the word *bhai* is used in the north of India, when a tinge of respect and civility is sought to be conveyed.

Rights and obligations of certain kin.

245 Of the rights and obligations of certain kin there is little to be said. The rights belong exclusively to males, and among males to male agnates. Obligations among Pathans are the obligations which rest on all males alike, such as the obligation to respect the person of a guest, while in his host's country, to carry on a feud, and the like. Among the non-Pathan tribes of Hazara, however, it is noted that the maternal uncle is bound to provide an ornament and clothes for a child on his birth, and to furnish part of the dowry for a niece or of the expenses of a nephew at marriage. At the death of a married woman the brothers and maternal uncles have to bear the greater part of the expense. Similarly among the Multani Pathans of the Dera Ismail Khan District it is the custom that on the birth of a first son the maternal grand parents of the child should give him a present of ornaments and clothing.

Birth customs.

246. This portion of the chapter may fitly close with some brief remarks on the subject of birth customs among the Mohammadans of the Province. The district reports contain mention of various beliefs which are current as to the possibility of predicting the sex of an unborn child. As an example of them it may be mentioned that it is generally believed that if the mother of the unborn child eats much meat, or if she is active over her household duties, she will give birth to a boy, while a lazy woman, or one who eats a purely vegetable diet, will become the mother of a girl. They do not, however, merit further mention here. Of more interest, as throwing light on the estimation in which sons and daughters respectively are held, is an account of the manner in which the news is received of the birth of a boy and of a girl. Among Pathans, when a woman's labour begins, all the men of the family are banished from the house, and take up their residence at the village *hujra* or guest house, till the period of purification (the 40th day after the child-birth) has passed. The custom is referred to in the saying quoted in Mr. Boyle's report on the birth customs of the Kohat trans-frontier, "*Ya ba dre shu, ya pa hujre shu*" *i. e.*, it is a question of staying at the *hujra* or of two becoming three. The birth of a son is notified at once to the father, who gives two or three rupees to the persons bringing news of the happy event. The relatives of both parents are then informed, and a feast is given. The birth of a daugter is regarded as a misfortune, and no unnecessary reference is made to it An account which has been furnished to me of the birth customs of the Mohammadans of Peshawar city contains in the case of some tribes a reference to a feast given on the birth of a daughter; but in such cases, where two goats are killed at that of a son, only one is slaughtered on the birth of a daughter. In view of the fact that among Mohammadans generally the possession of a daughter entails the certain prospect of receiving a solid sum in cash if she lives long enough to be married, it is curious that no satisfaction should be felt at her birth. In British territory the popular feeling on the subject would appear to be a survival from a state of society in which a family or a tribe could not survive without sons to withstand its enemies in the gate. In the unadministered portion of the Province, where tribal feuds are not generally noticed unless they lead to raids into British territory, it is no doubt still the case that the family which produces an undue proportion of daughters goes to the wall; and the birth of one is naturally no occasion for rejoicing. Nor, on reflection, when one considers the short time

which has elapsed since the British districts were in much the same, or in a still more unsettled, condition than tribal territory at present, need one be surprised that the same feeling has survived. The preference for sons, however, appears never to have gone so far as to lead to attempts to cause abortion where it is anticipated that a daughter will be born.

Seclusion of women after child birth.

247. Till the fortieth day after child-birth in theory the mother remains in her house with two or three of her near female relatives, and must only wash her hands and face. During this period she is considered impure, and is debarred from saying her prayers. In point of fact she probably in most cases goes out after eight or ten days, but it is not till forty days have elapsed that she is allowed to bathe her body, to braid her hair, and to put on clean clothes. Her husband then returns to his home, and her neighbours come and offer congratulations. A feast is also given, if the means of the parties permit of it. Among the Bangashes of Kohat it is noticed that during the period prior to purification a naked sword or dagger is placed by the woman's bed, with the object of warding off evil spirits. It is probably with some such object that in the Hangu tahsil some male relative takes a hatchet, and strikes with it a beam in the roof of the room where a woman who has given birth to a son is lying.

Name-giving.

248. Names are given to children much in the same way as in England, and the duty of selecting one is not laid on any specified relative. The near relatives on both sides are commonly consulted. Some tribes select for a boy a name which rhymes with that of his father. Thus the son of Feroz Gul will be called Nawaz Gul, Sher Jang's son will be called Mehr Jang, and the like. High sounding names famous in history are much in favour both for boys and girls. Sometimes the Mullah is consulted; there seems in fact to be no rule beyond the wishes of the parents.

Ear-piercing.

249. Ear-piercing is disliked by the Mullas, and is not commonly practised, though the ear is sometimes pierced, as it is considered lucky in the case of a child several of whose brothers and sisters have died.

Circumcision.

250. Circumcision is of course practised as among all Mohammadans. The age of the boy varies in different parts of the Province between three and ten years. Throughout the Province the circumcision of a child is made an occasion of rejoicing, and a feast is given to relatives and friends, or, at any rate, as in the case of poor people, sweetmeats are distributed.

Circumcision of women.

"There is a curious custom," wrote Sir Denzil Ibbetson in 1881: "among the Mussalman peasantry of the lower Indus, of circumcising their women by excision of the tip of the clitoris, not apparently with any idea of preserving their chastity, but as a religious rite." I am informed that at the present day the custom, though not a general one, is not unknown among the Mohammadans of Dera Ismail Khan. The operation is performed, if at all, by a *Nain* on a woman of marriageable age, generally with the object of facilitating conception. The tip of the clitoris is the part commonly cut off, but some women, writes a correspondent, "even cut the labia minora for the sake of necessity and sometimes for beauty (sic)." Religious motives do not appear to come in at all, except where the clitoris is very much prolonged and enlarged. In such cases it may be cut with the object of preventing the possibility of unnatural gratification. The custom has no special vogue among any particular tribe or clan. Infibulation is said never to occur.

PART II.—STATISTICAL.

251. The statistics of civil condition by age will be found in Table VII in Part II of this volume, while Table XIV gives those for civil condition by caste and main age periods. At the end of this chapter proportional figures are given in the following Subsidiary Tables :— Reference to statistics.

(*i*). Distribution by civil condition of 1,000 of each sex, religion and main age period at each of the last four Censuses.

(*ii*). Distribution by civil condition of 1,000 of each sex at certain age periods in each religion and natural division.

(*iii*). Distribution by main age periods and civil condition of 10,000 of each sex and religion.

(*iv*). Proportion of the sexes by civil condition at certain age periods for religions and natural divisions

(*v*). Distribution by civil condition of 1,000 of each sex at certain ages for selected castes.

252. It is hardly necessary to remark that Census statistics can not always be relied upon for absolute accuracy. For instance the age statistics are notoriously untrustworthy both in India and in Europe. The language return is vitiated in India by an entire ignorance among the uneducated of the difference between a language and a dialect, and a perfect indifference as to the name which is attached by the enumerator to the speech used in their homes. The figures for occupation, where they can be checked with departmental returns, are often found to be strikingly inaccurate But the statistics of civil condition may be accepted in the main as substantially correct. In the case of prostitutes and concubines, the instructions to supervisors, which directed that a person who has never been married must be entered as unmarried, may have been occasionally neglected, especially as the following sentence of the instructions, *viz.* that " persons who are recognised by custom as married are to be entered as such, even though they have not gone through the full ceremony ordinarily followed," leaves a loop-hole of escape ; for it may be difficult to say, in any particular case, whether a woman is recognised as married or not. But cases of doubt of this nature must have been exceedingly rare, especially seeing that among the Hindus, as among the Mohammadans of the Province, marriage is never presumed from cohabitation. If one may judge by the cases which come before the courts, in which one party commonly asserts that a marriage has taken place, while the other admits only a betrothal, it is probable that in the earlier age periods our figures for the married include a certain proportion of persons who have only been betrothed. But the degree of error arising from this cause must be small, and in the main I have no doubt that the enumerators' returns were correct. In tabulation also there was but little room for mistake. Civil condition was indicated by a symbol printed on the slips used, and after a few days the copyists were hardly ever found to make a mistake in the selection of the right slip When the time came for sorting, after the colour of the slip, the symbol printed on it was the first thing to catch the eye of the sorter, and here also errors were few and easily detected. The returns of civil condition by age are of course open to the same objections as the age returns themselves. Accuracy of the return.

253. The figures relating to marriage are best examined in comparison with those for other countries and provinces. It is obvious that in these matters we have no absolute standard. The comparative method is therefore that which will be adopted in considering the various questions which arise out of our figures. Statistics to be examined on the comparative method.

254. The first point in which our statistics are of interest is in the light they throw on the universality of marriage. I show in the margin the Universality of marriage. I.—At all ages.

proportion of persons who have been married (including the widowed) in the Province, in certain other Provinces of India, in India as a whole and in England respectively. The figures are for different years, those for England being according to the Census of 1891 and those for other Indian Provinces according to that of 1901, while the proportions for the North-West Frontier Province are calculated on the results of the present enumeration. In 20 years, however, no great change of social practice is effected, and the difference in the times at which the figures were compiled will have no appreciable effect.

Number of all ages who have been married per 1,000 of the sex concerned.

Area.	Male.	Female.
India	508	656
Berar	604	746
United Provinces	550	692
Central Provinces	533	651
Bengal	523	682
Punjab	470	625
Madras	448	610
North-West Frontier Province ...	418	546
England	380	404

(a) Among males.

255. To take first the figures for males, it will be seen that the proportion who have been married is very low in the North-West Frontier Province as compared with other parts of India. It approaches in fact very nearly to that for England, where prudential considerations restrict marriage to an extent which has no counterpart in the East. This comparative rarity of marriage is due to various causes. In the first place, as I have attempted to show in the first part of this chapter, the influence of Hinduism is practically nil. As a consequence, the belief of the Hindu that he can not ensure an advantageous rebirth, unless he has a son to perform the prescribed rites after his death, is absent; and with it a strong incentive to marriage is also lacking. A second cause is to be found in the low proportion of females which the Province contains. The subject has been discussed in the previous chapter to which the reader is referred for a statement of the facts. It is obvious that where the males considerably outnumber the females, especially in an area in which polygamy, if not widely practised, has at least some vogue, a certain percentage of men will be unable to obtain wives. The effect of these two causes will be seen more closely when we come to consider the statistics of marriage by age and religion. In considering the figures for the total population, it is obscured by that of the third reason which depresses the number of married persons, and which has undoubtedly the greatest influence of all, *viz*, the comparatively advanced age at which marriage takes place The consideration of this subject also belongs properly to the discussion of the statistics of marriage by age, but it must be referred to here.

(b) Among females.

256. In the case of females the comparatively low proportion of the married or widowed is largely due to the fact that the marriage of immature girls is almost unknown. But this does not explain it wholly, as we shall see when we examine the figures for persons aged 20 years and over. The absence of any religious obligation to get daughters married no doubt has some effect. In other parts of India, where Hindu sentiment is strong "if* a Hindu maiden is unmarried at puberty, her condition brings social obloquy on her family, and on a strict reading of certain texts entails retrospective damnation on three generations of ancestors." In the North-West Frontier Province on the other hand as far as I have been able to discover, the possession of an unmarried adult daughter is associated with the loss of no respect whatever; still less does it involve in popular imagination any more far reaching consequences. This fact, taken in conjunction with the absence of any religious inducement to males to marry, probably in part explains the comparatively high proportion of the unmarried among adult females. Other reasons are to be found in the frequency of widow re-marriage, which absorbs a certain number of husbands who would otherwise wed with virgins, and in the comparatively large degree to which the element of personal choice enters into matrimonial arrangements. In the rural areas of the Province strict *pardah* is practically unknown except among the well-to-do; and, as may be expected in a community where adult marriage is the rule, love matches are not uncommon. Lastly may be mentioned here the

* *Vide* India Census Report, 1901, paragraph 693.

faction feeling which exists in such force in those parts of the Province where Pathans predominate, and which has the effect of rendering impossible many marriages which might otherwise be concluded. In this connection it is interesting to notice (*vide* Subsidiary Table II appended to this chapter) that the proportion of unmarried females at the age periods '15 to 40' and '40 and over' is considerably higher in the Pathan area of the Province (the trans-Indus districts) than it is in Hazara, where Pathans form a small part only of the population.

Universality of marriage in different natural divisions.

257. The figures given in Subsidiary Table II at the end of this chapter show that females (*i.e.* the total female population of all ages) marry to exactly the same extent in the two natural divisions into which the districts of the Province have been divided In each the number of the unmarried females amounts to 45·4 per cent. In the case of males one per cent. more are married in the trans-Indus districts than in Hazara. The difference is no doubt due to the higher proportion of females who are to be found in the latter, where they amount to 881 per 1,000 males, as against a figure of 849 in the former, area.

Among the different religions.

258. The same table shows the varying degree to which marriage is universal among the followers of different religions. It will be convenient if I show in the margin the proportion who have been married (*i. e.*, married and widowed) among Mohammadans, Hindus and Sikhs respectively.

Number per 1,000 of all ages who have been married.

Religion.	Males.	Females.
Mohammadan	415	542
Hindu	468	605
Sikh	460	616

It will be seen that the figures for the two last vary little, while they are considerably in excess of those for Mohammadans. We are not, however, to suppose that marriage is really less common among Mohammadan males than among Hindus and Sikhs. Considering the great scarcity of females in the last mentioned communities, it would be strange if it were so. Among adults we shall find that Mohammadan males are more frequently married than Hindus or Sikhs, and the high proportion of bachelors found among the total Mohammadan population of all ages is due solely to the later age at which they marry. The variation in the age of marriage largely explains the different proportions for Mohammadans on the one hand and Hindus and Sikhs on the other in the case of females also. The peculiar circumstances of the followers of the last two religions in the North-West Frontier Province are clearly reflected in the marginal statement which shows how few are the married (or widowed) as compared with the figures for Hindus in India as a whole The difference is due partly to the later age for marriage in the Province, partly to the comparative weakness of Hindu sentiment, and in the case of males, to the low proportion of females.

Number who have been married per 1,000 of all ages.

Religion and area.	Males.	Females.
Hindus } N.-W. F. Province.	468	605
Sikhs } N.-W. F. Province.	460	616
Hindus India, 1901.	525	679

Universality of marriage. II.—For adults.

259. So far we have been discussing the proportion of married or widowed persons at all ages. Statistics based on the total population, however, are at best an imperfect guide. In order to realise the facts, we need to consider separately the figures for the different age periods. Looking at Subsidiary Table I at the end of this chapter it is at once apparent that it is not until after the age of 20 that marriage is common among males, and that a small proportion only of females under 15 have been married. I propose therefore to continue this discussion by considering the figures for adults only. By adults I mean in the case of females those who have attained or passed the age of 15, and in the case of males those aged 20 and over.

Among males aged 20 and over.

260. From Subsidiary Table I, at the close of this chapter, I extract certain figures, and place them by the side of corresponding ones for a number of Indian Provinces. The only figures for these last which are available

to me are those for the Census of 1901, and it will be best, therefore, if I compare with them those for the North-West Frontier Province in the same year (in no case do they differ from the proportions arrived at during the present Census by as much as one per cent.). The first point which strikes one is the very high proportion of bachelors which the North-West Frontier Province contains among men aged from 20 to 40. This is, no doubt, in a large degree due to the considerations mentioned in paragraph 255 above. At the same time it is also due in part to marriage being deferred, for marriage among men aged over 40 is more common in the Province than in the Punjab or the United Provinces, where the bachelors for the age period preceding it are considerably fewer than in the population with which we are concerned. Our figures show that for males who have not reached the age of 40 marriage is rarer than is commonly the case in other parts of India, but of those who survive that age a comparatively high proportion are found to have married.

Number of males unmarried per 1,000 at certain age periods (Census of 1901).

Area.	20—40.	40—60.	60 & over.
North-West Frontier Province.	311	53	30
Burma	298	88	83
Punjab	257	77	60
Madras	255	30	18
United Provinces ...	166	73	58
Bihar	102	30	24

Among females aged 15 and over.

261. The statistics for females we may examine in the same way, placing the figures for certain Indian provinces in 1901 by the side of those for the North-West Frontier Province in the same year. Except when contrasted with Burma, the Province is seen to possess a relatively high proportion of spinsters among adults. Our high figure for the age period '15 to 20' is of course largely due to the deferring of marriage till after the age of 20, but those for the remaining age periods can only be referred to the considerations I have mentioned in paragraph 256 above, when discussing the universality of marriage among the female population. At first sight one might suppose that where females are in defect, all would obtain husbands. And so they would, were there any strong social or religious grounds making marriage imperative. It is also curious to note that the high figure to which the bride price attains (*vide* paragraph 222 in the first part of this chapter), which is itself due to the scarcity of females, appears partially to defeat its own object by rendering marriage impossible, for lack of means, to a certain proportion of bachelors It looks in fact as if those who have daughters to dispose of had forced the market too high.

Number of females unmarried per 1,000 at certain age periods (Census of 1901).

Area.	15—20.	20—40.	40—60.	60 & over.
N.-W. F. Province ...	362	42	13	12
Burma	720	160	68	83
Punjab	237	21	5	5
Madras	286	28	12	9
United Provinces ...	99	23	12	10
Bihar	88	18	11	6

Marriage among adults of the different religions. (*a*) Males.

262. The figures for the different natural divisions appear to call for no remark. In the case of the different religions, however, the contrasts are too strong to be neglected. I show in the margin figures which throw light on the degree to which marriage is common among adult males of the three main religions in the Province, and among adult male Hindus and Mohammadans in India generally. It will be seen that Sikhs are considerably less married than Mohammadans in the Province, or than Hindus, or indeed Mohammadans, elsewhere. Hindus in the Province are also less married than Mohammadans after the age of 40, though before it, according to the figures of 1901, they have a lower proportion of bachelors. It is worth noticing here, however, that the proportions worked out on the figures of the

Number of bachelors per 1,000 at certain age periods for different religions (Census of 1901).

Religion and area.	20—30.	30—40.	40—60.	60 & over.
INDIA :—				
Mohammadans ...	290	77	38	29
Hindus ...	260	87	51	40
N.-W. F. Province—				
Mohammadans ...	303 (20—40)		49	27
Hindus ...	302 (20—40)		93	71
Sikhs ...	358 (20—40)		98	82

present Census show 302 Mohammadan and 330 Hindu bachelors per 1,000 aged between 20 and 40 years, and that the figures for the Censuses of 1881 and 1891 also show relatively more bachelors among Hindus of this age period than among Mohammadans. It may be assumed that a result given in common by three Censuses represents the actual state of affairs more nearly than a contrary one given by one only. The fact seems to be that the stronger inducement to marry, which Hindus and Sikhs possess, is in the North-West Frontier Province counterbalanced by the practical difficulty which stands in the way of their obtaining wives. It is curious also to notice that in our area the disproportion between the number of bachelors of the different religions is far more marked after the age of 40 than among adults before it. The figures for India in the marginal statement printed by the side of this paragraph show the same feature, *i. e.*, it is only for the age period '20 to 30' that Hindu males are more married than Mohammadan. The reason is perhaps to be found in the fact that, while with Hindus the main object of marriage is to become the father of a son, the Mohammadan in marrying is thinking of his personal comfort and is more likely to take a wife when the hope of begetting one is past. Also the disproportion of the sexes is far greater in the Province among Hindus and Sikhs than among Mohammadans. One result of this would be that while it is difficult for a Hindu or Sikh of any age to obtain a wife, one who is already elderly would find it well nigh impossible.

263. We must next consider how far marriage is common among adult females of the different religions, (*vide* marginal statement.) To look first at the figures for the Province only, the late age at which Mohammadan females marry is at once apparent. Of those between the ages of 15 and 20 over one-third are still unmarried, whereas in the case of Hindus the figure is less than one-sixth, and in that of Sikhs only one-fifteenth. Above the age of 20 also we find a considerably larger proportion of spinsters among Mohammadans than among the followers of the other two religions. This is a natural result of the greater scarcity of women among the latter. When we compare the figures for the Hindus of the Province with those of Hindus elsewhere in India, we see a similar cause producing a similar result for the age periods from 20 upwards. For the age period '15 to 20,' however, the influence of their Mohammadan environment is apparent in the higher proportion of spinsters in the North-West Frontier Province. Sikh females are even scarcer than Hindu, and the proportion unmarried is accordingly extremely small at all the age periods we are now considering. In the case of Mohammadans the late age at which marriage takes place is shown clearly by our figures. At the age period '15 to 20,' spinsters in the Province are proportionately more than twice as numerous as they are in India generally. The reason of the high proportion found at the succeeding age periods has already been discussed (*vide* paragraph 256 above). (*b*) Females.

Number of spinsters per 1,000 at certain age periods for different religions (Census of 1901).

Area and religion.	15—20.	20—30.	30—40.	40—60.	60 & over.
India :—					
Mohammadans...	161	33	17	12	10
Hindus ...	141	32	20	11	8
N.-W. F. P. :—					
Mohammadans...	379	43 (20—40)		14	13
Hindus ...	151	12 (20—40)		6	6
Sikhs ...	66	6 (20—40)		1	...

264. We have seen that, taking the population as a whole, it is not till after the age of 20 in the case of males, and after that of 15 in the case of females, that any high proportion is found to have been married. It remains to consider the figures for the population that has not reached those ages. It can be asserted at the outset that child marriage in its extremest form does not exist in the Province. No male under the age of 5 years has been recorded as married, and only 3 females (Mohammadans in Hazara). The latter figure is too small to be anything but accidental. For the next quinquennium the numbers who are other than unmarried are trifling, amounting to only two per mille in the case of males and 6 per mille in the case of females. As is to be Age of marriage. Child marriage.

expected, the numbers are higher among Hindus and Sikhs than among Mohammadans. Of 1,000 males of that religion aged from 5 to 10 years only 2 Mohammadans have been married, whereas 4 Hindus and 4 Sikhs are husbands or widowers. The figures illustrate the extent to which Hindus in the Province have been influenced by their environment, for in the total Hindu population of India at the last Census no less than 48 per mille of males of that age period had been married. Among females aged 5 to 10 the number who have been married is slightly larger, but it is still inconsiderable, being only ·5 per cent. in the case of Mohammadans, 1·1 per cent. in the case of Hindus and 1·4 per cent. in the case of Sikhs. The corresponding figures for India as a whole in 1901 were 7·3 per cent. in the case of Mohammadans and 12·8 per cent. in the case of Hindus.

These figures, which show the rarity of marriage either among male or female children of less than 10 years of age, exemplify also the freedom from Hindu influence which is to be found among the Mohammadans of the Province. Their practice in this respect affords an interesting commentary on the theory that infant marriage is most common where the difficulty of obtaining a husband is small, and the marriage ceremony inexpensive. We have here a community in which child marriage is unknown, while the marriage ceremony is so far from being expensive that the disposal of a daughter means the receipt of a solid sum in cash by her father. Infant marriage in India has been attributed in part to the influence of the climate which hastens the advent of puberty ; and it is no doubt partly as a result of climatic conditions that in the North-West Frontier Province it is virtually unknown. It is not only that the cold of winter is here intense and prolonged in comparison with those tracts where child marriage is common. A large proportion (see the figures for Pathans in Table XIII) of the population consists of settlers who, at various periods within the last three hundred years, have moved their habitations to their present homes. Even in the British districts puberty is no doubt reached later than, for example, in the torrid delta of the Ganges ; in the cold uplands which formed the Pathans' earlier homes this must undoubtedly have been the case, and the period which has elapsed since their migration has not been long enough to have witnessed any striking change in physiological conditions. On the other hand Kirchoff's theory that the age of marriage depends largely on the esteem in which marriage is held, and that this is bound to be low in a country where a man marries in order to gratify his animal desires and to obtain a household drudge, is not supported by the social customs of the Province. In an area where women are brought and sold, their position can not be said to be high ; but on the other hand the age of marriage is comparatively advanced.

Marriage during adolescence.

265. The figures for the remaining age periods, *viz.* '10 to 15' in the case of females, and '10 to 20' in the case of males, can be discussed summarily. At the age period '10 to 15,' as is to be expected, the proportion who have been married is higher in the case of females of all the three main religions than in the case of males ; and, as would be inferred from the preceding discussion, marriage is rarer in the North-West Frontier Province than among the bulk of the Indian population. Out of the total population of India aged '10 to 15' in 1901 86 per cent. of the males and only 55·9 per cent. of the females were unmarried. In the population we are dealing with of the same age period as many as 97·3 per cent. of the males and 88·3 of the females are unmarried. The married or widowed of this age are naturally more numerous among Hindus and Sikhs than among Mohammadans, but the variation is not very striking, and it is interesting to notice (*vide* marginal statement) how much less the Hindus of the Province marry their daughters at this age than Hindus elsewhere in India. Similarly for males of all religions aged '15 to 20' only 650 per mille in the total Indian population are unmarried, whereas the corresponding figure for the Province is 848.

Hindu females aged 10—15.

Area.	Number per 1,000 who are unmarried.
India, 1901 ...	511
N.-W. F. P., 1911 ...	809

Widow re-marriage.

266. The bride price appears to be due to the fact that, if the Census statistics from 1855 onwards are any guide, there is a marked deficiency of females in the population. A man naturally has to pay for what nature does not provide in sufficient abundance for all. Moreover in the circumstances he is not likely to limit the number of possible wives by forbidding widows to marry again. At any rate among the Mohammadans of the North-West Frontier Province no such prohibition is known; and where a widow is young and passably good looking the chances are in favour of her re-marriage. In the first place marriage is not regarded, as Hindus regard it, as an indissoluble tie, and divorce is common. In the second place, since a wife can only be obtained at a considerable cost, the family into whose possession she passed at marriage is naturally ready, should she be left a widow, to save further expenditure by handing her over to one of its unmarried males, or to recoup some or the whole of her initial cost by disposing of her hand to an outsider. It should be noticed that the bride price is paid for widows, as for virgins, the only difference being that it is generally higher in the case of the latter, and that in the case of the former it is recovered by the relatives of her deceased husband, and not by her father. The situation will be clearest if the taking of a wife is compared to the purchase of livestock. In the event of any further transaction in respect of the same woman, the price is naturally paid to the present owner (the relatives of her deceased husband), and not to the original one (her father).

Proportion of widows to total female population.

267. In the Province out of females of all ages, only 1 in 9 is widowed, whereas in the total female population of India, widows amount to 1 in 6. Our low proportion of widows is in part to be explained by the considerations referred to in the previous paragraph. But there are others. The number of widows is reduced by the number of those who marry a second time. It is also reduced if a small proportion of husbands die during the life-time of their wives. It is obvious that the earlier the age at which girls are married the more likely are they (unless, which is not the case in India, the marriage of child brides with adult husbands should be forbidden) to be left widows; and the more nearly the ages of husband and wife approximate to one another, the lower the proportion of widows is likely to be. In the comparatively advanced age at which girls in the Province are married, and the comparative identity of age between husbands and wives, we have a further reason for the low proportion of widows to be found in it. To say that it is also due to the greater universality of marriage in India as a whole is in some degree to repeat in different words an assertion already made; for the universality of marriage largely depends on the age at which it is undertaken. We have seen, however, that marriage is really less common in the Province than in India generally, even among the adult population, and to this cause partly may be attributed the small proportion of wives who have survived their husbands without marrying again. It is to be noticed that the proportion is relatively small at each of the age periods shown in Subsidiary Table I appended to this chapter.

Proportion of widows in population of different religions.

(a) Mohammadans.

(b) Hindus.

268. The proportion of widows is naturally smallest among the Mohammadan element of the population, where it amounts to 109 per 1,000 females. In England, where marriage is less common, and where the disparity of age between husband and wife is less, it is 75 per 1,000. Among the Hindus of the Province the proportion is higher, being 163 per 1,000. Even this figure is low when compared with that for Hindus elsewhere. The corresponding one for the Hindu female population of India as a whole in 1901 was 194. The difference is partly due to the fact that, even among Hindus, child marriage is almost unknown in our area. It is also due to their greater tolerance of widow re-marriage, which, though regarded with disfavour, is not prohibited by all castes*. The hill Brahmans of Hazara in particular have no objection to the practice, but hold that the marriage should be, if possible, with the deceased husband's younger brother. The Hindus of Swat hold the same view. The statistics of civil condition by caste which are given in Subsidiary

* At the marriage of a widow the ceremony is called *chadar andazi*, when, as described in Dera Ismail Khan, it consists in putting on the woman a white cloth dipped in *kesar*.

Even among the castes such as the Aroras and Khatris, the orthodox members of which will not give a widowed daughter in marriage a second time, there appears to be no objection, if a male marries a widow from an Arya Samaj family. I have heard of several such marriages.

Table V appended to this chapter have been prepared for the Province as a whole, and do not therefore clearly reflect the custom of the Brahmans of any particularly district. It is interesting, however, to notice that among them the proportion of widows is lower than among Khatris or Aroras, who comprise the other two most numerous Hindu castes of the Province.

(c) Sikhs.

269. The proportion of widows among Sikhs naturally approaches more nearly to that for Hindus than to that for the followers of the Prophet. The figure is, however, lower than among Hindus, chiefly as a result of the fact that Sikhs are mainly temporary immigrants to the Province; and of the women who are included among them, a small proportion only would be likely to be widowed.

Proportion of widowed in different religions at different age periods.

270. It is naturally at the earlier age periods that the proportion of the widowed varies most between the different religions, for it is during early life that the variation in the proportion of the married is greatest. Thus (*vide* Subsidiary Table II appended to this chapter) at the age period '5 to 10' Hindu widows are proportionately more than double, and Sikh widows nearly three times as numerous as, Mussalman. At the age period '10 to 15' the figure for Hindus and for Mohammadans is the same, though that for Sikhs is much higher, the proportion of the married also among Sikhs of that age period being correspondingly high. For the prime of life (15 to 40) also there is a great difference between the different religions, Hindu widows being twice as numerous proportionately as Mohammadan ones, while Sikh widows are little less numerous than Hindus. At the age period '40 and over' on the other hand the proportion of Mussalman widows amounts to more than two-thirds of that of Hindus, and nearly four-fifths that of Sikhs. The greater equality of the proportions in old and later middle age is no doubt due to the fact that at this period widows of whatever religion are seldom re-married, their continued widowhood being due, not to religious considerations, which vary in different areas, but to such as are in force the world over.

The remarriage of widowers.

271. The statement in the margin compares the proportion of widowers of the three main religions in the Province with those for Hindus and Mohammadans in India in 1901, and that for the male population of England in 1891. Looking first at the figures for the Province only, the comparatively low figure for Mohammadans is due, partly to the greater equality in the numbers of the two sexes of that religion, and partly to the fact that the followers of the Prophet do not, like Hindus, regard marriage as an indissoluble bond. The former reason appears to be required to explain a variation which, as the statement shows, is larger than that found between Mohammadans and Hindus in India generally. Similarly the high proportion of widowers among the Hindus of the Province, as compared with the total Hindu population of India, is to be explained by the difference in the sex distribution of the two groups; for the former have no stronger objection than the latter to the re-marriage of widowers, and the only other possible explanation, *viz.*, that female life is more insecure in the Province than elsewhere, is not borne out by the facts The small proportion of widowers to be found in England is due no doubt to the comparative rarity of marriage and the greater equality of age between husbands and wives In both these respects the conditions of the Province approach more nearly than do those of India generally to those of England, and the fact that in all religions the proportion of widowers is high appears to be wholly a matter of the distribution of the population by sex.

Religion and area.	Number of widowers per 1,000 males of all ages.
N.-W. F. PROVINCE—	
Mohammadan ...	45
Hindu ...	69
Sikh ...	67
INDIA, 1901—	
Mohammadan ...	42
Hindu ...	59
ENGLAND, 1891—	35

Polygamy.

272. Four wives are permitted to Mohammadans by the *Shariat*, though some of the tribes of the Province consider it lawful to have as many as seven. But in point of fact the bulk of the population are monogamous. Subsidiary Table IV printed at the end of this chapter gives some slight indication of the

prevalence of polygamy among the followers of the different religions. There are in the districts of the Province 103 Mohammadan wives to 100 husbands of all ages, as against only 74 Hindu and 62 Sikh wives per 100 husbands. The inference which the figures suggest, *viz.*, that polygamy is more prevalent among Mohammadans than among the other elements of the population is of course correct; for there are in the Province few, if any, Hindus or Sikhs who possess more than one wife. Beyond this the figures are little guide. We can not infer, for instance, as the figures taken by themselves suggest, that polyandry is largely practised by Sikhs. The reason for the low proportion of wives to husbands among Hindus and Sikhs is to be found in the fact that a large proportion of the followers of these religions are temporary immigrants, troops and the like, who are seldom accompanied by their wives. The figures for Mohammadans also are largely influenced by immigration. Temporary migrants (and a reference to Chapter III will show that the bulk of the migration to and from the Province is periodic or temporary in type) always contain a large excess of males, many of whom are naturally married; and while therefore an excess of emigrants tends to increase the proportion of wives to husbands in any given area, an excess of immigrants tends to decrease it. The working of these influences is seen when we look at the figures for the natural divisions taken separately. In Hazara, where emigration is in excess of immigration, there are 1,064 Mohammadan wives to every 1,000 Mohammadan husbands; whereas in the trans-Indus districts, where the reverse is the case, the wives among Mohammadans only exceed the husbands by 17 per 1,000. It must be remembered that the excess of males over females is larger among immigrants to Hazara than it is among immigrants to the trans-Indus districts of the Province, and the excess of immigrants over emigrants does not therefore decrease the proportion of wives to husbands in the trans-Indus districts so much as the excess of emigrants increases it in Hazara. The influence exerted on the statistics by migration prevents us from saying with accuracy what is the normal proportion of wives to husbands among Mohammadans, but the figure given in Subsidiary *Table IV*, according to which in the districts of the Province as whole wives exceed husbands by 3 in every hundred, is probably not far from the mark. Remembering, however, that a certain number of husbands have more than two wives, the proportion of husbands who possess more than one is not likely to be more than two per cent.

Variations at different Censuses in distribution of the population by civil condition.

(a) All religions.

273. Subsidiary Table I at the end of this chapter shows variations in the proportion of the unmarried, married and widowed by sex, age and religion at each of the last four Censuses. Except at the age period '10 to 15' the proportion of unmarried males of all religions has increased slightly in the last ten years. It increased also in the period 1891*—1901 except in the age period '60 and over,' in which there was a decrease of 1 per mille. The proportions for the year 1881 are nearer to those elicited by the present Census. On comparing the figures for 1881 with those for 1911 it will be seen that, while the proportion of bachelors aged under 20 years has increased, that of bachelors aged 20 and over has slightly fallen. It is doubtful how far 30 years is a long enough period to mark any change of social practice; but the figures suggest that, while increasing prosperity has made marriage more universal among adult males, public opinion tends to discourage it in the case of males who have not reached the age of 20. Among females, the unmarried at every age period are proportionately more numerous now than they were 30 years ago. Among females, as among males, the proportion unmarried was smaller in 1891 than it was ten years before, the change presumably marking the recovery from the period of scarcity, which in Kashmir took the form of severe famine, in 1878—1880; but, except at the age period '15 to 20' it has steadily increased since 1891. The increase since 1881 in the proportion of spinsters is probably due to the rise in the ratio borne by the female to the male population. The variations in the proportion of the married at the last four Censuses are small, and need not be remarked on. The proportionate number of widowers is much the same now as it was in 1901 and 1881, but is much lower than it was in 1891,

* It should be noticed that in 1891 the age statistics were prepared according to a method different from that of the other years (*vide* Chapter V, paragraph 179).

while that of widows has decreased steadily at each Census since 1881, except that it increased largely between the years 1881 and 1891. At each age period it is now, however, considerably lower than it was 30 years ago.

(b) For Hindus and Sikhs.

274. The variations in the case of Mohammadans need not be remarked on separately. Owing to their numbers they naturally govern the distribution of the total population of the Province. Among Hindu males the proportion unmarried at every age period has increased in the last 10 years; from the age of 20 onwards it is, however, lower now than it was in 1881. Widowed males have similarly increased proportionately since 1901, and also when compared with the figures of 1881. The proportion married is naturally therefore smaller now than in 1901 or in 1881. In the case of Hindu females the proportion married has decreased in the last ten years at every age period except the last shown in Subsidiary Table I, appended to this chapter, and widows are also proportionately less numerous than in 1901. The consequent rise in the proportion of unmarried females at each age period I find difficult to understand. Even more striking is the rise in the proportion of Sikh females who are unmarried. The variations can, I believe, only be explained if we regard them as accidental, and due to the smallness of the numbers with which we are concerned. It must be remembered that the Hindu females enumerated in the Province amount to under 50,000, and the Sikh to something over 10,000, souls only; and that the proportion of females to males is low, amounting to 680 per 1,000 in the case of the former, and 579 per 1,000 in the case of the latter. In this connection it is perhaps worth remarking that the rise in the proportion of the unmarried has coincided with a rise in the ratio borne to males by females, and that the rise in both respects is particularly marked in the case of Sikhs. In the marginal statement I show the sex distribution of Hindus and Sikhs at each Census from 1881 onwards. With reference to the variation shown in the case of the Hindus it must remembered that the figures for the Censuses previous to 1901 are calculated on the populations of the old districts of Bannu and Dera Ismail Khan, which included a large area cis-Indus, with a comparatively large Hindu population in which the proportions of the sexes were far more equal (as they are in the present Bannu and Dera Ismail Khan Districts) than is the case in the three northern districts of the Province. Considering therefore the small size and the migratory nature of the population of these two religions, and the fact that there has been so great a change in the area in which they were enumerated at different times, I believe nothing can be gained by subjecting the figures to further scrutiny.

Number of females per 1,000 males.

Year.	Religion.	
	Hindu.	Sikh.
1881 ...	669	284
1891 ...	723	345
1901 ...	640	343
1911 ...	680	519

Subsidiary Table I.—(For Province including Agencies).

Distribution by civil condition of 1,000 of each sex, religion, and main age period at each of the last four Censuses.

Religion, sex and age.	Unmarried.				Married.				Widowed.			
	1911	1901	1891	1881	1911	1901	1891	1881	1911	1901	1891	1881
1	2	3	4	5	6	7	8	9	10	11	12	13
All Religions (Males).												
0 and under 5 ...	1,000	1,000	999	999	...	...	1	1	...	...	...	...
5 " 10 ...	998	998	996		2	2	4		...	...	...	
10 " 15 ...	973	978	958	967	26	21	40	32	1	1	2	1
15 " 20 ...	848	843	737	805	146	150	251	188	6	7	12	7
20 " 40 ...	315	311	234	319	640	647	712	642	45	42	54	39
40 " 60 ...	59	53	44	66	827	833	800	817	114	114	156	117
60 and over ...	34	30	31	41	701	694	648	699	265	276	321	260
All Religions (Females).												
0 and under 5 ...	1,000	999	999	996	...	1	1	4	...	...	...	...
5 " 10 ...	994	994	989		6	6	11		...	...	...	
10 " 15 ...	883	881	778	816	114	116	218	180	3	3	4	4
15 " 20 ...	352	362	201	296	635	625	776	686	13	13	23	18
20 " 40 ...	50	42	24	36	878	884	858	877	72	74	118	87
40 " 60 ...	27	13	10	12	624	614	492	599	349	373	498	389
60 and over ...	16	12	11	9	261	244	207	254	723	744	782	737
Mohammadan (Males).												
0 and under 5 ...	1,000	1,000	1,000	999	...	...	...	1	...	...	...	...
5 " 10 ...	998	998	997		2	2	3		...	...	...	
10 " 15 ...	974	979	962	968	25	19	36	31	1	2	2	1
15 " 20 ...	855	854	745	813	139	139	243	181	6	7	12	6
20 " 40 ...	302	303	219	306	655	656	727	655	43	41	54	39
40 " 60 ...	55	49	38	60	835	841	810	827	110	110	152	113
60 and over ...	31	27	26	36	710	703	660	709	259	270	314	255
Mohammadan (Females).												
0 and under 5 ...	1,000	999	999	996	...	1	1	4	...	...	...	...
5 " 10 ...	995	995	989		5	5	11		...	...	...	
10 " 15 ...	888	891	790	822	109	106	206	174	3	3	4	4
15 " 20 ...	365	379	210	305	623	609	768	678	12	12	22	17
20 " 40 ...	51	43	25	38	881	887	861	879	68	70	114	83
40 " 60 ...	28	14	10	13	634	623	501	609	338	363	489	378
60 and over ...	17	13	12	10	266	249	214	260	717	738	774	730

SUBSIDIARY TABLE I—*contd.*—(For Province including Agencies).

Distribution by civil condition of 1,000 *of each sex, religion, and main age period at each of the last four Censuses.*

Religion, sex and age.	Unmarried.				Married.				Widowed.			
	1911	1901	1891	1881	1911	1901	1891	1881	1911	1901	1891	1881
1	2	3	4	5	6	7	8	9	10	11	12	13
Hindus (Males).												
0 and under 5 ...	1,000	999	998	998	...	1	2	2	...	...	...	...
5 „ 10 ...	996	996	992		4	4	7		...	...	1	
10 „ 15 ...	964	953	918	946	33	46	79	52	3	1	3	2
15 „ 20 ...	779	748	654	746	210	242	329	243	11	10	17	11
20 „ 40 ...	330	302	263	340	606	643	673	607	64	55	64	53
40 „ 60 ...	104	93	97	115	716	744	697	726	180	163	206	159
60 and over ...	82	71	95	102	563	559	501	579	355	370	404	319
Hindus (Females).												
0 and under 5 ...	1,000	998	997	993	...	2	3	7	...	...	...	...
5 „ 10 ...	988	985	976		11	14	22		1	1	2	
10 „ 15 ...	809	728	629	734	188	266	361	259	3	6	10	7
15 „ 20 ...	170	151	86	182	806	822	873	789	24	27	41	29
20 „ 40 ...	24	12	9	15	847	864	810	842	129	124	181	143
40 „ 60 ...	11	6	4	6	451	464	382	477	538	530	614	517
60 and over ...	8	6	4	5	166	163	118	171	826	831	878	824
Sikhs (Males).												
0 and under 5 ...	1,000	1,000	1,000	994	...	...	...	6	...	...	...	...
5 „ 10 ...	996	995	990		3	4	8		1	1	2	
10 „ 15 ...	967	931	918	926	32	68	79	74	1	1	3	...
15 „ 20 ...	792	734	671	620	194	257	317	368	14	9	12	12
20 „ 40 ...	405	358	340	426	531	607	620	528	64	35	40	46
40 „ 60 ...	95	98	87	130	756	764	738	752	149	138	175	118
60 and over ...	78	82	63	89	524	609	534	586	398	309	403	325
Sikhs (Females).												
0 and under 5 ...	1,000	998	995	993	...	2	5	7	...	...	...	...
5 „ 10 ...	986	982	956		14	17	41		...	1	3	
10 „ 15 ...	764	626	404	729	228	366	575	265	8	8	21	6
15 „ 20 ...	177	66	33	112	796	905	915	832	27	29	52	56
20 „ 40 ...	22	6	4	23	866	879	847	869	112	115	149	108
40 „ 60 ...	9	1	1	3	528	512	436	562	463	487	563	435
60 and over ...	26	...	...	...	170	183	180	178	804	817	820	822

SUBSIDIARY TABLE II.—*Distribution by Civil Condition of* 1,000 *each sex at certain ages in each religion and natural division.*

Religion and Natural Division.	Males.																	
	All ages.			0—5.			5—10.			10—15.			15—40.			40 and over.		
	Unmarried.	Married.	Widowed.	Unmarried.	Married.	Widowed.	Unmarried.	Married.	Widowed.	Unmarried.	Married.	Widowed.	Unmarried.	Married.	Widowed.	Unmarried.	Married.	Widowed.
1	2	3	4	5	6	7	8	9	10	11	12	13	14	15	16	17	18	19
N. W. F. P. (Total Districts).																		
All religions ...	582	371	47	1,000	...	...	998	2	...	973	26	1	423	540	37	52	793	155
Hindu ...	532	399	69	1,000	...	...	996	4	...	965	32	3	417	529	54	99	681	220
Mohammadan ...	585	370	45	1,000	...	...	998	2	...	974	25	1	417	548	35	48	801	151
Sikh ...	540	393	67	1,000	...	...	996	3	1	967	32	1	469	476	55	90	699	211
Christian ...	856	135	9	1,000	...	...	1,000	...	...	943	57	...	893	102	5	175	751	74
Hazara.																		
All religions ...	575	377	48	1,000	...	...	996	4	...	957	43	...	401	562	37	38	799	163
Hindu ...	568	370	62	1,000	...	...	999	1	...	975	24	1	501	462	37	110	661	229
Mohammadan ...	575	378	47	1,000	...	...	996	4	...	956	44	...	393	570	37	35	806	159
Sikh ...	560	370	70	1,000	...	...	993	7	...	972	28	...	447	495	58	62	718	220
Christian ...	600	400	...	1,000	...	...	...	...	...	...	...	...	671	329	...	200	800	...
Trans-Indus Districts.																		
All religions ...	585	369	46	1,000	...	...	998	2	...	981	19	...	431	532	37	57	790	153
Hindu ...	522	406	72	1,000	...	...	995	5	...	963	34	3	393	548	59	96	685	219
Mohammadan ...	589	367	44	1,000	...	...	999	1	...	982	17	1	425	540	35	53	799	148
Sikh ...	537	397	66	1,000	...	...	997	2	1	966	33	1	472	473	55	97	695	208
Christian ...	862	129	9	1,000	...	...	1,000	...	...	943	57	...	898	97	5	172	748	80

SUBSIDIARY TABLE II—*contd.—Distribution by civil condition of* 1,000 *of each sex at certain ages in each religion and natural division.*

Religion and Natural Division	Females.																	
	All ages.			0—5.			5—10.			10—15.			15—40.			40 and over.		
	Unmarried.	Married.	Widowed.	Unmarried.	Married.	Widowed.	Unmarried.	Married.	Widowed.	Unmarried.	Married.	Widowed.	Unmarried.	Married.	Widowed.	Unmarried.	Married.	Widowed.
1	2	3	4	5	6	7	8	9	10	11	12	13	14	15	16	17	18	19
N.-W. F. P. (Total Districts).																		
All religions ...	454	434	112	1,000	...	...	994	6	...	883	114	3	107	833	60	24	531	445
Hindu ...	395	442	163	1,000	...	..	989	11	...	809	188	3	54	838	108	11	382	607
Mohammadan ...	458	433	109	1,000	...	...	995	5	...	888	109	3	110	832	58	25	539	436
Sikh ...	384	467	149	1,000	...	...	986	14	...	763	229	8	54	851	95	14	423	563
Christian ...	464	490	46	1,000	...	..	1,000	...	...	982	18	...	230	747	23	133	594	273
Hazara.																		
All religions ...	454	449	97	1,000	...	...	991	9	...	869	128	3	88	860	52	13	567	420
Hindu ...	370	468	162	1,000	...	...	979	21	...	777	220	3	33	865	102	5	384	611
Mohammadan ...	458	448	94	1,000	...	...	991	9	...	873	124	3	91	860	49	14	574	412
Sikh ...	400	482	118	1,000	...	...	984	16	...	777	208	15	44	889	67	22	511	467
Christian ...	397	483	120	1,000	...	...	1,000	...	...	1,000	...	...	297	649	54	182	364	454
Trans-Indus Districts.																		
All religions ...	454	429	117	1,000	...	...	996	4	...	889	108	3	114	822	64	28	519	453
Hindu ...	401	436	163	1,000	...	...	990	9	1	817	180	3	59	832	109	12	382	606
Mohammadan ...	458	428	114	1,000	...	...	996	4	...	894	103	3	117	822	61	29	527	444
Sikh ...	380	463	157	1,000	...	...	987	13	...	758	237	5	56	842	102	12	400	588
Christian ...	467	491	42	1,000	...	..	1,000	...	...	982	18	...	225	754	21	129	614	257

SUBSIDIARY TABLE III.—(British Districts only).

Distribution by main age periods and civil condition of 10,000 of each sex and religion.

Religion or sex.	Number per 10,000 of sex concerned.											
	0—10.			10—15.			15—40.			40 and over.		
	Unmarried	Married.	Widowed.	Unmarried.	Married.	Widowed.	Unmarried.	Married.	Widowed.	Unmarried.	Married.	Widowed.
1	2	3	4	5	6	7	8	9	10	11	12	13
All Religions.												
Males ...	2,980	3	...	1,149	30	1	1,585	2,024	138	108	1,656	326
Females ...	3,225	9	...	861	112	2	406	3,169	232	48	1,053	883
Mohammadans.												
Males ...	3,074	3	...	1,172	30	1	1,503	1,977	127	101	1,692	320
Females ...	3,248	9	...	864	106	3	416	3,148	219	49	1,072	866
Hindus.												
Males ...	2,087	4	...	967	32	3	2,070	2,630	268	192	1,319	428
Females ...	2,877	15	1	830	193	3	222	3,473	447	21	741	1,177
Sikhs.												
Males ...	1,706	3	...	862	28	1	2,686	2,731	316	150	1,166	351
Females ...	2,829	19	...	759	228	8	227	3,607	403	27	812	1,081

SUBSIDIARY TABLE IV.—*Proportion of the sexes by civil condition at certain ages for religions and natural divisions.*

Natural division and religion.	Number of females per 1,000 males.														
	All ages.			0—10			10—15			15—40			40 and over.		
	Unmarried.	Married.	Widowed.	Unmarried.	Married.	Widowed.	Unmarried.	Married.	Widowed.	Unmarried.	Married.	Widowed.	Unmarried.	Married.	Widowed.
1	2	3	4	5	6	7	8	9	10	11	12	13	14	15	16
N.-W. F. P. (Total Districts).															
All religions	669	1,004	2,063	929	2,334	9,333	643	3,154	2,644	220	1,345	1,437	381	546	2,327
Mohammadans ...	688	1,030	2,137	929	2,310	11,500	649	3,076	2,988	243	1,401	1,516	427	557	2,382
Hindus	505	754	1,586	937	2,419	...	584	4,034	889	73	898	1,135	73	382	1,871
Sikhs	369	618	1,160	862	3,333	...	458	4,232	4,000	44	686	662	93	362	1,601
Christians ...	117	185	1,102	904		...	1,100	333	...	36	1,030	625	322	335	1,560
Hazara.															
All religions	697	1,050	1,771	951	2,299	...	667	2,179	5,176	209	1,460	1,332	265	522	1,932
Mohammadans ..	713	1,064	1,789	953	2,190	..	673	2,079	5,062	229	1,496	1,340	296	538	1,949
Hindus	416	810	1,662	911	13,000	...	563	6,485	3,000	34	965	1,418	33	386	1,773
Sikhs	460	838	1,091	827	1,667	...	490	4,583	...	56	1,025	667	220	442	1,317
Christians	319	583	...	900		...	...	...	...	193	857	...	400	200	...
Trans-Indus Districts.															
All religions	659	987	2,177	921	2,365	9,333	634	4,090	2,149	223	1,302	1,474	411	552	2,489
Mohammadans ...	679	1,017	2,283	920	2,432	11,500	639	4,154	2,500	248	1,365	1,584	461	565	2.568
Hindus	531	741	1.569	943	1,690	...	589	3,628	765	87	882	1.084	85	381	1,897
Sikhs	350	576	1,174	871	5,000	...	448	4,136	2,000	42	633	662	73	342	1,674
Christians	114	799	959	904	...	...	1.080	333	...	34	1,040	542	315	346	1,360

SUBSIDIARY TABLE V.—(For North-West Frontier Province including Agencies).

Distribution by civil condition of 1,000 of each sex at certain ages for selected castes.

Caste.	Distribution of 1,000 males of each age by civil condition.																	
	All ages.			0—5			5—12			12—20			20—40			40 and over.		
	Unmarried.	Married.	Widowed.	Unmarried.	Married.	Widowed.	Unmarried.	Married.	Widowed.	Unmarried.	Married.	Widowed.	Unmarried.	Married.	Widowed.	Unmarried.	Married.	Widowed.
1	2	3	4	5	6	7	8	9	10	11	12	13	14	15	16	17	18	19
Arora ...	551	369	80	1,000	...	...	997	3	...	874	119	7	282	653	65	80	697	223
Awan ...	586	368	46	1,000	...	...	995	5	...	912	86	2	307	644	49	40	808	152
Baghban ...	570	371	59	1,000	...	...	1,000	...	...	902	95	3	289	665	46	30	765	205
Baluch ...	548	405	47	1,000	...	...	999	1	...	871	126	3	246	714	40	30	805	165
Bhatiara ...	572	369	59	1,000	...	...	998	2	...	865	117	18	285	644	71	69	770	161
Brahman ...	549	373	78	1,000	...	...	998	2	...	888	102	10	336	596	68	105	655	240
Chamar ...	554	378	68	1,000	...	...	1,000	...	...	859	137	4	244	674	82	46	750	204
Chuhra ...	477	438	85	1,000	...	...	991	9	...	808	177	15	283	629	88	59	717	224
Dhobi ...	532	407	61	1,000	...	...	996	4	...	867	127	6	256	677	67	54	779	167
Dhund ...	584	381	35	1,000	...	...	995	5	...	886	112	2	233	737	30	28	837	135
Gakkhar ...	538	410	52	1,000	...	...	997	3	...	928	65	7	239	712	49	58	775	167
Gujar ...	583	373	44	1,000	...	...	995	5	...	911	87	2	313	645	42	40	817	143
Jat ...	557	395	48	1,000	...	...	997	3	...	858	137	5	318	631	51	46	789	165
Jhinwar ...	458	453	89	1,000	...	...	1,000	...	...	831	163	6	291	615	94	73	713	214
Jolaha ...	553	383	64	1,000	...	...	998	2	...	907	90	3	269	672	59	58	750	192
Karal ...	592	377	31	1,000	...	...	996	4	...	905	93	2	221	754	25	20	857	123
Kashmiri ...	540	402	58	1,000	...	...	998	2	...	930	65	5	260	679	61	42	795	163
Khatri ...	525	398	77	1,000	...	...	996	4	...	858	137	5	336	589	75	121	662	217
Kumhar ...	569	374	57	1,000	...	...	997	3	...	873	123	4	253	683	64	47	771	182
Lohar ...	585	366	49	1,000	...	...	996	4	...	876	120	4	289	659	52	37	799	164
Machhi ...	583	356	61	1,000	...	...	1,000	...	...	909	86	5	288	659	53	102	691	207
Maliar ...	548	389	63	1,000	...	...	997	3	...	924	71	5	267	667	66	50	770	180
Mallah ...	544	388	68	1,000	...	...	1,000	...	...	966	17	17	245	726	29	9	749	242
Mirasi ...	555	373	72	1,000	...	...	997	3	...	878	112	10	298	620	82	66	737	197
Mochi ...	556	384	60	1,000	...	...	996	4	...	852	138	10	242	703	55	35	758	207
Moghal ...	544	401	55	1,000	...	...	998	2	...	897	100	3	276	671	53	75	764	161
Musalli (with Kutana).	567	371	62	1,000	...	...	998	2	...	877	115	8	319	611	70	65	758	177
Nai ...	543	392	65	1,000	...	...	996	4	...	866	129	5	217	686	97	49	785	166
Paracha ...	573	368	59	1,000	...	...	998	2	...	894	105	1	291	645	64	46	777	177
Pathan ...	604	360	36	1,000	...	...	997	3	...	942	55	3	329	640	31	55	811	134
Qassab ...	583	368	49	1,000	...	...	988	12	...	884	112	4	267	673	60	58	788	154
Qureshi ...	566	381	53	1,000	...	...	992	8	...	902	96	2	276	673	51	61	771	168
Rajput ...	504	447	49	1,000	...	...	981	19	...	796	199	5	369	590	41	91	729	180
Saiad ...	572	383	45	1,000	...	...	997	3	...	908	90	2	277	683	40	44	803	153
Sarara ...	652	314	34	1,000	...	...	993	7	...	873	122	5	354	618	28	34	770	196
Shekh ...	515	414	71	1,000	...	...	994	6	...	874	121	5	292	639	69	53	741	206
Sonar ...	574	365	61	1,000	...	...	996	4	...	886	98	16	261	674	65	72	741	187
Swathi ...	591	372	37	1,000	...	...	998	2	...	941	56	3	271	694	35	37	840	123
Tanaoli ...	573	383	44	1,000	...	...	999	1	...	910	88	2	260	699	41	26	830	144
Tarkhan ...	558	386	56	1,000	...	...	1,000	...	...	866	131	3	237	700	63	49	777	174
Teli ...	564	379	57	1,000	...	...	993	7	...	874	126		273	[illegible]	66	73	756	171

SUBSIDIARY TABLE V—*contd.*—(For North-West Frontier Province including Agencies).

Distribution by civil condition of 1,000 of each sex at certain ages for selected castes.

Caste.	Distribution of 1,000 females of each age by civil condition																	
	All ages.			0—5			5—12			12—20			20—40			40 and over.		
	Unmarried.	Married.	Widowed.	Unmarried.	Married.	Widowed.	Unmarried	Married.	Widowed	Unmarried.	Married.	Widowed.	Unmarried.	Married.	Widowed.	Unmarried.	Married.	Widowed.
1	2	3	4	5	6	7	8	9	10	11	12	13	14	15	16	17	18	19
Arora ...	408	423	169	1,000	...	...	981	19	...	486	498	16	25	834	141	8	367	625
Awan ...	466	424	110	1,000	...	...	992	8	..	584	405	11	44	887	69	21	502	477
Baghban ...	450	150	100	1,000	...	...	990	10	..	583	413	4	44	887	69	23	607	370
Baluch ...	431	464	105	1,000	...	...	991	9	..	559	430	11	21	927	52	6	558	436
Bhatiara ...	481	414	105	1,000	...	...	987	13	.	629	357	14	78	865	57	44	513	443
Brahman ...	404	443	153	1,000	...	...	974	26	...	422	560	18	18	849	134	9	443	548
Chamar ...	451	450	99	1,000	...	...	994	6	...	696	300	4	77	870	53	60	587	353
Chuhra ...	389	510	101	1,000	...	...	981	19	...	473	516	11	50	850	100	39	586	375
Dhobi ...	445	449	106	1,000	...	...	992	8	...	553	441	6	54	868	78	45	562	393
Dhund ...	515	408	77	1,000	...	...	988	12	...	552	445	3	140	828	32	53	575	372
Gakkhar ...	451	443	106	1,000	...	...	991	9	...	530	462	8	37	883	80	12	540	439
Gujar ...	443	469	88	1,000	...	...	992	8	...	529	464	7	25	928	47	11	611	378
Jat ...	435	455	110	1,000	...	...	981	19	...	593	399	8	25	907	68	8	543	449
Jhinwar ...	474	411	115	1,000	...	...	983	17	...	655	345	..	80	826	94	46	500	454
Jolaha ..	453	444	103	1,000	...	...	990	10	...	601	392	7	56	869	75	-7	389	584
Karal ...	480	412	78	1,000	...	...	975	25	...	560	435	5	20	932	48	7	634	359
Kashmiri ...	444	435	121	1,000	...	...	993	7	...	617	377	6	42	8;8	80	12	539	449
Khatri ...	366	462	172	1,000	...	...	982	17	1	362	620	18	21	859	120	14	384	602
Kumhar ...	451	443	106	1,000	...	...	992	8	...	543	452	5	48	876	76	26	560	414
Lohar ...	490	424	86	1,000	...	...	983	17	...	586	406	8	67	875	58	21	566	413
Machhi ...	419	481	100	1,000	...	...	980	20	...	498	478	24	37	908	55	15	619	366
Maliar ...	449	443	108	1,000	...	...	991	9	...	574	418	8	38	883	79	22	578	400
Mallah ..	380	480	140	1,000	...	...	1,000	.	...	596	404	...	28	926	46	13	559	428
Mirasi ..	438	451	111	1,000	...	...	979	21	...	591	399	10	48	892	60	53	513	434
Mochi ...	462	443	95	1,000	...	...	991	9	...	527	463	10	40	895	65	24	552	424
Moghal ...	445	442	113	1,000	...	...	984	16	...	541	448	11	34	896	70	17	510	473
Musalli (with Kutana).	449	489	92	1,000	...	...	995	5	...	528	460	12	26	896	68	37	596	367
Nai ...	441	469	90	1 000	...	...	988	12	...	572	417	11	54	884	62	32	567	401
Paracha ...	457	424	119	1,000	...	...	992	6	2	640	349	11	81	848	71	56	523	421
Pathan ...	458	427	115	1,000	...	...	991	9	...	670	324	6	57	872	71	25	532	443
Qassab ...	472	420	108	1,000	...	...	984	16	..	639	338	23	89	842	69	52	534	414
Qureshi ...	470	423	107	1,000	...	...	984	16	..	571	413	16	72	856	72	29	515	456
Rajput ...	451	451	98	1,000	...	...	980	19	1	484	510	6	73	858	69	53	523	424
Saiad ...	470	419	111	1,000	...	...	989	11	..	685	309	6	51	872	77	27	544	429
Sarara ...	428	487	85	1,000	...	...	965	35	...	353	636	11	8	946	46	3	607	390
Shekh ...	431	449	120	1,000	...	...	995	4	1	570	425	5	61	854	85	43	488	469
Sonar ...	468	432	100	1,000	...	...	983	16	1	569	417	14	73	831	96	48	603	349
Swathi ...	488	411	101	1,000	...	...	992	8	...	544	451	5	120	814	66	9	542	449
Tanaoli ..	438	470	92	1,000	...	...	988	12	...	578	414	8	27	922	51	13	595	392
Tarkhan ...	456	448	96	1,000	...	...	990	10	...	560	431	9	32	899	69	-7	578	395
Teli ...	451	445	104	1,000	..	...	995	5	...	615	381	4	78	864	58	(8	532	400

CHAPTER VIII.

EDUCATION.

275. The statistics of education will be found in Tables VIII and IX in the second Part of this volume, the former of which shows education by age, religion and sex in the Province as a whole, as well as in the various districts and the trans-frontier posts which are included in it, while Table IX shows the extent to which literacy is to be found among the more numerous of the different tribes and castes. The information given in these two tables is amplified in the Subsidiary Tables printed at the end of this chapter, the first seven of which, showing proportional figures, are as under :— Reference to statistics.

I.—Education by age, sex and religion.
II.—Education by age, sex, and locality.
III.—Education by religion, sex and locality.
IV.—English education by age, sex, and locality.
V.—Progress of education since 1881.
V-A.—Progress of education since 1901 among the three main religions.
VI.—Education by caste.

Subsidiary Tables VII and VIII contain certain figures for the years of the last three Censuses compiled according to the returns of the Education Department, while two further tables give some information regarding the newspapers and books published in the Province.

276. At the present Census, as on previous occasions, the enumerators were directed to enter as literate only those persons who could both read and write. Where education is wide-spread, or almost universal, the preparation of a record of the people who possess these qualifications presents few difficulties. In England, for instance, the question as to whether a man can read or not can easily be answered one way or the other. Newspapers and publications of various descriptions are so common that a man is little likely to lose a proficiency in this direction which he ever possessed. If he could ever write, he has probably not forgotten the art. In rural India on the other hand all this is different. The ordinary peasant hardly ever has occasion either to write or to read, and some no doubt who have had some elementary education in their youth have forgotten with the lapse of years the little that they ever knew. If merely asked whether they can read and write, they may reply, speaking of a state of affairs which represents rather a memory than a fact, in the affirmative. The standard fixed on the present occasion was therefore something more definite than this. Under the instructions issued to the superior Census staff no one was to be recorded as literate, unless he could write a letter to a friend, and read the answer to it. If the backward condition of an area such as the North-West Frontier Province be borne in mind, it will be realised that such a standard is comparatively a high one. Scope of the return.

277. Of the total population of the Province only 20 per mille are literate according to the present Census. If the figure for males only be looked at, the proportion is found to be considerably higher, for the bulk of the female population possesses no tincture of education. The ratio per mille is 34 in the case of males, and 3 in the case of females. We have here figures which can only be compared with the low ratio recorded in Kashmir in 1901, where 38 males and 1 female per mille were reported to possess "the slight educational qualifications recognised at the last Census" (in paragraph 298 will be found a discussion of the difference in the standard recognised at the two Extent of literacy. (a) in the Province as a whole including the trans-frontier area.

enumerations). It must be remembered, however, that out of the total population of the Province (3,819,027 persons) on which the ratios given are calculated, no less than 1,622,094 resided in the trans-frontier portion, and that, out of these latter, only 13,528 were enumerated, the numbers of the remainder being based on an estimate. In estimating the numbers no attempt naturally could be made to discriminate between the literate and illiterate. Our low ratio may not, however, be expected to be due in any appreciable degree to this omission. In certain portions of the area, such as the Kurram* and Tochi valleys, and among the Sikhs who are to be found scattered in Tirah, literate persons no doubt exist, but the great bulk of the trans-frontier population is certainly wholly illiterate.

(*b*) in trans-frontier posts.

278. The figures for the Province as a whole can not usefully be subjected to further scrutiny. The statistics for those areas in which the population was enumerated on the regular schedule only lose their meaning, if there are included with them figures for an estimated population, among which, even if we assume that no literacy is to be found, the age distribution is unknown to us. The population brought within the scope of the regular Census consists of the inhabitants of the five British districts, together with a small number of persons enumerated in the British posts situated in the trans-frontier area These latter consist entirely of officials, or troops in the regular army and frontier militias, with a small number of followers and a few women and children. The agricultural community, which bulks so largely elsewhere, is almost entirely absent, the age distribution is abnormal, no less than 70 per cent. of the males being aged between 20 and 40 years, and the proportion of the sexes (71 females only per 1,000 males) is even farther removed from that found in the bulk of the Province. The statistics of literacy for this group can therefore be dismissed with a passing reference. It will be sufficient to note that, out of a total population of 13,338 persons, 2,448, or 18 per cent. were recorded as literate. The literate males amounted to 19, and the literate females to 7, per cent. of the population of that sex. The population presents therefore an abnormal aspect from the point of view of literacy also.

Literacy among the total enumerated population.

279. For among the total enumerated population of the Province literate males of all religions amount to only 6 (58 per mille) and literate females to ·6 per cent. (6 per mille). The figure for males indicates a very narrow diffusion of education, even for India. Only two† provinces showed in 1901 a lower one, *viz.* the Central Provinces (54 per mille) and the United Provinces (57 per 1,000). The figures for females are not so noticeably low when compared with those for other Indian areas. For India as a whole in 1901 literate females only amounted to 7 per 1,000 of the total female population, and Assam, Bengal, Berar the Central Provinces, the Punjab (including the North-West Frontier Province), and the United Provinces all showed in 1901 a lower proportion of literate females than we find in the North-West Frontier Province on the present occasion.

Literacy in the districts of the Province.

280. As I have noticed above, however, the condition of the population of the trans-frontier posts is abnormal in the possession of a comparatively high proportion of literates, and if the population of this group be left out of account, the figure will be found to be slightly lower. In the districts of the Province those persons who satisfy the requirements of the Census standard of literacy are only 33 per 1,000, 57 per 1,000 in the case of males, and 6 per 1,000 in the case of females. Between the different districts no very striking differences are to be found. Literate females vary from 9 per mille in Peshawar to only 2 per mille in Kohat, the variation being due partly to the larger urban population to be found in the former, and partly to the higher proportion of non-Muslims, particularly Europeans, which Peshawar includes.

---

*In 1901, when the population of the revenue paying portion of the Kurram valley was enumerated on the regular schedule, 1,010 persons were recorded as literate.

†For one portion of Bengal, *viz.* Chota Nagpur, however, the figure was only 49 per mille in 1901.

Dera Ismail Khan, with its high proportion of non-Muslims (considerably higher than is to be found in Peshawar, but with far fewer Europeans), comes next with 7 literate females per 1,000, while Bannu and Hazara each possess 3 only per mille. In the case of males the differences are slightly less. The highest proportion of literate males is found in Dera Ismail Khan (84 per 1,000). The pre-eminent position of the district is no doubt partly due to the high ratio of Hindus which it includes within its borders (*vide* Subsidiary Table II appended to Chapter IV). But, as we shall see when we come to consider the statistics of education by religion, the proportion of literate males in Dera Ismail Khan is higher than elsewhere, not only among Hindus, but also among Mussalmans. The Mohammadan population of the district therefore appears to take more kindly to education than do Mohammadans in other areas. The difference would seem to be partly due to a difference of race among the inhabitants, and partly to the trade centres which for so long a time have existed within it. The bulk of the population consists of Jats, Baluches and other non-Pathan tribes, less warlike and turning more readily to education and the arts of peace than does the Pathan, while the annual Powindah migration into the district has for a long time past provided its inhabitants with sources of livelihood other than are to be found in the cultivation of the soil. The two districts which follow after Dera Ismail Khan in respect of male literacy are Bannu and Peshawar, in each of which literate males amount to 61 per 1,000 of the whole. Mohammadans in Bannu (they are mainly Pathans) show no particular taste for education, even when compared with their fellow religionists elsewhere in the Province. The comparatively high figure here must be referred to the large proportion of Hindus which the district contains. The fact that literacy is as common in Peshawar as it is found to be is due to a combination of circumstances. In the first place, as a reference to Table VI (in the second Part of this volume) will show, there reside in it more than five-sixths of all the Christians enumerated in the Province. These are almost all Europeans, most of whom are of course literate. We have also to take into account the large commercial centres in the district, and the Cantonments of Peshawar, Nowshera and Mardan which are situated in it. The district also possesses a larger proportion of Sikhs than any other in the Province, and it will be seen that education is more widely diffused among them than among any other section of the community, if Christians be left out of account. It is in Peshawar that one would expect, considering all the circumstances, to find literacy most common, and it is rather necessary to look for an explanation of its being so rare than to give reasons for the district standing above Kohat and Hazara in this respect. Among males in Kohat there are 56 literates per 1,000 males. Mohammadans are more numerous proportionately in this district than in others, with the exception of Peshawar and Hazara. In Hazara literates also bear a smaller proportion to the whole, while its considerable urban population, as I have noted above, explains the higher figure for literacy of Peshawar. In Kohat our return is to be referred to the race, (mainly Pathan) religion (nearly all Mohammadans) and occupation (almost exclusively agricultural) of the population. The figures for Hazara require little explanation. Literates among males here amount only to 37 per 1,000, or 19 per mille fewer than are to be found elsewhere. To explain our figure we must look less to the race of the population than to the physical aspects of the district. The country is mountainous, and lies in a corner far removed from the beaten tract of industry or commerce. A certain amount of the Kashmir trade passes through it, but there are no large markets within it, and the transport of merchandise by road involves few educational qualifications among the persons who are engaged in it. Mohammadans make up as much as 95 per cent. of the total population, distances are long, communication is difficult, and the inhabitants are almost entirely graziers or agriculturists. It is, curiously enough, the only district in the Province in which the proportion of literate persons to the total population has increased in the last 10 years, but it can cause no surprise that, educationally, it is still the most backward.

Density and education.

281. No correspondence is to be traced between density and education. It is curious to note that literacy is most common in the district where density is lowest (Dera Ismail Khan), but the converse proposition is not true. The two set of facts have in reality, no relation with one another. The explanation is, I believe, to be found in a consideration of the figures for religion, but this will be adverted to in its proper place hereafter. It follows from what has been said in the previous paragraph that, of the two natural divisions into which the districts of the Province have been divided, education is considerably more common in the trans-Indus districts taken as a whole than in Hazara.

Density and education.

District.	Literates per 1,000 of total.	Density per square mile.
D. I. Khan	49	74
Bannu	34	149
Peshawar	37	332
Kohat	30	82
Hazara	21	207

Natural Division.	Density per square mile.	Literate per 1,000.
Hazara	202	21
Trans-Indus Districts ...	153	38

Educational facilities.

282. Similarly variations in educational facilities have not a great deal to say to the differences to be observed in our figures for districts. It will be interesting, however, to consider the relation borne by the schools of all kinds in existence to the male population of school-going age. If we regard as of school-going age the lowest possible figure, *viz* the male population aged from 10 to 15 years, we get the figures shown in the margin. I do not pretend that they possess any real value as indicating the extent to which opportunities for education exist in the various areas, for many boys no doubt begin to attend school before they have reached the age of 10, and some continue their studies after they have entered their 16th year. Nevertheless, in view of the circumstances of the Province, this age-period seems the most suitable that can be taken, and it at any rate furnishes a standard of comparison between different districts. It is in Bannu that schools are most numerous in proportion to the population, while in Peshawar one school only exists for nearly four times as many boys. Nevertheless the figure is the same for the one district as for the other, when the proportion borne by the literate to the total male population is looked at.

District.	No. of boys in total population aged 10-15 per school.	Literate per 1,000 males.	Literate per 1,000 males aged 10—15.
Hazara ...	188	37	25
Peshawar ...	243	61	36
Kohat ...	147	56	29
Bannu	64	61	41
D. I. Khan ...	70	84	75

Literacy by age.

283. The return of literacy by age calls for consideration next. The proportional figures will be found in Subsidiary Table II appended to this chapter. Among males 3 only per mille are literate under the age of 10 years. For the age period '10 to 15' the figure rises to 37. At the next age period shown, *viz* '15 to 20' there is a further rise to 82 per mille, and among 1,000 males aged '20 and over' as many as 89 fulfil the Census requirements of literacy. The proportions for females show a similar rise at each period up to the age group '15 to 20,' but the literates aged '20 and over' only amount to 7 per mille, as against 12 among the females whose age comes within the previous five years. The figure for male literacy in India as a whole at the last Census presented the same general features, *i. e.* an increase in the proportion returned as literate at the successive age periods. "This steady increase" wrote Mr. Gait* "at the successive age periods seems to show that, in spite of the instructions, the general tendency of the enumerators was to omit from the category of the literate persons who were still under instruction, even though they had passed beyond the preliminary stage of their education. The number of persons who first learn to read and write

* India Census Report, 1901, paragraph 266.

after attaining the age of 15 is infinitesimal, and unless (which is very unlikely) the persons enumerated at the age period '15 to 20' have enjoyed fewer educational opportunities than did those enumerated at all the higher ages when they passed through this period of life, the proportion of the literate amongst the former would be greater than, or at least equal to, the corresponding proportion at the higher ages." Among females throughout India in 1901, as on the present occasion in the North-West Frontier Province, literates were less numerous proportionally among those who had passed the age of 20 years than among those living during the quinquennium immediately preceding it.

Omissions of learners in 1901.

284. The explanation offered by Mr. Gait for the India figures in 1901 is not equally applicable to those of the North-West Frontier Province on the present occasion, and it is not, I believe, necessary. There was probably some tendency to omit learners at the recent Census, but there seems reason to suppose it to have been stronger in 1901 than in 1911. Especially in areas where enumerators and others employed on the Census consist largely of Government officials, there will always be a tendency for the instructions given at the previous Census to be followed, in spite of the fact that different ones may have been issued for the purpose of the subsequent operations In 1891 the rules laid down that persons should be returned as either literate, illiterate, or as learners; *i.e.* the literate were required to be distinguished from those under instruction. In 1901, on the other hand, literate or illiterate were the only returns required. The enumerator of 1901, with a recollection of the instructions of 1891 at the back of his head, would therefore be likely to omit the learners altogether. In 1891 they had to be recorded, but were required to be distinguished from the literate. In 1901 they were to be included among the literate, if already able both to read and write, but otherwise were to be omitted. What more natural then than that in 1901 they should tend to drop out altogether, without regard to the implied proviso, that they should be entered as literate, if their education had proceeded far enough to bring them up to the Census standard?

Fewer signs of omissions of learners at the recent Census.

285. But on the present occasion the number of enumerators who took part in the operations of 1891 must have been inconsiderable. Many, of course, had acted in a similar capacity in 1901, but the instructions then given were substantially the same as those issued in 1911, and we have here, if my surmise be correct, one reason at any rate why our figures should have been influenced to a comparatively small degree by the omission of school boys and others whose education had passed beyond the preliminary stage. But a stronger ground for believing that our statistics, in so far as they represent the literate to be more numerous proportionally among those who have passed the age of 20 than among those living during the five years previous, represent the actual facts, is to be found in the situation of the Province in regard to migration. Between three-fifths and two-thirds of all the persons recorded as literate are either Christians, Hindus, or Sikhs The Christians, of whom all but an inconsiderable minority are Europeans, do not generally enter the Province until after they have reached the age of 20; they are literate in nearly all cases, and the effect of their inclusion in our figures is solely in the direction of raising the proportion of adult literates. This is bound to be the result of including among the adults a body among whom literacy is far more common than among the bulk of the inhabitants of whatever age. Literates among Hindus are nearly eighteen, and among Sikhs twenty five, times as numerous, in proportion to the totals of their respective communities, as they are among Mohammadans, who constitute over ninety per cent. of the total population of the Province; and among both communities the proportion of immigrants is exceedingly high. Among Hindu males they amount to 32 per cent. of the total population of that sex and religion; among Sikhs to 48 per cent. When these facts are borne in mind, it will be realised that a large number from among the persons recorded as literate in the Province did not receive their education within it, but entered it for the first time, already able to read and write, after reaching what are called years of discretion.

In an area in which education is in any degree universal, the appearance of a considerable body of literate immigrants would of course have little effect on the proportions of the whole able to read and write at the various age periods. But in the North-West Frontier Province the bulk of the population are entirely illiterate, and figures as small as those with which we are here concerned are considerably affected by the appearance of a single regiment recruited outside the Province, and containing, as the majority of Indian regiments do to-day, a considerable proportion of literate men. I am not discussing the figures for literacy by religion, but it is necessary in this connection to refer to them here. If Subsidiary Table I, appended to this chapter, be turned to, it will be seen that among Mohammadans the proportion of literate persons (both males and females) who have passed the age of 20 is lower than among those aged '15 to 20,' the Mohammadan being of course the only one among the communities contained in the Province of which the figures are not affected by migration to any considerable extent.

Literacy among males of the age groups '10 to 15' and '15 to 20.'

286 It has been possible to explain the variations in the proportion of literate persons at the age periods '15 to 20,' and '20 and over' respectively. The rise shown in the proportion at the former period over those living at the previous quinquennium needs hardly so much explanation. "The number of persons", writes Mr. Gait in the passage quoted above, "who first learn to read and write after attaining the age of 15 is infinitesimal". But, in the first place, it must be remembered that the age-group shown as '10 to 15' includes only those persons whose age was returned as 10, 11, 12, 13 or 14 years, and that boys whose age is shown as 15 appear in the following age period. And secondly it is doubtful how large a proportion of scholars, of the class to be found in the bulk of the schools of the Province, are literate, in the Census meaning of the word, before attaining the age of 15,* and I do not think that our figures for these two age periods lead one to suppose that many learners have been omitted, provided that they had reached such a degree of proficiency as to bring them within the Census definition of literacy. Moreover, when the place comes to consider the figures for the present Census in relation to those of the previous one, it will be found that, while the proportion of the whole who are classed as literate above the age of 20 has decreased since 1901, the corresponding proportion for those aged '15 to 20' has gone up in the last 10 years.

Literacy by age in individual districts.

287. The returns of literacy by age in the different districts of the Province present no features of particular interest (*vide* Subsidiary Table II appended to this chapter), for they agree closely in nearly all cases with those which have been noticed in regard to the population of British Territory as a whole. It is worth noticing, however, that in Dera Ismail Khan, unlike the other districts, the proportion of the total male population of the age group concerned who have been shown as literate at the age of "20 and over" is lower than the corresponding figures for the period '15 to 20' and that the district where conditions are farthest removed from this is Kohat, where literate males, who are only 62 per 1,000 among those aged "15 to 20," amount to 93 per 1,000 among those aged '20 and over'. In Dera Ismail Khan, though the proportion of immigrants to the total population is higher than is found elsewhere in the Province, they enter the district mainly from the west, being Powindahs and others born in Afghanistan and tribal territory, and only an inconsiderable minority are able to read and write. On the other hand the proportion of literates among the native (*i. e.* district-born) population is higher than is to be found elsewhere. Of Hindu males (*vide* paragraph 83, Chapter III) 859 per 1,000 were born in the district, and presumably received their education within it; and it is in Dera Ismail Khan that education is most widely diffused among males of that religion. In Kohat, on the other hand, where more than half the total

*The Director of Public Instruction tells me they form a very small portion of the whole.

male literates are either Hindus or Sikhs, a very large proportion (of the males of these religions) are immigrants from outside, the extra-district born amounting to 439 per 1,000 in the case of the former religion, and to as high a figure as 857 per mille in the case of the latter. Of the total literates therefore a very large number must be supposed to have received their education outside the Province, and to have entered it, already able to read and write, after arriving at maturity. The figures for individual districts therefore support the view that the higher proportion of literates observed among adults than among those of school-going age is to be attributed, not to any omissions from our returns, but to the disturbing influence of migration, a factor which, it will have been noticed, has to be taken into account, from whichever point of view the statistics of the Province are regarded.

288. Turning to the statistics of education by religion, (*vide* Subsidiary Table I, appended to this chapter) it will be seen that, as might be expected, the first position, to which that held by no other religion is comparable, is taken by Christians, among whom as many as 851 per 1,000 of both sexes are literate. The actual number of literates is 5,720 persons (4,956 males and 764 females). Of these 5,421 (4,734 males and 687 females) are either Europeans or Anglo-Indians. The total number of native Christians therefore, who are able to read and write, amounts to 299 persons (222 males and 77 females), or 399 per 1,000 in the case of males, and 297 per 1,000 in the case of females. A large number of our native Christians are Goanese servants, the majority of whom can read and write some vernacular character, if not English, while conversion in the case of others is in many cases accompanied by the giving of some degree of education. Our figures for native Christians are, however, so small (552 males and 325 females in all) that it hardly seems worth while to devote any further consideration to them. Among Europeans and Anglo-Indians literates amount per mille to 952 in the case of males, and to 791 in the case of females, the variation being due to the fact that children of less than 12 years of age are far more numerous proportionately in the case of the latter sex than among the former. Among Sikhs 352 persons of both sexes are literate per 1,000; for Hindus the figure is 248, while among Mohammadans only 14 per mille are able to read and write. **Education by religion.**

289 The varying degrees of literacy found in the two sexes deprive the figures, however, of most of their interest, and I will consider them, as I have done throughout the chapter, for each sex separately. To take males first, among Sikhs nearly one-half, or 462 per 1,000 are able to read and write. This is considerably higher than our figure for Hindu males (375 per mille) and more than four times as high as the only figure for Sikhs elsewhere with which I can compare it, *i.e.*, Sikh males in the Punjab (British territory) in 1901*. In the same way the proportion of literate Hindus in the Province is strikingly large. For India as a whole it amounted to 94 per mille in 1901, and in Travancore, where the figure was higher than in any other unit of which the Census was taken separately, it only stood at 218. The peculiar circumstances of the Hindus and Sikhs in the Province explain the prevalence of literacy among them. Speaking broadly, it may be said that no member of either community is engaged in agriculture. The majority find a livelihood in trade, or in Government service, especially the army. A trader, unless he be a mere peddlar, is necessarily able to cypher, if not to read and write some character, and the proportion of literates among sepoys is now high. Mussalmans tend everywhere to be the most backward of the Indian communities in respect of education, if the Animist be excepted. But in the North-West Frontier Province the contrast between them and the followers of other religions is especially marked in this respect. Out of the total number of males, only 25 per 1,000, or one in forty, fulfil the Census requirements of literacy. For the area comprising the Punjab (British territory) and the North- **Literacy among males by religion.**

* 103 per mille.

West Frontier Province in 1901 the figure was 20, and in Kashmir it was only 13, but in all other areas it was higher, and in Burma, where Mohammadans are an alien and a trading community, it was as high as 194 per 1,000.

Mohammadans and education.

290. The backward condition of the Mohammadans in respect of education is due, partly to the past history of the Province, and perhaps still more to considerations of the race of its inhabitants, and the physical aspects and geographical position of the country. In point of fact all these factors are mutually inter-dependent. Geographical position, physical aspects and the character of the inhabitants have all helped to mould the history of the Province. The characteristics of the population are again largely due, one may surmise, to the natural features of the scenery amidst which they live. The physical aspects and geographical position of the country would not of themselves lead to the existence of a rude and illiterate population, if one may judge by the evidences which point to the country having enjoyed a considerable degree of civilization and prosperity in the time of its Greek and Buddhist governors, (*vide* paragraphs 38 and 39 *ante*). But superimpose upon these a population turning more readily to the foray than to the market, and the result is a foregone conclusion. And, for convenience, one may attribute the extreme rarity of education in the first place to historical, and in the second to racial, considerations. It is to be noticed that the areas included in the North-West Frontier Province, along with the Punjab, were among the latest, if we except Burma, to be brought under British rule. The country started behind the remainder of British India in the race for education, and, though Peshawar passed at the same time as Lahore under the control of the East India Company, educational effort was naturally later and more restricted in outlying areas than in the more central ones. We have here one reason for the backward condition of the Province. But a stronger one is to be found in the character of its inhabitants. Place the Burman in the North-West Frontier Province, and the picture would no doubt be widely different. But then the Burman, prior to the inclusion of Burma in the territories of the British Crown, had developed an indigenous system of education. The Pathan on the other hand has always despised education as fit only for Hindus and cowards. He had little need for spelling, but much for swordsmanship, and if the *hamsayah* of an alien creed, whom he employed to look after his money matters, cheated him so flagrantly that even his ignorant master could not overlook it, there was short shrift for the accountant, and a fresh start was made with a clean sheet. The establishment of settled government has put an end to the necessity, as to the possibility, of a pursuit of the arts of war to the exclusion of those of peace, and educational facilities have been provided to the inhabitants. But it is natural, considering their antecedents, that they should have shown no conspicuous eagerness to avail themselves of them, and our Census figures suggest that, even of the few boys who attend school, a good many leave before having reached the standard of literacy which is recognized in our statistics.

Literacy among females by religion.

291. Leaving on one side the Christian figures, which, as consisting almost entirely of Europeans, have little interest here, the Sikhs contain the highest proportion of literates for females also. Of the total number of females of this religion, as many as 133 per 1,000 are able to read and write. It will be seen that this is an extraordinarily high figure, when it is remembered that it is higher than was found in India as a whole in 1901 among Christians, who naturally included a large proportion of Europeans ; and much higher than was elicited even among Jain females in Bengal in the same year.* The actual numbers are, however, very small, literate Sikh females amounting to 1,380 souls only, though this is considerably in excess of the literate out of the vastly greater Mohammadan female population. The teaching of Guru Govind Singh, the founder of the militant faith of Sikhism, was in the direction of raising the position of women, but, even after making all due allowance for his influence, our figure here may at first occasion some surprise. I should be inclined to suspect some error in enumeration or in tabulation, were it not that the

* 83 per 1,000. This is a far larger proportion than was found among any other community in any part of India in 1901, if the Christians be excepted.

corresponding figure in 1901 was as high as 125 per 1,000, and the proportion arrived at as a result of the present operations exhibits therefore an increase which is in general agreement with that shown in respect of female education among the followers of other religions. The figures for Hindus also indicate what is comparatively a very high proportion of lit-rates among females (57 per 1,000). The figure most nearly approaching it, as disclosed by the Census of India in 1901, was that elicited for Burma, where literate females among Hindus amounted to 42 per mille of the whole. In Rajputana and the Central Provinces on the other hand, where the Hindu population is no doubt principally engaged in agriculture, the figure was only 1 per mille. It is to the occupations followed by their male relatives in the North-West Frontier Province that the high figure for female literacy among Hindus and Sikhs must be attributed. As we have seen, the bread winners are for the most part either traders, or in military employ, but the number of women accompanying those of the latter group, who are immigrants without exception, is trifling; and our females are largely composed of the relatives of traders. Of the total number of Hindus and Sikhs enumerated in the Province, as many as 77 per cent., are either Aroras, Brahmans or Khatris. To this fact, and to the entire absence from among them of graziers or agriculturists, is to be attributed the degree to which their women are found to be literate. Among the Mohammadans on the other hand we have a mainly agricultural population. We have seen that literacy is extremely rare among the males; among the females it is almost non-existent. Only one Mohammadan female out of a thousand in the Province is able to read and write. It is hardly necessary to quote statistics for other areas to show how low a figure this is.

Literacy by caste.

292. As regards the degree of literacy found among the members of the various tribes and castes little remains to be observed which has not been said by implication in the foregoing paragraphs. A consideration of the figures will, however, throw a clearer light on the conclusions which I have attempted to draw, and it is with this object in view that I refer to them here. I propose to arrange the various tribes and castes in groups according to the prevalence of literacy among the males included in each, at the same time drawing attention to the figures for females, where these appear disproportionate to those for males. I include in my first group figures for those caste or tribal units among whom literate males amount to more than 30 per cent. of the whole (*vide* margin). As will be expected, all the persons dealt with are either Hindus or Sikhs, and the bulk of them are engaged in or supported by trade. It is interesting to notice, as being at variance with the statistics of female literacy among the followers of the various religions as a whole, that the Khatris possess a higher proportion of literate females than either of the other two castes shown, although the Sikhs among them only amount to one in seven, while of Arora females one in five, and of Brahman females one in four, is a Sikh. My next group, *viz*, of those castes and tribes of whose total number of males more than 10 and less than 30 per cent. are literate, only contains two entries. Our Rajputs, of whom more than two-thirds are Mohammadans, were in the majority of cases born outside the Province. They are largely employed in the army, and the comparatively high proportion of literate males is thus easy to understand. The literate females are only 71 in number, (there are 527 Rajput females entered as Hindu or Sikh by religion) out of whom 25 are Mohammadans. It is curious to find that the caste which follows next in order of literacy is the Jhinwar. Of our Jhinwars, who include persons returned as Bhisti, 48 per cent. of the males are

Caste or tribe.	Number literate per thousand.	
	Males.	Females.
Arora ...	408	64
Khatri ...	407	92
Brahman ...	375	65

Caste or tribe.	Number literate per thousand.	
	Males.	Females.
Rajput ...	205	16
Jhinwar ...	116	19

Hindus or Sikhs, and of the 164 persons recorded as literate, only five (males) are Mohammadans. My next group consists mainly of persons belonging to what I may describe as the professional and commercial classes, together with (an odd addition) Chuhras. The comparatively high position which our Jats enjoy in order of literacy is due to the inclusion among the figures of a good many males in military employ, *e. g.*, in Sikh regiments, who are almost without exception immigrants to the Province. As regards the Chuhras it must be remembered that these are only found in urban areas, mainly in cantonments, the scavenger of the rural areas being the Mussalli, or Kutana, who appears next to the bottom of our list of castes arranged in their relative positions with regard to literacy. The position of these castes in regard to female literacy is much the same as with regard to male, except that among Sonar women education is far more common than among other tribes, who show a greater degree of male literacy. Our next group, which comprises 56 per cent. of the total population of the Province, includes the more numerically important of the agricultural tribes, (with the exception of Jat which has already appeared above) together with the Dhobis, who are confined to urban areas, and the Kashmiris, who are largely agricultural labourers rather than agriculturists proper, while some are engaged in the carrying trade which traverses the Hazara District. There are proportionately more literate females among the Kashmiris and Dhobis than among the other castes and tribes included in this group, but even among them the standard of female literacy is exceedingly low, only one in five hundred females being able to read and write. The remainder of the tribes and castes which are dealt with in Table IX are mainly of the village menial type, together with a few of the more backward of the agricultural tribes, such as the Tanaolis, Gujars, Dhunds, Karals, Baghbans and Maliars, the majority of whom are found in Hazara, where, as we have seen, education is even less common than elsewhere in the districts of the Province. It is curious to notice that the Bhatiaras (gram parchers) have as many as 5 literate females per 1,000, and that the Tanaolis have 2, while the corresponding proportion in the case of none of the other remaining castes is higher than 1 per 1,000. The actual figures are, however, in each case very small, only 11 Bhatiara and 48 Tanaoli females being able to read and write.

Caste or tribe.	Number literate per thousand.	
	Males.	Females.
Shekh ...	97	10
Qureshi ...	93	5
Jat ...	89	3
Paracha ..	74	2
Moghul ...	64	2
Saiad ...	55	4
Sonar ...	53	13
Gakkhar ...	48	...
Chuhra ...	40	2

Caste or tribe.	Number literate per thousand.	
	Males.	Females.
Kashmiri ..	27	2
Baluch ...	27	1
Swathi ...	24	1
Pathan ...	23	1
Awan ...	22	1
Dhobi ...	19	2

Literacy in English.

293. In Subsidiary Table I, appended to this chapter, will be found proportional figures showing the relative degree of literacy in English found among the various religions represented in the Province. Leaving on one side the Christian figures, which, for the reasons already noted, have little interest here, it will be seen that it is among Hindus that the greatest diffusion of English education is to be found. Of 1,000 males 35 are literate in English. Among Sikhs the corresponding figure is 25 per mille, while among Mohammadans only 2 per mille, or 1 male in 500, is able to read and write the English language. The Hindus and Sikhs of the North-West Frontier Province, as they are ahead of the bulk of their co-religionists elsewhere in India in vernacular, lead the way also in English, education. Of the total number of Hindu males enumerated in India in 1901 only 6 per mille were returned as knowing English, and the Sikh figure was even lower (5 per mille). On the other hand the Mohammadans of the Province show a smaller proportion of English-knowing literates now than the Mussalmans of India as a whole did in 1901. The causes which determine the position of the followers of the various religions in the

North-West Frontier Province in respect of education in vernacular languages, as compared with that of persons holding the same faith elsewhere, are the same as those which explain the relative degrees to which the knowledge of English is found in different areas. The man who is literate in his own language is by no means necessarily acquainted also with English, but a knowledge of one tongue is, for all intents and purposes, a necessary preliminary to his becoming acquainted with the other ; and where persons who can read and write their own language are most numerous, the greatest number of those who know English may also be expected to be found. Among the total enumerated population of all religions in the Province, as a reference to Subsidiary Table I will show, 8 males and 1 female per 1,000 of that sex are literate in this tongue.

Literacy in English by districts.

294. For local variations, and for the proportions living at the different age periods who are acquainted with English, a reference should be made to Subsidiary Table III appended to this chapter. Hazara, as would be expected from its position in regard to education in the vernacular, possesses the lowest proportion of English-knowing literates, the district which comes nearest to it, *viz.* Bannu, having one more than twice as large. The figure for Peshawar, (males) is strikingly high, amounting to 136 per 10,000. But if we omit Christians, it falls to 46 per 10,000. I show in the margin the proportion for each district separately, after deducting from the figures on which the calculation is based the Christian population in each case. The comparatively high proportion of males who know English in Dera Ismail Khan is intelligible enough, in view of the facts in regard to literacy in the vernacular. That our figure for Kohat is relatively so high seems to be accidental ; at any rate I can not point to the circumstances which explain it. Coming to the proportion recorded as literate in English at the different age periods, it will be noticed that this is higher among males aged '15 to 20' than among those aged '20 and over' in every district except Peshawar, where the large number of Europeans disturbs the figures. Judged by this standard a knowledge of English is seen to be growing rapidly, particularly in Bannu, where the proportion found at the earlier age period is nearly three times as high as that at the latter. The existence of an excellent Mission school there has no doubt contributed much to this result. The number of females who are literate in English is infinitesimal, and it hardly seems worth while subjecting the figures to examination in detail. The proportion of English literates found among the different castes and tribes similarly needs no discussion. It is highest in the case of the three castes, Brahman, Arora, and Khatri, among the members of which literacy in a vernacular is most common. There are only two other groups, of those dealt with in Table IX, in which the males who know English amount to more than one per cent. (Qureshi and Shekh), and among them also the ability to read and write their own language is comparatively common.

Males literate in English per 10,000 (Christians excepted).

District.	Literate in English per 10,000.
Hazara	22
Peshawar	46
Kohat	55
Bannu	47
D. I. Khan ...	67

Comparison with results of Census of 1901. (a) in the total area of the Province.

295. We have seen that, among females, literacy is more often found in the case of persons of the age group '15 to 20' than of those who have passed the latter year. In regard to Mohammadan males the same feature is to be noticed, and I have endeavoured to show that the contrary result which has been elicited in the case of the males belonging to other religions is due solely to migration. This fact points to education being on the increase ; in fact the inference which is to be drawn from it is too strong to be escaped from, unless we are to attribute the variation to the fact that a very large proportion of our adults have forgotten what they once knew, which is unlikely. In the circumstances it seems unnecessary to be unduly depressed by a comparison of the results of the present and of previous Censuses (*vide* Subsidiary table V appended to this chapter). At first sight, however, the figures are undoubtedly somewhat disheartening. The ratio borne to the whole by literate females has risen

everywhere since 1901, except in Peshawar and Kohat, where it shows a slight fall. But turning to the figures for males we are confronted by a very different picture. In the case of every district, except Hazara, the proportion of literate males has gone down in the last ten years, and the actual number of persons recorded as literate in 1911 (75,434) is less by 2,864 souls than that given in the Census tables for 1901. On an examination of the figures in detail, however, there seems reason to suppose that the decrease is apparent only. I show in the margin the number of literate persons enumerated in 1901 and 1911, respectively, in each district of the Province and in the trans-frontier area. It will be seen that proportionally the largest decrease is to be found in the area outside British territory, the figures for which have decreased from 4,285 in 1901 to 2,448 on the present occasion. The total population concerned was, however, very different in the two years. The figure for Kurram in 1901, represents the literates out of the total population of the revenue paying portion of the Agency (55,257 persons), whereas on the present occasion only the inhabitants of posts were enumerated (2,967 persons). The enumerated population of the Malakand Agency declined, owing to a decrease in the number of troops stationed within it, from 8,128 persons in 1901 to 4,435 in 1911. It should be noticed that, whereas our figure for literates in the trans-frontier area in 1911 represents those found in posts in all the five Agencies of the Province, the corresponding figure for 1911 only refers to the Malakand and Kurram Agencies, but to a far larger population. The figures shown against this portion of the Province in the two years respectively are in fact not comparable.

Education in 1911 and 1901.

District, etc.	Total literate.	
	1911.	1901.
Hazara	12,892	10,870
Peshawar	32,188	31,247
Kohat	6,912	9,093
Bannu	8,502	9,537
Dera Ismail Khan ...	12,492	13,266
Total districts ...	**72,986**	**74,013**
Trans-Frontier Posts ...	2,448	...
Kurram	...	1,010
Malakand	...	3,275
Total Trans-Frontier	**2,448**	**4,285**
Total Province ...	**75,434**	**78,298**

(b) in British territory.

296. This brings us to a consideration of the figures for literacy in the districts of the Province in the two years. Those for 1901 include the literate persons enumerated, not only in British territory, but also a small number found beyond the Border, *viz.* the figures for Peshawar include those of posts in the Khyber Agency, and the figures for Bannu and Dera Ismail Khan include those for posts in the Tochi and Wano respectively. On the present occasion the number of literate persons enumerated were, 125 in the Khyber, 255 in the Tochi, and 133 in Wano. Even if we assume that the figures were the same in 1901 as in 1911, we can reduce by 513 the number of persons shown as able to read and write in British territory in 1901. But in the Tochi and Wano Agencies the enumerated population was far larger than in 1911. A reference to the notes, printed below Table II in the second Part of this volume, will show that 9,206 persons (troops and followers stationed there in connection with the Mahsud Blockade) were enumerated in 1901 in the two agencies. From enquires I have made in the proper quarter I gather that 20 per cent. of these persons were probably literate, and if 936 literate persons are deducted from the 1901 figures for Bannu, and 904 from those for Dera Ismail Khan on this account, we shall probably be near the facts. We shall then be confronted with a small decrease in the case of Bannu, and a small rise in that of Dera Ismail Khan.

Special immigration in 1901.

297. From our figure for literates in British districts in 1901 (74,013) I believe then that we can deduct 1,965* persons on the ground that they were not present in those districts, and were only so shown for convenience in the Provincial Census tables of that year. In that case, instead of a decrease, we find a rise of 938 in the number of persons recorded as literate. This, it will be said, is a preposterously small increase to be the result of ten years of

*1,965. This figure is made up as follows :—125 (number of literate persons enumerated in 1911 in the Khyber) plus 936 (estimated number of literate persons enumerated in 1901 in the Tochi) plus 904 (estimated number of literate persons enumerated in 1901 in Wano).

administration, and so it would be, were there no special circumstances to explain it. It will be noticed from a reference to the marginal statement above that the most marked fall in the figures for literacy since 1901 is in Kohat. It is accompanied by a very large decrease in the population of Kohat cantonment, and a smaller one in that of the Kohat Municipal area (*vide* Table IV in Part II of this volume), while the Hindus of the district, as a reference to paragraph 115 above will show, are also less numerous than in 1901. All the decreases alike are largely to be attributed to the fact that in 1901 there was a large temporary immigration in connection with the building of the Khushalgarh-Thall railway line then under construction. The work was largely done by Pioneer regiments (though they were not present in the cantonment they are shown in the Census Tables of 1901 as forming a part of its population), which contain a higher percentage of literates than other branches of the native army, and the presence of a civil engineering staff must have had no small effect on the figures. If we could assume that the whole of the difference between the numbers recorded as literate in Kohat in 1901 and 1911 respectively is due to this special immigration in the former year, while finding education to be stationary in Kohat, in the districts of the Province taken as a whole we should be able to record a rise in the number of literate persons of something between four and five per cent.

Difference in instructions issued in 1901 and 1911.

298. But is it the fact that the progress of education in the last ten years has been no more than this? In any case the Hazara District is the only one which shows what may be regarded as a substantial advance. The literates there have increased in numbers by 19 per cent. But in Peshawar the increase is trifling only (3 per cent.), and in the other districts, even after making every possible allowance for the influence of migration, we are confronted either by a very small advance, or by actual retrogression. In this connection we come to a consideration of the instructions issued to the Census staff in 1901 and in 1911 respectively on the subject of the record of literacy. In 1901 it was merely laid down, in the instructions to enumerators printed on the cover in which the schedules were bound up, that those only should be recorded as literate who could both read and write. On the present occasion no change was made in the rules issued for the guidance of enumerators, but in the instructions to the superior Census staff it was added that a man was only to be shown as literate, if he could write a letter to a friend and read the answer to it. I am informed that in Kohat generally and over a large area of the Peshawar District this was in many cases interpreted as meaning that only those who had read up to the 3rd middle class, part of the curriculum of which consists of the writing of a letter, should be recorded as literate. In view of the fact that a large number, perhaps even the majority, of boys leave school before they have completed the primary course, this interpretation would eliminate many who would have been recorded as literate in 1901; and even where the instructions were not so precisely construed, it seems obvious that those issued on the present occasion have had the effect of raising the Census standard of literacy. In 1901 the enumerators were indeed told to record as literate only those who could both read and write, but this might mean merely the signing of one's name and the reading with difficulty of printed matter. A man literate in this sense would hesitate before asserting that he could read a letter and write an answer to it.

Variation by religion since 1901 in number of literates.

299. The considerations I have mentioned give a somewhat different complexion to our figures for literacy viewed in relation to those obtained in 1901. There is reason to think, though confessedly the point does not admit of proof, that the decrease is apparent only, and a difference in the instructions issued to the Census staff on the two occasions might be supposed to provide any further explanation required. We need not, however, rest satisfied with this. An examination of the figures by religion for the two years will throw some additional light on the question and proportional figures for Mohammadans, Hindus and Sikhs will be found in Subsidiary Table V (*a*) appended to this chapter.

(*a*) among Mohammadan males.

300. The actual figures for Mohammadan males by districts I give in the margin. It is after all in the Mohammadans that interest centres in the

North-West Frontier Province. It will be seen that in Hazara and Dera Ismail Khan the growth of literacy among Mohammadan males has exceeded the actual increase of population of that religion and sex, and that in the districts of the Province taken as a whole it only falls a trifle below it. In Peshawar the small increase (only 4 per cent.) in the number of the Mohammadan males who can read and write is to be attributed to the change in the instructions issued, some of the enumerators over large areas (*vide* paragraph 298) having interpreted the rules of the present Census as meaning that only those who had read up to the 3rd middle class were to be recorded as literate. In Kohat the decrease is partly to be attributed to the same cause, and, since school-boys were employed as enumerators in some tracts, it had here no doubt greater influence. Migration also has to be taken into account, for, of the literate immigrants present in the district in 1901 in connection with the building of the Khushalgarh-Thall railway, a certain number must have been Mohammadans. The figures for Bannu I find it difficult to explain. The higher standard of literacy required on the present occasion may have something to say to them, but the effect of this can hardly be expected to have been great, seeing that the Deputy Commissioner informs me that "no regard was paid to the school class in which individuals had read, in order to judge of their literacy." The inclusion in the 1901 figures of the troops stationed beyond the border, among whom many Mohammadans were no doubt to be found, has obviously contributed to the result. But I doubt whether either or both explanations are sufficient, and some carelessness in the record of literate persons on the present occasion would seem to be pointed at.*

DISTRICT.	Literate Mohammadans (males).		
	1911	1901	Variation per cent.
Hazara	4.995	4.475	+ 12
Peshawar... ...	11,678	11,183	+ 4
Kohat	3,107	3,162	— 2
Bannu	2,648	3,049	—13
Dera Ismail Khan ...	3,860	2,955	+31
TOTAL DISTRICTS * ...	26,288	24,824	+ 6

(*b*) among Mohammadan females.

301. A reference to Subsidiary Table V (*a*) will show that, unlike the case of females of other religions, the proportion of Mohammadan females who are literate has decreased since 1901 in the districts of the Province. To take individual districts, in Hazara it shows a rise (from ·4 to 1 per mille) and in Dera Ismail Khan it is found to be stationary. But to what are we to attribute the fall in the other three districts ?. It is unlikely in the extreme that female literacy is actually less common among Mohammadans now than ten years ago. Migration can have nothing to do with it, and I can only infer that the stress laid during the present enumeration on the power of writing a letter must have ruled out many women who would have been recorded as literate in 1901. It is well known that the majority of Mohammadan females confine their educational capacities, should they possess any, to a power to read the Koran, and I am informed by an officer who formed part of the Rawalpindi compilation office staff (where the schedules of Hazara, Peshawar and Kohat were dealt with) in 1901 that many women returned as "Koran Khwanda" were included as literate. The fact that in Dera Ismail Khan the proportion of literate females shows no change since 1901, and that in Hazara it has risen, are only in keeping with our statistics for males which show these to be the two districts in which education in the last ten years has made most progress.

(*c*) among Hindu males.

302. Of all the districts of the Province, it is only in Hazara that literates among Hindu males are proportionally more numerous now than was the case ten years ago. The male Hindu population of the Province has also largely decreased since 1901, the only district which shows a rise being Hazara. The decrease in the population of this religion has been attributed (*vide* paragraphs 115 and 119, Chapter IV) to migration. The fall in the proportion who are literate must be ascribed to the same cause. When we consider the classes from which the temporary immigrants of 1901 (now

District.	Hindu males.	
	1911	1901
Hazara ...	14,882	13.504
Peshawar ...	22,599	25.253
Kohat ...	6,758	10,317
Bannu ...	11,648	13,077
D. I. Khan...	15.510	16,677

* It is of course equally possible that the variation in this, as in other districts, is due to some error in the figures of 1901. It is worth remarking that in the Punjab, as in the North-West Frontier Province, the proportion of the male population recorded as literate at the recent Census was lower than in 1901.

no longer present) were drawn, and the cause of a temporary emigration of Hindus from the Province in 1911, the explanation suggested will be seen to fit in with the facts. The extraordinary immigrants of 1901 to the Kohat, Bannu and Dera Ismail Khan Districts were either troops, or were engaged in railway construction. None, or but few, Hindus employed on the latter can have been engaged in manual labour or in a menial capacity. Most must have been literate, being clerks, etc. Troops again, as we have seen, contain a high proportion of literates. The absence of temporary immigrants means therefore the absence of literate immigrants. Again the replacing of immigrants from outside by natives of the Province in Government offices and the like has meant largely the replacing of Hindus by Mohammadans. The Hindus who have gone were literate. The Hindus who remain have no such reason to be. When we come to the question of emigration we find the same state of affairs. It will be interesting to see, on the result of the next Census, whether the Hindu population of the Province continues to decrease, but certainly the facts as now before us point to the conclusion that the separation of the North-West Frontier Province from the Punjab tends to make the former a more and more Mohammadan country. But the people who have the power to move their habitations, (we are not here dealing with the migration of large sections of the population in response to demands for labour, or as a result of scarcity or the like) are the well-to-do, and consequently the literate. The temporary emigration of Hindus from the Province in consequence of fears of a collision between Hindus and Mohammadans at the time of the Census (*vide* paragraph 23 *supra*) is a case in point. It mainly affected Peshawar city, but had its influence also in areas outside it. The Hindus who could get away were those of means, prosperous traders, lawyers and the like, who were in nearly all cases educated. The poor (and consequently illiterate) Hindus all remained behind, and the result has naturally been to decrease the proportion who have been returned as literate.

303. But how far does the suggested explanation fit in with the fact that among females the proportion who are literate has increased since 1901? It must be remembered that the temporary immigration of 1901 was one almost exclusively of males, and the figures for female literacy are therefore not affected by this cause. The figures for the actual population of the two sexes in 1901 and in 1911 bear this out. Hindu males throughout the Province have decreased in number during the last ten years by 11 per cent. In the case of females the drop has been one of 5 per cent. only. In paragraph 114 (Chapter IV) it has been suggested that there has been no real decrease in the number of Hindu females found in the Province, and that the difference between the figures of 1901 and 1911 is probably due to the record on the present occasion as Sikhs of women who were recorded as Hindus at the previous one. But be this as it may, the point I wish to make here is that the figures for literacy among Hindu females are far less affected by migration than those for males of the same religion, and the tendency in favour of an extension of education among females therefore shows its natural effects. This tendency is far stronger among Hindus than among Mohammadans, and in the case of the latter I have stated my reason for thinking that our figures indicate no real retrogression. (*d*) among Hindu females.

304. The number of Sikhs resident in the Province is much smaller, and the figures for this religion deserve briefer treatment. They present the same general features as those for Hindus, *viz.* a rise (through a smaller one) in the proportion of females recorded as literate, and a fall (here a much larger one) in the proportion of literate males. The actual number of Sikh females, it is to be noticed, enumerated throughout the districts of the Province, has risen enormously* since 1901; that the number of literates among them should have increased even more quickly need occasion no surprise. It is merely in accordance with the general trend of events all over the world. On the other hand, while there has been a slight rise in the number of Sikh males enumerated in the districts of the Province, (*vide* margin), the number of literate Sikhs of this sex (*e*) among Sikhs.

Sikh males in British territory.

1911.	1901.
19,967	19,106

* But see previous paragraph. *It is doubtful how far the rise is real.*

has fallen. The decrease here is in part to be attributed to a change in the age distribution of the population. Of the total number of Sikh males enumerated in the Province 74 per cent in 1901 were aged '20 and over.' Now only 65 per cent. have reached or passed the age of 20 years.

In this connection it is worth while to examine the figures for literacy at the different age groups now and in 1901, (*vide margin*). The drop in the proportions shown as literate before reaching the age of 15 years is only what might be expected from the difference in the instructions issued now and in 1901, and I fancy that the figures arrived at during the present Census correspond closely enough with the actual facts. At the age group '15 to 20' our figure shows a satisfactory rise, while out of those aged '20 and over' 16 per thousand fewer are literate now than ten years ago. The fall here is probably in part accidental. Our Sikh population is in the main a shifting one; nearly one-half of our Sikh males were born outside the Province, and, with a population as little stable as this, the number of literate persons may be expected to show extraordinary variations. In part also the stricter definition of literacy issued on the present occasion may be considered responsible for the variation.

Sikh males enumerated in the North-West Frontier Province.

Age.	Literate per mille.	
	1911.	1901.
0—10 ...	44	60
10—15 ...	338	379
15—20 ...	466	374
20 and over ...	583	599
All ages ...	462	510

NOTE.—As the total figures are more easily accessible I include above those for Sikhs in trans-frontier posts, as well as in British districts.

Proportion recorded as literate at the different age periods in 1901 and 1911.

305. So much for the progress of education since 1901 among the followers of the various religions. It remains to consider the proportion of the whole recorded as literate at the different age periods. If Subsidiary Table V be referred to, it will be seen that in the districts as a whole the proportion of males aged '15 to 20' who can read and write is now 6 per thousand higher than it was ten years ago, and that the whole decrease has occurred among those aged '20 and over.' We see here the influence of migration, which has been referred to in discussing the variation since 1901 by religion. Immigrants especially literate immigrants, are nearly always at least 20 years of age, and the figures for literacy among persons who have not lived so long are therefore little affected by their presence. In Kohat and Bannu, it will be noticed, the advance of education has not kept pace with the growth of the male population living between the ages of 15 and 20. But, taking British territory as a whole, our figures are satisfactory, for the proportion of literate persons in this group affords the best indication as to the numbers who have attended school with advantage during the previous five years. As regards the proportion at the age period '20 and over' I have nothing to add to what has already been said.

Comparison with Censuses previous to 1901.

306. The materials on which to base any trustworthy comparison of the extent of literacy in 1901 with that at earlier enumerations are not very satisfactory. In 1881 and 1891 each person was recorded as literate, learning or illiterate. If we take as our basis of comparison the figures for the literate only, we shall omit many school boys and other students, who had already reached the Census standard of literacy; while if we compare with the figures of 1911 and 1901 those for the literate plus those under instruction in the earlier years, we shall include many who had not yet reached that standard. On the assumption that few persons learn to read and write after attaining the age of 15, and that most of those recorded as "learning," who had passed that age, were probably literate in the Census meaning of the term, the only satisfactory method of comparison would seem to be to compare the persons recorded as literate, plus those aged 15 and over who were recorded as learning, in the two earlier years. This has been done in Subsidiary Table V, appended to this chapter, except that, as the ages of persons returned as learning in 1881 were not tabulated, it has been necessary to count them all as literate. Another difficulty arises from the fact that the word "learners," seems to have

been widely misunderstood in 1891. Mr. Maclagan noticed, (*vide* paragraph 210, Punjab Census Report, 1891) that his figure for learners appeared to be exaggerated in Peshawar, and remarked that it no doubt included "many of the turbulent fanatics who hang about the mosques under pretence of studying theology, and term themselves Talib-ul-ilm, or searchers after learning." But the exaggeration does not appear to have been confined to Peshawar. Taking together the figures for the five districts now included in the Province, we find that among Mohammadan males of all ages, the learners amount to just over one-half of the literates. Both for 1881 and for 1891 therefore the figures for male literates are probably considerably higher than they should have been. The result of this conclusion is, however, only to render still more marked the rise in the number of literate males recorded in 1901.*

307. From whichever point of view we look at them, it is impossible to deduce from our figures any definite advance in education among males since 1901, though the increase of literacy among females seems satisfactory enough. It is also to be noticed (*vide* Subsidiary Table IV) that literacy in English shows a satisfactory advance. It is not perhaps surprising that no great enthusiasm for education yet appears in our statistics among the rural population, but it is worth while considering our figures along side of those compiled by the Education Department, in order to see whether the smallness of the former appears to be due to extensive omissions to record literacy in the Census returns. The total number of scholars shown in the departmental returns as attending school in 1911 is 31,891. Of these, however, 6,824 were pupils in schools which teach the Koran only, *i. e.* rote schools, the passing through which would entitle no one to be classed as literate in our sense of the word. The balance are distributed as shown in the margin. In primary and elementary schools the departmental returns show 15,747 pupils. Of these of course only a small proportion are literate in the Census meaning of the word. The Director of Public Instruction, with reference to a primary school (by no means an abnormal case) he had just inspected, wrote that nearly 75 per cent. of the boys were in one of the two lowest classes (in no sense literate). Probably many of the boys in the 3rd, 4th and 5th primary classes were not recorded as literate, and it will probably be a liberal estimate, if we assume 20 per cent. of the pupils with whom we are here concerned to be such. This will give us a figure of 3,149. If we add to these 9,320 pupils receiving instruction in secondary schools of one sort or another, we get 12,469 persons under instruction whom we may infer to be literate from the departmental returns. It remains to consider which of the figures arrived at during the Census we can set against this. Of the children of under 15 recorded as literate (7,487), the great majority must be at school, and we can set them, without hesitation, by the side of the departmental figures. But this does not by any means exhaust the pupils dealt with at the Census. Perhaps the majority of the boys in secondary schools are 15 years of age or over. The Director of Public Instruction tells me that a boy seldom enters a middle school till he is 14, and that the average age at which the 3rd middle class is reached (and we have seen that to have reached this class was in some areas held to be a necessary condition of being recorded as literate) is 16 years. The only figure obtained at the Census therefore which we can fitly compare with the number of literate pupils as shown in the departmental returns is that for literate persons of under 20 years of age. The former figure is 12,569, the latter 15,922. This clearly leaves a very small margin for boys who have left school, and for those persons (probably in the North-West

Comparison of Census statistics with returns of the Education Department.

Number of scholars shown for 1911 in departmental returns.

Total public institutions ...	**23,012**
Arts Colleges	22
Training schools	53
Secondary schools	8,128
Primary schools	14,809
Total private institutions ...	**2,055**
Advanced	1,108
Elementary	938
Others	9

* *Vide* footnote on page 182.

Frontier Province a small number only) who learn to read and write outside the institutions dealt with by the Education Department. On the other hand the figure I have given (12,469) for persons who may be inferred to be literate from the departmental returns is rather a high one. On the whole I do not think we can conclude from these latter that our Census returns are defective.* Moreover it is to be noted that at the age group '15 to 20', where the returns of the Education Department do perhaps seem to throw doubt on our figures, the proportion of literates has risen since 1901, in spite of the higher standard set on the present occasion.

308. The departmental statistics showing the number of educational institutions and scholars in 1911, 1901 and 1891, respectively, which are printed in Subsidiary Table VII are not entirely correct, owing to the fact that I have not been able to eliminate from the figures for Dera Ismail Khan in the two earlier years those for schools situated in the Leiah Tahsil, which was, previous to October 1901, included in the district.† Taking the figures as they stand, it will be seen that the total number of educational institutions, which increased largely between the years 1891 and 1901, has fallen during the last decade; and that the total number of scholars, which increased by 37 per cent. in the earlier decade, has risen by 17 per cent. only in the latter. This result is due, however, to a considerable decrease between the years 1901 and 1911 in the number of private institutions in existence, that of Government schools, together with the pupils under instruction in them, showing a marked rise everywhere. This does not suggest any real retrogression in education. Nor, I am inclined to think, is this to be inferred from the Census figures. I have given much anxious consideration to the question of the accuracy of those of 1911, but beyond the *a priori* improbability that the number of literate persons should have decreased, I can find no indications pointing to their incorrectness. The checking I had carried out for a whole district showed that inaccuracy, if inaccuracy there be, is not due to errors during tabulation. It will be noted that among females our statistics show literacy to have increased faster than the female population as a whole. Persons literate in English again are more numerous proportionally than they were in 1901, and the same is the case in regard to males aged '15 to 20.' It is only among males aged '20 and over' that the proportionate decrease is to be observed. The decrease here is, I believe, partly apparent and due to the stress laid, in the instructions issued on the present occasion, on the power of writing a letter. In so far as it is real, it is to be attributed to a decrease in the number of immigrants from the east (*vide* Subsidiary Table V, appended to Chapter III.) All the indications, whether we regard the statistics of birth-place, caste or religion, point to the fact that, since the formation of the Province, it has tended to grow more self-contained, and, education being rarer here than in the neighbouring provinces, this means that the percentage of literates to the whole has fallen. But the evidence which is available clearly suggests that among the population native to the Province education is spreading, and the figures obtained at the next Census should put this beyond doubt.

---

* The possibility of some error having occurred during tabulation struck me directly I saw the figures, and I had those for the Kohat District, where the decrease since last Census was greatest, compiled anew from the enumeration books on the tick system. The result was, however, to confirm the original figures.

† From the Bannu and Dera Ismail Khan figures in 1901 and 1891 I have deducted the schools situated in the other three tahsils now included in the Mianwali District of the Punjab, and from the Hazara figures for 1891 those for the Attock tahsil which was part of the district in that year.

SUBSIDIARY TABLE I.—(Total N.-W. F. Province including Agencies.)

Education by age, sex and religion.

Religion.	Number per mille who are literate.											Number per mille who are literate in English.		
	All ages.			0—10		10—15		15—20		20 and over.				
	Total.	Males.	Females.	Males.	Females.	Males.	Females.	Males.	Females.	Males.	Females.	Total.	Males.	Females.
1	2	3	4	5	6	7	8	9	10	11	12	13	14	15
All religions	**34**	**58**	**6**	**3**	**1**	**37**	**9**	**82**	**12**	**91**	**8**	**5**	**8**	**1**
Mohammadans	14	25	1	1	...	18	2	40	3	38	1	1	2	...
Hindus	248	375	57	28	14	305	92	450	105	492	65	21	35	1
Sikhs	352	462	132	44	32	338	190	466	206	583	163	17	25	1
Christians	851	897	640	281	203	607	411	656	594	951	852	830	879	603

SUBSIDIARY TABLE II.—*Education by age, sex and locality.*

District and Natural Division.	Number per mille who are literate.										
	All ages.			0—10		10—15		15—20		20 and over.	
	Total.	Males.	Females.	Males.	Females.	Males.	Females.	Males.	Females.	Males.	Females.
1	2	3	4	5	6	7	8	9	10	11	12
N.-W. F. P. (Districts) ...	**33**	**57**	**6**	**3**	**1**	**37**	**9**	**83**	**12**	**89**	**7**
Hazara	21	37	3	1	...	25	6	56	7	60	4
Trans-Indus Districts ...	**38**	**64**	**7**	**4**	**2**	**42**	**10**	**93**	**18**	**99**	**9**
Peshawar	37	61	9	4	3	36	11	91	17	93	12
Kohat	31	56	2	2	...	29	3	62	7	96	3
Bannu	34	61	3	3	...	41	5	88	5	99	3
Dera Ismail Khan ...	49	84	7	5	1	75	16	129	19	124	8

SUBSIDIARY TABLE III.—*Education by religion, sex and locality.*

District and Natural Division.	Number per mille who are literate.							
	Hindu.		*Mohammadan.*		*Christian.*		*Sikh.*	
	Males.	Females.	Males.	Females.	Males.	Females.	Males.	Females.
1	2	3	4	5	6	7	8	9
N.-W. F. P. Districts ...	**373**	**57**	**24**	**1**	**897**	**638**	**457**	**132**
Hazara	392	41	17	1	858	776	321	59
Trans-Indus Districts ...	**369**	**60**	**27**	**1**	**898**	**631**	**485**	**151**
Peshawar	340	124	27	1	915	616	450	180
Kohat	330	21	28	1	818	730	578	67
Bannu	351	13	22	...	603	639	572	90
Dera Ismail Khan	442	44	32	1	834	683	465	109

SUBSIDIARY TABLE IV.—*English education by age, sex and locality.*

District and Natural Division.	Literate in English per 10,000.													
	1911.										1901.		1891.	
	0—10		10—15		15—20		20 and over.		*All ages.*		*All ages.*		*All ages.*	
	Males.	Females.	Males.	Females.	Males.	Females.	Males.	Females.	Males.	Females.	Males.	Females.	Males.	Females.
1	2	3	4	5	6	7	8	9	10	11	12	13	14	15
N.-W. F. P. Districts ...	**3**	**2**	**32**	**2**	**130**	**6**	**134**	**12**	**83**	**7**	**72**	**6**	**46**	**3**
Hazara	...	...	16	...	64	2	36	4	25	2	13	1	14	1
Trans-Indus Districts ...	**4**	**3**	**39**	**3**	**156**	**7**	**169**	**15**	**104**	**10**	**93**	**8**	**55**	**4**
Peshawar	7	5	35	5	130	9	231	21	136	14	115	11	115	7
Kohat	1	...	23	2	123	7	107	11	65	6	75	4	31	4
Bannu	1	...	41	1	202	4	69	5	54	3	55	2	10	...
Dera Ismail Khan	2	1	65	1	231	4	105	9	80	5	75	5	12	2

SUBSIDIARY TABLE V.—*Progress of education since* 1881.

District and Natural Division	Number literate per mille.															
	All ages.								15—20				20 and over.			
	Males.				Females.				Males.		Females.		Males.		Females.	
	1911	1901	1891	1881	1911	1901	1891	1881	1911	1901	1911	1901	1911	1901	1911	1901
1	2	3	4	5	6	7	8	9	10	11	12	13	14	15	16	17
N.-W. F. P. Districts.	**57**	**62**	**61**	**58**	**6**	**5**	**2**	**1**	**82**	**76**	**12**	**10**	**89**	**98**	**7**	**7**
Hazara	37	35	43	31	3	1	1	...	56	49	7	3	60	57	4	2
Trans-Indus Districts.	**64**	**72**	**66**	**65**	**7**	**7**	**3**	**2**	**93**	**87**	**18**	**12**	**99**	**112**	**9**	**8**
Peshawar ...	61	65	71	80	9	10	5	4	91	74	17	17	93	103	12	12
Kohat ..	56	72	51	48	2	3	2	...	62	78	7	6	96	114	3	4
Bannu ..	61	73	52	50	3	2	1		88	94	5	4	99	114	3	3
Dera Ismail Khan	84	93	74	64	7	5	1	1	129	126	19	11	124	141	8	5

NOTE.—The figures for distribution by age being not available in 1881, all persons returned as 'under instruction' are treated as 'literate.' In the year 1891 all persons aged 15 and over who were recorded as 'learning' have been treated as 'literate.'

SUBSIDIARY TABLE V (*a*).—*Progress of education since* 1901 *by religion.*

District and Natural Division.	Number literate per mille.											
	Mohammadans.				*Hindus.*				*Sikhs.*			
	Males.		Females.		Males.		Females.		Males.		Females.	
	1911	1901	1911	1901	1911	1901	1911	1901	1911	1901	1911	1901
1	2	3	4	5	6	7	8	9	10	11	12	13
Total Districts N.-W. F. P.	**24**	**25**	**1**	**2**	**373**	**389**	**57**	**39**	**457**	**505**	**132**	**126**
Hazara ...	17	16	1	·4	392	387	41	18	321	333	59	20
Trans-Indus Districts	**27**	**28**	**1**	**2**	**369**	**389**	**61**	**43**	**485**	**530**	**151**	**160**
Peshawar ...	27	29	1	3	340	356	124	86	450	544	180	173
Kohat ...	28	29	·8	1	330	406	21	20	578	441	67	124
Bannu ...	22	27	·3	·8	351	360	13	13	572	575	90	121
Dera Ismail Khan ...	32	25	1	1	442	452	44	24	465	539	109	124

SUBSIDIARY TABLE VI.—*Education by Caste.*

CASTE.	NUMBER PER 1,000.						NUMBER PER 1,000 LITERATE IN ENGLISH.		
	LITERATE.			ILLITERATE.					
	Total.	Male.	Female.	Total.	Male.	Female.	Total.	Male.	Female.
1	2	3	4	5	6	7	8	9	10
Arora	253	408	64	747	592	936	145	261	3
Awan	13	22	1	987	978	999	11	19	...
Baghban	2	4	...	998	996	1,000	1	2	...
Baluch	15	27	1	985	973	999	22	39	...
Bhatiara	8	11	5	992	989	995	2	4	...
Brahman	249	375	65	751	625	935	293	486	9
Chamar	6	11	...	994	989	1,000	32	57	...
Chuhra	25	40	2	975	960	998	16	26	...
Dhobi	11	19	2	989	981	998	9	17	...
Dhund	5	9	...	995	991	1,000	3	6	...
Gakkhar	26	48	...	974	952	1,000	25	26	...
Gujar	6	10	...	994	990	1,000	3	5	...
Jat	52	89	3	948	911	997	23	40	...
Jhinwar	83	116	19	917	884	981	26	28	...
Jolaha	3	5	...	997	995	1,000	1	2	...
Karal	4	8	1	996	992	999	...	...	...
Kashmiri	16	27	2	984	973	998	17	33	...
Khatri	283	407	92	717	593	908	340	552	13
Kumhar	6	12	...	994	988	1,000	3	6	...
Lohar	7	12	...	993	988	1,000	2	4	...
Macchi	2	5	...	998	995	1,000	...	...	...
Maliar	3	4	1	997	996	999	1	1	...
Mallah	2	3	1	998	997	999	...	...	...
Mirasi	5	10	...	995	990	1,000	...	...	...
Mochi	5	8	1	995	992	999	2	3	...
Moghal	36	64	2	964	936	998	48	86	...
Musalli (with Kutana) ...	2	4	...	998	996	1,000	2	3	...
Nai	4	8	1	996	992	999	3	5	...
Paracha	41	74	2	959	926	998	29	54	...
Pathan	13	23	1	987	977	999	11	21	...
Qassab	7	13	1	993	987	999	5	9	...
Qureshi	52	93	5	948	907	995	57	107	1
Rajput	149	205	16	851	795	984	164	231	7
Saiad	31	55	4	969	945	996	31	60	...
Sarara	2	4	...	998	996	1,000	...	...	...
Shekh	59	97	10	941	903	990	118	209	3
Sonar	34	53	13	966	947	987	14	27	...
Swathi	13	24	1	987	976	999	3	6	...
Tanaoli	6	10	2	994	990	998	3	5	...
Tarkhan	7	13	1	993	987	999	3	6	...
Teli	7	13	...	993	987	1,000	...	...	...

SUBSIDIARY TABLE VII.—*Number of institutions and pupils according to the returns of the Education Department.*

Class of institution.	1911. Number of Institutions.	1911. Number of Scholars.	1901. Number of Institutions.	1901. Number of Scholars.	1891. Number of Institutions.	1891. Number of Scholars.
1	2	3	4	5	6	7
Total Institutions N.-W. F. Province ...	**976**	**31,891**	**1,199**	**27,184**	**684**	**19,891**
Total Public Institutions	**323**	**23,012**	**222**	**13,921**	**136**	**7,854**
Total Private Institutions	**653**	**8,879**	**977**	**13,263**	**548**	**12,037**
Hazara District Total Institutions ...	**217**	**7,075**	**195**	**4,260**	**23**	**1,108**
Total Public Institutions	**70**	**4,926**	**38**	**2,505**	**23**	**1,108**
Secondary Schools	7	1,442	5	751	3	321
Primary Schools	63	3,484	33	1,754	20	787
Total Private Institutions	**147**	**2,149**	**157**	**1,755**	...	...
Advanced	14	295	Not available.			
Elementary	11	199				
Teaching Qoran only	121	1,647				
Other Private Schools	1	8				
Peshawar District Total Institutions ...	**231**	**9,817**	**377**	**9,244**	**476**	**7,363**
Total Public Institutions	**108**	**7,795**	**81**	**4,774**	**54**	**3,040**
Arts Colleges	1	22	1	6	...	...
Secondary Schools	10	2,881	13	1,935	8	1,173
Primary Schools	96	4,839	67	2,833	46	1,867
Training Schools	1	53	...	...	...	...
Total Private Institutions	**123**	**2,022**	**296**	**4,470**	**422**	**4,323**
Advanced	8	87	36	549	144	1,616
Elementary	20	462	6	6	34	374
Teaching Qoran only	95	1,473	...	...	244	2,333
Other Private Schools	...	...	254	254	...	...
Kohat District Total Institutions ...	**89**	**2,655**	**72**	**1,691**	**134**	**2,331**
Total Public Institutions	**49**	**2,175**	**14**	**1,038**	**8**	**582**
Secondary Schools	3	707	1	392	1	332
Primary Schools	46	1,468	13	646	7	250
Total Private Institutions	**40**	**480**	**58**	**653**	**126**	**1,749**
Advanced	11	90	12	165	14	196
Elementary	2	50	3	28	...	...
Teaching Qoran only	27	340	43	460	112	1,553
Bannu District Total Institutions ...	**215**	**5,985**	**258**	**5,347**	**19**	**5,998**
Total Public Institutions	**50**	**3,806**	**32**	**2,073**	**19**	**917**
Secondary Schools	4	991	3	585	3	389
Primary Schools	46	2,815	29	1,488	16	528

SUBSIDIARY TABLE VII—concld.—*Number of institutions and pupils according to the returns of the Education Department.*

Class of institution.	1911. Number of		1901. Number of		1891. Number of	
	Institutions.	Scholars.	Institutions.	Scholars.	Institutions.	Scholars.
1	2	3	4	5	6	7
Total Private Institutions	**165**	**2.179**	**226**	**3.274**	...	**5.081**
Advanced	36	574	Not available.			
Teaching Qoran only	129	1,604				
Other Private Schools	...	1				
Dera Ismail Khan District Total Institutions	**224**	**6.359**	**297**	**6.642**	**32**	**3 091**
Total Public Institutions ...	**46**	**4 310**	**57**	**3.531**	**32**	**2 207**
Secondary Schools	6	2,107	8	1,194	5	155
Primary Schools	40	2,203	49	2,337	27	2,052
Total Private Institutions	**178**	**2 049**	**240**	**3,111**	...	**884**
Advanced	4	62	Not available.			
Elementary	6	227				
Teaching Qoran only	168	1,760				

The figures for Dera Ismail Khan for the years 1901 and 1891 include those for the Leiah tahsil, which now forms part of th Mianwali District of the Punjab.

SUBSIDIARY TABLE VIII.—*Main results of University examinations.*

Examination.	1911.		1901.		1891.	
	Candidates.	Passed.	Candidates.	Passed.	Candidates.	Passed.
1	2	3	4	5	6	7
Matriculation Entrance	228	120	164	105	42	26
F. A. or Intermediate examination	12	4	Not available.			
1st B. A. or 1st B. S. C.	...	...				
Degrees in Arts	3	...				
Degrees in Medicine	...	...				
Degrees in Law	...	...				
Degrees in Civil Engineering	...	...				

SUBSIDIARY TABLE IX.—*Number and circulation of news-papers.*

Language.	Class of news-paper (daily, weekly, etc.).	1911.		1901.		1891.	
		Number.	Circulation	Number.	Circulation.	Number.	Circulation.
1	2	3	4	5	6	7	8
Urdu	Weekly ...	1 (*a*)	475	2 {1 (*b*) + 1 (*c*)}	300	...	...
Urdu and Pushtu ...	" ...	1 (*d*)	2,500	...	...	...	...

(*a*) Published at Abbottabad.

(*b*) Was published at Dera Ismail Khan.

(*c*) Was published at Bannu.

(*d*) Published at Peshawar.

SUBSIDIARY TABLE X.—*Number of books published in each language.*

LANGUAGE.	NUMBER OF BOOKS PUBLISHED IN												
	1901	1902	1903	1904	1905	1906	1907	1908	1909	1910	Total of decade.		
											1901—1910	1891—1900	1881—1891
1	2	3	4	5	6	7	8	9	10	11	12	13	14
Arabic	...	...	...	...	...	2	..	2	12	1	17	...	3
English	...	...	...	...	...	1	...	...	2	...	3	...	...
Hindi	...	...	...	...	...	..	...	1	...	...	1	2	1
Panjabi	...	...	-	...	1	2	8	1	2	13	27	3	4
Pashto	...	...	...	...	...	9	1	1	8	1	20	1	2
Persian	...	...	...	...	...	3	4	2	11	..	20	3	1
Sanskrit	1	...	...	...	...	...	1	...	...	...	2	...	...
Urdu	1	1	...	...	...	3	4	1	4	6	20	7	4
Arabic and Panjabi	...	...	...	...	...	...	...	...	...	1	1	...	...
Arabic and Pashto	...	...	...	...	...	...	...	1	3	2	6	...	...
Arabic and Persian	...	...	...	...	...	4	1	1	1	...	7	...	...
Arabic and Urdu	...	...	...	...	...	1	...	..	1	...	2	...	...
Panjabi and Urdu	...	...	...	...	...	..	...	...	...	1	1	1	...
Pashto and Urdu	...	...	...	...	...	1	...	...	...	...	1	...	2
Persian and Urdu	...	...	...	...	...	...	...	1	...	...	1	...	...
Sanskrit and Hindi	...	...	...	...	...	1	...	...	...	...	1	...	...
Sanskrit and Marathi	...	...	...	...	...	1	...	...	...	...	1	...	...
Urdu and English	...	...	...	...	...	..	1	...	...	...	1	...	...
Urdu and Hindi	...	...	...	...	...	...	...	...	...	...	...	2	...
Arabic, Panjabi and Multani	...	...	...	...	...	...	...	...	...	...	...	...	1
Arabic, Persian and Pashto	...	...	...	...	...	6	...	1	1	...	8	...	...
Arabic, Persian and Urdu	...	...	...	...	...	...	...	...	1	...	1	...	...
English, Panjabi, Sanskrit, Urdu, Arabic, Persian Pashto and Latin.	...	...	...	...	...	-	...	...	...	...	...	...	1

CHAPTER IX.

LANGUAGE.

Reference to statistics. Classification of languages in Table X.

309. A return of the languages spoken in their homes by the people of the Province will be found in Table X in the second Part of this volume. The names appearing in the first column of that table are those actually recorded in the Census schedules, except that 14,288 persons in the Mansehra tahsil of the Hazara District, whose language was, obviously wrongly, recorded as Urdu, have been shown against Hindko, there being no doubt that they actually use a form of Lahnda or Western Punjabi. In a few cases where the name given is not that by which the language in question is commonly known, this latter has been added in brackets, thus Chitrali (Chitiari), Gorkhi (Naipali) and Dehgani (Pashai). The languages shown in the table have been classified according to the areas in which they are spoken, and not by linguistic families. The only exception to this rule is to be found in the case of various dialects, returned severally by an inconsiderable number of persons, the names of which, *e. g.*, Multani and Ponchi, are derived from areas situated outside the Province, but which, as representing forms of Lahnda or Western Punjabi, the most widespread, after Pashto, of the languages spoken within it, have been entered under the main heading of 'Provincial Vernaculars.' Similar considerations explain the appearance of Pashai, which is spoken in Afghanistan, under the heading of 'Vernaculars of India-Extra Provincial.'

Classification in subsidiary tables to the chapter.

310. In Subsidiary Tables I (*a*) and I (*b*), appended to this chapter, languages will be found arranged under the main heads given in Dr. G. A. Grierson's classified scheme. In the former are shown the variations since 1901 in the number of speakers of each. In the latter the figures as obtained from the schedules have been re-arranged to bring them into accord with the conclusions of the Linguistic Survey. The classification of languages as now made by Dr. Grierson "follows generally," writes the Census Commissioner, "the scheme drawn up by him for last Census, but a few changes have been made in accordance with the latest conclusions arrived at in the course of the Linguistic Survey." The only ones with which we are concerned here are in connection with Lahnda, which is now held to be "a distinct language of the North-Western group of Sanscritic languages, while Punjabi proper is placed with Western Hindi, Rajasthani and Gujerati, in the Western group of these languages"; and with the re-classification of Kashmiri and Kohistani which will be noted in the following pages. In Subsidiary Table II proportionate figures are given showing the degree to which each of the main languages is spoken in the districts and natural divisions of the Province.

The accuracy of the return of language. Difficulties in the way.

311. Before proceeding to discuss the figures some consideration must be given to the question of the accuracy of the return; and it may be premised that our language table, in so far as it attributes to Punjabi, if by that term the true Punjabi is understood, 848,218 speakers, is glaringly incorrect. The degree of error will be returned to later. What I wish to point out here is the nature of the difficulty which arises in attempting to prepare a trustworthy record of language. A large part of the population enumerated have no idea of the name of their mother tongue. As Mr. Maclagan put it in 1891, 'the peasant as little knows that he is talking Punjabi or Hindi as M. Jourdain knew that he was talking prose'. Dr. Grierson's remarks in the chapter on language in the last India Census Report are worth quoting in full in this connection: "As a rule," he observed, "in Northern India natives do not grasp the idea connoted by the word language. They understand that connoted by dialect readily enough, but their minds are not trained to grasp the conception, so familiar to us, of a general term embracing a number of interconnected dialects. It is as though we in England spoke of 'Somersetshire' and 'Yorkshire'

dialects, but never used the term 'English language.' Moreover the average native rarely knows the name of his own dialect, though he can recognise without difficulty the dialect spoken by a stranger. It follows that in Northern India the language names have generally been invented by the English," and, he might have added, are in some cases not even recognised by their speakers.

312. In the language of the bulk of the population of the Province who do not speak Pashto we have a case in point. It was for long supposed to be a form of Punjabi, though in 1881 Sir Denzil Ibbetson noted that the dialects of the Derajat had more affinity with Sindhi than with Punjabi. But as early as 1901 it had been established that it was quite distinct from Punjabi; and Dr. Grierson, though classifying it, with Punjabi, under the Indian (Sanscritic) branch of the Indo-European linguistic family, now places it in a group of languages (the North-Western) quite distinct from that to which the true Punjabi belongs. But while, according to the conclusions of the Linguistic Survey, it has a separate entity, it possesses (except among philologists, by whom it is styled Lahnda or Western Punjabi) no separate name. There are indeed local terms in use, such as Hindki in Hazara, Hindko* in Peshawar, Kohat and Bannu, and Derawal in Dera Ismail Khan. But, partly because none of these names appeared in the specimen schedule, and partly because the language is popularly supposed to be a branch of Punjabi, while, of the alternative names, Hindko at any rate is somewhat disliked as conveying some suggestion of inferiority, the name Punjabi has been almost universally returned. Although the use of a general name tends to obliterate the existence of local variations of dialect, its return would not have been of much importance, had it not been that there are within the Province a certain number of persons who speak the true Punjabi. As it is, we are driven to sources of information outside the language table in order to estimate the actual linguistic distribution of the population.

The return of Punjabi.

313. In the case of one other language shown some doubt arises as to the correctness of our return. This is Gujari, returned by 25,619 persons, mainly in the Hazara District. The chief reason for distrusting our figure lies in the fact that it amounts to something less than one-half of that obtained at the previous Census. It is to be noted that the language, which is the tribal speech of the Gujars of the hills, was not returned at all in 1891; its speakers are believed to be largely bilingual, and it appears to be to some extent a matter of chance whether Gujari on the one hand, or Hindki or Punjabi on the other, is returned. As regards the other entries, although our figure for Urdu is considerably different from that first compiled from the schedules, the language table may be assumed to be substantially correct.

Gujari.

314. To deal first with the languages as classified in Table X, only a trifling number of persons (33,849) have been recorded as speaking extra-Provincial vernaculars. According to the figures given in that table only one person in 65 speaks a foreign tongue. It is to be noticed, however, that Punjabi has been shown as a Provincial vernacular. Of the language referred to by most of the people who made the return this classification is perfectly correct. But Punjabi proper is not a language native to the Province. It is spoken within it by immigrants only. The method by which the calculation has been arrived at will be explained later; it is sufficient to mention here that about 25,000 persons (*vide* Subsidiary Table I (*b*) appended to this chapter) are probably speakers of the true Punjabi, and, if this figure be added to the number given above, it will be found that the speakers of foreign languages in the Province are to the total population roughly in the ratio of one to thirty-seven.

Distribution of population by language.
(*a*) As classified by area in which spoken.

315. In an area where immigrants are as numerous relatively as they are found to be in the districts of the Province, this figure is of course very low. The explanation lies in the fact that the Province is situated on the boundary line between areas in which two distinct languages are spoken. To the west we find Pashto, to the east Lahnda;† and in the

Small number of speakers of extra-Provincial vernaculars.

*It is also called Peshawari in Peshawar and Kohati in Kohat.

†Dr. Grierson is indifferent whether the language be referred to as Lahnda or as Western Punjabi; but as the use of the latter name may lead to confusion with Punjabi proper, the former term appears to be preferable. It may be noted, however, that in the Province the word Lahnda as applied to a language is not understood.

Province itself (British territory), though Pashto speakers are a good deal the more numerous, we find the two languages spoken side by side. Our immigrants come mainly from the areas contiguous to the Province on either side, and in such cases their tongue is of course just as much a vernacular of the Province as of their homes. Of the speakers of foreign languages, nearly all use those native to India, principally Punjabi and Urdu. Naipali* is spoken by 5,179 persons, being Gurkha sepoys and their families stationed within the Province, the bulk of whom are found in Abbottabad, and Kashmiri speakers amount to 561 persons. Vernaculars of Asiatic countries beyond India are represented by 3,843 persons, most of whom speak Persian, and European languages by 5,888, of whom nearly all are, naturally, speakers of English.

Distribution of population by language. (b) As classified by linguistic families.

316. Coming to languages as classified by linguistic families, we find (*vide* Subsidiary Table I (*b*)) that all but 53 persons, out of the total population of the Province, speak tongues of the Indo-European family. The languages appearing in our schedules which do not belong to that family are Tamil (with Madrasi), Arabic, Chinese and Turki, an entry which, from the birth-places of the persons returning it, *viz*. Bokhara, Samarkand, etc., appears to refer to Turkish dialects. The numbers concerned are too small to have any great interest, and represent merely faint signs of the great interchange of population which is going on all over the world, and which sweeps the Chinaman as far afield as to Peshawar. Of the Indo-European family, languages of the Eranian branch, (notably Pashto) are those which are most widely spoken. The Indian (Non-Sanscritic) branch is represented by 735 speakers only, most of whom speak Kashmiri, and the Indian (Sanscritic) branch accounts for the whole of the remainder, with the exception of the 5,888 persons who speak English and other European languages.

Local distribution of speakers of each language.

317. In Subsidiary Table II will be found proportionate figures showing the distribution by language of the population, of each district and natural division, and of the districts as a whole. In this table only the languages most commonly spoken have been shown, with the exception of English and Naipali, which, as being spoken solely by immigrants living in groups dissociated from the bulk of the population, have less interest in this connection than the others. In the Province as a whole (British territory) 56 per cent. of the population speak Pashto. If we include the tribal territory, however, the preponderance of Pashto will be found to be much greater, nearly the whole of the persons living in this area being Pashto speakers. In trans-frontier posts, notably among the troops stationed in the Malakand Agency, other languages are spoken, but we can assume that in that portion of the Province which is not included in British India, Pashto is spoken by 80 per cent. of the inhabitants. A few speakers of foreign tongues, who were enumerated in British posts, are shown in Table X, and the balance is composed of persons in the Malakand Agency who use Gujari, Kohistani, Chitiari and the other little known tongues which are current in that secluded corner of the world. Little less common than Pashto in British territory is Lahnda. Owing to the erroneous and universal entry of this tongue as Punjabi, which I have referred to above, the separation of speakers of each is matter for estimate only and in Subsidiary Table II I have therefore shown the two languages together. Between them they account for 42 per cent. of the population. Urdu is spoken by ·8 and Gujari by just over 1, per cent. Speakers of other languages comprise a trifling proportion only of the whole.

318. But though the language most commonly met with in the Province as a whole, Pashto is not everywhere the dominant tongue. In Hazara no more than 483 persons per 10,000 speak it, and in Dera Ismail Khan it is only the vernacular of something over a quarter of the population. According to the present Census the district where it is most common is Bannu, where Pashto speakers amount to 8,751 per 10,000 of the whole. Kohat comes next with 8,684 per 10,000, while in Peshawar they amount to just over 82 per cent. (8,202 per 10,000). Under the head Punjabi with Hindko (*vide* Subsidiary Table II) we find the largest proportion in Hazara (8,990 per 10,000). In Dera Ismail Khan the

*Nepal is not strictly regarded as forming part of India, and the entry of Naipali should perhaps have appeared under head C in Table X 'Vernaculars of Asiatic countries beyond India.'

figure is not very much smaller (7,111 per 10,000) while in Peshawar, Kohat and Bannu (in that order) something over 16 per cent. of the total population speaks one or other of these two tongues. The other languages shown in Subsidiary Table II are spoken by comparatively small numbers of persons. Hindostani is naturally commonest in the district (Peshawar) which posesses the head-quarters of the Province, and the largest trade centres within it. It is least common, as we should expect, in the mountainous district of Hazara, which posesses less attraction to immigrants than any of the others. Gujari is found only in Hazara (with the exception of 27 speakers of the tongue recorded in Peshawar); while nearly all our Persian speakers are in either Peshawar or Kohat, mainly the former. In both cases the presence of the language is to be attributed to the proximity of the district to Kabul, where Persian is commonly spoken, and to the fact that the Kabul trade takes routes (the Khyber and the Kurram) which debouch on one or other of them.

Pashto.

319. After this general review, we can proceed to consider separately each of the languages recorded at the Census. Pashto naturally claims first attention. No account of it, or of its two main dialects is necessary. By Europeans (at any rate among civil officers) serving here it is perhaps the best known of the languages of the Province. Its genius seems to be more akin to that of English than is the case of any other Indian vernacular; and among Europeans there are at least one or two distinguished representatives who have mastered it so thoroughly that it is commonly asserted that a Pathan, if he could not see the speaker, would be unable to distinguish him from one of his own people. Those who require a detailed account of the language, its origin and linguistic affinities, with some mention of its literature, are referred to paragraphs 475 foll: of the India Census Report, 1901. With Pashto speakers are included 10 persons who returned their tongue as Ormuri, and 8 who recorded it as Kabuli. The latter is stated by Dr. Grierson to be one of the names by which Pashto is known, but it seems equally possible that it refers to Persian, which is the language used by the upper classes in Kabul. Regarding Ormuri a few words are necessary. Dr. Grierson wrote * of it in 1901:— "Pashto exhibits many points of connection with the Ghalchah languages of the Pamirs, but still more closely related to these last is the curious isolated little speech, known as Ormuri or Bargista (the speech of Barak, which is the tongue of a few thousand people near Kaniguram in Waziristan, a locality outside the Census area." (It has been included on the present occasion in the area of which the population was estimated). "They have an impossible tradition that they came from Yaman in Arabia, and that their language was invented for them by a very old and learned man, named 'Umar Laban', some four hundred years ago. They claim to be descended from a certain Mir Barak, from whom one of the names of their tribe and of their language is derived..................The language is certainly an East Eranian one, and deserves more study than it has yet recieved. It does not appear to have any literature, but the Arab-Persian alphabet as adapted for Pashto has been employed in writing it." I find no trace of the return of the language in 1901. It was returned in 1891, but the numbers using it were merged in Pashto, and were not separately shown in the Punjab Census Report for that year.

Ormuri.

Comparison of number of Pathans and of Pashto speakers.

320. As is well known, Pashto is the national language of the Pathans. It has, however, been returned by a good many persons who did not record themselves as Pathan in the column of caste, tribe or race. Pashto speakers (including Ormuri) are 1,229,599 persons, while the persons who are shown in Table XIII as Pathans amount to 845,183 only. No doubt the record was correct in the case of a good many Saiads, Qureshis, Swathis, Tanaolis and others; but I fancy that large numbers must have recorded it, in spite of the fact that in their homes the language in use is Lahnda. The Awans, for instance, of the Peshawar District, are bilingual; they can speak Pashto as readily as Lahnda, but they use the latter in their homes. From the fact, however, that Pashto is the tongue of the dominant community, there would be a natural tendency to return it rather than any other.

* *Vide* paragraph 476 India Census Report, 1901.

Increase in number of Pashto speakers since 1901.

321. For the same reason the increase in the number of Pashto speakers since 1901 has been comparatively large (8 per cent.), as against an increase of 7 per cent. in the population of the districts of the Province as a whole, and one of 4 per cent. only in the number of persons who have shown their language as Punjabi or Hindko. The number of Pathans recorded in British territory has increased since 1901 by 6 per cent. only. The difference is no doubt in part due to the greater care taken on the present occasion in preparing a record of caste (*e. g.* circulation of caste index and the like); and it may be suspected that fewer persons have been wrongly recorded as Pathans on the present occasion than on the last. But I think that in any case our figures for Pashto are somewhat higher than they should be. At first sight one might suppose that Pashto speakers would tend to increase more slowly than speakers of languages in use in the vast and populous regions to the east of the Province; that the larger civilization would tend to absorb the smaller. In support of this view one might point to the fact that the books used in elementary schools are written in Urdu for boys and in Hindi or Gurmukhi for girls. But in actual fact, at any rate since the separation of the Province from the Punjab, development seems to be taking an opposite direction. The number of immigrants from the Punjab is now considerably smaller than was the case ten years ago, it is the indigenous tribes who have increased in numbers and not the foreign groups, and during the last decade the Province appears every year to have grown more self-supporting and self-centred. The use of Urdu books in schools, the language of which has to be learnt by the pupils before they can master their contents, appears as yet to have had little effect. Even a pupil who has perfectly mastered this tongue, returns on leaving school to a society where it is another language that he hears daily around him. Even if he does not forget what he has learnt, he probably goes on speaking Pashto at home; and, whatever he speaks there, he will, for the reason above given, record his language as Pashto, if he thinks there is the slightest chance of his assertion being believed.

Proportional numbers of Pashto speakers now and in 1901.

322. In the districts of the Province as a whole Pashto speakers now amount to 5,562 per 10,000 of the total population. In 1901 (*vide* Subsidiary Table II, appended to Chapter VI, Punjab Census Report, 1901) they only amounted to 5,408·5 per 10,000. But the general increase in the spread of Pashto which these figures denote is not found equally in all the districts of the Province. As the figures in the margin show, in Hazara and Dera Ismail Khan Pashto speakers are less numerous proportionately now than was the case ten years ago, and it is only in the three central districts, and notably in Kohat, that the reverse is the case. This development is in accordance with *a priori* probabilities. In Hazara and Dera Ismail Khan Pathans are in a minority, in the former district in an insignificant minority; whereas in the three central districts they dominate the total population. Pathan sentiment, and the desire to imitate Pathan customs, are naturally much weaker in the districts which form the north and south extremities of the Province than elsewhere; and in them the natural tendency for the larger civilization to absorb the less is showing its full effects. In the central districts on the other hand the influence of an outside civilisation has, at any rate for the time being, received a set back in the last ten years. One may suspect, however, that before many decades have passed the course of events will be found to be taking the opposite direction. Pride of birth and the vitality of the Pathan will, however, no doubt preserve Pashto for far longer than other local languages when pressed upon by more cultivated tongues.

Pashto speakers per 10,000 of population in 1901 and 1911.

District	1901.	1911.
Hazara.	563·4	483
Peshawar	7,848·6	8,202
Kohat	7,799·4	8,684
Bannu	8,459·7	8,751
Dera Ismail Khan ...	2,897·8	2,773

Proportion of Pashto speakers in Hazara, Peshawar and Kohat since 1881.

323. In this connection it will be interesting to notice the ratio borne by Pashto speakers to the total population at the Censuses prior to 1901. The figures for Bannu and Dera Ismail Khan in those years can not usefully be compared with the statistics obtained at later enumerations; for previous to

1901 both districts included large areas cis-Indus in which Pashto is little spoken, and we have no figures for the distribution of the population by language for units smaller than the district. I show in the margin the proportion of Pashto speakers enumerated in the three northern districts of the Province since 1881. It will be seen that in Hazara, though there was a slight rise in the proportion of Pashto speakers in 1891 as compared with ten years before, the general tendency has been for the language to become less common as the years go on. In Peshawar and Kohat on the other hand the proportion of Pashto speakers did not vary by more than 3 per cent. at any time between the years 1881 and 1901, and showed no continuous tendency in either direction. It is only the last decade, in which took place the separation of the Province from the Punjab, which has seen a marked rise in the proportion of persons returned as speaking Pashto. A consideration of the figures for the last 30 years therefore only confirms the conclusions which we arrived at on a review of the statistics for the years 1901 and 1911, *viz.* that the decrease in the use of Pashto in Hazara may be expected to persist, while it is unlikely that the language will continue largely to extend the number of its speakers in the central districts. The comparatively rapid growth which it has shown in the last decade is due to special circumstances, the effect of which is likely to be temporary only.

Pashto speakers 10,000 *of total population.*

District.	1881.	1891.	1901.	1911.
Hazara ...	650	659	563	483
Peshawar ...	7,731	7,996	7,849	8,202
Kohat ...	7,848	7,790	7,799	8,684

324. Proceeding with individual languages in the order in which they are dealt with in Subsidiary Table I we may next consider the figures for Persian. Persian speakers amount to 3,811 persons, of whom the bulk (3,286) were enumerated in Peshawar. 155 were found in Kohat, and 357, mainly in Kurram, in the trans-frontier posts. The persons we are here concerned with are largely immigrants, traders and the like, from Kabul, though a certain number consist of permanent residents. The Qazzilbash "a * name applied to descendants of certain Turki tribes who came in with or after Nadir Shah" speak Persian, and any one unacquainted with the city of Peshawar would be astonished at the extent to which Persian is spoken among its inhabitants. Many Persian speakers are found in the lowest orders, and I remember a Chamar who used that tongue. He was born in Kabul, and stated that by caste he was a Quresh. The largest increase recorded is in Peshawar, where persons giving their language as Persian, who in 1901 amounted to 1,890 souls only, are now as many as 3,280. The figures of 1901 do not, however, appear to be entirely free from suspicion. The number recorded in 1891 was 3,408, and there is hardly likely to have been so great a fluctuation in ten years. In Kohat also it appears possible that there was in 1901 some confusion between the use of *Farsi* as denoting Urdu, and as indicating the true Persian; for the Persian speakers recorded, who amounted to 398 persons in 1891 and to 155 only on the present occasion, are shown as being as many as 801 in 1901. The numbers are small, and the fluctuations are not of great interest. It is clear that outside of Peshawar city the language is hardly spoken at all. **Persian.**

325. The only other language of the Eranian branch of the Indo-European family, appearing in Subsidiary Table I, is Balochi, which was returned by 124 persons in 1901, mainly in Dera Ismail Khan. It has not been returned on the present occasion; and the presence of a small number of Balochi speakers in the Province ten years ago was no doubt accidental only. The figures for †Kashmiri (which is now classified as belonging to the Indian, non-Sanscritic branch, of the Indo-European family), call for rather fuller **Balochi.** **Kashmiri.**

* Maclagan's Census Report, page 314.

†Kashmiri was classed in 1901 by Dr. Grierson as one of the North-Western group of the Sanscritic languages of the Indo-European family. On re-consideration he has re-classified it as stated in the text.

comment. It is to be noticed that in 1901, as at the recent Census, the numbers concerned were trifling only. In both years they form but a small part of the persons who recorded their caste as Kashmiri, or their birthplace as Kashmir. On the present occasion 4,655 persons showed themselves as having been born in the state, and no less than 15,198 appear as Kashmiri in the table of caste. In 1891 Mr. Maclagan * pointed "to the neglect of the language by Kashmiri settlers in the second or third generation" as one of the causes of the decrease in the number of Kashmiri speakers enumerated in the Punjab in that year as compared with ten years earlier. The decrease which has now been recorded is no doubt partly due to this cause ; in part also it is to be attributed to a shrinkage of immigration from the state (*vide* Subsidiary Table V, appended to Chapter III).

Other languages of the Indian (non-Sanscritic) branch of the Indo-European family.

326. Other languages of the Indian (non-Sanscritic) branch of the Indo-European family are spoken by 174 persons only. The languages included under this general head are Chitiari, with which I have grouped Kashkari, with Kohistani, and Dehgani, or, to use the name by which it is more commonly known, Pashai. The corresponding figures for 1901 require no comment. One person only was shown in that year as speaking Chitiari. To turn to the figures of the present Census, Chitiari, which was actually recorded as Chitrali, was returned by 10 persons in Peshawar, and Kashkari by 31 souls in the same district. All were immigrants from the Malakand Agency. Of the Kunar river Sir Thomas Holdich writes † "from this point" (*i.e.* Mustaj) "you may call it the Chitral river or Kashkar, for it now flows past Chitral, and through the district known to the hill people as Kashkar;" and from this the name of the language appears to be taken. Kohistani was shown as their mother tongue by 117 persons, of whom 85 were found in Hazara and the balance in Peshawar. The little known group of dialects to which the name is applied is spoken by the inhabitants of the Indus Kohistan, and by those dwellers in the Swat and Panjkora Kohistans who have not abandoned their original tongue in favour of Pashto. Kohistani, which Dr. Grierson classed in 1901 as one of the North-West group of the Sanscritic languages, he now groups, like Kashmiri and Chitiari, with the non-Sanscritic sub-branch. Its speakers are of course immigrants into the districts in which they have been enumerated, although their speech, as being current in an area included in the sphere politically subject to the Local Administration, has been shown in Table X as one of the Provincial vernaculars. The other language coming under the common head with which this paragraph is concerned is that returned by its speakers as Dehgani, but more readily recognizable as Pashai. Of this tongue little is known. "Pashai properly speaking," says Dr. Grierson‡, "is the speech of the Dehgans of Laghman, and of the country to the east of it as far as the Kunar. It is also called Laghmani, from the tract where it is spoken (the abode of the Lambagai of Ptolemy) and Dehgani because most of its speakers belong to the Dehgani tribe. The boundaries of the language are said to be, roughly, on the west the Laghman river, on the north the boundary of the Kafirs, on the east the Kunar River, and on the south the Kabul River, although the riverain villages on the left bank of the Kabul speak Pashto. It has two well marked dialects, an eastern and a western. This language, the most western outpost of Indo-Aryan speech, is thus spoken in the heart of Afghanistan, and is of more than ordinary interest both to ethnologists and philologists." Our Dehgani (or Pashai) speakers are of course immigrants from the west. They recorded their race as "Afghan Kohistani" and their birthplace as Kohistan ; terms which (Koh means a hill in Persian) are used loosely in the Province for any hilly country and its inhabitants. Their tongue, as being a branch of Indo-Aryan speech, has been included in Table X under the heading of "Extra Provincial Vernaculars of India," in spite of the fact that it is actually spoken in an area (Afghanistan) which is entirely beyond the sphere of control of the Indian Government.

Chitiari.

Kohistani.

Pashai.

---

* *Vide* Punjab Census Report, 1891, paragraph 241.

† The Indian Borderland, page 244.

‡ *Vide* paragraph 485, India Census Report, 1901.

327. This brings us to a consideration of the various languages which are grouped together in Subsidiary Table I as falling under the Indian (Sanscritic) branch of the Indo-European linguistic family. Owing to the unfortunate use of Punjabi as a general term for the dialects locally known as Hindko, Hindki and Derawal, which I have referred to in paragraph 312 above, it will be best in the first place to consider together languages which belong in reality to two entirely separate groups. These are Hindko, and its dialects (Lahnda) which belongs, with Sindhi and others, to the North-Western, and Punjabi, which is classed by philologists, along with Western Hindi, Rajasthani, Gujerati, Khandeshi, Western Pahari and Bhil languages, in the Western group of the sub-branch of the Indo-European family with which we are here concerned. As I have pointed out, we are driven to sources of information other than the table of language in order to estimate how many of our population who returned themselves as using Punjabi are speakers of Punjabi proper, and how many, when they recorded Punjabi, meant something quite different. I will attempt presently to discriminate between the speakers of the two tongues; for the present I will consider both taken together.

Languages of the Indian (Sanscritic) branch of the Indo-European linguistic family.
Punjabi and Hindko.

328. The two languages, or groups of languages, are spoken (*vide* Subsidiary Table II) by something over two-fifths of the population of the British territory included in the Province. The exact proportion is 4,168 per 10,000. In Kohat and Bannu Punjabi plus Hindko (or it would be more in accordance with their relative importance in the Province to say Hindko plus Punjabi) are spoken by only 12 per cent. of the total population, and in Peshawar by only 16 per cent. But in Dera Ismail Khan, where, as we have seen, Pashto is comparatively so little used, the speakers of one or other of these two languages amount to 71, and in Hazara to as much as 90, per cent. of the whole As will have been observed, the variations between the different localities are due to differences of race in their inhabitants, the Pathans speaking Pashto, and tribes of Indian origin mainly using some form of Lahnda. As I have noticed, however, the use of Pashto extends considerably beyond the Pathan population in the three central districts of the Province.

Extent of population by whom spoken in different districts.

329. In the margin I show the proportionate numbers of the speakers of those two languages in each district in 1901 and 1911, respectively. Just as in the case of Pashto, the language has become more common in the last ten years in those areas where it is spoken by the bulk of the population, while in the central districts, where its occurrence is comparatively rare, it has given ground to Pashto. In speaking of the language in the singular I am of course merely employing a convenient form of speech. There are two languages; and this is the place at which some attempt must be made to distinguish the speakers of each.

Lahnda plus Punjabi.

Speakers of Lahnda plus Punjabi.

District.	Number per 10,000 of population.	
	1901.	1911.
Hazara ...	8,415	8,990
Peshawar ...	1,947	1,560
Kohat ...	1,961	1,224
Bannu ...	1,453	1,195
Dera Ismail Khan ...	6,922	7,111

330. In separating the speakers of the true Punjabi from among the large numbers who have returned it, obviously the best guide to follow is the table of birth-place. We can not of course say with any certainty of various tracts whether the language of their inhabitants will be Punjabi or Lahnda. There is, as is only to be expected, a fringe of debateable ground where the area of one language meets another. But we shall probably be making at any rate a reasonable approximation to the facts if we say that the speakers of the true Punjabi are not much more numerous than the persons enumerated within

Punjabi.

the Province who showed as their birth-place one or other of the Punjab districts and States shown in the margin. It must be remembered of course that all the persons shown in the marginal statement did not necessarily return their language as Punjabi. They may, for instance, have returned Urdu. Nor is it certain that some from among them have not, with their change of residence, given up the use of Punjabi in favour of Lahnda. At the same time in view of the fact that the immigrants with whom we are here concerned are for the most part purely temporary residents of the Province, such as troops and followers, it may be assumed that they still speak Punjabi proper. We also have to remember that a certain number of speakers of the true Punjabi are also no doubt to be found outside the districts which I have noted as Punjabi speaking. Taking into account the uncertain character of the indications on which the calculation has to be based, I have preferred to estimate the number of the Punjabi speakers at something above the number of persons shown in the marginal statement, and, for the purpose of Subsidiary Table I (*b*) appended to this chapter, I have put the number at 25,000. To these I have added the 46 persons who returned their language as Dogri, which is one of the dialects of the Punjabi tongue.

District, etc.	No. of immigrants from.
Sialkot ..	3,974
Gujranwala ..	1,864
Lahore ..	1,525
Montgomery ...	16
Gurdaspur ...	2,324
Amritsar ..	3,073
Ferozepur ...	618
Kangra	1,578
Hoshiarpur ...	2,046
Jalandhar ..	1,379
Ludhiana ...	1,639
Ambala	880
Karnal	213
Rohtak ..	758
Hissar ...	185
Kalsia ...	8
Kapurthala ..	74
Jhind ...	16
Patiala ...	1,111
Faridkot ...	18
Malerkotla ...	142
Nabha ...	212
TOTAL ..	23,653

Variation in the number of Punjabi speakers since 1901.

331. In the figures for Punjabi speakers obtained at the Census of 1901 we have nothing which we can fitly compare with the number which I have suggested. In 1901 the language commonly returned in Hazara was Hindki, and in Dera Ismail Khan Derawal. The persons who made these returns are properly included under the head of Lahnda. But elsewhere, as on the present occasion, the language commonly returned was Punjabi, and in the Punjab Census Report, 1901, Punjabi, by which the true Punjabi is meant, is credited with close on three hundred thousand speakers in the North-West Frontier Province. This is obviously incorrect. The language of Peshawar, Kohat and Bannu, when it is not Pashto, is just as far removed from Punjabi proper as that of Hazara and Dera Ismail Khan. It is in fact virtually the same language as is spoken in those two districts The degree of variation I will note when I consider the figures for Lahnda.

332. As perhaps throwing further light on the correctness of my calculations, and also because the figures will be useful at a further Census, when, it is hoped, the blunder * I have made may not be repeated, I show in the margin the figures by districts for immigrants from the Punjabi speaking districts, given in the marginal statement against paragraph 330, by the side of the persons recorded as speaking Punjabi in 1901. It is, I think, plain that though the most common entries in 1901 were Hindki for Hazara, and Derawal for Dera Ismail Khan, in that year too there was considerable confusion between

District.	Recorded as speaking Punjabi 1901.	Immigrant from Punjabi speaking districts 1911.
1	2	3
Hazara ..	43,165	1,460
Peshawar	149,346	12,149
Kohat ...	39,317	3,003
Bannu ...	31,112	2,680
Dera Ismail Khan ...	30,815	1,552

* The way to avoid it would of course be to enter freely in the specimen schedule entries of Hindko, Hindki and Derawal, and to lay stress in the instructions to supervisors on the necessity of seeing that Punjabi is only returned by persons who speak the true Punjabi, who will nearly always be immigrants from the Central Punjab.

these languages and Punjabi, while in the three central districts Punjabi has been recorded wholesale in place of Hindko. It is largely because the 1901 figures are so high that I have put the number of true Punjabi speakers on the present occasion at so numerous a figure as 25,000 ; but it is at least open to question whether the estimate is not unduly large.

333. As I have said, the language of the bulk of the population who do not speak Pashto is Lahnda. Regarding the origin of this language, with the other tongues of the Sanscritic Indo-Aryan Group, I would refer the reader to Dr. Grierson's remarks in paragraphs 486 foll : of the last India Census Report. As regards the language itself, in view of its importance in the Province, it will be fitting that I give some account here, though I can contribute little beyond quotations from Dr. Grierson himself. "Lahnda", he remarks * "is a language the existence of which has long been recognized, but under many names. In the last Census Report it was called Jatki, but this, like Multani, Western Punjabi and other titles given to it, has the disadvantage of not being sufficiently comprehensive. It is not spoken only by Jats; it is not peculiar to Multan ; and it is not a Western dialect of the Punjabi of the Manjh. I therefore think it best to give it the name which is indicated by the natives of the Punjab themselves †, *i.e.,* Lahnda or the language of the west (Punjabi, *Lahnde-di-Boli*). It has no literature, and has no standard form, so that it is rather a group of connected dialects than a language with a definite standard. The eastern boundary of Lahnda may be taken as the river Chenab from the Kashmir Frontier down to the town of Ramnagar in the district of Gujranwala. Thence it runs in a straight line to the north-west corner of Montgomery and across that district to the south-west corner......................Its northern boundary may be taken as coinciding on the east with the range of mountains forming the southern limit of the Kashmir Valley, while to the west it skirts that valley and reaches as far north as the watershed dividing the Indus from the Jhelam Valley. Here it is bounded on the west by the Kohistani of the Indus Valley, till we reach the Hazara District. Thence the western boundary may be roughly taken as the Indus itself. These eastern and western boundaries are, however, very indefinite. Pashto is spoken in several places close to the Indus, and from the Indus westwards up to the Afghan mountain country we find Lahnda also spoken, but principally by Hindus, the Mussalman language being Pashto. As we get further south into the Derajat, Lahnda more than holds its own, and is the principal language of the plains, west of the Indus." Lahnda.

334. The statement that west of the Indus, if the Derajat be excepted, Lahnda is principally spoken by Hindus, is not quite accurate. In Peshawar, however much freedom they possess in expressing themselves in Pashto, the non-Pathan tribes, such as the Awan, habitually use Lahnda among themselves, in spite of the fact that they are composed of Mohammadans. This, however, is a digression. Dr. Grierson describes Lahnda as a group of connected dialects rather than as a language. The following remarks regarding the different forms taken by it are derived from some unpublished notes on the language written by the Reverend Trevor Bomford which he has kindly permitted me to use : "With regard to the variation", he writes, "in words, spelling, pronunciation, grammar and in the meanings of the words which exist in different parts it must be remembered that the language is spoken over a tract of country some 450 miles long by 100 broad, and that many of those parts were formerly completely isolated from one another. The northern section too is separated from the southern by the Salt Hills range. Under these circumstances one would expect variations, and they exist, but the differences are hardly as great as those between Sussex and Yorkshire or between Devonshire and Norfolk. Another thing to be kept in mind is that while the different dialects of English were free from any contact with foreign languages, those of Western Punjabi come into close contact with Sindhi, Pashto, Kashmiri and Punjabi, and that in different parts there is a tendancy to

* *Vide* paragraph 517, India Census Report, 1901.

† Persons living in the North-West Frontier Province naturally do not recognize it by this name. To them it is rather the language of the east than that of the west.

borrow from the contiguous dialects." But in spite of the division into northern and southern groups of dialects, with the Salt Range as a boundary between them, and of the reasons for the variations within each group which are glanced at above, "the general resemblance", writes Mr. Bomford, "is so great that a Muzaffargarh Jat had no difficulty in making himself understood in Hazara," when he spoke his own dialect.

335. This is not the place, nor have I the necessary knowledge, to attempt to give any account of the points in which Lahnda resembles or differs from Punjabi, Sindhi or any other tongue. Moreover I can refer the reader to no published grammar of the language. I will therefore pass on to consider the local distribution of its speakers, among whom, in dealing with each district separately, I include all those persons who returned their language as Punjabi who are not shown, in the marginal statement printed against paragraph 331, as having been born in an area in the Punjab where the true Punjabi is spoken. On this assumption the figures for Lahnda by districts are as shown in the margin. I have attributed here to this language only those persons whom we know to have been born in areas where the true Punjabi is spoken, and have not taken, as in the case of the figures for the Province as a whole which are printed in Subsidiary Table I (*b*), a round number somewhat in excess of the figures derived from the birth-place table. The figures here given, though they do not profess to be accurate, are at any rate a reasonable approximation to the number of Lahnda speakers who are to be found in the Province. It is not worth comparing them with those obtained at the Census of 1901; for these latter, as follows from the conclusion stated in paragraph 331, are vitiated by the confusion existing in the minds of the enumerators between Punjabi and Lahnda, while no attempt was made in the text of the Census Report to qualify or explain the results actually obtained from the schedules.

Lahnda speakers.

District.	Number	Percentage of total population.
Hazara ...	540,671	89
Peshawar ...	122,813	14
Kohat ...	24,255	11
Bannu ...	27,195	11
D. I. Khan ...	180,587	71

Hindostani.

336 The next language with which, following the order of Subsidiary Table I (*a*), I will deal, is Urdu, with which are included the returns of Hindostani. Other names returned by small numbers only, which I have dealt with under this head, are Dakhani, Hindi, Bhasha, Gwaliori and Bhopali. As is well known, Urdu and Hindostani are not to be distinguished, the two names being used almost indiscriminately. Dakhani is a form of the same tongue as spoken in the south. Hindi in our area probably refers to western Hindi, the common name of the various forms of this language, Bhasha is properly the name of a script and not a language, and Gwaliori and Bhopali are not the names of recognised linguistic forms. But all three probably refer to Hindostani. The total number of persons using this tongue is not large, amounting only to 17,455 persons, of whom 11,224 were enumerated in the Peshawar District. In Dera Ismail Khan there are 2,531 Hindostani speakers; in no other district do they amount to 1,600 souls, and in Hazara they are only 515. The language is used, in fact, only by a small number of educated people, many of whom are immigrants. Hindostani speakers are not only actually, but also relatively, far more numerous in Peshawar than elsewhere. In that district they amount to 130 per 10,000 of the total population. In Dera Ismail Khan the proportion is 99 per 10,000, and in Hazara it is only 9.

Since 1901 speakers of Hindostani have increased by 4 per cent only, a rate of increase considerably below that of the population as a whole. This is a result in general accordance with development as recorded in other columns of the Census schedule which show, for example, the spread of education to have been trifling, and a considerable fall in the number of immigrants from Hindustani speaking areas, and from the east generally.

Gujari.

337. With Gujari (25,668 speakers) I have included in Table X, 49 persons who recorded their language as Pahari. Of the total number all but 27 were enumerated in the Hazara District. I have already mentioned (*vide*

paragraph 313) the great decrease in the number of Gujari speakers since 1901. The explanation would seem to lie in the fact that, as the people we are concerned with are largely bilingual, it is to a large extent a matter of chance whether Gujari or Punjabi (properly Hindki) is returned; and in support of this view it may be mentioned that Gujrai was not returned at all in 1891. This language is a dialect of western Hindi and appears to have affinities with Rajasthani. "Before finally leaving the consideration of Rajasthani" wrote * Dr. Grierson in the last India Census Report, "it is necessary to mention the interesting tribe of Gujjars, or Gujars, who appear to have entered India from the north-west in about the 5th century A. D. There are two branches of them, a northern and a southern. The southern Gujars occupy Gujerat and gave their name to that country. The northern spread over the Punjab, (where they gave their name to two districts) and the western part of the United Provinces....................The Gujars of the Punjab proper speak the languages of the people among whom they live, but those of the Himalaya have a tongue of their own, which in its grammar is indistinguishable from that of the language of Jaipur. Whether they got their language from the western Pahari tribes...............or whether the Jaipuris got their language from the Gujars of Gujerat, I am not yet in a position to say, as the Linguistic Survey has not yet reached those parts of India; but it is a curious and noteworthy fact that we find in the mountains of Kashmir a dialect of a language spoken so many hundred miles to their south-east." Gujari has been returned almost without exception by the Gujars of Mansehra, the most northerly of the tahsils of the Hazara District, which marches with Kashmir on the east for the whole of its length.

Naipali.

338. The other languages which have been returned can be dismissed with a few words. The natives of Nepal serving in Gurkha Battalions stationed in the Province (in Abbottabad and the Malakand Agency) have shown their tongue as Gorkhi, which refers to the language more usually known as Naipali. This language is classed in accordance with the conclusions of the Linguistic Survey as forming one of the northern group of languages belonging to the Indian (Sanscritic) branch of the Indo-European Family. It has little interest here. It is used solely by immigrants; and the number of its speakers depends entirely on the strength of the Gurkha force which happens to form part of the garrison of the Province. Fluctuations in the number of persons using English similarly depend almost entirely on the number and strength of the British Regiments to be found in cantonments; and for this reason they have no great interest. European languages other than English are represented by only 49 persons, of whom 34 returned their language as Portuguese, being no doubt Goanese servants.

English.

European languages other than English.

Vernaculars of India not before dealt with.

339. Vernaculars not mentioned in the foregoing paragraphs have been returned by 840 persons only (*vide* head 'Others' under the Indian (Sanscritic) branch of the Indo-European family, in Subsidiary Table I (*a*), together with 23 who returned their language as Tamil or as Madrasi. The entries included under the former head are Sindhi, Marathi, Oriya, Bengali, Purbi, Gujerati, Marwari and Odki. Purbi was returned by 359, Marathi, (with Goai and Konkani) by 219, Gujerati (with Parsi) by 97, and Odki by 95 persons. The other entries concerned refer to a trifling number of speakers only in each case. It appears odd at first sight that Bengali, for instance, was returned as their language by only 17 persons, seeing that the birth-place table shows 209 to have been born in Bengal. The explanation lies in the fact that the persons in question were members of tribes native to the Province, who were born during their parents' sojourn outside it. Our Marathi speakers are mainly men in a Bombay regiment serving at the time of the Census in Kohat. Purbi was returned mainly by Purbias employed as domestic servants in Peshawar. Gujerati was shown as their native tongue by a few Parsis and Borahs engaged in retail trade in Peshawar and Hazara, and Odki only appears in the returns of Dera Ismail Khan. It is impossible (*vide* notes to Subsidiary Table I (*a*)) to compare for each of the languages dealt with in this paragraph the figures in 1901 and on the present occasion respectively. It is worth noticing, however, that taken as a whole they are noticeably smaller than was the case ten years ago. This result is in accordance with the statistics of birth-place for the two years, immigrants from outside into the Province being now considerably less numerous than in 1901.

* *Vide* India Census Report 1901, paragraph 586.

SUBSIDIARY TABLE I.—*Distribution of the total population by language, (a) according to Census.*

Language.	Total number of speakers. 1911.	1901.	Number per mille of population of Province (1911).	Where chiefly spoken.
1	2	3	4	5
Indo-European family	**2,210 418**	**2,111,617**	**999.9**	
ERANIAN BRANCH	1,233,410	1,145 425	558·9	
Pashto	1,229,599 (a)	1,142,011	556·3	P. K. B.
Persian	3,811	3,290	1·7	P.
Balochi	...	124	...	
INDIAN BRANCH—NON-SANSCRITIC	735	827	·3	
Kashmiri	561	826	·2	P.
Others	174 (b)	1 (*)	·1	
INDIAN BRANCH—SANSCRITIC	970,385	960,621	438·9	
NORTH-WESTERN GROUP—				
Hindko and its dialects (Lahnda)	72,979 (c)	582,571 (d)	33·01	H.
WESTERN GROUP—				
Hindostani and other forms of Western Hindi ...	17,455 (e)	16,775 (f)	7·9	H. P.
Gujari (with Pahari)	25,668	53,310	11·6	H.
Punjabi (with Dogri)	848,264	300,587	383·5	H. D.
NORTHERN GROUP—				
Gorkhi (Naipali)	5,179	7,378 (h)	2·3	H.
Others	840 (g)		·4	
EUROPEAN BRANCH	5,888	4,744	2·7	
English	5,839	4,724	2·7	P.
Others...	49 (i)	20	·02	
Languages of other families	**53** (j)	**258** (k)	**·02**	
Not returned	...	**1,239**	...	
Total ...	**2,210,471**	**2,113,109**	**1,000**	

NOTE.—In column 5, H=Hazara, P=Peshawar, K=Kohat, B=Bannu and D=Dera Ismail Khan.

NOTE.—The figures given in column 3 of the table work up to the total population given in Table X, Part IV, of the Punjab Census Report, 1901, less the population of the Sherani country 1901 (12,371 persons). The references given in the notes referring to the same column are to the details of languages shown in the same table Punjab Census Report, 1901.

(a) Includes Ormuri.

(b) Includes Chitiari (with Kashkari), Kohistani, and Dehgani (Pashai).

(c) Includes Peshawari, Tinaoli, Pothwari, Multani, Derawal, Malwai and Ponchi.

(d) Includes Lahnda (or Jatki), Derawal, Chinawar, Hindki, Peshawari, Pothwari, Multani, Bahawalpuri, Awankari, Dhanni, Ghebi, Tinaoli, Chachi and Kohati.

(e) Includes Urdu, Dakhani, Hindi, Bhasha, Gwaliori and Bhopali.

(f) Includes Urdu, Hindostani and Hariani.

(g) Includes Sindhi, Marathi (with Goai and Konkani), Oriya, Bengali, Purbi, Gujerati (with Parsi), Marwari and Odki.

(h) Includes Sindhi, Odki and "Other Indian Vernaculars" (less Sindhi, Brahui and Kashmiri). The last entry no doubt includes some languages not belonging to the Indo-European Family, but it is impossible to distinguish these from the rest.

(i) Includes Armenian, Portuguese, Russian, Irish, French, Danish and German.

(j) Includes Tamil (with Madrasi), Arabic, Chinese and Turki, (Turkish).

(k) Includes Brahui and "Other Asiatic Vernaculars" (not Persian).

(*) Chitiari.

Subsidiary Table I.—(*b*) *according to Linguistic Survey.*

Language.	Total number of speakers, (1911).	Number per mille of population of Province.	Where chiefly spoken.
1	2	3	4
Indo-European Family	**2,210,418**	**999·9**	
ERANIAN BRANCH	1,233,410	558·9	
Pashto	1,229,599	556·3	P. K. B.
Persian	3,811	1·7	P.
INDIAN BRANCH—NON-SANSCRITIC ...	735	·3	
Kashmiri	561	·2	P.
Others	174	·1	
INDIAN BRANCH—SANSCRITIC	970,385	438·9	
North-Western Group—			
Hindko and its dialects (Lahnda)	886,197	400·9	H. D.
Western Group—			
Hindostani and other forms of Western Hindi ...	17,455	7·9	H. P.
Gujari (with Pahari)	25,668	11·6	H.
Panjabi (with Dogri)	25,046	11·3	H. D.
Northern Group—			
Gorkhi (Naipali)...	5,179	2·3	H.
Others	840	·4	
EUROPEAN BRANCH	5,888	2·7	
English	5,839	2·7	P.
Others	49	·02	
Languages of other families	**53**	**·02**	
Total ...	**2,210,471**	**1,000**	

Note.—In column 4, H=Hazara, P=Peshawar, K=Kohat, B=Bannu, D=Dera Ismail Khan.

Subsidiary Table II.—*Distribution by language of the population of each district.*

District and Natural Division.	Number per 10,000 of population speaking					
	Pashto.	Punjabi with Hindko.	Hindostani, etc.	Gujari with Pahari.	Persian.	Others.
1	2	3	4	5	6	7
N.-W. F. P. Total Districts	**5,562**	**4,168**	**78**	**118**	**16**	**58**
Hazara	483	8,990	9	425	...	93
Trans-Indus Districts	**7,483**	**2,348**	**103**	...	**22**	**44**
Peshawar	8,202	1,560	130	...	38	70
Kohat	8,684	1,224	68	...	7	17
Bannu	8,751	1,195	48	...	...	6
Dera Ismail Khan	2,773	7,111	99	...	...	17

CHAPTER X.

INFIRMITIES.

Introductory.

340. The statistics of infirmities will be found in Tables XII and XII-A in the second Part of this volume. The former shows the distribution of the infirm by age and by the area of enumeration, while the latter exhibits the numbers recorded as belonging to each of the castes and tribes which in 1901 contributed more than two per mille to the total population of the Province. At the end of this chapter are printed proportional figures showing :—

I.—The distribution of the infirm by districts at each of the last four Censuses.

II.—The distribution of the infirm by age at each of the last four Censuses.

III.—The number afflicted at each age period, and the proportion of females to males.

IV.—The proportion afflicted in each of the castes and tribes shown in Table XII-A, with the proportion of females to males in each case.

It is to be noted that in trans-frontier posts, where the population consists entirely of officials and troops or Militia, with a few women, children and followers, no infirmities were recorded; and the proportions shown in the Subsidiary Tables have been worked out on the population of British territory only.

Accuracy of the statistics.

341. The infirmities recorded on the present occasion, as on previous ones, were insanity, deaf-mutism, blindness and leprosy. Owing partly to the impossibility of accurate diagnosis, and in part to intentional concealment, the securing of correct figures is here perhaps more difficult than in the case of any of the other statistics collected during the Census. It is particularly necessary therefore to explain the principles on which they were obtained, and the instructions given to the Census staff for the purpose. The instructions printed on the cover of the enumeration book, in which the schedules for each block were bound up, and which were therefore in the hands of every enumerator, were as follows :—"Column 16. If any person be blind of both eyes, or insane, or suffering from corrosive leprosy, or deaf and dumb from birth, enter the name of the infirmity in this column. Do not enter those who are blind of one eye only, or who are suffering from white leprosy only, or who have become deaf and dumb after birth." In the instructions which were given to the superior Census staff it was added that "Care is needed to prevent the entry of persons suffering from leucoderma or white leprosy, and other infirmities not falling within the scope of column 16."

Insanity.

342. To take the infirmities in the order in which they appear in Table XII, it is to be noted that our enumerators are not of the class to distinguish between the weak-minded, and those who are actually insane. Nor are there, so far as I am aware, separate words in the vernaculars of the Province for these different degrees of mental derangement. The word used in translating insane was '*pagal*,' which refers to either. In 1891 the word '*bawala*' was employed; and probably the same was used in 1901. This again has no precise signification, but is, as Mr. Maclagan remarked (paragraph 189, Punjab Census Report, 1891) "a vague term corresponding fairly well to our phrase of unsound mind." It must be remembered therefore that our figures for the insane include the persons whom we class as idiots, as well as those suffering from insanity properly so called. An attempt to eliminate the former was, however, made during compilation; and persons returned as "*kam-aqal*,"

which we may translate by the colloquial word 'wanting', do not appear in our tables. The distribution by age in 1901 of the infirm in the North-West Frontier Province is not given in the Punjab Census Report of that year. On comparing the figures of the present Census with those of 1881 and 1891, however, (*vide* Subsidiary Table II, appended to this chapter), it will be seen that the proportions returned as insane both of males and females under the age of 10 years are now considerably lower than in the earlier years, a fact which points to fewer of the congenitally weak-minded having been included in the statistics of the present Census.

343. But inaccuracy in our figures may be due not only to errors of diagnosis. The possibility of intentional concealment has also to be taken into account. The better classes at any rate do not willingly admit that their family circle contains an insane person. In rural areas this factor has probably little weight. The persons who made the preliminary enumeration, *viz.* the Patwaris, are probably pretty well acquainted with the existence of the insane. In towns, however, where enumerators in many cases can have had no personal knowledge of the persons residing in the blocks for which they were responsible, a certain number of cases may be expected not to have been reported. The urban population does not include of course a large proportion of the total inhabitants of the Province. But from whatever cause, whether owing to the greater stress of town life, or to the numbers of beggars who congregate in them, the number of the insane is proportionally higher in urban than in rural areas. I give in the margin the proportional figures for persons suffering from this infirmity within municipal limits and in the villages respectively of the tahsils which contain the head-quarters of districts. Abbottabad town is a small place which possesses few urban characteristics, and we find the figures here to be lower than in the neighbouring villages, but in all other head-quarter tahsils the reverse is the case. The difference is not, however, very marked except in Bannu. The proportion of the sexes found among the insane, however, throws some light on the question. The number of females is relatively very low, for they amount to only 39 per cent. of the males. The corresponding figure for India as a whole in 1901 was 60 per cent. It is in the case of females that the temptation, and the opportunity, to omit to return infirmities is greatest; and if the figures of 1901 can be taken as a guide, there is reason to suspect that our return here is defective in no small degree.

Tahsil.	Area.	Number insane per 1,000.
Abbottabad ...	Rural ...	·4
" ...	Municipal ...	·2
Peshawar ...	Rural ...	·2
" ...	Municipal ...	·8
Kohat ...	Rural ..	·4
" ...	Municipal ...	·5
Bannu ...	Rural ...	·5
" ...	Municipal ...	1·2
D. I. Khan ...	Rural ...	·3
" ...	Municipal ...	·6

344. The instructions explained that only the congenitally deaf and dumb should be recorded; but I fancy that this was a refinement not much regarded by the enumerators. I found it necessary, after Table XII had first been compiled, to strike out a certain number of persons who were recorded as deaf only; but probably many, who had become deaf from old age or the like, were returned as '*bahra-gunga*,' and these of course find a place in our returns. The degree to which this has been the case can be inferred from the proportional figures showing the prevalence of this infirmity among the persons living at the successive age groups. The lives of the true deaf-mutes are relatively short, and the ratio borne by persons suffering from this defect to the total number living at each successive age period should therefore show a steady decline. Unfortunately the tendency which they show in this direction is but slight (*vide* Subsidiary Table III.) It is true that in the case of males, as in that of females, the proportion contributed to the whole by deaf-mutes is smaller at each of the later age groups than at "15 to 20." Among females the highest ratio found is at the age group "10 to 15," and that for the last group "(60 and over)" is slightly lower than the proportion of the total female population. But even in the case of this sex our figures are only explicable on the assumption that many beside the congenitally deaf-mute are included. How otherwise are we to explain the proportion among females aged '60 and over Deaf-mutism.

being higher than that for either of the two preceding age groups, and the proportion at the age group '45 to 50' being higher than that found at any earlier group until we come to '15 to 20'? In the case of males the figures are even more open to similar objections. Some indications of intentional concealment may also be found in our statistics. Among persons suffering from this infirmity only 57 females have been recorded per 100 males, the corresponding figure for India as a whole in 1901 having been 65. Moreover, since in the North-West Frontier Province women are often not married till they have reached the age of 20, the fact that deaf-mutes are comparatively so rare at the age group '20 to 25' must give rise to suspicion. The very low proportion found among children of both sexes who have not yet reached the age of 5 is of course explicable, as pointed out by Mr. Maclagan in 1891, by the fact that, until the age for speech is reached, it is obviously impossible to attribute inability to deaf-mutism, and that parents are naturally disinclined to believe that it will prove permanent, even in the case of those who have left that age behind. Our statistics for deaf-mutism have all the appearance of being vitiated by concealment as well as by errors of diagnosis and by misunderstanding of the instructions; they are in fact perhaps among the most unsatisfactory of those obtained at the Census.

Blindness.

345. The figures for the blind are probably far more trustworthy. Our tables profess to show only those persons who are totally blind of both eyes. At previous Censuses it has been noticed that the enumerators "are prone to enter as blind persons who have lost the sight of one eye only, as well as those whose sight has become dim in old age." Our statistics no doubt include a certain proportion of persons belonging to the latter class, witness the striking difference in the proportion of the whole returned as blind after the age of 60 as compared with the proportion found at the previous quinquennium. But the inclusion of those who are blind of one eye only is rendered unlikely by the fact that the word used in Hindostani (in which language the Census record was prepared) for the one-eyed (*kana*) is distinct from that employed for those who can not see at all (*andha*); and entries of the former it was easy to eliminate during compilation. As blindness is a defect due generally to accident, disease (such as small-pox), exposure or advancing years, it is easily intelligible that the proportion to the whole borne by the blind among the population of each age period should show in the case of both sexes a continuous rise with each quinquennium of life. The only exceptions (*vide* Subsidiary Table III) are at the age group, '20 to 25' in the case of females and at that from 25 to 30 years in the case of males. In the case of females the aberration occurs at the same age as a similar one which I noticed above with regard to deaf-mutes, and it is doubtless to be attributed to the same cause. In the case of males the comparatively low figure we find at the age group '25 to 30' is due to the fact that at this age immigrants are extremely numerous, many of whom, as for example men in military employ, are necessarily free from physical defects. It will be noticed that in the case of lepers and deaf-mutes also the males returned at this age period bear a smaller proportion to the total than those at either the preceding or the succeeding quinquennium, while in the case of the insane the figure is considerably lower than that at the previous group, and no higher than that found at the following one. In so far as the proportion of the sexes is any guide the return for this infirmity is that which has the least appearance of being vitiated by intentional concealment, 807 females having been returned as blind for every 1,000 males. At the same time the figure here is considerably lower than that recorded for India as a whole in 1901; and lower than that (87 per cent.) obtained in the North-West Frontier Province in the same year. It is unlikely, though not of course impossible, that the enumeration of 1901 was more accurate than that of 1911: and I am inclined to believe that the variation corresponds with the actual facts, the increased proportion of males on the present occasion being due to the larger numbers of residents of tribal territory, among whom of course males naturally predominate, who visit the districts of the Province to seek in its hospitals and dispensaries relief for eye trouble. In the case of insanity, deaf-mutism and blindness alike the sufferers recorded on the present occasion bear a larger proportion to the total population of both sexes than they did in 1901. The

increase has, however, been greater among males than among females, and the proportion of the latter to the former has consequently fallen. It is hardly likely that there has been more concealment of the defects of women on the present occasion than in 1901, and errors of diagnosis or misunderstanding of the instructions might be expected to affect both sexes equally. It would appear therefore that females suffering from these three infirmities are actually less numerous relatively to males than they were in 1901.

Leprosy.

346. It is in the case of leprosy that the danger of wilful concealment is greatest, especially where the leper is a female of respectable status. In India as a whole in 1901 the number of females per 100 males (34) was lower among lepers than among persons suffering from either of the other three infirmities dealt with at the Census. We find the same feature now in the statistics of the North-West Frontier Province. Female lepers amount to 382 only per 1,000 males. Errors of diagnosis also no doubt detract from the accuracy of our figures, for it is often difficult to distinguish leprosy from other diseases which exhibit similar symptoms, such as leucoderma and syphilis. In this connection, however, it is interesting to observe that this is the only infirmity which, according to our record, is less prevalent now than was the case ten years ago.

Variation in numbers suffering from the various infirmities since 1881.

347. In the statement printed in the margin I show the numbers of persons suffering from each infirmity at each of the last four Censuses. The area of the districts now included in the Province was considerably larger in the two earlier years than in the two later ones, the Mianwali District of the Punjab, with a population in 1901 of 424,588 persons, having been formed in that year from portions of the Bannu and Dera Ismail Khan Districts. The figures for 1881 and 1891 are not therefore properly comparable with those for the two later years. A reference to Subsidiary Table I (first line) appended to this chapter, in which proportional figures are given, will furnish a better survey of the facts. It will be seen that, taking the last decade only, all * infirmities except leprosy show a considerable increase. For the whole period of 30 years, however, the results are not so uniform. Insanity decreased from 1881 to 1891, but since then the proportion shows a rise to 1911, with an intermediate drop at the Census of 1901. In the case of deaf-mutes we find a continuous rise from 1881 to 1911, except that among males they were relatively less numerous in 1901 than in 1891. Blindness on the other hand has shown a marked decrease since 1881, though the figures of 1911, which are considerably lower than those of 1891, are somewhat higher than those of ten years ago. In the case of leprosy we can find no persistent tendency in either direction, the present figure, which is lower than that recorded in 1881 and 1901, being higher than that elicited as a result of the operations of 1891.

Number of persons (of both sexes) suffering from infirmities since 1881.

Infirmity.	1911.	1901.	1891.	1881.
Insane ...	884	606	752	1,083
Deaf-mute ...	2,100	1,807	2,059	1,648
Blind ...	3,440	2,668	5,017	6,183
Lepers ...	282	294	276	344
Total ...	6,706	5,375	8,104	9,258

348 In India as a whole "up to 1901", writes the Census Commissioner, "there was a steady decrease in the number of persons afflicted. This has been ascribed partly to a progressive improvement in the accuracy of diagnosis; partly to an improvement in the material condition of the people, better sanitation, and, (especially in the case of blindness) cures effected with the aid of modern medical and surgical science; and partly (in the decade ending in 1901) to a relatively high mortality of lepers, etc., in the famine years". In the area with which we are concerned increased accuracy of diagnosis since 1881 has certainly not resulted in any fall in the prevalence of deaf-mutism. In so far as this factor may be supposed to have affected the figures its influence seems to have been in the other direction. In the case of the insane a steady decrease was found from 1881 to 1901, but the figures of the present Census again record a rise, though, as observed in paragraph 342 above, in so far

* Female deaf-mutes, however, bear the same proportion to the total population of that sex as they did in 1901.

as the distribution of the insane by age in the two years is any guide, our figures may be conjectured to contain a smaller proportion of the congenitally weak-minded than those of 1891. The decrease in the prevalence of blindness may with confidence be attributed in part to "cures effected with the aid of modern medical and surgical science", and in part to better sanitation and the growth of some realization of the importance of personal cleanliness. Famine, it is to be noticed, is responsible for none of the fluctuations occurring since 1881 in our statistics of infirmities. "A slight alteration of the instructions, which made it clear that the words 'from birth' referred only to deaf-mutes, and not to the other infirmities" may be responsible for some small part of the rise noticed in the number of the insane.

Variations since 1881 in the number of the insane.

349. The discussion can best be continued if the figures for each infirmity are considered separately. If Subsidiary Table I be referred to, it will be seen that in the districts of the Province as a whole, both among males and females, insanity is more common now than was the case in 1901 or 1891, 54 males and 25 females per 100,000 having been recorded as insane. Kashmir and Burma showed a higher figure in the case of males in 1901, and the same two areas, along with Assam and the Punjab, also exceeded in 1901 our proportion for females. In all other Provinces and States in India, however, this infirmity was found to be less prevalent than our statistics now show. The rise since 1901 has occurred in the case of all districts alike, but it is more marked in the trans-Indus districts than in Hazara. In Hazara there has been since 1881 a consistent increase at a rate in excess of the rate of growth of the population as a whole. In the trans-Indus districts on the other hand the rise now recorded follows on a considerable decrease shown at the end of the decade 1891—1901. The largest proportionate increase has occurred in Bannu, where for every 100,000 males there are now 43 more with unhinged minds than were found ten years ago.

350. The variations here are not easy to explain. Famine and scarcity, with their attendant consequences, can not account for them; for nothing of the kind has been experienced during the last thirty years. Nor is there reason to suppose that the material condition of the people has altered for the worse. If, as Mr. Maclagan suggests, the main reason for the comparative rarity of mental derangement in eastern, as contrasted with western, countries, "lies in the greater placidity of oriental existence", the more strenuous attitude towards life which marks every passing year may be expected to lead to an increase of insanity. But this factor could hardly account in ten years for so striking a rise as we are confronted with here. Even if the explanation be accepted for the Hazara District, and no sane person could regard it as sufficient in itself, it can hardly be applicable to the other districts of the Province, where insanity decreased between the years 1891—1901, only to rise again at the end of the following decade. One explanation which has been suggested to me is that the variation is due to an increased use of *charas* and other intoxicants, following on the rise in prices which has occurred in the last ten years. This is mere hypothesis, however; and I believe the explanation is more likely to lie in the fact that the insane, or those recorded as such, are largely composed of religious, or *quasi*-religious mendicants, who wander about from place to place, and the numbers of whom, in a small area such as the North-West Frontier Province, naturally vary greatly from year to year. Such mendicants are commonly referred to as *lewanai* (mad), for they often either can not or will not speak at all, or only jibber. They are not in all cases, it is to be noticed, actually insane. This explanation fits in with the fact that the increase has occurred principally in the case of males, the figures for females having exhibited no very striking variations since 1891.

351. The distribution of the insane by age (*vide* Subsidiary Table II) points to the inclusion in our figures for males of a large proportion of persons who, even if they are actually mad, are probably religious mendicants. The latter class are usually men of more than 20 years of age. Whereas in 1891 (the distribution of the infirm by age in 1901 is not available) of the total number of males recorded as insane, 463 per mille were of under 20 years of

age, at the recent Census only 315 per mille were under 20. On the other hand in the case of females, the figures for whom are little disturbed by the religious mendicant element, the age distribution of the insane in 1891 and in 1911 is far more equal, and in both years the proportion of the whole aged less than 20 years is far higher than among males on the present occasion.

352. Referring to the Census of the Punjab in 1891, Mr. Maclagan, (Census Report paragraph 184), after noting that of 100 insane persons only 33 were females, remarked: "The life of women in this country is, among the upper classes, one of considerable seclusion, and among the lower orders it is a life very monotonous in its tenour. The women's thoughts are limited to petty subjects, and their education is a by-word. Being women, they are not dull; but being cut off from variety, they are not excitable. In childhood they are less indulged than the men; in youth they are more restrained from excesses; and in mature life they are less addicted to the intoxication of drugs or liquor. They are as a rule less exposed to hardship and hunger, and when they work out of doors, their work is less harassing than that of the men. These three, excitement, excess and exposure, are the occasion of a very large part of the insanity in the world, and their comparative absence among women in this country accounts no doubt for the comparative immunity of the women from unsoundness of mind." The proportion of the sexes noticed by Mr. Maclagan, which works out to 49 females per 100 males, is considerably lower than that elicited for India as a whole in 1901, (when in Coorg indeed insane females were found to be as numerous as insane males), but considerably higher than that (39 females per 100 males) obtained for the North-West Frontier Province at the present Census. The considerations mentioned by Mr. Maclagan in the passage above quoted, and in particular the use of drugs and liquors, are no doubt causes for insanity being actually commoner among men than women. At the same time I do not think that our figures for the Province correctly represent the real facts. In the first place I do not believe for one moment that mental unsoundness is usually returned in the case of women who live behind the *pardah*. In the second our figures for males are exaggerated by the inclusion of a number of persons whose actual insanity is by no means beyond question. In the case of females on the other hand this is a factor which can be left out of account.

Proportion of the sexes among the insane.

353. It is doubtful how far our returns for insanity are sufficiently accurate to render profitable the subjection to any critical examination of the figures showing the relative prevalence of insanity at the various age periods (*vide* Subsidiary Table III). Among males, with some fluctuations, insanity tends to become more common up to the age of 50 years, after which, probably owing to the shorter lives of the insane, it is of rarer occurrence. The highest figure previous to the quinquennium closing at the age of 50 is that recorded among males aged '20 to 25,' the period of excesses. The figures for females are more perplexing. If they are correct, it is difficult to understand why the proportion at the age period '55 to 60' should be so strikingly high, and why *e. g.*, that at the age period '25 to 30' should be only half of that found at the quinquenniums preceding and following it. The high figure among females aged '55 to 60' is probably more accurate than that found at some of the earlier age periods, at which intentional concealment has more influence on the statistics. It is interesting to notice, however, that the next highest figure we find at the age period '15 to 20'.

Insanity by age.

354. The aberrations which appear in our returns for infirmities are no doubt in part due to the very small numbers concerned. This is still more the case when we come to consider the statistics for insanity by caste. The castes and tribes showing the highest proportionate figures for male insanity are Arora-98, Brahman-76, Machhi-92, Mallah-111, Moghal-97, Paracha-111, Qureshi-109 and Sonar-119, per 100,000. The actual numbers are probably too small to be other than accidental. Of Arora males only 37 are insane, of Brahman 6, of Machhi 2, of Mallah 3, of Moghal 8, of Paracha 7, of Qureshi 12, and of Sonar 6. At the same time it is curious that Brahmans, Aroras and Khatris should all show a higher proportion of insane persons among

Insanity by caste.

males than we find among the male population of the Province as a whole. All belong to the trading or professional classes, among whom the conditions of life should be more easy than is the rule in others. Possibly in the case of all three, as consisting largely of educated persons, the returns were more carefully made than in that of the Chuhras, Musallis, and Sararas, among whom no person of either sex was recorded as insane.

Variation in he prevalence of deaf-mutism since 1881.

355. The number of deaf-mutes recorded in the Province is relatively very large, (in the case of males 113, and in that of females 75, per 100,000 of that sex). The only areas in India in which the corresponding figures were higher in 1901 were Kashmir in the case of males, and Kashmir and the Native States of the Punjab in the case of females. In paragraph 344 above I have given reasons for thinking that our figures include a considerable number of persons who are not congenital deaf-mutes; but there is no reason to suppose that this source of error is more marked in one part of the Province than in another, or that it affects the figures of the present Census more than those of previous ones. The different sets of figures are therefore comparable, even if the value of none be very great. It is to be noticed that both among males and females deaf-mutes are relatively far more numerous in Hazara than in the trans-Indus districts. The same was the case in 1901, but whereas in Hazara the proportion suffering from this infirmity has risen since that time, in the trans-Indus districts there has been a decrease at each of the last two Censuses. In fact at each Census taken since 1881 deaf-mutism has been recorded with more frequency in the hilly district of Hazara than in the plains lying west of the Indus. In the Punjab in 1881, as in 1891, the infirmity was found to be more prevalent in the hill tracts than elsewhere. Mr. Maclagan, while admitting that the reason for this did not appear to be satisfactorily settled, suggested that the disease might be "connected with the syphilis so prevalent in the hills, or with the effect on the ear of the rareness of the air in the higher altitudes, or with some other characteristic of the hill climate." Our figures do not suggest that high altitudes have great influence in this connection, for the percentage of deaf-mutes in Mansehra, the most elevated tahsil of the Hazara district, is no larger than that found in Haripur or Abbottabad. If, as Mr. Maclagan suggests, "this infirmity is the outcome, generally speaking, of dirt and want and low living," we may have, in the first, one of the causes of the greater prevalence of deaf-mutism in Hazara. In a cold climate such as is to be found there people undoubtedly have a greater objection to washing than in the warmer atmosphere of the plains; but it is discouraging to find that our figures show a rise since 1901. Probably the Census record was prepared less accurately in the district than elsewhere in the Province. The standard of education among the population is very low, or, to speak more accurately, education is almost non-existent. Distances are long, roads are bad, and at the time of the Census large areas were under snow. Supervision was therefore more difficult here than in other parts of the Province, and a high degree of accuracy can not be hoped to have been attained, either on the present, or on any previous occasion. I make the suggestion with great diffidence, but it is at least possible that the record contains fewer omissions now than in the earlier years; and we may have here one reason for the variation since last Census. That the record contains congenital deaf-mutes only, however, as I have said above, I should hesitate to affirm.

356. In the trans-Indus districts deaf-mutes, both male and female, bear a smaller proportion to the total population of that sex than they did ten years ago. The figures of 1901 again showed a decreasing ratio when compared with those for 1891, and these latter showed persons suffering from the infirmity to be only slightly more numerous, relatively, than they were in 1881. It is probable that the figures of each successive Census have included a smaller number of persons not actually suffering from this congenital defect. But the chief reason for the decrease is, I believe, to be found in the improved material condition of the people. The importance of cleanliness is probably more appreciated year by year.

Deaf-mutism by caste.

357. The value of the statistics of this infirmity by caste is of course subject to the same qualifications as I referred to above in the case of insanity. The fact that the proportion of deaf-mutes is so high among Bhatiara males

(2·7 per mille) is probably merely accidental. Only 6 males of this caste have been recorded as suffering from this defect, and no females. At the same time it is no doubt more than a coincidence that tribes also showing very high proportions among males are the Kashmiris and Swathis, the former of whom were born, or are descended from persons born, in an area where the defect is so common, while the latter live almost entirely in the Hazara District, which marches with Kashmir, and appears to share in this respect some of the characteristics of that state.

Blindness. Distribution by districts and natural divisions.

358. In the districts of the Province as a whole 161 males and 151 females per 100,000 have been recorded as blind. The corresponding figures for the whole of India in 1901 were 121 in the case of males and 120 in that of females. The figures of this infirmity are lower in Hazara than in the plain districts. This is intelligible enough. Heat, dust and glare are undoubtedly fruitful causes of eye trouble, and these conditions, which are prevalent for a large part of year in the latter area, are entirely absent over the greater portion of the former. Coming to the individual districts which lie west of the Indus again we find figures such as might *a priori* be expected. The driest, and the hottest and the dustiest district is Dera Ismail Khan, and here blindness is relatively far more common than in the other districts lying west of the Indus. After Dera Ismail Khan the district in which the greatest degree of heat and glare is to be found is Kohat; for in Bannu and Peshawar, though the thermometer registers high degrees of temperature, there is a large amount of irrigation, and there is always plenty of verdure to rest the eye. Peshawar, however, with its large urban centres, naturally contains a larger proportion of the blind than either of the other two districts, to which there is little to attract the wandering mendicant.

Natural division.	Blind per 100,000.	
	Males.	Females.
Hazara ...	120	112
Trans-Indus districts	176	166

District.	Blind per 100,000.	
	Males.	Females.
Dera Ismail Khan ...	263	325

District.	Blind per 100,000.	
	Males.	Females.
Peshawar ...	182	154
Kohat ...	122	111
Bannu ...	113	99

Variations in the prevalence of blindness since 1881.

359. In the whole area of British territory the blind of both eyes form a larger proportion of the whole than they did in 1901, (*vide* Subsidiary Table I), but a smaller one than that contributed in 1891 and 1881. As compared indeed with the figures for the earliest year (1881) the decrease is particularly marked. The numbers concerned are probably too small for us to infer that the variation shown between the years 1901 and 1911 is other than accidental. But the persistent tendency to decrease which our figures show over the whole period from 1881 to 1911 is no doubt more than accidental, and may be attributed to an improvement in the material condition of the people, to cures effected by modern surgical science, and to an extension of vaccination, which, as reducing the spread of small-pox, may naturally be expected to restrict the blindness which not uncommonly attends upon it. I have found it impossible to obtain any trustworthy statisticts showing the numbers of persons vaccinated, or of those who have undergone operations for cataract, in the various decades respectively. The Civil Surgeon of Peshawar writes: "Though vaccination has certainly been carried on more vigorously during the last ten years, at the same time small-pox is an epidemic disease and we have unfortunately no record of cases during the periods in question; but taking deaths from small-pox as an indication as to the presence of the disease I find that from 1891 to 1900 there were 5,603 deaths, and from 1901 to 1910 there were 5,701. So I think we may fairly assume that the number of cases was probably about equal over these decades. With regard to successful cataract operations again the information at my disposal is most incomplete. The returns available show that from 1891 to 1900, 527 operations were performed, and from 1901 to 1910, 877; but how many of these were successful, and how many were

double cataracts is not recorded. The number seems to me to be too small to have any influence on the total." From the other districts the information supplied to me is so incomplete as not to be worth reproducing here. It may, however, be assumed that surgical and medical science is more readily accessible to the people to-day than it was ten years ago.

360. Between the two natural divisions included in the Province (British territory) no striking differences are to be found. In both blindness was less common in 1891 than in 1881; and was found again to have decreased in 1901. In both the proportion of the whole recorded as blind is now higher than was the case in 1901; but whereas in the trans-Indus districts our proportional figure for both sexes is lower than that recorded in 1891, in Hazara the blind among males are now slightly more numerous, relatively, than they were in that year. In only one district in the Province has the proportion of the blind to the whole decreased steadily since 1881, *viz.* Bannu. The presence in the district of a large body of comparatively recent settlers from tribal territory, and the existence of an excellent mission hospital with a wide reputation for the relief of eye trouble are probably the factors which have determined our figures here. The Wazirs who have taken up their abode in Bannu during the last 40 or 50 years may be expected to have been the latest to obtain some glimmering of the importance of cleanliness in this connection; and accordingly the results of this acquisition of knowledge may be seen more clearly here than elsewhere. At the same time, for the reasons I have indicated above, the district at every Census since 1881 has been found to be comparatively little afflicted with blindness. Its great prevalence in Dera Ismail Khan is in part due to the conditions I have referred to above as being characteristic of that area. In this connection I would also refer to the description of the district quoted in paragraph 13 above. The fact that the conditions of life are so hard is naturally reflected also in our statistics of infirmities. Except in the case of insanity, the figures for which I can not explain, all infirmities are more prevalent here than in any other area west of the Indus. It is, however, in the case of blindness that the difference is most marked.

Leprosy.

361. Leprosy is the only infirmity the proportionate figures for which have decreased since 1901. The actual numbers also show a fall from 294 in 1901 to 282 at the present Census. The disease is three times as common in Hazara as in the trans-Indus districts. In no area of the Province, however, is the proportionate number of lepers so high as it was found to be throughout India in 1901; and even in Hazara we have a far lower one than was recorded in 1901 in the neighbouring state of Kashmir. In Hazara, Peshawar and Kohat the proportion of lepers, both male and female, has fallen since 1901. On the other hand in Kohat and Dera Ismail Khan we are confronted with a quite startling rise.

Proportionate numbers of lepers.

Area.	Number per 100,000.	
	Males.	Females.
India, 1901 ...	48	17
Hazara, 1911 ...	33	11
N.-W .F. P., 1911 ...	17	8
Kashmir, 1901 ...	72	36
Trans-Indus Districts N.W. F.P. 1911. ...	11	7

362. The greater prevalence of leprosy in the hills, which our figures for Hazara indicate, is in keeping with the results of the Census of the Punjab in 1891, when this disease was found to be six times as common in the hill tracts as in any of the other natural divisions of the Province. Whether this result is to be regarded as connecting leprosy with syphilis, which is known to be common in the hills, or whether the variation is due to differences in the food eaten I find it impossible to say. The causes which predispose to the disease do not seem to have been accurately determined; and no correspondence could be traced between the physical and climatic characteristics, or between the race and staple diet of their inhabitants, of those tracts in India in which leprosy was found to be specially common in 1901.

Variation since 1901.

363. As to the causes of the variation since 1901 in the numbers of lepers recorded in the different areas of the Province, it is difficult to find an explanation which will fit in with the fact that, while we find a fall in Hazara, we find a rise in the trans-Indus districts. In the latter area indeed the variations are

not uniform. It is, however, perhaps significant that it is just those districts which showed a particularly low population of lepers in 1901 (Kohat and Dera Ismail Khan) in which the figures for the present occasion show a striking rise. But even if we assume that the lowness of the figures in these districts in 1901 was due to omissions from the record, it still remains to explain why those obtained at the present Census should be considerably higher than we find in the neighbouring districts. I doubt personally whether in the trans-Indus area the disease is sufficiently well known to allow of our statistics possessing very much value. The enumerators were warned, as on previous occasions, not to record as lepers those suffering from leucoderma or white leprosy only. But Mr. Gait noted (paragraph 260 India Census Report, 1901) that he was informed by an expert "that in the earlier stages of real leprosy it is very difficult to distinguish it from leucoderma, and that even a trained medical man has to make a very careful examination before he can satisfy himself as to the diagnosis." It is of course in areas where the disease is least common that errors of diagnosis on the part of enumerators are most likely to be made. On the subject of leprosy in Kohat, where our figures show so large a rise (though it will be noted that even on the present occasion only 30 lepers were recorded in the district), the Civil Surgeon writes, "I have personally so far not come across a leper in the district. Only one Assistant Surgeon reports having seen a case this year, and the patient came from Independent Territory. Tahsildars and Police Inspectors who have been referred to all state that they have neither seen nor heard of any case of leprosy. I am of opinion that many cases of so-called 'white leprosy' (otherwise leucoderma) must have been entered as leprosy by the enumerators."

364. In the circumstances I doubt whether we can infer from our figures that there has been any real increase of leprosy in the trans-Indus districts since 1901. It must be admitted that there is no reason why mistaken entries should have been more common at the recent Census than ten years ago; but if the view be taken that our statistics contain any large proportion of them, they are not of much use for purposes of comparison, however doubtful the figures with which we compare them may be. It may be admitted that leprosy plus various forms of skin discolouration are slightly more common than was the case ten years ago. Beyond this I doubt whether any inference can be drawn. Coming to the figures for Hazara the variation requiring explanation is precisely in the opposite direction. To accept our figures here as correct, because they show leprosy to be, relatively, on the decrease, after rejecting another set of figures which tells a different story, appears at first sight to savour of an optimism too determined to be well-founded. At the same time there is something more in the argument than this. The figures for each Census since 1881 show conclusively that leprosy is far more common in Hazara than in the other districts of the Province. As being more common, the disease may be expected to be more readily recognised in Hazara than elsewhere, and mistakes of diagnosis should be rarer. I think we can assume that at the Census of 1901, as on the present occasion, they have not affected the figures to any appreciable extent. We can then assume the decrease in leprosy to be real, and to be due to the improved material condition of the people at large.

Proportion of the sexes among lepers.

365. 382 women have been recorded as lepers per 1,000 males. In 1901 the figure was 480 females per 1,000 males: while in India as a whole in the same year the number was 340. The only age period at which female lepers are found to be as numerous as male is, curiously enough, '10 to 15' which is certianly one of the groups at which we should have supposed concealment in the case of females to be most likely to take place. On the other hand at the age group '60 and over', at which *a priori* there would seem to be little likelihood of concealment, there are only 281 female lepers per 1,000 males, *i. e.* a considerably lower figure than that arrived at for lepers of all ages. In the circumstances I do not think our statistics point to any serious omission of females suffering from this disease. It must, however, be conceded, for whatever the admission may be worth, that our figures show the decrease in the prevalence of leprosy to be somewhat more marked in the case of females than in that of males. As to the reason of this I can offer no explanation. It is likely, however, that, especially in the case of numbers so small as those with which we are here concerned, variations in the sex proportions should actually occur from time to time.

SUBSIDIARY TABLE I.—*Number afflicted per* 100,000 *of the population at each of the last four Censuses.*

District and Natural Division.	Insane.								Deaf-mutes.							
	Males.				Females.				Males.				Females.			
	1911	1901	1891	1881	1911	1901	1891	1881	1911	1901	1891	1881	1911	1901	1891	1881
1	2	3	4	5	6	7	8	9	10	11	12	13	14	15	16	17
N.-W. F. P. Total Districts.	**54**	**37**	**41**	**70**	**25**	**21**	**24**	**38**	**113**	**100**	**109**	**104**	**75**	**75**	**69**	**61**
Hazara	50	37	23	61	23	22	21	41	166	111	125	108	120	92	81	64
Trans-Indus Districts ...	**55**	**37**	**46**	**72**	**25**	**20**	**25**	**37**	**93**	**95**	**103**	**102**	**58**	**68**	**66**	**61**
Peshawar	52	38	45	66	20	18	18	31	80	88	107	89	48	56	65	47
Kohat	45	31	28	63	27	25	18	27	117	111	87	131	73	91	61	74
Bannu	74	31	45	61	37	19	35	32	84	72	111	101	58	61	78	59
Dera Ismail Khan ...	54	32	55	92	28	18	28	53	129	104	99	109	79	71	58	75

District and Natural Division.	Blind.								Lepers.							
	Males.				Females.				Males.				Females.			
	1911	1901	1891	1881	1911	1901	1891	1881	1911	1901	1891	1881	1911	1901	1891	1881
1	18	19	20	21	22	23	24	25	26	27	28	29	30	31	32	33
N.-W. F. P. Total Districts.	**161**	**128**	**198**	**295**	**151**	**132**	**245**	**341**	**17**	**18**	**16**	**23**	**8**	**10**	**7**	**11**
Hazara	120	73	114	181	112	71	114	186	33	44	44	56	11	18	14	21
Trans-Indus Districts ...	**176**	**148**	**223**	**324**	**166**	**156**	**284**	**383**	**11**	**8**	**8**	**15**	**6**	**7**	**5**	**8**
Peshawar	182	153	200	267	154	141	246	304	9	11	17	20	5	7	6	9
Kohat	122	92	150	276	111	119	175	339	18	2	6	15	9	5	7	2
Bannu	113	116	196	259	99	120	258	296	7	8	12	11	5	7	5	8
Dera Ismail Khan ...	263	199	308	470	325	248	402	569	19	4	2	10	12	6	5	8

SUBSIDIARY TABLE II.—*Distribution of the infirm by age per* 10,000 *of each sex.*

Age.	Insane. Males. 1911	1901	1891	1881	Insane. Females. 1911	1901	1891	1881	Deaf-mutes. Males. 1911	1901	1891	1881	Deaf-mutes. Females. 1911	1901	1891	1881
1	2	3	4	5	6	7	8	9	10	11	12	13	14	15	16	17
0—5 ...	237	Not available.	319	402	320	Not available.	438	475	554	Not available.	900	798	759	Not available.	895	917
5—10 ...	883		1,397	1,247	1,280		1,476	1,335	1,782		1,808	1,768	1,584		2,011	2,129
10—15 ...	1,104		1,457	1,193	1,320		1,235	1,632	1,355		1,365	1,233	1,610		1,267	1,174
15—20 ...	931		1,457	1,354	1,440		1,832	1,721	1,220		1,073	1,106	942		1,281	991
20—25 ...	1,246		1,496	2,239	1,160		1,076	1,691	816		915	1,242	681		689	1,450
25—30 ...	1,167		1,496		600		1,076		621		900		956		909	
30—35 ...	1,230		679	1,528	1,280		676	1,157	943		638	1,224	982		523	1,119
35—40 ...	725		660		280		756		599		518		484		620	
40—45 ...	726		200	992	600		320	920	576		360	1,006	720		220	715
45—50 ...	584		479		440		556		307		465		340		455	
50—55 ...	489		60	442	440		279	564	471		165	580	367		179	624
55—60 ...	189		140		320		240		157		450		78		441	
60 and over	489		160	603	520		40	505	599		443	1,043	497		510	881

Age.	Blind.								Lepers.							
	Males.				Females.				Males.				Females.			
	1911	1901	1891	1881	1911	1901	1891	1881	1911	1901	1891	1881	1911	1901	1891	1881
1	18	19	20	21	22	23	24	25	26	27	28	29	30	31	32	33
0—5 ...	284	Not available.	491	366	247	Not available.	346	306	196	Not available.	303	120	385	Not available.	513	...
5—10 ...	625		844	852	508		610	599	686		455	522	1,282		641	842
10—15 ...	593		667	706	514		524	494	539		555	442	1,410		1,283	526
15—20 ...	478		753	582	508		695	547	882		858	723	769		1,154	632
20—25 ...	562		545	1,018	507		419	882	981		859	1,727	897		766	2,211
25—30 ...	551		655		547		734		686		909		385		1,026	
30—35 ...	772		479	1,189	697		373	1,139	1,079		606	2,048	1,282		641	1,368
35—40 ...	594		762		430		796		981		1,566		385		1,026	
40—45 ...	767		377	1,161	801		443	1,254	784		657	1,647	769		641	2,000
45—50 ...	499		852		573		1,099		490		1,061		385		1,154	
50—55 ...	877		368	1,390	1,016		342	1,560	784		505	1,245	641		257	1,474
55—60 ...	320		1,200		397		1,503		343		555		256		385	
60 and over	3,078		2,007	2,736	3,255		2,116	3,219	1,569		1,111	1,526	1,154		513	947

Subsidiary Table III.—*Number afflicted per* 100,000 *persons of each age period, and number of females afflicted per* 1,000 *males in the North-West Frontier Province.*

Age.	Number afflicted per 100,000.								Number of females afflicted per 1,000 males.			
	Insane.		*Deaf-mutes.*		*Blind.*		*Lepers*		Insane.	Deaf-mutes.	Blind.	Lepers.
	Males.	Females.	Males.	Females.	Males	Females	Males.	Females.				
1	2	3	4	5	6	7	8	9	10	11	12	13
0—5 ...	9	5	44	35	32	23	2	2	533	784	704	750
5—10 ...	30	20	129	75	64	48	8	6	571	508	655	714
10—15 ...	50	33	129	122	81	80	8	11	471	680	699	1,000
15—20 ...	63	50	175	99	98	107	19	8	610	442	857	333
20—25 ...	85	34	118	61	116	92	22	8	367	477	729	350
25—30 ...	74	17	83	84	105	96	14	3	203	880	800	214
30—35 ...	74	34	120	79	140	113	21	16	410	595	728	455
35—40 ...	73	15	128	77	180	138	32	6	152	462	584	150
40—45 ...	64	23	107	84	204	188	22	9	326	714	842	375
45—50 ...	95	37	106	88	244	297	26	10	297	634	926	300
50—55 ...	60	26	122	67	322	371	31	12	355	444	934	312
55—60 ...	67	62	116	47	338	475	39	16	667	286	1,000	286
60 and over ...	46	25	117	74	860	969	47	17	419	475	853	281
All ages ...	**53**	**25**	**112**	**75**	**159**	**151**	**17**	**8**	**394**	**572**	**807**	**382**

SUBSIDIARY TABLE IV.—*Number afflicted per* 100,000 *persons of each caste, and number of females afflicted per* 1,000 *males.*

CASTE.	NUMBER AFFLICTED PER 100,000 PERSONS.								NUMBER OF FEMALES AFFLICTED PER 1,000 MALES.			
	Insane.		*Deaf-mutes.*		*Blind.*		*Lepers.*		Insane.	Deaf-mutes.	Blind.	Lepers.
	Males.	Females.	Males.	Females.	Males.	Females.	Males.	Females.				
1	2	3	4	5	6	7	8	9	10	11	12	13
Arora	98	32	129	115	187	160	5	3	270	735	904	500
Awan	61	26	191	69	164	162	15	10	363	305	833	522
Baghban ...	18	52	64	73	156	115	9	...	2,500	1,000	647	...
Baluch	28	17	111	133	332	556	28	8	500	1,000	1,396	250
Bhatiara ...	...	47	272	...	91	236	...	47	...	...	2,500	...
Brahman ...	76	19	115	19	229	168	13	...	167	111	500	...
Chamar ...	...	50	76	...	38	50	...	...	...	...	1,000	...
Chuhra	...	...	...	45	...	315	28	...	...	...	...	...
Dhobi	49	30	74	162	148	384	12	...	500	1,833	2,167	...
Dhund	13	20	101	163	101	82	32	41	1,500	1,500	750	1,200
Gakkhar ...	54	...	109	160	109	96	...	32	...	1,250	750	...
Gujar	52	35	131	67	87	75	39	13	562	432	722	292
Jat	33	19	94	62	182	250	18	13	437	500	1,045	556
Jhinwar	...	...	154	145	77	727	77	...	...	500	5,000	...
Jolaha	70	23	165	63	170	138	25	6	286	333	706	200
Karal	71	19	133	74	80	74	141	9	250	533	889	62
Kashmiri ...	53	37	217	149	158	111	7	...	625	606	625	...
Khatri	69	14	65	57	162	107	5	14	133	571	429	2,000
Kumhar ...	34	18	111	100	179	192	9	...	500	846	1,000	...
Lohar	26	53	111	91	91	151	...	8	1,750	706	1,429	...
Machhi	92	162	231	...	92	970	46	...	1,500	...	9,000	...
Maliar	58	...	144	94	346	178	...	...	...	600	472	...
Mallah	111	...	111	...	111	...	...	...	...	...	...	...
Mirasi	51	...	203	29	279	350	...	88	...	125	1,091	...
Mochi	81	56	121	150	323	206	8	...	600	1,067	550	...
Moghal	97	15	145	61	181	106	36	15	125	333	467	333
Musalli (with Kutana)	...	...	110	84	137	201	14	...	...	625	1,200	...
Nai	54	26	138	77	168	145	8	...	428	500	773	...
Paracha ...	111	19	48	38	64	133	16	...	143	667	1,750	...
Pathan	51	22	98	53	168	107	14	6	377	478	560	375
Qassab	44	...	88	120	132	192	22	...	...	1,250	1,333	...
Qureshi ...	109	20	163	142	190	182	9	10	167	778	857	1,000
Rajput	28	...	113	177	66	420	9	...	...	667	2,714	...
Saiad	66	33	120	114	145	173	15	6	462	872	1,088	333
Sarara	...	...	43	26	87	77	87	...	...	500	750	...
Shekh	70	25	110	127	120	216	10	...	286	909	1,417	...
Sonar	119	21	99	171	219	128	...	...	167	1,600	545	...
Swathi	54	39	238	176	109	105	45	...	636	667	864	...
Tanaoli	54	26	114	88	111	95	24	10	444	711	784	375
Tarkhan ...	35	25	163	96	154	166	13	5	625	514	943	333
Teli	27	...	190	184	218	277	...	...	...	857	1,125	...

CHAPTER XI.

CASTE.

Reference to statistics.

366. The main statistics of caste will be found in Table XIII, in which are shown the numbers by sex and religion of those groups which in 1901 contributed more than 1 per mille of the population of the Province. Table IX shows the number of literate persons found among certain tribes and castes. Table XII-A gives statistics of infirmities, and Table XIV of civil condition by age, among the same groups as are dealt with in Table IX. In the last three mentioned tables no tribe or caste has been included, the numbers of which did not, at the Census of 1901, amount to 2 per mille out of the total population. In Subsidiary Table I, appended to this chapter, the various groups shown in Table XIII will be found arranged according to their traditional occupations; while Subsidiary Table II is intended to show variations in their numbers in different years. Owing to great changes since 1891 in the boundaries of Bannu and Dera Ismail Khan, and the fact that statistics of caste for areas smaller than districts are not available, I have divided Subsidiary Table II into two parts. Part A shows the numbers in 1901 and 1911 of each group in the districts of the Province as a whole, while Part B shows variations since 1881 in the three northern districts only, the boundaries of which have not been seriously modified since that year.

Method of caste classification.

367. Some explanation is needed as to the manner in which the figures have been arrived at. A list of the castes and tribes to be dealt with in each table was of course prepared before the work of tabulation was begun. At the same time, in order to avoid the temptation of classing all those which could not readily be identified under the head of "minor and unspecified," I classified every entry actually made in the schedules; and only at the end lumped together under that heading the names which did not appear in my lists as originally prepared. No one without experience of the classification of the entries of caste made in Census schedules will realise the difficulties and perplexities which arise during such a task. I certainly had no conception myself how troublesome the work would prove to be. Before the schedules were filled up, a caste index was prepared and circulated among the superior Census staff. It was divided into two parts. The first contained a list of all but a few unimportant groups to be found in the Province, together with a brief note of the religion and occupation, so far as a common occupation existed, of each, and of the area in which it was most generally to be found. The second part contained names of titles and occupational names which there seemed reason to expect might be, wrongly, found to be entered in the caste column, with a note of the true caste group to which each referred. There is every likelihood that the caste index did something to reduce the amount of confusion which is apt to occur; but in spite of it the schedules contained an enormous number of entries which were not what was wanted. The chief difficulty arises in the large number of cases in which people record as their caste, not the main group to which we commonly regard them as belonging, but some minor one falling under the general head, the identification of which is more or less difficult. If a man records himself as a Golra, a Janjua or an Utradhi, we have little difficulty in identifying him as an Awan, a Rajput or an Arora respectively; though Janjua, generally known as a sub-division of Rajputs, appears among the sub-sections of many other castes also. But in a great number of cases the name recorded is one which is entirely unknown to fame; and it is then difficult to decide on what lines to proceed. In dealing with such cases I found of great assistance the caste index which was prepared by Mr. Maclagan in the course of the Punjab Census, 1891. In that year sub-divisions, as well as main castes, were recorded and tabulated; and a mass of material was thus obtained

which could not be collected by asking, as we asked on the present occasion, for the entry of the name of the main group only. But however much trouble be taken, if one is to get the work done within a reasonable time, one has to do a good deal of very rough classification. Where I had nothing else to guide me, I looked at the occupation column and determined the caste to which the name was to be attributed by this; and I believe, for the reasons which I shall set forth in their due place, that this was the best indication which, in the circumstances, I could have followed. In many cases I was able in this way to identify the name returned. Thus, finding caste returned as Sapal and occupation as tailor, I looked up the list of sub-castes returned in 1891 under Darzi, and found that, as I expected, Sapal was one of them.

Classification of Pathan tribes.

368. In the case of tribes of Indian origin the explanation which has been suggested for the appearance of names like Bhatti and Khokhar as sub-castes of a tribe of high social status like the Rajputs on the one hand, and of menial and professional castes like the Nais on the other, is that the latter, *i.e.*, the Khokhar or Bhatti Nais, were originally servants of Bhatti or Khokhar Rajputs. (Khokhar, it may be noticed, which is best known as a division of the Rajputs, refers, in the north of our area at any rate, in most cases to Awans). In the case of the sub-sections of Pathans the position is different. The *Khels* or *Zais* derive their names in all cases from their actual or traditional ancestor; and seeing that the number of Mohammadan names is limited it is only to be expected that the same one should recur in many different tribes. Thus the Ali Khel is a clan of the Bangash, of the Mohammadzai, of the Mohmand and of the Orakzai; almost every tribe possesses a Khankhel; and names like Hassankhel and Akkakhel are constantly met with. In many cases the locality from which the name was returned was a sufficient indication of the group to which it belonged. Where the identification was doubtful I have included the entry under "Other Pathans." As a basis for my list of Pathan tribes, the numbers of which are shown separately in Table XIII, I took those tabulated by Mr. Maclagan in 1891; for the names appearing in the tables of 1901 are nothing but a welter of clan and tribal designations, some being those of main tribes and others those of tribal sections. Thus Adam Khel and Afridi appear side by side, and there is no indication of the fact that the one should be included in the other. To Mr. Maclagan's list I added a few names, such as Mohammadzai, which, from the number of the persons returning them and the distinct position accorded to them as tribal units, deserve to be separately shown. The tribes appearing in Table XIII are nearly all such as possess numerical importance within British Territory, and those which have been returned by small numbers only, such as Daur, Mangal, Mullagori, Shirani, and Turi, bear names famous across the border if not in the British districts of the Province. The difficulty of determining to what main section many Pathans belong is indicated by the fact that those whom I had to show under the vague heading "Other Pathans" amount to as much as 12 per cent. of the whole. There are of course included among these a good many persons who recorded themselves as 'Pathan' merely.

Accuracy of the statistics.

369. Considering the nature of the data with which we have to deal no meticulous measure of accuracy is to be expected in our statistics. It will be well if I give here an example of the way in which the returns have been modified during tabulation *i.e.*, the extent to which entries other than the names appearing in Table XIII have been included under them. Out of our 276,511 Awans,* 6,877 or something between 2 and 3 per cent. returned some other name. Some of the names such as Bhatti (19), Sial (31), Chauhan (71) and Janjua (55) are those found among other tribes also, such as the Rajput and the Jat, but which, from the area of enumeration and from the occupations of the persons returning them, probably refer to Awans in the present instance. The majority of the names, such as Golra (168), Abdal (134), Badan (533), Barsin (193), Pothwari (563), Jaswal (424), Dhanial (248), Qutbshahi (323), Mangrial (315), Pakhral (229), Shadwal (272), can be identified with certainty as being those of Awan sections. But in other cases it is impossible to be so sure.

* The Awan is the tribe in which the greatest number of miscellaneous entries have been included, if the general heading 'Other Pathans' be excluded.

Hindki (213) is a general term applied to any non-Pathan. In the case of persons enumerated, as were those in question, in the Peshawar District, there is a greater likelihood of their belonging to the Awan than to any other tribe, and among Awans I have included them. It is for the same reason that I have included Gilkar (75), Gadba (89),* Sarwan (42),* Sarban (134), Zemindar (7), and Chachhi (30). All but the last properly indicate occupations only, while the last is a local name. The above instances I quote here merely to illustrate the methods which have been followed in tabulation. There is no need for me to go into fuller detail. Those who wish to refer to it will find in the administrative volume prepared in connection with the Census a complete list of all the names which have been included in each group. That the classification made has been correct in every case I do not for one moment assert. I can myself detect many mistakes in it, and a fuller knowledge would no doubt enable me to indicate many more. All I contend is that the table is as accurate as, with the time at my disposal, I could make it, and further that, for all practical purposes, it is as correct as it has any need to be.

Caste hardly exists in the North-West Frontier Province.

370. The subject of caste, in the sense in which the word is understood in India, is one which has little interest in the North-West Frontier Province. As a system, however far non-Hindus have been influenced by it, it is the creation of Hindus, and Hindus, as we have seen, form but a trifling element in our population. Even they, as I have attempted to show in dealing with their marriage customs, obey caste rules with a laxity which is to be attributed to their Mussalman environment. Those persons therefore who are subject to the caste system as known elsewhere in India are for the most part not natives of the Province, and even those who were born within it, in so far as they are guided by caste rules, obey injunctions which have taken their form in, and derive their main interest from, areas outside it. As to the Mohammadans, all eat together, intermarriage between different groups is not uncommon, and, as I will attempt to show in the next paragraph, there is no necessary identity of occupation between the members of the various units.

Community of occupation not necessarily found among most of the groups shown in Table XIII.

371. Whatever theory be adopted, and many have been propounded, of the origin of caste, it will be readily admitted that one of its outstanding features is community of occupation among the members of each group. We have here a feature which is present in a comparatively unimportant degree in the North-West Frontier Province. Certain occupations are indeed associated with many of the various groups shown in Table XIII. The Pathan, for instance, is generally the land-owner or cultivator. The same may be said of the Awans, and other tribes, such as the Swathis, Tanaolis, Dhunds and Sararas of Hazara, and the Jats and Baluches of Dera Ismail Khan. Certain menial occupations, such as that of the Mussallis and Kutanas (Mohammadan sweepers) are restricted to certain groups, and, from the degradation with which they are associated in the popular imagination, no member of one of those of superior social status would engage in them. But there is no general objection, such as is found in India generally, to a member of one group adopting the occupation of another. The freedom with which Pathans enlist in the army may be placed on one side in this connection. It is no greater than is found in the case of other groups, such as the Jats and Rajputs of the Punjab, who, however, it may be noticed, represent rather tribal than caste groups proper. But other instances can readily be found. Trade and agriculture for instance are not usually found side by side among the members of one and the same caste. Yet our figures for Pathans include large numbers, notably the Powindahs of the Derajat, whose presence in the Province is mainly due to their position as traders. It is not necessary here to go into the question as to the correctness of our common classification as Pathans of Pathans proper on the one hand and Afghans, Ghilzais, Hazaras, and Tajaks on the other. Taking the persons classified as Pathans as they stand, while most of them are agriculturists, large numbers are traders, carriers, sepoys and others in service, public or private, landless labourers and graziers. The range of occupations followed by the Awans is probably even wider; and, with the exception of the small numbers belonging to the Hindu castes proper, the same may be said of others of the groups appearing in Table XIII.

* In the north of the Province. In Dera Ismail Khan Sarwan and Sarban have been tabulated as Baluch.

The tribal type of caste.

372. It is not of course contended that our figures are alone in consisting in the main of tribal rather than caste groups. The same statement is true of a large portion of the population of the Punjab. In that province also what Sir Denzil Ibbetson calls the tribal type of caste is largely in evidence. "The purest type" he wrote (*vide* Punjab Census Report, 1881, paragraph 342) "of the ethnic or national caste are the Pathans and Biloches, both untainted by any admixture of Hindu feeling or custom. Here the fiction which unites the caste, race, nation, or whatever you may chose to call it, is that of common descent from a traditional ancestor. In the main it is something more than a fiction, for if the common ancestor be mythical, as he probably is, there is a very real bond of common origin, common habitat, common customs and modes of thought, and tribal association continued through several centuries, which holds these people together . . . . Throughout the Western plains, and in a somewhat lower degree throughout the cis-Indus Salt range tract, where Islam has largely superseded Brahmanism and where the prohibition against intermarriage with another caste is almost universally neglected, we find the distribution of the land-owning classes based upon tribe rather than upon caste." The reference here is to such well known groups as the Jat and the Rajput.

Community of occupation the only common link between the members of many of our caste groups.

373. But though the members of our largest tribal groups are not, in many cases, bound together by community of occupation, in the case of some of our other groups the name returned in the column of caste is in effect a return of occupation and nothing more. "So too," writes Sir Denzil Ibbetson, "the lines which separate occupations from one another are relaxed. In the case of impure occupations, which render those who follow them outcast, this is not indeed the case. The Pathan who should become a scavenger would no longer be recognised as a Pathan, though he might still claim the name; indeed, as already pointed out in the chapter on Religion, the prejudice is carried into the very mosque, and the outcast who has adopted Islam is not recognised as a Mussalman, unless at the same time he abandons his degrading occupation. But the taint is not so markedly hereditary, nor is the prejudice against menial occupations or handicrafts generally so strong. A Pathan who became a weaver would still remain a Pathan, and would not be thought to be polluted; though, as in all countries, he would be thought to have fallen in the social scale, and the better class of Pathan would not give him his daughter to wife. In fact the difference between a Pathan who took to weaving on the frontier and the Rajput who took to weaving in the Delhi territory would be precisely that between caste in India and social standing in Europe. The degradation would not in the case of the former be ceremonial or religious, nor would it be hereditary, save in the sense that the children would be born into a lower condition of life, but the immediate and individual loss of position would be as real as among the strictest castes of the Hindus. Thus we find on the frontier men of all castes engaging from poverty or other necessity in all occupations save those of an actually degrading nature."

374. Thus our Mohammadan Dhobis, our Mohammadan Darzis, our Mohammadan syces are recruited from men of various origins. The tum-tum driver of Peshawar is never a Kori or Jaiswara or a man of the traditional syce caste. He may be a Pathan, he is very commonly an Awan. In these two instances indeed he will not hesitate to return Pathan or Awan in the caste column of the schedule. But in the case of other occupations, such as Dhobi, Darzi or Bhisti (classed with Jhinwar in Table XIII), in fact in the case of all groups the names of which denote an occupation as well as a caste, he probably returns the occupational name. We have here examples of what Sir Denzil Ibbetson calls the trades-guild type of caste. It is to be noted that all the names I have specified are those of menial or artisan castes. Sir Denzil Ibbetson questions whether in the case of these the real caste is not something smaller than the group which is described by the common name; whether it is not in fact the smaller unit which he calls the section. "If", he writes, "the numerous agricultural tribes of the Indus who are included under the generic term Jat, observed caste distinctions and refused to eat together and intermarry, we should have a state of things corresponding exactly with what we find throughout the Province among the industrial classes, where each

so called caste comprises under a common occupational term a number of sections of different geographical origin and of different habits, who refuse to hold communion with one another, and are for all practical purposes separate castes." The difference between what Sir Denzil Ibbetson describes as the position of the occupational castes in the Punjab, and that of similar (Mohammadan) groups in this Province is that here not only are there no endogamous sections within each, but intermarriage takes place between the different occupational units. A man first looks for a wife in his own tribe or occupational section; in fact, if a bride is available within his circle of immediate relatives and connections, he does not look any further. But if not successful here, he regards it as '*taqdir ka muamla*', and marries a woman of another tribe or from a family engaged in another occupation.

Groups shown in Table XIII fall into four main classes.

375. For the purposes of our discussion we may divide the names appearing in Table XIII into four main groups. We have first the units which are professedly tribal in character, in which the bond which binds the members together is a claim to common origin. By far the most important of these is of course the Pathan; others are the Awans, Gujars and various other agricultural tribes, such as the Jats, Swathis, Baluches, Tanaolis and the like. Next we have the Mohammadan occupational groups, such as the Darzis, Dhobis, and Jolahas, which comprise men of very different origin and antecedents. Thirdly we have those Hindu castes, such as the Arora and the Khatri, which from long residence among a Mohammadan population have lost much of their respect for the characteristic injunctions of their religion; and lastly we have the Hindu castes, the appearance of which in the Province has been of a date so recent that, helped by the spread of means of communication, they have continued to model their lives on the pattern of their fellow religionists in the areas which formed their original homes. A good instance of a caste of the last mentioned group is the Dhobi Our Hindu Dhobis (they only amount to 970 souls in all) were in most cases born within the Province, but they are essentially a foreign group. Their fathers or grand-fathers were born in the United Provinces, and they have retained the customs and language of their country of origin. They will tell you they are Purbis; their religion they return as Kanaujia, and they intermarry only with persons of the same origin as themselves, *i.e*, with other Purbia Dhobis.

The tribal group. Pathans.

376. The tribal group is represented in its clearest form by the major sub-divisions of the Pathans. The tie which unites together the members of each group is an assertion of common descent, and, in a certain degree, common ownership of land. How far tribal genealogies represent actual facts I find it impossible to say. In some cases they are admittedly fictitious, as, for instance, in the case of the Bannuchis, who are undoubtedly of very mixed composition. "The tribe" says* Sir Denzil Ibbetson, "is probably far more homogeneous in its composition among the Pathans than among the Biloches. Saiyad, Turk and other clans have occasionally been affiliated to it; but as a rule people of foreign descent preserve their tribal individuality, becoming merely associated, and not intermingled, with the tribes among whom they have settled. Even then they generally claim Pathan origin on the female side, and the tribe is generally descended in theory at least from a common ancestor. The *hamsaya* custom, by which strangers are protected by the tribe with which they dwell, is in full force among the Pathans as among the Biloches. But with the former, though it does protect in many cases families of one tribe who have settled with another, it seldom accounts for any considerable proportion of the tribe; and its action is generally confined to the traders, menials and other dependants of foreign extraction, who are protected by but not received into the tribe." And in another place the same writer remarks: "the Pathan genealogies, which were probably concocted not more than 400 years ago, teem with obvious absurdities. But they are based upon existing affinities of the people whom they trace back to Kais"

---

*Punjab Census Report, 1881, paragraph 393.

Other tribal groups.

377. The bulk of the remainder also of the population of the Province are divided up into groups which pertain to the tribe rather than to the caste. I note in the margin the names other than Pathan appearing in Table XIII which can be identified at once as belonging to the tribal type of caste, if indeed 'caste' is not in this connection entirely a misnomer. Gurkha and Kashmiri are indeed rather local than tribal names. They are used in the Province to describe groups composed of elements which in their homes are separated clearly from one another. But as being national rather than caste divisions I include them here. The Rajputs, except in Hazara, are not a tribe native to the Province, and may seem out of place in a list composed almost entirely of indigenous groups. At the same time, though the bulk of them come from another area, the Punjab, they possess a tribal rather than a caste organization. The figures for Jats represent a by no means homogeneous group. In the Mohammadan Jats, the great majority of whom are found in Dera Ismail Khan, we have an indigenous group which, however heterogeneous in origin, is to be clearly distinguished from our Hindu and Sikh Jats, who are present in the Province as immigrants only, the majority of those who have returned their religion as Sikh being employed in the army. With the exception of the foreign groups just referred to, the names shown are without exception those of agricultural tribes.

Awan.
Baluch.
Dhund.
Gakkhar.
Gujar.
Gurka.
Jat.
Karal.
Kashmiri.
Khokhar.
Mishwani.
Moghal.
Qureshi.
Rajput.
Saiad
Saram.
Swathi.
Tanaoli.
Turk.

Occupational groups.

378. I have found it most difficult to determine the actual position of those castes the names of which indicate also an occupation. When a man says, for instance, that his *qaum* is Darzi, one has not advanced far towards an understanding of what he actually means. It is undoubtedly the case that the occupation of the tailor is one which in the North-West Frontier Province may be taken up by any one, and which is in fact recruited from many and various sources. Our Darzi, who stated his *qaum* to be such, is very likely on further questioning to say that he is an Awan who has taken to tailoring. And at the first blush one is strongly tempted to say that names like Darzi, Dhobi and Lohar, when returned by Mohammadans, give no information beyond the occupations of the persons returning them. In a sense this is true ; but it is by no means the whole truth. The work of a tailor is one which implies no degradation ; and, except in so far as the possession of land has always been held to be the most honourable status which a man can enjoy, and in losing this he would lose in public estimation, an Awan (*i. e.*, a member of an agricultural tribe) who took to tailoring would lose nothing of the respect of his fellows. And yet our Awan who has become a tailor quickly ceases to call himself an Awan. It is the other Darzis of his quarter who come to his house on occasions of sorrow and rejoicing; it is the daughter of a Darzi that he probably takes to wife ; it is the Darzis who in fact become his caste-fellows.

379. I show in the margin the occupational groups which are represented in our tables I am only dealing here with the Mohammadans of the Province, and in the case of those units which include the followers of other religions also I have shown M against the names to indicate that it is only of their Mohammadan members that I am now speaking. The list contains mainly persons of the professional and menial castes, (*kasbi* and *kamin*), and each name denotes an occupation. The status possessed by the members of the different groups varies considerably. In the Arain, the Baghban and the Maliar, all of which seem merely to be names locally in use in different places for what is virtually one group, we have castes the position of which is little, if at all, lower than that of other agriculturists. The people in question grow vegetables ; and, possibly because of the use of night-soil as manure in market gardens, the caste is somewhat contemned. Passing downwards through the various grades we come to the Kumhar. the Teli, the Chamar (or Mochi; it is difficult to distinguish the two groups) and the Jolaha.

Arain.	
Baghban.	
Bhatiara	M.
Chamar	M.
Darzi	M.
Dhobi	M.
Jhinwar	M.
Jolaha	M.
Kumhar	M.
Lohar	M.
Machhi.	
Maliar.	
Mallah.	
Mochi	M.
Nai	M.
Qassab.	
Rangrez.	
Sonar	M.
Tarkhan	M.
Teli	M.

Of the origin of all these castes it is difficult to speak with any certainty. The same group in almost every case will be found to consist of two distinct elements. First we have members of the true caste concerned, who are all immigrants or descendants of immigrants from the east; and secondly we have the indigenous article, the man of a tribe native to the Province who has taken to the occupation indicated by the name. Thus I have met a Chamar (by occupation) who said his *quam* was Qureshi, and a Darzi, who was undoubtedly a Madda Khel, one of the trans-frontier branches of the great Yusafzai tribe. The two elements strive to keep distinct, the Punjabi Chamars intermarrying with the Punjabi Chamars, and Chamars of tribes native to the Province with their own brotherhood. But I fancy the fusion of the two has gone pretty far.

Line of cleavage between tribal and occupational groups.

380. We have then two sets of tribal groups, one consisting of Pathans, and the other of non-Pathan stock. Below these we have the occupational communities, consisting in part of comparatively recent immigrants from the east, and in part of a miscellaneous collection of persons who claim at any rate to be by origin members of the agricultural tribes superior to them and indigenous to the Province. That the inferior classes are recruited partly from those above them there can be no doubt. There is no insuperable obstacle, religious or social, to a Pathan, for instance, taking to weaving. No one would deny that he was a Pathan because he had adopted an occupation which is held in low repute; but he would naturally lose in social status. He would no longer find it possible to obtain a wife from a landowning stock, and would perforce look for one in the community which he had chosen to join. His son would probably cease to call himself a Pathan; at least no one else would admit the claim.

Other Mohammadan groups.

381. Leaving on one side the Chuhra (or Mehtar), to whom Hindu prejudice has been strong enough even on the Frontier to deny the title of Mussalman, the other Mohammadan groups are the Faqir, Khoja, the Mirasi, the Musalli, the Paracha (including the Banjara) and the Shekh. Faqir is nothing but a convenient name under which to group a miscellaneous collection of beggars who can give no more definite account of their origin. The Khoja I suspect strongly of being nothing more than the Paracha who has grown rich. Neither group is native to the Province; both are strongly permeated with Hindu sentiment, and possess something, or at any rate the desire for something far more nearly resembling a caste organisation than is to be found in any of the indigenous Mohammadan groups. The Mirasi and the Musalli (one the musician and genealogist, the other the scavenger and grain winnower) I have included here, and not among the profesional and menial classes of which a list is given in paragraph 379, because there does seem to be some clear line of cleavage between them and the groups superior to them. The Shekhs form a by no means homogeneous community, Shekh being the new designation adopted by those persons who, when embracing Islam, choose a new caste name.

Causes of the preservation of the separate social units.

382. Taking the Mohammadan population as a whole we can say with confidence that its division is into tribes and not into castes. In the first place, as I have attempted to show in Chapter VII, there is no hard and fast line forbidding intermarriage between the different groups That the tribes remain as distinct from one another as is found to be the case appears to be due to the preference for marriage with near relatives. A man will rarely marry his daughter outside his own tribe, or, in the case of the occupational groups, outside his own occupation, and he will never, except under the direst compulsion, permit her union with a group of inferior status to his own. But if the proposed bridegroom be of a position better than his own, there are no caste prejudices to stand in the way. Men commonly marry women of a tribe into which they would not permit their daughter to marry, especially when they are taking a second wife. The result of this is bound to be that the strains of the various caste and tribal groups have got largely mixed; and the small difference in the appearance of the various groups must often have been noticed. In the second place there is no rule forbidding the adoption by any individual of any

occupation he pleases. But as men naturally follow their father's occupation this does not produce the same fusion of the groups following different occupations as is the case in Europe. If there are any exceptions to the general assertions made above, they exist in the case of the Parachas and Khojas, who are still sufficiently Hinduised for their prejudices in regard to marriage to have persisted, and in that of the Mirasis and Musallis, with whom other tribes will not as a rule ally themselves. Even the Mirasis moreover probably contain a considerable percentage of persons who represent, not a distinct group, like the Punjabi Mirasis who are to be found in the Province, but a collection of individuals of diverse origin who are bound together by nothing beyond a common occupation, and the community of interests and of habitation which a common occupation in India implies.

Pride of race tends to keep pure the groups of highest social status.

383. So far then we may say that the Mohammadan groups shown in Table XIII represent tribes in the one set of cases, and occupations in the other, rather than castes. Marriage being determined by considerations of social status, and these being much the same as in Europe, it follows that the higher the estimate in which any group is held, the more homogeneous its composition is likely to remain. It is thus naturally the Pathans who have best been able to preserve their national type. Looking down on all other communities, they will not give their daughters in marriage to them. A Pathan who takes to a menial occupation does not, *ipso facto*, cease to be a Pathan, but he will find it difficult to obtain a wife of his own race, and in one or two generations will find himself divorced completely from it. Yet many Pathans have taken non-Pathan wives, and thus introduced a foreign strain; and that more have not done so is no doubt due to the fact that they live for the most part in the midst of their fellow Pathans; and the opportunity or the desire to marry into an alien group does not arise. And the strong prejudice in favour of marrying a near relative has also had a powerful influence in keeping the stock pure. Exactly the same circumstances have tended to keep free from admixture of outside blood all the agricultural tribes which are represented in considerable numbers in the Province. They too live for the most part in villages in which the whole, or the greater part, of the community belongs to the same tribe as themselves. They too prefer a wife from the circle of their immediate relatives. There is no theoretical objection to a marriage outside the tribal unit; still less is there any prohibition, outside the ordinary social one, against the adoption of any means of livelihood, however low it may be held in popular estimation. It is only that, in practice, circumstances combine to keep each group distinct. In our agricultural tribes therefore we have groups which, if they have little in common with castes, at any rate represent sufficiently distinct communities.

Causes of the preservation of distinct occupational groups.

384. In the occupational groups the intermixture which occurs is naturally greater. As possessing a low social status pride of blood does not operate to prevent fusion. They live largely in isolated homes, or in small communities of ten or a dozen houses. This again hinders marriage within the community composed of their fellow craftsmen. Social conventions operate to prevent unions between a landowner and a member of the menial and professional classes; but not between members of different occupational groups. The preference for a marriage within the circle of the immediate relatives is indeed the main factor which tends to make the *tarkhan*, for instance, a member of a community of *tarkhans* in a sense that a carpenter in England is not a member of a society consisting exclusively of carpenters. Moreover, even in the North-West Frontier Province, a man generally follows the profession of his father. Given occupations generally hereditary, and a strong bias in favour of marriage within the family circle, and you have sufficient explanation of the existence of occupational units more or less distinct from one another. At the same time the impulse tending to keep them separate appears, as society becomes more complex, to be decreasing in force year by year, and men tend more and more to desert the occupations of their fathers in favour of whatever happens best to suit their own particular circumstances.

Hindu and Sikh castes.
(*a*) the indigenous castes.

385. In more or less strong contrast with the position of the various units which go to make up the Mohammadan population is that of the Hindus (and with the Hindus I include the Sikhs) who are to be found in the Province.

I have said that these consist of immigrant or foreign groups on the one hand, and of indigenous ones on the other. Among the latter may be included the bulk of our Aroras, Hindu Sonars, Bhatias, Brahmans and Khatris, though there are also to be found among them a certain number of foreign-born, who have brought with them the customs of the land of their birth. Now these represent castes in something approaching the generally accepted meaning of the word. Their choice of occupation is more restricted than among the Mohammadans, and probably does not vary much from that open to them, for instance, in the Delhi District of the Punjab. The field within which they can marry is again (*vide* paragraph 234, Chapter VII) not much wider than in areas where Hindu sentiment has far greater strength. But beyond this I fancy that few traces of caste restrictions remain. For instance commensality between different Hindu castes is the rule. In rural areas Brahmans, Khatris, Aroras and Bhatias eat together; and celebrate in common the various occasions, whether of joy or mourning, which arise among them. Child marriage (*vide* paragraph 264, Chapter VII) in its extreme form is not to be found. No distinct caste government exists; and the *panchayat*, which is merely a gathering of co-religionists to celebrate weddings and funerals, is not composed of Brahmans alone or of Khatris alone, but of the whole Hindu community, of whatever caste, to be found in the village.

(*b*) The foreign castes.

386. Lastly we have the castes the members of which are either immigrants to the Province, or the descendants of comparatively recent settlers. Of our immigrant Hindus the majority are either Rajputs or Jats. Most of these, however, are in military employ. They are seldom accompanied by their families, and they are only stationed here for comparatively short terms of years. Of more interest are the customs of the permanent immigrants, who are composed almost entirely of members of the menial castes, such as Dhobis, Bhatiaras, Jhinwars, Mochis and Nais. Their appearance in the Province dates from annexation only, and they are found almost entirely in cantonments, whither they followed the troops of the East India Company when first they were stationed here. They have not been long enough in the Province to have given up the customs of the country of their birth; and their caste restrictions and caste organisation vary little from those found among them in the United Provinces, from which they, or their fathers, have generally found their way. The Hindu Dhobis and Saises, for instance, in many cases obtain their brides from their original homes; and find it necessary to make enquiries in various and far distant places to ensure that they do not marry into a group with which inter-marriage is forbidden. But perhaps in strongest contrast with the customs of the other inhabitants of the Province is their system of caste government.

System of caste government. (*a*) Among Hindus.

387. The system of caste government among the various groups was one of the subjects on which an attempt was made to collect detailed information at the present Census. With reference to our immigrant Hindus the enquiry is not without pertinence. The Dhobis, for instance, have their caste *panchayat*, which, in the cases which have come to my notice, met together formally to expel from the brotherhood a caste-fellow who had married a Mehtar woman, and to assess the fine to be levied annually on another who was employed as 'bearer' to a European. (The objection here was to the fact that as 'bearer' he was required to clean his master's leather shoes). Such menial groups live collected together in cantonments in comparatively large communities, and the caste *panchayat* in their case has the opportunity of existing in something more than name. But outside them, even among Hindus, my questions as to caste government were simply not understood. There is in fact, even among the Hindus whom I have described as indigenous to the Province, no system of caste government at all. I have mentioned how, owing to their small numbers, the *panchayat* to be found in any village in the Province is not a caste gathering but a gathering of all Hindus, whatever their caste. But more than this, it exists, even so, only in name. The *panchayat* is merely a gathering of persons of the same religion to celebrate occasions either joyful or the reverse. It possesses no disciplinary powers. Even if a member embraces Islam, there is no gathering of the community formally to out-cast him. He merely drops out, *ipso motu*; though if he were to present himself at the house of any of his former caste-fellows, he would of course be refused admittance.

(*b*) Among Mohammadans.

388. Among Mohammadans, with the possible exception of the Khojas and Parachas, there is nothing corresponding to the system of caste government found among Mohammadans, as among Hindus, in other parts of India. In the case of certain of the occupational groups traces exist of an organisation of the type of the trades-guild. This I will return to in a subsequent paragraph. But as regards the agricultural tribes, who make up the bulk of the population of the Province, my enquiries were met in most cases by the simple rejoinder that there was nothing to report. Even among Pathans, the *jirga*, or tribal council, has been replaced by our courts of law as a method of settling disputes (though, as everywhere else, people will be found who take things into their own hands), and in its present form, as found in the British districts, is merely a jury called into existence under our legal system to assess damages or to offer a finding of fact.

The jirga in the trans-frontier area of the Province.

389. Across the border on the other hand the *jirga* is the controlling authority of the tribe or section. If it be a full one, it consists of all the male adults of the tribe. In the ordinary course it represents merely the section of the tribe concerned; but in the rare event of a whole tribe combining for a common end, the action to be taken would be decided upon by a *jirga* representative of the whole body of tribesmen. As regards its disciplinary powers against individuals, and it is only cases such as those mentioned by him that would come within its purview, the following notes have been furnished to me by Mr. Boyle, Commandant of the Samana Rifles. Writing of the trans-frontier area subject to the political control of the Deputy Commissioner of Kohat Mr. Boyle, says, "Neglect to keep the fast is said to be unknown in the Kohat Pass. The authorities consulted by me among the Pass *Maliks* are unable to suggest the punishment that would meet the case. It would, however, probably follow the lines of the treatment accorded to offenders in Tirah *i.e.*, expulsion from tribal councils followed by a disciplinary visit from the Mullas and their *lashkar*" (*lashkar* means properly an armed gathering of tribesmen), "of seekers after knowledge" (*talib-ilms*, the disorderly rabble who hang about the mosques under pretence of studying theology) "which after all is a cloak to enrich the priestly coffers. Refusal to comply with their demands would entail a feud with the tribe at large, and would probably end in a heavy fine and the burning of the defaulter's homestead. This would also be followed by the usual pennance recognised by Mohammadan law, *i.e.*, a fast for a period double the amount of neglect. The use of alcoholic liquors is also denied, as facilities for such depravity do not exist among the trans-frontier tribes, The drunkard, however, is looked upon as a pervert, and the threat held out by the Mullas appears to consist in the gate of paradise and its concomitant joys being barred for ever. The possiblity of the penitent sinner has not been considered apparently, and no disciplinary measures appear customary. The taking of interest, althougn forbidden in Mohammadan law, is universal. It may figure in the form of deferred payment at usurious rates, or in the bald form and calculation of the Hindu usurer; but there are few people who pay any heed to the eternal fire, which is the future fate laid down in the Koran for the usurer."

No central authority exists among tribal groups in British territory.

390. In the passage above quoted Mr. Boyle has given some account of the powers possessed by the central controlling authority over the individual members of a Pathan tribe in the trans-frontier area of the Province. The power of the *jirga* is here far greater than is the case in British territory. Even in the tribal area it does not interfere with the mass of details of which a true caste *panchayat* takes cognizance. And in the administered districts its powers virtually amount to nothing at all. The points with which it deals in tribal territory are largely matters of inter-tribal politics. Its powers are in fact political rather than social; and in British territory inter-tribal politics simply can not exist. If A, belonging to one section of a tribe, steals cattle belonging to B, who belongs to another section, it is to the Sirkar, and not to his fellow tribesmen, that the latter looks for redress. The blood-feud unfortunately still exists in British territory; but its scope is considerably restricted, as, under any system of civilized government, it necessarily must be. And just as among the Pathan tribes their inclusion in the Indian Empire has weakened, has in fact reduced to nothing, the power of any authority existing

within the tribe, so among the tribes of Indian origin their intercourse with the Pathan and their adoption of Islam has put an end to the inquisitorial interference with the actions of the individual which is to be found in the caste groups which have their habitation to the south and east. There is no need for me to discuss here the origin of the various groups, whether Pathan or otherwise, with which we are here concerned. I could contribute nothing beyond extracts from Sir Denzil Ibbetson's great Report of 1881. It is sufficient if I mention that among the non-Pathan tribes also the actions of individual members are controlled by nothing more than legal enactment and a public opinion which, however different its judgments, works in much the same way as public opinion in Europe.

Caste government in the occupational groups.

391. If anything resembling caste government exists in the Province at all (excepting always our purely immigrant Hindu groups, such as the Dhobi) it is to be found among certain occupational communities the organisation of which appears closely to resemble that of the trade guilds of mediæval Europe. The matters of which cognizance is taken by the caste *panchayat* are those not affecting individuals as individuals, as in the case, for instance, of the Dhobi who took to cleaning his master's shoes, but affecting the common interests of his fellow craftsmen. Thus among the *bakar-qasais* (mutton butchers) of Peshawar city, there is a common fund, to which all the members of the occupational group contribute. Among other objects on which this fund would be expended is a 'grant-in-aid' to a butcher who, for instance, is required to provide meat at a camping ground. The Qassab *chaudhris* issue orders as to the closing of shops; and any Qassab who fails to obey the instructions is fined. The community subject to this central control is one, it is to be noticed, composed of diverse elements, Awans, Gujars and others, bound together by community of occupation and nothing else. The Telis, or oil-pressers, similarly have a caste organisation of the trades-guild type. The amount of soap which individual Telis may turn out in a year, for instance, is settled by the caste *panchayat*, and a fine is imposed on a member who makes more than the amount fixed. As in the case of the Qassabs this control, which seems to be concerned originally with matters affecting the common occupation of the members, or the conditions under which it is to be followed, is extended also to the purely social sphere, and a Teli who, when summoned to a feast, does not attend, or arrives late, is fined by order of the controlling authority of the brotherhood. It is to be noticed, however, that the Teli who gave me the above information, was the grandson of a man who settled in Peshawar from the Gujranwala District of the Punjab, and formed one of a group, which though settled here for two or three generations, is still essentially a foreign one. The Kumhars have a *panchayat* which determines the rates at which, vessels shall be sold, and by these rates all the potters of Peshawar city are bound, in spite of the fact that in origin they include many different groups, some of them being *asli kumhars* coming originally from the Punjab, while others are Awans, Kashmiris and the like, who are Kumhars by occupation only. It is only in the case of these three groups *viz*, the Qassabs, the Telis and the Kumhars that I have succeeded in finding any trace of the existence of a caste organisation, and in all it is with the interests of the trade followed that the caste *panchayat* is principally concerned. In all the other groups with reference to which the word *panchayat* is understood at all, it means merely a gathering of the brotherhood on occasions of sorrow or joy. But among the bulk of the population, as it was tersely expressed to me, "*har sok khpal de kor badshah dai*" (every man is master of his own house).

Variations in the numbers of the various tribes and castes.

392. With this very imperfect sketch, which owes any merits it may possess mainly to the labours of the late Sir Denzil Ibbetson, I must leave the consideration of the character of the various units shown in Table XIII, and pass on to discuss in outline the variations which have taken place in their numbers since 1881. The necessary statistics will be found in Subsidiary Table II appended to this chapter. For this purpose I will consider the figures not for single units, but for groups of them, devoting some further attention to those castes or tribes which seem to demand it, when I deal, at the end of this chapter, with some individual entries in the Table. The Subsidiary Table, in

the form prescribed by the Census Commissioner, is intended to show the numbers recorded under each group at each successive Census since the year 1881 in the Province as a whole. In the case of the North-West Frontier Province, however, owing to the alteration of the boundaries of the Bannu and Dera Ismail Khan Districts which has taken place since 1891, a table in this form would be misleading. I have therefore divided it into two parts. In the first are shown the numbers recorded as belonging to each tribe or caste in the total area of the Province in 1901 and 1911, respectively. In the second will be found the figures for each Census since 1881 for the three northern districts only, the boundaries of which have remained virtually unchanged since that year.

393. To compare first the figures of 1901 with those of the present Census, the marginally noted tribes and castes are those which have shown in the last ten years the largest percentage of increase (20 per cent. and over). The Bhatias and Parachas are traders, the Gurkhas are in military employ, and the Qassabs are menials or shop-keepers, in whichever way you chose to regard them. The large increase shown in the number of Bhatias (who are Hindus or Sikhs) is due to a mistake at last Census which I will refer to later. The figures for Gurkhas depend entirely on the strength and number of the Gurkha battalions, and their variations have little interest here. The point which merits notice is that of the other tribes showing the largest increases, all but the Parachas and Qassabs are agriculturists, and that all are indigenous to the Province, or have been settled here for so long as to be virtually native to it. This result is in keeping with the statistics of birthplace, which show the increase of population since 1901 to have occurred wholly among the native born population, the number of immigrants having largely decreased. (a) since 1901.

Baghban.
Bhatia.
Dhund.
Gakkhar.
Gurkha.
Karal.
Paracha.
Qassab.
Qureshi.
Turk.

394. The next largest rate of increase (*viz.* from 10 to 20 per cent.) is found among the Kumhars, Mishwanis, Sararas, Swathis, Awans, Kashmiris and Rangrezes. The Kumhars and Rangrezes are menials, the names of which denote an occupation as well as a caste, and it is as much to the greater demand for pottery and dyed stuffs as to any increase in the numbers of the members of the these castes that we must refer our figures. The same remark applies also to the Qassabs, but not, I understand, to the Parachas. Any one can become a Qassab by merely opening a butcher's shop, but an Awan who takes to selling the articles commonly sold by a Paracha will not thereby become one. The Kashmiris are not of course by origin native to the Province, but most of those enumerated here on the present occasion were born within it, and appear to be a prolific race. The other tribes mentioned in this paragraph, *viz*, the Mishwanis, Sararas, Swathis and Awans, are all agricultural tribes, the first three being practically confined to the Hazara District.

395. In my next group of tribes, the increase among which since last Census varies from 1 to 10 per cent., is included the bulk of the population of the Province. The tribes and castes are as shown in the margin. In all we have groups native to the Province, or, if by origin not indigenous, such as have been domiciled here for a long period and are included in the permanent, as opposed to the immigrant, population. The Aroras and Khatris make up the bulk of the non-Mussalman element. Almost without exception they are engaged in trade, though a few are clerks in Government service and the like. In the Chamars, Lohars, Mirasis, Nais and Tarkhans we have members of professional or menial groups supplying needs which naturally increase with a growing population. Our Gujars and Moghals are partly agriculturists, and partly engaged in miscellaneous occupations. All the other groups shown are agricultural tribes, and the increases found in their numbers are the natural result of the growth of the rural population since 1901.

Arain.
Arora.
Baluch.
Chamar.
Gujar.
Jat.
Khatri
Lohar.
Mirasi.
Mochi.
Moghal.
Nai.
Pathan.
Salad.
Tanaoli.
Tarkhan.

396. Coming to the groups the numbers of which have decreased since last Census, a fall of under 10 per cent. is found in the case of the Bhatiaras, Dhobis, Jolahas, Machhis, Mallahs and Shekhs. The Shekhs are partly agriculturists, partly, in the cases where the term merely means any new convert to Islam, of mixed occupations. The native population of the Province, however, contains few new converts, and a decrease in the number of immigrants we might expect to find accompanied by a fall in the figures for Shekh. The other groups here referred to are all of the professional and menial class, and, as the number of persons following the occupations which these terms denote are not likely to have actually decreased, to quote Mr. Rose's comment in the Punjab Census Report, 1901, "the only explanation possible is that the occupational caste and the actual occupation are by no means one and the same thing, and that at each Census caste and occupation are confused, but in varying degrees." The same remark applies to the Mallahs and Sonars, the numbers of whom, along with those of the Brahmans and Khojas have decreased since 1901 by amounts varying from 10 to 20 per cent. As regards the Sonars the explanation no doubt partly lies in the fact that it is only our Hindu Sonars who have decreased in numbers, and the Mussalmans engaged in goldsmith's work are particularly likely to return some other name as that of their *quam*. The decrease in the number of Brahmans is only what might be expected from the decrease of the number of Hindus; that in the number of Khojas is probably to be explained by a rise in the number of Parachas.

Darzi.
Chuhra.
Faqir.
Jhinwar.
Khokhar.
Maliar.
Rajput.
Teli.

397. Finally may be mentioned, (*vide* marginal list) those castes and tribes the numbers of which have fallen since 1901 by more than 20 per cent. The loss among Maliars is counterbalanced by the gain among Baghbans. The circulation of a caste index has had the effect of largely reducing the number of Faqirs, Faqir not being the name of a caste or tribe, but merely a convenient term under which all sorts of beggars and vagrants can be shown without further enquiry. The other castes, *viz.* the Darzis, Chuhras, Jhinwars, Khokhars, Rajputs and Telis, in so far as they are representatives of castes as distinct from occupations, are all strangers to the Province. There are few Rajputs, other than sepoys, except in Hazara, and the variation here is accidental only. Khokhar has been classed with Awan in the three northern districts on the present occasion, and this fact has not a little to do with the variation. The decrease in Darzis, Jhinwars and Telis appears also to be accidental, and to be due to the fact that the names indicate occupations rather than castes. The various occupations of the Jhinwar, water-carrying, bread-baking and *doolie*-bearing are followed, if necessary, by the Pathan and other tribes, and the same may be said of the avocation of the tailor and the oil-presser. The first annexation of the districts of the Province was followed by a great influx of the menial castes of Hindostan and the Punjab, who found employment, and satisfied needs which had not before existed, in the towns and cantonments. Now the native born population is taking more and more to forms of employment which, before annexation, were not open to them. The Darzis proper, *i.e.* the Darzi caste from the east, are being replaced by men who are tailors by occupation only. The same is true of the Jhinwar and the Teli. The Chuhra figures I find it difficult to understand. The Chuhra as a caste, and the scavenger as an occupation, hardly existed in the Province previous to the advent of British rule, and it is to be expected that a considerable number of the immigrant Chuhras have embraced Islam and ceased to return themselves as Chuhras by caste. But the Musallis and Kutanas, who correspond to the Chuhra in the local social economy, have also fallen in numbers. We should expect our Chuhras to re-appear as Musallis, but they have apparently not done so.

(*b*) since 1881.

398. Some further light on the variations since 1901 in the numbers for the various castes and tribes will be thrown by the figures given in Subsidiary Table II (*b*), in which are shown the numbers and variation in each in the three northern districts of the Province from 1881 onwards. Those for Bannu and Dera Ismail Khan in 1881 and 1891 are not, as I have pointed out

above, properly comparable with those of the two subsequent Censuses. It will be noticed that in many cases (*vide* list printed in the margin) a notable rise or fall in the last decade has followed an equally striking development in the opposite direction during the one preceding it. Nearly all the groups mentioned are occupational units, the names of which in other parts of India indicate castes proper, but which, in the North-West Frontier Province, primarily denote occupations. I have already indicated (*vide* paragraph 396) what I believe to be the reason of the variations here. The fact seems to be that no profit is to be obtained from any detailed analysis of the variations of most of our caste, as distinct from tribal, groups. Castes proper as distinct from tribes, are hardly represented in the Province except by the Aroras, Bhatias, Brahmans and Khatris. In the three northern districts the numbers of Aroras have increased steadily since 1881, through the high rate of increase shown between 1891 and 1901 has not been maintained during the last decade. Our Brahmans are now more numerous than in 1891, but fewer than in 1901, in which year their numbers seem to have been abnormally (and presumably temporarily) swollen. The variation since 1901 in the number of Bhatias is capable of clear explanation. The caste has never been represented in anything but insignificant numbers in the three northern districts. I show in the margin the number enumerated in Bannu and Dera Ismail Khan at each of the last three Censuses, from which it may reasonably be inferred that the Bhatias of Dera Ismail Khan were confused with some other group (possibly with Bhatti) in 1901, and consequently did not appear at all in the statistics of that year. The Khatris show in the last decade the highest rate of increase of any of our Hindu groups. In the three northern districts of the Province the growth of population in the caste has been at a rate equal to that of the population as a whole, and the much greater one recorded during the decade 1891-1901 points to abnormal temporary immigration in 1901, if indeed, considered in conjunction with the variations in other castes also, it does not suggest some inaccuracy in the caste tables of that year. Regarded in the light of the statistics for religion and for immigration, however, a small rate of increase, or an actual decrease, since 1901 in the numbers of the Hindu castes has all the appearance of corresponding with the actual facts; while the Khatris, as being the largest of the native groups, have naturally been affected least by migration, and show most clearly the growth of population due to natural increase.

Baghban.
Brahman.
Darzi.
Dhobi.
Dhund.
Faqir.
Gakkhar.
Julaha.
Kashmiri.
Kumhar.
Maliar.
Mochi.
Sonar.
Teli.
Turk.

Bhatias.

District.	Number enumerated in.		
	1891.	1901.	1911.
Bannu ...	2,173	1,934	2,033
Dera Ismail Khan	1,791	...	1,798

Variations recorded in the numbers of the agricultural tribes since 1901.

399. For the reasons I have indicated above, I do not propose to devote here any further attention to variations in the numbers of the Mohammadan occupational castes. Looking, however, at the tribes proper as shown in Subsidiary Table II (*a*) (and by tribes proper I mean those groups indigenous to the Province and mainly engaged in agriculture, who are united by an assertion, if no more, of common descent) we may arrange them, as shown in the margin, in the order of the rate of increase recorded during the last decade in the Province as a whole (British territory). The figures for Tanaolis depend primarily on the population enumerated in Feudal Tanawal in the Hazara District; and the statistics here (*vide* paragraph 58 *supra*) are not to be trusted The figures for Saiads there is no reason to suspect; and, except in so far as the circulation of a caste index may be expected to have directed more attention to the record of caste, and to have led to the record of persons as Saiads with more discrimination than on earlier occasions, can only be explained on the supposition that this part of it is increasing less quickly than the community as a whole. The Gujars are mainly to be found in

Tribe.		*Variation per cent.*
Tanaoli	...	+3·51
Saiad	...	+4·1
Gujar	...	+5·3
Pathan	...	+6·2
Jat	...	+6·8
Moghal	...	+9·1
Baluch	...	+9·6
Swathi	...	+14·6
Awan	...	+14·8
Sarara	...	+16·0
Mishwani	...	+19·2
Dhund	...	+20·7
Gakkhar	...	+22·1
Karal	...	+38·6
Qureshi	...	+49·0
Turk	...	+88·9

Hazara; and the comparatively small expansion shown in their numbers since 1901 is probably due in part to the tendency to emigrate which forms so marked a characteristic of the inhabitants of that district. At the same time it is to be noticed that nearly all our Swathis, Sararas, Mishwanis, Dhunds, Gakkhars, Karals and Turks have also been enumerated in Hazara, and that of the Moghals nearly two-thirds live in the same district, while all show a rate of increase in advance of that of the population of the Province as a whole. Sarara was not recorded at all in Hazara in 1891, and only in trifling numbers in Peshawar and Kohat, and it is impossible to say how steady has been the rate of growth among Sararas in the last 20 years. The figures for Dhunds now are roughly the same as was the case in 1891, and the large increase recorded in the last decade is largely due to the considerable decrease shown as having taken place in the one preceding it. The same is the case in regard to the Gakkhars and Turks, the latter of whom, though nearly twice as numerous as they were shown as being in 1901, are still fewer than they were ten years previously. The figures for Jats and Baluches require little comment. The rates of increase shown by each exhibit little variation from the normal, though both are names used very loosely in the Province, and comprehend widely diverse elements. Looking at the entries in columns 7 to 9 of Subsidiary Table II (*b*) it will be seen that in the three northern districts of the Province the rate of increase among Pathans was abnormally high between the years 1891 and 1901, and that in the last decade it has been abnormally low. The rate of growth recorded in the one decade naturally depends largely on that recorded in the other, and suggests that the term Pathan was used more comprehensively on the last occasion than it has been on this. In the case of Awan the reverse seems to have been the case; while Qureshis were included with Shekhs in 1881 and 1891, and we are unable therefore to base any conclusions as to how far the high percentage of increase recorded since 1901 corresponds with the actual facts on a consideration of the variations elicited by the Censuses taken previous to that date.

Position of the menial and professional groups.

400. On the subject of the tribes proper, as on that of the castes proper, little remains for me to say. As regards their origin, their characteristics and their hereditary occupations I would refer the reader to Sir Denzil Ibbetson's Census Report, Punjab for 1881. But some information can perhaps be usefully included here on the subject of the position held in the village community by the members of the professional and menial groups. The *hamsaya* custom, under which it is defined, is characteristic of the Province, and I have come across no detailed account of it.

401. Characteristic examples of *hamsaya* groups are to be found in the castes of which a list is given in the margin. The members of them live in villages by permission of the proprietors, and often in houses provided for them rent free. They are not in all cases village menials; but their position is always *de jure* that of dependants, though *de facto* that, *e g.* of the Hindu money-lender, is often very much the reverse. But even if they are shop-keepers or artisans of the ordinary type, selling their wares to whomsoever choses to buy, they are usually compelled to sell at preferential rates to the land-holders of the village. Beginning at the top of the social scale, we may consider first the shop-keeping and trading castes, the Aroras, Bhatias, Khatris and Parachas; though it is to be noticed that all but the last, as being Hindus, are in one sense treated with less respect than the lowest of the Mohammadan menial groups, such as the Musallis and the Jolahas.

Arora.
Bhatia.
Bhatiara.
Chamar.
Dhobi.
Jolaha.
Khatri.
Kumhar.
Lohar.
Mirasi (or Dum).
Musalli (with Kutana)
Nai.
Paracha.
Qassab.
Rangrez.
Sonar.
Tarkhan.
Teli.

The trading castes.

402. In relation to non-proprietors, the position of the trading castes is much the same in rural areas in the North-West Frontier Province as elsewhere. But their relation to the land-holding community is distinct from this. Instead of paying cash for their houses and shops, and for permission to reside in the village, they have certain services to perform. They take food,

if required, to guests of the landlords; provide oil and tobacco in the *hujra*, go to the city to make purchases, weigh goods for the proprietors, etc. They also receive certain dues like other *hamsayas*, each man getting 4 or 5 sers of grain from each threshing floor; and their inferior position is marked by their being required to take a gift of sweets, or of a similar nature, to the proprietors on the occasion of a wedding, getting in return a gift of. equal value. In the Agror Valley in Hazara to this day dues are paid in cash by Hindus to the Khan, whenever they celebrate a marriage in their houses.

403. The Bhatiara similarly, and to an even greater degree, is the servant of all the proprietors of the village. He brings water for drinking to the harvest field and the threshing floor, and for cooking and drinking at marriages and funerals. He pours water on newly made graves, carries *doolies* at weddings, and does miscellaneous *begar* when required. In return for these services he gets Rs 2 or more in cash at each wedding, 4 sers of grain from each threshing floor, and a head load of produce from each field as it is reaped. Besides this he probably brings water daily to the houses of the richest proprietors; but this is a matter of private arrangement between the parties, and the payment takes the form of an allowance of grain. The Chamar, who is not to be distinguished from the Mochi, is partly an artisan, who sells the shoes he makes, and partly a village menial, who mends the old shoes of the proprietors, and does miscellaneous *begar*, getting in return a share of grain from each harvest field and each threshing floor. Bhatiara. Chamar.

404. The Dhobi (not commonly to be found in villages) and the Dum, though *hamsayas*, are not village menials. The Jolaha (also commonly returned as Bafinda and Paoli) is regarded as perhaps the lowest of Mohammadan groups, and *begar* is taken from him more freely than from any other caste. At the same time he is not a village menial in the sense that the Chamar, for instance, is. He serves the one proprietor whose *hamsaya* he is; and weaves for him at a cheaper rate than for others. Other employers, however, pay him, in cash or kind, for each separate task he performs for them. The Kumhar (or Kulal) on the other hand is a servant of the community pure and simple For marriages and funerals he makes all the earthen vessels required. He furnishes a large *ghara* to hold water in the *hujra*, and the smaller vessels to drink from, as well as a vessel to hold water for ablutions in the mosque. In return he gets Rs 2 in cash on the occasion of each wedding he assists at, and a head load of the produce from each field. In addition he sells his wares to all who choose to buy from him. Jolaha. Kumhar.

405. The Lohar and the Tarkhan (also frequently returned as Karigar, Najjar and Kamangar) may be dealt with together. The two groups are hardly distinguishable, and if carpenter's and blacksmith's work are not ordinarily done by one and the same person, the sons of the one, as of the other, seem to take indifferently to either occupation. The Tarkhan and the Lohar make and repair between them the agricultural implements required in the village, receiving the necessary materials from the proprietors. The Tarkhan also plasters walls and roofs with mud, and repairs them when necessary. In return both Tarkhan and Lohar get a share of grain per plough, and sometimes a piece of land free of revenue. Water mills in the same way they keep in repair, getting a fixed percentage of the grain or sugar ground or extracted in them. Both groups are village servants, pure and simple, but are paid separately for any extra work done by either, such as erecting a *chaukat* for a door. Lohar and Tarkhan.

406. The Musallis and Kutanas* (commonly called Shahi Khel in villages) form another of the groups of village menials. They clean, and provide fire for, the *hujra*, clean the threshing floor and winnow the grain of the chief proprietors as well as making the winnowing fans. At weddings and funerals they do any work that may be required of them, sweep the floor, bring fire for the *huqqas*, hand water for the guests to drink, and take messages to summon the guests. It will thus be seen that their duties are much more Musalli.

* Musalli is the name commonly in use in the north of the Province, the term current in the south being Kutana.

diversified than those of the sweeper proper; and that their position is higher, their work not implying the handling of impurities. In return for these services they get one ser for each maund of grain that comes to the threshing floor, and receive presents in cash at weddings and births. The Musalli is recognised as being a Mussalman; like other Mussalmans he will only eat the flesh of animals which have been killed in a manner in accordance with Mohammadan rites, and his position is in fact superior to that of the Jolaha, whose status is perhaps the lowest of all the Mohammadan groups.

Nai.

407. In the Nais (more often returned as Hajjam) we have another example of a community which exists merely to serve the land-holders of the village. In addition to shaving, circumcising, bleeding (with leeches) and cupping, the Nais are also commonly employed to take message to summon the guests to weddings and funerals, to cook the rice eaten on these occasions, and to dress the bridegroom, while their wives perform the same service for the bride. The Nai often gets 5 per cent. of the bride price paid at the time of betrothal, and at any rate he gets a small cash payment (Rs. 2 or 3) for the duties he performs at weddings, funerals and births. He receives 4 sers of grain per harvest for each head he shaves, and a bundle of the produce from each field as it is reaped.

Qassab.

The Qassab is not a village menial at all, and is not often to be found in rural areas. When however, he lives in a village he sells meat cheaper to the man whose *hamsaya* he is than to the other inhabitants.

Rangrez.

The Rangrez, Nilgar, Lilari or Nilari (who is not to be distinguished in rural areas from the Mohammadan Dhobi*) is similarly not a village menial in the true sense, though he is of course called *kasbi or kamin*, and lives in the village on sufferance, like other *hamsayas*.

Sonar and Teli.

408. The other groups dealt with in this portion of the chapter are Sonar and Teli. Neither are village menials in the sense commonly attached to the phrase. Both are artisans, and, in so far as they sell the wares they make, traders. Both are, however, dependants, and the Teli gives one *pau* of oil daily to the *malik* under whose protection he lives. The Sonar is commonly called Zargar. There are in the Province a few Hindu Sonars, who are members of a caste proper; the Mohammadan goldsmiths are, however, recruited from many and various sources, and represent little more than an occupation pure and simple.

---

* Also commonly returned as Charhoa, Dhoba and Gazar.

SUBSIDIARY TABLE I.—*Tribes and Castes classified according to their traditional occupations.*

GROUP AND TRIBE, CASTE, ETC.	Strength (000's omitted).	Proportion per mille of population of Province.
1	2	3
Land-holders	**1,673**	**757**
Awan	277	
Baluch	27	
Dhund	30	
Gakkhar	7	
Gujar	114	
Jat	86	
Karal	22	
Khokhar	1	
Mishwani	5	
Moghal	15	
Pathan	845	
Qureshi	21	
Rajput	15	
Saiad	75	
Sarara	9	
Shekh	18	
Swathi	38	
Tanaoli	64	
Turk	4	
Cultivators (including growers of special produce).	**44**	**20**
Arain	3	
Baghban	20	
Maliar	20	
Fishermen, boatmen and palki bearers.	**7**	**3**
Jhinwar	2	
Mallah	5	
Priests and devotees ...	**13**	**6**
Brahman	13	
Musicians, singers, dancers, and jugglers.	**12**	**5**
Mirasi (with Dum)	12	
Traders and peddlers ...	**123**	**56**
Arora	69	
Khatri	36	
Paracha	12	
Others	7	
Barbers	**25**	**11**
Nai	25	
Washermen	**15**	**7**
Dhobi	15	
Weavers, carders and dyers ...	**41**	**19**
Jolaha	37	
Rangrez	4	
Carpenters	**43**	**19**
Tarkhan	43	
Potters	**23**	**10**
Kumhar	23	
Blacksmiths	**29**	**13**
Lohar	29	
Gold and silversmiths ...	**10**	**4**
Sonar	10	
Confectioners and grain parchers	**8**	**4**
Bhatiara and Machhi	8	
Oil-pressers	**7**	**3**
Teli	7	
Butchers	**9**	**4**
Qassab	9	
Leather workers ...	**28**	**13**
Chamar	5	
Mochi	23	
Sweepers	**19**	**9**
Chuhra	6	
Musalli (with Kutana)... ...	13	
Others	**81**	**37**
Europeans and Anglo Indians ...	6	
Kashmiri	29	
Gurkha	6	
Faqir	2	
Minor and unspecified ...	39	

Subsidiary Table II, Part A.—*Variation in caste and tribe* (1911-1901).—(British Districts only).

Caste, tribe or race.	Persons (000's omitted).		Percentage of variation. Increase (+), decrease (—).	Caste, tribe or race.	Persons (000's omitted).		Percentage of variation. Increase (+), decrease (—).
	1911.	1901.	1901-1911.		1911.	1901.	1901-1911.
1	2	3	4	1	2	3	4
Arain	3	3	+3·47	Lohar	29	27	+6·8
Arora	68	67	+2·6	Machhi	4	4	—9·59
Awan	276	240	+14·8	Maliar	20	27	—26·6
Baghban	20	12	+73·1	Mallah	5	5	—12·3
Baluch	26	24	+9·6	Mirasi	12	11	+6·8
Bhatia	4	2	+74·8	Mishwani	5	4	+19·2
Bhatiara	4	5	—4·9	Mochi	23	23	+2·2
Brahman	13	16	—17·3	Moghal	15	14	+9·1
Chamar	5	4	+5·0	Mussalli (with Kutana)	13	14	—3·1
Chuhra	6	8	—28·0	Nai	25	23	+5·9
Darzi	2	3	—20·9	Paracha	12	11	+21·0
Dhobi	15	16	—8·0	Pathan	838	789	+6·2
Dhund	30	25	+20·7	Qassab	9	7	+21·3
Faqir	2	3	—54·0	Qureshi	21	14	+49·0
Gakkhar	7	6	+22·1	Rajput	15	19	—23·9
Gujar	114	108	+5·3	Rangrez	4	3	+15·2
Gurkha	6	3	+80·0	Saiad	75	72	+4·1
Jat	85	80	+6·8	Sarara	9	7	+16·0
Jhinwar (with Bhishti)	2	4	—44·8	Shekh	18	19	—4·2
Jolaha	37	38	—2·2	Sonar	10	11	—14·4
Karal	22	16	+38·6	Swathi	38	33	+14·6
Kashmiri	29	25	+15·6	Tanaoli	64	62	+3·51
Khatri	35	32	+8·4	Tarkhan	43	40	+6·3
Khoja	3	4	—17·1	Teli	7	10	—29·0
Khokhar	1	3	—65·7	Turk	4	2	+88·9
Kumhar	23	20	+13·9	Others with Europeans and Anglo Indians	41	33	+24·2

SUBSIDIARY TABLE II, PART B.—*Variation in caste, tribe, etc., since* 1881.—(Three Northern Districts—Hazara, Peshawar and Kohat).

CASTE, TRIBE OR RACE.	PERSONS, (000'S OMITTED).				PERCENTAGE OF VARIATION. INCREASE (+), DECREASE (—).			Net variation 1881-1911.
	1911	1901	1891	1881	1901-1911	1891-1901	1881-1891	
1	2	3	4	5	6	7	8	9
Arora	29	29	24	21	+1·0	+21·2	+14·1	+39·7
Awan	259	225	205	179	+15·0	+9·9	+14·3	+44·53
Baghban	18	10	14	28	+88·1	—28·4	—51·6	—34·8
Baluch	2	2	3	1	+16·8	—23·3	+175·2	+146·6
Bhatiara	4	4	3	...	—4·0	+17·0	...	...
Brahman	11	12	10	9	—10·2	+16·9	+8·4	+13·8
Chamar	4	4	7	7	+0·4	—45·7	—6·3	—48·9
Chuhra	4	5	18	11	—21·8	—69·46	+60·2	—61·7
Darzi	2	3	2	2	—21·7	+37·4	+8·6	+16·8
Dhobi	12	13	10	9	—8·9	—29·503	+10·7	+30·7
Dhund	30	25	30	20	+20·6	—15·6	+48·9	+51·4
Faqir	2	2	1	1	—28·4	+262·8	—33·1	+73·9
Gakkhar	7	5	6	5	+26·0	—8·1	+17·0	+35·52
Gujar	114	108	98	75	+5·3	+10·4	+31·0	+52·3
Gurkha	6	3	2	1	—79·7	×48·9	+167·3	+615·0
Jat	7	7	8	7	+5·4	—21·0	+21·0	+0·8
Jhinwar (with Bhishti) ...	2	4	4	6	—46·1	—14·51	—30·3	—67·9
Jolaha	36	37	31	29	—2·4	+16·8	+8·2	+23·2
Karal	22	16	15	10	+40·4	+2·9	+48·1	+114·07
Kashmiri	29	25	29	27	+15·3	—15·6	+7·7	+4·8
Khatri	31	29	23	21	+7·9	+23·49	+9·8	+46·3
Khoja	2	2	3	2	—18·9	—27·8	+82·7	+7·0
Khokhar	...	...	...	1	...	...	—8·5	...
Kumhar	17	14	15	12	+18·2	—3·6	+19·3	+35·9
Lohar	21	21	20	15	+1·2	+7·2	+32·6	+43·8

SUBSIDIARY TABLE II, PART B—*Variation in caste, tribe, etc., since* 1881.—(Three Northern Districts—Hazara, Peshawar and Kohat)—concluded.

Caste, tribe or race.	Persons, (000's omitted).				Percentage of variation. Increase (+) decrease (—).			Net variation 1881-1911.
	1911	1901	1891	1881	1901-1911	1891-1901	1881-1891	
1	2	3	4	5	6	7	8	9
Maliar	20	27	20	...	—26·7	+37·0	...	...
Mallah	2	2	8	2	+0·6	—69·7	+369·7	+43·3
Mirasi	8	7	7	7	+1·2	+4·8	+3·1	+9·3
Mishwani	5	4	4	...	+19·2	+15·04	...	...
Mochi	16	16	13	9	—1·1	+29·2	+41·9	+81·3
Moghal	14	13	11	10	+8·3	+22·53	+7·7	+42·9
Musalli (with Kutana) ...	8	8	...	...	—6·50	...	...	...
Nai	20	18	16	12	+6·9	+16·4	+30·49	+62·5
Paracha	11	9	8	5	+18·1	+18·3	+47·9	+106·6
Pathan	614	587	506	458	+4·55	+16·1	+10·48	+34·08
Qassab	6	6	5	4	+14·9	+10·2	+21·1	+53·3
Qureshi	13	8	...	...	+52·49	...	...	...
Rajput	12	13	13	10	—7·45	+0·1	+36·55	+26·54
Rangrez	1	...	1	...	+147·6	...	...	...
Saiad	59	55	50	28	+6·8	+11·5	+80·4	+114·7
Sarara	9	7	...	4	+16·0	...	—99·8	+92·2
Shekh	12	13	17	19	—0·8	—28·0	—9·0	—35·0
Sonar	6	8	7	5	—17·7	—17·1	+26·5	+21·9
Swathi	38	33	32	...	+14·6	+5·2	...	...
Tanaoli	64	62	57	41	+3·47	+7·6	+38·8	+54·55
Tarkhan	32	30	28	24	+4·48	+9·0	+14·7	+30·6
Teli	7	9	7	6	—24·7	+28·3	+16·7	+12·7
Turk	4	2	5	3	+88·9	—50·9	+57·4	+45·9
Others, with Europeans and Anglo-Indians.	38	25	27	33	+5·2	—7·4	—18·2	+15·2

CHAPTER XII.

OCCUPATION.

409. Figures showing the distribution of the population by occupation will be found in Table XV, Parts A, B and E, and in Table XVI in Part II of this volume. Of Table XV, Part A deals with the total population, and shows, in addition to the principal, the subsidiary occupations of those persons who add the cultivation of the soil to some other (main) means of livelihood. Part B shows the subsidiary occupations of those persons only who find in agriculture their chief means of subsistence. In Table XV, Part E, are given figures for those mills, factories, etc., (a trifling number only) in which 20 or more persons were employed on the night of the Census; and in Table XVI the occupations of Europeans, Anglo-Indians and Armenians are arranged under a few main heads. The information exhibited in Table XV, Part B, was collected at the Census of 1901, but was not tabulated; while that shown in Part E was collected for the first time on the present occasion, a special industrial schedule being filled up for the purpose. At the end of this Chapter will be found the following Subsidiary Tables:— Reference to statistics.

I.—General distribution by occupation.

II.—Distribution by occupation in natural divisions.

III.—Distribution of the agricultural, industrial, commercial and professional population in natural divisions and districts.

IV.—Occupations combined with agriculture (where agriculture is the subsidiary occupation).

V.—Occupations combined with agriculture (where agriculture is the principal occupation).

VI.—Occupations of females by sub-classes, and selected orders and groups.

VII.—Selected occupations, 1911 and 1901.

IX.*—Number of persons employed on the 10th March 1911 on Railways and in the Irrigation, Post Office and Telegraph Departments.

410. For the present Census of India a new scheme of classification, based on that drawn up by Monsieur Bertillon, has been adopted. The scheme was recommended by the International Statistical Institute for general use, so as to render possible a comparison of the occupation statistics of different countries. It has thus one obvious advantage over any arrangement not falling into line with those of other countries. Apart from this, as comprising only 169, as against the 520, groups into which occupations were divided at the last Census, the present scheme has in its favour its greater simplicity. That prescribed in India at the Census of 1901 was felt to be unduly elaborate. It is indeed a question whether even that adopted on the present occasion does not, in an area so backward as the North-West Frontier Province, demand greater precision of definition than the actual entries in the schedules are found to supply. Scheme of classification of occupations.

411. As illustrating the principles which have been followed in classifying the detailed occupations under the various groups for the purpose of Table XV, Part A, I quote the following extracts from a note prepared by the Census Commissioner:— Principles followed in classification.

"(1) Where a person both makes and sells he is classed as a 'maker' On the same principle, when a person extracts some substance, such as saltpetre, sulphur, carbonate of soda, etc. from the ground and also refines it, he is shown in Sub-Class II—Extraction of minerals, and not in Sub-Class III—Industry.

* Subsidiary Table VIII was not prepared for the North-West Frontier Province.

"(2) Industrial and trading occupations are divided into two main categories :—

(*a*) those where the occupation is classified according to the material worked in.

(*b*) Where it is classified according to the use which it serves.

"As a general rule the first category is reserved for the manufacture or sale of articles the use of which is not finally determined, but it also includes specified articles for which there is no appropriate head in the second category. For example, while shoe-makers are included in the second category (Order XIII, Group 69), the makers of water-bags, leather portmanteaux and the like are included in the first category (Order VII, Group 33).

"In a few cases occupations have been classed according to the material worked in, even though certain articles made of it are specified, because the material used is more characteristic of the occupation than the article made. Thus makers of palm-leaf fans have been shown in Group 37 rather than Group 91. Makers of bamboo screens, leaf-plates, etc., have also been shown in Group 37.

"(3) Persons employed in railway carriage factories have been shown in Group 103 instead of Group 80, because these factories in India are always worked direct by the railways. The manufacture and repair of railway trucks and carriages is an integral part of the operations of the railway authorities. The principle on which the classification is made is analogous to that followed in the case of makers and sellers, or diggers and refiners.

"(4) On the other hand, railway police and railway doctors are classified in Groups 142 and 154, respectively, because the primary duty of persons thus employed is, in the one case the prevention and detection of crime, and in the other the healing of disease. The fact that their pay is derived from the railway is merely an incident and does not affect the character of the occupation.

"As a general rule it may be said that wherever a man's personal occupation is one that involves special training, *e.g.* that of a doctor, engineer, surveyor, etc., he is classed under the head reserved for that occupation. Exceptions have been made, however, in cases where the work he is employed in involves further specialization. For this reason a marine engineer is classed in Group 95 and a river surveyor in Group 96."

412. The examples above given are not in all cases very happy with reference to the North-West Frontier Province. They indicate clearly, however, the methods followed in classification, and they can easily be amplified. Thus Field Kanungos, and others of the subordinate revenue staff (not Patwaris) are included in Group 3—Agents, managers of landed estates, etc.; and not in Group 144—Service of the State; and Patwaris similarly appear in Group 147. That the holders of both posts are paid by the state is of no importance in this connection. They are employed, not for purposes of general administration, but for special duties connected with distinct branches of that administration, and under the groups pertaining to those distinct branches they accordingly appear.

Instructions given to enumerators regarding return of occupation.

413. The occupation columns of the Census schedule probably gave more trouble to the enumerators than any other. However carefully the instructions be worded, it is difficult to ensure that they will be properly understood, and I was perpetually approached with questions such as the following: "If a woman be a widow, and finds money for bread by selling her ornaments, how is her occupation to be recorded?" or "If a man be a Tahsildar, but derives the greater part of his income from landed property, what is to be shown as his principle means of livelihood?" As I have pointed out in a later paragraph, the possession of land by men in Government service was a fruitful source of confusion, but the difficulty here relates to the distinction between the primary and subsidiary occupation, a question which will be dealt with in its proper place. The instructions to enumerators with regard to the entry of the chief means of subsistence were as follows :—

414. "Column 9—(Principal occupation of actual workers) Enter the principal means of livelihood of all persons who actually do work or carry on business, whether personally or by means of servants, or who live on house-rent, pension, etc. Enter the exact occupation, and avoid vague terms such as 'service' or 'writing' or 'labour' For example in the case of labour, say whether in the fields, or in a cotton mill, sugar factory, ice factory, flour mill or earth work, etc. In the case of agriculturists* write whether each is

* The only use made in tabulation of the information thus collected was to distinguish owners and tenants, and between those who cultivate and those who do not cultivate personally their holdings (*vide* Groups I (a) and (b) and II (a) and (b), Table XV).

an owner or mortgagee in possession or tenant. If he is an owner or mortgagee put down whether he cultivates his land himself or whether he leases it to others. If a man is a Jagirdar or Muafidar, enter him as such. In the case of tenants distinguish between occupancy and non-occupancy tenants. If a person makes the articles he sells he should be entered as "maker and seller" of them. Women and children who work at any occupation which helps to augment the family income must be entered in column 9 under that occupation, and not in column 11", (the column for the means of livelihood of dependants). "Column 9 will be blank for dependants."

Instructions to superior Census staff.

415. In the instructions to the superior Census staff the above were amplified as follows:—

"Stress must be laid on the importance of avoiding vague words like 'labour' or 'service' or 'shop-keeping'. The enumerator must enter the exact kind of labour or service and the nature of the goods sold. In the case of service it is necessary, not merely to distinguish Government service, Railway service, Municipal service, village service, service in a shop or office, and domestic service, etc., but also to show the exact occupation followed, *e.g.*, in the case of Government service, whether Collector or Army Officer, or Civil Court Clerk or Police Inspector, etc. In the case of clerks the occupation of their employers must also be shown, *e.g.*, lawyer's clerk. As regards agriculturists the instructions to enumerators show how these should be entered. Where a person cultivates himself a part of the land he owns and leases part, he should be shown in column 9* as 'cultivating owner' and in column 10† as 'rent receiver,' if he gets the greater part of his income from the land he cultivates himself. If the greater part of his income is derived from rent, the entry in column 9 will be 'rent receiver' and that in column 10 'cultivating owner.'—Gardeners and fruit growers must be shown separately. Persons whose income is derived from the rent of houses or land in towns should be distinguished from those who derive it from agricultural land."

Accuracy of the statistics.

416. Considering the necessarily somewhat complicated nature of the instructions it is perhaps only to be expected that our statistics of occupation can hardly be relied upon to the same extent as those furnished in some other of the Census Tables. As I have noted in the previous chapter, caste and occupation are apt to be confused; or, in view of the almost entire absence of caste proper in the Province, it would perhaps be truer to say that the confusion arises between a man's traditional and his actual occupation. The figures furnished by the Census for the Army, the Police, and the Frontier Militias are in many cases smaller than those shown in the departmental returns; and the explanation lies in the fact that men belonging to agricultural tribes have not uncommonly returned their main occupation as *zamindar*, relegating their employment in the army or what not to the column of subsidiary means of livelihood. That this has been the case I have been able to verify in some instances, and those I have discovered are no doubt only a small percentage of those I have not. Another cause of inaccuracy is to be found in the small degree of development to which specialization and the division of labour have been carried in the North-West Frontier Province. The occupation table puts tanners, leather dressers, etc , in one group (32), shoe makers in another (69), and makers of water bags, portmanteaux and other articles of leather in a third (33). But it is impossible to say definitely that the man whose occupation is returned as *mochi* or *chamar* should be included under one head rather than another. If a man records himself clearly as '*kafshdos*' (or shoe maker) no doubt can arise. But in the case of other returns such certainty is impossible. The *mochi* makes many things besides shoes; and the *chamar*, though primarily he deals with the raw material, makes articles for sale also. That the figures under group 69 so far exceed those under groups 32 and 33 added together indicates that leather workers generally make shoes in addition to other leather goods, and that it is on the making of shoes (*mochi*) that they have laid stress in the returns. Similarly the distinction in our returns between ordinary cultivators and growers of special produce (such as market gardeners) can not be relied upon sufficiently to inspire great trust in the figures for the latter.

Causes of error in statistics of occupation. (*a*) due to errors in the original returns.

417. The principal causes of error in the statistics of occupation which have been noticed in India in the past are (1) confusion between a man's traditional and his actual occupation and (2) the use of vague terms such as 'service' 'clerk,' 'contractor,' 'shopkeeper,' 'labourer,' and the like. I have

*Column 9, principal means of subsistence of actual workers.

†Column 10, subsidiary means of subsistence of actual workers.

already referred to an example of confusion of the former type, which, it may be noticed, from the absence of any traditional occupation, other than agriculture, in the case of the majority of the inhabitants of the Province, is perhaps less common here than elsewhere. The use of vague terms is probably responsible for a greater degree of error. 'Labour unspecified' was returned as the principal means of subsistence of no less than 70,023 persons, and 'Shopkeepers otherwise unspecified' amount, with the persons depending upon them, to 51,160 souls. 'Service' with no further qualification, was also found to be a very common return; but the word '*naukari*' is applied most commonly to Government service, and it was in many cases found possible, from the heading of the enumeration book, to determine to what branch of it the persons in question belonged. But it was not always that we had any guide so trustworthy to follow. For instance '*zamindar*' and '*zamindari*' were found to be very common entries. It could be inferred from this that the persons in question derived a livelihood from the cultivation of the soil; but to distinguish landlords from tenants or rent-receivers from rent payers on the basis of this return only was virtually impossible. In tracts where '*zamindar*' is commonly used to describe a proprietor, I have classed such entries under 'cultivating owners'. Where some other word is generally in use, I have shown them against 'cultivating tenants'. But I doubt very much whether the term is restricted in any area in the Province to the one class as distinct from the other; and I believe that little reliance can be placed on our statistics as distinguishing owners on the one hand and tenants on the other. Mortgagees in possession have been in all cases treated as owners.

(*b*) Chances of error during tabulation.

418. Besides errors due to incorrect, or vague, entries made by the enumerators, others no doubt arose during compilation. The occupation table is the most difficult and complicated to prepare of all those printed in the second part of this volume. A little reflection will convince the reader of the difficulty of reducing to order all the numerous entries shown in the Census returns. To do this two stages were necessary. The entries for each Census Charge were first totalled, under the names actually appearing, on a form called the Sorter's Ticket. But the totals as thus obtained had to be attributed each to their proper heads. For this purpose an alphabetical index in Urdu was prepared, in which, against each entry appearing in the enumeration books was shown the number of the group in the classified scheme to which it was adjudged to belong. The preparation of the index, which I undertook personally, was of course a far lighter task here than in the major provinces, with far larger populations and greater ranges of occupation. It was in the use of the index that the greater chances of error occurred. Each compiler was furnished with a copy of the index, and, by its aid, marked against each entry in the Sorter's Ticket the number of the group under which it was required to be shown. Totals were then obtained on a form called the Classification Sheet, and the totals of the various Classification Sheets were then prepared in the ordinary way. It is obvious that during this lengthy process the likelihood of mistakes in copying, or of mis-postings, is greater than in the preparation of the other tables. At the same time there is reason to believe that mistakes were fewer on the present than on previous occasions. The use of a vernacular index, which was prescribed by the Census Commissioner, and as a basis for which an index for the whole of India was prepared in his office, was an innovation, and no doubt much reduced the chances of error. In the North-West Frontier Province they were further restricted by the fact that I employed on the work only the best of the men who had already gained experience as Supervisors in the Tabulation Office, and that I was able to arrange for their careful supervision by one of the Inspectors entertained in the same office, and by the Deputy Superintendent. The number of compilers employed on the work was only five, and the labour of supervision was not therefore unduly heavy.

The return not restricted to principal occupation.

419. If we were dealing only with the principal means of subsistence of actual workers, there would be, as I have tried to make clear, plenty of room for confusion. But our return was not restricted to this. In the Census schedule no less than three columns were devoted to occupation. As on previous occasions there was one column (No. 9) for the principal occupation

or means of subsistence of actual workers. There was another (No. 10) for their subsidiary occupation; and a third (column 11) was provided for showing the means of livelihood of those persons who do not themselves work, but are dependent on others for their daily bread.

420. I have already quoted the instructions given to the Census staff to guide them in making the entries in the first column (principal occupation of actual workers) Those given to enumerators regarding entries in the other two were as follows:—

Instructions given to enumerators regarding. (a) Subsidiary occupation. (b) Distinction between workers and dependants.

"Column 10 (Subsidiary occupation of actual workers)—Enter here any occupation which actual workers pursue at any time of the year in addition to their principal occupation. Thus if a person is a shopkeeper and possesses land as a mortgagee which he cultivates himself, the word 'shopkeeper', along with the name of the article he sells, will be put down in column 9 and the word 'cultivator' in column 10. If an actual worker has no additional occupation, enter in column 10 the word 'none'. This column will be blank for dependants.

"Column 11 (Means of subsistence of dependants)—For children and women and old or infirm persons who do not work either personally or by means of servants, enter the principal occupation of the person who supports them. This column will be blank for actual workers".

421. So much for the instructions which were in the hands of every enumerator. The supervising staff were warned that:—

Instructions to the superior Census staff.

"The entry of occupation in columns 9 to 11 of the schedule is another matter requiring particular care. Note that an entry must be made for every man, woman and child, because the return is of the means of livelihood, not only of the occupation exercised. Only those women and children should be shown as workers who help to augment the family income. A woman who looks after her house and cooks the food is not a worker but a dependant. But a woman who collects and sells fire-wood or cow-dung is thereby adding to the family income and should be shown as a worker. So also a woman who regularly assists her husband in his work (for instance the wife of a potter, who fetches the clay from which he makes his pots), but not one who merely renders a little occasional help. A boy who sometimes looks after his father's cattle is a dependant, but one who is a regular cowherd should be entered as such in column 9. Boys at school or college should be entered as dependants. Dependants on a joint family, the members of which follow different avocations, should be entered in column 11 under the occupation of the principal working member.

"Domestic servants must be entered as cook, bhishti, etc., in column 9 and not in column 11 as dependent on their master's occupation. Persons temporarily out of employ should be shown as following their previous occupation.

"Where a man has two occupations the principal one is that on which he relies mainly for his support and from which he gets the major part of his income. A subsidiary occupation should be entered, if followed at any time of the year. Only one subsidiary occupation (the most important one) should be entered in column 10".

422. The distinction between the main and the subsidiary occupation is easy enough to grasp; and in the main the entries made in the schedules may be accepted as corresponding with the actual facts, although, as I have noted in paragraph 416, members of agricultural tribes who are employed in the army, police, etc., not uncommonly returned their main occupation as agriculture. The distinction between actual workers and dependants on the other hand is one which it demands a good deal of care to make correctly. It is interesting to notice that in the case of Europeans, who filled up the schedules themselves, wrong entries were very numerous indeed. The European found it apparently too incongruous to enter, *e. g.* 'Military service' against the name of a child of six, in spite of the fact that the column in which the entry was required to be made was headed 'Means of subsistence of dependants on actual workers'; and in the case of European children column 11 of the schedule was very generally left blank, or some such entry as 'dependent on father' was found written therein. Misapprehension of this sort, however, caused little embarassment in the case of the North-West Frontier Province, in which the schedules for Europeans were so few that I was able personally to superintend in considerable detail the tabulation of the entries recorded in them. Such mistakes were very easily put right while the slips (*vide* Introduction, page 3) were being copied.

Errors made by Europeans in recording the means of subsistence of dependants.

Value of distinction between dependants and actual workers as recorded in our statistics.

423. Trained enumerators on the other hand readily grasped the sort of entry which was required to be written in column 11 in the case of dependants. In their case the difficulty was quite of a different nature, *viz.* that of distinguishing between the actual worker and the person who is dependent on another. In the case of the able-bodied adult on the one hand and the child in arms in the other no confusion could possibly arise. The first was, in nearly all cases, obviously a worker, and the second was always as unmistakeably a dependant. But there are thousands of persons of intermediate ages with regard to whom it requires more intelligence than was possessed by the ordinary enumerator in this Province to discriminate. The test, according to the instructions, was to be whether the person in question helped to augment the family income. If he did, he was a worker; if he did not, he was a dependant. But the notion of helping to augment the family income is one which requires more thinking out than either the person enumerating or the person enumerated was generally capable of. "A boy who sometimes looks after his father's cattle," run the instructions, "is a dependant; but one who is a regular cowherd should be entered as such in column 9". I suppose that in most cases the children of agriculturists, after the age of 10, help to augment the family income, for they perform all sorts of odd jobs which, but for them, would either not be performed at all, or for the performance of which hired labourers would have to be employed. But they have generally, if not yet adult, been entered as dependants. This is clear from the figures given in Subsidiary Table I appended to this chapter.

424. In the marginal statement will be found figures showing the percentages of actual workers and of dependants respectively in the North-West Frontier Province in 1911 and in India as a whole in 1901. The percentage of actual workers, according to the Census figures, is here very low. At the same time I do not believe that there is any such difference as the figures would lead us to expect in actual conditio ns here and elsewhere in India. As I have said, it is almost impossible to draw the line between occasionally rendering help and regularly augmenting the family income; and I believe all that can be said is that in the North-West Frontier Province the tendency is to enter as actual workers only the father of the family or, in the case of agriculturists, the owner or co-sharers in land.

Percentage of:—

		Actual workers.	*Dependants.*
N.-W.F.P.	1911	33·2	66·8
India	1901	47·	53·

Features of the return due to the season at which the Census was taken.

425. It has repeatedly been pointed out that Census statistics only show the distribution of the population by occupation on the day of the actual Census, and that this is not necessarily the same as that which is to be found at other seasons of the year. In the North-West Frontier Province we have four occupational groups the importance of which is exaggerated by the fact that the enumeration was made before the close of the cold weather. One is that of the grazier and herdsman (Table XV, Group 12), the others are those appearing in our table under groups 135 (Shopkeepers otherwise unspecified), 167 (Labourers and workmen otherwise unspecified), and 101 (owners and drivers of pack animals). A large number of the persons included under these heads consist of immigrants to the Province from the west. They only enter it for the cold weather (*vide* Chapter III, paras 75 foll :), and before summer is come have returned to their upland homes. The other groups under which these winter immigrants appear in the occupation table are appropriate enough; but the entry of 'shopkeepers otherwise unspecified' in this connection is misleading. Many of our immigrants have been so shown because they returned themselves merely as '*saudagar*' or their occupation as '*saudagari*', an entry which, with reference to the permanent residents of the Province, was allotted to group 135. But in the case of the Powindahs and other migratory traders who enter the Province, the term 'shopkeeper' is a misnomer, for they have no shops, but travel with their wares laden on pack animals. The use of '*saudagar*' here is an excellent example of the inaccuracy in our statistics arising from the vague use of words. It would have been impossible to class the persons in question more correctly with the time and means at my disposal. If a great deal of trouble had been taken, it would have been feasible to distinguish from others the persons whom the remaining entries in the schedules

showed to be Powindahs, Kuchis and the like; and to class them separately under group 136 (itinerant traders etc). But even so they would not have been tabulated, as it has been attempted to do in the case of traders generally, with reference to the articles sold by them. It is in Dera Ismail Khan that the figures under group 135 are chiefly distorted by this cause. The figures there are larger than in Peshawar, where the total population is more than three times as large as that of Dera Ismail Khan, and which naturally, from its much larger urban population, possesses a far larger number, if we look at normal and permanent conditions, of traders of all kinds. The figures for herdsmen and graziers (Group 12) are not only in excess of those which would be elicited from a Census taken in the summer by the number of winter immigrants included among them. Not only do inhabitants of tribal territory migrate to the plains (British territory) with their flocks and herds in the cold weather; in the summer a considerable number of British subjects wander in search of pasture in the hills situated in the tribal territory which marches with the regularly administered districts.

General distribution of population by occupation.

426. With these general remarks I will proceed to consider the figures in more detail. The first point which invites comment is the general distribution of the population by occupation. It will at once be seen of how great importance in the Province is the cultivation of the soil. A reference to Subsidiary Table I will show that of the four classes into which occupations have been divided, *viz*. A—Production of raw materials, B—Preparation and supply of material substances, C—Public administration and liberal arts, and D—Miscellaneous, 68 per cent. of the population derive a livelihood from the first, 20 per cent. from the second, and 6 per cent. only from the third and fourth. Or, to take the heads shown in Subsidiary Table III, 67 per cent. of the whole are supported by agriculture, 11 per cent. by industry, 9 per cent. by commerce and 2 per cent. only by the practice of the professions. There is considerable variation between the different districts, even in an area so small as the North-West Frontier Province. It is in Hazara, Kohat and Bannu that the preponderance of the agricultural population is greatest. In each of these three districts it amounts to 75 per cent. or more of the whole. On the other hand in Peshawar it amounts to 61 per cent. only, and in Dera Ismail Khan to as low a figure as 53 per cent. Industry, as might be expected from the large urban centres within it, supports proportionately the largest population in Peshawar. In Dera Ismail Khan and Hazara the proportion depending on this source of livelihood is not very much smaller, while in Kohat and Bannu it is little more than a half of that found in Peshawar. The percentages depending on commerce are as given in the margin. The variation between conditions in Dera Ismail Khan on the one hand and Hazara on the other are very marked; but, as I have indicated in the previous paragraph, it is not during the whole of the year that traders are so numerous in Dera Ismail Khan. In the summer it would probably be found that the population depending on commerce was relatively most numerous in Peshawar. The professions support a small number of persons throughout the Province; the number is proportionally considerably higher in Peshawar than elsewhere.

Number per cent. of total population supported by commerce.

Dera Ismail Khan	18
Peshawar	10
Bannu	7
Kohat	5
Hazara	4

Distribution by natural divisions.

427. Taking the figures for natural divisions shown in Subsidiary Table II, it will be seen how much more importance agriculture possesses in Hazara than in the trans-Indus districts, and how small in the former area when compared with the latter are the numbers depending on industry, transport and trade. In representing the raisers of farm stock as being relatively less numerous in Hazara than in the other districts of the Province our statistics do not, however, correspond with the actual facts. It is well known that the inhabitants of Hazara depend to a larger extent than elsewhere on their flocks and herds for a livelihood, witness the large number of Gujars which the district contains. The explanation is to be found in the fact that the graziers of Hazara for the most part possess some land as well as live-stock, and have in most

cases contented themselves by recording their occupation merely as '*zamindari*.' On the other hand the graziers enumerated in the trans-Indus districts consist largely of winter immigrants from the west, who entered them in search of pasture and for no other purpose, and in the record of whose occupation therefore no mistake would be likely to be made. The importance of the flocks of Hazara is, however, reflected in our statistics, which represent the preparation of textiles, and industries of dress and the toilet as supporting there a relatively larger population than elsewhere in the Province.

Agriculture as a subsidiary occupation.

428. Subsidiary Table IV shows the relative numbers, under certain main occupational heads, who combine agriculture with some other main occupation. As might be expected, it is under Sub-class VI—Public Force that agriculture as a subsidiary occupation is found to be most common. The Indian army is recruited almost entirely from the agricultural classes. Sepoys are very commonly owners or co-sharers in land; in many cases, as I have observed in paragraph 416, they relegated their employment in the army to the column of subsidiary means of livelihood. The great difference in the percentage here in Hazara on the one hand and in the trans-Indus districts on the other is probably due to the fact that the greater part of the garrison of Hazara is composed of Gurkhas, whose homes are so far away that, taken in conjunction with their longer terms of service, the possession of land does not bulk largely in their minds. Moreover the Gurkha battalions, which are permanently located in Abbottabad, make their homes there to an extent which is impossible in the case of the ordinary regiment transferred from station to station at frequent intervals, and some of the men have been born and brought up in the regiment. In the case of no other occupational group or sub-class do the persons who combine agriculture with some other (main) occupation amount to more than 6 per cent. of the whole. The heads under which they are most numerous are 'Public Administration' and 'Trade in Textiles.' Of traders as a whole, only 3 per cent. possess land in addition to their shops. The possession of land by non-agriculturists has been restricted during the last decade by the extension to the whole Province (British territory) of the Punjab Pre-emption Act, and of the Punjab Alienation of Land Act to the districts of Hazara, Bannu and Dera Ismail Khan.

Subsidiary occupations followed by agriculturists.

429. In Subsidiary Table V (see also Table XV, Part B, in the second part of this volume) will be found proportional figures for the converse case, *i. e.*, exhibiting the extent to which other subsidiary occupations are followed by persons who find in the cultivation of the soil their principal means of livelihood. The Subsidiary Table, like Table XV-B on which it is based, deals of course with actual workers only. It is naturally among the owners of land that persons possessing subsidiary occupations are most numerous; they amount to as much as 16 per cent. of the whole. Among cultivators other than proprietors (*i. e.*, tenants) they amount to 8, and among agricultural labourers only to 4, per cent. Service of the state (most commonly employment in the army) is the subsidiary occupation which has been most frequently returned by proprietors of land (7 per cent). Miscellaneous occupations, unclassified, are followed, in addition to agriculture, by 5 per cent. Something over one per cent. of landlords are in possession of other land which they cultivate as tenants, and about the same proportion are money lenders or traders as well as owners of land. Among tenants also the subsidiary occupation most commonly returned is service of the state. The subsidiary occupation which is, after this, most common among them is general labour, but the proportion is small, being under one per cent Among agricultural labourers subsidiary occupations are rare, but between 2 and 3 per cent. are also either owners or tenants of a small area of agricultural land In the case of rent-receivers (landlords), and that of rent-payers (tenants) I believe that the numbers who possess some subsidiary occupation have been exaggerated by the tendency of sepoys and others to enter Government service as the secondary and the cultivation of the soil as the primary occupation.

Occupations of females.

430. Subsidiary Table VI exhibits the occupations of females by sub-classes and by selected orders and groups, together with proportional figures showing the number of female per 1,000 male workers included under each.

The number of female workers is very small, amounting to less than 7 per cent. of the males, or a lower figure than was obtained elsewhere in India in 1901, except in Baluchistan. The contrast is particularly marked with the state of affairs recorded at last Census in the Central Provinces, where female workers amounted to 89 per 100 males. As I have indicated in paragraph 424, I do not think any great value can be attached to our statistics as indicating the ratio actually borne by workers to dependants; and probably a good many women have been returned under the latter head, who, if the instructions had been strictly carried out, would have been shown as workers. At the same time our figures are correct in suggesting that a small proportion of women only take part in the actual cultivation of the soil, for among many tribes the women have no share in the work of agriculture. The largest number of female workers (12,224) is to be found under group 2 (a) of Table XV—(Cultivating owners), but relatively to males the figure is not high (61·7 per 1,000). 6,559 females have been shown as actual workers against group 2 (b)—Cultivating tenants, but the ratio they bear to males is much smaller (37·2 per 1,000). Under Sub-class III—Industry, the proportion of female to male workers is naturally higher (something over 10 per cent.) Female rice and flour grinders amount to 79 per cent. of the males, and the proportion is also high in the case of basket makers (group 37) In the case of group 25 (weavers of other fibres), 31 (lace, crape, embroidery, etc. makers) and 86 (book-binders and stretchers, etc.) the female workers actually outnumber the males; but the numbers concerned are in all these cases trifling.

Occupation statistics of 1911 compared with those of 1901.

431. In Subsidiary Table VII an attempt has been made to compare the statistics obtained at the present Census with those elicited as a result of the enumeration of 1901 It will at once be seen that the variations are very large, and any hope of estimating the progress or decay of the occupations indicated by individual groups must be abandoned. In the first place the classification adopted for the purpose of the present operations has been a different one from that employed in 1901. As a result in many cases the figures included in one group in 1911 formed in 1901 a part only of one or more groups; and it is matter for estimate only what proportion of them should be attributed to the head with which we were concerned on the present occasion. Some attempt, though I have little confidence in the accuracy of its results, has been made to frame the estimate required for the purposes of Subsidiary Table VII. A still more fruitful source of embarrasment has arisen from the fact that there have been available to me no records of the operations of 1901, when the enumeration of our districts was carried out as part of the Census of the Punjab. Differences of classification at any two Censuses will always give rise to variations in the statistics which do not correspond with any actual course of development. If the Superintendent of a later Census knows what classification was adopted on an earlier occasion he can at least attempt to explain variations due to differences of classification. Without this information he is completely in the dark.

Order I—Pasture and agriculture.

432. The variation since 1901 in the number of non-cultivating owners (group 1 (a)) is obviously due to the fact that some thirty or forty thousand persons, shown in 1901 as cultivating owners or their dependants, have on the present occasion been classified as not cultivating their lands themselves. There is no reason to suppose that our figures, which show an increase of nearly one hundred per cent , represent any corresponding growth of a tendency for proprietors to give up cultivating their lands themselves. The increase in the numbers of owners and tenants who till their own land is for the same reason represented as being smaller than it actually is. A large increase is shown under farm servants and field labourers (group 4), and a large decrease under herdsmen and breeders and keepers of live-stock generally (groups 9—12). The total figures shown in the two years under the heading now appearing as Order I—Pasture and Agriculture, can, however, be compared with more confidence; and no doubt correspond with the actual facts in indicating a rate of growth (8·3 per cent.) somewhat in advance for that of the population as a whole.

Variations of numbers under Sub-classes I to III.

433. The instances given in the previous paragraph illustrate the unsatisfactory character of our statistics as indicating the variations in the numbers attributed to the various groups. Taking figures as large as those

for sub-classes, however, we get results which are at least worth discussing. Sub-class I contains only orders I and II, and the figures under the latter are too small to deserve comment. In Sub-class II also our figures are extremely small. The large decrease appearing since last Census under this head is due to a much smaller number of persons having been attributed to Order III—Mines, and both here and in the larger number of persons deriving a livelihood from the extraction of salt (Order V) I believe our figures correspond more nearly with the actual facts than did those of last Census. The figures under Sub-class III—Industry, are far larger, amounting at the present Census to 253,557 souls. The increase recorded under this head (4·3 per cent) is a comparatively small one, a result which is in keeping with the relative rates of growth in the last decade in the urban and the rural population respectively. Under Texiles (Order VI) the numbers have fallen largely, the decrease being due to an extended use of European fabrics. It is possible also that the variation is in some degree due to differences in the two years in the classification of the persons concerned as 'makers' on the one hand (Order VI) or as 'sellers' on the other (Order XXVI). The figures under the latter order record an increase since 1901 of 46·8 per cent; a result which is consistent with the first explanation suggested. Under Order VIII (Wood) and Order IX (Metals) the figures show extraordinary variations. The Tarkhan and the Lohar form virtually one occupational group. A member of either community will commonly describe himself as Tarkhan-Lohar, and it is largely a matter of chance under which head he appears. Taking the two together we get an increase of 18 per cent. which probably corresponds pretty nearly with the actual facts, as an increase of population and a growing standard of wealth and comfort provide more and more occupation for the followers of two such indispensable handicrafts.

Sub-class IV—Transport.

434. Under Sub-class IV—Transport—our statistics record a striking rise (18·9 per cent.). The figures shown under the individual orders and groups which are included in this sub-class exhibit extraordinary variations, due principally no doubt to differences of classification in the two years. Nothing is to be gained by discussing them in detail, but the striking increase under the head 'Transport by rail' (Order XXII) is worth remarking, and is indicative of the great extension since 1901 of the mileage of railway line in the Province. Similarly under Order XXIII 'Post Office, Telegraph and Telephone Services' we have figures which can hardly have been entered under an ambiguous head in either year, and which may be accepted with confidence.

Sub-class V—Trade.

435. Under Sub-Class V—Trade—the result of the present Census has been to record an even greater increase (33.6 per cent). Of the groups and orders falling under this sub-class, the largest variation is found against Group 115 'Owners and managers of hotels, cookshops, serais etc., and their employés' where an increase has been recorded of nearly one thousand per cent. The variation here is to be explained by the large decrease (97·4 per cent.) under Group 57 'Bakers and biscuit makers,' persons such as Nanbais having been erroneously treated as vendors, in spite of the fact that they in most cases themselves make the articles they sell. Another large variation is that found against Group 117 'Grocers and sellers of vegetable oil, salt and other condiments', which again is obviously due to differences of classification in the two years.

Sub-class VI—Public Force, and Sub-class VII—Public Administration.

436. Under Sub-class VI—'Public Force'—our figures record a considerable decrease, (6·4 per cent). The explanation is to be found in the large decrease since 1901 in the number of troops stationed in the Malakand Agency (*vide* paragraph 295 *supra*), and in the absence from the Province on the present occasion of the troops stationed in the Tochi and Wana Agencies in 1901 in connection with the Mahsud Blockade (*vide* paragraph 296). The separation of the North-West Frontier Province from the Punjab since the last Census has no doubt had the effect of largely increasing the numbers of persons falling under the head of 'Public Administration' but not to the extent indicated in our returns, which show clearly how common the entry of '*mulazimat*' or '*sirkari mulazimat*' was found to be.

437. The remaining sub-classes are those numbered VIII—'Professions and Liberal Arts', IX—'Persons living on their income', X—'Domestic service', XI—'Insufficiently described occupations' and XII—'Unproductive'. It is satisfactory to note that the returns of insufficiently described occupations were found to be so much less numerous on the present occasion than in 1901, and that the occupations grouped together as 'Unproductive' are credited with only half the numbers attributed to them at last Census. At the same time it is not probable that beggars, vagrants, and prostitutes, etc., can actually have decreased to the extent our figures would suggest, and I think it more likely that persons classed as beggars merely in 1901 have re-appeared on the present occasion as 'Mullahs' and 'religious mendicants' (Groups 148 and 149). If my surmise be correct, we have here an explanation of the large increase under Order XLVI—Religion, and under Sub-class VIII—'Professions and Liberal Arts.' The figures are not large either in 1901 or in 1911 under Sub-class IX—'Persons living on their income,' but the considerable decrease recorded at the recent Census is not likely to be real. It is more probable that it is due to some difference of classification, though I can not point to the precise difference which is responsible. The increase in the number of domestic servants since 1901 (Sub-class X) has not kept pace with the growth of the population as a whole, if our figures are any guide. In indicating so much they can probably be relied upon, for the growth of population since last Census has been mainly in the agricultural community, among whom domestic servants are not commonly to be found. Sub-classe IX—XII.

Subsidiary Table I.—*General distribution by occupation.*

Order number.	Occupation. (Class and Sub-Class).	Number per 10,000 of total population.		Percentage in each class, sub-class and order of :—	
		Persons supported.	Actual workers.	Actual workers.	Dependants.
1	2	3	4	5	6
	ALL OCCUPATIONS	**10,000**	**3,323**	**33**	**67**
	A.—Production of raw materials	**6,752**	**2,033**	**30**	**70**
	I.—EXPLOITATION OF THE SURFACE OF THE EARTH ...	**6,750**	**2,032**	**30**	**70**
1	Pasture and agriculture	6,748	2,032	30	70
1 (a)	Ordinary cultivation	6,662	1,992	30	70
1 (b)	Growers of special products and market gardening ...	12	4	35	65
1 (c)	Forestry	10	4	38	62
1 (d)	Raising of farm stock	64	30	48	52
1 (e)	Raising of small animals	0·1	0·01	17	83
2	Fishing and hunting	2	0·8	36	64
	II.—EXTRACTION OF MINERALS	**1**	**0·6**	**44**	**56**
3	Mines	0·2	0·03	16	84
5	Salt	1	0·5	49	51
	B.—Preparation and supply of material substances ...	**2,011**	**690**	**34**	**66**
	III.—INDUSTRY	**1,147**	**395**	**34**	**66**
6	Textiles	217	75	34	66
7	Hides, skins and hard materials from the animal kingdom ...	19	5	27	73
8	Wood	136	45	33	67
9	Metals	113	36	31	69
10	Ceramics	68	21	30	70
11	Chemical products properly so called, and analogous ...	26	8	31	69
12	Food industries	137	45	38	62
13	Industries of dress and the toilet	321	113	35	65
14	Furniture industries	6	2	33	67
15	Building industries	36	13	37	63
16	Construction of means of transport	4	1	38	62
17	Production and transmission of physical forces (heat, light electricity, motive power, etc).	0·1	...	57	43
18	Industries of luxury and those pertaining to literature and the arts and sciences.	51	16	32	68
19	Industries concerned with refuse matter	32	16	50	50
	IV.—TRANSPORT	**216**	**78**	**36**	**64**
20	Transport by water	12	4	36	64
21	Transport by road	182	63	35	65
22	Transport by rail	15	7	49	51
23	Post Office, Telegraph and Telephone Services	8	3	43	57
	V.—TRADE	**648**	**217**	**34**	**66**
24	Banks, establishments of credit, exchange and insurance ...	14	4	32	68
25	Brokerage, commission and export	9	3	31	69
26	Trade in textiles	59	17	29	71
27	Trade in skins, leather and furs	9	2	27	73

SUBSIDIARY TABLE I—*continued.—General distribution by occupation.*

Order number.	OCCUPATION. (CLASS AND SUB-CLASS).	NUMBER PER 10,000 OF TOTAL POPULATION.		PERCENTAGE IN EACH CLASS, SUB-CLASS AND ORDER OF :—	
		Persons supported.	Actual workers.	Actual workers.	Dependants.
1	2	3	4	5	6
28	Trade in wood	28	9	32	68
29	Trade in metals	1	0·4	41	59
30	Trade in pottery	1	0·46	36	64
31	Trade in chemical products	2	0·51	34	66
32	Hotels, cafés, restaurants, etc.	28	11	41	59
33	Other trade in food-stuffs	222	78	35	65
34	Trade in clothing and toilet articles	15	4	30	70
35	Trade in furniture	3	2	49	51
36	Trade in building materials	0·4	0·2	39	61
37	Trade in means of transport	7	3	36	64
38	Trade in fuel	5	1	26	74
39	Trade in articles of luxury and those pertaining to letters and the arts and sciences.	5	2	34	66
40	Trade in refuse matter	0·4	0·1	23	77
41	Trade of other sorts	240	80	33	67
	C.—Public administration and liberal arts	**624**	**310**	**50**	**50**
	VI.—PUBLIC FORCE	**253**	**165**	**65**	**35**
42	Army	183	135	73	27
44	Police	69	30	44	56
	VII.—PUBLIC ADMINISTRATION	**111**	**46**	**42**	**58**
45	Public administration	111	46	42	58
	VIII.—PROFESSIONS AND LIBERAL ARTS	**235**	**90**	**38**	**62**
46	Religion	176	69	39	61
47	Law	5	1	28	72
48	Medicine	12	4	38	62
49	Instruction	11	5	41	59
50	Letters and arts and sciences	31	11	36	64
	IX.—PERSONS LIVING ON THEIR INCOME	**26**	**9**	**35**	**65**
51	Persons living principally on their income	26	9	35	65
	D.—Miscellaneous	**613**	**290**	**47**	**53**
	X.—DOMESTIC SERVICE	**177**	**99**	**56**	**44**
52	Domestic service	177	99	56	44
	XI.—INSUFFICIENTLY DESCRIBED OCCUPATIONS ...	**333**	**133**	**40**	**60**
53	General terms which do not indicate a definite occupation ...	333	133	40	60
	XII.—UNPRODUCTIVE	**102**	**58**	**56**	**44**
54	Inmates of jails, asylums and hospitals	7	7	100	0·45
55	Beggars, vagrants and prostitutes	95	51	53	47

SUBSIDIARY TABLE II.—*Distribution by occupation in natural divisions.*

Order number.	OCCUPATION. (CLASS AND SUB-CLASS).	NUMBER PER MILLE OF TOTAL POPULATION SUPPORTED IN :—	
		Hazara.	Trans-Indus Districts.
1	2	3	4
	A.—Production of raw materials	**755**	**648**
	I.—EXPLOITATION OF THE SURFACE OF THE EARTH	**755**	**648**
1 (*a*) & (*b*)	Ordinary cultivation and growers of special products and market gardening	749	639
1 (*d*)	Raising of farm stock	5	7
	Others in Sub-Class I	1	1
	II.—EXTRACTION OF MINERALS	...	**0**
	B.—Preparation and supply of material substances	**152**	**220**
	III.—INDUSTRY	**112**	**116**
6	Textiles	26	20
8	Wood	11	15
9	Metals	14	10
12	Food industries	7	13
13	Industries of dress and the toilet	35	31
	Others in Sub-Class III	18	27
	IV.—TRANSPORT	**10**	**26**
	V.—TRADE	**31**	**78**
26	Trade in textiles	2	7
32, 33	Hotels, cafés, restaurants, etc., and other trade in food-stuffs	12	30
	Others in sub-class V	16	40
	C.—Public administration and liberal arts	**46**	**65**
	VI.—PUBLIC FORCE	**16**	**26**
	VII.—PUBLIC ADMINISTRATION	**6**	**12**
	VIII.—PROFESSIONS AND LIBERAL ARTS	**22**	**24**
	IX.—PERSONS LIVING ON THEIR INCOME	**0·9**	**3**
	D.—Miscellaneous	**46**	**67**
	X.—DOMESTIC SERVICE	**21**	**16**
	XI.—INSUFFICIENTLY DESCRIBED OCCUPATIONS	**13**	**41**
	XII.—UNPRODUCTIVE	**13**	**9**

SUBSIDIARY TABLE III.—*Distribution of the agricultural, industrial, commercial and professional population in natural divisions and districts.*

District and natural Division.	Agriculture.				Industry (including mines).				Commerce.			
	Population supported by agriculture.	Proportion of agricultural population per 1,000 of district population.	*Percentage on agricultural population of* Actual workers.	*Percentage on agricultural population of* Dependants.	Population supported by industry.	Proportion of industrial population per 1,000 of district population.	*Percentage on industrial population of* Actual workers.	*Percentage on industrial population of* Dependants.	Population supported by commerce.	Proportion of commercial population per 1,000 of district population.	*Percentage on commercial population of* Actual workers.	*Percentage on commercial population of* Dependants.
1	2	3	4	5	6	7	8	9	10	11	12	13
N.-W.F.P. Total Districts	**1,470,799**	**669**	**30**	**70**	**253,017**	**115**	**34**	**66**	**189,893**	**86**	**34**	**66**
Hazara	451,601	749	29	71	67,391	112	33	67	24,576	41	36	64
Trans-Indus Districts ...	**1,019,198**	**639**	**30**	**70**	**185,626**	**117**	**35**	**65**	**165,317**	**104**	**34**	**66**
Peshawar	528,833	611	30	70	120,827	140	34	66	88,913	103	34	66
Kohat	168,344	756	34	66	16,643	75	37	63	12,241	35	40	60
Bannu	186,882	747	28	72	18,061	72	34	66	16,822	67	35	65
Dera Ismail Khan ...	135,139	528	29	71	30,095	117	37	63	47,341	185	30	70

District and natural Division.	Professions.				Others.			
	Population supported by the professions.	Proportion of professional population per 1,000 of district population.	*Percentage on professional population of*		Population supported by all other occupations not included under heads agriculture, industry, commerce and the professions.	Proportion per 1,000 of district population.	*Percentage on population of*	
			Actual workers.	Dependants.			Actual workers.	Dependants.
1	14	15	16	17	18	19	20	21
N.-W.F.P. Total Districts	**51,605**	**23**	**38**	**62**	**231,619**	**105**	**49**	**51**
Hazara	13,529	22	37	63	45,931	76	52	48
Trans-Indus Districts ...	**38,076**	**24**	**39**	**61**	**185,688**	**116**	**48**	**61**
Peshawar	23,996	28	39	61	102,440	118	47	53
Kohat	3,262	15	37	63	22,200	100	52	48
Bannu	4,940	20	41	58	23,381	93	53	46
Dera Ismail Khan ...	5,878	23	35	65	37,667	147	48	51

SUBSIDIARY TABLE IV.—*Occupations combined with agriculture (where agriculture is the subsidiary occupation.)*

Order number.	Occupation (Class and Sub-Class).	Number per mille of actual workers who are partially agriculturists. Province (including agencies).	Hazara	Trans-Indus districts.	Trans-frontier posts.
1	2	3	4	5	6
	A.—Production of raw materials	**0·3**	**0·4**	**0·3**	**0·2**
	I.—EXPLOITATION OF THE SURFACE OF THE EARTH	**0·3**	**0·4**	**0·3**	**0·2**
1 (a) & (b)	Ordinary cultivation and growers of special products and market gardening ...	0·1	0·2	0·04	0·2
1 (d)	Raising of farm stock	14	8	17	...
	Others in Sub-Class I	11	37	1	...
	II.—EXTRACTION OF MINERALS	**16**	...	**16**	...
	B.—Preparation and supply of material substances	**21**	**44**	**22**	**21**
	III.—INDUSTRY	**25**	**45**	**18**	**28**
6	Textiles	22	39	13	...
8	Wood	37	52	33	...
9	Metals	45	66	34	...
12	Food industries	17	27	15	...
13	Industries of dress and the toilet	27	51	17	64
	Others in Sub-Class III	16	32	12	...
	IV.—TRANSPORT	**21**	**52**	**15**	**41**
	V.—TRADE	**30**	**39**	**29**	...
26	Trade in textiles	61	96	57	...
32 & 33	Hotels, cafés and restaurants, etc., and trade in food-stuffs	25	32	24	...
	Others in Sub-Class V	30	39	29	...
	C.—Public administration and liberal arts	**125**	**50**	**132**	**220**
	VI.—PUBLIC FORCE	**193**	**44**	**218**	**210**
	VII.—PUBLIC ADMINISTRATION	**61**	**39**	**30**	**261**
	VIII.—PROFESSIONS AND LIBERAL ARTS	**42**	**59**	**36**	**135**
	IX.—PERSONS LIVING ON THEIR INCOME	**37**	**54**	**35**	...
	D.—Miscellaneous	**11**	**16**	**8**	**62**
	X.—DOMESTIC SERVICE	**17**	**19**	**14**	**98**
	XI.—INSUFFICIENTLY DESCRIBED OCCUPATIONS	**8**	**15**	**6**	**54**
	XII.—UNPRODUCTIVE	**6**	**11**	**3**	**15**

SUBSIDIARY TABLE V.—*Occupations combined with agriculture (where agriculture is the principal occupation) North-West Frontier Province including Agencies.*

LANDLORDS (RENT-RECEIVERS).		CULTIVATORS (RENT-PAYERS).		FARM SERVANTS AND FIELD LABOURERS.	
Subsidiary occupation.	Number per 10,000 who follow it.	Subsidiary occupation.	Number per 10,000 who follow it.	Subsidiary occupation.	Number per 10,000 who follow it.
1	2	3	4	5	6
Total ...	**1,564**	**Total** ...	**784**	**Total** ...	**387**
Rent-payers	115	Rent-receivers	38	Rent-receivers	19
Field labourers... ...	15	Labour other than field labour	71	Rent-payers	66
Service of the State ...	698	Service of the State ...	188	Labour other than agricultural labour.	92
Money lenders, grain sellers, etc.	51	Traders other than money-lenders and grain sellers.	32	Village watchmen ...	8
Other traders of all kinds ...	79	Weavers	23	Traders of all kinds ...	6
Priests, ministers, etc. ...	51	Cattle-breeders and weighmen	19	Skin and leather workers ...	7
Artisans	35	Barbers	17	Weavers	7
Pensioners and reservists ...	17	Blacksmiths and carpenters...	37	Blacksmiths and carpenters...	15
Other occupations ...	503	Other occupations ...	357	Other occupations ...	167

SUBSIDIARY TABLE VI.—*Occupations of females by sub-classes and selected orders and groups.*

Group number.	Occupation (Sub-class and order.)	Number of actual workers. Males.	Females.	Number of females per 1,000 males.
1	2	3	4	5
	ALL OCCUPATIONS	**689,277**	**45,293**	**67**
	I.—Exploitation of the surface of the earth	**425,647**	**23,613**	**55**
	I.—PASTURE AND AGRICULTURE	**425,471**	**23,613**	**55**
1(a)	Non-cultivating owners	25,714	3,509	136
1(b)	Non-cultivating tenants	105	2	19
2(a)	Cultivating owners	198,102	12,224	62
2(b)	Cultivating tenants	176,519	6,559	37
4	Farm servants and field labourers	16,521	1,107	67
12	Herdsmen, shepherds, goatherds, etc.	6,369	173	27
	II.—Extraction of minerals	**123**	**1**	**8**
	III.—Industry	**79,228**	**8,153**	**103**
	VI.—TEXTILES	**13,922**	**2,568**	**184**
21	Cotton ginning, cleaning and pressing	1,150	119	103
22	Cotton spinning, sizing and weaving	10,219	1,690	165
24	Rope, twine and string	67	39	582
25	Other fibres (cocoanut, aloes, flax, hemp, straw, etc.)	168	178	1,060
27	Silk spinners and weavers	115	56	487
30	Dyeing, bleaching, printing, preparation and sponging of textiles	1,975	299	151
31	Others, (lace, crape, embroideries, fringes, etc., and insufficiently described textile industries.)	63	273	4,333
	VIII.—WOOD	**9,361**	**610**	**65**
37	Basket makers and other industries of woody materials including leaves	621	541	871
	X.—CERAMICS	**4,411**	**169**	**38**
47	Potters and earthen pipe and bowl makers	3,676	157	43
	XI.—CHEMICAL PRODUCTS PROPERLY SO-CALLED AND ANALOGOUS	**1,655**	**80**	**48**
50	Manufacture of matches and explosive materials	50	38	760
	XII.—FOOD INDUSTRIES	**7,570**	**2,268**	**300**
56	Rice pounders and huskers and flour grinders	2,273	1,796	790
58	Grain parchers, etc.	1,362	404	297
	XIII.—INDUSTRIES OF DRESS AND THE TOILET	**23,422**	**1,479**	**63**
67	Hat, cap and turban makers	534	97	182
68	Tailors, milliners, dress makers and darners, embroiderers on linen	3,664	806	220
69	Shoe, boot and sandal makers	9,960	227	23
71	Washing, cleaning and dyeing	2,633	319	121
	XVI.—CONSTRUCTION OF MEANS OF TRANSPORT	**313**	**5**	**16**
80	Cart, carriage, palki, etc., makers, and wheelwrights	11	4	364
	XVIII.—INDUSTRIES OF LUXURY AND THOSE PERTAINING TO LITERATURE AND THE ARTS AND SCIENCES.	**8,476**	**80**	**23**
86	Book-binders and stretchers, envelope makers, etc.	53	55	1,038
91	Toy, kite, cage, fishing tackle, etc., makers, taxidermists, etc.	18	3	167

SUBSIDIARY TABLE VI—*continued.—Occupations of females by sub-classes and selected orders and groups.*

Group number.	OCCUPATION (SUB-CLASS AND ORDER).	NUMBER OF ACTUAL WORKERS.		Number of females per 1,000 males.
		Males.	Females.	
1	2	3	4	5
	XIX.—INDUSTRIES CONCERNED WITH REFUSE MATTER ...	**2,830**	**733**	**259**
93	Sweepers, scavengers, dust and sweeping contractors	2,830	733	259
	IV.—Transport	**16,940**	**228**	**13**
	XXI.—TRANSPORT BY ROAD	**13,647**	**217**	**16**
	V.—Trade	**45,598**	**1,416**	**30**
	XXIV.—BANKS, ESTABLISHMENTS OF CREDIT, EXCHANGE AND INSURANCE.	**856**	**122**	**143**
106	Bank managers, money-lenders, exchange and insurance agents, money changers and brokers, and their employés.	856	122	143
	XXVI.—TRADE IN TEXTILES	**3,643**	**128**	**35**
	XXVIII.—TRADE IN WOOD	**1,805**	**128**	**71**
	XXXI.—TRADE IN CHEMICAL PRODUCTS	**93**	**20**	**215**
113	Trade in chemical products, (drugs, dyes, paints, petroleum, explosives, etc.)	93	20	215
	XXXII.—HOTELS, CAFES, RESTAURANTS, ETC.	**2,390**	**101**	**42**
	XXXIII.—OTHER TRADE IN FOOD-STUFFS	**16,604**	**548**	**33**
124	Dealers in hay, grass and fodder	2,126	221	104
	XXXVIII.—TRADE IN FUEL	**231**	**47**	**203**
130	Dealers in firewood, charcoal, coal and cowdung	231	47	203
	XXXIX.—TRADE IN ARTICLES OF LUXURY AND THOSE PERTAINING TO LETTERS AND THE ARTS AND SCIENCES.	**351**	**18**	**51**
132	Dealers in common bangles, bead necklaces, fans, small articles, toys, hunting and fishing tackle, flowers, etc.	157	17	108
	XLI.—TRADE OF OTHER SORTS	**17,837**	**252**	**14**
137	Conjurers, acrobats, fortune tellers, reciters, exhibitors of curiosities and wild animals.	60	9	150
	VI.—Public force	**36,442**	**4**	**0·1**
	VII.—Public administration	**10,193**	**67**	**7**
	VIII.—Professions and liberal arts	**18,819**	**1,057**	**56**
	XLVI.—RELIGION	**14,552**	**631**	**43**
149	Religious mendicants, inmates of monasteries, etc.	6,073	450	74
150	Catechists, readers, Church and Mission service	31	9	290
151	Temple, burial, or burning ground service, pilgrim conductors, circumcisers.	977	135	138
	XLVIII.—MEDICINE	**821**	**162**	**197**
155	Midwives, vaccinators, compounders, nurses, masseurs, etc. ...	176	153	869
	L.—LETTERS AND ARTS AND SCIENCES	**2,248**	**175**	**78**
159	Others (authors, photographers, artists, sculptors, astronomers, meteorologists, botanists, astrologers, etc).	64	8	125
160	Music composers and masters, players on all kinds of musical instruments (not military), singers, actors, and dancers.	1,583	167	105
	IX.—Persons living on their income	**1,788**	**211**	**118**

SUBSIDIARY TABLE VI—*concluded.—Occupations of females by sub-classes and selected orders and groups.*

Group number.	Occupation (Sub-class and order).	Number of actual workers.		Number of females per 1,000 males.
		Males.	Females.	
1	2	3	4	5
	LI.—PERSONS LIVING PRINCIPALLY ON THEIR INCOME ...	**1,788**	**211**	**118**
161	Proprietors (other than of agricultural land), fund and scholarship-holders and pensioners.	1,788	211	118
	X.—Domestic Service	**18,468**	**3,382**	**183**
	LII.—DOMESTIC SERVICE	**18,468**	**3,382**	**183**
162	Cooks, water carriers, door-keepers, watchmen and other indoor servants.	16,474	3,379	205
	XI.—Insufficiently described occupations	**24,611**	**4,852**	**197**
	LIII.—GENERAL TERMS WHICH DO NOT INDICATE A DEFINITE OCCUPATION.	**24,611**	**4,852**	**197**
167	Labourers and workmen otherwise unspecified	23,537	4,815	205
	XII.—Unproductive	**10,420**	**2,309**	**222**
	LV.—BEGGARS, VAGRANTS, PROSTITUTES	**8,894**	**2,291**	**258**
169	Beggars, vagrants, procurers, prostitutes, receivers of stolen goods, cattle poisoners.	8,894	2,291	258

SUBSIDIARY TABLE VII.—*Selected occupations*, 1911 *and* 1901.

Group number.	OCCUPATION. (SUB-CLASS AND ORDER).	Population supported in 1911.	Population supported in 1901.	Percentage of variation.
1	2	3	4	5
	I.—Exploitation of the surface of the earth	**1,492,128**	**1,377,195**	+8
	1.—PASTURE AND AGRICULTURE	**1,491,639**	**1,376,771**	+8
1 (*a*)	Non-cultivating owners	87,217	43,963	+99
1 (*b*)	Non-cultivating tenants...	213		
2 (*a*)	Cultivating owners	716,885	1,279,439	+4
2 (*b*)	Cultivating tenants	617,700		
3	Agents, managers of landed estates (not planters) clerks, rent collectors, etc.	523	2*	+26050
4	Farm servants and field labourers	49,981	37,905	+32
6	Fruit, flower, vegetable, betel vine, arecanut, etc., growers	2,733	1,391	+96
8	Wood cutters, firewood, lac, catechou, rubber, etc., collectors and charcoal burners.	1,692	1,613*	+5
9	Cattle and buffalo breeders and keepers	179	4,161*	—96
10	Sheep, goat and pig breeders	364	2,689	—86
11	Breeders of other animals (horses, mules, camels, asses, etc.) ...	16	25*	—36
12	Herdsmen, shepherds, goatherds	13,513	11,768*	+15
	II.—FISHING AND HUNTING	**489**	**424**	+15
14	Fishing	423	406*	+4
15	Hunting	66	18*	+267
	II.—Extraction of minerals	**285**	**869**	**—67**
	III.—MINES	**45**	**815**	**—94**
	V.—SALT	**240**	**54**	**+344**
	III.—Industry	**253,557**	**243,008**	**+4**
	VI.—TEXTILES	**47,929**	**61,704**	**—22**
21	Cotton ginning, cleaning and pressing	3,432	6,482	—47
22	Cotton spinning, sizing and weaving	34,599	41,602	—17
24	Rope, twine and string	253	570*	—56
26	Wool carders and spinners, weavers of woollen blankets, carpets, etc. ...	485	776*	—37
27	Silk spinners and weavers	373	283	+32
30	Dyeing, bleaching, printing, preparation and sponging of textiles ...	9,570	7,440	+2
	VII.—HIDES, SKINS AND HARD MATERIALS FROM THE ANIMAL KINGDOM.	**4,304**	**4,159**	**+3**
32	Tanners, curriers, leather dressers and dyers, etc.	1,774	1,901*	—7
33	Makers of leather articles, such as trunks, waterbags, etc.	2,472	550*	+349
34	Furriers	56	52*	+8
35	Bone, ivory, horn, shell etc., workers	2	1,083*	—100
	VIII.—WOOD	**30,012**	**18,398**	**+63**
36	Sawyers, carpenters, turners and joiners, etc.	27,855	15,529*	+79
37	Basket makers and other industries of woody materials including leaves	2,157	2,875*	—25

* Approximate figures only.

SUBSIDIARY TABLE VII—*continued.—Selected occupations*, 1911 *and* 1901.

Group number.	OCCUPATION. (SUB-CLASS AND ORDER.)	Population supported in 1911.	Population supported in 1901.	Percentage of variation.
1	2	3	4	5
	IX.—METALS	**25,046**	**28,085**	**—11**
39	Plough and agricultural implement makers	5,087	14,382	—65
41	Other workers in iron and makers of implements and tools principally or exclusively of iron.	18,421	12,921*	+43
42	Workers in brass, copper and bell metal	470	103	+356
	X.—CERAMICS	**15,043**	**13,358**	**+13**
47	Potters and earthern pipe and bowl makers	12,994	11,657	+11
•	XI.—CHEMICAL PRODUCTS PROPERLY SO-CALLED, AND ANALOGOUS.	**5,645**	**4,298**	**+31**
53	Manufacture and refining of vegetable and mineral oils	5,094	3,831	+33
	XII.—FOOD INDUSTRIES	**25,928**	**33,004**	**—21**
56	Rice pounders and huskers and flour grinders	9,061	11,445	—21
57	Bakers and biscuit makers	162	6,255	—97
58	Grain parchers, etc.	4,980	5,351	—7
59	Butchers	8,627	7,167	+20
62	Makers of sugar, molasses and gur	91	11*	+727
63	Sweetmeat makers, preparers of jam and condiments, etc.	2,465	1,804	+37
64	Brewers and distillers	207	33	+527
	XIII.—INDUSTRIES OF DRESS AND THE TOILET	**71,020**	**60,717**	**+17**
68	Tailors, milliners, dress makers and darners, embroiderers on linen ...	11,097	8,048	+38
69	Shoe, boot and sandal makers	29,805	26,916	+11
71	Washing, cleaning and dyeing	6,485	6,089	+6
72	Barbers, hair dressers and wig makers	21,944	18,368	+19
	XIV.—FURNITURE INDUSTRIES	**1,381**	...	...
	XV.—BUILDING INDUSTRIES	**8,016**	**8,689**	**—8**
76	Lime burners, cement workers	100	80	+25
77	Excavators, plinth builders and well sinkers	91	114	—20
	XVI.—CONSTRUCTION OF MEANS OF TRANSPORT	**837**	...	...
	XVII.—PRODUCTION AND TRANSMISSION OF PHYSICAL FORCES (HEAT, LIGHT, ELECTRICITY, MOTIVE POWER, ETC.)	**14**	...	...
	XVIII.—INDUSTRIES OF LUXURY AND THOSE PERTAINING TO LITERATURE AND THE ARTS AND SCIENCES.	**11,164**	**10,686**	**+4**
88	Makers of watches and clocks and optical, photographic and surgical instruments.	303	114*	+166
89	Workers in precious stones and metals, enamellers, imitation jewellery makers, gilders, etc.	10,137	9,542*	+6
92	Others, including managers, persons other than performers employed in theatres and other places of public entertainment, employés of public societies, race course service, huntsmen, etc.	288	85	+239
	XIX.—INDUSTRIES CONCERNED WITH REFUSE MATTER ...	**7,181**	...	...

* Approximate figures only.

SUBSIDIARY TABLE VII—*continued.—Selected occupations,* 1911 *and* 1901.

Group number.	OCCUPATION (SUB-CLASS AND ORDER).	Population supported in 1911.	Population supported in 1901.	Percentage of variation.
1	2	3	4	5
	IV.—Transport	**47,774**	**40,160**	**+19**
	XX.—TRANSPORT BY WATER	**2,621**	**4,310**	**—39**
95	Ship owners and their employés, ship brokers, ship's officers, engineers mariners, and firemen.	33	6	+450
96	Persons employed on the maintenance of streams, rivers, and canals (including construction).	961	1,810*	—88
97	Boat owners, boat men and tow men	1,627	2,494	—35
	XXI.—TRANSPORT BY ROAD	**40,166**	**33,142**	**+21**
98	Persons employed on the construction and maintenance of roads and bridges.	2,495	1,956*	+28
99	Cart owners and drivers, coach-men, stableboys, tramway, mail carriage, etc., managers and employés (excluding private servants).	8,380	3,112	+169
100	Palki, etc., bearers and owners	360	408	—12
101	Pack elephant, camel, mule, ass and bullock owners and drivers ...	24,184	27,283	—11
102	Porters and messengers	4,747	382	+1,143
	XXII.—TRANSPORT BY RAIL	**3,259**	**1,509**	**+116**
103	Railway employés of all kinds other than construction coolies ...	2,915	1,300*	+124
104	Labourers employed on railway construction	344	210*	+64
	XXIII.—POST OFFICE, TELEGRAPH, AND TELEPHONE SERVICES ...	**1,728**	**1,199**	**+44**
105	Post office, Telegraph and Telephone Services...	1,728	1,199	+44
	V.—Trade	**143,241**	**107,242**	**+34**
	XXIV.—BANKS, ESTABLISHMENTS OF CREDIT, EXCHANGE AND INSURANCE.	**3,037**	**2,879**	**+5**
106	Bank managers, money lenders, exchange and insurance agents, money changers and brokers and their employés.	3,037	2,879	+5
	XXV.—BROKERAGE, COMMISSION AND EXPORT	**2,058**	**2,877**	**—3**
107	Brokers, commission agents, commercial travellers, warehouse owners and employés.	2,058	2,877*	—3
	XXVI.—TRADE IN TEXTILES	**13,056**	**8,895**	**+47**
108	Trade in piece goods, wool, cotton, silk, hair and other textiles ...	13,056	8,895	+47
	XXVII.—TRADE IN SKINS, LEATHER AND FURS...	**2,071**	**1,713**	**+21**
109	Trade in skins, leather, furs, feathers, horn, etc.	2,071	1,713*	+21
	XXVIII.—TRADE IN WOOD	**6,095**	**6,121**	**—0·4**
	XXIX.—TRADE IN METALS	**229**	**227**	**+0·9**
111	Trade in metals, machinery, knife, tool, etc., sellers	229	227*	+0·9
	XXX.—TRADE IN POTTERY	**284**	**221**	**+28**
112	Trade in pottery	284	221	+28
	XXXI.—TRADE IN CHEMICAL PRODUCTS	**337**	**553***	**—39**
113	Trade in chemical products (drugs, dyes, paints, petroleum, explosives, etc.)	337	553*	—39
	XXXII.—HOTELS, CAFES, RESTAURANTS, ETC.	**6,120**	**1,321**	**+363**
114	Vendors of wine, liquors, ærated waters, etc.	641	873*	—27
115	Owners and managers of hotels, cook-shops, serais, etc. and their employés.	5,479	510*	+974

* Approximate figures only.

SUBSIDIARY TABLE VII—*continued.—Selected occupations,* 1911 *and* 1901.

Group number.	OCCUPATION. (SUB-CLASS AND ORDER).	Population supported in 1911.	Population supported in 1901.	Percentage of variation.
1	2	3	4	5
	XXXIII.—OTHER TRADE IN FOOD-STUFFS	**49,072**	**33,828**	**+45**
116	Fish dealers	14	300	—95
117	Grocers and sellers of vegetable oil, salt and other condiments ...	25,073	8,052	+211
118	Sellers of milk, butter, ghee, poultry, eggs, etc.	6,056	1,150*	+423
119	Sellers of sweetmeats, sugar, gur and molasses	1,460	1,363*	+7
120	Cardamom, betel-leaf, vegetables, fruit, and arecanut sellers ...	6,338	8,666	—27
121	Grain and pulse dealers...	3,655	6,451	—43
122	Tobacco, opium, ganja, etc., sellers...	674	1,377*	—51
123	Dealers in sheep, goats and pigs	232	1,792*	—87
124	Dealers in hay, grass and fodder	5,570	4,405	+26
	XXXIV.—TRADE IN CLOTHING AND TOILET ARTICLES	**3,237**	**2,088***	**+55**
125	Trade in ready-made clothing and other articles of dress and the toilet (hats, umbrellas, socks, ready-made shoes, perfumes, etc.)	3 237	2,088*	+55
	XXXV.—TRADE IN FURNITURE	**725**	**2,057**	**—65**
127	Hardware, cooking utensils, porcelain, crockery, glassware, bottles, articles for gardening, the cellar, etc.	39	1,002*	—96
	XXXVI.—TRADE IN BUILDING MATERIALS	**88**	**66**	**+33**
128	Trade in building materials (stones, bricks, plaster, cement, sand, tiles, thatch, etc.)	88	66	+33
	XXXVII.—TRADE IN MEANS OF TRANSPORT	**1,553**	**1,658***	**—6**
129	Dealers and hirers of elephants, camels, horses, cattle, asses, mules, etc., sellers (not makers) of carriages, saddlery, etc.	1,553	1,658*	—6
	XXXVIII.—TRADE IN FUEL	**1,069**	**107***	**+900**
130	Dealers in firewood, charcoal, coal, cowdung, etc.	1,069	107*	+900
	XXXIX.—TRADE IN ARTICLES OF LUXURY AND THOSE PERTAINING TO LETTERS AND THE ARTS AND SCIENCES.	**1,093**	**1,264**	**—13**
131	Dealers in precious stones, jewellery (real and imitation), clocks, optical instruments, etc.	403	524*	—23
132	Dealers in common bangles, bead necklaces, fans, small articles, toys, hunting and fishing tackle, flowers, etc.	427	598*	—29
	XL.—TRADE IN REFUSE MATTER	**86**	...	...
	XLI.—TRADE OF OTHER SORTS	**53,031**	**40,171**	**+32**
135	Shopkeepers otherwise unspecified	51,160	37,072	+38
138	Other trades (including farmers of pounds, tolls, and markets) ...	142	366*	—61
	VI.—Public force	**55,829**	**59,658**	**—6**
	XLII.—ARMY	**40,555**	**45,913**	**—12**
139	Army (Imperial)	40,555	45,913	—12
	XLIV.—POLICE	**15,274**	**13,715**	**+11**
142	Police	8,631	8,364*	+4
143	Village watchmen	6,643	6,457*	+3
	VII.—Public Administration	**24,634**	**11,057**	**+123**
	XLV.—PUBLIC ADMINISTRATION	**24,634**	**11,057**	**+123**
144	Service of the State	17,588	2,901*	+506
145	Service of Native and Foreign States	1,589	1,731	—8

* Approximate figures only.

SUBSIDIARY TABLE VII—*concluded.*—*Selected occupations,* 1911 *and* 1901.

Group number.	OCCUPATION (SUB-CLASS AND ORDER).	Population supported in 1911.	Population supported in 1901.	Percentage of variation.
1	2	3	4	5
146	Municipal and other local (not village) service	2,191	2,719	—19
147	Village officials and servants other than watchmen	3,266	3,696*	—12
	VIII.—Professions and liberal arts	**51,795**	**38,973**	**+33**
	XLVI.—RELIGION	**38,923**	**26,470**	**+47**
148	Priests, ministers, etc.	22,972	7,499	+206
149	Religious mendicants, inmates of monasteries, etc.	12,854	407	+3,058
150	Catechists, readers, Church and Mission service	71	15,679*	—99
151	Temple, burial, or burning ground service, pilgrim conductors, circumcisers.	3,026	2,884*	+49
	XLVII.—LAW	**1,141**	**1,283**	**—11**
152	Lawyers of all kinds, including kazis, law agents and mukhtiars ...	240	153*	+57
153	Lawyers' clerks, petition writers, etc.	901	1,130	—20
	XLVIII.—MEDICINE	**2,555**	**2,755**	**—7**
154	Medical practitioners of all kinds, including dentists, oculists and veterinary surgeons.	1,901	1,667*	+14
155	Midwives, vaccinators, compounders, nurses, masseurs, etc. ...	654	1,088	—40
	XLIX.—INSTRUCTION	**2,432**	**2,872**	—15
156	Professors and teachers of all kinds † and clerks and servants connected with education.	2,432	2,872*	—15
	L.—LETTERS AND ARTS AND SCIENCES	**6,744**	**5,593**	**+21**
159	Others (authors, photographers, artists, sculptors, astronomers, meteorologists, botanists, astrologers, etc.).	165	140*	+11
160	Music composers and masters, players on all kinds of musical instruments (not military), singers, actors, and dancers.	5,140	4,253	+21
	IX.—Persons living on their income	**5,750**	**13,191**	**—56**
	LI.—PERSONS LIVING PRINCIPALLY ON THEIR INCOME ...	**5,750**	**13,191**	**—56**
161	Proprietors (other than of agricultural land), fund and scholarship holders and pensioners.	5,750	13,191*	—56
	X.—Domestic service	**39,208**	**38,313**	**+2**
	LII.—DOMESTIC SERVICE	**39,208**	**38,313**	**+2**
162	Cooks, water carriers, door-keepers, watchmen and other indoor servants	35,676	38,902	—8
163	Private grooms, coachmen, dog boys, etc.	3,532	4,706	—25
	XI.—Insufficiently described occupations	**73,643**	**90,073**	**—18**
	LIII.—GENERAL TERMS WHICH DO NOT INDICATE A DEFINITE OCCUPATION.	**73,643**	**90,073**	**—18**
164	Manufacturers, business men, and contractors otherwise unspecified ...	2,839	1,158	+145
165	Cashiers, accountants, book-keepers, clerks and other employés in unspecified offices, warehouses and shops.	424	4,100*	—90
167	Labourers and workmen otherwise unspecified	70,023	84,815	—17
	XII.—Unproductive	**22,627**	**43,583**	**—48**
	LIV.—INMATES OF JAILS, ASYLUMS, AND HOSPITALS	**1,551**	**1,388**	**+12**
168	Inmates of jails, asylums and hospitals	1,551	1,388	+12
	LV.—BEGGARS, VAGRANTS, AND PROSTITUTES	**21,076**	**42,195**	**—50**
169	Beggars, vagrants, procurers, prostitutes, receivers of stolen goods, cattle poisoners.	21,076	42,195	—50

* Approximate figures only.
† Except law, medicine, music, dancing and drawing.

SUBSIDIARY TABLE IX.*—*Number of persons employed on the 10th March 1911 on Railways and in the Irrigation, Post Office and Telegraph Departments.*

CLASS OF PERSONS EMPLOYED.	Europeans and Anglo-Indians.	Indians.	REMARKS.
1	2	3	4
RAILWAYS.			
Total number of persons employed	**23**	**4,224**	
Persons directly employed	23	2,529	
Officers	7	...	
Subordinates drawing more than Rs. 75 per mensem	15	17	
" " from Rs. 20 to 75 "	1	338	
" " under Rs. 20 "	...	2,174	
Persons indirectly employed	...	1,695	
Contractors	...	83	
Contractors' regular employés	...	102	
Coolies	...	1,510	
IRRIGATION DEPARTMENT.			
Total number of persons employed	**26**	**11,283**	
Persons directly employed	26	2,206	
Officers	13	5	
Upper Subordinates	13	20	
Lower "	...	208	
Clerks	...	70	
Peons and other servants	...	745	
Coolies	...	1,158	
Persons indirectly employed	...	9,077	
Contractors	...	250	
Contractors' regular employés	...	307	
Coolies	...	(a) 8,520	(a) 4,623 of these were employed on the Upper Swat River Canal in the Malakand Agency.
POSTAL DEPARTMENT.			
Total number of persons employed	**6**	**974**	
Supervising officers	2	4	
Postmasters	4	(b) 119	(b) Include 30 signallers.
Miscellaneous agents	...	131	
Clerks	...	(c) 118	(c) Include 23 signallers.
Postmen, etc.	...	363	
Road Establishment	...	184	
Railway Mail Service	...	22	
Clerks and Sorters	...	13	
Mail Guards, etc.	...	9	
Combined Offices	...	33	
Signallers	...	6	
Messengers, etc.	...	27	
TELEGRAPH DEPARTMENT.			
Total number of persons employed	**52**	**253**	
Administrative establishment	1	...	
Signalling	51	12	
Clerks	...	4	
Skilled labour	...	63	
Unskilled labour	...	89	
Messengers, etc.	...	85	

* Subsidiary Table VIII has not been prepared for the North-West Frontier Province.

PART II.

TABLE I.

Area, Houses and Population.

The areas shown in this Table of the Districts of Hazara, Kohat, Bannu, and Dera Ismail Khan differ from those shown in the Census Report, Punjab, 1901. The present figures are derived from the Revenue records, and the changes are due to more accurate measurements taken during the recent Settlement operations.

The Table includes, besides the enumerated population of the five districts and of British posts across the border, the estimated population of the whole trans-frontier area.

Population statistics for tahsils will be found in Provincial Tables I and II at the end of this volume.

TABLE I.

Area, Houses and Population.

District, Agency, etc.	Area in square miles.	Towns.	Villages.	Occupied houses. Total.	Occupied houses. In towns.	Occupied houses. In villages.
1	2	3	4	5	6	7
N.-W. F P. Total ...	**38,918**	**19**	**3,033**	**435,161**	**57,471**	**377,690**
Districts ...	**13,418**	**19**	**3,033**	**435,161**	**57,471**	**377,690**
Hazara	2,984	4	1,156	126,848	6,056	120,792
Peshawar	2,605	9	792	165,581	32,043	133,538
Kohat	2,695	1	290	42,144	3,864	38,280
Bannu	1,674	2	377	45,874	4,520	41,354
Dera Ismail Khan	3,460	3	418	54,714	10,988	43,726
Agencies and Tribal Areas ...	**25,500**	...	...	...	...	...
Agencies.						
Malakand (Dir, Swat and Chitral)	...	...	...	...	...	...
Khyber	...	...	...	...	...	...
Kurram	...	...	...	...	...	...
Tochi	...	...	...	...	...	...
Wano	...	...	...	...	...	...
Tribal area under the political cont ol of the Deputy Commis sioner of —						
Hazara	...	...	...	...	...	...
Peshawar	...	...	...	...	...	...
Kohat	...	...	...	...	...	...
Bannu	...	...	...	...	...	...
Dera Ismail Khan ...	...	...	...	...	...	...

TABLE I.

Area, Houses and Population.

Population.								
Persons.			*Males.*			*Females.*		
Total.	Urban.	Rural.	Total.	Urban.	Rural.	Total.	Urban.	Rural.
8	9	10	11	12	13	14	15	16
3,819,027	**291,714**	**3,527,313**	**2,046,978**	**179,449**	**1,867,529**	**1,772,049**	**112,265**	**1,659,784**
2,196,933	**291,714**	**1,905,219**	**1,182,102**	**179,449**	**1,002,653**	**1,014,831**	**112,265**	**902,566**
603,028	29,744	573,284	320,465	18,313	302,152	282,563	11,431	271,132
865,009	167,168	697,841	470,421	102,686	367,735	394,588	64,482	330,106
222,690	22,654	200,036	119,081	14,429	104,652	103,609	8,225	95,384
250,086	21,788	228,298	133,707	14,126	119,581	116,379	7,662	108,717
256,120	50,360	205,760	138,428	29,895	108,533	117,692	20,465	97,227
1,622,094	...	**1,622,094**	**864,876**	...	**864,876**	**757,218**	...	**757,218**
576,433	...	576,433	300,710	...	300,710	275,723	...	275,723
181,134	...	181,134	97,077	...	97,077	84,057	...	84,057
98,692	...	98,692	54,271	...	54,271	44,421	...	44,421
144,379	...	144,379	78,477	...	78,477	65,902	...	65,902
101,416	...	101,416	55,350	...	35,350	46,066	...	46,066
98,302	...	98,302	52,351	...	52,351	45,951	...	45,951
240,250	...	240,250	127,838	...	127,838	112,412	...	112,412
144,000	...	144,000	78,423	...	78,423	65,577	...	65,577
17,884	...	17,884	9,631	...	9,631	8,253	...	8,253
19,604	...	19,604	10,748	...	10,748	8,856	...	8,856

TABLE II.

Variation in population since 1881.

The differences between the figures here shown and those shown in the Punjab Census Report, 1901 (population of Bannu in 1901 and of Dera Ismail Khan in 1901 and 1891) are explained in footnotes at the foot of the Table.

The Table includes, for the first time, an estimate of the population of the whole trans-border portion of the Province. The figures given for the Malakand, Tochi and Wano Agencies in 1901 represent only the population of British posts. The figures for posts in the Khyber in that year are included in the population of Peshawar. The figures for the Kurram in 1901 show the population of the revenue paying portion of the Agency only. Previous to 1901 no part of the trans-frontier population was estimated or enumerated with the exception of troops and followers in the Khyber Pass in 1881, who are included (*vide* footnote to table) in the population of the Peshawar district for that year.

TABLE II.

Variation in population since 1881.

District, Agency, etc.	Persons.				Males.			
	1911	1901	1891	1881	1911	1901	1891	1881
1	2	3	4	5	6	7	8	9
N.-W. F. P. Total	**3.819.027**	**2.125.496**	**1.857.519**	**1,575,943**	**2,046,978**	**1,159,317**	**1,007.653**	**866,333**
Districts	**2.196.933**	**2.041.534**	**1.857.519**	**1,575.943**	**1,182.102**	**1,105,709**	**1,007,653**	**866,333**
Hazara	603,028	560,288	516,288	407,075	320,465	299.708	278,265	218,616
Peshawar	865,009	788,707	711,795	§ 607.625	470,421	428,582	387,214	341,115
Kohat	222,690	217,865	193,148	174,762	119,081	122,174	108,625	97,748
Bannu	250,086	* 226,801	204,469	182,740	133,707	121,991	109,989	99,441
Dera Ismail Khan	256,120	† 247,873	‡ 229,819	203,741	138,428	133,259	‡ 123,560	109,413
Agencies and Tribal Areas ...	**1.622.094**	**83.962**	...	...	**864.876**	**53.608**	...	...
Agencies.								
Malakand (Dir, Swat and Chitral)	576,433	8,128	...	...	300,710	8,037	...	...
Khyber	181,134	...	...	...	97,077	...	...	...
Kurram	98,692	54,257	...	...	54,271	29,734	...	...
Tochi	144,379	4,684	...	...	78,477	4,669	...	...
Wano	101,416	4,522	...	...	55,350	4,522	...	...
Tribal area under the political control of the Deputy Commissioner of :—								
Hazara	98,302	...	...	...	52,351	...	...	...
Peshawar	240,250	...	...	...	127,838	...	...	...
Kohat	144,000	...	...	...	78,423	...	...	...
Bannu	17,884	...	...	...	9,631	...	...	...
Dera Ismail Khan	19,604	12,371	...	...	10,748	6,646	...	...

* Excludes a population of 4,684 (4,669 males + 15 females) enumerated in the Tochi Agency. It has been shown against the

† Excludes a population of 4,522 (males) enumerated in the Wano Agency and includes 16 persons (11 males + 5 females), population against the Wano Agency.

‡ Includes 15 persons (10 males + 5 females) population of Naranji in 1891. The village was uninhabited in 1881.

§ Includes 8,173 persons (7,970 males and 203 females) enumerated in the Khyber Pass.

T A L

Variation in population since 1881.

Females.				Variation: Increase (+), Decrease (—)			Net variation in period 1881--1911. Increase (+). Decrease (—).
1911	1901	1891	1881	1901 to 1911.	1891 to 1901.	1881 to 1891.	
10	11	12	13	14	15	16	17
1,772,049	**966,179**	**849,866**	**709,610**	**+1,693,531**	**+267,977**	**+281,576**	**+2,243,084**
1,014,831	**935,825**	**849,866**	**709,610**	**+155,399**	**+184,015**	**+281,576**	**+620,990**
282,563	260,580	238,023	188,459	+42,740	+44,000	+109,213	+195,953
394,588	360,125	324,581	266,510	+76,302	+76,912	+104,170	+257,384
103,609	95,691	86,523	77,014	+4,825	+22,717	+20,386	+47,928
116,379	104,810	94,480	83,299	+23,285	+22,332	+21,729	+67,346
117,692	114,619	‡ 106,259	94,328	+8,247	+18,054	+26,078	+52,379
757,218	**30,354**	...	...	**+1,538,132**	...	...	...
275,723	91	...	...	+568,305	...	...	...
84,057	...	...	...	...	...	...	...
44,421	24,523	...	...	+44,435	...	...	...
65,902	15	...	...	+139,695	...	...	...
46,066	...	...	...	+96,894	...	...	...
45,951	...	...	...	...	...	...	...
112,412	...	...	...	...	...	...	...
65,577	...	...	...	...	...	...	...
8,253	...	...	...	...	...	...	...
8,856	5,725	..	...	+7,233	...	...	...

Tochi Agency.

in 1901 of Naranji village transferred to Dera Ismail Khan from Dera Ghazi Khan in 1902. The figure 4,522 (males) has been shown

TABLE III.

Towns and villages classified by population.

No statistics are available of the number of villages situated in the trans-border area. This Table deals therefore with the five British Districts only.

In this Table the persons enumerated in encampments, boats, trains, etc., are separately shown, and the figures for individual towns do not therefore in all cases agree with those shown in Tables IV and V.

TABLE III.

Towns and villages classified by population.

Inhabited towns and villages.			Total Districts, N.-W. F. P.	Districts. Hazara.	Peshawar.	Kohat.	Bannu.	D. I. Khan.
1			2	3	4	5	6	7
Total Number			**3.052**	**1.160**	**801**	**291**	**879**	**421**
Population			**2.196.933**	**603.028**	**865.009**	**222.690**	**250.086**	**256.120**
Number and population of towns and villages.	Under 500.	Number	**1.902**	802	394	177	236	291
		Population	**401.919**	151,478	95,935	39,142	56,735	58,629
	500—1,000.	Number	**604**	214	181	56	72	81
		Population	**424.922**	148,791	130,114	37,938	53,149	54,930
	1,000—2,000.	Number	**334**	97	124	37	51	25
		Population	**463.319**	137,547	168,258	49,307	74,131	34,076
	2,000—5,000.	Number	**183**	42	89	16	18	18
		Population	**541.890**	128,246	268,380	49,304	43,526	52,434
	5,000—10,000.	Number	**21**	4	10	4	1	2
		Population	**133.392**	25,460	67,260	24,341	5,680	10,651
	10,000—20,000.	Number	**4**	1	1	...	1	1
		Population	**49.532**	11,506	10,982	...	16,865	10,179
	20,000—50,000.	Number	**3**	...	1	1	...	1
		Population	**83.282**	...	25,498	22,653	...	35,131
	50,000—100,000.	Number	**1**	...	1	...	...	...
		Population	**97.707**	...	97,707	...	...	...
Encampments, boat, and railway population unclassed.			**970**	...	875	5	...	90

TABLE IV.

Towns classified by population with variation since 1881.

TABLE IV.

Towns classified by population with variation since 1881.

TOWN.	District.	Municipality, Suburbs, Cantonment, etc.	Population. 1911.	1901.	1891.	1881.
1	2	3	4	5	6	7
Total Urban	**Population N.-W. F. Province**	...	**291.714**	**258.930**	**233.485**	**194.490**
CLASS I.—100.000 & over—NIL.						
CLASS II.—50.000 to 100,000.						
Peshawar	Peshawar	Total ...	97,935	95,147	84,191	79,982
		*Municipality ...	74.062	73,343	63,079	59,292
		Cantonment ...	23,873	21,804	21,112	20,690
CLASS III.—20,000 to 50,000.						
Dera Ismail Khan	Dera Ismail Khan ...	Total ...	35,131	31,737	26,884	22,164
		Municipality ...	29,401	28,287	23,246	18,988
		Cantonment ...	5.730	3,450	3,638	3,176
Nowshera	Peshawar	Total ...	25,498	9,518	6,885	5,473
		Cantonment ...	14,543	9,518	6,885	5,473
		Notified Area ...	10,955	...	...	...
Kohat	Kohat	Total ...	22,654	30,762	27.003	18,179
		Municipality ...	16,697	18,092	14.347	13.490
		Cantonment ...	5,957	12,670	12,656	4,689
CLASS IV.—10,000 to 20,000.						
Edwardesabad	Bannu	Total ...	16,865	14,291	8,817	8,960
		Municipality ...	11,751	10,070	6.550	5,260
		Cantonment ...	5,114	4,221	2,267	3,700
Abbottabad	Hazara	Total ...	11,506	7,764	10,163	4,189
		Municipality ...	4,003	3,395	2,413	1,808
		Cantonment ...	7,503	4,369	7,750	2,381
Prang	Peshawar	...	10,982	10,235	12,327	8,874
Kulachi	Dera Ismail Khan ...	Municipality ...	10,179	9,125	9,447	7,834
CLASS V.—5,000 to 10,000.						
Tangi	Peshawar	...	9,907	9,095	9,909	9,037
Charsadda	Peshawar	...	9,178	9,119	10,619	8,363
Mardan	Peshawar	Total ...	8,929	3,572	3,537	2,766
		Cantonment ...	2,795	3,572	3,537	2,766
		Notified Area ...	6,134	...	...	...
Buffa	Hazara	Notified Area ...	7,384	7,029	7,437	5,410
Haripur	Hazara	Municipality ...	6,193	5,578	5,419	4,884
Tank	Dera Ismail Khan ...	Notified Area ...	5,050	4,402	...	...
CLASS VI.—Under 5,000.						
Lakki	Bannu	Notified Area...	4,923	5,218	4.488	4,068
Nawanshahr	Hazara	Notified Area...	4,661	4,114	5,298	4,307
Ressalpura	Peshawar	Cantonment ...	3,167	...	...	...
Jamrud	Peshawar	Cantonment ...	1,452	1,848	744	...
Cherat	Peshawar	Cantonment ...	120	376	317	...

* In this table figures for Civil Lines are in all cases included in the population of Municipalities.

TABLE IV.

Towns classified by population with variation since 1881.

Variation: Increase (+), Decrease (—). 1901 to 1911.	1891 to 1901.	1881 to 1891.	Variation in period 1881—1911. Increase (+), Decrease (—).	Males. 1911	1901	1891	Females. 1911	1901	1891
8	9	10	11	12	13	14	15	16	17
+32,784	**+25,445**	**+38,995**	**+97,224**	**179,449**	**159,724**	**146,313**	**112,265**	**99,206**	**87,172**
+2,788	+10,956	+4,209	+17,953	59,680	57,526	51,264	38,255	37,621	32,927
+719	+10,264	+3,787	+14,770	40,993	40,870	34,599	33,069	32,473	28,480
+2,069	+692	+422	+3,183	18,687	16,656	16,665	5,186	5,148	4,447
+3,394	+4,853	+4,720	+12,967	21,844	18,526	16,314	13,287	13,211	10,570
+1,114	+5,041	+4,258	+19,413	16,829	15,545	13,092	12,572	12,742	10,154
+2,280	—188	+462	+2,554	5,015	2,981	3,222	715	469	416
+15,980	+2,633	+1,412	+20,025	16,829	7,198	5,185	8,669	2,320	1,700
+5,025	+2,633	+1,412	+9,070	11,068	7,198	5,185	3,475	2,320	1,700
...	...	...	...	5,761	...	...	5,194	...	...
—8,108	+3,759	+8,824	+4,475	14,429	22,492	20,042	8,225	8,270	6,961
—1,395	+3,745	+857	+3,207	9,295	10,508	7,999	7,402	7,584	6,348
—6,713	+14	+7,967	+1,268	5,134	11,984	12,043	823	686	613
+2,574	+5,474	—143	+7,905	11,561	9,791	6,116	5,304	4,500	2,701
+1,681	+3,520	+1 290	+6,491	6,908	6,036	4,119	4,843	4,034	2,431
+893	+1,954	—1.433	+1,414	4,653	3,755	1,997	461	466	270
+3,742	—2,399	+5,974	+7,317	8,491	5,400	8,666	3,015	2,364	1,497
+608	+982	+605	+2,195	2,620	2,271	1,747	1,383	1,124	666
+3,134	—3,381	+5,369	+5,122	5,871	3,129	6,919	1,632	1.240	831
+747	—2,092	+3,453	+2,108	5,869	5,362	6,686	5,113	4,873	5,641
+1,054	—322	+1,613	+2,345	5,071	4,471	4,790	5,108	4,654	4,657
+812	—814	+872	+870	5,178	4,760	5,300	4,729	4,335	4,609
+ 59	—1,500	+2,256	+815	5,115	4,887	5,823	4,063	4,232	4,796
+5,357	+35	+771	+6,163	6,012	2,854	2,907	2,917	718	630
—777	+35	+771	+29	2,177	2,854	2.907	618	718	630
...	—	...	...	3,835	...	...	2,299	...	...
+355	—408	+2,027	+1,974	3,892	3,774	3,936	3.492	3,255	3,501
+615	+159	+535	+1,309	3,477	3,039	3,091	2,716	2,539	2,328
+648	...	...	...	2,980	2,561	...	2,070	1,841	...
—295	+730	+420	+855	2,565	2,791	2.384	2.358	2,427	2.104
+547	—1,184	+991	+354	2,453	2,222	2,798	2,208	1,892	2,500
...	...	...	...	2,639	...	...	528	...	...
—396	+1,104	...	...	1,268	1,711	715	184	137	29
—256	+59	...	...	96	359	296	24	17	21

TABLE V.

Towns arranged territorially with population by religion.

TABLE V.

Towns arranged territorially with population by Religion.

District.	Town, Municipality, Cantonment, etc.	Population.			Mohammadans.		
		Persons.	Males.	Females.	Persons.	Males.	Females.
1	2	3	4	5	6	7	8
Total Urban Population N.-W. F. P. ...		**291.714**	**179.449**	**112.265**	**203.742**	**121.374**	**82.368**
Hazara	Buffa	7,384	3,892	3 492	6,530	3,427	3,103
	Nawanshahr	4,661	2,453	2,208	3,404	1,767	1,637
	Abbottabad	11,506	8,491	3,015	3,729	2,688	1,041
	**Municipality*	4,003	2,620	1,383	2,556	1,695	861
	Cantonment	7,503	5,871	1,632	1,173	993	180
	Haripur	6,193	3,477	2,716	3,515	1,985	1,530
Peshawar	Tangi	9,907	5,178	4,729	9,436	4,917	4,519
	Mardan	8,929	6,012	2,917	5,477	3,599	1,878
	Cantonment	2,795	2,177	618	1,181	937	244
	Notified Area	6,134	3,835	2,299	4,296	2,662	1,634
	Charsadda	9,178	5,115	4,063	8,650	4,794	3,856
	Prang	10,982	5,869	5,113	10,906	5,825	5,081
	Ressalpura	3,167	2,639	528	2,268	1,887	381
	Nowshera	25,498	16,829	8,669	16,177	9,717	6,460
	Cantonment	14,543	11,068	3,475	5,809	4,300	1,509
	Notified Area	10,955	5,761	5,194	10,368	5,417	4,951
	Peshawar	97,935	59,680	38,255	73,198	42,963	30,235
	Municipality	74,062	40,993	33,069	61,845	33,758	28,087
	Cantonment	23,873	18,687	5,186	11,353	9,205	2,148
	Jamrud	1,452	1,268	184	1,293	1,152	141
	Cherat	120	96	24	62	54	8
Kohat	Kohat	22,654	14,429	8,225	15,930	9,684	6,246
	Municipality	16,697	9,295	7,402	13,372	7,401	5,971
	Cantonment	5,957	5,134	823	2,558	2,283	275
Bannu	Edwardesabad	16,865	11,561	5,304	6,340	4,932	1,408
	Municipality	11,751	6,908	4,843	3,816	2,563	1,253
	Cantonment	5,114	4,653	461	2,524	2,369	155
	Lakki	4,923	2,565	2,358	3,411	1,817	1,594
Dera Ismail Khan	Tank	5,050	2,980	2,070	3,837	2,326	1,511
	Kulachi	10,179	5,071	5,108	7,820	3,984	3,836
	Dera Ismail Khan	35,131	21,844	13,287	21,759	13,856	7,903
	Municipality	29,401	16,829	12,572	18,317	10,777	7,540
	Cantonment	5,730	5,015	715	3,442	3,079	363

* The populations of Civil Lines are included in those of Municipalities in each case.

TABLE V.

Towns arranged territorially with population by Religion.

Hindus.			Sikhs.			Christians.			Others.		
Persons.	Males.	Females.	Persons.	Males.	Females.	Persons.	Males.	Females.	Persons.	Males.	Females.
9	10	11	12	13	14	15	16	17	18	19	20
64,771	**40,682**	**24,089**	**16,685**	**12,023**	**4,662**	**6,451**	**5,324**	**1,127**	**65**	**46**	**19**
801	434	367	53	31	22	...	...	...	...	...	...
1,069	560	509	188	126	62	...	...	...	...	...	...
6,828	5,031	1,797	785	662	123	164	110	54	...	...	...
1,110	697	413	292	206	86	45	22	23	...	...	...
5,718	4,334	1,384	493	456	37	119	88	31	...	...	...
2,250	1,236	1,014	423	252	171	5	4	1	...	...	...
302	162	140	169	99	70	...	...	...	...	...	...
1,892	1,351	541	1,465	1,012	453	95	50	45	...	...	...
984	744	240	554	455	99	76	41	35	...	...	...
908	607	301	911	557	354	19	9	10	...	...	...
201	128	73	326	192	134	1	1	...	...	...	...
73	41	32	3	3	...	...	...	...	...	...	...
716	579	137	177	167	10	6	6	...	...	...	...
5,468	3,751	1,717	1,808	1,573	235	2,044	1,788	256	1	...	1
4,926	3,431	1,495	1,763	1,549	214	2,044	1,788	256	1	...	*1
542	320	222	45	24	21	...	...	...	...	...	...
16,328	10,408	5,920	5,026	3,455	1,571	3,332	2,813	519	51	†41	‡10
9,180	5,501	3,679	2,966	1,693	1,273	71	41	30	...	...	...
7,148	4,907	2,241	2,060	1,762	298	3,261	2,772	489	51	†41	‡10
64	55	9	18	18	...	77	43	34	...	...	...
33	17	16	25	25	...	...	...	...	...	...	...
4,850	3,365	1,485	1,693	1,271	422	168	104	64	$13	5	8
2,577	1,482	1,095	743	410	333	5	2	3	...	...	...
2,273	1,883	390	950	861	89	163	102	61	$13	5	8
7,714	4,726	2,988	2,585	1,730	855	226	173	53	...	...	...
6,011	3,257	2,754	1,838	1,034	804	86	54	32	...	...	...
1,703	1,469	234	747	696	51	140	119	21	...	...	...
1,130	563	567	382	185	197	...	...	...	...	...	...
1,130	605	525	75	44	31	8	5	3	...	...	...
2,306	1,012	1,194	153	75	78	...	...	...	...	...	...
11,716	6,658	5,058	1,331	1,103	228	325	227	98	...	...	...
10,632	5,794	4,838	343	210	133	109	48	61	...	...	...
1,084	864	220	988	893	95	216	179	37	...	...	...

* Parsi.
† 40 Parsis, 1 Jain.
‡ 7 Parsis, 2 Jains, 1 Jew.
$ All Jews.

TABLE VI.

Religion.

In this and in the following tables is shown only the population enumerated on the regular schedule, *viz.* that of the five Districts and of British Posts in Agencies and Tribal Areas.

TABLE VI.

Religion.

District or Agency.	Population.			Mohammedans.		
	Persons.	Males.	Females.	Persons.	Males.	Females.
1	2	3	4	5	6	7
Total N.-W. F. Province ...	**2,210,471**	**1,194,743**	**1,015,728**	**2,049,599**	**1,094,422**	**955,177**
Total Districts ...	**2,196,933**	**1,182,102**	**1,014,831**	**2,039,994**	**1,085,276**	**954,718**
Hazara	603,028	320,465	282,563	572,972	302,124	270,848
Peshawar	865,009	470,421	394,588	807,788	432,422	375,366
Kohat	222,690	119,081	103,609	208,868	110,101	98,767
Bannu	250,086	133,707	116,379	225,374	119,513	105,861
Dera Ismail Khan	256,120	138,428	117,692	224,992	121,116	103,876
Total agencies and tribal areas. Population of posts only	**13,538**	**12,641**	**897**	**9,605**	**9,146**	**459**
Agencies.						
Malakand (Dir, Swat and Chitral)	4,435	4,228	207	1,849	1,784	65
Khyber	1,672	1,585	87	1,560	1,489	71
Kurram	2,967	2,397	570	2,288	1,985	303
Tochi	1,879	1,854	25	1,516	1,503	13
Wano	1,986	1,985	1	1,924	1,923	1
Tribal area under the political control of the Deputy Commissioner of:—						
Hazara	52	52	...	52	52	...
Bannu	44	38	6	44	38	6
Dera Ismail Khan	503	502	1	372	372	...

TABLE VI.

Religion.

Hindus.			Sikhs.			Christians.			Others.		
Persons.	Males.	Females.	Persons.	Males.	Females.	Persons.	Males.	Females.	Persons.	Males.	Females.
8	9	10	11	12	13	14	15	16	17	18	19
122,628	**73,732**	**48,896**	**31,459**	**21,017**	**10,442**	**6,718**	**5,524**	**1,194**	**67**	**48**	**19**
119,942	**71,397**	**48,545**	**30,345**	**19,967**	**10,378**	**6,585**	**5,414**	**1,171**	**67**	**48**	**19**
24,389	14,882	9,507	5,489	3,339	2,150	178	120	58	...	...	...
35,367	22,599	12,768	16,196	10,630	5,566	5,604	4,727	877	54	*43	†11
10,848	6,758	4,090	2,739	2,069	670	222	148	74	‡13	5	8
20,721	11,648	9,073	3,746	2,362	1,384	245	184	61	...	...	...
28,617	15,510	13,107	2,175	1,567	608	336	235	101	...	...	...
2,686	**2,335**	**351**	**1,114**	**1,050**	**64**	**133**	**110**	**23**	...	...	...
1,763	1,656	107	732	715	17	91	73	18	...	...	...
56	48	8	47	41	6	9	7	2	...	...	...
554	328	226	114	76	38	11	8	3	...	...	...
219	210	9	132	129	3	12	12	...	...	...	...
52	52	...	...	...	...	10	10	...	...	...	...
...	...	...	...	...	...	...	...	...	...	...	...
...	...	...	...	...	...	...	...	...	...	...	...
42	41	1	89	89	...	...	...	...	...	...	...

* Parsis 41 and Jains 2.
† Parsis 8, Jains 2 and Jew 1.
‡ All Jews.

CORRIGENDA TO TABLE VII.

PAGE XXIV.

Line 6, column 2 *for* 334,681 *read* 334,678.

" " " 3 *for* 167,930 *read* 167,927.

" 41, " 1 *for* "70 and under" *read* "70 and over."

PAGE XXV.

Line 17, column 1 *for* "56 and under 60" *read* "55 and under 60."

PAGE XXVIII.

Against Total—Dera Ismail Khan

Column 8 *for* 105,816 *read* 105,814.

TABLE VII.

Age, Sex and Civil Condition.

PART I.—Provincial Totals.

TABLE VII.

Age, Sex and Civil Condition.—Part I.—Provincial Totals.

Age.	Population.			Unmarried.			Married.			Widowed.		
	Persons.	Males.	Females.	Persons.	Males.	Females.	Persons.	Males.	Females.	Persons.	Males.	Females.
1	2	3	4	5	6	7	8	9	10	11	12	13
ALL RELIGIONS.												
0 and under 1 ...	84,638	42,923	41,715	84,638	42,923	41,715	...	...	...	...	...	...
1 " 2 ...	31,397	15,740	15,657	31,397	15,740	15,657	...	...	...	...	...	...
2 " 3 ...	66,954	32,891	34,063	66,954	32,891	34,063	...	...	...	...	...	...
3 " 4 ...	75,570	37,446	38,124	75,570	37,446	38,124	...	...	...	...	...	...
4 " 5 ...	76,119	38,927	37,192	76,116	38,927	37,189	3	...	3	...	...	...
Total 0 and under 5	**334.681**	**167.930**	**166 751**	**334.675**	**167.927**	**166 748**	**3**	...	**3**	...	...	...
5 and under 10 ...	346,834	185,110	161,718	345,493	184,715	160,778	1,310	398	912	31	3	28
10 " 15 ...	238,834	139,789	99,045	223,504	136,071	87,433	14,948	3,611	11,337	382	107	275
15 " 20 ...	165,708	93 055	72,653	104,424	78,873	25,551	59,734	13,602	46,132	1,550	580	970
20 " 25 ...	177,029	92,444	84,585	61,838	54,386	7,452	110,527	35,994	74.533	4,664	2,064	2,600
25 " 30 ...	187,449	100,229	87,220	38,385	34,692	3,693	140,337	61,662	78,675	8,727	3,875	4,852
30 " 35 ...	199,527	105,011	94,516	21,249	18,140	3,109	163,912	80,895	83,017	14,366	5,976	8,390
35 " 40 ...	110,407	62,618	47,789	7,715	6,329	1,386	91,725	52,027	39,698	10,967	4,262	6,705
40 " 45 ...	137,075	71,709	65,366	7,426	5,483	1,943	107,525	59,813	47,712	22,124	6,413	15,711
45 " 50 ...	68,489	38,865	29,624	3,261	2,284	977	51,344	32,433	18,911	13,884	4,148	9,736
50 " 55 ...	93,881	51,831	42,050	3,037	2,219	818	63,321	42,454	20,867	27,523	7,158	20,365
55 " 60 ...	30,878	18,039	12,839	859	599	260	20,540	14,483	6,057	9.479	2,957	6.522
60 " 65 ...	63,625	35,630	27,995	1,703	1,295	408	35,029	20,743	8,286	26,893	7,592	19,301
65 " 70 ...	14,050	8,101	5,949	407	250	157	7,470	5.790	1,680	6,173	2,061	4,112
70 and over ...	42,007	24,379	17,628	1,078	796	282	18,671	15,202	3,469	22,258	8,381	13,877
Total N.-W. F. P. ...	**2.210.471**	**1.194.743**	**1.015.728**	**1.155,054**	**694.059**	**460.995**	**886.396**	**445.107**	**441.289**	**169.021**	**55.577**	**113.444**
MUHAMMADANS.												
0 and under 1 ...	79,593	40.299	39.294	79.593	40.299	39.294	...	...	...	...	...	...
1 " 2 ...	29,630	14.795	14,835	29,630	14,795	14,835	...	...	...	...	...	...
2 " 3 ...	63,325	31,091	32,234	63,325	31,091	32,234	...	...	...	...	...	...
3 " 4 ...	71,670	35,465	36.205	71,670	35.465	36,205	...	...	...	...	...	...
4 " 5 ...	72.440	37,089	35.351	72 437	37,089	35.348	3	...	3	...	...	...
Total 0 and under 5	**316.658**	**158.739**	**157.919**	**316.655**	**158.739**	**157.916**	**3**	...	**3**	...	...	...
5 and under 10 ...	328.528	175.430	153.098	327.328	175.070	152,258	1,175	358	817	25	2	23
10 " 15 ...	223,619	130.688	92.931	209.823	127,298	82,525	13,459	3,304	10,155	337	86	251
15 " 20 ...	151,229	83,631	67.598	96,143	71,485	24,658	53,770	11,675	42,095	1,316	471	845
20 " 25 ...	155,179	76,918	78,261	51,927	44,731	7,196	99.433	30,561	68,872	3,819	1,626	2,193
25 " 30 ...	168,471	86,969	81,502	32,802	29,243	3.559	128 200	54.506	73,694	7,469	3,220	4,249
30 " 35 ...	184,903	95,492	89.411	18.986	16,010	2,976	153,141	74,323	78,818	12,776	5,159	7,017
35 " 40 ...	100,571	55.953	44,618	6 665	5,336	1,329	84,330	47,037	37,293	9,576	3,580	5,996
40 " 45 ...	127,759	65,960	61,799	6,754	4,851	1,903	101,135	55,515	45,620	19,870	5 594	14,276
45 " 50 ...	63,088	35,547	27,541	2,930	1,975	955	47,825	29,943	17 882	12,333	3.629	8,704
50 " 55 ...	87,900	48,219	39,681	2,573	1,796	777	60,139	40,005	20,134	25,188	6,418	18,770
55 " 60 ...	28,757	16,677	12.080	746	496	250	19,387	13.563	5.824	8,624	2.618	6.006
60 " 65 ...	60,024	33,580	26,444	1,524	1,136	388	33,492	25.488	8.004	25.008	6.956	18,052
65 " 70 ...	13,079	7,497	5.582	359	207	152	7,078	5,482	1.596	5,642	1,808	3,834
70 and under ...	39,834	23,122	16,712	952	680	272	17,948	14.591	3.357	20,934	7,851	13,083
Total N.-W. F. P. ...	**2,049.599**	**1.094.422**	**955.177**	**1.076.137**	**639.053**	**437.114**	**820.515**	**406.351**	**414.164**	**152.917**	**49.018**	**103.899**
HINDUS.												
0 and under 1 ...	4,057	2.098	1,959	4,057	2,098	1,959	...	...	...	...	...	...
1 " 2 ...	1,408	761	647	1.408	761	647	...	...	...	...	...	...
2 " 3 ...	2,913	1,427	1,486	2,913	1,427	1,486	...	...	...	...	...	...
3 " 4 ...	3.105	1.575	1,530	3.105	1,575	1.530	...	...	...	...	...	...
4 " 5 ...	2,951	1,448	1.503	2,951	1.448	1.503	...	...	...	...	...	...
Total 0 and under 5	**14.434**	**7.309**	**7.125**	**14.434**	**7.309**	**7.125**	...	...	...	...	...	...
5 and under 10 ...	14,781	7,760	7,021	14.668	7,727	6,941	108	33	75	5	...	5
10 " 15 ...	12,260	7,243	5,017	11,038	6,981	4,057	1,187	243	944	35	19	16
15 " 20 ...	11,250	7,160	4,090	6,275	5,580	695	4.797	1.500	3,297	178	80	98
20 " 25 ...	14.696	9 617	5,079	5,475	5,311	164	8,540	3,989	4,557	675	317	358
25 " 30 ...	13,340	8,821	4 519	2,904	2,814	90	9,441	5,522	3,919	995	485	510
30 " 35 ...	10,878	6,796	4,082	1,338	1.238	100	8,289	4,945	3,344	1,251	613	638
35 " 40 ...	7,335	4 839	2,496	609	576	33	5 648	3 761	1,887	1,078	502	575
40 " 45 ...	7,387	4,449	2,938	503	473	30	4,979	3,296	1,683	1,905	680	1,225
45 " 50 ...	4,330	2,651	1,679	270	254	16	2,763	1,973	790	1,297	424	873
50 " 55 ...	4,910	2,912	1,998	375	344	31	2,546	1,947	599	1,989	621	1,368
55 " 60 ...	1,740	1,112	628	89	85	4	935	743	192	716	284	432
60 " 65 ...	2,870	1,668	1,202	143	136	7	1.245	1,024	221	1,482	508	974
65 " 70 ...	702	421	281	32	28	4	305	236	69	365	157	208
70 and over	1,715	974	741	96	88	8	542	463	79	1,077	423	654
Total N.-W. F. P. ...	**122.628**	**73.732**	**48.896**	**58.249**	**38.944**	**19.305**	**51.331**	**29.675**	**21 656**	**13.048**	**5.113**	**7.935**

TABLE VII.

Age, Sex and Civil Condition.—Part I—Provincial Totals.

Age.	Population.			Unmarried.			Married.			Widowed.		
	Persons.	Males.	Females.	Persons.	Males.	Females.	Persons.	Males.	Females.	Persons.	Males.	Females.
1	2	3	4	5	6	7	8	9	10	11	12	13
SIKHS												
0 and under 1 ...	878	468	410	878	468	410	...	...	...	...	...	...
1 „ 2 ...	273	133	140	273	133	140	...	...	...	...	...	...
2 „ 3 ...	646	332	314	646	332	314	...	...	...	...	...	...
3 „ 4 ...	714	366	348	714	366	348	...	...	...	...	...	...
4 „ 5 ...	637	339	298	637	339	298	...	...	...	...	...	...
Total 0 and under 5	**3,148**	**1,638**	**1,510**	**3,148**	**1,638**	**1,510**	...	...	...	...	...	...
5 and under 10 ...	3,271	1,803	1,468	3,243	1,795	1,448	27	7	20	1	1	...
10 „ 15 ...	2,842	1,803	1,040	2,537	1,742	795	295	58	237	10	2	8
15 „ 20 ...	3,035	2,141	894	1,853	1,695	158	1,129	417	712	53	29	24
20 „ 25 ...	4,847	3,746	1,101	2,267	2,224	43	2,415	1,406	1,009	165	116	49
25 „ 30 ...	3,882	2,869	1,013	1,216	1,204	12	2,414	1,503	911	252	162	90
30 „ 35 ...	2,964	2,108	856	493	477	16	2,138	1,429	709	333	202	131
35 „ 40 ...	2,065	1,503	562	243	236	7	1,525	1,096	429	297	171	126
40 „ 45 ...	1,704	1,123	581	123	119	4	1,245	875	370	336	129	207
45 „ 50 ...	949	576	373	43	40	3	659	445	214	247	91	156
50 „ 55 ...	993	653	340	78	75	3	592	467	125	323	111	212
55 „ 60 ...	355	233	122	17	14	3	204	166	38	134	53	81
60 „ 65 ...	709	374	335	36	23	13	281	225	56	392	126	266
65 „ 70 ...	256	177	79	15	15	...	81	67	14	160	95	65
70 and over ...	439	271	168	28	26	2	168	139	29	243	106	137
Total N.-W. F. P.	**31,459**	**21,017**	**10,442**	**15,340**	**11,323**	**4,017**	**13,173**	**8,300**	**4,873**	**2,946**	**1,394**	**1,552**
CHRISTIANS.												
0 and under 1 ...	107	57	50	107	57	50	...	...	...	...	...	...
1 „ 2 ...	86	51	35	86	51	35	...	...	...	...	...	...
2 „ 3 ...	69	40	29	69	40	29	...	...	...	...	...	...
3 „ 4 ...	81	40	41	81	40	41	...	...	...	...	...	...
4 „ 5 ...	90	50	40	90	50	40	...	...	...	...	...	...
Total 0 and under 5	**433**	**238**	**195**	**433**	**238**	**195**	...	...	...	...	...	...
5 and under 10 ...	252	122	130	252	122	130	...	...	...	...	...	...
10 „ 15 ...	112	56	56	105	50	55	7	6	1	...	...	...
15 „ 20 ...	191	122	69	152	112	40	36	10	26	3	...	3
20 „ 25 ...	2,292	2,153	139	2,160	2,111	49	127	37	90	5	5	...
25 „ 30 ...	1,741	1,557	184	1,457	1,425	32	273	124	149	11	8	3
30 „ 35 ...	772	608	164	429	413	16	338	193	145	5	2	3
35 „ 40 ...	431	319	112	197	180	17	219	130	89	15	9	6
40 „ 45 ...	222	174	48	46	40	6	163	124	39	13	10	3
45 „ 50 ...	119	89	30	17	14	3	96	71	25	6	4	2
50 „ 55 ...	76	46	30	11	4	7	44	35	9	21	7	14
55 „ 60 ...	25	16	9	7	4	3	13	10	3	5	2	3
60 „ 65 ...	22	8	14	...	...	...	11	6	5	11	2	9
65 „ 70 ...	12	5	7	1	...	1	6	5	1	5	...	5
70 and over ...	18	11	7	1	1	...	13	9	4	4	1	3
Total N.-W. F. P.	**6,718**	**5,524**	**1,194**	**5,268**	**4,714**	**554**	**1,346**	**760**	**586**	**104**	**50**	**54**
PARSIS.												
2 years ...	1	1	...	1	1	...	...	...	...	...	...	...
5 and under 10	1	1	...	1	1	...	...	...	...	...	...	...
15 „ 20 ...	2	1	1	1	1	...	1	...	1	...	...	...
20 „ 25 ...	12	10	2	9	9	...	3	1	2	...	...	...
25 „ 30 ...	12	10	2	6	6	...	6	4	2	...	...	...
30 „ 35 ...	7	6	1	2	2	...	5	4	1	...	...	...
35 „ 40 ...	5	4	1	1	1	...	3	3	...	1	...	1
40 „ 45 ...	3	3	...	...	...	...	3	3	...	...	...	...
45 „ 50 ...	1	1	...	1	1	...	...	...	...	...	...	...
50 „ 55 ...	2	1	1	...	...	...	...	...	...	2	1	1
55 „ 60 ...	1	1	...	...	...	...	1	1	...	...	...	...
65 „ 70 ...	1	1	...	...	...	...	...	...	...	1	1	...
70 and over ...	1	1	...	1	1	...	...	...	...	...	...	...
Total N.-W. F. P.	**49**	**41**	**8**	**23**	**23**	...	**22**	**16**	**6**	**4**	**2**	**2**
JEWS.												
0 and under 1 ...	3	1	2	3	1	2	...	...	...	...	...	...
4 „ 5 ...	1	1	...	1	1	...	...	...	...	...	...	...
5 „ 10 ...	1	...	1	1	...	1	...	...	...	...	...	...
10 „ 15 ...	1	...	1	1	...	1	...	...	...	...	...	...
20 „ 25 ...	3	...	3	...	...	...	3	...	3	...	...	...
25 „ 30 ...	1	1	...	...	...	...	1	1	...	...	...	...
30 „ 35 ...	2	1	1	1	...	1	1	1	...	...	...	...
45 „ 50 ...	2	1	1	...	...	...	1	1	...	1	...	1
Total N.-W. F. P.	**14**	**5**	**9**	**7**	**2**	**5**	**6**	**3**	**3**	**1**	...	**1**
JAINS.												
15 and under 20 ...	1	...	1	...	...	...	1	...	1	...	...	...
25 „ 30 ...	2	2	...	...	...	...	2	2	...	...	...	...
30 „ 35 ...	1	...	1	...	...	...	...	...	...	1	...	1
Total N.-W. F. P.	**4**	**2**	**2**	...	...	...	**3**	**2**	**1**	**1**	...	**1**

TABLE VII.

PART II.—District Tables.

Showing the distribution by age, sex and civil condition of the total population of all religions and for the principal religions in each district and in trans-frontier posts.

TABLE VII.

Age, Sex and Civil Conditions.—Part II.—District Tables.—All religions.

Age.	Population.			Unmarried.			Married.			Widowed.		
	Persons.	Males.	Females.	Persons.	Males.	Females.	Persons	Males.	Females.	Persons.	Males.	Females.
1	2	3	4	5	6	9	8	9	10	11	12	13
HAZARA.												
0 and under 5 ...	93,901	46,875	47,026	93,898	46,875	47,023	3	...	3	...	...	...
5 „ 10 ...	95,364	50,000	45,364	94,760	49,816	44,944	604	184	420	...	...	...
10 „ 15 ...	70,865	40,869	29,996	65,165	39,092	26,073	5,595	1,760	3,835	105	17	88
15 „ 20 ...	47,847	25,476	22,371	28,218	21,736	6,482	19,189	3,612	15,577	440	128	312
20 „ 40 ...	174,649	88,427	86,222	27,067	23,983	3,084	138,150	60,339	77,811	9,432	4,105	5,327
40 „ 60 ...	83,614	47,073	36,541	2,565	2,070	495	64,000	39,498	24,502	17,049	5,505	11,544
60 and over ...	36,788	21,745	15,043	743	546	197	20,242	15,498	4,744	15,803	5,701	10,102
Total ...	**603,028**	**320,465**	**282,563**	**312,416**	**184,118**	**128,298**	**247,783**	**120,891**	**126,892**	**42,829**	**15,456**	**27,373**
PESHAWAR.												
0 and under 5 ...	128,866	65,223	63,643	128,866	65,223	63,643	...	...	...	...	...	...
5 „ 10 ...	127,316	69,013	58,303	127,154	68,956	58,198	159	57	102	3	...	3
10 „ 15 ...	94,492	56,190	38,302	90,308	55,533	34,775	4,064	620	3,444	120	37	83
15 „ 20 ...	64,751	36,642	28,109	44,045	32,565	11,480	20,207	3,911	16,296	499	166	333
20 „ 40 ...	264,424	141,483	122,941	58,019	50,680	7,339	191,896	85,256	106,640	14,509	5,547	8,962
40 „ 60 ...	135,101	73,255	61,846	6,866	4,360	2,506	99,233	61,460	37,773	29,002	7,435	21,567
60 and over ...	50,059	28,615	21,444	1,335	973	362	25,594	20,636	4,958	23,130	7,006	16,124
Total ...	**865,009**	**470,421**	**394,588**	**456,593**	**278,290**	**178,303**	**341,153**	**171,940**	**169,213**	**67,263**	**20,191**	**47,072**
KOHAT.												
0 and under 5 ...	35,784	17,612	18,172	35,784	17,612	18,172	...	...	...	...	...	...
5 „ 10 ...	39,772	20,892	18,880	39,573	20,827	18,746	101	63	128	8	2	6
10 „ 15 ...	22,650	13,106	9,544	20,666	12,593	8,073	1,918	494	1,424	66	19	47
15 „ 20 ...	15,757	8,752	7,005	9,012	6,827	2,185	6,545	1,858	4,687	200	67	133
20 „ 40 ...	66,037	35,879	30,158	11,755	10,350	1,405	50,162	23,774	26,388	4,120	1,755	2,365
40 „ 60 ...	31,982	17,095	14,887	1,520	1,231	289	23,049	13,801	9,248	7,413	2,063	5,350
60 and over ...	10,708	5,745	4,963	358	278	80	5,214	3,839	1,375	5,136	1,628	3,508
Total ...	**222,690**	**119,081**	**103,609**	**118,668**	**69,718**	**48,950**	**87,079**	**43,829**	**43,250**	**16,943**	**5,534**	**11,409**
BANNU.												
0 and under 5 ...	38,654	19,041	19,613	38,654	19,041	19,613	...	...	...	...	...	...
5 „ 10 ...	44,947	23,690	21,257	44,747	23,656	21,091	189	34	155	11	...	11
10 „ 15 ...	23,929	13,734	10,195	22,461	13,354	9,107	1,421	362	1,059	47	18	29
15 „ 20 ...	17,254	9,975	7,279	10,775	7,993	2,782	6,312	1,898	4,414	167	84	83
20 „ 40 ...	78,017	41,658	36,359	14,545	12,089	2,456	58,652	27,375	31,277	4,820	2,194	2,626
40 „ 60 ...	37,527	20,156	17,371	1,778	1,382	396	26,794	16,154	10,640	8,955	2,620	6,335
60 and over ...	9,758	5,453	4,305	368	270	98	4,523	3,508	1,015	4,867	1,675	3,192
Total ...	**250,086**	**133,707**	**116,379**	**133,328**	**77,785**	**55,543**	**97,891**	**49,331**	**48,560**	**18,867**	**6,591**	**12,276**
DERA ISMAIL KHAN.												
0 and under 5 ...	37,161	19,006	18,155	37,161	19,006	18,155	...	...	...	...	...	...
5 „ 10 ...	39,137	21,338	17,799	38,967	21,283	17,684	161	54	107	9	1	8
10 „ 15 ...	26,547	15,615	10,932	24,584	15,246	9,338	1,922	356	1,566	41	13	28
15 „ 20 ...	18,505	10,695	7,810	11,175	8,569	2,606	7,148	2,052	5,096	182	74	108
20 „ 40 ...	82,086	44,001	38,085	13,951	12,606	1,345	62,640	29,157	33,483	5,495	2,238	3,257
40 „ 60 ...	40,511	21,396	19,115	1,668	1,357	311	28,447	17,133	11,314	10,396	2,906	7,490
60 and over ...	12,173	6,377	5,796	373	263	110	5,496	4,158	1,338	6,304	1,956	4,348
Total ...	**256,120**	**138,428**	**117,692**	**127,879**	**78,330**	**49,549**	**105,816**	**52,910**	**52,904**	**22,427**	**7,188**	**15,239**
TRANS-FRONTIER POSTS.												
0 and under 5 ...	312	170	142	312	170	142	...	...	...	...	...	...
5 „ 10 ...	298	183	115	202	177	115	6	6	...	...	...	...
10 „ 15 ...	351	275	76	320	253	67	28	19	9	3	3	...
15 „ 20 ...	1,594	1,515	79	1,199	1,183	16	333	271	62	62	61	1
20 „ 40 ...	9,199	8,854	345	3,850	3,839	11	5,001	4,677	324	348	338	10
40 „ 60 ...	1,588	1,469	119	186	185	1	1,207	1,137	70	195	147	48
60 and over ...	196	175	21	11	11	...	101	96	5	84	68	16
Total ...	**13,538**	**12,641**	**897**	**6,170**	**5,818**	**352**	**6,676**	**6,206**	**470**	**692**	**617**	**75**

TABLE VII.

Age, Sex and Civil Condition—Part II.—District Tables—Muhammadans.

Age.		Population.			Unmarried.			Married.			Widowed.		
		Persons.	Males.	Females.	Persons.	Males.	Females.	Persons.	Males.	Females.	Persons.	Males.	Females.
1		2	3	4	5	6	7	8	9	10	11	12	13
						HAZARA.							
0 and under 5	...	90,391	45,052	45,339	90,388	45,052	45,336	3	...	3	...	...	...
5 " 10	...	91,994	48,205	43,789	91,426	48,026	43,400	568	179	389	...	...	...
10 " 15	...	67,815	39,059	28,756	62,437	37,328	25,109	5,281	1,715	3,566	97	16	81
15 " 20	...	44,838	23,527	21,311	26,494	20,134	6,360	17,944	3,280	14,664	400	113	287
20 " 40	...	163,230	80,908	82,322	23,932	20,911	3,021	130,679	56,256	74,423	8,619	3,741	4,878
40 " 60	...	79,430	44,564	34,866	2,284	1,806	478	61,406	37,715	23,691	15,740	5,043	10,697
60 and over	...	35,274	20,809	14,465	653	460	193	19,600	14,962	4,638	15,021	5,387	9,634
Total	...	**572,972**	**302,124**	**270,848**	**297,614**	**173,717**	**123,897**	**235,481**	**114,107**	**121,374**	**39,877**	**14,300**	**25,577**
						PESHAWAR.							
0 and under 5	...	123,147	62,250	60,897	123,147	62,250	60,897	...	...	...	...	...	...
5 " 10	...	121,711	66,024	55,687	121,588	65,981	55,607	120	43	77	3	...	3
10 " 15	...	89,837	53,254	36,583	86,247	52,710	33,537	3,483	513	2,970	107	31	76
15 " 20	...	59,689	33,246	26,443	41,118	29,888	11,230	18,172	3,236	14,936	399	122	277
20 " 40	...	238,770	122,490	116,280	48,634	41,515	7,119	177,426	76,480	100,946	12,710	4,495	8,215
40 " 60	...	127,133	68,058	59,075	6,172	3,715	2,457	94,210	57,773	36,437	26,751	6,570	20,181
60 and over	...	47,501	27,100	20,401	1,193	851	342	24,592	19,800	4,792	21,716	6,449	15,267
Total	...	**807,788**	**432,422**	**375,366**	**428,099**	**256,910**	**171,189**	**318,003**	**157,845**	**160,158**	**61,686**	**17,667**	**44,019**
						KOHAT.							
0 and under 5	...	34,344	16,864	17,480	34,344	16,864	17,480	...	...	...	...	...	...
5 " 10	...	38,225	20,125	18,100	38,043	20,064	17,979	175	60	115	7	1	6
10 " 15	...	21,401	12,363	9,038	19,572	11,890	7,682	1,773	461	1,312	56	12	44
15 " 20	...	14,470	7,910	6,560	8,279	6,172	2,107	6,012	1,679	4,333	179	59	120
20 " 40	...	60,002	31,430	28,572	10,127	8,764	1,363	46,233	21,175	25,058	3,642	1,491	2,151
40 " 60	...	30,149	15,920	14,229	1,402	1,123	279	21,835	12,905	8,930	6,912	1,892	5,020
60 and over	...	10,277	5,489	4,788	350	272	78	5,032	3,693	1,339	4,895	1,524	3,371
Total	...	**208,868**	**110,101**	**98,767**	**112,117**	**65,149**	**46,968**	**81,060**	**39,973**	**41,087**	**15,691**	**4,979**	**10,712**
						BANNU.							
0 and under 5	...	35,283	17,405	17,878	35,283	17,405	17,878	...	...	...	...	...	...
5 " 10	...	41,326	21,824	19,502	41,155	21,801	19,354	163	23	140	8	...	8
10 " 15	...	21,358	12,213	9,145	20,089	11,877	8,212	1,229	321	908	40	15	25
15 " 20	...	15,111	8,624	6,487	9,527	6,940	2,587	5,446	1,614	3,832	138	70	68
20 " 40	...	69,460	36,461	32,999	13,076	10,683	2,393	52,309	23,957	28,352	4,075	1,821	2,254
40 " 60	...	33,958	18,027	15,931	1,608	1,227	381	24,518	14,546	9,972	7,832	2,254	5,578
60 and over	...	8,878	4,959	3,919	325	231	94	4,187	3,246	941	4,366	1,482	2,884
Total	...	**225,374**	**119,513**	**105,861**	**121,063**	**70,164**	**50,899**	**87,852**	**43,707**	**44,145**	**16,459**	**5,642**	**10,817**
						DERA ISMAIL KHAN.							
0 and under 5	...	33,344	17,090	16,254	33,344	17,090	16,254	...	...	...	...	...	...
5 " 10	...	35,104	19,144	15,960	34,951	19,093	15,858	146	50	96	7	1	6
10 " 15	...	23,015	13,640	9,375	21,291	13,339	7,952	1,689	291	1,398	35	10	25
15 " 20	...	15,862	9,096	6,766	9,735	7,375	2,360	5,982	1,669	4,313	145	52	93
20 " 40	...	71,106	37,676	33,430	11,841	10,682	1,159	54,882	25,168	29,714	4,383	1,826	2,557
40 " 60	...	35,694	18,754	16,940	1,401	1,111	290	25,649	15,250	10,399	8,644	2,393	6,251
60 and over	...	10,867	5,716	5,151	310	205	105	5,033	3,790	1,243	5,524	1,721	3,803
Total	...	**224,992**	**121,116**	**103,876**	**112,873**	**68,895**	**43,978**	**93,381**	**46,218**	**47,163**	**18,738**	**6,003**	**12,735**
						TRANS-FRONTIER POSTS.							
0 and under 5	...	149	78	71	149	78	71	...	...	...	...	...	...
5 " 10	...	168	108	60	165	105	60	3	3	...	...	...	...
10 " 15	...	193	159	34	187	154	33	4	3	1	2	2	...
15 " 20	...	1,259	1,228	31	990	976	14	214	197	17	55	55	...
20 " 40	...	6,556	6,367	189	2,770	2,765	5	3,575	3,391	184	211	211	...
40 " 60	...	1,140	1,080	60	136	136	...	868	837	31	136	107	29
60 and over	...	140	126	14	4	4	...	74	70	4	62	52	10
Total	...	**9,605**	**9,146**	**459**	**4,401**	**4,218**	**183**	**4,738**	**4,501**	**237**	**466**	**427**	**39**

TABLE VII.

Age, Sex and Civil Condition—Part II.—District Tables—Hindus.

Age.	Population.			Unmarried.			Married.			Widowed.		
	Persons	Males.	Females.	Persons.	Males.	Females.	Persons.	Males.	Females.	Persons.	Males.	Females.
1	2	3	4	5	6	7	8	9	10	11	12	13
HAZARA.												
0 and under 5 ...	2,851	1,477	1,374	2,851	1,477	1,374	...	...	...	...	...	...
5 „ 10 ...	2,659	1,393	1,266	2.631	1,391	1,240	28	2	26	...	...	...
10 „ 15 ...	2,352	1,378	974	2,101	1,344	757	247	33	214	4	1	3
15 „ 20 ...	2,531	1,669	862	1,470	1,374	96	1,029	285	744	32	10	22
20 „ 40 ...	9,402	6,204	3.198	2,608	2,568	40	6,120	3,354	2,766	674	282	392
40 „ 60 ...	3,403	2,022	1,381	240	231	9	2,027	1,395	632	1,136	396	740
60 and over ...	1,191	739	452	74	73	1	503	431	72	614	235	379
Total ...	**24.389**	**14.882**	**9.507**	**11.975**	**8.458**	**3.517**	**9.954**	**5.500**	**4.454**	**2,460**	**924**	**1.536**
PESHAWAR.												
0 and under 5 ...	3,728	1,906	1,822	3,728	1,906	1,822	...	...	...	...	...	...
5 „ 10 ...	3,754	2,013	1,741	3,726	2,001	1,725	28	12	16	...	...	...
10 „ 15 ...	3,231	2,058	1,173	2,816	1,979	837	407	75	332	8	4	4
15 „ 20 ...	3,381	2,223	1,158	1,876	1,743	133	1,440	451	989	65	29	36
20 „ 40 ...	14,145	9,846	4,299	3,460	3,360	100	9,470	5,766	3,704	1,215	720	495
40 „ 60 ...	5,450	3,544	1,906	473	439	34	3,363	2,465	898	1,614	640	974
60 and over ...	1,678	1,009	669	87	80	7	685	565	120	906	364	542
Total ...	**35.367**	**22.599**	**12.768**	**16.166**	**11.508**	**4.658**	**15.393**	**9.334**	**6.059**	**3.808**	**1.757**	**2.051**
KOHAT.												
0 and under 5 ...	1,217	627	590	1,217	627	590	...	...	...	...	...	...
5 „ 10 ...	1,322	601	661	1,309	658	651	13	3	10	...	...	...
10 „ 15 ...	1,054	611	443	918	575	343	126	29	97	10	7	3
15 „ 20 ...	1,007	644	363	562	497	65	428	142	286	17	5	12
20 „ 40 ...	4.375	3,051	1,324	935	908	27	3,075	1,966	1,109	365	177	188
40 „ 60 ...	1,521	947	574	92	83	9	978	720	258	451	144	307
60 and over ...	352	217	135	8	6	2	142	123	19	202	88	114
Total ...	**10.848**	**6.758**	**4.090**	**5.041**	**3.354**	**1.687**	**4.762**	**2.983**	**1.779**	**1.045**	**421**	**624**
BANNU.												
0 and under 5 ...	2,911	1,419	1,492	2,911	1.419	1,492	...	...	...	...	...	...
5 „ 10 ...	3,112	1,555	1,557	3,084	1,544	1,540	25	11	14	3	...	3
10 „ 15 ...	2,116	1,212	904	1,943	1,174	769	167	35	132	6	3	3
15 „ 20 ...	1,650	978	672	906	739	167	719	228	491	25	11	14
20 „ 40 ...	7,079	4,210	2,869	1,179	1,128	51	5,264	2,774	2,490	636	308	328
40 „ 60 ...	3,076	1,836	1,240	151	140	11	1,961	1,381	580	964	315	649
60 and over ...	777	438	339	35	31	4	308	239	69	434	168	266
Total ...	**20,721**	**11,648**	**9.073**	**10 209**	**6 175**	**4.034**	**8.444**	**4.668**	**3.776**	**2.068**	**805**	**1.263**
DERA ISMAIL KHAN.												
0 and under 5 ...	3,597	1,803	1,794	3,597	1,803	1,794	...	...	...	...	...	...
5 „ 10 ...	3,833	2,082	1,751	3,819	2,079	1,740	12	3	9	2	...	2
10 „ 15 ...	3,383	1,895	1,488	3,156	1,832	1,324	221	60	161	6	3	3
15 „ 20 ...	2 432	1,438	994	1,306	1,074	232	1,093	345	748	33	19	14
20 „ 40 ...	9,573	5,205	4,368	1,557	1,389	168	6,994	3,464	3,530	1,022	352	670
40 „ 60 ...	4,552	2,463	2,089	247	229	18	2,614	1,753	861	1,691	481	1,210
60 and over ...	1,247	624	623	61	56	5	435	347	88	751	221	530
Total ...	**28,617**	**15,510**	**13.107**	**13.743**	**8.462**	**5.281**	**11.369**	**5.972**	**5.397**	**3.505**	**1.076**	**2.429**
TRANS-FRONTIER POSTS.												
0 and under 5 ...	130	77	53	130	77	53	...	...	...	...	...	...
5 „ 10 ...	101	56	45	99	54	45	2	2	...	...	...	...
10 „ 15 ...	124	89	35	104	77	27	19	11	8	1	1	...
15 „ 20 ...	249	208	41	155	153	2	88	49	39	6	6	...
20 „ 40 ...	1,675	1,557	118	587	586	1	1,001	893	108	87	78	9
40 „ 60 ...	365	312	53	34	34	...	280	245	35	51	33	18
60 and over ...	42	36	6	6	6	...	19	18	1	17	12	5
Total ...	**2,686**	**2.335**	**351**	**1.115**	**987**	**128**	**1.409**	**1.218**	**191**	**162**	**130**	**82**

TABLE VII.

Age, Sex and Civil Condition.—Part II—District Totals—Sikhs.

Age.	Population.			Unmarried.			Married.			Widowed.		
	Persons.	Males.	Females.	Persons.	Males.	Females.	Persons.	Males.	Females.	Persons.	Males.	Females.
1	2	3	4	5	6	7	8	9	10	11	12	13
HAZARA.												
0 and under 5 ...	642	336	306	642	336	306	...	...	...	...	...	...
5 " 10 ...	709	402	307	701	399	302	8	3	5	...	...	...
10 " 15 ...	697	432	265	626	420	206	67	12	55	4	...	4
15 " 20 ...	472	277	195	250	225	25	214	47	167	8	5	3
20 " 40 ...	1,901	1,233	668	463	450	13	1,301	701	600	137	82	55
40 " 60 ...	750	464	286	34	28	6	546	370	176	170	66	104
60 and over ...	318	195	123	16	13	3	136	103	33	166	79	87
Total ...	**5,489**	**3,339**	**2,150**	**2,732**	**1,871**	**861**	**2,272**	**1,236**	**1,036**	**485**	**232**	**253**
PESHAWAR.												
0 and under 5 ...	1,684	896	788	1,684	896	788	...	...	...	...	...	...
5 " 10 ...	1,642	873	769	1,631	871	760	11	2	9	...	...	...
10 " 15 ...	1,334	837	497	1,159	806	353	170	29	141	5	2	3
15 " 20 ...	1,536	1,085	451	935	851	84	568	219	349	33	15	18
20 " 40 ...	6,935	5,006	1,929	2,070	2,024	46	4,302	2,665	1,637	563	317	246
40 " 60 ...	2,231	1,449	782	167	165	2	1,454	1,071	383	610	213	397
60 and over ...	834	484	350	52	40	12	291	254	37	491	190	301
Total ...	**16,196**	**10,630**	**5,566**	**7,698**	**5,653**	**2,045**	**6,796**	**4,240**	**2,556**	**1,702**	**737**	**965**
KOHAT.												
0 and under 5 ...	193	107	86	193	107	86	...	...	...	...	...	...
5 " 10 ...	219	103	116	215	102	113	3	...	3	1	1	...
10 " 15 ...	192	131	61	173	127	46	19	4	15	...	...	...
15 " 20 ...	271	193	78	165	154	11	102	36	66	4	3	1
20 " 40 ...	1,516	1,301	215	624	618	6	782	598	184	110	85	25
40 " 60 ...	269	195	74	18	18	...	207	153	54	44	24	20
60 and over ...	79	39	40	...	...	...	40	23	17	39	16	23
Total ...	**2,739**	**2,069**	**670**	**1,388**	**1,126**	**262**	**1,153**	**814**	**339**	**198**	**129**	**69**
BANNU.												
0 and under 5 ...	426	196	230	426	196	230	...	...	...	...	...	...
5 " 10 ...	491	301	190	490	301	189	1	...	1	...	...	...
10 " 15 ...	446	302	144	420	296	124	25	6	19	1	...	1
15 " 20 ...	468	352	116	320	295	25	144	54	90	4	3	1
20 " 40 ...	1,354	892	462	230	221	9	1,021	610	411	103	61	42
40 " 60 ...	458	263	195	18	14	4	285	201	84	155	48	107
60 and over ...	103	56	47	8	8	...	28	23	5	67	25	42
Total ...	**3,746**	**2,362**	**1,384**	**1,912**	**1,331**	**581**	**1,504**	**894**	**610**	**330**	**137**	**193**
DERA ISMAIL KHAN.												
0 and under 5 ...	179	91	88	179	91	88	...	...	...	...	...	...
5 " 10 ...	185	109	76	182	108	74	3	1	2	...	...	...
10 " 15 ...	142	76	66	130	71	59	12	5	7	...	...	...
15 " 20 ...	206	159	47	131	118	13	72	38	34	3	3	...
20 " 40 ...	1,184	949	235	410	407	3	690	485	205	84	57	27
40 " 60 ...	221	146	75	13	12	1	155	108	47	53	26	27
60 and over ...	58	37	21	2	2	...	28	21	7	28	14	14
Total ...	**2,175**	**1,567**	**608**	**1,047**	**809**	**238**	**960**	**658**	**302**	**168**	**100**	**68**
TRANS-FRONTIER POSTS.												
0 and under 5 ...	24	12	12	24	12	12	...	...	...	...	...	...
5 " 10 ...	25	15	10	24	14	10	1	1	...	...	...	...
10 " 15 ...	31	24	7	29	22	7	2	2	...	...	...	...
15 " 20 ...	82	75	7	52	52	...	29	23	6	1	...	1
20 " 40 ...	868	845	23	422	421	1	396	375	21	50	49	1
40 " 60 ...	72	68	4	11	11	...	53	50	3	8	7	1
60 and over ...	12	11	1	1	1	...	7	7	...	4	3	1
Total ...	**1,114**	**1,050**	**64**	**563**	**533**	**30**	**458**	**458**	**30**	**63**	**59**	**4**

TABLE VII.

Age, Sex and Civil Condition.—Part II.—District Totals.—(Christians).

Age.	Population.			Unmarried.			Married.			Widowed.		
	Persons.	Males.	Females.	Persons.	Males.	Females.	Persons.	Males.	Females.	Persons.	Males.	Females.
1	2	3	4	5	6	7	8	9	10	11	12	13
HAZARA.												
0 and under 5 ...	17	10	7	17	10	7	...	...	...	...	...	...
5 " 10 ...	2	...	2	2	...	2	...	...	...	...	...	...
10 " 15 ...	1	...	1	1	...	1	...	...	...	...	...	...
15 " 20 ...	6	3	3	4	3	1	2	...	2	...	...	...
20 " 40 ...	116	82	34	64	54	10	50	28	22	2	...	2
40 " 60 ...	31	23	8	7	5	2	21	18	3	3	...	3
60 and over ...	5	2	3	...	...	...	3	2	1	2	...	2
Total ...	**178**	**120**	**58**	**95**	**72**	**23**	**76**	**48**	**28**	**7**	..	**7**
PESHAWAR.												
0 and under 5 ...	306	170	136	306	170	136	...	...		...	...	...
5 " 10 ...	208	102	106	208	102	106	...	...	...	...	...	...
10 " 15 ...	90	41	49	86	38	48	4	3	1	...	...	...
15 " 20 ...	142	87	55	115	82	33	25	5	20	2	...	2
20 " 40 ...	4,534	4,109	425	3,836	3,763	73	679	331	348	19	15	4
40 " 60 ...	280	198	82	53	40	13	202	147	55	25	11	14
60 and over ...	44	20	24	2	1	1	26	17	9	16	2	14
Total ..	**5,804**	**4,727**	**877**	**4,606**	**4,196**	**410**	**936**	**503**	**433**	**62**	**28**	**34**
KOHAT.												
0 and under 5 ...	26	12	14	26	12	14	...	...	...	..	...	...
5 " 10 ...	5	3	2	5	3	2	...	...	...	...	...	...
10 " 15 ...	2	1	1	2	1	1	...	...	...	...	...	...
15 " 20 ...	9	5	4	6	4	2	3	1	2	...	...	...
20 " 40 ...	139	95	44	69	60	9	67	33	34	3	2	1
40 " 60 ...	41	32	9	8	7	1	28	22	6	5	3	2
60 and over ...	...	...	...	...	...	...	...	...	...	...	...	...
Total ...	**222**	**148**	**74**	**116**	**87**	**29**	**98**	**56**	**42**	**8**	**6**	**8**
BANNU.												
0 and under 5 ...	34	21	13	34	21	13	..	...	...	...	...	...
5 " 10 ...	18	10	8	18	10	8	...	...	...	...	...	...
10 " 15 ...	9	7	2	9	7	2	...	...	...	...	...	...
15 " 20 ...	25	21	4	22	19	3	3	2	1	...	...	...
20 " 40 ...	124	95	29	60	57	3	58	34	24	6	4	2
40 " 60 ...	35	30	5	1	1	...	30	26	4	4	3	1
60 and over ...	...	...	...	...	...	...	...	...	...	...	...	...
Total ...	**245**	**184**	**61**	**144**	**115**	**29**	**91**	**62**	**29**	**10**	**7**	**3**
DERA ISMAIL KHAN.												
0 and under 5	41	22	19	41	22	19	...	..	...	...	..	...
5 " 10	15	3	12	15	3	12	.	...	...	...	...	...
10 " 15	7	4	3	7	4	3	...	...	...	..	...	...
15 " 20	5	2	3	3	2	1	1	...	1	1	...	1
20 " 40 ...	223	171	52	143	128	15	74	40	34	6	3	3
40 " 60 ...	44	33	11	7	5	2	29	22	7	8	6	2
60 and over	1	...	1	...	...	...	...	...	...	1	...	1
Total ..	**336**	**235**	**101**	**216**	**164**	**52**	**104**	**62**	**42**	**16**	**9**	**7**
TRANS-FRONTIER POSTS.												
0 and under 5 ...	9	3	6	9	3	6	...	..	...	...	...	...
5 " 10 .	4	4	...	4	4	...	...	...	..	...	..	...
10 " 15 .	3	3	...	..	...	...	3	3	...	...	...	...
15 " 20 ..	4	4	...	2	2	...	2	2		...	...	...
20 " 40 ...	100	85	15	71	67	4	29	18	11	...	...	...
40 " 60 ...	11	9	2	5	4	1	6	5	1	...	...	...
60 and over ...	2	2	...				1	1	...	1	1	...
Total ...	**133**	**110**	**23**	**91**	**80**	**11**	**41**	**29**	**12**	**1**	**1**	...

Corrigenda to Table VIII.

PART I.

PAGE xxxiv.--LINE 11 column 5 *for* "41,146" *read* "14,146."

TABLE VIII.

Education by religion and age.

PART I.—General Table.

Showing the total literate population of the Province (*a*) all for religions (*b*) for each religion.

The figures for Christians (total literate) include 302 Native Christians (223 males and 79 females), of whom 163 (128 males and 35 females) are literate in English.

TABLE VIII.

Education by Religion and Age.—Part I.—General Table.

Religion.	Age.	Population. Total. Persons	Population. Total. Males.	Population. Total. Females.	Population. Literate. Persons.	Population. Literate. Males.	Population. Literate. Females.	Population. Illiterate. Persons.	Population. Illiterate. Males.	Population. Illiterate. Females.	Literate in English. Persons.	Literate in English. Males.	Literate in English. Females.
1	2	3	4	5	6	7	8	9	10	11	12	13	14
All Religions	0 & under 10	681,512	353,043	328,469	1,437	1,013	424	680,075	352,030	328,045	171	108	63
	10 „ 15	238,834	139,789	99,045	6,050	5,186	864	232,784	134,603	98,181	472	448	24
	15 „ 20	165,708	93,055	72,653	8,535	7,656	879	157,173	85,399	71,774	1,243	1,202	41
	20 & over ...	1,124,417	608,856	515,561	59,412	55,516	3,896	1,065,005	553,340	511,665	8,966	8,322	644
	Total ...	**2,210,471**	**1,194,743**	**1,015,728**	**75,434**	**69,371**	**6,063**	**2,135,037**	**1,125,372**	**1,009,665**	**10,852**	**10,080**	**772**
Muhammadan ...	0 & under 10	645,186	334,169	311,017	408	344	64	644,778	333,825	310,953	10	10	..
	10 „ 15	223,619	130,688	92,931	2,515	2,336	179	221,104	128,352	92,752	196	195	1
	15 „ 20	151,229	83,631	67,598	3,577	3,353	224	147,652	80,278	67,374	494	491	3
	20 & over ...	1,029,565	545,934	483,631	21,680	20,995	685	1,007,885	524,939	482,946	1,393	1,381	12
	Total ...	**2,049,599**	**1,094,422**	**955,177**	**28,180**	**27,028**	**1,152**	**2,021,419**	**1,067,394**	**954,025**	**2,093**	**2,077**	**16**
Hindu ...	0 & under 10	29,215	15,069	41,146	613	415	198	28,602	14,654	13,948	6	5	1
	10 „ 15	12,260	7,243	5,017	2,671	2,207	464	9,589	5,036	4,553	202	199	3
	15 „ 20	11,250	7,160	4,090	3,654	3,225	429	7,596	3,935	3,661	562	553	9
	20 & over ...	69,903	44,260	25,643	23,466	2,1793	1,673	46,437	22,467	23,970	1,844	1,830	14
	Total ...	**122,628**	**73,732**	**48,896**	**30,404**	**27,640**	**2,764**	**92,224**	**46,092**	**46,132**	**2,614**	**2,587**	**27**
Sikh ...	0 & under 10	6,419	3,441	2,978	249	153	96	6,170	3,288	2,882	...	...	...
	10 „ 15	2,842	1,802	1,040	807	609	198	2,035	1,193	842	30	30	...
	15 „ 20	3,035	2,141	894	1,181	997	184	1,854	1,144	710	84	84	...
	20 & over ...	19,163	13,633	5,530	8,847	7,945	902	10,316	5,688	4,628	416	407	9
	Total ...	**31,459**	**21,017**	**10,442**	**11,084**	**9,704**	**1,380**	**20,375**	**11,313**	**9,062**	**530**	**521**	**9**
Christian ...	0 & under 10	685	360	325	167	101	66	518	259	259	155	93	62
	10 „ 15	112	56	56	57	34	23	55	22	33	44	24	20
	15 „ 20	191	122	69	121	80	41	70	42	28	102	73	29
	20 & over ...	5,730	4,986	744	5,375	4,741	634	355	245	110	5,276	4,667	609
	Total ...	**6,718**	**5,524**	**1,194**	**5,720**	**4,956**	**764**	**998**	**568**	**430**	**5,577**	**4,857**	**720**
Parsi ...	0 & under 10	2	2	...	...	...	...	2	2	...	...	...	...
	10 „ 15	...	...	...	...	...	...	...	...	...	...	...	...
	15 „ 20	2	1	1	1	1	...	1	...	1	1	1	...
	20 & over ...	45	38	7	39	38	1	6	...	6	35	35	...
	Total ...	**49**	**41**	**8**	**40**	**39**	**1**	**9**	**2**	**7**	**36**	**36**	...
Jew ...	0 & under 10	5	2	3	...	...	...	5	2	3	...	...	...
	10 „ 15	1	...	1	...	...	...	1	...	1	...	...	...
	15 „ 20	...	...	...	...	...	...	...	...	...	...	...	...
	20 & over ...	8	3	5	3	2	1	5	4	4	2	2	...
	Total ...	**14**	**5**	**9**	**3**	**2**	**1**	**11**	**3**	**8**	**2**	**2**	...
Jain ...	0 & under 10	...	...	...	...	...	...	...	...	...	...	...	...
	10 „ 15	...	...	...	...	...	...	...	...	...	...	...	...
	15 „ 20	1	...	1	1	...	1	...	...	...	...	...	...
	20 & over ...	3	2	1	2	2	...	1	...	1	...	...	...
	Total ...	**4**	**2**	**2**	**3**	**2**	**1**	**1**	—	**1**	...	...	...

TABLE VIII.

PART II.—District Tables.

In this part are shown the figures for all religions and for each of the main religions only.

TABLE VIII.

Education by Religion and Age.—Part II—District Tables.—All religions.

District, etc.	Age.	Population. Total. Persons.	Total. Males.	Total. Females.	Literate. Persons.	Literate. Males.	Literate. Females.	Illiterate. Persons.	Illiterate. Males.	Illiterate. Females.	Literate in English. Persons.	Literate in English. Males.	Literate in English. Females.
1	2	3	4	5	6	7	8	9	10	11	12	13	14
Hazara ...	0 and under 10	189,265	96,875	92,390	151	111	40	189,114	96,764	92,350	...	...	...
	10 „ 15	70,865	40,869	29,996	1,195	1,029	166	69,670	39,840	29,830	66	65	1
	15 „ 20	47,847	25,476	22,371	1,600	1,439	161	46,247	24,037	22,210	166	162	4
	20 and over ...	295,051	157,245	137,806	9,946	9,421	525	285,105	147,824	137,281	615	564	51
	Total ...	**603,028**	**320,465**	**282,563**	**12,892**	**12,000**	**892**	**590,136**	**308,465**	**281,671**	**847**	**791**	**56**
Peshawar ...	0 and under 10	256,182	134,236	121,946	813	500	313	255,369	133,736	121,633	153	95	58
	10 „ 15	94,492	56,190	38,302	2,447	2,023	424	92,045	54,167	37,878	214	195	19
	15 „ 20	64,751	36,642	28,109	3,803	3,329	474	60,948	33,313	27,635	501	475	26
	20 and over ...	449,584	243,353	206,231	25,125	22,651	2,474	424,459	220,702	203,757	6,068	5,632	436
	Total ...	**865,009**	**470,421**	**394,588**	**32,188**	**28,503**	**3,685**	**832,821**	**441,918**	**390,903**	**6,836**	**6,397**	**639**
Kohat ...	0 and under 10	75,556	38,504	37,052	78	70	8	75,478	38,434	37,044	2	2	...
	10 „ 15	22,650	13,106	9,544	416	385	31	22,234	12,721	9,513	32	30	2
	15 „ 20	15,757	8,752	7,005	593	545	48	15,164	8,207	6,957	113	108	5
	20 and over ...	108,727	58,719	50,008	5,825	5,653	172	102,902	53,066	49,836	687	631	56
	Total ...	**222,690**	**119,081**	**103,609**	**6,912**	**6,653**	**259**	**215,778**	**112,428**	**103,350**	**834**	**771**	**63**
Bannu ...	0 and under 10	83,601	42,731	40,870	144	132	12	83,457	42,599	40,858	3	3	...
	10 „ 15	23,929	13,734	10,195	612	559	53	23,317	13,175	10,142	57	56	1
	15 „ 20	17,254	9,975	7,279	916	876	40	16,338	9,099	7,239	204	201	3
	20 and over ...	125,302	67,267	58,035	6,830	6,627	203	118,472	60,640	57,832	490	461	29
	Total ...	**250,086**	**133,707**	**116,379**	**8,502**	**8,194**	**308**	**241,584**	**125,513**	**116,071**	**754**	**721**	**33**
Dera Ismail Khan ...	0 and under 10	76,298	40,344	35,954	248	198	50	76,050	40,146	35,904	12	7	5
	10 „ 15	26,547	15,615	10,932	1,345	1,166	179	25,202	14,449	10,753	103	102	1
	15 „ 20	18,505	10,695	7,810	1,523	1,378	145	16,982	9,317	7,665	250	247	3
	20 and over ...	134,770	71,774	62,996	9,376	8,892	484	125,394	62,882	62,512	807	752	55
	Total ...	**256,120**	**138,428**	**117,692**	**12,492**	**11,634**	**858**	**243,628**	**126,794**	**116,834**	**1,172**	**1,108**	**64**
Trans-Frontier Posts	0 and under 10	610	353	257	3	2	1	607	351	256	1	1	...
	10 „ 15	351	275	76	35	24	11	316	251	65	...	...	...
	15 „ 20	1,594	1,515	79	100	89	11	1,494	1,426	68	9	9	...
	20 and over ...	10,983	10,498	485	2,310	2,272	38	8,673	8,226	447	299	282	17
	Total ...	**13,538**	**12,641**	**897**	**2,448**	**2,337**	**61**	**11,090**	**10,254**	**836**	**309**	**292**	**17**

TABLE VIII.

Education by Religion and Age.—Part II.—District Tables.—Muhammadans.

District etc.	Age.	Population. Total. Persons.	Total. Males.	Total. Females.	Literate. Persons.	Literate. Males.	Literate. Females.	Illiterate. Persons.	Illiterate. Males.	Illiterate. Females.	Literate in English. Persons.	Literate in English. Males.	Literate in English. Females.
1	2	3	4	5	6	7	8	9	10	11	12	13	14
Hazara ...	0 and under 10...	182,385	93,257	89,128	69	53	16	182,316	93,204	89,112	...	...	...
	10 „ 15...	67,815	39,059	28,756	643	577	66	67,172	38,482	28,690	37	37	...
	15 „ 20...	44,838	23,527	21,311	677	602	75	44 161	22.925	21,236	88	86	2
	20 and over ...	277,934	146,281	131,653	3,937	3,763	174	273,997	142,518	131,479	237	233	4
	Total ...	**572.972**	**302.124**	**270.848**	**5.326**	**4,995**	**331**	**567.646**	**297.129**	**270.517**	**362**	**356**	**6**
Peshawar ...	0 and under 10...	244,858	128,274	116,584	194	158	36	244,664	128,116	116,548	5	5	...
	10 „ 15...	89,837	53,254	36,583	1,101	1,023	78	88,736	52,231	36,505	92	91	1
	15 „ 20...	59,689	33,246	26,443	1,903	1,810	93	57,786	31,436	26,350	221	220	1
	20 and over ...	413,404	217,648	195,756	9,037	8,687	350	404,367	208,961	195,406	399	393	6
	Total ...	**807,788**	**432.422**	**375.366**	**12.235**	**11.678**	**557**	**795.553**	**420.744**	**374.809**	**717**	**709**	**8**
Kohat ...	0 and under 10...	72,569	36,989	35,580	31	27	4	72,538	36,962	35,576	...	...	...
	10 „ 15...	21,401	12,363	9,038	182	171	11	21,219	12,192	9,027	16	16	...
	15 „ 20...	14,470	7,910	6,560	270	253	17	14,200	7,657	6,543	74	74	...
	20 and over ...	100,428	52,839	47,589	2,700	2,656	44	97,728	50,183	47,545	234	232	2
	Total ...	**208.868**	**110.101**	**98.767**	**3.183**	**3.107**	**76**	**205.685**	**108.994**	**98.691**	**324**	**322**	**2**
Bannu ...	0 and under 10...	76,609	39,229	37,380	42	39	3	76,567	39,190	37,377	...	...	...
	10 „ 15...	21,358	12,213	9,145	198	197	1	21,160	12,016	9,144	17	17	...
	15 „ 20...	15,111	8,624	6,487	228	222	6	14,883	8,402	6,481	22	22	...
	20 and over ...	112,296	59,447	52,849	2,210	2,190	20	110,086	57,257	52,829	129	129	...
	Total ...	**225.374**	**119.513**	**105.861**	**2.678**	**2.648**	**30**	**222.696**	**116.865**	**105.831**	**168**	**168**	...
Dera Ismail Khan	0 and under 10...	68,448	36,234	32,214	71	66	5	68,377	36,168	32,209	5	5	...
	10 „ 15...	23,015	13,640	9,375	378	359	19	22,637	13,281	9,356	34	34	...
	15 „ 20...	15,862	9,096	6.766	452	419	33	15,410	8,677	6,733	85	85	...
	20 and over ...	117,667	62,146	55,521	3,104	3,016	88	114,563	59,130	55,433	274	274	...
	Total ...	**224.992**	**121.116**	**103 876**	**4.005**	**3.860**	**145**	**220.987**	**117.256**	**103.731**	**398**	**398**	...
Trans-frontier posts.	0 and under 10...	317	186	131	1	1	...	316	185	131	...	...	...
	10 „ 15...	193	159	34	13	9	4	180	150	30	...	...	...
	15 „ 20...	1,259	1,228	31	47	47	...	1,212	1,181	31	4	4	...
	20 and over ...	7,836	7,573	263	692	683	9	7,144	6,890	254	120	120	...
	Total ...	**9.605**	**9.146**	**459**	**753**	**740**	**13**	**8.852**	**8,406**	**446**	**124**	**124**	...

TABLE VIII.

Education by Religion and Age.—Part II.—District Tables.—Hindus.

District etc.	Age.	Population. Total. Persons.	Total. Males.	Total. Females.	Literate. Persons.	Literate. Males.	Literate. Females.	Illiterate. Persons.	Illiterate. Males.	Illiterate. Females.	Literate in English. Persons.	Literate in English. Males.	Literate in English. Females.
1	2	3	4	5	6	7	8	9	10	11	12	13	14
Hazara ...	0 and under 10 ..	5,510	2,870	2,640	42	33	9	5,468	2,837	2,631	...	...	...
	10 " 15...	2,352	1,378	974	436	356	80	1,916	1,022	894	22	22	...
	15 " 20...	2,531	1,669	862	781	715	66	1,750	954	796	67	67	...
	20 and over ...	13,996	8,965	5,031	4,959	4,725	234	9,037	4,240	4,797	191	189	2
	Total ...	**24,389**	**14,882**	**9,507**	**6,218**	**5,829**	**389**	**18,171**	**9,053**	**9,118**	**280**	**278**	**2**
Peshawar ...	0 and under 10 ..	7,482	3,919	3,563	307	164	143	7,175	3,755	3,420	4	3	1
	10 " 15...	3,231	2,058	1,173	816	622	194	2,415	1,436	979	77	75	2
	15 " 20 ..	3,381	2,223	1,158	1,122	896	226	2,259	1,327	932	154	147	7
	20 and over ...	21,273	14,399	6,874	7,011	5,993	1,018	14,262	8,406	5,856	934	929	5
	Total ...	**35,367**	**22,599**	**12,768**	**9,256**	**7,675**	**1,681**	**26,111**	**14,924**	**11,187**	**1,169**	**1,154**	**15**
Kohat ...	0 and under 10...	2,539	1,288	1,251	26	25	1	2,513	1,263	1,250	1	1	..
	10 " 15...	1,054	611	443	164	149	15	890	462	428	9	8	1
	15 " 20...	1,007	644	363	232	213	19	775	431	344	25	23	2
	20 and over ...	6,248	4,215	2,033	1,889	1,840	49	4,359	2,375	1,984	219	215	4
	Total ...	**10,848**	**6,758**	**4,090**	**2,311**	**2,227**	**84**	**8,537**	**4,531**	**4,006**	**254**	**247**	**7**
Bannu ...	0 and under 10...	6,023	2,974	3,049	81	75	6	5,942	2,899	3,043	...	...	...
	10 " 15...	2,116	1,212	904	310	282	28	1,806	930	876	29	29	...
	15 " 20...	1,650	978	672	489	481	8	1,161	497	664	158	158	...
	20 and over ..	10,932	6,484	4,448	3,320	3,247	73	7,612	3,237	4,375	185	184	1
	Total ...	**20,721**	**11,648**	**9,073**	**4,200**	**4,085**	**115**	**16,521**	**7,563**	**8,958**	**372**	**371**	**1**
Dera Ismail Khan	0 and under 10...	7,430	3,885	3,545	156	118	38	7,274	3,767	3,507	1	1	...
	10 " 15...	3,383	1,895	1,488	935	789	146	2,448	1,106	1,342	65	65	...
	15 " 20...	2,432	1,438	994	995	894	101	1,437	544	893	154	154	...
	20 and over ...	15,372	8,292	7,080	5,341	5,048	293	10,031	3,244	6,787	268	266	2
	Total ...	**28,817**	**15,510**	**13,107**	**7,427**	**6,849**	**578**	**21,190**	**8,661**	**12,529**	**488**	**486**	**2**
Trans-frontier posts.	0 and under 10...	231	133	98	1	...	1	230	133	97	...	...	...
	10 " 15...	124	89	35	10	9	1	114	80	34	...	...	...
	15 " 20 ..	249	208	41	35	26	9	214	182	32	4	4	...
	20 and over ...	2,082	1,905	177	946	940	6	1,136	965	171	47	47	...
	Total ...	**2,686**	**2,335**	**351**	**992**	**975**	**17**	**1,694**	**1,360**	**334**	**51**	**51**	...

TABLE VIII.

Education by Religion and Age—Part II.—District Tables.—Sikhs.

District, etc.	Age.	Population: Total: Persons.	Males.	Females.	Literate: Persons.	Males.	Females.	Illiterate: Persons.	Males.	Females.	Literate in English: Persons.	Males.	Females.
1	2	3	4	5	6	7	8	9	10	11	12	13	14
Hazara ...	0 and under 10 ...	1,351	738	613	40	25	15	1,311	713	598	...	...	...
	10 " 15 ...	697	432	265	115	96	19	582	336	246	6	6	...
	15 " 20 ...	472	277	195	139	121	18	333	156	177	9	9	...
	20 and over ...	2,969	1,892	1,077	906	831	75	2,063	1,061	1,002	49	45	4
	Total ...	**5.489**	**3.339**	**2.150**	**1.200**	**1.073**	**127**	**4.289**	**2.266**	**2,023**	**64**	**60**	**4**
Peshawar ...	0 and under 10 ...	3,326	1,769	1,557	163	87	76	3.163	1,682	1,481	...	...	...
	10 " 15 ...	1,334	837	497	490	354	136	844	483	361	9	9	...
	15 " 20 ...	1,536	1,085	451	679	554	125	857	531	326	41	41	...
	20 and over ...	10,000	6,939	3,061	4,454	3,787	667	5,546	3,152	2,394	186	182	4
	Total ...	**16.196**	**10.630**	**5.566**	**5.786**	**4.782**	**1.004**	**10.410**	**5.848**	**4.562**	**236**	**232**	**4**
Kohat ...	0 and under 10 ...	412	210	202	20	17	3	392	193	199	...	...	...
	10 " 15 ...	192	131	61	68	64	4	124	67	57	5	5	...
	15 " 20 ...	271	193	78	86	77	9	185	116	69	9	9	...
	20 and over ...	1,864	1,535	329	1,067	1,038	29	797	497	300	65	65	...
	Total ...	**2.739**	**2.069**	**670**	**1.241**	**1.196**	**45**	**1.498**	**873**	**625**	**79**	**79**	...
Bannu ...	0 and under 10 ...	917	497	420	15	13	2	902	484	418	...	...	...
	10 " 15 ...	446	302	144	97	75	22	349	227	122	9	9	...
	15 " 20 ...	468	352	116	189	167	22	279	185	94	18	18	...
	20 and over ...	1,915	1,211	704	1,173	1,095	78	742	116	626	61	61	...
	Total ...	**3.740**	**2.362**	**1.334**	**1.474**	**1.350**	**124**	**2.272**	**1.012**	**1.260**	**88**	**88**	...
Dera Ismail Khan ...	0 and under 10 ...	364	200	164	11	11	...	353	189	164	...	...	...
	10 " 15 ...	142	76	66	25	14	11	117	62	55	1	1	...
	15 " 20 ...	206	159	47	71	63	8	135	96	39	6	6	...
	20 and over ...	1,463	1,132	331	688	641	47	775	491	284	34	33	1
	Total ...	**2.175**	**1.567**	**608**	**795**	**729**	**66**	**1.380**	**838**	**542**	**41**	**40**	**1**
Trans-frontier posts ...	0 and under 10 ...	49	27	22	...	...	...	49	27	22	...	...	...
	10 " 15 ...	31	24	7	12	6	6	19	18	1	...	...	...
	15 " 20 ...	82	75	7	17	15	2	65	60	5	1	1	...
	20 and over ...	952	924	28	559	553	6	393	371	22	21	21	...
	Total ...	**1.114**	**1.050**	**64**	**588**	**574**	**14**	**526**	**476**	**60**	**22**	**22**	...

TABLE VIII.

Education by Religion and Age.—Part II.—District Tables—Christians.

District, etc.	Age.	Population: Total: Persons.	Total: Males.	Total: Females.	Literate: Persons.	Literate: Males.	Literate: Females.	Illiterate: Persons.	Illiterate: Males.	Illiterate: Females.	Literate in English: Persons.	Literate in English: Males.	Literate in English: Females.
1	2	3	4	5	6	7	8	9	10	11	12	13	14
Hazara ...	0 and under 10 ...	19	10	9	...	...	...	19	10	9	...	...	...
	10 " 15 ...	1	...	1	1	...	1	...	...	...	1	...	1
	15 " 20 ...	6	3	3	3	1	2	3	2	1	2	...	2
	20 and over ...	152	107	45	144	102	42	8	5	3	138	97	41
	Total ...	**178**	**120**	**58**	**148**	**103**	**45**	**30**	**17**	**13**	**141**	**97**	**44**
Peshawar ...	0 and under 10 ...	514	272	242	149	91	58	365	181	184	144	87	57
	10 " 15 ...	90	41	49	40	24	16	50	17	33	36	20	16
	15 " 20 ...	142	87	55	97	68	29	45	19	26	84	66	18
	20 and over ...	4,858	4,327	531	4,581	4,144	437	277	183	94	4,514	4,093	421
	Total ...	**5,604**	**4,727**	**877**	**4,867**	**4,327**	**540**	**737**	**400**	**337**	**4,778**	**4,266**	**512**
Kohat	0 and under 10 ...	31	15	16	1	1	...	30	14	16	1	1	...
	10 " 15 ...	2	1	1	2	1	1	...	...	...	2	1	1
	15 " 20 ...	9	5	4	5	2	3	4	3	1	5	2	3
	20 and over ...	180	127	53	167	117	50	13	10	3	167	117	50
	Total ...	**222**	**148**	**74**	**175**	**121**	**54**	**47**	**27**	**20**	**175**	**121**	**54**
Bannu ...	0 and under 10 ...	52	31	21	6	5	1	46	26	20	3	3	...
	10 " 15 ...	9	7	2	7	5	2	2	2	...	2	1	1
	15 " 20 ...	25	21	4	10	6	4	15	15	...	6	3	3
	20 and over ...	159	125	34	127	95	32	32	30	2	115	87	28
	Total ...	**245**	**184**	**61**	**150**	**111**	**39**	**95**	**73**	**22**	**126**	**94**	**32**
Dera Ismail Khan ...	0 and under 10 ...	56	25	31	10	3	7	46	22	24	6	1	5
	10 " 15 ...	7	4	3	7	4	3	...	...	...	3	2	1
	15 " 20 ...	5	2	3	5	2	3	...	—	...	5	2	3
	20 and over ...	268	204	64	243	187	56	25	17	8	231	179	52
	Total ...	**336**	**235**	**101**	**265**	**196**	**69**	**71**	**39**	**32**	**245**	**184**	**61**
Trans-frontier posts ...	0 and under 10 ...	13	7	6	1	1	...	12	6	6	1	1	...
	10 " 15 ...	3	3	...	...	...	...	3	3	...	...	...	...
	15 " 20 ...	4	4	...	1	1	...	3	3	...	...	...	...
	20 and over ...	113	96	17	113	96	17	...	...	...	111	94	17
	Total ...	**133**	**110**	**23**	**115**	**98**	**17**	**18**	**12**	**6**	**112**	**95**	**17**

TABLE IX.

Education by selected Tribes, Castes or Races.

This table, the figures in which are for the whole Province, is intended to show the extent to which literacy is to be found among the different tribes and castes living therein. It deals only with those groups which in 1901 contributed more than 2 per mille to the total population. The figures for the total population of particular tribes and castes will not always be found to agree with those shown in Table XIII, owing to the inclusion in the figures of the later table of entries added during the course of compilation. In most cases a reference to Table XIII will show the additional entries which have been included in it : *e. g.* Mirasi (with Dum.)

TABLE IX.

Education by selected tribes, castes or races.

Tribe, Caste or Race.	Population.									Literate in English.		
	Total.			Literate.			Illiterate.					
	Persons.	Males.	Females.	Persons.	Males.	Females.	Persons.	Males.	Females.	Persons.	Males.	Females.
1	2	3	4	5	6	7	8	9	10	11	12	13
Arora ...	69,144	37,909	31,235	17,474	15,472	2,002	51,670	22,437	29,233	1,001	991	10
Awan ...	275,711	149,550	126,161	3,474	3,306	168	272,237	146,244	125,993	291	290	1
Baghban ...	20,471	10,881	9,590	41	39	2	20,430	10,842	9,588	2	2	...
Baluch ...	26,513	14,466	12,047	397	388	9	26,116	14,078	12,038	57	57	...
Bhatiara ...	4,331	2,209	2,122	36	25	11	4,295	2,184	2,111	1	1	...
Brahman ...	13,208	7,856	5,352	3,290	2,943	347	9,918	4,913	5,005	387	382	5
Chamar ...	4,658	2,649	2,009	29	29	...	4,629	2,620	2,009	15	15	...
Chuhra ...	5,750	3,530	2,220	144	140	4	5,606	3,390	2,216	9	9	...
Dhobi ...	14,877	8,100	6,777	166	152	14	14,711	7,948	6,763	14	14	...
Dhund ...	30,464	15,773	14,691	145	141	4	30,319	15,632	14,687	10	10	...
Gakkhar ...	6,807	3,676	3,131	176	176	...	6,631	3,500	3,131	17	17	...
Gujar ...	113,871	61,711	52,160	636	610	26	113,235	61,101	52,134	29	29	...
Jat ...	86,097	48,873	37,224	4,502	4,363	139	81,595	44,510	37,085	197	196	1
Jhinwar ...	1,987	1,299	688	164	151	13	1,823	1,148	675	5	5	...
Jolaha ...	37,390	19,999	17,391	110	107	3	37,280	19,892	17,388	4	4	...
Karal ...	22,106	11,316	10,790	98	92	6	22,008	11,224	10,784	...	...	...
Kashmiri ...	28,631	15,198	13,433	445	415	30	28,186	14,783	13,403	50	50	...
Khatri ...	35,720	21,662	14,058	10,108	8,819	1,289	25,612	12,843	12,769	1,213	1,195	18
Kumhar ...	22,664	11,705	10,959	140	135	5	22,524	11,570	10,954	7	7	...
Lohar ...	28,589	15,331	13,258	187	181	6	28,402	15,150	13,252	6	6	...
Machhi ...	4,019	2,163	1,856	10	10	...	4,009	2,153	1,856	...	...	...
Maliar ...	19,950	10,412	9,538	51	46	5	19,899	10,366	9,533	1	1	...
Mallah ...	4,805	2,696	2,109	11	9	2	4,794	2,687	2,107	...	...	...
Mirasi ...	7,366	3,940	3,426	38	38	...	7,328	3,902	3,426	...	...	...
Mochi ...	23,040	12,383	10,657	105	96	9	22,935	12,287	10,648	4	4	...
Moghal ...	14,865	8,269	6,596	540	526	14	14,325	7,743	6,582	71	71	...
Musalli (with Kutana)	13,254	7,287	5,967	28	26	2	13,226	7,261	5,965	2	2	...
Nai ...	24,777	13,075	11,702	107	100	7	24,670	12,975	11,695	7	7	...
Paracha ...	11,553	6,278	5,275	475	466	9	11,078	5,812	5,266	34	34	...
Pathan ...	845,183	449,500	395,683	10,672	10,420	252	834,511	439,080	395,431	941	937	4
Qassab ...	8,721	4,559	4,162	61	58	3	8,660	4,501	4,159	4	4	...
Qureshi ...	20,939	11,058	9,881	1,079	1,033	46	19,860	10,025	9,835	119	118	1
Rajput ...	15,157	10,637	4,520	2,255	2,184	71	12,902	8,453	4,449	249	246	3
Saiad ...	75,115	39,230	35,885	2,321	2,171	150	72,794	37,059	35,735	239	237	2
Sarara ...	8,507	4,616	3,891	21	21	...	8,486	4,595	3,891	...	...	...
Shekh ...	17,892	10,013	7,879	1,051	976	75	16,841	9,037	7,804	211	209	2
Sonar ...	9,714	5,033	4,681	326	265	61	9,388	4,768	4,620	14	14	...
Swathi ...	38,329	20,181	18,148	494	478	16	37,835	19,703	18,132	12	12	...
Tanaoli ...	63,985	33,349	30,636	373	325	48	63,612	33,024	30,588	17	17	...
Tarkhan ...	42,618	22,764	19,854	307	295	12	42,311	22,469	19,842	13	13	...
Teli ...	6,932	3,678	3,254	47	47	...	6,885	3,631	3,254	...	...	...

TABLE X.

Language.

In this table languages have been classified according to the locality in which they are spoken ; and no attempt has been made to arrange them by linguistic families. The names appearing in column 1 are those which were returned in the Census Schedules. In the case of the language shown as Punjabi the name returned is misleading, for the bulk of the persons who returned their language as 'Punjabi' are not speakers of dialects of the true Punjabi, but of the (quite distinct) tongue, styled in accordance with the classification of the Linguistic Survey, 'Lahnda' or Western Punjabi. As far as concerns the majority of its speakers, Punjabi in this table is the same as 'Hindko' or 'Hindki.' For an estimate of the number of persons whose language is Punjabi proper, a reference should be made to Chapter IX of this Report.

TABLE X.

Language.

Language.	N.-W. F. P.			Hazara.			Peshawar.		
	Persons.	Males.	Females.	Persons.	Males.	Females.	Persons.	Males.	Females.
1	2	3	4	5	6	7	8	9	10
All Languages.	**2,210,471**	**1,194,743**	**1,015,728**	**603,028**	**320,465**	**282,563**	**865,009**	**470,421**	**394,588**
A.—Provincial Vernaculars—Total.	**2,176,622**	**1,171,116**	**1,005,506**	**597,008**	**315,572**	**281,436**	**844,527**	**457,527**	**387,000**
Pushto (with Ormuri) (*a*) ...	1,229,599	655,759	573,840	29,151	14,645	14,506	709,465	378,778	330,687
Punjabi ...	848,218	462,859	385,359	483,518	256,184	227,334	130,663	75,420	55,243
Hindko (or Hindki) (*b*) ...	72,939	37,158	35,781	58,583	29,510	29,073	4,296	3,229	1,067
Gujari (with Pahari) (*c*) ...	25,668	15,183	10,485	25,641	15,156	10,485	27	27	...
Chitrali (Chitiari) (*d*) ...	41	41	...	...	...	...	41	41	...
Kohistani ...	117	87	30	85	56	29	32	31	1
Others (*e*) ...	40	29	11	30	21	9	3	1	2
B.—Vernaculars of India—Extra Provincial—Total.	**24,120**	**16,343**	**7,777**	**5,863**	**4,788**	**1,075**	**12,112**	**6,605**	**5,507**
Urdu (with Hindostani) (*f*) ...	17,455	10,675	6,780	515	292	223	11,224	5,809	5,415
Gorkhhi (Naipali) ...	5,179	4,359	820	5,140	4,350	790	38	8	30
Kashmiri ...	561	473	88	136	77	59	378	349	29
Purbi ...	359	333	26	3	3	...	318	311	7
Odki ...	95	82	13	...	...	...	...	...	...
Gujarati (with Parsi) (*g*) ...	97	89	8	37	37	...	45	38	7
Dogri ...	46	43	3	17	14	3	27	27	...
Marathi (with Goai) (*h*) ...	219	204	15	14	14	...	21	15	6
Marwari ...	49	39	10	...	...	...	17	14	3
Dehgani (Pashai) ...	16	16	...	...	...	...	16	16	...
Others (*i*) ...	44	30	14	1	1	...	28	18	10
C.—Vernaculars of Asiatic countries beyond India—Total.	**3,843**	**2,266**	**1,577**	**11**	**11**	...	**3,309**	**1,865**	**1,444**
Persian ...	3,811	2,247	1,564	9	9	...	3,280	1,848	1,432
Turki ...	16	13	3	...	...	...	16	13	3
Others (*j*) ...	16	6	10	2	2	...	13	4	9
D.—European Languages—Total	**5,886**	**5,018**	**868**	**146**	**94**	**52**	**5,061**	**4,424**	**637**
English ...	5,839	4,975	864	144	92	52	5,028	4,395	633
Portuguese ...	34	34	...	...	...	...	22	22	...
Others (*k*) ...	13	9	4	2	2	...	11	7	4

TABLE X.

Language.

Kohat.			Bannu.			Dera Ismail Khan.			Trans-frontier posts.			Remarks.
Persons.	Males.	Females.	Persons.	Males.	Females.	Persons.	Males.	Females.	Persons.	Males.	Females.	
11	12	13	14	15	16	17	18	19	20	21	22	23
222,690	**119,081**	**103,609**	**250,086**	**133,707**	**116,379**	**256,120**	**138,428**	**117,692**	**13,538**	**12,641**	**897**	
220,641	**117,628**	**103,013**	**248,720**	**132,583**	**116,137**	**253,154**	**135,961**	**117,193**	**12,572**	**11,845**	**727**	
193,383	101,487	91,896	218,845	114,890	103,955	71,015	38,610	32,405	7,740	7,349	391	
20,924	13,549	7,375	28,148	16,657	11,491	180,184	96,577	83,607	4,781	4,472	309	
6,334	2,592	3,742	1,727	1,036	691	1,950	769	1,181	49	22	27	
...	...	...	...	...	...	...	...	...	...	...	...	
...	...	...	...	...	...	...	...	...	...	...	...	
...	...	...	...	...	...	...	...	...	...	...	...	
...	...	...	...	...	...	5	5	...	2	2	...	
1,705	**1,226**	**479**	**1,237**	**1,027**	**210**	**2,713**	**2,278**	**435**	**490**	**419**	**71**	
1,521	1,051	470	1,204	1,004	200	2,531	2,129	402	460	390	70	
...	...	...	...	...	...	1	1	...	...	...	...	
8	8	...	...	...	...	11	11	...	28	28	...	
2	2	...	16	7	9	20	10	10	...	...	...	
...	...	...	...	...	...	95	82	13	...	...	...	
6	5	1	...	...	...	9	9	...	...	...	...	
...	...	...	...	...	...	2	2	...	...	...	...	
164	156	8	16	15	1	4	4	...	...	...	...	
2	2	...	...	...	...	30	23	7	...	...	...	
...	...	...	...	...	...	...	...	...	...	...	...	
2	2	...	1	1	...	10	7	3	2	1	1	
155	**103**	**52**	**7**	**5**	**2**	**4**	**4**	...	**357**	**278**	**79**	
155	103	52	6	5	1	4	4	...	357	278	79	
...	...	...	...	...	...	...	...	...	...	...	...	
...	...	...	1	...	1	...	...	...	...	...	...	
189	**124**	**65**	**122**	**92**	**30**	**249**	**185**	**64**	**119**	**99**	**20**	
180	115	65	121	91	30	247	183	64	119	99	20	
9	9	...	1	1	...	2	2	...	...	...	...	
...	...	...	...	...	...	...	...	...	...	...	...	

(*a*) 'Ormuri' was returned by 20 persons only (10 males, 10 females) in the Dera Ismail Khan District. Under Pashto also are included 8 persons (2 males and 6 females in Peshawar) who returned their language as 'Kabuli.'

(*b*) Includes 'Peshawari' (2 males and 11 females in Peshawar and 1 male in Trans-frontier posts.)

(*c*) 'Pahari' was returned by 49 persons (26 males and 1 female in the Hazara District and 22 males in the Peshawar District).

(*d*) Includes 31 persons (males in the Peshawar District) who returned their language as Kashkari.

(*e*) The languages included under this head are :— 'Tinaoli' (20 males in Hazara), 'Pothwari' (2 males in Trans-frontier posts), 'Multani' (4 males in Dera Ismail Khan), 'Derawal' (2 females in Peshawar and 1 male in Dera Ismail Khan), 'Malwai' (1 male and 9 females in the Hazara District) and 'Ponchi' (1 male in the Peshawar District), all dialects of Lahnda or Western Punjabi.

(*f*) Under this head are included 5 males who returned their language as 'Bhopali,' 1 male who returned it as 'Gwaliori' and 26 males who returned it as 'Bhasha.' There are included also 4 speakers of 'Dakhini' (males) and 24 speakers of 'Hindi' (17 males and 7 females.)

(*g*) 'Parsi' was returned by 3 persons (2 males and 1 female.)

(*h*) 'Goai' was returned by 13 persons (12 males and 1 female.) Includes 3 males and 1 female who returned their language as 'Konkani.'

(*i*) Includes 'Tamil' (2 males and 2 females), 'Madrasi' (11 males and 8 females), 'Sindhi' (2 females), 'Oriya' (2 males), 'Bengali' (15 males and 2 females).

(*j*) Includes 'Arabic' (3 males and 9 females), 'Chinese' (1 male and 1 female), and 'Armenian' (2 males).

(*k*) Includes 'Russian' (1 female)' 'Irish' (1 male), 'French' (2 males and 2 females), 'Danish' (1 male and 1 female), and 'German' (5 males).

TABLE XI.

Birth Place.

TABLE XI.

Birth Place.

DISTRICT &c. WHERE

Serial number.	District, State, Province or country where born.	N.-W. F. P. Persons.	N.-W. F. P. Males.	N.-W. F. P. Females.	Hazara. Persons.	Hazara. Males.	Hazara. Females.	Peshawar. Persons.	Peshawar. Males.	Peshawar. Females.
	1	2	3	4	5	6	7	8	9	10
	TOTAL ...	**2,210,471**	**1,194,743**	**1,015,728**	**603,028**	**320,465**	**282,563**	**865,009**	**470,421**	**394,588**
(a)	**Districts, agencies and tribal areas within the N.-W. F. P.**	**2,075,126**	**1,096,591**	**978,535**	**589,816**	**311,162**	**278,654**	**805,094**	**425,555**	**379,539**
1	Hazara	588,335	310,877	277,458	585,019	308,130	276,889	2,167	1,812	355
2	Peshawar	776,153	408,335	367,818	392	274	118	772,408	405,057	367,351
3	Kohat	200,255	104,125	96,130	28	21	7	595	378	217
4	Bannu	234,634	122,205	112,429	16	13	3	192	156	36
5	Dera Ismail Khan ...	215,571	112,875	102,696	42	27	15	327	205	122
6	Agencies and tribal areas ...	60,166	38,168	21,998	4,319	2,697	1,622	29,393	17,941	11,452
7	N.-W. F. P. unspecified ...	12	6	6		...	...	12	6	6
(b)	**Provinces and States in India beyond N.-W. F. P.**	**82,139**	**62,560**	**19,579**	**8,365**	**5,306**	**3,059**	**39,161**	**29,786**	**9,375**
	Provinces	**73,415**	**55,340**	**18,075**	**6,286**	**3,83[illegible]**	**2,450**	**35,142**	**26,417**	**8,725**
8	Punjab	67,132	50,774	16,358	5,964	3,639	2,325	32,057	24,406	7,651
9	*Attock*	11,489	8,692	2,797	1,254	655	599	7,585	5,995	1,590
10	*Rawalpindi*	10,746	7,893	2,853	2,428	1,274	1,154	5,320	4,063	1,257
11	*Mianwali*	7,829	5,541	2,288	7	4	3	1,064	960	104
12	*Jhelum*	6,712	5,602	1,110	586	417	169	4,041	3,373	668
13	*Other Punjab Districts* ..	30,356	23,046	7,310	1,689	1,289	400	14,047	10,015	4,032
14	Ajmer Merwara	16	11	5	1	1	...	14	9	5
15	Andamans	11	4	7	1	...	1	7	3	4
16	Baluchistan	269	226	43	2	1	1	59	43	16
17	Bengal	209	128	81	17	14	3	113	54	59
18	Bombay	558	433	125	30	22	8	228	160	68
19	Burma	29	12	17	8	1	7	5	2	3
20	Central Provinces and Berar ...	86	52	34	2	...	2	37	21	16
21	Eastern Bengal and Assam ...	110	55	55	10	10	...	88	41	47
22	Madras	72	41	31	2	1	1	43	19	24
23	United Provinces	4,923	3,604	1,319	249	147	102	2,491	1,659	832
	States	**8,411**	**6,999**	**1,412**	**2,035**	**1,438**	**597**	**3,834**	**3,254**	**580**
24	Punjab States	1,761	1,523	238	119	100	19	906	748	158
25	Baroda	11	11	...	1	1	...	...	...	...
26	Bombay States	108	108	...	...	...	...	104	104	...
27	Central India Agency ...	91	72	19	1	...	1	25	16	9
28	Central Provinces States .	1	1	...	...	...	...	1	1	...
29	Eastern Bengal and Assam States	10	3	7	...	...	...	10	3	7
30	Hyderabad	94	62	32	6	1	5	79	55	24
31	Kashmir	4,655	3,804	851	1,783	1,228	555	2,078	1,836	242
32	Travancore	2	1	1	...	...	...	2	1	1
33	Mysore	45	32	13	2	2	...	22	13	9
34	Rajputana Agency ..	1492	1,282	210	121	105	16	502	402	100
35	United Provinces States ...	141	100	41	2	1	1	105	75	30
	India unspecified ...	**211**	**123**	**88**	**31**	**19**	**12**	**136**	**68**	**68**
	§ French and Portugese Settlements.	**102**	**98**	**4**	**13**	**13**	...	**49**	**47**	**2**

§ All the persons here shown were born in Goa.

TABLE XI.

Birth Place.

ENUMERATED.

Kohat.			Bannu.			Dera Ismail Khan.			Trans-Frontier Posts.			Serial number.
Persons.	Males.	Females.	Persons.	Males.	Females.	Persons.	Males.	Females	Persons.	Males.	Females.	
11	12	13	14	15	16	17	18	19	20	21	22	
222.690	**119.081**	**103.609**	**250.086**	**133.707**	**116.379**	**256.120**	**138.428**	**117.692**	**13.538**	**12.641**	**897**	
211.120	**109.968**	**101.152**	**239.077**	**125.267**	**113.810**	**221.756**	**117.023**	**104.733**	**8.263**	**7.616**	**647**	(a)
473	398	75	339	214	125	109	99	10	228	224	4	1
889	753	136	619	513	106	893	820	73	952	918	34	2
197,097	101,803	95,294	1,486	964	522	153	95	58	896	864	32	3
465	217	248	231,459	120,174	111,285	2,257	1,406	851	245	239	6	4
125	86	39	815	527	288	214,052	111,827	102,225	210	203	7	5
12,071	6,711	5,360	4.359	2,875	1,484	4,292	2.776	1,516	5.732	5,168	564	6
...	...	...	...	...	...	...	...	...	...	...	...	7
9.515	**7.658**	**1.857**	**7.859**	**6.354**	**1.505**	**13.108**	**9.560**	**3.548**	**4.131**	**3.896**	**235**	(b)
8.564	**6.794**	**1.770**	**7.440**	**5.981**	**1.459**	**12.378**	**8.940**	**3.438**	**3.605**	**3.372**	**233**	
7.674	6,029	1,645	6,585	5,280	1,305	11,500	8,277	3,223	3,352	3,143	209	8
1,628	1,137	491	358	322	36	.209	155	54	455	428	27	9
1,179	841	338	573	539	34	566	520	46	680	656	24	10
315	215	100	1,548	1,175	373	4,708	3,011	1,697	187	176	11	11
710	599	111	465	446	19	738	625	113	172	142	30	12
3,842	3,237	605	3,641	2,798	843	5,279	3,966	1,313	1,858	1,741	117	13
...	...	...	...	...	...	1	1	...	...	...	...	14
1	1	...	2	...	2	...	...	...	...	...	...	15
...	...	...	37	31	6	102	83	19	69	68	1	16
52	38	14	4	2	2	17	14	3	6	6	...	17
241	201	40	14	14	...	36	27	9	9	9	...	18
7	7	...	1	1	...	8	1	7	...	...	...	19
10	7	3	26	18	8	10	5	5	1	1	...	20
2	...	2	...	...	...	1	1	...	9	3	6	21
8	7	1	4	1	3	6	4	2	9	9	...	22
569	504	65	767	634	133	697	527	170	150	133	17	23
831	**846**	**85**	**394**	**351**	**43**	**702**	**537**	**105**	**515**	**513**	**2**	
149	147	2	102	84	18	164	124	40	321	320	1	24
10	10	...	...	...	...	...	...	...	...	...	...	25
...	...	...	3	3	...	1	1	...	...	...	..	26
31	28	3	9	7	2	24	20	4	1	1	...	27
...	...	...	...	...	...	...	...	...	...	...	...	28
...	...	...	...	...	...	...	...	...	...	...	...	29
...	...	...	...	...	...	9	6	3	...	...	...	30
147	117	30	188	180	8	293	278	15	166	165	1	31
...	...	...	...	...	...	...	...	...	...	...	...	32
6	5	1	3	...	3	8	8	...	4	4	...	33
585	536	49	75	68	7	192	154	38	17	17	...	34
3	3	...	14	9	5	11	6	5	6	6	...	35
7	**5**	**2**	**10**	**8**	**2**	**16**	**12**	**4**	**11**	**11**	...	
13	**13**	...	**15**	**14**	**1**	**12**	**11**	**1**	...	...	...	

TABLE XI.

Birth Place.

Serial number.	District, State, Province or country where born.	DISTRICT &c., WHERE								
		N.-W. F. P.			HAZARA.			PESHAWAR.		
		Persons.	Males.	Females.	Persons.	Males.	Females.	Persons.	Males.	Females.
	1	2	3	4	5	6	7	8	9	10
(c)	**Countries in Asia beyond India.**	**48,234**	**31,107**	**17,127**	**4,769**	**3,947**	**822**	**16,290**	**10,972**	**5,318**
1	Afghanistan	42,480	26,209	16,271	99	67	32	15,973	10,711	5,262
2	Arabia	31	20	11	...	...	...	24	15	9
3	Asia Minor	1	1	...	...	...	...	1	1	...
4	Bhutan	1	1	...	...	...	...	...	...	...
5	Ceylon	16	9	7	...	...	...	14	8	6
6	China	8	5	3	3	3	...	3	...	3
7	Hong Kong — ...	2	2	...	1	1	...	1	1	...
8	Nepal	5,653	4,834	819	4,663	3,873	790	238	216	22
9	Persia	5	5	...	1	1	...	4	4	...
10	Russia in Asia	19	11	8	...	...	...	19	11	8
11	Straits Settlements ...	10	6	4	2	2	...	7	3	4
12	Tibet ...	3	3	...	...	...	...	1	1	...
13	Turkey in Asia	5	1	4	...	...	...	5	1	4
(d)	**Countries in Europe** ...	**4,891**	**4,430**	**461**	**68**	**45**	**23**	**4,411**	**4,070**	**341**
14	United Kingdom	4,836	4,390	446	64	41	23	4,362	4,035	327
15	*England and Wales* ...	3,672	3,339	333	56	34	22	3,304	3,066	238
16	*Scotland*	192	156	36	3	2	1	144	118	26
17	*Ireland* ...	962	890	72	4	4	...	906	848	58
18	*Channel Islands and Isle of Man*	10	5	5	1	1	...	8	3	5
19	Austria Hungary	1	1	...	1	1	...	...	...	...
20	Cyprus	2	2	...	...	...	...	2	2	...
21	Denmark	1	...	1	...	...	...	1	...	1
22	France	10	7	3	...	...	...	10	7	3
23	Germany	8	6	2	...	...	...	6	5	1
24	Gibraltar	4	2	2	...	...	...	4	2	2
25	Italy	1	1	...	...	...	...	1	1	...
26	Malta	10	8	2	1	1	...	9	7	2
28	Portugal	1	1	...	...	...	...	1	1	...
27	Russia	2	1	1	...	...	...	2	1	1
29	Spain	8	6	2	...	...	...	8	6	2
30	Switzerland	3	2	1	...	...	...	3	2	1
31	Turkey in Europe ...	3	2	1	2	2	...	1	...	1
32	Europe unspecified ...	1	1	...	...	...	...	1	1	...
(e)	**Countries in Africa** ...	**24**	**13**	**11**	**5**	**2**	**3**	**16**	**8**	**8**
33	Cape Colony	3	2	1	...	...	...	2	1	1
34	Egypt	2	1	1	...	...	...	2	1	1
35	Natal	6	3	3	5	2	3	1	1	...
36	St. Helena	1	1	...	...	...	...	...	...	...
37	Africa unspecified	12	6	6	...	...	...	11	5	6
(f)	**Countries in America** ...	**26**	**21**	**5**	**1**	...	**1**	**20**	**17**	**8**
38	Bermudas	2	1	1	...	...	...	1	1	...
39	Canada	8	7	1	1	...	1	5	5	...
40	Cuba	1	1	...	...	...	...	1	1	...
41	Honduras	1	1	...	...	...	...	...	...	...
42	Jamaica	2	2	...	...	...	...	1	1	...
43	Newfoundland	3	2	1	...	...	...	3	2	1
44	West Indies	2	1	1	...	...	...	2	1	1
45	America unspecified ...	7	6	1	...	...	...	7	6	1
(g)	**Countries in Australasia** ...	**28**	**20**	**8**	**3**	**2**	**1**	**16**	**13**	**3**
46	Australia	18	12	6	2	2	...	10	8	2
47	Tasmania	3	2	1	1	...	1	1	1	...
48	New Zealand	7	6	1	...	...	...	5	4	1
(h)	**At Sea**	**3**	**1**	**2**	**1**	**1**	...	**1**	...	**1**

TABLE XI.

Birth Place.

ENUMERATED.

Kohat.			Bannu.			Dera Ismail Khan.			Trans-Frontier Posts.			Serial number.
Persons.	Males.	Females.	Persons.	Males.	Females.	Persons.	Males.	Females.	Persons.	Males.	Females.	
11	12	13	14	15	16	17	18	19	20	21	22	
1,955	**1,388**	**567**	**3,079**	**2,030**	**1,049**	**21,073**	**11,703**	**9,370**	**1,068**	**1,067**	**1**	(c)
1,954	1,387	567	3,077	2,029	1,048	21,060	11,698	9,362	317	317	...	1
...	...	...	...	...	...	3	1	2	4	4	...	2
...	...	...	...	...	...	...	...	...	...	...	...	3
...	...	...	...	...	...	...	...	...	1	1	...	4
...	...	...	2	1	1	...	...	...	...	...	...	5
...	...	...	...	...	...	1	1	...	1	1	...	6
...	...	...	...	...	...	...	...	...	...	...	...	7
1	1	...	...	...	...	9	3	6	742	741	1	8
...	...	...	...	...	...	...	...	...	...	...	...	9
...	...	...	...	...	...	...	...	...	...	...	...	10
...	...	...	...	...	...	...	...	...	1	1	...	11
...	...	...	...	...	...	...	...	...	2	2	...	12
...	...	...	...	...	...	...	...	...	...	...	...	13
95	**64**	**31**	**68**	**54**	**14**	**178**	**140**	**38**	**71**	**57**	**14**	(d)
93	63	30	68	54	14	178	140	38	71	57	14	14
67	44	23	54	42	12	139	109	30	52	44	8	15
14	12	2	7	7	...	14	10	4	10	7	3	16
12	7	5	7	5	2	25	21	4	8	5	3	17
...	...	...	...	...	...	...	...	...	1	1	...	18
...	...	...	...	...	...	...	...	...	...	...	...	19
...	...	...	...	...	...	...	...	...	...	...	...	20
...	...	...	...	...	...	...	...	...	...	...	...	21
...	...	...	...	...	...	...	...	...	...	...	...	22
2	1	1	...	...	...	...	...	...	...	...	...	23
...	...	...	...	...	...	...	...	...	...	...	...	24
...	...	...	...	...	...	...	...	...	...	...	...	25
...	...	...	...	...	...	...	...	...	...	...	...	26
...	...	...	...	...	...	...	...	...	...	...	...	27
...	...	...	...	...	...	...	...	...	...	...	...	28
...	...	...	...	...	...	...	...	...	...	...	...	29
...	...	...	...	...	...	...	...	...	...	...	...	30
...	...	...	...	...	...	...	...	...	...	...	...	31
...	...	...	...	...	...	...	...	...	...	...	...	32
...	...	...	**1**	**1**	...	...	...	...	**2**	**2**	...	(e)
...	...	...	...	...	...	...	...	...	1	1	...	33
...	...	...	...	...	...	...	...	...	...	...	...	34
...	...	...	...	...	...	...	...	...	...	...	...	35
...	...	...	1	1	...	...	...	...	...	...	...	36
...	...	...	...	...	...	...	...	...	1	1	...	37
2	**1**	**1**	...	...	...	...	...	...	**3**	**3**	...	(f)
1	...	1	...	...	...	...	...	...	...	...	...	38
...	...	...	...	...	...	...	...	...	2	2	...	39
...	...	...	...	...	...	...	...	...	...	...	...	40
...	...	...	...	...	...	...	...	...	1	1	...	41
1	1	...	...	...	...	...	...	...	...	...	...	42
...	...	...	...	...	...	...	...	...	...	...	...	43
...	...	...	...	...	...	...	...	...	...	...	...	44
...	...	...	...	...	...	...	...	...	...	...	...	45
3	**2**	**1**	**2**	**1**	**1**	**4**	**2**	**2**	...	...	...	(g)
2	1	1	2	1	1	2	...	2	...	...	...	46
...	...	...	...	...	...	1	1	...	...	...	...	47
1	1	...	...	...	...	1	1	...	...	...	...	48
...	...	...	...	...	...	**1**	...	**1**	...	...	...	(h)

TABLE XII.

Infirmities.

PART I.—Distribution by Age.

In this part is shown the total number of afflicted persons enumerated in the Province.

PART II.—Distribution by Districts.

No afflicted persons were enumerated in trans-frontier posts.

TABLE XII.

Infirmities.

Part I--Distribution by Age.

Age.	Population afflicted.			Insane.			Deaf-mutes.			Blind.			Lepers.		
	Persons.	Males.	Females.	Persons.	Males.	Females.	Persons.	Males.	Females.	Persons.	Males.	Females.	Persons.	Males.	Females.
1	2	3	4	5	6	7	8	9	10	11	12	13	14	15	16
0 and under 1 ...	16	9	7	2	2	...	5	2	3	8	5	3	1	...	1
1 „ 2 ...	8	6	2	...	...	...	2	1	1	6	5	1	...	...	...
2 „ 3 ...	44	16	28	1	...	1	16	3	13	26	13	13	1	...	1
3 „ 4 ...	86	57	29	12	8	4	45	31	14	28	17	11	1	1	...
4 „ 5 ...	100	59	41	8	5	3	64	37	27	24	14	10	4	3	1
Total 0 and under 5 ...	**254**	**147**	**107**	**23**	**15**	**8**	**132**	**74**	**58**	**92**	**54**	**38**	**7**	**4**	**3**
5 and under 10 ...	668	427	241	88	56	32	359	238	121	197	119	78	24	14	10
10 „ 15 ...	621	375	246	103	70	33	304	181	123	192	113	79	22	11	11
15 „ 20 ...	523	331	192	95	59	36	235	163	72	169	91	78	24	18	6
20 „ 25 ...	481	315	166	108	79	29	161	109	52	185	107	78	27	20	7
25 „ 30 ...	451	276	175	89	74	15	156	83	73	189	105	84	17	14	3
30 „ 35 ...	597	373	224	110	78	32	201	126	75	254	147	107	32	22	10
35 „ 40 ...	372	259	113	53	46	7	117	80	37	179	113	66	23	20	3
40 „ 45 ...	484	285	199	61	46	15	132	77	55	269	146	123	22	16	6
45 „ 50 ...	311	183	128	48	37	11	67	41	26	183	95	88	13	10	3
50 „ 55 ...	477	277	200	42	31	11	91	63	28	323	167	156	21	16	5
55 „ 60 ...	178	101	77	20	12	8	27	21	6	122	61	61	9	7	2
60 „ 65 ...	477	253	224	26	15	11	57	38	19	371	183	188	23	17	6
65 „ 70 ...	136	73	63	3	3	...	12	6	6	118	62	56	3	2	1
70 and over	676	403	273	15	13	2	49	36	13	597	341	256	15	13	2
All ages	**6,706**	**4,078**	**2,628**	**884**	**634**	**250**	**2,100**	**1,336**	**764**	**3,440**	**1,904**	**1,536**	**282**	**204**	**78**

Part II--Distribution by Districts.

District.	Population afflicted.			Insane.			Deaf-mutes.			Blind.			Lepers.		
	Persons.	Males.	Females.	Persons.	Males.	Females.	Persons.	Males.	Females.	Persons.	Males.	Females.	Persons.	Males.	Females.
1	2	3	4	5	6	7	8	9	10	11	12	13	14	15	16
Total N.-W. F. P. ...	**6,706**	**4,078**	**2,628**	**884**	**634**	**250**	**2,100**	**1,336**	**764**	**3,440**	**1,904**	**1,536**	**282**	**204**	**78**
Hazara	1,936	1,183	753	227	161	66	870	531	339	703	386	317	136	105	31
Peshawar	2,413	1,520	893	325	245	80	563	375	188	1,465	858	607	60	42	18
Kohat	587	359	228	82	54	28	215	139	76	260	145	115	30	21	9
Bannu	603	371	232	142	99	43	180	112	68	266	151	115	15	9	6
Dera Ismail Khan ...	1,167	645	522	108	75	33	272	179	93	746	364	382	41	27	14

TABLE XII—A.

Infirmities by selected Tribes, Castes or Races.

This table, like Table IX, has been prepared only for those tribes and castes which in 1901 contributed more than 2 per mille to the total population of the Province. As in Table IX, the title page of which should be referred to in this connection, the figures given in columns 2, 3 and 4 for particular tribes and castes will not always be found to agree with those given in Table XIII.

TABLE XII—A.

Infirmities by selected tribes, castes or races.

Caste or Tribe.	Population dealt with.			Insane.			Deaf Mutes.			Blind.			Lepers		
	Persons.	Males.	Females.	Persons.	Males.	Females.	Persons.	Males.	Females.	Persons.	Males.	Females.	Persons.	Males.	Females
1	2	3	4	5	6	7	8	9	10	11	12	13	14	15	16
Arora ...	69,144	37,909	31,235	47	37	10	85	49	36	121	71	50	3	2	1
Awan ...	275,711	149,550	126,161	124	91	33	372	285	87	449	245	204	35	23	12
Baghban ...	20,471	10,881	9,590	7	2	5	14	7	7	28	17	11	1	1	...
Baluch ...	26,513	14,466	12,047	6	4	2	32	16	16	115	48	67	5	4	1
Bhatiara ...	4,331	2,209	2,122	1	...	1	6	6	...	7	2	5	1	...	1
Brahman ...	13,208	7,856	5,352	7	6	1	10	9	1	27	18	9	1	1	...
Chamar ...	4,658	2,649	2,009	1	...	1	2	2	...	2	1	1	...	...	...
Chuhra ...	5,750	3,530	2,220	...	...	...	1	...	1	7	...	7	1	1	...
Dhobi ...	14,877	8,100	6,777	6	4	2	17	6	11	38	12	26	1	1	...
Dhund ...	30,464	15,773	14,691	5	2	3	40	16	24	28	16	12	11	5	6
Gakkhar ...	6,807	3,676	3,131	2	2	...	9	4	5	7	4	3	1	...	1
Gujar ...	113,871	61,711	52,160	50	32	18	116	81	35	93	54	39	31	24	7
Jat ...	86,097	48,873	37,224	23	16	7	69	46	23	182	89	93	14	9	5
Jhinwar ...	1,987	1,299	688	...	...	...	3	2	1	6	1	5	1	1	...
Jolaha ...	37,390	19,999	17,391	18	14	4	44	33	11	58	34	24	6	5	1
Karal ...	22,106	11,316	10,790	10	8	2	23	15	8	17	9	8	17	16	1
Kashmiri ...	28,631	15,198	13,433	13	8	5	53	33	20	39	24	15	1	1	...
Khatri ...	35,720	21,662	14,058	17	15	2	22	14	8	50	35	15	3	1	2
Kumhar ...	22,664	11,705	10,959	6	4	2	24	13	11	42	21	21	1	1	...
Lohar ...	28,589	15,331	13,258	11	4	7	29	17	12	34	14	20	1	...	1
Machhi ...	4,019	2,163	1,856	5	2	3	5	5	...	20	2	18	1	1	...
Maliar ...	19,950	10,412	9,538	6	6	...	24	15	9	53	36	17	...	...	...
Mallah ...	4,805	2,696	2,109	3	3	...	3	3	...	3	3	...	...	...	...
Mirasi ...	7,366	3,940	3,426	2	2	...	9	8	1	23	11	12	3	...	3
Mochi ...	23,040	12,383	10,657	16	10	6	31	15	16	62	40	22	1	1	...
Moghal ...	14,865	8,269	6,596	9	8	1	16	12	4	22	15	7	4	3	1
Musalli (with Kutana)	13,254	7,287	5,967	...	...	...	13	8	5	22	10	12	1	1	...
Nai ...	24,777	13,075	11,702	10	7	3	27	18	9	39	22	17	1	1	...
Paracha ...	11,553	6,278	5,275	8	7	1	5	3	2	11	4	7	1	1	...
Pathan ...	845,183	449,500	395,683	318	231	87	649	439	210	1,178	755	423	88	64	24
Qassab ...	8,721	4,559	4,162	2	2	...	9	4	5	14	6	8	1	1	...
Qureshi ...	20,939	11,058	9,881	14	12	2	32	18	14	39	21	18	2	1	1
Rajput ...	15,157	10,637	4,520	3	3	...	20	12	8	26	7	19	1	1	...
Saiad ...	75,115	39,230	35,885	38	26	12	88	47	41	119	57	62	8	6	2
Sarara ...	8,507	4,616	3,891	...	...	...	3	2	1	7	4	3	4	4	...
Shekh ...	17,892	10,013	7,879	9	7	2	21	11	10	29	12	17	1	1	...
Sonar ...	9,714	5,033	4,681	7	6	1	13	5	8	17	11	6	...	...	...
Swathi ...	38,329	20,181	18,148	18	11	7	80	48	32	41	22	19	9	9	...
Tanaoli ...	63,985	33,349	30,636	26	18	8	65	38	27	66	37	29	11	8	3
Tarkhan ...	42,618	22,764	19,854	13	8	5	56	37	19	68	35	33	4	3	1
Teli ...	6,932	3,678	3,254	1	1	...	13	7	6	17	8	9	...	...	...

TABLE XIII.

Caste, Tribe, Race or Nationality.

This table includes figures for the total population which was enumerated on the regular schedule, with the exception of Europeans and Anglo-Indians, for the numbers of whom a reference should be made to Table XVIII. The more numerically important of the various Pathan tribes are shown separately. Of other tribes and castes, separate figures are given only for those groups which in 1901 contributed more than 1 per mille to the population of the Province, the remainder being included under one designation *viz.*, minor and unspecified. For an explanation of differences between the total population of particular castes and tribes as given in this table and as given in Tables IX, XII-A and XIV a reference should be made to the title page of Table IX.

TABLE XIII.

Caste, Tribe, Race or Nationality.

Caste or Tribe.	Total N.-W. F. P.		Hazara.		Peshawar.	
	Males.	Females.	Males.	Females.	Males.	Females.
1	2	3	4	5	6	7
TOTAL (omitting Europeans and Anglo-Indians.)	**1,189,771**	**1,014,859**	**320,373**	**282,513**	**466,023**	**393,948**
Arain (*Mohammadan*)	1,797	1,546	...	...	70	44
Arora	37,977	31,238	1,853	1,295	10,344	7,872
Hindu	30,343	25,370	1,604	1,125	5,719	4,319
Sikh	7,634	5,868	249	170	4,625	3,553
Awan (with Khokhar) * *Mohammadan*	150,029	126,482	54,160	48,753	75,692	61,878
Baghban (*Mohammadan*)... ...	10,881	9,590	—	...	9,452	8,309
Baluch (*Mohammadan*)	14,466	12,047	100	79	713	612
Bhatia	2,095	1,991	10	10	74	149
Hindu	1,956	1,830	10	10	26	57
Sikh	139	161	...	...	48	92
Bhatiara	2,209	2,122	21	22	1,645	1,612
Mohammadan	2,101	2,029	21	22	1,537	1,519
Hindu	39	22	...	...	39	22
Sikh	69	71	...	...	69	71
Brahman	7,856	5,352	3,496	2,734	2,456	1,276
Hindu	5,839	3,901	1,878	1,476	2,105	1,110
Sikh	2,017	1,451	1,618	1,258	351	166
Chamar	2,674	2,012	159	144	1,775	1,282
Mohammadan	2,410	1,923	159	144	1,624	1,196
Hindu ... —	259	89	...	...	147	86
Sikh	5	...	...	—	4	—
Chuhra (with Mehtar)	3,536	2,257	205	167	2,005	1,373
Mohammadan	533	346	31	10	291	192
Hindu	2,978	1,906	152	152	1,711	1,181
Sikh	25	5	22	5	3	...
Darzi	1,278	1,000	565	509	590	427
Mohammadan	1,265	1,000	565	509	583	427
Hindu	6	...	...	...	...	...
Sikh	7	...	...	...	7	...
Dhobi	8,100	6,777	1,558	1,333	4,483	3,581
Mohammadan	7,533	6,369	1,514	1,268	4,107	3,337
Hindu	562	408	44	65	375	244
Sikh	5	...	...	...	1	...
Dhund (*Mohammadan*)	15,773	14,691	15,664	14,674	56	2
Faqir	769	839	...	...	691	823
Mohammadan	666	800	...	...	628	784
Hindu	58	...	...	...	18	...
Sikh	45	39	...	...	45	39
Gakkhar ... — ...	3,676	3,131	3,270	3,024	148	75
Mohammadan	3,675	3,131	3,270	3,024	147	75
Sikh ... —	1	...	...	...	1	...
Gujar	61,711	52,160	51,312	43,722	9,914	8,301
Mohammadan	61,418	52,080	51,312	43,722	9,828	8,233
Hindu	265	80	...	...	85	68
Sikh	28	...	...	...	1	...

* In the Hazara, Peshawar and Kohat Districts, where Khokhar is the name of a well-known sub-division of Awans. Elsewhere Khokhar has been treated as a distinct tribe.

TABLE XIII.

Caste, Tribe, Race or Nationality.

Kohat.		Bannu.		Dera Ismail Khan.		Trans-frontier posts.	
Males.	Females.	Males.	Females.	Males.	Females.	Males.	Females.
8	9	10	11	12	13	14	15
118.966	**103.544**	**133.617**	**116.349**	**138.249**	**117.628**	**12.543**	**877**
18	12	390	247	1,319	1,243	...	...
4,481	3,517	8,975	7,919	11,788	10,414	536	221
3,721	3,023	7,586	6,715	11,343	10,010	370	178
760	494	1,389	1,204	445	404	166	43
10,088	8,443	6,610	5,429	2,846	1,936	633	43
213	225	1,216	1,053	...	3	...	...
390	537	488	386	12,719	10,432	56	1
...	...	1,077	956	922	876	12	...
...	...	991	888	919	875	10	...
...	...	86	68	3	1	2	...
229	219	282	244	32	25	...	...
229	219	282	244	32	25	...	...
...	...	...	...	...	...	...	...
...	...	...	...	...	...	...	...
324	286	541	346	932	693	107	17
321	282	519	334	924	689	92	10
3	4	22	12	8	4	15	7
127	143	576	440	31	3	6	...
127	143	494	440	6	...	...	...
...	...	81	...	25	3	6	...
...	...	1	...	...	...	...	...
355	164	247	104	567	434	157	15
1	...	36	20	167	124	7	...
354	164	211	84	400	310	150	15
...	...	...	...	...	...	...	...
96	61	15	3	4	...	8	...
96	61	9	3	4	...	8	...
...	...	6	...	...	...	...	...
...	...	...	...	...	...	...	...
576	464	140	86	1,271	1,302	72	11
528	425	96	54	1,242	1,281	46	4
47	39	44	32	28	21	24	7
1	...	...	...	1	...	2	...
11	15	33	...	...	...	9	...
4	...	23	5	49	11	2	—
...	...	23	5	15	11	...	...
4	...	...	...	34	...	2	...
...	...	...	...	...	...	...	...
69	18	83	11	61	3	45	—
69	18	83	11	61	3	45	...
...	...	...	...	...	...	...	...
343	111	50	10	61	8	31	8
137	99	49	10	61	8	31	8
179	12	1	...	...	...	...	...
27	...	...	...	...	...	...	...

TABLE XIII.

Caste, Tribe, Race or Nationality.

Caste or Tribe.	Total N.-W. F. P.		Hazara.		Peshawar.	
	Males.	Females.	Males.	Females.	Males.	Females.
1	2	3	4	5	6	7
Gurkha (*Hindu*)	5,163	1,180	4,173	1,146	243	28
Jat	48,873	37,224	597	168	3,649	693
Mohammadan	41,486	36,584	148	139	715	351
Hindu	1,223	121	...	...	210	44
Sikh	6,164	519	449	29	2,724	298
Jhinwar (with Bhisti)	1,524	803	428	368	742	320
Mohammadan	786	564	396	353	315	142
Hindu	599	198	25	15	338	137
Sikh	139	41	7	...	89	41
Iolaha	19,999	17,391	7,419	6,421	10,658	9,162
Mohammadan	19,995	17,389	7,419	6,421	10,658	9,162
Hindu	4	2	...	...	...	...
Karal (*Mohammadan*)	11,316	10,790	11,304	10,790	...	...
Kashmiri (*Mohammadan*) ...	15,198	13,433	8,211	7,651	6,817	5,668
Khatri	21,662	14,058	7,735	6,042	10,166	5,702
Hindu	17,947	12,086	6,858	5,404	7,831	4,541
Sikh	3,715	1,972	877	638	2,335	1,161
Khoja (*Mohammadan*)	1,676	1,298	574	415	518	423
Khokhar (*Mohammadan*) ...	639	540	...	...	...	...
Kumhar	11,705	10,959	2,579	2,383	5,200	4,957
Mohammadan	11,625	10,951	2,563	2,383	5,184	4,952
Hindu	76	7	16	...	16	4
Sikh	4	1	...	...	...	1
Lohar	15,331	13,258	4,744	4,122	4,792	4,067
Mohammadan	15,307	13,253	4,742	4,122	4,782	4,064
Hindu	24	5	2	...	10	3
Machhi (*Mohammadan*)	2,175	1,856	...	...	47	70
Maliar (*Mohammadan*)	10,412	9,538	3,649	3,246	6,460	5,888
Mallah	2,696	2,109	350	193	926	817
Mohammadan ...	2,693	2,109	350	193	923	817
Hindu	3	...	...	...	3	...
Mirasi (with Dum) *Mohammadan* ...	6,134	5,656	1,054	1,010	2,408	2,167
Mishwani (*Mohammadan*) ...	2,404	2,484	2,404	2,484	...	...
Mochi	12,526	10,683	4,571	4,139	3,152	2,526
Mohammadan	12,323	10,660	4,569	4,136	3,014	2,526
Hindu	203	23	2	3	138	...
Moghal (*Mohammadan*)	8,269	6,596	5,136	4,324	2,607	1,989
Musalli (with Kutana) (*Mohammadan*)	7,287	5,967	1,351	1,261	2,654	2,232
Nai	13,075	11,702	3,541	3,317	4,900	4,250
Mohammadan	12,907	11,659	3,526	3,309	4,824	4,216
Hindu	136	42	15	8	62	33
Sikh	32	1	...	...	14	1
Paracha (with Banjara) (*Mohammadan*)	6,670	5,660	282	192	4,717	4,068

TABLE XIII.

Caste, Tribe, Race or Nationality.

Kohat.		Bannu.		Dera Ismail Khan.		Trans-frontier posts.	
Males.	Females.	Males.	Females.	Males.	Females.	Males.	Females.
8	9	10	11	12	13	14	15
1	...	...	...	3	6	743	...
1,581	267	6,670	4,908	35,615	31,175	761	13
170	193	5,643	4,858	34,760	31,036	50	7
421	23	543	10	28	44	21	...
990	51	484	40	827	95	690	6
123	63	98	24	62	28	71	...
25	42	2	1	48	26	...	...
87	21	81	23	...	2	68	...
11	...	15	...	14	...	3	...
1,081	1,046	450	403	389	359	2	...
1,080	1,046	447	403	389	357	2	...
1	...	3	...	...	2	...	...
...	...	12	...	...	...	...	...
64	99	34	7	27	6	45	2
908	512	852	669	1,202	987	799	146
710	407	761	643	1,117	952	670	139
198	105	91	26	85	35	129	7
5	22	...	...	568	437	11	1
...	...	47	27	592	513	...	...
945	859	1,308	1,342	1,648	1,418	25	...
908	857	1,300	1,341	1,648	1,418	22	...
37	2	4	1	...	—	3	...
...	...	4	...	...	...	...	...
1,782	1,765	2,534	2,247	1,460	1,056	19	1
1,780	1,765	2,525	2,245	1,460	1,056	18	1
2	...	9	2	...	...	1	...
36	2	80	97	2,012	1,687	...	...
279	387	3	...	11	13	10	4
13	15	73	68	1,334	1,016	...	...
13	15	73	68	1,334	1,016	...	...
...	...	...	...	...	...	...	...
422	490	1,183	1,072	1,019	917	48	...
...	...	...	...	...	...	...	...
932	813	1,050	894	2,792	2,310	29	1
888	799	1,041	894	2,792	2,304	19	1
44	14	9	...	...	6	10	...
154	60	4	16	300	199	68	8
215	186	599	541	2,392	1,729	76	18
1,854	1,743	1,414	1,240	1,341	1,152	25	...
1,828	1,743	1,381	1,239	1,331	1,152	17	...
23	...	30	1	1	—	5	...
3	...	3	...	9	...	3	...
995	801	442	369	223	223	11	7

TABLE XIII.

Caste, Tribe, Race or Nationality.

Caste or Tribe.	Total N.-W. F. P.		Hazara		Peshawar.	
	Males.	Females.	Males.	Females.	Males.	Females.
1	2	3	4	5	6	7
Pathan (*Mohammadan*)	449,500	395,683	27,577	25,022	219,047	195,053
Afridi	14,852	10,309	41	28	9,552	6,989
Bangash	13,815	12,062	381	335	215	136
Bannuchi	16,945	17,660	...	...	21	...
Bhitanni	6,238	4,242	...	...	...	...
Daudzai	5,452	5,284	...	...	5,447	5,284
Daur	234	185	...	...	...	...
Dilazak	1,859	1,806	1,066	931	793	875
Durrani	2,533	1,836	19	24	2,440	1,786
Gadun (Jadun)	14,394	13,152	12,615	11,515	1,769	1,637
Ghilzai	17,163	13,448	...	...	4,170	2,844
Gigiani	7,468	5,289	...	...	7,468	5,289
Khalil	8,613	8,433	...	...	8,600	8,433
Khattak	77,795	70,757	209	117	27,738	26,787
Khugiani	660	691	...	...	594	677
Mangal	126	33	...	...	30	12
Marwat	39,436	37,582	...	...	3	...
Mohammadzai	15,889	14,341	135	82	15,711	14,243
Mohmand	36,934	32,572	34	38	36,417	32,396
Mullagori	423	185	...	...	423	185
Niazi	3,285	3,121	...	...	18	6
Orakzai	7,568	5,961	...	...	317	333
Shinwari	1,033	456	...	...	712	447
Shirani	454	358	...	...	...	...
Tarin	1,428	1,421	1,020	976	391	419
Tarklanri	631	680	...	...	610	654
Turi	612	93	...	...	...	...
Usterana	1,098	1,120	...	...	...	...
Utmankhel	3,853	3,411	...	...	3,853	3,411
Wazir (Total)	18,844	15,430	...	...	66	42
Wazir Darwesh Khel ...	15,896	13,818	...	...	...	...
" *Mahsud*	2,255	1,177	...	...	...	...
Yusafzai	67,652	62,374	7,303	7,468	58,775	54,690
Zadran	567	398	...	...	...	...
Zaimusht	563	521	...	...	...	...
Other Pathans	56,845	46,664	4,754	3,478	32,873	27,443
Qassab (*Mohammadan*)	4,559	4,162	201	204	2,455	2,236
Qureshi (*Mohammadan*)	11,058	9,881	2,768	2,451	2,201	1,867
Rajput	10,715	4,548	3,400	2,800	3,855	984
Mohammadan	6,921	4,021	3 349	2,785	1,595	713
Hindu	3,571	480	30	13	2,180	230
Sikh	223	47	21	2	80	41
Rangrez	2,198	1,735	83	64	245	409
Mohammadan	2,194	1,735	83	64	245	409
Sikh	4	...	...	...	...	...
Saiad (*Mohammadan*)	39,230	35,885	13,010	12,286	13,036	11,782
Sarara (*Mohammadan*)	4,616	3,891	4,611	3,890	4	...
Shekh (*Mohammadan*)	10,013	7,879	2,089	1,810	4,063	3,202
Sonar	5,033	4,681	294	400	2,495	2,189
Mohammadan	4,376	4,071	218	293	2,219	1,981
Hindu	507	484	31	62	194	141
Sikh	150	126	45	45	82	67

TABLE XIII.

Caste, Tribe, Race or Nationality.

Kohat.		Bannu.		Dera Ismail Khan.		Trans-frontier posts.	
Males.	Females.	Males.	Females.	Males.	Females.	Males.	Females.
8	9	10	11	12	13	14	15
77,541	69,542	77,558	70,439	40,791	35,349	6,986	278
3,294	3,091	372	50	375	151	1,218	...
12,814	11,512	58	23	45	37	302	19
...	...	16,693	17,601	228	59	3	...
17	14	2,676	1,220	3,545	3,008	...	...
...	...	...	...	...	...	5	...
...	...	143	99	91	86	...	...
...	...	...	...	...	...	...	...
18	7	4	3	52	16	...	...
...	...	...	...	...	...	10	...
511	326	2,043	1,363	10,231	8,882	208	33
...	...	...	...	...	...	...	...
...	...	1	...	...	...	12	...
45,178	40,713	3,550	3,070	505	66	615	4
...	...	...	...	...	...	66	14
24	21	...	...	...	...	72	...
93	64	33,220	32,189	6,046	5,328	74	1
43	16	...	...	...	...	...	...
59	78	119	44	42	10	263	6
...	...	...	...	...	...	...	...
2,608	2,644	451	311	208	160	...	...
6,576	5,540	155	10	325	78	195	...
110	...	7	4	...	...	204	5
...	...	...	...	454	358	...	...
...	...	...	...	17	26	...	...
4	12	5	5	12	9	...	...
64	93	...	...	...	...	548	...
...	...	...	...	1,098	1,120	...	...
...	...	...	...	...	...	...	...
908	828	14,580	13,116	2,107	1,443	1,183	1
358	500	13,584	12,471	1,070	846	884	1
6	6	996	645	954	526	299	...
227	23	331	99	353	84	663	10
...	...	567	398	...	...	...	...
563	518	...	...	...	3	...	...
4,430	4,042	2,521	808	10,965	10,708	1,302	185
714	669	505	427	682	626	2	...
1,548	1,675	3,747	3,212	713	666	81	10
1,085	334	725	167	1,196	246	454	17
648	281	296	28	751	199	282	15
413	52	418	137	377	46	153	2
24	1	11	2	68	1	19	...
94	93	1,649	981	127	188	...	...
94	93	1,645	981	127	188	...	...
...	...	4	...	...	...	...	...
4,708	4,287	5,541	5,073	2,722	2,443	213	14
...	...	1	...	...	...	...	1
742	519	817	640	2,168	1,680	134	28
497	502	1,293	1,110	451	479	3	1
428	449	1,153	1,003	358	345	...	...
59	43	128	104	92	134	3	...
10	10	12	3	1	...	...	1

TABLE XIII.

Caste, Tribe, Race or Nationality

Caste or Tribe.	Total N. W. F. P.		Hazara.		Peshawar.	
	Males.	Females.	Males.	Females.	Males.	Females.
1	2	3	4	5	6	7
Swathi (*Mohammadan*) ...	20,181	18,148	20,010	17,756	159	391
Tanaoli (*Mohammadan*)	33,349	30,636	31,156	28,734	2,136	1,899
Tarkhan	22,764	19,854	5,488	4,556	8,852	7,792
Mohammadan	22,559	19,808	5,488	4,556	8,759	7,771
Hindu	32	5	...	...	19	5
Sikh	173	41	...	...	74	16
Teli (*Mohammadan*)	3,678	3,254	1,447	1,264	2,074	1,846
Turk (*Mohammadan*)	2,309	2,190	2,255	2,144	47	46
Minor and unspecified ...	20,999	16,012	3,509	2,994	14,582	11,609
Mohammadan	18,022	14,912	3,388	2,955	13,003	10,827
Hindu	1,939	657	42	28	1,130	515
Sikh	438	99	51	3	77	19
Christian	552	325	28	8	329	237
Parsi	41	8	...	...	41	8
Jew	5	9	...	...	...	1
Jain	2	2	...	...	2	2
Caste not returned (*Mohammadan*)	8	...	...	...	8	...

TABLE XIII.

Caste, Tribe, Race or Nationality.

Kohat.		Bannu.		Dera Ismail Khan.		Trans-frontier posts.	
Males.	Females.	Males.	Females.	Males.	Females.	Males.	Females.
8	9	10	11	12	13	14	15
...	...	...	...	...	...	12	1
30	3	21	...	4	...	2	...
2,749	2,411	3,137	2,693	2,504	2,395	34	7
2,703	2,406	3,080	2,673	2,499	2,395	30	7
4	...	3	...	2	...	4	...
42	5	54	20	3	...	...	...
96	80	24	20	37	44	...	...
3	...	...	...	...	...	4	...
445	84	1,000	424	1,262	898	201	3
77	59	500	285	886	786	168	...
330	8	220	99	217	7	...	...
...	...	186	9	103	68	21	...
33	9	94	31	56	37	12	3
...	...	...	...	...	...	...	...
5	8	...	...	...	...	...	...
...	...	...	...	...	...	...	...
...	...	...	...	...	...	...	...

TABLE XIV.

Civil Condition by age for Selected Castes.

THIS table, like Tables IX and XII-A., deals only with those tribes and castes which in 1901 contributed more than 2 per mille to the total population of the Province. The figures given are those for the total population for the Province of each caste and tribe dealt with. For an explanation of discrepancies between the figures here given and those shown in Table XIII a reference should be made to the title page of Table IX.

TABLE XIV.

Civil Condition by age for Selected Castes.

Caste, Tribe or Race.	Sex.	Population dealt with.	Unmarried.							Serial number.
			Total.	0—5	5—12	12—15	15—20	20—40	40 & over	
1	2	3	4	5	6	7	8	9	10	
Arora	M	37,909	20,906	4,608	6,580	2,834	2,717	3,546	621	1
	F	31,235	12,725	4,559	5,551	1,804	506	255	50	2
Awan	M	149.550	87,591	21,283	28,463	13,349	10,140	13,064	1,292	3
	F	126,161	58,795	22,522	23,241	7,517	3,316	1,715	484	4
Baghban	M	10,881	6,207	1,554	2,202	852	642	885	72	5
	F	9,590	4,310	1,684	1,773	479	200	126	48	6
Baluch	M	14,466	7,927	2,047	2,871	1,100	732	1,088	89	7
	F	12.047	5,195	1,970	2,245	614	272	79	15	8
Bhatiara ...	M	2,209	1,264	297	467	146	150	169	35	9
	F	2,122	1,020	346	376	147	85	48	18	10
Brahman ...	M	7,856	4,313	790	1,195	585	626	937	180	11
	F	5,352	2,161	820	956	285	62	28	10	12
Chamar... ...	M	2,649	1,467	458	418	210	173	181	27	13
	F	2,009	907	319	317	132	63	48	28	14
Chuhra	M	3,530	1,686	368	434	229	192	421	42	15
	F	2,220	864	273	360	130	45	42	14	16
Dhobi	M	8,100	4,313	1,081	1,426	556	535	611	104	17
	F	6,777	3,026	1,122	1,136	405	191	109	63	18
Dhund	M	15,773	9,211	2,618	3,329	1,275	919	984	86	19
	F	14,691	7,561	2,472	3,144	882	340	582	141	20
Gakkhar ...	M	3,676	1,977	431	675	247	282	299	43	21
	F	3,131	1.411	529	569	163	108	35	7	22
Gujar	M	61,711	35,997	8,961	11,947	5,067	4,326	5,138	558	23
	F	52,160	23,128	8,717	10,098	2,655	1,138	410	110	24
Jat	M	48,873	27,212	5,951	8,953	2,780	3,145	6,010	373	25
	F	37,224	16,184	5,769	7,589	1,732	728	309	57	26
Jhinwar... ...	M	1,299	594	98	165	66	72	173	20	27
	F	688	326	108	119	56	20	17	6	28
Jolaha	M	19,999	11,060	2,601	3,764	1,490	1,444	1,476	285	29
	F	17,391	7,883	2,916	3,111	997	459	304	96	30
Karal	M	11,316	6,702	1,844	2,580	924	675	635	44	31
	F	10,790	5,181	2,010	2,215	601	282	60	13	32
Kashmiri ...	M	15,198	8,199	1,963	2,678	1,215	1,038	1,151	154	33
	F	13,433	5,962	2,056	2,440	904	362	166	34	34
Khatri	M	21,662	11,365	2,033	2,854	1,477	1,595	2,833	573	35
	F	14,058	5,145	1,924	2,279	628	176	95	43	36
Kumhar ...	M	11.705	6.664	1,821	2,262	941	696	829	115	37
	F	10,959	4,940	1,882	2,014	543	283	162	56	38
Lohar	M	15,331	8,969	2,291	3,209	1,197	944	1,208	120	39
	F	13,258	6,498	2,474	2,622	710	370	277	45	40
Machhi	M	2,163	1,260	285	437	179	128	184	47	41
	F	1,856	777	291	335	91	33	21	6	42

TABLE XIV.

Civil Condition by age for Selected Castes.

Serial number.	Married.							Widowed.						
	Total.	0—5	5—12	12—15	15—20	20—40	40 & over	Total.	0—5	5—12	12—15	15—20	20—40	40 & over.
	11	12	13	14	15	16	17	18	19	20	21	22	23	24
1	14,405	...	19	109	645	8,192	5,440	2,598	...	1	9	36	813	1,739
2	13,221	...	110	449	1,917	8,530	2,215	5,289	...	...	12	62	1,441	3,774
3	55,041	...	146	384	1,825	27,342	25,344	6,918	...	1	7	51	2,086	4,773
4	53,446	...	178	1,093	6,408	34,116	11,651	13,920	...	2	36	177	2,638	11,067
5	4,033	...	...	14	144	2,033	1,842	641	...	...	1	3	142	495
6	4,317	...	18	69	412	2,578	1,240	963	...	1	2	3	201	756
7	5,859	...	4	34	231	3,158	2,432	680	...	...	...	6	175	499
8	5,592	...	21	90	591	3,555	1,335	1,260	...	...	1	17	201	1,041
9	815	...	1	11	29	381	393	130	...	...	1	5	42	82
10	879	...	5	24	108	530	212	223	...	...	4	1	35	183
11	2,929	...	3	23	117	1,663	1,123	614	...	...	3	10	190	411
12	2,370	...	26	104	357	1,413	470	821	...	...	3	12	224	582
13	1,000	...	...	10	51	501	438	182	...	...	...	2	61	119
14	903	...	2	19	65	543	274	199	...	...	...	1	33	165
15	1,545	...	4	15	77	934	515	299	...	...	...	8	130	161
16	1,131	...	7	28	163	721	212	225	...	...	2	2	85	136
17	3,294	...	6	32	128	1,612	1,516	493	...	...	1	7	160	325
18	3,036	...	9	55	421	1,765	786	715	...	...	1	5	159	550
19	6,008	...	16	56	220	3,110	2,606	554	...	...	...	6	126	422
20	6,001	...	37	184	800	3,450	1,530	1,129	...	...	2	5	134	988
21	1,509	...	2	6	31	891	579	190	...	...	1	3	61	125
22	1,388	...	5	36	200	831	316	332	...	...	1	3	75	253
23	22,986	...	66	140	751	10,592	11,437	2,728	...	...	3	20	701	2,004
24	24,477	...	79	654	2,671	15,023	6,050	4,555	...	1	12	38	755	3,749
25	19,315	...	30	105	839	11,898	6,443	2,346	...	...	1	37	960	1,348
26	16,922	1	144	303	1,352	11,197	3,925	4,118	...	...	2	32	837	3,247
27	589	...	...	6	21	366	196	116	...	...	...	1	56	59
28	283	...	2	15	25	176	65	79	...	...	...	...	20	59
29	7,668	...	8	49	243	3,693	3,675	1,271	...	...	...	8	322	941
30	7,719	...	33	141	808	4,681	2,056	1,789	...	1	...	16	403	1,369
31	4,266	...	10	31	133	2,169	1,923	348	...	...	1	2	68	277
32	4,773	...	57	130	555	2,826	1,205	836	...	...	...	7	146	683
33	6,115	...	4	24	135	3,005	2,947	884	...	...	2	9	270	603
34	5,847	...	18	98	677	3,501	1,553	1,624	...	...	3	10	319	1,292
35	8,615	...	12	73	417	4,970	3,143	1,682	...	...	1	15	638	1,028
36	6,496	...	39	336	1,043	3,915	1,163	2,417	...	2	5	36	548	1,826
37	4,375	...	6	32	199	2,242	1,896	666	...	...	2	5	210	449
38	4,857	...	16	127	561	2,939	1,214	1,162	...	...	1	6	256	899
39	5,611	...	12	40	253	2,747	2,559	751	...	...	...	9	216	526
40	5,616	...	46	117	630	3,603	1,220	1,144	...	...	...	15	238	891
41	771	...	...	5	24	422	320	132	...	...	2	...	34	96
42	893	...	7	24	95	515	252	186	...	...	...	6	31	149

TABLE XIV.

Civil Condition by age for Selected Castes.

Caste Tribe or Race.	Sex.	Population dealt with.	Unmarried. Total.	0—5	5—12	12—15	15—20	20—40	40 & over	Serial number.
1	2	3	4	5	6	7	8	9	10	
Maliar	M	10,412	5,706	1,365	1,848	811	764	793	125	1
	F	9,538	4,281	1,639	1,658	559	275	106	44	2
Mallah	M	2,696	1,467	309	349	334	279	190	6	3
	F	2,109	801	304	242	177	55	15	8	4
Mirasi	M	3,940	2,186	521	730	294	241	337	63	5
	F	3,426	1,500	548	560	202	100	52	38	6
Mochi	M	12,383	6,884	1,836	2,450	868	768	871	91	7
	F	10,657	4,919	1,804	2,099	562	280	130	44	8
Moghal	M	8,269	4,501	1,012	1,535	571	537	700	146	9
	F	6,596	2,932	1,041	1,272	351	178	69	21	10
Musalli (with Kutana)	M	7,287	4,133	1,015	1,319	519	475	700	105	11
	F	5,967	2,678	876	1,201	359	135	65	42	12
Nai	M	13,075	7,097	1,952	2,430	968	804	796	147	13
	F	11,702	5,486	2,006	2,196	687	334	198	65	14
Paracha	M	6,278	3,597	845	1,308	528	382	465	69	15
	F	5,275	2,411	800	966	281	167	131	66	16
Pathan	M	449,500	271,356	67,797	83,860	42,389	29,453	42,851	5,006	17
	F	395,683	181,373	64,079	71,282	27,144	9,772	7,048	2,048	18
Qassab	M	4,559	2,657	683	935	320	336	327	56	19
	F	4,162	1,963	638	776	246	145	114	44	20
Qureshi	M	11,058	6,254	1,524	2,217	744	744	875	150	21
	F	9,881	4,647	1,643	1,897	529	306	221	51	22
Rajput	M	10,637	5,364	830	1,023	491	839	2,038	143	23
	F	4,520	2,039	650	851	272	122	101	43	24
Saiad	M	39,230	22,459	4,935	7,720	3,768	2,568	3,100	368	25
	F	35,885	16,855	5,824	6,316	2,825	1,157	534	199	26
Sarara	M	4,616	3,010	744	1,078	361	284	524	19	27
	F	3,891	1,667	663	797	149	47	9	2	28
Shekh	M	10,013	5,152	1,178	1,488	628	683	1,058	117	29
	F	7,879	3,394	1,125	1,334	457	251	162	65	30
Sonar	M	5,033	2,887	687	1,035	366	352	369	78	31
	F	4,681	2,190	782	855	264	143	101	45	32
Swathi	M	20,181	11,933	2,977	4,398	1,595	1,404	1,394	165	33
	F	18,148	8,867	2,918	3,832	991	438	659	29	34
Tanaoli	M	33,349	19,120	4,808	6,914	2,594	2,348	2,260	196	35
	F	30,636	13,421	5,076	5,564	1,701	735	267	78	36
Tarkhan	M	22,764	12,711	3,369	4,336	1,746	1,468	1,562	230	37
	F	19,854	9,054	3,393	3,737	1,119	508	197	100	38
Teli	M	3,678	2,074	478	720	304	229	282	61	39
	F	3,254	1,466	472	547	206	115	79	47	40

TABLE XIV.

Civil Condition by age for Selected Castes.

Serial number.	Married. Total.	0—5	5—12	12—15	15—20	20—40	40 & over	Widowed. Total.	0—5	5—12	12—15	15—20	20—40	40 & over.
	11	12	13	14	15	16	17	18	19	20	21	22	23	24
1	4,047	...	6	15	106	1,977	1,943	659	...	...	1	8	196	454
2	4,224	...	15	88	520	2,435	1,166	1,033	...	...	1	10	217	805
3	1,047	...	...	2	9	562	474	182	...	...	...	7	22	153
4	1,013	...	...	10	147	503	353	295	...	...	...	...	25	270
5	1,469	...	2	7	61	700	699	285	...	...	...	6	92	187
6	1,547	...	12	33	171	965	366	379	...	...	1	4	65	309
7	4,751	...	9	39	226	2,527	1,950	748	...	...	3	17	196	532
8	4,721	...	20	142	597	2,936	1,026	1,017	...	...	1	15	214	787
9	3,315	...	3	11	113	1,702	1,486	453	...	...	...	4	136	313
10	2,917	...	21	60	378	1,818	640	747	...	...	...	11	143	593
11	2,703	...	2	10	120	1,338	1,233	451	...	...	1	8	154	288
12	2,738	...	6	93	337	1,625	676	551	...	...	...	11	123	417
13	5,121	...	10	37	226	2,513	2,335	857	...	...	3	7	355	492
14	5,166	...	27	132	612	3,263	1,132	1,050	...	...	5	14	231	800
15	2,310	...	2	30	77	1,031	1,170	371	...	...	...	1	103	267
16	2,239	...	6	34	210	1,369	620	625	...	2	...	8	115	500
17	161,692	...	282	654	3,583	83,432	73,741	16,452	...	1	38	170	4,032	12,211
18	168,804	...	620	3,148	14,726	106,539	43,771	45,506	...	14	76	262	8,643	36,511
19	1,677	...	11	17	66	826	757	225	...	...	...	3	74	148
20	1,750	...	13	51	156	1,083	447	449	...	...	4	10	89	346
21	4,220	...	17	27	131	2,136	1,909	584	...	...	1	3	163	417
22	4,183	...	31	138	466	2,640	908	1,051	...	...	5	19	224	803
23	4,754	...	20	143	189	3,254	1,148	519	...	...	...	9	227	283
24	2,038	...	16	82	333	1,185	422	443	...	1	...	5	95	342
25	15,020	...	27	108	518	7,633	6,734	1,751	...	...	1	13	449	1,288
26	15,042	...	67	250	1,544	9,203	3,978	3,988	...	1	4	30	815	3,138
27	1,450	...	8	16	74	916	436	156	...	...	...	4	41	111
28	1,895	...	29	71	282	1,095	418	329	...	...	...	6	54	269
29	4,148	...	9	30	151	2,321	1,637	713	...	...	...	7	251	455
30	3,540	...	6	117	411	2,268	738	945	...	2	...	6	227	710
31	1,839	...	4	13	66	955	801	307	...	...	1	12	92	202
32	2,021	...	14	58	240	1,143	566	470	...	1	2	8	132	327
33	7,510	...	10	20	160	3,573	3,747	738	...	...	...	8	179	551
34	7,455	...	29	153	1,034	4,488	1,751	1,826	...	...	3	10	364	1,449
35	12,778	...	7	154	323	6,073	6,221	1,451	...	...	...	12	359	1,080
36	14,405	...	65	335	1,412	9,155	3,438	2,810	...	...	1	34	508	2,267
37	8,798	...	2	126	361	4,623	3,686	1,255	...	...	2	10	416	827
38	8,904	...	37	200	1,052	5,495	2,120	1,896	...	...	4	22	421	1,449
39	1,393	...	5	10	67	683	628	211	...	...	...	...	69	142
40	1,449	...	3	23	176	877	370	339	...	...	...	2	59	278

TABLE XV.

Occupation or means of livelihood.

PART A.—General Table.

In this table occupations are arranged into 4 Classes, marked A, B, C and D, respectively. The Classes are sub-divided into Sub-classes, of which there are 12. The Sub-classes are divided again into 55 Orders, and below the Orders the occupations returned have been tabulated in 169 groups. The serial numbers have been omitted of those groups which indicate occupations which have not been returned in the North-West Frontier Province, *e.g.*, group 139—Army (Imperial) is followed directly by group 142—(Police), as no representatives of group 140—Army (Native States) and group 141—Navy were enumerated. The groups which have thus been omitted are :—5—Tea, coffee, cinchona and indigo plantations. 18—Other minerals (jade, diamonds, limestone, etc.) 23—Jute spinning, pressing and weaving. 28—Hair, camel and horse hair, bristles work, brush makers, etc. 29—Persons occupied with feathers. 38—Forging and rolling of iron and other metals. 49—Others (mosaic, talc, mica, alabaster, etc., workers). 52—Manufacture of dyes, paint and ink. 54—Manufacture of paper, card board and papier maché. 60—Fish curers. 65—Toddy drawers. 94—Harbour works, dock-yards and pilots. 140—Army (Native States). 141—Navy. The omission of group 18 involves the omissions of Order IV—Quarries of hard rock, and the omission of group 141 that of Order XLIII—Navy, as no other groups fall under either order.

TABLE XV.

Occupation or means of livelihood—Part A.—General Table.

Number of Group.	Occupation.	N.-W. F. P. (Total). Total workers and dependants.	Actual Workers. Total. Males.	Actual Workers. Total. Females.	Actual Workers. Partially agriculturists. Males.	Actual Workers. Partially agriculturists. Females.	Dependants.	HAZARA. Total workers and dependants.	Actual Workers. Total. Males.	Actual Workers. Total. Females.
	1	2	3	4	5	6	7	8	9	10
	ALL OCCUPATIONS ...	**2.210.471**	**689.277**	**45,293**	**13.267**	**169**	**1.475.901**	**693,028**	**180.605**	**11,557**
	Total Class A.—Production of raw materials.	**1,492,413**	**425,770**	**23.614**	**149**	**1**	**1.043,029**	**455,190**	**127,662**	**6,688**
	TOTAL SUB-CLASS I.—EXPLOITATION OF THE SURFACE OF THE EARTH.	**1,492.128**	**425,647**	**23,613**	**147**	**1**	**1,042,868**	**455.188**	**127,660**	**6,683**
	Total Order I.—Pasture and Agriculture.	**1.491.639**	**425.471**	**23.613**	**147**	**1**	**1,042,555**	**455,186**	**127,660**	**6,688**
	Total Order I (a).—Ordinary cultivation.	**1,472,519**	**417,117**	**23,401**	**13**	...	**1,032,001**	**451,176**	**125,021**	**6,667**
	Income from rent of agricultural land—									
1 (a)	Non-cultivating owners	87,217	25,714	3,509	..	...	57,994	4 570	1,073	365
(b)	Non-cultivating tenants	213	105	2	...	...	106	30	20	...
	Ordinary cultivators—									
2 (a)	Cultivating owners	716,885	198,102	12,224	...	...	506,559	194,386	54,345	3,545
(b)	Cultivating tenants	617,700	176,519	6,559	...	...	434,622	240,041	65,385	2,671
3	Agents, managers of landed estates (not planters), clerks, rent collectors, etc.	523	156	...	13	...	367	121	46	...
4	Farm servants and field labourers ...	49,981	16,521	1,107	...	...	32,353	12,028	4 152	86
	Total Order I (b).—Growers of special products and market gardening.	**2,733**	**958**	**11**	**28**	**1**	**1,764**	**425**	**156**	...
6	Fruit, flower, vegetable, betel-vine, areca-nut, etc., growers.	2,733	958	11	28	1	1,764	425	156	...
	Total Order I (c).—Forestry ...	**2,297**	**840**	**22**	**11**	...	**1,435**	**655**	**267**	...
7	Forest officers, rangers, guards, etc. ...	605	254	...	11	...	351	478	208	...
8	Wood cutters, firewood, lac, catechou, rubber, etc., collectors and charcoal burners.	1,692	586	22	...	...	1,084	177	59	...
	Total Order I (d).—Raising of farm stock.	**14,072**	**6,553**	**179**	**95**	...	**7,340**	**2,919**	**2,214**	**21**
9	Cattle and buffalo breeders and keepers	179	78	...	...	...	101	56	46	...
10	Sheep, goat and pig breeders ...	364	121	6	...	...	237	106	50	4
11	Breeders of other animals (horses, mules, camels, asses, etc.)	16	7	...	...	...	9	4	...	...
12	Herdsmen, shepherds, goatherds, etc. ...	13,513	6,347	173	95	...	6,993	2,753	2,118	17
	Total Order I (e).—Raising of small animals.	**18**	**3**	...	...	...	**15**	**11**	**2**	...
13	Birds, bees, silkworms, etc. ...	18	3	...	...	...	15	11	2	...
	Total Order II.—Fishing and hunting...	**489**	**176**	...	...	...	**313**	**2**	...	...
14	Fishing	423	143	...	...	...	280	2	...	...
15	Hunting	66	33	...	...	...	33	...	...	...
	TOTAL SUB-CLASS II.—EXTRACTION OF MINERALS.	**285**	**123**	**1**	**2**	...	**161**	**2**	**2**	...
	Total Order III.—Mines	**45**	**7**	...	...	...	**38**	**2**	**2**	...
16	Coal mines and petroleum wells ...	5	2	...	...	...	3	2	2	...
17	Mines and metallic minerals (gold, iron, manganese), etc.	40	5	...	...	...	35	—	...	...
	Total Order V.—Salt	**240**	**116**	**1**	**2**	...	**123**	...	...	...
19	Rock, sea, and marsh salt	211	107	1	2	...	103	...	...	...
20	Extraction of saltpetre, alum and other substances soluble in water.	29	9	...	...	...	20	...	...	...

TABLE XV.

Occupation or means of livelihood.—Part A.—General Table.

RA.			PESHAWAR.						KOHAT.						
KERS.				ACTUAL WORKERS.						ACTUAL WORKERS.					
Partially agricul-turists.				*Total.*		*Partially agricul-turists.*				*Total.*		*Partially agricul-turists.*			
Males.	Females.	Dependants.	Total workers and depen-dants.	Males.	Females.	Males.	Females.	Dependants.	Total workers and depen-dants.	Males.	Females.	Males.	Females.	Dependants.	Number of Group.
11	12	13	14	15	16	17	18	19	20	21	22	23	24	25	
2,230	**38**	**410,866**	**865,009**	**270,023**	**16,214**	**4,471**	**67**	**578,772**	**222,690**	**70,884**	**10 313**	**1,832**	**27**	**141,493**	
57	...	**320,840**	**534,848**	**152,981**	**6,511**	**62**	...	**375,356**	**170,132**	**50,222**	**8,045**	**5**	**1**	**111,865**	
57	...	**320,840**	**534,773**	**152,965**	**6,511**	**62**	...	**375,297**	**169,924**	**50,117**	**8,044**	**3**	**1**	**111,763**	
57	...	**320,833**	**534,392**	**152,827**	**6,511**	**62**	...	**375,054**	**169,918**	**50,115**	**8,044**	**3**	**1**	**111,759**	
7	...	**319,488**	**527,427**	**150,522**	**6,481**	**1**	...	**370,424**	**168,134**	**49,375**	**7,959**	...	...	**110,800**	
...	...	3,132	24,425	7,568	1,591	...	...	15,266	23,021	8,233	238	...	...	14,550	1 (a)
...	...	10	24	2	2	...	...	20	7	1	...	...	...	6	(b)
...	...	136,496	249,108	69,171	2,414	...	...	177,523	104,375	28,593	5,737	...	...	70,045	2 (a)
...	...	171,985	222,306	63,350	1,642	...	...	157,314	40,352	12,387	1,956	...	...	20,009	(b)
7	...	75	172	39	...	1	...	133	24	8	...	...	...	16	3
...	...	7,790	31,392	10,392	832	...	...	20,168	355	153	28	...	...	174	4
22	...	**269**	**1,406**	**466**	**9**	**2**	...	**931**	**210**	**82**	**1**	**3**	**1**	**127**	
22	...	269	1,406	466	9	2	...	931	210	82	1	3	1	127	6
10	...	**388**	**753**	**192**	**3**	**1**	...	**658**	**404**	**117**	**13**	...	...	**274**	
10	...	270	98	38	...	1	...	60	28	8	...	...	...	20	7
...	...	118	655	154	3	...	...	498	376	109	13	...	...	254	8
18	...	**684**	**4,803**	**1,646**	**18**	**58**	...	**3,139**	**1,170**	**541**	**71**	...	...	**558**	
...	...	10	73	25	...	...	...	48	...	...	...	...	...	...	9
...	...	52	250	66	2	...	...	182	...	...	...	...	...	...	10
...	...	4	2	2	...	...	...	...	1	...	...	...	...	1	11
18	...	618	4,478	1,553	16	58	...	2,909	1,169	541	71	...	...	557	12
...	...	**9**	**3**	**1**	...	...	...	**2**	...	...	...	...	...	...	
...	...	9	3	1	...	...	...	2	...	...	...	...	...	...	13
...	...	**2**	**381**	**138**	...	...	...	**243**	**6**	**2**	...	...	...	**4**	
...	...	2	333	113	...	...	...	220	6	2	...	...	...	4	14
...	...	...	48	25	...	...	...	23	...	...	...	...	...	...	15
...	...	...	**75**	**16**	...	...	...	**59**	**208**	**105**	**1**	**2**	...	**102**	
...	...	...	**43**	**5**	...	...	...	**38**	...	...	...	...	...	...	
...	...	...	3	...	...	...	...	3	...	...	...	...	...	...	16
...	...	...	40	5	...	...	...	35	—	—	...	...	...	...	17
...	...	...	**32**	**11**	...	...	...	**21**	**208**	**105**	**1**	**2**	...	**102**	
...	...	...	3	2	...	...	...	1	208	105	1	2	...	102	19
...	...	...	29	9	...	...	...	20	...	...	...	...	...	...	20

TABLE XV.

Occupation or means of livelihood—Part A.—General Table.

Number of Group.	OCCUPATION.	BANNU.					
		Total workers and dependants.	ACTUAL WORKERS.				Dependants.
			Total.		*Partially agriculturists.*		
			Males.	Females.	Males.	Females.	
	1	26	27	28	29	30	31
	ALL OCCUPATIONS	**250 086**	**74.846**	**3,237**	**1,392**	**36**	**172.003**
	Total Class A.—Production of raw materials.	**188,211**	**50.904**	**1.304**	**5**	...	**136,003**
	TOTAL SUB-CLASS I.—EXPLOITATION OF THE SURFACE OF THE EARTH.	**188,211**	**50.804**	**1.304**	**5**	...	**136,003**
	TOTAL ORDER I.—PASTURE AND AGRICULTURE.	**188.208**	**50.902**	**1.304**	**5**	...	**136,002**
	TOTAL ORDER I (*a*).—ORDINARY CULTIVATION.	**186.518**	**50.142**	**1.253**	**2**	...	**135,123**
	Income from rent of agricultural land—						
1 (*a*)	Non-cultivating owners	16,655	3.995	715	...	...	11,945
(*b*)	Non-cultivating tenants	80	46	...	...	...	34
	Ordinary cultivators—						
2 (*a*)	Cultivating owners	113.577	29.484	358	...	...	83.735
(*b*)	Cultivating tenants	52,001	15.376	138	...	...	36,487
3	Agents, managers of landed estates (not planters), clerks, rent collectors, etc.	97	37	...	2	...	60
4	Farm servants and field labourers ...	4.108	1,204	42	...	...	2,862
	TOTAL ORDER I (*b*).—GROWERS OF SPECIAL PRODUCTS AND MARKET GARDENING.	**364**	**114**	...	...	...	**250**
6	Fruit, flower, vegetable, betel-vine, areca-nut, etc., growers.	364	114	...	...	...	250
	TOTAL ORDER I (*c*).—FORESTRY ...	**308**	**187**	...	...	...	**121**
7	Forest officers, rangers, guards, etc. ...	—	...	...	...	...	...
8	Wood-cutters, fire-wood, lac, catechou, rubber, etc. collectors, and charcoal burners.	308	187	...	...	...	121
	TOTAL ORDER I (*d*).—RAISING OF FARM STOCK.	**1.018**	**459**	**51**	**3**	...	**508**
9	Cattle and buffalo breeders and keepers	1	...	...	...	...	1
10	Sheep. goat and pig breeders ...	...	...	...	...	...	...
11	Breeders of other animals (horses, mules, camels, asses, etc.)	7	3	...	...	...	4
12	Herdsmen, shepherds, goatherds, etc. ...	1,010	456	51	3	...	503
	TOTAL ORDER I (*e*).—RAISING OF SMALL ANIMALS.	...	...	...	...	...	...
13	Birds, bees, silkworms, etc. ...	...	...	...	...	...	...
	TOTAL ORDER II.—FISHING AND HUNTING...	**3**	**2**	...	...	...	**1**
14	Fishing	...	...	...	...	...	—
15	Hunting	3	2	...	...	...	1
	TOTAL SUB-CLASS II.—EXTRACTION OF MINERALS.	...	...	...	...	...	...
	TOTAL ORDER III.—MINES	...	...	...	...	...	...
16	Coal mines and petroleum wells ...	...	...	...	...	...	...
17	Mines and metallic minerals (gold, iron, manganese), etc.	...	...	...	...	...	...
	TOTAL ORDER V.—SALT	...	...	...	...	...	...
19	Rock, sea, and marsh salt	...	...	...	...	...	...
20	Extraction of saltpetre, alum and other substances soluble in water.	...	...	...	...	...	...

TABLE XV.

Occupation or means of livelihood.—Part A.—General Table.

DERA ISMAIL KHAN.						TRANS-FRONTIER POSTS.						
Total workers and dependants.	Actual Workers. Total. Males.	Actual Workers. Total. Females.	Actual Workers. Partially agriculturists. Males.	Actual Workers. Partially agriculturists. Females.	Dependants.	Total workers and dependants.	Actual Workers. Total. Males.	Actual Workers. Total. Females.	Actual Workers. Partially agriculturists. Males.	Actual Workers. Partially agriculturists. Females.	Dependants.	Number of Group.
32	33	34	35	36	37	38	39	40	41	42	43	
256.120	80.769	3.949	2.017	1	**171.402**	13.538	**12.150**	**23**	1.325	...	1.365	
139.577	**39.654**	1.065	19	...	98.858	**4.455**	4.347	1	1	...	107	
139.577	39.654	1.065	19	...	98.858	**4.455**	**4.347**	1	1	...	**107**	
139.480	39.620	1.065	**19**	...	98.795	**4.455**	**4.347**	1	1	...	**107**	
134.816	**37.715**	1.040	2	...	**96.061**	**4.448**	**4.342**	1	1	...	**106**	
18,189	4,500	600	...	...	13,089	357	345	...	...	...	12	1 (a)
72	36	...	...	...	36	...	...	...	...	...	...	(b)
53,152	14,297	169	...	...	38,686	2,289	2,213	1	...	...	75	2 (a)
61,200	18,238	152	...	...	42,810	1,798	1,782	...	...	...	16	(b)
105	24	...	2	...	81	4	2	...	1	...	2	3
2,098	620	119	...	...	1,359	...	...	...	...	...	...	4
323	**135**	**1**	**1**	...	**187**	**5**	**5**	...	...	...	...	
323	135	1	1	...	187	5	5	...	...	...	...	6
177	**77**	**6**	...	...	**94**	...	...	...	...	...	...	
1	...	...	...	...	1	...	...	...	...	...	...	7
176	77	6	...	...	93	...	...	...	...	...	...	8
4.160	**1.693**	**18**	**16**	...	**2.449**	**2**	...	...	...	...	**2**	
49	7	...	...	...	42	...	...	...	...	...	...	9
8	5	...	...	...	3	...	...	...	...	...	...	10
2	2	...	...	...	...	...	...	...	...	...	...	11
4,101	1,679	18	16	...	2,404	2	...	...	...	...	2	12
4	...	...	...	...	**4**	...	...	...	...	...	...	
4	...	...	...	...	4	...	...	...	...	—	...	13
97	**34**	...	...	...	**63**	...	...	...	...	...	...	
82	28	...	...	...	54	...	...	...	...	...	...	14
15	6	...	...	...	9	...	...	...	...	...	...	15
...	...	...	...	...	...	...	...	...	...	...	...	
...	...	...	...	...	...	...	...	...	...	...	...	
...	...	...	...	...	...	...	...	...	...	...	...	16
...	...	...	...	...	...	...	...	...	...	...	...	17
...	...	...	...	...	...	...	...	...	...	...	...	
...	...	...	...	...	...	...	...	...	...	...	...	19
...	...	...	...	...	...	...	...	...	...	...	...	20

TABLE XV.

Occupation or means of livelihood—Part A.—General Table.

Number of Group.	Occupation.	N.-W. F. P. (Total). Total workers and dependants.	Actual Workers. Total. Males.	Actual Workers. Total. Females.	Actual Workers. Partially agriculturists. Males.	Actual Workers. Partially agriculturists. Females.	Dependants.	Haza[ra] Total workers and dependants.	Actual Wor[kers]. Total. Males.	Actual Wor[kers]. Total. Females.
	1	2	3	4	5	6	7	8	9	10
	Total Class B.—Preparation and supply of material substances.	**444 572**	**142.766**	**9.797**	**3.954**	**80**	**292.009**	**91.965**	**29.743**	**1.542**
	TOTAL SUB-CLASS III.—INDUSTRY...	**253.557**	**79.228**	**8.153**	**2.147**	**66**	**166.176**	**67.389**	**21.025**	**1.332**
	TOTAL ORDER VI.—TEXTILES	**47.929**	**13.922**	**2.568**	**351**	**11**	**31.439**	**15.971**	**4.984**	**577**
21	Cotton ginning, cleaning, and pressing	3,432	1,150	119	31	2	2,163	1,292	148	25
22	Cotton spinning, sizing and weaving ...	34,599	10,219	1,690	261	9	22,690	12,431	3,882	498
24	Rope, twine and string	253	67	39	...	...	147	1	...	...
25	Other fibres (cocoanut, aloes, flax, hemp, straw, etc.).	569	168	78	...	...	323	3	1	...
26	Wool carders and spinners, weavers of woollen blankets, carpets, etc.	485	165	14	2	...	306	79	37	...
27	Silk spinners and weavers... ...	373	115	56	...	...	202	4	1	3
30	Dyeing, bleaching, printing, preparation and sponging of textiles.	7,590	1,975	299	57	...	5,316	2,161	615	51
31	Others (lace, crape, embroideries, fringes, etc., and insufficiently described textile industries.)	628	63	273	...	...	292	...	...	...
	TOTAL ORDER VII.—HIDES, SKINS AND HARD MATERIALS FROM THE ANIMAL KINGDOM.	**4.304**	**1,135**	**44**	**21**	...	**3.125**	**1.000**	**265**	**15**
32	Tanners, curriers, leather dressers and dyers, etc.	1,774	415	17	17	...	1,342	88	19	4
33	Makers of leather articles, such as trunks. water bags, etc.	2,472	698	27	4	...	1,747	912	246	11
34	Furriers	56	20	...	...	...	36	...	...	...
35	Bone, ivory, horn, shell, etc. workers ...	2	2	...	...	...	...	...	...	...
	TOTAL ORDER VIII.—WOOD	**30.012**	**9,361**	**610**	**358**	**7**	**20.041**	**6.523**	**2,051**	...
36	Sawyers, carpenters, turners, and joiners, etc.	27,855	8,740	69	357	7	19,046	6,508	2,048	...
37	Basket makers and other industries of woody material including leaves.	2,157	621	541	1	...	995	15	3	...
	TOTAL ORDER IX.—METALS	**25.046**	**7.823**	**25**	**356**	...	**17.198**	**8.667**	**2.759**	...
39	Plough and agricultural implement makers.	5,087	1,448	...	129	...	3,639	2,495	725	...
40	Makers of arms, guns, etc.... ..	123	50	...	4	..	73	13	8	...
41	Other workers in iron and makers of implements and tools principally or exclusively of iron.	18,421	5,764	21	220	...	12,636	6,084	2,005	...
42	Workers in brass, copper and bell metal.	470	188	1	...	...	281	18	5	...
43	Workers in other metals (tin, zinc, lead, quick-silver, etc.).	930	370	2	3	...	558	57	16	...
44	Workers in mints, die-sinkers, etc. ...	15	3	1	...	...	11	...	...	...
	TOTAL ORDER X.—CERAMICS	**15.043**	**4.411**	**169**	**59**	**2**	**10.463**	**3,617**	**1,095**	**61**
45	Makers of glass and crystal ware ...	86	40	...	...	...	46	...	...	...
46	Makers of porcelain and crockery ...	45	30	...	...	...	15	...	...	...
47	Potters and earthern pipe and bowl makers.	12,994	3,676	157	57	2	9,161	3,535	1,090	61
48	Brick and tile makers	1,918	665	12	2	...	1,241	32	5	...
	TOTAL ORDER XI.—CHEMICAL PRODUCTS PROPERLY SO-CALLED, AND ANALOGOUS.	**5.645**	**1.655**	**80**	**77**	...	**3.910**	**2.258**	**699**	**61**
50	Manufacture of matches and explosive materials.	248	50	38	1	...	160	126	22	31
51	Manufacture of ærated and mineral waters.	184	48	...	...	...	136	...	...	...
53	Manufacture and refining of vegetable and mineral oils.	5,094	1,514	41	76	...	3,539	2,130	677	30
55	Others (soap, candles, lac, cutch, perfumes, and miscellaneous drugs).	119	43	1	...	...	75	2	...	...

TABLE XV.

Occupation or means of livelihood.—Part A.—General Table.

RA.			PESHAWAR.						KOHAT.						
KERS.				ACTUAL WORKERS.						ACTUAL WORKERS.					
Partially agricul-turists.				Total.		Partially agricul-turists.				Total.		Partially agricul-turists.			
Males.	Females.	Dependants.	Total workers and dependants.	Males.	Females.	Males.	Females.	Dependants.	Total workers and dependants.	Males.	Females.	Males.	Females.	Dependants.	Number of Group.
11	12	13	14	15	16	17	18	19	20	21	22	23	24	25	
1.367	**22**	**60.680**	**209.665**	**66.637**	**5.011**	**1.228**	**35**	**138.017**	**28.676**	**9.579**	**1.289**	**141**	**2**	**17.808**	
1.000	**9**	**45,032**	**120,752**	**36.924**	**4.263**	**737**	**25**	**79.565**	**16.435**	**5.032**	**976**	**98**	**2**	**10.427**	
214	**8**	**10.410**	**23.294**	**6.267**	**1.598**	**94**	**8**	**15.429**	**1.981**	**632**	**85**	**7**	...	**1.264**	
20	...	819	1,790	594	52	8	2	1,144	140	57	4	2	...	79	21
168	3	8,051	16,919	4,574	1,018	65	6	11,327	1,373	484	23	3	...	866	22
...	...	1	46	18	...	...	...	28	39	...	39	...	...	...	24
...	...	2	414	99	70	...	...	245	39	12	1	...	...	26	25
...	...	42	204	64	...	...	...	140	29	5	12	1	...	12	26
...	...	...	341	108	53	...	...	180	28	6	...	...	...	22	27
26	...	1,495	2,965	748	133	21	...	2,084	322	67	5	1	...	250	30
...	...	...	615	62	272	...	...	281	11	1	1	...	...	9	31
2	...	**720**	**2.130**	**526**	**18**	**1**	...	**1.586**	**194**	**59**	**9**	**2**	...	**126**	
...	...	65	1,001	197	9	...	...	795	172	52	3	2	...	117	32
2	...	655	1,071	307	9	1	...	755	22	7	6	...	...	9	33
...	...	...	56	20	...	...	...	36	...	...	...	...	...	...	34
...	...	...	2	2	...	...	...	...	...	...	...	...	...	...	35
107	...	**4.472**	**12.609**	**3.957**	**157**	**111**	**7**	**8,495**	**3.506**	**1.054**	**436**	**38**	...	**2.016**	
107	...	4,460	11,385	3,490	36	110	7	7,859	2,821	987	30	38	...	1,804	36
...	...	12	1,224	467	121	1	...	636	685	67	406	...	...	212	37
182	...	**5.908**	**10.298**	**3.238**	**9**	**131**	...	**7.051**	**1.344**	**399**	**8**	**27**	...	**937**	
85	...	1,770	2,225	605	...	41	...	1,620	113	38	...	...	...	75	39
...	...	5	90	36	...	3	...	54	11	2	...	...	...	9	40
95	...	4,079	7,151	2,280	7	87	...	4,864	1,138	320	8	27	...	810	41
...	...	13	355	132	...	...	...	223	58	31	...	...	...	27	42
2	..	41	462	182	1	...	...	279	24	8	...	...	...	16	43
...	...	...	15	3	1	...	...	11	...	...	...	...	...	...	44
27	...	**2.461**	**7.504**	**2.134**	**67**	**26**	**2**	**5.303**	**806**	**207**	**4**	**3**	...	**595**	
...	...	...	...	...	...	...	...	...	...	...	...	...	...	...	45
...	...	...	45	30	...	...	...	15	...	...	...	...	...	...	46
27	...	2,434	6,139	1,653	57	25	2	4,429	732	178	4	3	...	550	47
...	...	27	1,320	451	10	1	...	859	74	29	...	...	...	45	48
31	...	**1.498**	**2.630**	**718**	**14**	**39**	...	**1.898**	**161**	**27**	**2**	...	...	**132**	
1	...	73	102	21	7	...	...	74	6	1	...	...	...	5	50
...	...	...	154	41	...	...	...	113	16	...	...	...	...	16	51
30	...	1,423	2,258	613	7	39	...	1,638	139	26	2	...	...	111	53
...	...	2	116	43	...	...	...	73	...	...	...	...	...	...	55

TABLE XV.

Occupation or means of livelihood.—Part A.—General Table.

Number of Group.	Occupation.	BANNU. Total workers and dependants.	Actual Workers. Total. Males.	Actual Workers. Total. Females.	Actual Workers. Partially agriculturists. Males.	Actual Workers. Partially agriculturists. Females.	Dependants.
	1	26	27	28	29	30	31
	Total Class B.—Preparation and supply of material substances.	**34.883**	**11.245**	**769**	**699**	**31**	**22.869**
	TOTAL SUB-CLASS III.—INDUSTRY...	**18.061**	**6.474**	**615**	**157**	**30**	**11.972**
	TOTAL ORDER VI.—TEXTILES	**2.478**	**737**	**94**	**20**	...	**1.647**
21	Cotton ginning, cleaning, and pressing	143	31	38	...	...	74
22	Cotton spinning, sizing and weaving ...	1,308	423	46	19	...	839
24	Rope, twine and string	1	1	...	...	...	...
25	Other fibres (cocoanut, aloes, flax, hemp, straw, etc.).	1	1	...	...	...	...
26	Wool carders and spinners, weavers of woollen blankets, carpets, etc.	133	47	1	1	...	85
27	Silk spinners and weavers	...	...	...	...	...	...
30	Dyeing, bleaching, printing, preparation and sponging of textiles.	892	234	9	...	...	649
31	Others (lace, crape, embroideries, fringes, etc., and insufficiently described textile industries.)	...	...	...	...	...	...
	TOTAL ORDER VII.—HIDES, SKINS AND HARD MATERIALS FROM THE ANIMAL KINGDOM.	**599**	**157**	**2**	**16**	...	**440**
32	Tanners, curriers, leather dressers and dyers, etc.	474	127	1	15	...	346
33	Makers of leather articles, such as trunks, water bags, etc.	125	30	1	1	...	94
34	Furriers	...	...	...	...	...	...
35	Bone, ivory, horn, shell, etc. workers ...	...	...	...	...	...	...
	TOTAL ORDER VIII.—WOOD	**3,039**	**857**	**5**	**69**	...	**2.177**
36	Sawyers, carpenters, turners, and joiners, etc.	3,032	856	2	69	...	2,174
37	Basket makers and other industries of woody material including leaves.	7	1	3	...	...	3
	TOTAL ORDER IX.—METALS	**2.641**	**772**	**1**	...	...	**1.868**
39	Plough and agricultural implement makers.	137	47	...	...	...	90
40	Makers of arms, guns, etc.... ...	...	...	...	...	...	...
41	Other workers in iron and makers of implements and tools principally or exclusively of iron.	2,430	698	...	...	...	1,732
42	Workers in brass, copper and bell metal.	1	1	...	...	...	...
43	Workers in other metals (tin, zinc, lead, quick-silver, etc.).	73	26	1	...	...	46
44	Workers in mints, die-sinkers, etc. ...	...	...	...	...	...	...
	TOTAL ORDER X.—CERAMICS	**1.099**	**331**	**19**	...	...	**749**
45	Makers of glass and crystal ware ...	...	...	...	...	...	...
46	Makers of porcelain and crockery ...	...	...	...	...	...	...
47	Potters and earthern pipe and bowl makers.	992	276	19	...	...	697
48	Brick and tile makers	107	55	...	...	...	52
	TOTAL ORDER XI.—CHEMICAL PRODUCTS PROPERLY SO-CALLED, AND ANALOGOUS.	**46**	**13**	...	...	...	**33**
50	Manufacture of matches and explosive materials.	...	...	...	...	...	...
51	Manufacture of ærated and mineral waters.	...	...	...	...	...	...
53	Manufacture and refining of vegetable and mineral oils.	46	13	...	...	...	33
55	Others (soap, candles, lac, cutch, perfumes, and miscellaneous drugs).	...	...	...	...	...	...

TABLE XV.

Occupation or means of livelihood.—Part A.—General Table.

DERA ISMAIL KHAN.						TRANS-FRONTIER POSTS.						
Total workers and dependants.	ACTUAL WORKERS.				Dependants.	Total workers and dependants.	ACTUAL WORKERS.				Dependants.	Number of Group.
	Total.		*Partially agriculturists.*				*Total.*		*Partially agriculturists.*			
	Males.	Females.	Males.	Females.			Males.	Females.	Males.	Females.		
32	33	34	35	36	37	38	39	40	41	42	43	
77.436	**24.312**	**1,167**	**492**	...	**51.957**	**1.947**	**1.250**	**19**	**27**	...	**678**	
30.095	**10,194**	**948**	**138**	...	**18.953**	**825**	**579**	**19**	**17**	...	**227**	
4.199	**1.300**	**214**	**16**	...	**2.685**	**6**	**2**	...	...	...	**4**	
66	19	...	1	...	47	1	1	...	...	...	...	21
2,567	855	105	6	...	1,607	1	1	...	...	...	...	22
166	48	...	...	...	118	...	...	...	...	...	...	24
112	55	7	...	...	50	...	...	...	...	...	...	25
40	12	1	...	...	27	...	...	...	...	...	...	26
...	...	...	...	...	...	...	...	...	...	...	...	27
1,246	311	101	9	...	834	4	...	...	...	...	4	30
2	...	...	...	...	2	...	...	...	...	...	...	31
381	**128**	...	...	...	**253**	...	...	...	...	...	...	
39	20	...	...	...	19	...	...	...	...	...	...	32
342	108	...	...	...	234	...	...	...	...	...	...	33
...	...	...	...	...	...	...	...	...	...	...	...	34
...	...	...	...	...	...	...	...	...	...	...	...	35
4.268	**1.384**	**12**	**33**	...	**2.872**	**67**	**58**	...	...	...	**9**	
4,042	1,301	1	33	...	2,740	67	58	...	...	...	9	36
226	83	11	...	...	132	...	...	...	...	...	...	37
2.057	**631**	**6**	**16**	...	**1.420**	**39**	**24**	**1**	...	...	**14**	
117	33	...	3	...	84	...	...	...	...	...	...	39
6	1	...	1	...	5	3	3	...	...	...	...	40
1,589	441	5	11	...	1,143	29	20	1	...	...	8	41
35	18	1	...	...	16	3	1	...	...	...	2	42
310	138	...	1	...	172	4	...	...	...	...	4	43
...	...	...	...	...	...	...	...	...	...	...	...	44
2.000	**633**	**18**	**3**	...	**1.349**	**17**	**11**	...	...	...	**6**	
86	40	...	...	...	46	...	...	...	...	...	...	45
...	...	...	...	...	...	...	...	...	...	...	...	46
1,533	469	16	2	...	1,048	13	10	...	...	...	3	47
381	124	2	1	...	255	4	1	...	...	...	3	48
550	**198**	**3**	**7**	...	**349**	...	...	...	...	...	...	
14	6	...	...	...	8	...	...	...	...	...	...	50
14	7	...	...	...	7	...	...	...	...	...	...	51
521	185	2	7	...	334	...	...	...	...	...	...	53
1	...	1	...	...	...	...	...	...	...	...	...	55

TABLE XV.

Occupation or means of livelihood—Part A.—General Table.

Number of Group.	OCCUPATION.	N.-W. F. P. (TOTAL). Total workers and dependants.	Actual Workers. Total. Males.	Actual Workers. Total. Females.	Actual Workers. Partially agriculturists. Males.	Actual Workers. Partially agriculturists. Females.	Dependants.	HAZA[RA] Total workers and dependants.	Actual Wor[kers]. Total. Males.	Actual Wor[kers]. Total. Females.
	1	2	3	4	5	6	7	8	9	10
	TOTAL ORDER XII.—FOOD INDUSTRIES ...	**25,928**	**7,570**	**2,268**	**135**	**35**	**16,090**	**4,472**	**1,458**	**174**
56	Rice pounders and huskers and flour grinders.	9,061	2,273	1,796	41	32	4,992	2,150	695	47
57	Bakers and biscuit makers... ...	162	50	1	1	...	111	57	24	...
58	Grain parchers, etc.	4,980	1,362	404	48	2	3,214	909	258	119
59	Butchers	8,627	2,517	55	36	1	6,055	895	286	6
61	Butter, cheese and ghee makers ...	22	9	...	...	...	13	...	...	...
62	Makers of sugar, molasses, and gur ...	91	44	...	...	...	47	...	...	...
63	Sweetmeat makers, preparers of jam and condiments, etc.	2,465	1,118	2	3	...	1,345	370	163	...
64	Brewers and distillers ...	207	76	...	...	...	131	...	...	...
66	Manufacturers of tobacco, opium, and ganja.	313	121	10	6	...	182	91	32	2
	TOTAL ORDER XIII.—INDUSTRIES OF DRESS AND THE TOILET.	**71,057**	**23,422**	**1,479**	**660**	**5**	**46,153**	**20,927**	**6,425**	**334**
67	Hat, cap and turban makers ...	1,608	534	97	6	1	977	16	8	1
68	Tailors, milliners, dress makers and darners, embroiderers on linen.	11,097	3,664	806	44	1	6,627	3,461	1,058	245
69	Shoe, boot and sandal makers ...	29,805	9,960	227	320	...	19,618	10,086	3,185	...
70	Other industries pertaining to dress gloves, socks, gaiters, belts, buttons, umbrellas, canes, etc.	95	54	...	...	...	41	2	2	...
71	Washing, cleaning, and dyeing	6,485	2,633	319	20	1	3,533	755	212	69
72	Barbers, hair dressers, and wig makers	21,944	6,554	30	270	2	15,360	6,607	1,960	19
73	Other industries connected with the toilet, tattooers, shampooers, bath-houses, etc.	23	23	...	...	.	...	...	...	...
	TOTAL ORDER XIV.—FURNITURE INDUSTRIES.	**1,381**	**435**	**24**	**29**	...	**922**	**478**	**153**	**16**
74	Cabinet makers, carriage painters, etc.	1,290	407	24	26	...	859	475	152	16
75	Upholsterers, tent makers, etc. ...	91	28	...	3	...	63	3	1	...
	TOTAL ORDER XV.—BUILDING INDUSTRIES	**8,016**	**2,867**	**68**	**15**	...	**5,081**	**571**	**150**	...
76	Lime burners, cement workers ...	100	48	...	...	...	52	...	...	...
77	Excavators, plinth builders and well sinkers.	91	40	...	4	...	51	...	...	...
78	Stone and marble workers, masons and brick-layers.	4,005	1,464	27	8	..	2,514	289	53	...
79	Others (thatchers, building contractors, house painters, tilers, plumbers, lock-smiths, etc.)	3,820	1,315	41	3	...	2,464	282	97	...
	TOTAL ORDER XVI.—CONSTRUCTION OF MEANS OF TRANSPORT.	**837**	**313**	**5**	**3**	...	**519**	**130**	**77**	...
80	Cart, carriage, palki, etc., makers and wheelwrights.	80	11	4	...	...	65	...	...	...
81	Saddlers, harness makers, whip and lash makers.	580	248	1	3	...	331	130	77	...
82	Ship and boat builders	177	54	...	...	...	123	...	...	...
	TOTAL ORDER XVII.—PRODUCTION AND TRANSMISSION OF PHYSICAL FORCES (HEAT, LIGHT, ELECTRICITY, MOTIVE POWER, ETC.)	**14**	**8**	...	...	...	**6**	...	..	...
83	Gas works, electric light and ice factories.	14	8	...	...	...	6	...	...	...
	TOTAL ORDER XVIII.—INDUSTRIES OF LUXURY AND THOSE PERTAINING TO LITERATURE AND THE ARTS AND SCIENCES.	**11,164**	**3,476**	**80**	**75**	**3**	**7,608**	**1,647**	**491**	...
84	Printers, lithographers, engravers, etc....	114	46	...	...	...	68	4	1	...
85	News-paper and magazine managers and editors, journalists, etc.	3	3	...	...	...	...	...	...	...
86	Book-binders and stitchers, envelope makers, etc.	218	53	55	1	...	110	11	3	...

TABLE XV.

Occupation or means of livelihood.—Part A.—General Table.

RA.			PESHAWAR.						KOHAT.						
KERS.			Total workers and dependants.	Actual Workers.				Dependants.	Total workers and dependants.	Actual Workers.				Dependants.	Number of Group.
Partially agriculturists.		Dependants.		Total.		Partially agriculturists.				Total.		Partially agriculturists.			
Males.	Females.			Males.	Females.	Males.	Females.			Males.	Females.	Males.	Females.		
11	12	13	14	15	16	17	18	19	20	21	22	23	24	25	
40	**4**	**2.840**	**15.694**	**4.516**	**1,100**	**59**	**1**	**10.078**	**1.491**	**405**	**150**	**1**	...	**936**	
22	1	1,408	5,004	1,302	986	11	1	2,716	426	90	87	1	...	249	56
1	...	33	56	17	1	...	...	38	4	2	...	...	...	2	57
9	2	532	2,844	798	71	20	...	1,975	320	61	60	...	...	109	58
8	1	603	6,322	1,774	33	20	...	4,515	515	147	3	...	...	305	59
...	...	...	14	2	...	...	...	12	...	...	...	...	...	...	61
...	...	...	91	44	...	...	...	47	...	...	...	...	...	...	62
...	...	207	1,141	490	1	2	...	650	226	105	...	...	...	121	63
...	...	...	...	...	...	...	...	...	...	...	..	...	...	...	64
...	...	57	222	89	8	6	...	125	...	...	...	...	...	...	66
344	**1**	**14.168**	**30.306**	**9.989**	**855**	**222**	**4**	**19.462**	**5.074**	**1.550**	**140**	**15**	...	**3.284**	
1	...	7	1,592	526	96	5	1	970	...	...	...	...	...	...	67
20	...	2,158	5,413	1,703	464	7	1	3,246	606	243	12	...	...	346	68
183	...	6,901	11,774	4,109	91	96	...	7,574	1,477	443	99	2	...	935	69
...	...	...	88	49	...	...	...	39	4	2	...	...	...	2	70
9	...	474	2,943	1,066	196	6	1	1,681	402	145	29	1	...	228	71
131	1	4,628	8,473	2,513	8	108	1	5,952	2,585	712	...	12	...	1,873	72
...	...	...	23	23	...	...	...	...	...	...	...	...	...	...	73
26	...	**309**	**847**	**257**	**8**	...	...	**582**	...	...	...	...	...	...	
26	...	307	778	236	8	...	...	534	...	...	...	...	...	...	74
...	...	2	69	21	...	...	...	48	...	...	...	..	...	...	75
4	...	**421**	**5.260**	**1.896**	**24**	**8**	...	**3.340**	**223**	**76**	**18**	...	...	**129**	
...	...	...	67	34	...	...	...	33	...	...	...	...	...	...	76
...	...	...	55	29	...	4	...	26	...	...	...	...	...	...	77
4	...	236	2,996	1,138	13	4	...	1,845	149	67	9	...	...	73	78
..	...	185	2,142	695	11	...	...	4,436	74	9	9	...	...	56	79
3	...	**63**	**698**	**232**	**5**	...	...	**461**	**3**	...	...	...	...	**3**	
...	...	...	80	11	4	...	...	65	...	...	...	...	...	...	80
3	...	53	441	167	1	...	...	273	3	...	...	...	...	3	81
...	...	...	177	54	...	...	...	123	...	...	...	...	...	...	82
...	...	...	**5**	**4**	...	...	...	**1**	...	...	...	...	...	...	
...	...	...	5	4	...	...	...	1	...	...	...	...	...	...	83
17	...	**1.156**	**5.817**	**1,750**	**68**	**43**	**3**	**3.999**	**919**	**330**	**10**	**3**	...	**579**	
...	...	3	78	35	...	...	...	43	17	7	...	...	...	10	84
...	...	...	3	3	...	...	...	...	...	...	...	...	...	...	85
...	...	8	148	21	55	...	...	72	...	...	...	...	...	...	86

TABLE XV.

Occupation or means of livelihood—Part A.—General Table.

Number of Group.	Occupation.	BANNU. Total workers and dependants.	Actual Workers. Total. Males.	Actual Workers. Total. Females.	Actual Workers. Partially agriculturists. Males.	Actual Workers. Partially agriculturists. Females.	Dependants.
	1	26	27	28	29	30	31
	Total Order XII.—Food Industries ...	**1,820**	**484**	**396**	**30**	**30**	**940**
56	Rice pounders and huskers and flour grinders.	631	81	294	7	30	256
57	Bakers and biscuit makers... ...	4	2	...	...	...	2
58	Grain parchers, etc.	640	186	96	18	...	358
59	Butchers	235	100	6	4	...	129
61	Butter, cheese and ghee makers ...	...	...	...	...	...	...
62	Makers of sugar, molasses, and gur ...	...	...	...	...	...	...
63	Sweetmeat makers, preparers of jam and condiments, etc.	107	43	...	1	...	64
64	Brewers and distillers	203	72	...	...	...	131
66	Manufacturers of tobacco, opium, and ganja.	...	...	...	...	...	...
	Total Order XIII.—Industries of dress and the toilet.	**4,383**	**1,425**	**21**	**10**	...	**2,937**
67	Hat, cap and turban makers ...	...	...	...	...	...	...
68	Tailors, milliners, dress makers and darners, embroiderers on linen.	544	199	10	10	...	335
69	Shoe, boot and sandal makers ...	1,549	506	2	...	...	1,041
70	Other industries pertaining to dress, gloves, socks, gaiters, belts, buttons, umbrellas, canes, etc.	...	...	...	...	...	...
71	Washing, cleaning, and dyeing ...	158	69	9	...	...	80
72	Barbers, hair dressers, and wig makers	2,132	651	...	...	...	1,481
73	Other industries connected with the toilet, tattooers, shampooers, bath-houses, etc.	...	...	...	...	...	...
	Total Order XIV.—Furniture Industries.	**20**	**8**	...	...	...	**12**
74	Cabinet makers. carriage painters, etc.	20	8	...	...	...	12
75	Upholsterers, tent makers, etc. ...	...	...	...	...	...	...
	Total Order XV.—Building Industries	**568**	**207**	**4**	...	...	**357**
76	Lime burners, cement workers ..	2	2	...	...	...	...
77	Excavators, plinth builders and well sinkers.	...	...	...	...	...	...
78	Stone and marble workers, masons and brick-layers	427	148	4	...	...	275
79	Others (thatchers, building contractors, house painters, tilers, plumbers, lock-smiths, etc.)	139	57	...	...	...	82
	Total Order XVI.—Construction of means of transport.	**4**	**2**	...	...	...	**2**
80	Cart, carriage. palki, etc, makers and wheelwrights.	...	...	...	...	...	...
81	Saddlers, harness makers, whip and lash makers.	4	2	...	...	...	2
82	Ship and boat builders	...	...	...	...	...	...
	Total Order XVII.—Production and transmission of physical forces (heat, light, electricity, motive power, etc.)	**9**	**4**	...	...	...	**5**
83	Gas works, electric light and ice factories.	9	4	...	...	...	5
	Total Order XVIII.—Industries of luxury and those pertaining to literature and the arts and sciences.	**855**	**276**	...	**12**	...	**579**
84	Printers, lithographers. engravers, etc...	15	3	...	...	...	12
85	Newspaper and magazine managers and editors, journalists, etc.	...	...	...	...	...	...
86	Book-binders and stitchers, envelope makers, etc.	42	21	...	1	...	21

TABLE XV.

Occupation or means of livelihood.—Part A.—General Table.

DERA ISMAIL KHAN.						TRANS-FRONTIER POSTS.						
Total workers and dependants.	Actual Workers. Total. Males.	Actual Workers. Total. Females.	Actual Workers. Partially agriculturists. Males.	Actual Workers. Partially agriculturists. Females.	Dependants.	Total workers and dependants.	Actual Workers. Total. Males.	Actual Workers. Total. Females.	Actual Workers. Partially agriculturists. Males.	Actual Workers. Partially agriculturists. Females.	Dependants.	Number of Group.
32	33	34	35	36	37	38	39	40	41	42	43	
2,377	**670**	**448**	**5**	...	**1,259**	**74**	**37**	...	...	...	**37**	
850	105	382	...	...	363	...	...	...	...	...	...	56
41	5	...	...	...	36	...	...	...	...	...	...	57
267	59	58	1	...	150	...	...	...	...	...	...	58
621	194	7	4	...	420	39	16	...	...	...	23	59
8	7	...	...	...	1	...	...	...	...	...	...	61
...	...	...	...	...	...	...	...	...	...	...	...	62
586	296	1	...	...	289	35	21	...	...	...	14	63
4	4	...	...	...	...	...	...	...	...	...	...	64
...	...	...	...	...	...	...	...	...	...	...	...	66
10,007	**3,772**	**123**	**52**	...	**6,112**	**360**	**261**	**6**	**17**	...	**93**	
...	...	...	...	...	...	...	...	...	...	...	...	67
925	337	75	...	...	513	148	119	...	7	...	29	68
4,856	1,675	35	35	...	3,146	63	42	...	4	...	21	69
1	1	...	...	...	...	...	...	...	...	...	...	70
2,124	1,076	10	4	...	1,038	103	65	6	...	...	32	71
2,101	683	3	13	...	1,415	46	35	...	6	...	11	72
...	...	...	...	...	...	...	...	...	...	...	...	73
36	**17**	...	**3**	...	**19**	...	...	...	...	...	...	
17	11	...	...	...	6	...	...	...	...	...	...	74
19	6	...	3	...	13	...	...	...	...	...	...	75
1,359	**523**	**22**	**3**	...	**814**	**35**	**15**	...	...	...	**20**	
31	12	...	...	...	19	...	...	...	...	...	...	76
36	11	...	...	...	25	...	...	...	...	...	...	77
109	43	1	...	...	65	35	15	...	...	...	20	78
1,183	457	21	3	...	705	...	...	...	...	...	...	79
2	**2**	...	...	...	...	...	...	...	...	...	...	
...	...	...	...	...	...	...	...	...	...	...	...	80
2	2	...	...	...	...	...	...	...	...	...	...	81
...	...	...	...	...	...	...	...	...	...	...	...	82
...	...	...	...	...	...	...	...	...	...	...	...	
...	...	...	...	...	...	...	...	...	...	...	...	83
1,906	**610**	**2**	...	...	**1,294**	**20**	**19**	...	...	...	**1**	
...	...	...	...	...	...	...	...	...	...	...	...	84
...	...	...	...	...	...	...	...	...	...	...	...	85
17	8	...	...	...	9	...	...	...	...	...	...	86

TABLE XV.

Occupation or means of livelihood—Part A.—General Table.

Number of Group.	Occupation.	N.-W. F. P. (Total). Total workers and dependants.	N.-W. F. P. (Total). Actual Workers. Total. Males.	N.-W. F. P. (Total). Actual Workers. Total. Females.	N.-W. F. P. (Total). Actual Workers. Partially agriculturists. Males.	N.-W. F. P. (Total). Actual Workers. Partially agriculturists. Females.	N.-W. F. P. (Total). Dependants.	HAZA[RA] Total workers and dependants.	HAZA[RA] Actual Wor[kers]. Total. Males.	HAZA[RA] Actual Wor[kers]. Total. Females.
	1	2	3	4	5	6	7	8	9	10
87	Makers of musical instruments ...	28	14	...	...	...	14	...	...	...
88	Makers of watches and clocks and optical, photographic and surgical instruments.	303	117	...	1	...	186	12	5	...
89	Workers in precious stones and metals, enamellers, imitation jewellery makers, gilders, etc.	10,137	3,113	22	73	3	7,002	1,620	482	...
90	Makers of bangles, rosaries, bead and other necklaces, spangles, lingams and sacred threads.	31	14	...	...	...	17	...	...	...
91	Toy, kite, cage, fishing tackle, etc., makers, taxidermists, etc.	42	18	3	...	...	21	...	...	...
92	Others, including managers, persons other than performers employed in theatres and other places of public entertainment, employés of public societies, race course service, huntsmen, etc.	288	98	...	...	...	190	...	...	...
	Total Order XIX.—Industries concerned with refuse matter.	**7,181**	**2,830**	**733**	**8**	**3**	**3,618**	**1,128**	**418**	**94**
93	Sweepers, scavengers, dust and sweeping contractors.	7,181	2,830	733	8	3	3,618	1,128	418	94
	TOTAL SUB-CLASS IV.—TRANSPORT	**47,774**	**16,940**	**228**	**366**	**2**	**30,606**	**5,951**	**2,336**	**6**
	Total Order XX.—Transport by water	**2,621**	**946**	**5**	**15**	...	**1,670**	**177**	**66**	...
95	Ship owners and their employés, ship brokers, ship's officers, engineers, mariners, and firemen.	33	22	...	...	...	11	...	...	...
96	Persons employed on the maintenance of streams, rivers, and canals (including construction).	961	365	3	1	...	593	6	3	...
97	Boat owners, boat men, and tow men ...	1,627	559	2	14	...	1,066	171	63	...
	Total Order XXI.—Transport by road...	**40,166**	**13,647**	**217**	**261**	**2**	**26,302**	**5,339**	**2,103**	**6**
98	Persons employed on the construction and maintenance of roads and bridges.	2,495	1,015	31	15	...	1,449	420	208	...
99	Cart owners and drivers, coach-men, stableboys, tramway, mail carriage etc., managers and employes (excluding private servants).	8,380	3,096	13	84	...	5,271	1,360	725	...
100	Palki etc., bearers and owners	360	190	5	...	...	165	90	17	...
101	Pack elephant, camel, mule, ass and bullock owners and drivers.	24,184	7,679	40	117	2	16,465	3,256	1,096	5
102	Porters and messengers	4,747	1,667	128	45	...	2,952	213	57	1
	Total Order XXII.—Transport by rail	**3,259**	**1,602**	**2**	**65**	...	**1,655**	**178**	**61**	...
103	Railway employés of all kinds other than construction coolies.	2,915	1,371	2	50	...	1,542	177	60	...
104	Labourers employed on railway construction.	344	231	...	15	...	113	1	1	...
	Total Order XXIII.—Post office, Telegraph, and Telephone services.	**1,728**	**745**	**4**	**25**	...	**979**	**257**	**106**	...
105	Post Office, Telegraph and Telephone Services.	1,728	745	4	25		979	257	106	...
	TOTAL SUB-CLASS V.—TRADE ...	**143,241**	**46,598**	**1,416**	**1,441**	**22**	**95,227**	**18,625**	**6,382**	**204**
	Total Order XXIV.—Banks, establishments of credit, exchange and insurance.	**3,037**	**856**	**122**	**67**	**12**	**2,059**	**1,371**	**378**	**25**
106	Bank managers, money lenders, exchange and insurance agents, money changers and brokers and their employes.	3,037	856	132	67	12	2,059	1,371	378	25

TABLE XV.

Occupation or means of livelihood—Part A.—General Table.

RA.			PESHAWAR.						KOHAT.						
KERS.			Total workers and dependants.	Actual Workers.				Dependants.	Total workers and dependants.	Actual Workers.				Dependants.	Number of Group.
Partially agriculturists.				Total.		Partially agriculturists.				Total.		Partially agriculturists.			
Males.	Females.	Dependants.		Males.	Females.	Males.	Females.			Males.	Females.	Males.	Females.		
11	12	13	14	15	16	17	18	19	20	21	22	23	24	25	
...	...	...	28	14	..	...	...	14	...	...	...	...	...	...	87
...	...	7	121	39	...	...	...	82	105	44	...	...	...	61	88
17	...	1,138	5,173	1,545	10	43	3	3,618	789	278	10	3	...	501	89
...	...	...	31	14	...	...	..	17	...	...	...	...	...	...	90
...	...	...	42	18	3	...	...	21	...	...	...	..	..	...	91
...	...	...	193	61	...	...	...	132	8	1	...	...	...	7	92
3	**1**	**616**	**3,660**	**1,440**	**340**	**3**	...	**1,880**	**733**	**293**	**114**	**2**	**2**	**326**	
3	1	616	3,660	1,440	340	3	.	1,880	733	293	114	2	2	326	93
122	...	**8,609**	**23,669**	**8,067**	**105**	**88**	**2**	**15,497**	**2,599**	**1,073**	**75**	**32**	...	**1,451**	
1	...	**111**	**1,948**	**676**	**5**	**12**	..	**1,267**	**6**	**4**	...	...	...	**2**	
...	...	...	9	3	...	..	...	6	...	...	...	...	...	...	95
1	.	3	849	318	3	...	.	528	1	...	...	...	...	1	96
...	...	108	1,090	355	2	12	...	733	5	4	...	...	...	1	97
116	...	**8,230**	**18,980**	**6,188**	**98**	**49**	**2**	**12,694**	**1,681**	**601**	**73**	**2**	...	**1,007**	
10	...	212	907	356	7	4	...	544	196	83	5	1	...	108	98
33	...	635	5,406	1,706	12	20	...	3,688	334	140	...	...	...	194	99
...	...	73	97	51	1	...	...	45	61	11	4	...	...	46	100
73	...	2,155	8,424	2,580	13	16	2	5,831	936	350	4	1	...	582	101
...	...	155	4,146	1,495	65	9	...	2,586	154	17	60	...	...	77	102
2	...	**117**	**1,972**	**898**	**1**	**23**	...	**1,073**	**786**	**407**	**1**	**23**	...	**378**	
2	...	117	1,833	817	1	23	...	1,015	715	384	1	23	...	330	103
...	...	...	139	81	...	...	...	58	71	23	...	...	...	48	104
3	...	**161**	**769**	**305**	**1**	**4**	...	**463**	**126**	**61**	**1**	**7**	...	**64**	
3	...	151	769	305	1	4	...	463	126	61	1	7	...	64	105
245	**13**	**12,039**	**65,244**	**21,646**	**643**	**403**	**8**	**42,955**	**9,642**	**3,474**	**238**	**11**	...	**5,930**	
44	**12**	**968**	**899**	**272**	**57**	**12**	...	**670**	**128**	**38**	**1**	**1**	...	**89**	
44	12	968	899	272	57	12	...	570	128	38	1	1	...	89	160

TABLE XV.

Occupation or means of livelihood—Part A.—General Table.

Number of Group.	Occupation.	BANNU.					
		Total workers and dependants.	Actual Workers.				Dependants.
			Total.		Partially agriculturists.		
			Males.	Females.	Males.	Females.	
	1	26	27	28	29	30	31
87	Makers of musical instruments ...	...	...	...	...	...	...
88	Makers of watches and clocks and optical, photographic and surgical instruments.	22	7	...	1	...	15
89	Workers in precious stones and metals, enamellers, imitation jewellery makers, gilders, etc.	689	209	...	10	...	480
90	Makers of bangles, rosaries, bead and other necklaces, spangles, lingams and sacred threads.	...	...	...	...	...	...
91	Toy, kite, cage, fishing tackle, etc., makers, taxidermists, etc.	...	...	...	...	...	...
92	Others, including managers, persons other than performers employed in theatres and other places of public entertainment, employés of public societies, race course service, huntsmen, etc.	87	36	...	...	...	51
	TOTAL ORDER XIX.—INDUSTRIES CONCERNED WITH REFUSE MATTER.	**500**	**201**	**73**	...	...	**226**
93	Sweepers, scavengers, dust and sweeping contractors.	500	201	73	...	...	226
	TOTAL SUB-CLASS IV.—TRANSPORT	**2.860**	**1.246**	**11**	...	...	**1.603**
	TOTAL ORDER XX.—TRANSPORT BY WATER	**42**	**12**	...	...	...	**30**
95	Ship owners and their employés, ship brokers, ship's officers, engineers, mariners, and firemen.	...	...	...	...	...	...
96	Persons employed on the maintenance of streams, rivers, and canals (including construction).	42	12	...	...	...	30
97	Boat owners, boat men, and tow men ...	...	...	...	...	...	...
	TOTAL ORDER XXI.—TRANSPORT BY ROAD...	**2.468**	**1.007**	**9**	**41**	...	**1.452**
98	Persons employed on the construction and maintenance of roads and bridges	302	93	2	...	...	207
99	Cart owners and drivers, coach-men, stableboys, tramway. mail carriage etc., managers and employés (excluding private servants).	569	267	...	16	...	302
100	Palki etc., bearers and owners ...	10	10	...	...	...	...
101	Pack elephant, camel, mule, ass and bullock owners and drivers.	1,495	603	5	24	...	887
102	Porters and messengers	92	34	2	1	...	56
	TOTAL ORDER XXII.—TRANSPORT BY RAIL	**201**	**160**	...	**17**	...	**41**
103	Railway employés of all kinds other than construction coolies.	73	39	...	2	...	34
104	Labourers employed on railway construction.	128	121	...	15	...	7
	TOTAL ORDER XXIII.—POST OFFICE, TELEGRAPH, AND TELEPHONE SERVICES.	**149**	**67**	**2**	...	...	**80**
105	Post Office, Telegraph and Telephone Services.	149	67	2	...	...	80
	TOTAL SUB-CLASS V.—TRADE ...	**13.962**	**4.525**	**143**	**484**	**1**	**9.294**
	TOTAL ORDER XXIV.—BANKS, ESTABLISHMENTS OF CREDIT, EXCHANGE AND INSURANCE.	**75**	**26**	**1**	...	...	**48**
106	Bank managers, money lenders, exchange and insurance agents, money changers and brokers and their employés.	75	26	1	...	...	48

TABLE XV.

Occupation or means of livelihood.—Part A.—General Table.

DERA ISMAIL KHAN.						TRANS-FRONTIER POSTS.						
Total workers and dependants.	Actual Workers.				Dependants.	Total workers and dependants.	Actual Workers.				Dependants.	Number of Group
	Total.		*Partially agriculturists.*				Total.		*Partially agriculturists.*			
	Males.	Females.	Males.	Females.			Males.	Females.	Males.	Females.		
32	33	34	35	36	37	38	39	40	41	42	43	
...	...	...	...	...	...	...	...	...	...	...	...	87
42	21	...	...	...	21	1	1	...	...	...	...	88
1,847	581	2	...	...	1,264	19	18	...	...	...	1	89
...	...	...	...	...	...	...	...	...	...	...	...	90
...	...	...	...	...	...	...	...	...	...	...	...	91
...	...	...	...	...	...	...	...	...	...	...	...	92
953	**326**	**100**	...	...	**527**	**207**	**152**	**12**	...	...	**43**	
953	326	100	...	...	527	207	152	12	...	...	43	93
12.385	**3.973**	**31**	**56**	...	**8.381**	**310**	**245**	...	**10**	...	**65**	
431	**174**	...	**2**	...	**257**	**17**	**14**	...	...	...	**3**	
24	19	...	...	...	5	...	...	...	...	...	...	95
46	18	...	...	...	28	17	14	...	...	...	3	96
361	137	...	2	...	224	...	...	...	...	...	...	97
11.534	**3.607**	**13**	**46**	...	**7.896**	**164**	**141**	...	**7**	...	**23**	
646	252	17	...	...	377	24	23	...	...	...	1	98
680	241	1	8	...	438	31	17	...	7	...	14	99
...	...	...	...	...	...	102	101	...	...	...	1	100
10 070	3,050	13	3	...	7,007	3	...	...	...	...	3	101
138	64	...	35	...	74	4	...	...	...	...	4	102
29	**12**	...	...	...	**17**	**93**	**64**	...	...	...	**29**	
29	12	...	...	...	17	88	59	...	...	...	29	103
...	...	...	...	...	...	5	5	...	...	...	...	104
391	**180**	...	**8**	...	**211**	**36**	**26**	...	**3**	...	**10**	
391	180	...	8	...	211	36	26	...	3	...	10	105
34.956	**10.145**	**188**	**298**	...	**24.623**	**812**	**426**	...	...	...	**386**	
564	**142**	**38**	**10**	...	**384**	...	...	...	...	...	...	
564	142	38	10	...	384	...	...	...	...	...	...	106

TABLE XV.

Occupation or means of livelihood—Part A.—General Table.

Number of Group.	Occupation.	N.-W. F. P. (Total). Total workers and dependants.	Actual Workers. Total. Males.	Actual Workers. Total. Females.	Actual Workers. Partially agriculturists. Males.	Actual Workers. Partially agriculturists. Females.	Dependants.	HAZA[RA] Total workers and dependants.	Actual Wor[kers]. Total. Males.	Actual Wor[kers]. Total. Females.
	1	2	3	4	5	6	7	8	9	10
	Total Order XXV.—Brokerage, commission and export.	**2,058**	**640**	**1**	**8**	...	**1,417**	**47**	**13**	...
107	Brokers, commission agents, commercial travellers, warehouse owners and employés.	2,058	640	1	8	...	1,417	47	13	...
	Total Order XXVI.—Trade in textiles	**13,056**	**3,643**	**128**	**230**	...	**9,285**	**1,220**	**389**	**8**
108	Trade in piece goods, wool, cotton, silk, hair, and other textiles.	13,056	3,643	128	230	...	9,285	1,220	389	8
	Total Order XXVII.—Trade in skins, leather and furs.	**2,071**	**544**	**16**	**13**	...	**1,511**	**444**	**143**	**1**
109	Trade in skins, leather, furs, feathers, horn, etc.	2,071	544	16	13	...	1,511	444	143	1
	Total Order XXVIII.—Trade in wood	**6,095**	**1,805**	**128**	**6**	...	**4,162**	**896**	**230**	**3**
110	Trade in wood (not firewood), cork, bark, etc.	6,095	1,805	128	6	...	4,162	896	230	3
	Total Order XXIX.—Trade in metals.	**229**	**93**	...	...	...	**136**	**6**	...	...
111	Trade in metals, machinery, knife, tool, etc., sellers.	229	93	...	...	...	136	6	...	...
	Total Order XXX.—Trade in pottery	**284**	**99**	**3**	**1**	...	**182**	...	...	...
112	Trade in pottery	284	99	3	1	...	182	...	...	...
	Total Order XXXI.—Trade in chemical products.	**337**	**93**	**20**	...	...	**224**	**68**	**18**	...
113	Trade in chemical products (drugs, dyes, paints, petroleum, explosives, etc.).	337	93	20	...	...	224	68	18	...
	Total Order XXXII.—Hotels, cafes, restaurants, etc.	**6,120**	**2,390**	**101**	**25**	...	**3,629**	**475**	**139**	**7**
114	Vendors of wine, liquors, ærated waters, etc.	641	267	1	10	...	373	126	34	...
115	Owners and managers of hotels, cookshops, sarais, etc., and their employés.	5,479	2,123	100	15	...	3,256	349	105	7
	Total Order XXXIII.—Other trade in food stuffs.	**49,072**	**16,604**	**548**	**462**	**6**	**31,920**	**7,011**	**2,823**	**83**
116	Fish dealers	14	9	...	...	...	5	4	1	...
117	Grocers and sellers of vegetable oil, salt, and other condiments.	25,073	8,477	199	388	5	16,397	5,577	2,254	73
118	Sellers of milk, butter, ghee, poultry, eggs, etc.	6,056	1,813	44	20	...	4,199	202	80	1
119	Sellers of sweatmeats, sugar, gur and molasses.	1,460	565	12	6	...	883	8	1	...
120	Cardamom, betel-leaf, vegetables, fruit, and arecanut sellers.	6,338	2,162	61	11	1	4,115	399	157	7
121	Grain and pulse dealers	3 655	1,133	11	14	...	2,511	226	56	2
122	Tobacco, opium, ganja, etc., sellers ...	674	202	...	1	...	472	79	31	...
123	Dealers in sheep, goats and pigs ...	232	117	...	1	...	115	41	19	...
124	Dealers in hay, grass and fodder ...	5,570	2,126	221	21	...	3,223	475	224	...
	Total Order XXXIV.—Trade in clothing and toilet articles ...	**3,237**	**949**	**27**	**25**	**3**	**2,261**	**90**	**26**	**1**
125	Trade in ready-made clothing and other articles of dress and the toilet (hats, umbrellas, socks, ready-made shoes, perfumes, etc.).	3,237	949	27	25	3	2,261	90	26	1
	Total Order XXXV.—Trade in furniture.	**725**	**353**	...	**19**	...	**372**	**4**	**3**	...
126	Trade in furniture, carpets, curtains and bedding.	686	335	...	19	...	351	1	1	...

TABLE XV.

Occupation or means of livelihood.—Part A.—General Table.

RA.			PESHAWAR.						KOHAT.						
KERS.				ACTUAL WORKERS.						ACTUAL WORKERS.					
Partially agricul-turists.				*Total.*		*Partially agricul-turists.*				*Total.*		*Partially agricul-turists.*			
Males.	Females.	Dependants.	Total workers and depen-dants.	Males.	Females.	Males.	Females.	Dependants.	Total workers and depen-dants.	Males.	Females.	Males.	Females.	Dependants.	Number of Group.
11	12	13	14	15	16	17	18	19	20	21	22	23	24	25	
...	...	**34**	**1.673**	**532**	**1**	**6**	...	**1.140**	**125**	**36**	...	...	...	**89**	
...	...	34	1,673	532	1	6	...	1,140	125	36	...	...	...	89	107
38	...	**823**	**3.974**	**1.244**	**24**	**45**	...	**2.706**	**524**	**103**	**95**	...	...	**326**	
38	...	823	3,974	1,244	24	45	...	2,706	524	103	95	...	...	326	108
4	...	**300**	**927**	**236**	**14**	**9**	...	**677**	**290**	**56**	**1**	...	...	**233**	
4	...	300	927	236	14	9	...	677	290	56	1	...	...	233	109
1	...	**663**	**2.417**	**770**	**26**	...	...	**1.621**	**352**	**67**	**60**	...	...	**225**	
1	...	663	2,417	770	26	...	...	1,621	352	67	60	...	...	225	110
...	...	**6**	**103**	**47**	...	...	...	**56**	**1**	...	...	...	...	**1**	
...	...	6	103	47	...	...	...	56	1	...	...	...	...	1	111
...	...	...	**242**	**85**	**3**	...	...	**154**	**36**	**13**	...	...	...	**23**	
...	...	...	242	85	3	...	...	154	36	13	...	...	...	23	112
...	...	**50**	**168**	**44**	**17**	...	...	**107**	**49**	**17**	**3**	...	...	**29**	
...	...	50	168	44	17	...	...	107	49	17	3	...	...	29	113
8	...	**329**	**4.627**	**1.817**	**48**	**9**	...	**2.762**	**181**	**55**	**3**	**1**	...	**123**	
4	...	92	273	126	1	...	...	146	14	3	...	1	...	11	114
4	...	237	4,354	1,691	47	9	...	2,616	167	52	3	...	...	112	115
89	**1**	**4.105**	**28.337**	**8.951**	**307**	**168**	**5**	**19.079**	**2.797**	**1.197**	**36**	...	...	**1.564**	
...	...	3	8	6	...	...	...	2	...	...	...	...	...	...	116
77	...	3,250	10,558	3,299	65	120	5	7,194	1,370	522	7	...	...	841	117
...	...	121	5,131	1,522	29	19	...	3,580	100	17	1	...	...	82	118
...	...	7	1,342	533	12	6	...	797	72	12	...	...	...	60	119
1	1	235	5,152	1,649	53	5	...	3,450	142	68	...	...	...	74	120
...	...	168	2,300	658	7	10	...	1,635	156	45	1	...	...	110	121
...	...	48	527	155	...	1	...	372	5	2	...	...	...	3	122
1	...	22	81	26	...	...	...	55	...	...	...	...	...	...	123
10	...	251	3,238	1,103	141	7	...	1,994	952	531	27	...	...	394	124
2	...	**63**	**2.362**	**644**	**22**	**17**	**3**	**1.696**	**61**	**24**	...	...	...	**37**	
2	...	63	2,362	644	22	17	3	1,696	61	24	...	...	...	37	125
...	...	**1**	**301**	**127**	...	**2**	...	**174**	**21**	**2**	...	...	...	**19**	
...	...	...	265	111	...	2	...	154	21	2	...	...	...	19	126

TABLE XV.

Occupation or means of livelihood—Part A.—General Table.

Number of Group.	Occupation.	BANNU.					
		Total workers and dependants.	Actual Workers.				Dependants.
			Total.		Partially agriculturists.		
			Males.	Females.	Males.	Females.	
	1	26	27	28	29	30	31
	Total Order XXV.—Brokerage, commission and export.	**103**	**27**	...	**2**	...	**76**
107	Brokers, commission agents, commercial travellers, warehouse owners and employés.	103	27	...	2	...	76
	Total Order XXVI.—Trade in textiles	**879**	**355**	...	**126**	...	**524**
108	Trade in piece goods, wool, cotton, silk, hair, and other textiles.	879	355	...	126	...	524
	Total Order XXVII.—Trade in skins, leather and furs	**105**	**30**	...	...	...	**75**
109	Trade in skins, leather, furs, feathers, horn, etc.	105	30	...	...	...	75
	Total Order XXVIII.—Trade in wood	**1.007**	**283**	**15**	**4**	...	**709**
110	Trade in wood (not firewood), cork, bark, etc.	1,007	283	15	4	...	709
	Total Order XXIX.—Trade in metals.	...	...	...	...	...	...
111	Trade in metals, machinery, knife, tool, etc., sellers.	...	...	...	...	...	...
	Total Order XXX.—Trade in pottery	**2**	**1**	...	**1**	...	**1**
112	Trade in pottery	2	1	...	1	...	1
	Total Order XXXI.—Trade in chemical products.	**1**	**1**	...	...	...	...
113	Trade in chemical products (drugs, dyes, paints, petroleum, explosives, etc.).	1	1	...	...	...	...
	Total Order XXXII.—Hotels, cafes, restaurants, etc.	**272**	**97**	**26**	...	...	**149**
114	Vendors of wine, liquors, ærated waters, etc.	3	2	...	...	...	1
115	Owners and managers of hotels, cookshops, sarais, etc., and their employés.	269	95	26	...	...	148
	Total Order XXXIII.—Other trade in food stuffs.	**3.651**	**1.072**	**50**	**81**	...	**2.529**
116	Fish dealers	...	...	...	...	...	...
117	Grocers and sellers of vegetable oil, salt, and other condiments.	2,993	842	7	73	...	2,144
118	Sellers of milk, butter, ghee, poultry, eggs, etc.	88	29	8	...	...	51
119	Sellers of sweatmeats, sugar, gur and molasses	16	2	...		...	14
120	Cardamom, betel-leaf, vegetables, fruit, and arecanut sellers.	96	44	...	4	...	52
121	Grain and pulse dealers	25	10	...		...	15
122	Tobacco, opium, ganja, etc., sellers	1	1	...		...	...
123	Dealers in sheep, goats and pigs	14	5	...	...	...	9
124	Dealers in hay, grass and fodder	418	139	35	4	...	244
	Total Order XXXIV.—Trade in clothing and toilet articles	**104**	**25**	...	**1**	...	**79**
125	Trade in ready-made clothing and other articles of dress and the toilet (hats, umbrellas, socks, ready-made shoes, perfumes, etc.).	104	25	...	1	...	79
	Total Order XXXV.—Trade in furniture.	**80**	**23**	...	**17**	...	**57**
126	Trade in furniture, carpets, curtains and bedding	80	23		17	...	57

TABLE XV.

Occupation or means of livelihood.—Part A.—General Table.

DERA ISMAIL KHAN.						TRANS-FRONTIER POSTS.						
Total workers and dependants.	Actual Workers.				Dependants.	Total workers and dependants.	Actual Workers.				Dependants.	Number of Group
	Total.		Partially agriculturists.				Total.		Partially agriculturists.			
	Males.	Females.	Males.	Females.			Males.	Females.	Males.	Females.		
32	33	34	35	36	37	38	39	40	41	42	43	
109	**31**	...	...	...	**78**	**1**	**1**	...	...	...	...	
109	31	...	...	...	78	1	1	...	...	...	...	107
6,419	**1,534**	**1**	**21**	...	**4,884**	**40**	**18**	...	...	...	**22**	
6,419	1,534	1	21	...	4,884	40	18	...	...	...	22	108
305	**79**	...	...	...	**226**	...	...	...	...	...	...	
305	79	...	...	...	226	...	...	...	...	...	...	109
1,421	**453**	**24**	**1**	...	**944**	**2**	**2**	...	...	...	...	
1,421	453	24	1	...	944	2	2	...	...	...	...	110
119	**46**	...	...	...	**73**	...	...	...	...	...	...	
119	46	...	...	...	73	...	...	...	...	...	...	111
4	...	...	...	...	**4**	...	...	...	...	...	...	
4	...	...	...	...	4	...	...	...	...	...	...	112
51	**13**	...	...	...	**38**	...	...	...	...	...	...	
51	13	...	...	...	38	...	...	...	...	...	...	113
508	**249**	**17**	**7**	...	**242**	**57**	**33**	...	...	...	**24**	
180	78	...	5	...	102	45	24	...	...	...	21	114
328	171	17	2	...	140	12	9	...	...	...	3	115
7,188	**2,520**	**72**	**124**	...	**4,596**	**88**	**41**	...	...	...	**47**	
2	2	...	...	...	...	...	...	...	...	...	...	116
4,561	1,551	47	118	...	2,963	14	9	...	...	...	5	117
496	159	5	1	...	332	39	6	...	...	...	33	118
22	17	...	...	...	5	...	...	...	...	...	...	119
544	243	1	1	...	300	5	1	...	...	...	4	120
925	346	1	4	...	578	23	18	...	...	...	5	121
60	11	...	...	...	49	2	2	...	...	...	...	122
96	67	...	...	...	29	...	...	...	...	...	...	123
482	124	18	...	...	340	5	5	...	...	...	...	124
613	**225**	**4**	**5**	...	**384**	**7**	**5**	...	...	...	**2**	
613	225	4	5	...	384	7	5	...	...	...	2	125
319	**198**	...	...	...	**121**	...	...	...	...	...	...	
319	198	...	...	...	121	...	...	...	...	...	...	126

TABLE XV.

Occupation or means of livelihood—Part A.—General Table.

Number of Group.	Occupation.	N.-W. F. P. (Total). Total workers and dependants.	Actual Workers. Total. Males.	Actual Workers. Total. Females.	Actual Workers. Partially agriculturists. Males.	Actual Workers. Partially agriculturists. Females.	Dependants.	Haza[ra] Total workers and dependants.	Actual Wor[kers]. Total. Males.	Actual Wor[kers]. Total. Females.
	1	2	3	4	5	6	7	8	9	10
127	Hardware, cooking utensils, porcelain crockery, glassware, bottles, articles for gardening, the cellar, etc.	39	18	...	...	...	21	3	2	...
	Total Order XXXVI.—Trade in building materials.	**88**	**34**	...	...	...	**54**	...	...	...
128	Trade in building materials (stones, bricks, plaster, cement, sand, tiles, thatch, etc.)	88	34	...	...	...	54	...	...	...
	Total Order XXXVII.—Trade in means of transport.	**1,553**	**556**	**5**	**7**	...	**992**	**232**	**87**	**4**
129	Dealers and hirers of elephants, camels, horses, cattle, asses, mules, etc; sellers (not makers) of carriages, saddlery, etc.	1,553	556	5	7	...	992	232	87	4
	Total Order XXXVIII.—Trade in fuel	**1,069**	**231**	**47**	**1**	...	**791**	**4**	...	...
130	Dealers in firewood, charcoal, coal, cowdung, etc.	1,069	231	47	1	...	791	4	...	...
	Total Order XXXIX.—Trade in articles of luxury and those pertaining to letters and the arts and sciences.	**1,093**	**351**	**18**	**5**	...	**724**	**106**	**41**	**1**
131	Dealers in precious stones, jewellery (real and imitation), clocks, optical instruments, etc.	403	130	...	4	...	273	13	5	...
132	Dealers in common bangles, bead necklaces, fans, small articles, toys, hunting and fishing tackle, flowers, etc.	427	157	17	1	...	253	63	25	1
133	Publishers, booksellers, stationers, dealers in music, pictures, musical instruments and curiosities.	263	64	1	...	...	198	30	11	...
	Total Order XL.—Trade in refuse matter.	**86**	**20**	...	...	...	**66**	...	...	...
134	Dealers in rags, stable refuse, etc. ...	86	20	...	...	...	66	...	...	...
	Total Order XLI.—Trade of other sorts.	**53,031**	**17,337**	**252**	**572**	**1**	**35,442**	**6,651**	**2,092**	**71**
135	Shopkeepers otherwise unspecified ...	51,160	16,701	237	570	1	34,222	6,368	2,018	67
136	Itinerant traders, pedlars, hawkers, etc.	1,534	539	6	1	...	989	238	67	2
137	Conjurors, acrobats, fortune tellers, reciters, exhibitors of curiosities and wild animals.	195	60	9	...	...	126	29	4	2
138	Other trades (including farmers of pounds, tolls, and markets.)	142	37	...	1	...	105	16	3	...
	Total Class C.—Public administration and liberal arts.	**1,38,008**	**67,242**	**1,339**	**8,533**	**34**	**69,427**	**27,860**	**11,382**	**294**
	TOTAL SUB-CLASS VI.—PUBLIC FORCE.	**55,829**	**36,442**	**4**	**7,020**	**6**	**19,383**	**9,958**	**5,149**	...
	Total Order XLII.—Army	**40,555**	**29,778**	...	**6,587**	**6**	**10,777**	**7,038**	**4,066**	...
139	Army (Imperial)	40,555	29,778	...	6,587	6	10,777	7,038	4,066	...
	Total Order XLIV.—Police ...	**15,274**	**6,664**	**4**	**433**	...	**8,606**	**2,920**	**1,083**	...
142	Police	8,631	4,105	3	293	...	4,523	1,316	388	...
143	Villagewatchmen	6,643	2,559	1	140	...	4,083	1,604	695	...
	TOTAL SUB-CLASS VII.—PUBLIC ADMINISTRATION.	**24,634**	**10,193**	**67**	**627**	**1**	**14,374**	**3,828**	**1,316**	**5**
	Total Order XLV.—Public administration.	**24,634**	**10,193**	**67**	**627**	**1**	**14,374**	**3,828**	**1,316**	**5**
144	Service of the state	17,588	7,759	25	506	1	9,804	1,546	570	...

TABLE XV.

Occupation or means of livelihood—Part A.—General Table.

RA. — ...kers. Partially agriculturists. Males.	Females.	Dependants.	PESHAWAR. Total workers and dependants.	Actual Workers. Total. Males.	Females.	Partially agriculturists. Males.	Females.	Dependants.	KOHAT. Total workers and dependants.	Actual Workers. Total. Males.	Females.	Partially agriculturists. Males.	Females.	Dependants.	Number of Group.
11	12	13	14	15	16	17	18	19	20	21	22	23	24	25	
...	...	1	36	16	...	...	...	20	...	...	...	...	...	...	127
...	...	...	**88**	**34**	...	...	...	**54**	...	...	...	...	...	...	
...	...	...	88	34	...	...	...	54	...	...	...	...	...	...	128
...	...	**141**	**757**	**215**	**1**	**7**	...	**541**	**125**	**91**	...	...	...	**34**	
...	...	141	757	215	1	7	...	541	125	91	...	...	...	34	129
...	...	**4**	**793**	**137**	**42**	**1**	...	**614**	**47**	**23**	**3**	...	...	**12**	
...	...	4	793	137	42	1	...	614	47	23	3	...	...	21	130
...	...	**64**	**783**	**256**	**16**	**5**	...	**511**	**35**	**6**	...	...	...	**29**	
...	...	8	242	83	...	4	...	159	12	2	...	...	...	10	131
...	...	37	349	129	15	1	...	205	...	...	...	...	...	...	132
...	...	19	192	44	1	...	...	147	23	4	...	...	...	19	133
...	...	...	**86**	**20**	...	...	...	**66**	...	...	...	...	...	...	
...	...	...	86	20	...	...	...	66	...	...	...	...	...	...	134
59	...	**4.488**	**16.707**	**6.215**	**65**	**122**	...	**10.427**	**4.870**	**1.746**	**36**	**9**	...	**3.088**	
57	...	4,283	15,590	5,832	61	122	...	9,697	4,801	1,718	36	9	...	3,047	135
1	...	169	909	323	4	...	...	582	67	26	...	...	...	41	136
...	...	23	143	46	...	...	...	97	2	2	...	...	...	...	137
1	...	13	65	14	...	...	...	51	...	...	...	...	...	...	138
580	**2**	**16,184**	**60.521**	**28.175**	**720**	**2.989**	**19**	**31.626**	**14.126**	**7.573**	**64**	**1.643**	**9**	**6.489**	
226	...	**4.809**	**22.972**	**14.339**	**4**	**2.538**	**2**	**8.629**	**7.500**	**5.174**	...	**1.578**	**4**	**2.326**	
138	...	**2.972**	**16.599**	**11.545**	...	**2.329**	**2**	**5.054**	**6.044**	**4.564**	...	**1.556**	**4**	**1.480**	
138	...	2,972	16,599	11,545	...	2,329	2	5,054	6,044	4,564	...	1,556	4	1,480	139
88	...	**1.837**	**6.373**	**2.794**	**4**	**209**	...	**3.575**	**1.456**	**610**	...	**22**	...	**846**	
36	...	928	3,402	1,741	3	165	...	1,658	1,026	421	...	21	...	605	142
52	...	909	2,971	1,053	1	44	...	1,917	430	189	...	1	...	241	143
52	...	**2.507**	**10.660**	**4.316**	**50**	**111**	**1**	**6.294**	**2.966**	**1.109**	...	**11**	...	**1.857**	
52	...	**2.507**	**10.660**	**4.316**	**50**	**111**	**1**	**6.294**	**2.966**	**1.109**	...	**11**	...	**1.857**	
38	...	976	8,040	3,415	15	68	1	4,610	2,697	996	...	10	...	1,701	144

TABLE XV.

Occupation or means of livelihood.—Part A.—General Table.

Number of Group.	Occupation.	BANNU					
		Total workers and dependants.	Actual Workers				Dependants.
			Total.		Partially agriculturists.		
			Males.	Females.	Males.	Females.	
	1	26	27	28	29	30	31
127	Hardware, cooking utensils, porcelain crockery, glassware, bottles, articles for gardening, the cellar, etc.	...	...	...	...	...	...
	Total Order XXXVI.—Trade in building materials.	...	...	...	...	...	...
128	Trade in building materials (stones, bricks, plaster, cement, sand, tiles, thatch, etc.)	...	...	...	...	...	...
	Total Order XXXVII.—Trade in means of transport.	**124**	**56**	...	...	...	**68**
129	Dealers and hirers of elephants, camels, horses, cattle, asses, mules, etc; sellers (not makers) of carriages, saddlery, etc.	124	56	...	...	...	68
	Total Order XXXVIII.—Trade in fuel	**219**	**68**	**2**	...	...	**149**
130	Dealers in firewood, charcoal, coal, cowdung, etc.	219	68	2	...	...	149
	Total Order XXXIX.—Trade in articles of luxury and those pertaining to letters and the arts and sciences.	**14**	**7**	...	...	..	**7**
131	Dealers in precious stones, jewellery (real and imitation), clocks, optical instruments, etc.	9	2	..	...	...	7
132	Dealers in common bangles, bead necklaces, fans, small articles, toys, hunting and fishing tackle, flowers, etc.	3	3	...	...	...	...
133	Publishers, booksellers, stationers, dealers in music, pictures, musical instruments and curiosities.	2	2	...	...	...	...
	Total Order XL.—Trade in refuse matter.	...	...	...	...	...	...
134	Dealers in rags, stable refuse, etc. ...	...	...	...	...	...	...
	Total Order XLI.—Trade of other sorts.	**7,326**	**2,454**	**49**	**252**	**1**	**4,823**
135	Shopkeepers otherwise unspecified ..	7,144	2,383	49	252	1	4,712
136	Itinerant traders, pedlars, hawkers, etc.	121	51	...	...	...	70
137	Conjurors, acrobats, fortune tellers, reciters, exhibitors of curiosities and wild animals.	...	...	...	...	...	...
138	Other trades (including farmers of pounds, tolls, and markets.)	61	20	...	...	...	41
	Total Class C.—Public administration and liberal arts.	**11,844**	**6,091**	**88**	**634**	**3**	**5,665**
	TOTAL SUB-CLASS VI.—PUBLIC FORCE.	**4,481**	**3,306**	...	**468**	...	**1,175**
	Total Order XLII.—Army	**2,560**	**2,357**	...	**428**	...	**203**
139	Army (Imperial)	2,560	2,357	...	428	...	203
	Total Order XLIV.—Police ...	**1,921**	**949**	...	**40**	...	**972**
142	Police ..	1,007	633	...	14	...	464
143	Villagewatchmen	824	316	...	26	...	508
	TOTAL SUB-CLASS VII.—PUBLIC ADMINISTRATION.	**2,184**	**745**	**6**	**52**	...	**1,433**
	Total Order XLV.—Public administration	**2,184**	**745**	**6**	**52**	...	**1,433**
144	Service of the state ...	1,511	516	5	27	..	990

TABLE XV.

Occupation or means of livelihood.—Part A.—General Table.

DERA ISMAIL KHAN.						TRANS-FRONTIER POSTS.						
Total workers and dependants.	ACTUAL WORKERS.				Dependants.	Total workers and dependants.	ACTUAL WORKERS.				Dependants.	Number of Group.
	Total.		*Partially agriculturists.*				*Total.*		*Partially agriculturists.*			
	Males.	Females.	Males.	Females.			Males.	Females.	Males.	Females.		
32	33	34	35	36	37	38	39	40	41	42	43	
...	...	...	...	...	...	...	...	...	...	...	...	127
...	...	...	..	...	...	...	...	...	...	...	...	
...	...	...	...	...	...	...	...	...	...	...	...	128
315	**107**	...	...	...	**208**	...	...	...	...	...	...	
315	107	...	...	...	208	...	...	...	...	...	...	129
6	**3**	...	...	...	**3**	...	...	...	...	...	...	
6	3	...	...	...	3	...	...	...	...	...	...	130
142	**39**	**1**	...	...	**102**	**13**	**2**	...	...	...	**11**	
127	38	...	...	...	89	...	...	...	...	...	...	131
12	...	1	...	...	11	...	...	...	...	...	...	132
3	1	...	...	...	2	13	2	...	...	...	11	133
...	...	...	...	...	...	...	...	...	...	...	...	
...	...	...	...	...	...	...	...	...	...	...	...	134
16.873	**4.506**	**31**	**130**	...	**12.336**	**604**	**324**	...	...	...	**280**	
16,653	4,426	24	130	...	12,203	604	324	...	...	...	280	135
199	72	...	...	...	127	...	...	...	...	...	...	136
21	8	7	...	...	6	...	...	...	...	...	...	137
...	...	...	...	...	...	...	...	...	...	...	...	138
17.770	**8.389**	**172**	**1.447**	**1**	**9.209**	**5.887**	**5.632**	**1**	**1,240**	...	**254**	
6.681	**4.298**	...	**1.332**	...	**2.383**	**4.237**	**4.176**	...	**878**	...	**61**	
4.238	**3.221**	...	**1.259**	...	**1.017**	**4.076**	**4.025**	...	**877**	...	**51**	
4,238	3,221	...	1,259	...	1,017	4,076	4,025	...	877	...	51	139
2.443	**1,077**	...	**73**	...	**1.366**	**161**	**151**	...	**1**	...	**10**	
1,668	801	...	57	...	867	122	121	...	...	...	1	142
775	276	...	16	...	499	39	30	...	1	...	9	143
3,561	**1.390**	**6**	**57**	...	**2.165**	**1.435**	**1.317**	...	**344**	...	**118**	
3.561	**1.390**	**6**	**57**	...	**2.165**	**1.435**	**1.317**	...	**344**	...	**118**	
2,396	981	5	48	...	1,410	1,398	1,281	...	315	...	117	144

TABLE XV.

Occupation or means of livelihood—Part A.—General Table.

Number of Group.	OCCUPATION.	N.-W. F. P. (TOTAL).						HAZA		
		Total workers and dependants.	ACTUAL WORKERS. Total. Males.	ACTUAL WORKERS. Total. Females.	Partially agriculturists. Males.	Partially agriculturists. Females.	Dependants.	Total workers and dependants.	ACTUAL WOR Total. Males.	ACTUAL WOR Total. Females.
	1	2	3	4	5	6	7	8	9	10
145	Service of Native and Foreign States ...	1,589	519	5	9	...	1,065	1,498	469	5
146	Municipal and other local (not village) service.	2,191	750	19	15	...	1,422	306	101	...
147	Village officials and servants other than watchmen.	3,266	1,165	18	97	...	2,083	478	176	...
	TOTAL SUB CLASS VIII.—PROFESSIONS AND LIBERAL ARTS.	**51,795**	**18,819**	**1,057**	**820**	**20**	**31,919**	**13,529**	**4,787**	**272**
	TOTAL ORDER XLVI.—RELIGION ...	**38,923**	**14,525**	**631**	**615**	**14**	**23,767**	**10,767**	**3,856**	**172**
148	Priests, ministers, etc.	22,972	7,444	37	418	8	15,491	6,420	1,941	...
149	Religious mendicants, inmates of monasteries, etc.	12,854	6,073	450	167	5	6,331	1,929	1,137	78
150	Catechists, readers, Church and mission service.	71	31	9	...	...	31	...	...	...
151	Temple, burial, or burning ground service, pilgrim conductors, circumcisers.	3,026	977	135	30	1	1,914	2,418	778	94
	TOTAL ORDER XLVII.—LAW	**1,141**	**313**	**3**	**28**	**1**	**825**	**139**	**39**	...
152	Lawyers of all kinds, including kazis, law agents and mukhtiars.	240	55	3	11	1	182	29	5	...
153	Lawyer's clerks, petition writers, etc. ...	901	258	...	17	...	643	110	34	...
	TOTAL ORDER XLVIII.—MEDICINE ...	**2,555**	**821**	**162**	**56**	**1**	**1,572**	**283**	**104**	**17**
154	Medical practitioners of all kinds, including dentists, oculists and veterinary surgeons.	1,901	645	9	44	...	1,247	177	66	...
155	Midwives, vaccinators, compounders, nurses, masseurs, etc.	654	176	153	12	1	325	106	38	17
	TOTAL ORDER XLIX.—INSTRUCTION ...	**2,432**	**912**	**86**	**47**	**2**	**1,434**	**451**	**170**	**11**
156	Professors and teachers of all kinds* and clerks and servants connected with education.	2,432	912	86	47	2	1,434	451	170	11
	TOTAL ORDER L.—LETTERS AND ARTS AND SCIENCES.	**6,744**	**2,248**	**175**	**74**	**2**	**4,321**	**1889**	**618**	**72**
157	Public scribes, stenographers, etc. ...	270	97	...	1	...	173	24	7	...
158	Architects, surveyors, engineers, and their employés.	1,169	504	...	35	...	665	183	98	...
159	Others (authors, photographers, artists, sculptors, astronomers, meteorologists, botanists, astrologers, etc.).	165	64	8	5	...	93	39	4	7
160	Music composers and masters, players on all kinds of musical instruments (not military), singers, actors, and dancers.	5,140	1,583	167	33	2	3,390	1,643	509	65
	TOTAL SUB-CLASS IX.—PESRONS LIVING ON THEIR INCOME.	**5,750**	**1,788**	**211**	**66**	**7**	**3,751**	**545**	**130**	**17**
	TOTAL ORDER LI.—PERSONS LIVING PRINCIPALLY ON THEIR INCOME.	**5,750**	**1,788**	**211**	**66**	**7**	**3,751**	**545**	**130**	**17**
161	Proprietors (other than of agricultural land), fund and scholarship holders and pensioners.	5,750	1,788	211	66	7	3,751	545	130	17
	Total Class D.—Miscellaneous ...	**135,478**	**53,499**	**10,543**	**631**	**44**	**71,436**	**28,013**	**11,818**	**3,033**
	TOTAL SUB-CLASS X.—DOMESTIC SERVICE.	**39,208**	**18,468**	**3,382**	**351**	**15**	**17,358**	**12,469**	**5,972**	**1,387**
	TOTAL ORDER LII.—DOMESTIC SERVICE ...	**39,208**	**18,468**	**3,382**	**351**	**15**	**17,358**	**12,469**	**5,972**	**1,387**
162	Cooks, water carriers, doorkeepers, watchmen and other indoor servants	35,676	16,474	3,379	288	15	15,823	12,179	5,830	1,387
163	Private grooms, coachmen, dog boys, etc.	3,532	1,994	3	63	..	1,535	290	142	...

* Except law, medicine, music, dancing and drawing.

TABLE XV.

Occupation or means of livelihood—Part A.—General Table.

...RA.			PESHAWAR.						KOHAT.						
...KERS.				ACTUAL WORKERS.						ACTUAL WORKERS.					
Partially agriculturists.				Total.		Partially agriculturists.				Total.		Partially agriculturists.			
Males.	Females.	Dependants.	Total workers and dependants.	Males.	Females.	Males.	Females.	Dependants.	Total workers and dependants.	Males.	Females.	Males.	Females.	Dependants.	Number of Group.
11	12	13	14	15	16	17	18	19	20	21	22	23	24	25	
1	...	1,024	84	50	...	8	...	34	...	...	...	...	...	...	145
3	...	205	1,382	487	17	10	...	878	69	30	...	...	...	39	146
10	...	302	1,154	364	18	25	...	772	200	83	...	1	...	117	147
295	**1**	**8.470**	**23.996**	**8.815**	**531**	**300**	**13**	**14.650**	**3.260**	**1.159**	**54**	**54**	**5**	**2.049**	
256	**1**	**6.739**	**18.805**	**7.227**	**333**	**237**	**8**	**11.345**	**2.603**	**919**	**32**	**28**	**4**	**1.652**	
174	...	4,479	9,849	3,229	10	149	4	6,610	2,015	623	6	27	4	1,386	148
55	...	714	8,054	3,868	319	86	4	4,467	518	269	24	1	...	225	149
...	...	...	48	24	...	...	...	24	3	1	2	...	...	...	150
27	1	1,546	254	106	4	2	...	144	67	26	...	...	...	41	151
2	...	**100**	**565**	**146**	**3**	**16**	**1**	**416**	**76**	**28**	...	...	...	**48**	
...	...	24	92	26	3	10	1	63	4	1	...	...	...	3	152
2	...	76	473	120	...	6	...	353	72	27	...	...	...	45	153
6	...	**162**	**1.234**	**337**	**66**	**10**	...	**831**	**125**	**49**	**14**	**18**	**1**	**62**	
2	...	111	938	258	7	6	...	673	97	44	...	18	...	53	154
4	...	51	296	79	59	4	...	158	28	5	14	...	1	9	155
14	...	**270**	**1.093**	**398**	**59**	**19**	**2**	**636**	**169**	**62**	**5**	...	...	**102**	
14	...	270	1,093	398	59	19	2	636	169	62	5	...	...	102	156
17	...	**1.199**	**2.299**	**707**	**70**	**18**	**2**	**1.522**	**289**	**101**	**3**	**8**	...	**185**	
...	...	17	154	46	...	1	...	108	3	3	...	...	...	...	157
10	...	85	495	167	...	6	...	328	69	41	...	2	...	28	158
...	...	28	49	24	1	5	...	24	1	1	...	...	...	...	159
7	...	1,069	1,601	470	69	6	2	1,062	216	56	3	6	...	157	160
7	**1**	**398**	**2.893**	**705**	**135**	**40**	**3**	**2.053**	**398**	**131**	**10**	...	...	**257**	
7	**1**	**398**	**2.893**	**705**	**135**	**40**	**3**	**2.053**	**398**	**131**	**10**	...	...	**257**	
7	1	398	2,893	705	135	40	3	2,053	398	131	10	...	...	257	161
226	**14**	**13.162**	**59.975**	**22.230**	**3.972**	**192**	**13**	**33.773**	**9.756**	**3.510**	**915**	**43**	**15**	**5.331**	
135	**8**	**5.110**	**17.458**	**7.825**	**1.430**	**116**	**2**	**8.203**	**2.186**	**1.171**	**135**	**41**	**5**	**880**	
135	**8**	**5.110**	**17.458**	**7.825**	**1.430**	**116**	**2**	**8.203**	**2.186**	**1.171**	**135**	**41**	**5**	**880**	
112	8	4,962	15,389	6,632	1,427	90	2	7,330	1,702	866	135	35	5	701	162
23	...	148	2,069	1,193	3	26	...	873	484	305	...	6	...	179	163

TABLE XV.

Occupation or means of livelihood—Part A.—General Table.

Number of Group.	Occupation.	BANNU. Total workers and dependants.	Actual Workers. Total. Males.	Actual Workers. Total. Females.	Actual Workers. Partially agriculturists. Males.	Actual Workers. Partially agriculturists. Females.	Dependants.
	1	26	27	28	29	30	31
145	Service of Native and Foreign States...	4	...	...	...	...	4
146	Municipal and other local (not village) service.	146	41	1	1	...	104
147	Village officials and servants other than watchmen.	523	188	...	24	...	335
	TOTAL SUB-CLASS VIII.—PROFESSIONS AND LIBERAL ARTS.	**4,940**	**1,979**	**71**	**100**	...	**2,890**
	TOTAL ORDER XLVI.—RELIGION ...	**3,424**	**1,441**	**49**	**59**	...	**1,934**
148	Priests, ministers, etc.	2,578	1,051	2	43	...	1,525
149	Religious mendicants, inmates of monasteries, etc.	717	373	10	16	...	334
150	Catechists, readers, Church and mission service.	9	5	...	...	...	4
151	Temple, burial, or burning ground service, pilgrim conductors, circumcisers.	120	12	37	...	...	71
	TOTAL ORDER XLVII.—LAW	**111**	**25**	...	**8**	...	**86**
152	Lawyers of all kinds, including kazis, law agents and mukhtiars.	27	4	...	...	...	23
153	Lawyer's clerks, petition writers, etc. ...	84	21	...	8	...	63
	TOTAL ORDER XLVIII.—MEDICINE ...	**294**	**128**	**16**	**11**	...	**150**
154	Medical practitioners of all kinds, including dentists, oculists and veterinary surgeons.	226	112	...	11	...	114
155	Midwives, vaccinators, compounders, nurses, masseurs, etc.	68	16	16	...	...	36
	TOTAL ORDER XLIX.—INSTRUCTION ...	**275**	**111**	**4**	**13**	...	**160**
156	Professors and teachers of all kinds* and clerks and servants connected with education.	275	111	4	13	...	160
	TOTAL ORDER L.—LETTERS AND ARTS AND SCIENCES.	**836**	**274**	**2**	**9**	...	**560**
157	Public scribes, stenographers, etc. ..	18	7	...	...	...	11
158	Architects, surveyors, engineers, and their employés.	101	39	...	5	...	62
159	Others (authors, photographers, artists, sculptors, astronomers, meteorologists, botanists, astrologers, etc.).	22	15	...	...	...	7
160	Music composers and masters, players on all kinds of musical instruments (not military), singers, actors, and dancers.	695	213	2	4	...	480
	TOTAL SUB-CLASS IX.—PESRONS LIVING ON THEIR INCOME.	**239**	**61**	**11**	**14**	**3**	**167**
	TOTAL ORDER LI.—PERSONS LIVING PRINCIPALLY ON THEIR INCOME.	**239**	**61**	**11**	**14**	**3**	**167**
161	Proprietors (other than of agricultural land), fund and scholarship holders and pensioners.	239	61	11	14	3	167
	Total Class D.—Miscellaneous ...	**15,148**	**6,606**	**1,076**	**54**	**2**	**7,466**
	TOTAL SUB-CLASS X.—DOMESTIC SERVICE.	**2,333**	**1,166**	**174**	**14**	...	**993**
	TOTAL ORDER LII.—DOMESTIC SERVICE ...	**2,333**	**1,166**	**174**	**14**	...	**993**
162	Cooks, water carriers, doorkeepers, watchmen and other indoor servants	2,226	1,104	174	10	...	948
163	Private grooms, coachmen, dog boys, etc.	107	62	...	4	...	45

TABLE XV.

Occupation or means of livelihood.—Part A.—General Table.

DERA ISMAIL KHAN.						TRANS-FRONTIER POSTS.						
Total workers and dependants.	ACTUAL WORKERS.				Dependants.	Total workers and dependants.	ACTUAL WORKERS.				Dependants.	Number of Group.
	Total.		*Partially agriculturists.*				*Total.*		*Partially agriculturists.*			
	Males.	Females.	Males.	Females.			Males.	Females.	Males.	Females.		
32	33	34	35	36	37	38	39	40	41	42	43	
3	...	...	...	...	3	...	...	...	...	...	...	145
281	85	1	1	...	195	7	6	...	...	...	1	146
881	324	...	8	...	557	30	30	...	29	...	...	147
5,878	**1.947**	**128**	**53**	**1**	**3,803**	**190**	**132**	**1**	**18**	...	**57**	
3,292	**1,061**	**45**	**34**	**1**	**2,186**	**32**	**21**	...	**1**	...	**11**	
2,087	585	19	24	...	1,483	23	15	...	1	...	8	148
1,030	440	19	9	1	591	6	6	...	...	...	...	149
11	1	7	...	...	3	...	...	...	...	...	...	150
164	55	...	1	...	109	3	...	...	...	...	3	151
250	**75**	...	**2**	...	**175**	...	...	...	...	...	...	
88	19	...	1	...	69	...	...	...	...	...	...	152
162	56	...	1	...	106	...	...	...	...	...	...	153
567	**173**	**48**	**6**	...	**346**	**52**	**30**	**1**	**5**	...	**21**	
423	143	2	6	...	278	40	22	...	1	...	18	154
144	30	46	...	...	68	12	8	1	4	...	3	155
429	**162**	**7**	**1**	...	**260**	**15**	**9**	...	...	...	**6**	
429	162	7	1	...	260	15	9	...	...	...	6	156
1,240	**476**	**28**	**10**	...	**836**	**91**	**72**	...	**12**	...	**19**	
71	34	...	...	...	37	...	...	...	...	...	...	157
247	104	...	...	...	143	74	55	...	12	...	19	158
54	20	...	...	...	34	...	...	...	...	...	...	159
968	318	28	10	...	622	17	17	...	...	...	...	160
1.650	**754**	**38**	**5**	...	**858**	**25**	**7**	...	...	...	**18**	
1.650	**754**	**38**	**5**	...	**858**	**25**	**7**	...	...	...	**18**	
1,650	754	38	5	...	858	25	7	...	...	...	18	161
21 337	**8.414**	**1.545**	**59**	...	**11.378**	**1.249**	**921**	**2**	**57**	...	**326**	
4.399	**2,061**	**254**	**18**	...	**2,084**	**363**	**273**	**2**	**27**	...	**88**	
4.399	**2.061**	**254**	**18**	...	**2,084**	**363**	**273**	**2**	**27**	...	**88**	
3,865	1,803	254	14	...	1,808	315	239	2	27	...	74	162
534	258	...	4	...	276	48	34	...	...	...	14	163

TABLE XV.

Occupation or means of livelihood.—Part A.—General Table.

Number of Group.	Occupation.	N.-W. F. P. (Total.) Total workers and dependants.	Actual Workers. Total. Males.	Actual Workers. Total. Females.	Actual Workers. Partially agriculturists. Males.	Actual Workers. Partially agriculturists. Females.	Dependants.	HAZA[RA] Total workers and dependants.	Actual Wor[kers]. Total. Males.	Actual Wor[kers]. Total. Females.
	1	2	3	4	5	6	7	8	9	10
	TOTAL SUB CLASS XI.—INSUFFICIENTLY DESCRIBED OCCUPATIONS.	**73.643**	**24.611**	**4.852**	**207**	**28**	**44.180**	**7.658**	**2.502**	**855**
	TOTAL ORDER LIII.—GENERAL TERMS WHICH DO NOT INDICATE A DEFINITE OCCUPATION.	**73.643**	**24.611**	**4.852**	**207**	**28**	**44.180**	**7.658**	**2 502**	**855**
164	Manufacturers, business men, and contractors otherwise unspecified.	2,839	751	36	36	10	2,052	440	129	...
165	Cashiers, accountants, book-keepers, clerks and other employés in unspecified offices, warehouses and shops.	424	170	1	5	...	253	17	6	...
166	Mechanics otherwise unspecified ...	357	153	...	4	...	204	...	...	...
167	Labourers and workmen otherwise unspecified.	70,023	23,537	4,815	162	18	41,671	7.201	2,367	855
	TOTAL SUB-CLASS XII.—UNPRODUCTIVE.	**22.627**	**10.420**	**2.309**	**73**	**1**	**9.898**	**7,886**	**3,344**	**791**
	TOTAL ORDER LIV.—INMATES OF JAILS, ASYLUMS, AND HOSPITALS.	**1.551**	**1.526**	**18**	**2**	...	**7**	**187**	**185**	**2**
168	Inmates of jails, asylums and hospitals	1,551	1,526	18	2	...	7	187	185	2
	TOTAL ORDER LV.—BEGGARS, VAGRANTS, PROSTITUTES.	**21.076**	**8.894**	**2.291**	**71**	**1**	**9.891**	**7.699**	**3.159**	**789**
169	Beggars, vagrants, procurers, prostitutes, receivers of stolen goods, cattle poisoners.	21,076	8,894	2,291	71	1	9,891	7,699	3,159	789

TABLE XV.

Occupation or means of livelihood—Part A.—General Table.

RA. — [Actual Wor]kers. — Partially agriculturists. — Males.	Partially agriculturists. — Females.	Dependants.	PESHAWAR. — Total workers and dependants.	Actual Workers. — Total. — Males.	Actual Workers. — Total. — Females.	Actual Workers. — Partially agriculturists. — Males.	Actual Workers. — Partially agriculturists. — Females.	Dependants.	KOHAT. — Total workers and dependants.	Actual Workers. — Total. — Males.	Actual Workers. — Total. — Females.	Actual Workers. — Partially agriculturists. — Males.	Actual Workers. — Partially agriculturists. — Females.	Dependants.	Number of Group.
11	12	13	14	15	16	17	18	19	20	21	22	23	24	25	
45	**6**	**4,301**	**37,004**	**11,638**	**2,073**	**70**	**11**	**23,293**	**6,321**	**1,786**	**645**	**1**	**10**	**3,890**	
45	**6**	**4,301**	**37,004**	**11,638**	**2,073**	**70**	**11**	**23,293**	**6,321**	**1,786**	**645**	**1**	**10**	**3,890**	
13	...	311	1,539	372	21	11	10	1,146	245	66	15	...	...	164	164
...	...	11	289	120	...	4	...	169	13	11	...	1	...	2	165
...	...	...	159	99	...	3	...	60	19	10	...	...	...	9	166
32	6	3,979	35,017	11,047	2,052	52	1	21,918	6,044	1,699	630	...	10	3,715	167
46	...	**3,751**	**5,513**	**2,767**	**469**	**6**	...	**2,277**	**1,249**	**553**	**135**	**1**	...	**561**	
...	...	...	**490**	**482**	**8**	...	...	...	**151**	**146**	...	...	...	**5**	
...	...	...	490	482	8	...	...	...	151	146	...	...	...	5	168
46	...	**3,751**	**5,023**	**2,285**	**461**	**6**	...	**2,277**	**1,098**	**407**	**135**	**1**	...	**556**	
46	...	3,751	5,023	2,285	461	6	...	2,277	1,098	407	135	1	...	556	169

TABLE XV.

Occupation or means of livelihood.—Part A.—General Table.

Number of Group.	Occupation.	BANNU					
		Total workers and dependants.	Actual Workers				Dependants.
			Total.		*Partially agriculturists.*		
			Males.	Females.	Males.	Females.	
	1	26	27	28	29	30	31
	TOTAL SUB-CLASS XI.—INSUFFICIENTLY DESCRIBED OCCUPATIONS.	**10,169**	**4,094**	**549**	**28**	**1**	**5,526**
	TOTAL ORDER LII.—GENERAL TERMS WHICH DO NOT INDICATE A DEFINITE OCCUPATION.	**10,169**	**4,094**	**549**	**28**	**1**	**5,526**
164	Manufacturers, business men, and contractors otherwise unspecified.	278	84	...	12	...	194
165	Cashiers, accountants, book-keepers, clerks and other employes in unspecified offices, warehouses and shops.	28	5	...	...	...	23
166	Mechanics otherwise unspecified	152	32	...	1	...	120
167	Labourers and workmen otherwise unspecified.	9,711	3,973	549	15	1	5,189
	TOTAL SUB-CLASS XII.—UNPRODUCTIVE.	**2,646**	**1,346**	**353**	**12**	**1**	**947**
	TOTAL ORDER LIV.—INMATES OF JAILS, ASYLUMS, AND HOSPITALS.	**321**	**313**	**6**	...	...	**2**
168	Inmates of jails, asylums and hospitals	321	313	6	...	...	2
	TOTAL ORDER LV—BEGGARS, VAGRANTS, PROSTITUTES.	**2,325**	**1,033**	**347**	**12**	**1**	**945**
169	Beggars, vagrants, procurers, prostitutes, receivers of stolen goods, cattle poisoners.	2,325	1,033	347	12	1	945

TABLE XV.

Occupation or means of livelihood.—Part A.—General Table.

DERA ISMAIL KHAN.						TRANS-FRONTIER POSTS.						
Total workers and dependants.	ACTUAL WORKERS.				Dependants.	Total workers and dependants.	ACTUAL WORKERS.				Dependants.	Number of Group.
	Total.		Partially agriculturists.				Total.		Partially agriculturists.			
	Males.	Females.	Males.	Females.			Males.	Females.	Males.	Females.		
32	33	34	35	36	37	38	39	40	41	42	43	
11,795	4,074	730	35	...	6,991	696	517	...	28	...	179	
11.795	4,074	730	85	...	6.991	696	517	...	28	...	179	
284	82	...	...	...	202	53	18	...	...	...	35	164
69	27	1	...	...	41	8	1	...	...	...	7	165
27	12	...	...	...	15	...	...	...	...	...	...	166
11,415	3,953	729	35	...	6,733	635	498	...	28	...	137	167
6.143	2.279	561	6	...	2.303	90	131	...	2	...	69	
341	339	2	...	...	...	6	61	...	2	...	...	
341	339	2	...	...	...	61	61	...	2	...	—	168
4.802	1.940	559	6	...	2,303	129	70	...	...	...	69	
4,802	1,940	559	6	...	2,303	129	70	...	...	...	59	169

TABLE XV.

Occupation or means of livelihood.

PART B.—Subsidiary Occupations of Agriculturists. Actual workers only.

In this Part Agriculturists are classed as (i) Rent receivers, *i.e.*, those persons shown in Groups 1 (*a*) and 1 (*b*) of Part A of this table; (ii) Rent payers, *i.e.*, the persons shown in Groups 2 (*a*) and 2 (*b*) of Part A of this Table; and (iii) Farm servants and field labourers (Group 4 of Table XV, Part A). The figures for dependants are not shown in this Part.

TABLE XV.

Occupation or means of livelihood. Part B.—Subsidiary occupations of Agriculturists—Actual workers only.

(i) Rent receivers.

District, etc.	Total number of rent receivers (Actual workers).		Number of actual workers who returned subsidiary occupations.		Details of — Rent payers.		Field labourers.		Service of
	Males.	Females.	Males.	Females.	Males.	Females.	Males.	Females.	Males.
1	2	3	4	5	6	7	8	9	10
Total N.-W. F. P. ...	**25,819**	**3,511**	**4,439**	**147**	**241**	**96**	**42**	**3**	**2,035**
Hazara	1,093	365	231	22	26	14	3	...	53
Peshawar	7,570	1,593	1,257	29	42	...	21	3	471
Kohat	8,234	238	438	...	82	...	2	...	259
Bannu	4,041	715	1,535	92	34	82	9	...	728
Dera Ismail Khan ..	4,536	600	653	4	57	...	7	...	216
Trans-Frontier Posts ...	345	...	325	...	...	...	...	...	308

(ii) Rent payers.

District, etc.	Total number of rent payers (Actual workers).		Number of actual workers who returned subsidiary occupations.		Details of — Rent receivers.		Labour other than field labour.		Service of
	Males.	Females.	Males.	Females.	Males.	Females.	Males.	Females.	Males.
1	2	3	4	5	6	7	8	9	10
Total N.-W. F. P. ...	**374,616**	**18,781**	**30,610**	**219**	**1,497**	**10**	**2,789**	**19**	**7,374**
Hazara	119,730	6,214	11,180	65	570	7	1,434	15	923
Peshawar	132,521	4,056	10,414	114	337	1	749	2	3,063
Kohat	40,979	7,693	2,395	32	80	...	286	1	495
Bannu	44,856	496	2,511	4	264	2	193	...	52
Dera Ismail Khan ...	32,535	321	1,286	4	246	...	86	1	131
Trans-Frontier Posts ...	3,095	1	2,824	...	...	...	41	...	2,710

(iii) Farm servants and field labourers.

District, etc.	Total number of farm servants and field labourers (Actual workers).		Number of actual workers who returned subsidiary occupations.		Details of — Rent receivers.		Rent payers.		Labour agricultural
	Males.	Females.	Males.	Females.	Males.	Females.	Males.	Females.	Males.
1	2	3	4	5	6	7	8	9	10
Total N.-W. F. P. ...	**16,521**	**1,107**	**668**	**15**	**33**	...	**117**	...	**162**
Hazara	4,152	86	273	...	19	...	82	...	80
Peshawar	10,392	832	331	13	12	...	30	...	82
Kohat	153	28	44	2	...	...	...	...	...
Bannu	1,204	42	18	...	2	...	4	...	...
Dera Ismail Khan ...	620	119	2	...	...	...	1	...	...
Trans-Frontier Posts ...	...	...	...	...	...	...	...	...	...

TABLE XV.

Occupation or means of livelihood. Part B --Subsidiary occupations of Agriculturists—Actual workers only.

(i) Rent receivers.

SUBSIDIARY OCCUPATIONS RETURNED

...state.	Money lenders & wheat sellers.		Other traders of all kinds.		Priests, ministers, etc.		Artisans.		Pensioners and reservists.		Other occupations.	
Females.	Males.	Females.	Males.	Females.	Males.	Females.	Males.	Females.	Males.	Females.	Males.	Females.
11	12	13	14	15	16	17	18	19	20	21	22	23
13	**149**	...	**228**	**3**	**149**	...	**100**	**2**	**50**	**1**	**1,445**	**29**
5	5	...	18	...	10	...	28	...	1	...	87	3
8	8	...	44	1	71	...	37	1	44	1	519	15
...	5	...	1	...	1	...	5	...	1	...	82	...
...	72	...	94	...	52	...	9	...	4	...	533	10
...	59	...	71	2	15	...	21	1	...	...	207	1
...	...	...	...	...	...	...	...	...	...	...	17	...

(ii) Rent payers.

SUBSIDIARY OCCUPATIONS RETURNED.

...state.	Traders other than money lenders and wheat sellers.		Weavers.		Cattle breeders and weighmen.		Barbers.		Blacksmiths and carpenters.		Other occupations.	
Females.	Males.	Females.	Males.	Females.	Males.	Females.	Males.	Females.	Males.	Females.	Males.	Females.
11	12	13	14	15	16	17	18	19	20	21	22	23
21	**1,237**	**19**	**891**	**9**	**765**	**1**	**687**	**2**	**1,453**	**4**	**13,317**	**134**
14	478	1	624	...	448	...	299	1	774	...	5,630	27
3	506	17	212	9	228	1	278	1	463	2	4,578	78
4	48	...	17	...	8	...	22	...	62	2	1,377	25
...	119	1	21	...	7	...	43	...	119	...	1,693	1
...	79	...	17	...	74	...	40	...	35	...	578	3
...	7	...	...	...	...	...	5	...	...	...	61	...

(iii) Farm servants and field labourers.

SUBSIDIARY OCCUPATIONS RETURNED.

...other than labour.	Village watchmen.		Traders of all kinds.		Skin and leather workers.		Weavers.		Blacksmiths and carpenters.		Other occupations.	
Females.	Males.	Females.	Males.	Females.	Males.	Females.	Males.	Females.	Males.	Females.	Males.	Females.
11	12	13	14	15	16	17	18	19	20	21	22	23
...	**15**	...	**10**	...	**13**	...	**13**	...	**21**	**5**	**284**	**10**
...	6	...	10	...	6	...	7	...	1	...	62	...
...	9	...	...	...	...	...	6	...	2	5	190	8
...	...	...	...	...	7	...	...	...	18	...	19	2
...	...	...	...	...	...	...	...	...	...	...	12	...
...	...	...	...	...	...	...	...	...	...	...	1	...
...	...	...	...	...	...	...	...	...	...	...	...	...

[NOTE.—Parts C and D of Table XV have not been prepared for the North-West Frontier Province.]

TABLE XV.

Occupation or means of livelihood.

PART E.—Statistics of Industries.

In this part figures are given for those factories, mills, etc., only in which 20 or more persons were employed on March 10th, 1911. All the establishments shown are situated in the Peshawar District.

TABLE XV.

Occupation or means of livelihood.—Part E.—Statistics of Industries.

Description of Factory, etc.	Classification of factory, etc., according to number of persons employed (including management),	Number of factories.	Total number of persons employed.		Classification of persons employed.											
					Direction, Supervision and Clerical Work.				Skilled workmen.				Unskilled labourers.			
					Europeans and Anglo-Indians.		*Indians.*		*Europeans and Anglo-Indians.*		*Indians.*		*Age 14 and over.*		*Age under 14.*	
			Males.	Females.	Males.	Females.	Males.	Females.	Males.	Females.	Males.	Females.	Males.	Females.	Males.	Females.
1	2	3	4	5	6	7	8	9	10	11	12	13	14	15	16	17
Cotton-ginning factories :—																
	Total ...	**2**	**63**	...	...	..	**25**	...	...	...	**14**	...	**24**	...	...	...
Mills in which mechanical power is used.	From 20—50 persons	(*a*) 2	63	...	...	...	25	...	...	...	14	...	24	...	...	...
Sugar factory :—																
	Total ...	**1**	**62**	...	...	...	**4**	...	...	...	**18**	...	**40**	...	...	...
Factories in which mechanical power is used.	From 50—100 persons	(*a*) 1	62	...	...	...	4	...	...	...	18	...	40	...	...	...
Carriage building establishments :—																
	Total ...	**3**	**63**	...	...	...	**3**	...	...	...	**27**	...	**32**	...	**1**	...
Factories in which mechanical power is not used.	From 20—50 persons	(*b*) 3	63	...	...	...	3	...	...	...	27	...	32	...	1	...
Printing Presses :—																
	Total ...	**2**	**77**	...	**1**	...	**6**	...	**1**	...	**50**	...	**19**	...	...	...
Presses in which mechanical power is not used.	From 20—50 persons	(*c*) 2	77	...	1	...	6	...	1	...	50	...	19	...	...	...

(*a*) Motive power steam. State of business at time of Census—Normal.

(*b*) State of business at time of Census—1 factory slacker than usual, 1 brisker than usual, 1 normal.

(*c*) State of business—normal.

TABLE XVI.

Occupations of Europeans, Anglo-Indians and Armenians.

In this table are shown actual workers only. In addition the following numbers of dependants were enumerated :—Europeans 992 ; Anglo Indians 61 ; Armenians 5.

TABLE XVI.

Occupations of Europeans, Anglo-Indians and Armenians.

Occupations of actual workers.	Europeans.		Anglo-Indians.		Armenians.	
	Males.	Females.	Males.	Females.	Males.	Females.
1	2	3	4	5	6	7
Provincial Total.	**4,643**	**92**	**36**	**3**	**9**	..
I.—Exploitation of the surface of the earth—						
Agents and managers of landed estates, etc.	1	...	...	...	...	...
II.—Extraction of minerals—						
Owners, managers, Clerks, etc. ...	5	1	1	...	...	...
III.—Industries—						
Owners, Managers, Clerks, etc. ...	6	...	...	...	...	...
Artisans and other workmen ...	1	...	1	...	...	...
IV.—Transport—						
Owners, Managers, etc.	37	...	12	...	...	...
V.—Trade	15	2	1	...	5	...
VI.—Public Force—						
Commissioned and Gazetted Officers ...	554	...	...	...	...	...
Others	3,869	...	1	...	...	...
VII.—Public Administration—						
Gazetted Officers ...	33	...	...	...	...	...
Others	16	...	6	...	1	...
VIII.—Arts and Professions—						
Religious ...	14	4	...	...	...	...
Lawyers, doctors and teachers ...	61	11	11	...	...	...
Others ...	18	10	1	...	...	...
IX.—Persons living on their income	7	17	2	1	...	...
X.—Domestic service ...	...	47	...	2	1	...
XI.—Contractors, etc., otherwise unspecified ...	2	...	...	...	2	...
XII.—Occupation not returned ...	4	...	...	...	...	...

TABLE XVII.

Christians by sect and race.

The table includes 5 persons who returned themselves in the column of religion as Agnositc. They have been shown under the heading "Indefinite Beliefs."

The 8 persons shown under the head Minor Protestant Denominations returned themselves as belonging to the American Mission.

212 persons (of whom 187 are native Christians), who returned themselves simply as Protestants, have been shown under the heading Anglican Communion, in view of the fact that the only Protestant Missionary establishments in the Province belong to that denomination.

TABLE XVII.

Territorial distribution of the Christian population by sect and race.

District, etc.	Total.			Distribution by race.						Total.			Distribution by race.					
				European and allied races.		*Anglo-Indians.*		*Native.*					*European and allied races.*		*Anglo-Indians.*		*Native.*	
	Persons.	Males.	Females.	Males.	Females.	Males.	Females.	Males.	Females.	Persons.	Males.	Females.	Males.	Females.	Males.	Females.	Males.	Females.
1	2	3	4	5	6	7	8	9	10	11	12	13	14	15	16	17	18	19
	All Denominations.									**Anglican Communion.**								
TOTAL N.-W. F. P. ...	**6,718**	**5,624**	**1,194**	**4,922**	**819**	**50**	**50**	**552**	**325**	**4,462**	**3,628**	**834**	**3,346**	**590**	**28**	**36**	**254**	**208**
Districts ...	**6,585**	**5,414**	**1,171**	**4,825**	**799**	**49**	**50**	**540**	**322**	**4,357**	**3,541**	**816**	**3,264**	**575**	**27**	**36**	**250**	**205**
Hazara	178	120	58	89	48	3	2	28	8	121	83	38	(a) 77	35	2	1	4	2
Peshawar	5,604	4,727	877	4,359	599	39	41	329	237	3,636	3,056	580	2,880	407	19	32	157	141
Kohat	222	148	74	111	61	4	4	33	9	170	112	58	92	53	3	1	17	4
Bannu	245	184	61	90	30	...	...	94	31	167	113	54	70	25	...	...	43	29
Dera Ismail Khan ...	336	235	101	176	61	3	3	56	37	263	177	86	145	55	3	2	29	29
Trans-frontier posts ...	**133**	**110**	**23**	**97**	**20**	**1**	...	**12**	**3**	**105**	**87**	**18**	**82**	**15**	**1**	...	**4**	**3**
	Methodist.									**Presbyterian.**								
TOTAL N.-W. F. P. ...	**243**	**220**	**23**	**212**	**17**	**2**	...	**6**	**6**	**193**	**135**	**58**	**130**	**50**	**4**	**4**	**1**	**4**
Districts ...	**243**	**220**	**23**	**212**	**17**	**2**	...	**6**	**6**	**182**	**128**	**54**	**123**	**46**	**4**	**4**	**1**	**4**
Hazara	...	...	...	...	...	...	...	...	...	8	3	5	3	4	...	1	...	...
Peshawar	241	218	23	210	17	2	...	6	6	145	105	40	101	36	4	3	...	1
Kohat	...	...	...	...	...	...	...	...	...	11	6	5	5	2	...	...	1	3
Bannu	...	...	...	...	...	...	...	...	...	4	4	...	4	...	...	...	...	...
Dera Ismail Khan ...	2	2	...	2	...	...	...	...	...	14	10	4	10	4	...	...	...	...
Trans-frontier posts ...	...	...	...	...	...	...	...	...	...	**11**	**7**	**4**	**7**	**4**	...	...	...	...
	Sect not returned.									**Baptist.**								
TOTAL N.-W. F. P. ...	**295**	**213**	**82**	**45**	**10**	**5**	**3**	**163**	**69**	**32**	**27**	**5**	**27**	**5**	...	...	...	...
Districts ...	**286**	**204**	**82**	**44**	**10**	**5**	**3**	**155**	**69**	**31**	**26**	**5**	**26**	**5**	...	...	...	...
Hazara	22	15	7	4	2	...	...	11	5	...	...	...	...	...	...	...	...	...
Peshawar	183	118	65	(b) 24	(c) 8	5	3	89	54	30	25	5	25	5	...	...	...	...
Kohat	10	8	2	5	...	...	...	3	2	...	...	...	...	...	...	...	...	...
Bannu	55	53	2	5	...	...	...	48	2	...	...	...	...	...	...	...	...	...
Dera Ismail Khan ...	16	10	6	6	...	...	...	4	6	1	1	...	1	...	...	...	...	...
Trans-frontier posts ...	**9**	**9**	...	**1**	...	...	...	**8**	...	**1**	**1**	...	**1**	...	...	...	...	...
	Syrian.									**Quaker.**								
TOTAL N.-W. F. P. ...	**1**	...	**1**	...	**1**	...	...	...	...	**2**	**1**	**1**	**1**	**1**	...	...	...	...
Districts ...	**1**	...	**1**	...	**1**	...	...	...	...	...	...	...	...	...	...	...	...	...
Hazara	...	...	...	...	...	...	...	...	...	...	...	...	...	...	...	...	...	...
Peshawar	1	...	1	...	1	...	...	...	...	...	...	...	...	...	...	...	...	...
Kohat	...	...	...	...	...	...	...	...	...	...	...	...	...	...	...	...	...	...
Bannu	...	...	...	...	...	...	...	...	...	...	...	...	...	...	...	...	...	...
Dera Ismail Khan ...	...	...	...	...	...	...	...	...	...	...	...	...	...	...	...	...	...	...
Trans-frontier posts ...	...	...	...	...	...	...	...	...	...	**2**	**1**	**1**	**1**	**1**	...	...	...	...

(a)—Includes 2 Armenians.
(b)— " 7 "
(c)— " 5 "

TABLE XVII.

Territorial distribution of the Christian population by sect and race.

Total.			Distribution by race.					
			European and allied races.		Anglo-Indians.		Native.	
Persons.	Males.	Females.	Males.	Females.	Males.	Females.	Males.	Females.
20	21	22	23	24	25	26	27	28
Roman Catholic.								
1,444	**1,277**	**167**	**1,148**	**132**	**11**	**7**	**118**	**28**
1,439	**1,272**	**167**	**1,143**	**132**	**11**	**7**	**118**	**28**
27	19	8	5	7	1	...	13	1
1,325	1,183	142	1,107	114	9	3	67	25
28	21	7	8	4	1	3	12	...
19	14	5	11	5	...	...	3	...
40	35	5	12	2	...	1	23	2
5	**5**	...	**5**	...	...	...	...	...
Lutheran.								
7	**3**	**4**	**3**	**4**	...	...	...	...
7	**3**	**4**	**3**	**4**	...	...	...	...
...	...	...	...	...	...	...	...	...
6	3	3	3	3	...	...	...	...
1	...	1	...	1	...	...	...	...
...	...	...	...	...	...	...	...	...
...	...	...	...	...	...	...	...	...
...	...	...	...	...	...	...	...	...
Indefinite Beliefs.								
5	**3**	**2**	**3**	**2**	...	...	...	...
5	**3**	**2**	**3**	**2**	...	...	...	...
...	...	...	...	...	...	...	...	...
5	3	2	3	2	...	...	...	...
...	...	...	...	...	...	...	...	...
...	...	...	...	...	...	...	...	...
...	...	...	...	...	...	...	...	...
...	...	...	...	...	...	...	...	...
....								
...	...	...	...	...	...	...	...	...
...	...	...	...	...	...	...	...	...
...	...	...	...	...	...	...	...	...
...	...	...	...	...	...	...	...	...
...	...	...	...	...	...	...	...	...
...	...	...	...	...	...	...	...	...
...	...	...	...	...	...	...	...	...
...	...	...	...	...	...	...	...	...

Total.			Distribution by race.					
			European and allied races.		Anglo-Indians.		Native.	
Persons.	Males.	Females.	Males.	Females.	Males.	Females.	Males.	Females.
29	30	31	32	33	34	35	36	37
Greek.								
14	**8**	**6**	**1**	**1**	...	...	**7**	**5**
14	**8**	**6**	**1**	**1**	...	...	**7**	**5**
...	...	...	...	...	...	...	...	...
12	7	5	...	...	...	...	7	5
2	1	1	1	1	...	...	...	...
...	...	...	...	...	...	...	...	...
...	...	...	...	...	...	...	...	...
...	...	...	...	...	...	...	...	...
Congregationalist.								
12	**6**	**6**	**6**	**6**	...	...	...	...
12	**6**	**6**	**6**	**6**	...	...	...	...
...	...	...	...	...	...	...	...	...
12	6	6	6	6	...	...	...	...
...	...	...	...	...	...	...	...	...
...	...	...	...	...	...	...	...	...
...	...	...	...	...	...	...	...	...
...	...	...	...	...	...	...	...	...
Minor Protestant Denominations.								
8	**3**	**5**	...	...	...	...	**3**	**5**
8	**3**	**5**	...	...	...	...	**3**	**5**
...	...	...	...	...	...	...	...	...
8	3	5	...	...	...	...	3	5
...	...	...	...	...	...	...	...	...
...	...	...	...	...	...	...	...	...
...	...	...	...	...	...	...	...	...
...	...	...	...	...	...	...	...	...
....								
...	...	...	...	...	...	...	...	...
...	...	...	...	...	...	...	...	...
...	...	...	...	...	...	...	...	...
...	...	...	...	...	...	...	...	...
...	...	...	...	...	...	...	...	...
...	...	...	...	...	...	...	...	...
...	...	...	...	...	...	...	...	...
...	...	...	...	...	...	...	...	...

TABLE XVIII.

Europeans, Armenians and Anglo-Indians by race and age.

14 Armenians are included in the figures for Europeans, other than British subjects (*vide* footnotes to table).

TABLE XVIII.

Europeans, Armenians and Anglo-Indians by race and age.

District, etc.	Total.			European and Allied — British subjects.																Oth[er]				
				All ages.			0—12		12—15		15—30		30—50		50 & over		All ages.			0—12	
	Total.	Males.	Females.	Total.	Males.	Females.	Males.	Females.	Males.	Females.	Males.	Females.	Males.	Females.	Males.	Females.	Total.	Males.	Females.	Males.	Females.
1	2	3	4	5	6	7	8	9	10	11	12	13	14	15	16	17	18	19	20	21	22
Total N.-W.F.P.	**5,841**	**4,972**	**869**	**5,698**	**4,898**	**800**	**258**	**220**	**5**	**9**	**3,575**	**249**	**1,020**	**282**	**40**	**31**	**43**	**24**	**19**	**2**	**2**
Total Districts	**5,723**	**4,874**	**849**	**5,581**	**4,801**	**780**	**253**	**224**	**5**	**9**	**3,531**	**243**	**978**	**274**	**34**	**30**	**43**	**24**	**19**	**2**	**2**
Hazara ...	142	92	50	133	85	48	6	8	...	1	38	16	40	18	1	5	4	4	..	1	...
Peshawar ...	5,038	4,398	640	4,924	4,340	584	210	182	5	8	3,323	180	778	197	24	17	34	19	15	1	(c)2
Kohat ...	180	115	65	170	110	60	10	14	..	...	40	22	57	21	3	3	2	1	1	...	...
Bannu ..	120	90	30	118	90	28	12	4	..	...	38	12	37	11	3	1	2	...	2	...	...
D. I. Khan ...	243	179	64	236	176	60	15	16	..	...	92	13	66	27	3	4	1	...	1	...	...
Trans-frontier Posts.	**118**	**98**	**20**	**117**	**97**	**20**	**5**	**5**	...	..	**44**	**6**	**42**	**8**	**6**	**1**	...	...	...	...	...

(a)—Includes 1 Armenian.

(b)—Armenian.

(c)—Includes 1 Armenian.

(d)—Includes 3 Armenians.

(e)—Includes 2 Armenians.

(f)—Includes 2 Armenians.

(g)—Includes 2 Armenians.

TABLE XVIII.

Europeans, Armenians and Anglo-Indians by race and age.

RACES.								ANGLO-INDIANS.												
ERS.																				
12—15		15—30		30—50		50 & over.		All ages.			0—12		12—15		15—30		30—50		50 & over.	
Males.	Females.	Males.	Females.	Males.	Females.	Males.	Females.	Total.	Males.	Females.	Males.	Females.	Males.	Females.	Males.	Females.	Males.	Females.	Males.	Females.
23	24	25	26	27	28	29	30	31	32	33	34	35	36	37	38	39	40	41	42	43
...	...	**7**	**10**	**7**	**4**	**8**	**3**	**100**	**50**	**50**	**12**	**12**	...	**5**	**19**	**16**	**18**	**14**	**1**	**3**
...	...	**7**	**10**	**7**	**4**	**8**	**3**	**99**	**49**	**50**	**12**	**12**	...	**5**	**18**	**16**	**18**	**14**	**1**	**3**
...	...	...	...	(a) 2	...	(b) 1	...	5	3	2	...	...	...	...	1	1	2	1	...	...
...	...	(d) 7	7	(e) 4	(f) 3	(g) 7	(h) 3	80	39	41	11	11	...	5	17	13	10	10	1	2
...	...	...	1	1	...	...	...	8	4	4	1	1	...	...	...	1	3	2	...	...
...	...	...	2	...	...	...	...	...	...	...	...	...	...	...	...	...	...	...	...	...
...	...	...	...	...	1	...	...	6	3	3	...	...	...	...	...	1	3	1	...	1
...	...	...	...	...	...	...	...	**1**	**1**	...	...	...	...	...	**1**	...	...	...	...	...

PROVINCIAL TABLE I.

Area and Population of Tehsils.

PROVINCIAL TABLE I.

Area and Population of Tehsils.

District	Tehsil	Area in square miles.	Number of Towns.	Number of Villages.	Number of occupied houses.
	1	2	3	4	5
HAZARA.	Mansehra	1,427	1	242	37,080
	Abbottabad	689	2	364	45,940
	Haripur	664	1	302	36,794
	Amb*	204	...	111	5,538
	Phulra*		...	137	1,496
PESHAWAR.	Peshawar	450	2	258	43,093
	Charsadda	379	3	167	28,916
	Mardan	609	1	130	32,297
	Swabi	465	...	97	32,592
	Nowshera	702	3	140	28,683
KOHAT.	Kohat	751	1	85	14,630
	Teri	1,528	...	162	18,688
	Hangu	416	...	43	8,826
BANNU.	Bannu	464	1	228	26,448
	Marwat	1,210	1	149	19,426
DERA ISMAIL KHAN.	Dera Ismail Khan	1,733	1	267	34,326
	Tank	638	1	77	9,261
	Kulachi	1,089	1	74	11,127

* Form the area known as Feudal Tanawal.

PROVINCIAL TABLE I.

Area and Population of Tehsils.

Population.				Percentage of variation.		Number of persons per square mile in 1911.
1911.			1901 both sexes.	1901 to 1911.	1891 to 1901.	
Persons.	Males.	Females.				
6	7	8	9	10	11	12
196,712	104,286	92,426	182,396	+7·8	+10·3	138
221,052	118,135	102,917	194,632	+13·6	+10·8	321
157,705	82,362	75,343	151,638	+4	+6·1	237
20,212	11,602	8,610	24,956	−19	−5·1	135
7,347	4,080	3,267	6,666	+10·2	+9·4	
261,642	146,030	115,612	248,060	+5·5	+8·9	581
159,105	86,366	72,739	142,756	+11·5		420
153,333	82,604	70,729	137,215	+11·7	+30·5	252
153,723	80,643	73,080	144,513	+6·4	+10·6	331
137,206	74,778	62,428	116,163	+18·1	+7·4	195
74,162	41,045	33,117	79,601	−6·8	+13·7	99
104,462	54,222	50,240	94,363	+10·7	+10·4	68
44,066	23,814	20,252	43,901	+·4	+10·6	106
142,311	77,603	64,708	130,469	+9·1	+8·4	307
107,775	56,104	51,671	96,332	+11·9	+14·5	89
153,396	83,752	69,644	144,337	+6·3	+7·9	89
47,500	25,697	21,803	48,467	−2·0	+10·8	74
55,224	28,979	26,245	55,069	+·3	+5·3	51

PROVINCIAL TABLE II.

Population of Tehsils by religion and education.

PROVINCIAL TABLE II.

Population of Tehsils by Religion and Education.

	Tehsil.	DISTRIBUTION BY					
		Mohammadans.		Hindus.		Sikhs.	
		Males.	Females.	Males.	Females.	Males.	Females.
	1	2	3	4	5	6	7
Hazara.	Mansehra ...	101,440	90,363	2,416	1,797	429	263
	Abbottabad ...	107,592	97,009	8,186	4,421	2,244	1,433
	Haripur ...	77,695	71,794	3,995	3,094	666	454
	Amb* ...	11,367	8,446	235	164	...	...
	Phulra* ...	4,030	3,236	50	31	...	...
Peshawar.	Peshawar ...	127,627	106,345	11,368	6,600	4,134	2,103
	Mardan ...	77,121	67,529	3,235	1,817	2,182	1,325
	Swabi ...	78,019	71,026	1,300	992	1,321	1,061
	Charsadda ...	84,118	71,364	1,392	800	853	573
	Nowshera ...	65,537	59,102	5,304	2,559	2,140	504
Kohat.	Kohat ...	35,531	30,695	4,045	1,907	1,356	442
	Teri ...	52,670	48,946	1,379	1,175	165	116
	Hangu ...	21,900	19,126	1,334	1,008	548	112
Bannu.	Bannu ...	67,594	58,033	7,832	5,586	1,994	1,029
	Marwat ...	51,919	47,828	3,816	3,487	368	355
Dera Ismail Khan.	Dera Ismail Khan ...	71,120	60,174	11,121	8,994	1,282	378
	Tank ...	23,719	20,139	1,855	1,595	118	66
	Kulachi ...	26,277	23,563	2,534	2,518	167	164

* Form the area known as Feudal Tanawal.

PROVINCIAL TABLE II.

Population of Tehsils by Religion and Education.

RELIGION.				NUMBER OF LITERATE PERSONS.					
CHRISTIANS.		OTHERS.		0—15		15—20		20 and over.	
Males.	Females.	Males.	Females.	Males.	Females.	Males.	Females.	Males.	Females.
8	9	10	11	12	13	14	15	16	17
1	3	...	...	375	51	367	60	2,273	161
113	54	...	...	390	86	651	47	4,558	189
6	1	...	...	360	47	414	43	2,458	159
...	...	...	...	11	13	4	6	91	11
...	...	...	...	4	9	3	5	41	5
2,860	554	41	10	1,204	508	1,383	304	10,608	1,448
65	58	1	...	639	103	930	48	3,209	422
2	1	1	...	183	36	154	40	1,472	139
3	2	...	...	150	20	193	16	1,601	76
1,797	262	...	1	347	70	669	66	5,761	389
108	65	5	8	302	35	334	44	3,689	143
8	3	...	...	108	3	97	2	868	18
32	6	...	...	45	1	119	2	1,096	11
183	60	...	...	454	50	652	28	5,099	170
1	1	...	...	237	15	224	12	1,528	33
229	98	...	...	968	198	973	109	6,086	412
5	3	...	...	132	19	169	16	1,199	23
1	...	...	...	264	12	236	20	1,607	49

INDEX
TO
PART I—REPORT.

A.

Abbottabad Cantonment, growth of since 1901, p. 23.
Abbottabad Cantonment, proportion of the sexes in, p. 25.
Abbottabad, municipal area, insane per 1,000 in, p. 343.
Abbottabad, rural area, insane per 1,000 in, p. 343.
Abbottabad Tahsil, density in, p. 11.
Abbottabad Tahsil, description of, p. 2.
Abbottabad Tahsil, growth of population in, p 58.
Abbottabad Tahsil, Hindus and Sikhs in, p. 108.
Abbottabad Town, situation of, p. 2.
Abbottabad Town, small trade importance of, p. 108.
Abdal, p. 369.
Abdul Qaiyum, Sahibzada, pp. 88, 164, 169.
Abdur Rahman, Amir of Kabul, p. 88.
Abortions, causing of, p. 197.
Abu Bakr, p. 123.
Abul Fazl, p. 144.
Accuracy of enumeration, increase of since 1855, p. 49.
Accuracy of statistics, age, p. 175.
Accuracy of statistics, caste, p. 369.
Accuracy of statistics, civil condition, p. 252.
Accuracy of statistics, education, p. 298.
Accuracy of statistics, infirmities, p. 341.
Accuracy of statistics, language, p. 311.
Accuracy of statistics, movement of population, p. 54.
Accuracy of statistics, occupation, p. 416.
Accuracy of statistics, sex, p. 206.
Accuracy of vital statistics, p. 64.
Acharaj, p. 143.
Actual population, proportion of sexes in, p. 192.
Actual population, proportion of sexes in, different religions, p. 193.
Actual population, variations in, since 1901, pp. 56, 62.
Actual and traditional occupation, p. 417.
Actual workers and dependants, distinction between, p. 423.
Actual workers, percentage of, p 424.
Actual workers, percentage of, in India, p. 424.
Actual workers, percentage of, in N.-W. F. P, p. 424.
Adam Khel, p. 368.
Adigranth, p. 146.
Administration, public, persons employed in, p. 436.
Administrative divisions of N.-W. F. P., p. 1
Adolescence, marriage during, p. 265.
Adults, marriage of, p. 259.
Advanced schools, number of scholars in, p. 307.
Afghanistan, graziers from, pp. 32, 60, 77, 90.
Afghanistan, immigration from, pp. 67, 70, 74, 75, 78, 79, 85, 87, 88, 89.
Afghanistan, immigration from, variations in, pp. 87, 91.
Afghanistan, trade from, p. 22.
Afghans, p 371.
Afridi, pp. 2, 43, 368.
Agarwal, p. 132.
Age, average, p. 188.
Age, completed and current year of, p. 180.
Age distribution of population, p. 182.
Age distribution of population by caste, p 187
Age distribution of population by religion, variation in, p. 186.
Age, instructions regarding record of, p. 179.
Age, literacy by, p. 283.
Age, mean, p. 188.
Age, mean, variations in, p. 189.
Age, mis-statement of, p. 204.
Age, mis-statement of young females, p. 177.
Age of literate immigrants, p. 305.
Age of literates, pp. 295, 305.
Age of males, exaggeration of, p. 178.
Age returns inaccuracy of, in males, p. 205.
Age, school going, p. 307.
Age statistics, true birth and death rates calculated from, p. 190.
Age, understatement of by middle aged, p. 176.
Age variations in, distribution of population by, p. 179.
Agha Abbas, p. 163.
Agha Khan, p. 129.
Agha Khani, p. 147.
Agriculture and pasture, persons dependent on, p. 432.
Agriculture as a subsidiary occupation, p. 428.
Agriculture, population supported by, p. 426.
Agriculturists, subsidiary occupations of, p. 429.
Ahata, as compared with 'house,' p. 35.
Ahl-i-Hadis, pp. 122, 127.
Ahl-i-Kitab, p. 156.
Ahl-i-Qoran, p. 129.
Ahmadiyas, p. 128.
Ahmad Shah, p. 41.
Ajmer Merwara, population of (1911), p. 7.
Akbar, p. 126.
Akka Khel, p. 368.
Alexander of Macedon, pp. 38, 39.
Ali, p. 123.
Alienation of Land Act, Punjab, pp. 96, 428.
Ali Khel, p. 368.
All ages, distribution of population by civil condition at, p. 273.
All ages, universality of marriage at, p. 254.
All ages, universality of marriage at, among females, p. 256
All ages, universality of marriage at, among males, pp. 255, 262.
Alms giving, p. 159.
Amarnathi, p. 143.
Amir Abdur Rahman, pp. 88, 91.
Amulets, faith in, p. 166.
Anand, p. 234.
Andha, p. 345.
Androor, p. 243.
Andror, pp. 241, 242.
Anglican Communion, p. 120.
Anglo-Indians, literates among, p. 288.
Annexation, state of Province at, p. 44.
Arab, p. 129.
Arabic, p. 316.
Arain, p. 379.
Arains, variations in numbers of since 1901, p. 395.
Area, average of, each village, p. 11.
Area, culturable, p. 10.
Area, culturable, density per square mile in, pp. 12, 61.
Area, irrigated, p. 10.
Area of N.-W. F. Province, pp. 1, 8.
Area trans-border, p. 2.
Area trans-border, boundaries of, p. 2.
Area trans-frontier, literacy in, p. 278.
Area, urban and rural, distinction between, p. 16.
Arms traffic, effects of, on immigration from Afghanistan, p. 90.
Arora, pp. 132, 140, 172, 231, 234, 268, 291, 292, 294, 367, 375, 385.
Aroras insane per 100,000 among, p. 354.
Aroras literacy among, p. 292.
Aroras, variations since 1901 in numbers of, p. 395.
Arts colleges, scholars in, p. 307.
Arya, p. 148.
Arya Samaj, pp. 136, 145, 148, 149, 268.
Ashram, p. 143.
Asoka, pp. 38, 39.
Audas, p. 157.
Auge, p. 241.
Aukhe, p 241.
Avartars, p. 138.
Average size of towns, p. 18.
Awan, pp. 4, 236, 292, 320, 334, 367, 369, 371, 375, 377, 391.
Awan, Abdal, p. 369.
Awan, Badan, p. 369.
Awan, Barsin, p. 369.
Awan, Chachhi, p. 369.
Awan, Dhanial, p. 369.
Awan, Gadha, p. 369.
Awan, Gilkar, p. 369.
Awan, Golra, p. 369.
Awan, Jasmal, p. 369.
Awan, Mangrial, p. 369.
Awan, Pakhral, p. 369.
Awan, Pothwari, p. 369.
Awan, Qutbshahi, p. 369.
Awan, Sarban, p. 369.
Awan, Sarwan, p. 369.
Awan, Shadwal, p. 369.
Awan, Zamindar, p. 369.
Awans, literacy among, p. 292.
Awans, variations in numbers of, since 1901, pp. 394, 399.
Azan, pp. 129, 158, 170.

B.

Baba, pp. 238, 244.
Baba Kalu, p. 146.
Baba Khem Singh, p. 146.
Baba Kirtar Singh, p. 146.
Baba Kirtar Singh Sanatni, p. 155.
Baba Lalajasrai, p. 141.
Baba Mula, p. 146.
Baba Nanak, pp. 105, 155.
Baba Narsingh, p. 138.
Babar on the Gorkhatri, p. 144.
Babar on the Peshawar district, p. 40.
Baccha, dud pita, p. 175.
Baccha, shirkhwar, p. 175.
Bactria, Greek princes of, pp. 38, 39.
Badan, p 369.
Baghban, pp. 292, 379.
Baghbans, variations in numbers of since 1881, p. 398.
Baghbans, variations in numbers of since 1901, p. 393.
Bahra Gunga, p. 344.
Bairagi, p. 140.
Bajra, p. 10.
Bakar Qasai, p. 391.
Balashahi, p. 151.
Balmiki, pp. 103, 151.
Balochi, pp. 325, 334.
Baluch, pp. 4, 280, 292, 325, 371, 375, 377.
Baluches, literacy among, p. 292.
Baluches, variations in numbers of since 1901, p. 395.
Baluches, variations in numbers of since 1881, p. 399.
Baluchistan, p. 1, 2.
Baluchistan, density in, p. 9.
Baluchistan, emigrants to, pp. 98, 99.
Baluchistan. population of (1911), p. 7.
Baluchistan, sex proportions in, p. 215.
Baluchistan, urban population of, p. 20.
Bangash, pp. 12, 125, 126, 225, 247, 368.
Bannuchis, pp. 223, 376.
Bannuchis, Sir Herbert Edwardes on the, pp. 42, 163.
Bannu, before annexation, p. 42.
Bannu, blindness in, pp. 358, 360.
Bannu Cantonment, proportion of the sexes in, p. 25.
Bannu, density in, p. 11.
Bannu, description of, p. 2.
Bannu, growth of population in, p. 61.
Bannu, houses in, p. 32.
Bannu, Lahnda speakers in, p. 335.
Bannu, literacy in, pp. 280, 295.
Bannu, literate per 1,000 in, pp. 281, 282, 295.
Bannu, literates in English in, p. 294.
Bannu, municipal area, insane per 100,000 in, p. 343.
Bannu, Pashto speakers in, p. 322.
Bannu, proportionate number of speakers of Punjabi plus Lahnda in, p. 329.
Bannu, religious distribution of population of, p. 107.
Bannu tahsil, density in, p. 11.
Bannu tahsil, growth of population in, p. 61.
Bannu, variations among Bhatias in, p. 398.
Bannu, villages in, p. 29.
Barak, p 319.
Barawafat, pp. 23, 94.
Bargista, p. 319.
Baroda, area of, compared with that of N.-W. F. P., p. 8.
Barsin, p. 369.
Basin, p. 234.
Bawajogi, p. 144.

Bawala, p. 342.
Bawanja, p. 234.
Bazaar, p. 25.
Bazid, p. 126.
Bedi, pp. 146, 155.
Begar, pp. 403, 404.
Behar, civil condition in, pp. 260, 261.
Bellew on the Powindahs, p. 76.
Bellew on the Yusafzais, pp. 40, 157, 159, 160, 162.
Bengal, civil condition in, p. 254.
Bengal, emigrants to, pp. 98, 99.
Bengal, sex proportions in, p. 215.
Bengali, pp. 132, 339.
Berar, civil condition in, p. 254.
Betrothal, binding nature of, p. 224.
Betrothal, ceremonies of, p. 223.
Betrothal, power to make contract of, p. 228.
Bhagat, pp. 142, 143.
Bhagatrani, p. 142.
Bhagavarta, p. 134.
Bhagti, pp. 135, 137.
Bhagwatgita, pp. 128, 129.
Bhagwati, p. 142.
Bhai, pp. 240, 244.
Bhai Dyal Dass, p. 146.
Bhangi, p. 151.
Bhanwiya, p. 241.
Bhasha, p. 336.
Bhat, pp. 132, 379.
Bhatacharaj, p. 143.
Bhatia, pp. 385, 386.
Bhatiara, pp 132, 292.
Bhatiaras, deaf-mutism among, p. 357.
Bhatiaras, variations in numbers of since 1901, p. 396.
Bhatias, pp. 172, 231, 385.
Bhatias in Bannu, variations in numbers of, p. 398.
Bhatti, pp. 368, 369.
Bhavani, p. 142.
Bhil, p. 327.
Bhisti, pp. 132, 374.
Bhogarmang valley, vital statistics not recorded in, p. 54.
Bhopali, p. 336.
Bhra, pp. 240, 243.
Bilochis, p. 376.
Birth and death rates, calculated from age statistics, p. 190.
Birth and death rates, compared with other provinces, p. 54.
Birth customs, Mohammadan, p. 246.
Birth-place, statistics for, in British districts only, p. 70.
Blind, number of, in 1911, p. 347.
Blindness, at different age periods, p. 345.
Blindness, accuracy of statistics of, p. 345.
Blindness, causes of, p. 345.
Blindness, decrease in, p 348
Blindness in Bannu, pp 358, 360.
Blindness, increase in, p. 345.
Blindness in D. I. Khan, pp. 358, 360.
Blindness in Hazara, p. 358.
Blindness in Kohat, p. 358.
Blindness in Peshawar, p. 358.
Blindness in trans-Indus districts, p. 358.
Blindness, variations in numbers for, pp. 347, 359.
Blockade, Mahsud, pp. 62, 65, 91, 113, 296.
Bodies, heavenly, veneration of, p. 133.
Bombay, area of, compared with that of N.-W. F. P., p. 8.
Bombay, immigrants to, pp. 98, 99.
Bomford, Rev., T., on Lahnda, p. 334.
Bonjai, pp. 233, 234.
Borahs, p. 339.
Boundaries of the N.-W. F. Province, p. 2.
Boyle, Mr., R. C., on birth customs, p. 246.
Boyle, Mr., R. C., on tribal Government in trans-frontier area, p. 389.
Brahman, pp. 132, 172, 231, 268, 291, 292, 294, 385.
Brahmans, insane per 100,000 among, p. 354.
Brahmans, literacy among, p. 292.
Brahmans of Hazara, widow re-marriage among, p. 268.
Brahmanpanthi, p. 150.
Brahmo, p. 150.
Brahmo Samaj, p. 150.
Brahm Samaj, p. 150.
Bride price, pp. 199, 222, 235, 261, 266.
British territory, density in, p. 9.
British territory, proportion of the sexes in, p. 192.
Budha, worshippers of, p. 133.
Buddhism, pp. 38, 39.
Budhwar, p. 133.
Burma, civil condition in, pp. 260, 261.
Burma, density in, p. 9.
Burma, Hindu females in, literates among, p. 291.
Burma, Musalmans in, literates among, p. 289.
Burma, sex proportions in, p. 215.
Byzantines, p. 38.

C.

Calcutta devi, p. 142.
Cantonments, growth of, p. 21.
Cantonments, population of, p. 21.
Caste, age distribution by, p. 187.
Caste and tribes, variations in, p. 392.
Caste classification, method of, p. 367.
Caste, education by, p. 292.
Caste, existence of, p. 370.
Caste, foreign, p. 386.
Caste government in occupational groups, p. 391.
Caste government, system of, p. 387.
Caste government, system of, among Hindus, p. 387.
Caste government, system of, among Mohammadans, p. 388.
Caste, Hindu, p. 385.
Caste, identity of occupation among members of, p 371.
Caste index, divided in two parts, p. 387.
Caste index, preparation of, p. 367.
Caste, indigenous, p. 385.
Caste organisation among Kumhars, p. 391.
Caste organisation among Qassabs, p. 391.
Caste organisation among Telis, p. 391.
Caste, Sikh, p. 385.
Caste statistics, accuracy of, p. 369.
Caste, trading, p. 402.
Caste, tribal groups of, p. 375.
Caste, tribal type of, p. 372.
Casual migration, p. 71.
Caucasus, sex proportions in, p. 191.
Census staff, superior, instructions to, regarding record of occupations, p. 415.
Central Asia trade, pp. 12, 22.
Central Provinces, civil condition in, p. 254.
Central Provinces, density in, p 9.
Central Provinces, Hindu females in, literate among, p. 291.
Central Provinces, literacy in, p. 279.
Central Provinces, sex proportions in, p. 191.
Chacha, p. 238
Chachhi, p. 369.
Chadarandazi, p. 268.
Chadda, p. 234.
Chah Narain. p. 138.
Chamar, pp. 132, 324, 379, 404, 412.
Chamar and Mochi, occupation of, p 416.
Chamars, variations in numbers of, p. 395.
Chamkani chief, p. 43.
Chanda, p. 234.
Chandiok, p. 234.
Chandragupta, p. 38.
Charas, p. 350.
Chargarhi Khatris, p. 234.
Charhoa, p. 407.
Charms and spells, p. 167.
Charsadda tahsil, density in, p. 11
Charsadda tahsil, growth of population in, p. 59
Chaudhris, p. 391.
Chauhan, p. 369.
Chauk, p. 29
Chaukat, p. 405.
Child-birth, seclusion of women after, p. 197, 247.
Child-marriage, pp. 235, 264, 385.
Children, inaccuracy of age returns for, p. 175.
Children, increase in, p. 183.
Chinese, p. 316.
Chishtis, p. 129.
Chitiari, pp. 309, 317, 326.
Chitral, description of, p. 2.
Chitrali, pp. 309, 317, 326.
Chitral, miscellaneous superstitions in, p. 171.
Chhokra, p 234
Christians, p 120.
Christians as Goanese servants, p, 288.
Christians, literacy in English among, p. 293.
Christians, education among, p. 288.
Christians, occupations of, p. 26.
Christians, proportion of, in urban areas, p. 26.
Chuhra, pp. 103, 132, 151, 292, 381.
Chuhra and Mehtar, p 151.
Chuhras, Hindu figures for, p. 103.
Chuhras, literacy among, p. 292.
Chuhras, none insane among, p 354.
Chuhras, their inclusion among Hindus, p. 103.
Chuhras, variations in numbers of, p. 397.
Chulha as compared with 'house,' pp. 33, 34, 35.
Circumcision, p. 250.
Circumcision among women, p. 250.
Civil condition, accuracy of returns of, p. 252.
Civil condition, distribution of population by, p. 273.
Civil condition, distributton of population by, at all ages, p. 273.
Civil condition, distribution of population by, for Hindus and Sikhs, p. 274.
Civil condition, symbol of, on slips, p. 252.
Classes, scavenger, p. 103.
Classes of occupation, p. 426.
Clerk, returns of, p. 417.
Classification of Pathan tribes, p. 368.
Classification scheme of occupations, pp. 410, 411.
Climate, influence of, on age of marriage, p. 264.
Close marriages, p 218.
Close marriages among Mohammadans, p. 234.
Colleges, arts, scholars in, p. 307.
Commensality, relaxation of rules of, among Hindus, pp. 231, 385.
Commerce, percentage of population supported by, p. 426.
Commerce, percentage of population supported by, in Bannu, p. 426.
Commerce, percentage of population supported by, in D. I. Khan, p. 426.
Commerce, percentage of population supported by, in Hazara, p. 426.
Commerce, percentage of population supported by, in Kohat, p. 426.
Commerce, percentage of population supported by, in Peshawar, p. 426.
Communication, means of, p. 52.
Concealment of females, p. 206.
Conditions, agricultural, p. 51.
Contractor, returns of, p. 417.
Coorg, population of, in 1911, p. 7.
Coorg, sex proportions in, p. 191.
Crosthwaite, Capt., on the Daman of D. I. Khan District, p. 13.
Cultivated area, density calculated on, pp. 12, 61.
Cultivated area, influence of, on density, p. 10.
Customs, at birth, p. 246.

D.

Dada, pp. 237, 242, 244.
Dadi, p. 242.
Dahlij, p. 35.
Dakhhani, p 336.
Dakhna, p. 234.
Daman, climate of, p. 13.
Daman, want of water in, p. 29.
Darani, p. 242.
Dargai, railway to, pp. 22, 52, 66.
Daryapanthi, p. 133.
Darzis, pp. 367, 374, 375, 378, 379.
Darzis, variations in numbers of, since 1901, p. 397.
Darzis, variations in numbers of, since 1881, p. 398.
Daughter, birth of, misfortune, p. 246.
Daur, p. 368.
Deaf-mutes in 1911, p. 347.
Deaf-mutism, p. 344.
Deaf-mutism among Bhatiaras, p. 357.
Deaf-mutism among children, p. 344.
Deaf-mutism among Kashmiris, p. 357.
Deaf-mutism among Swathis, p. 357.
Deaf mutism at successive age periods, p 344.
Deaf-mutism by caste, p. 357.
Deaf-mutism, concealment of, from record, p. 344.
Deaf-mutism, decrease in, p. 356.
Deaf-mutism in Hazara, p. 355.
Deaf-mutism in Trans-Indus districts, p. 355.
Deaf-mutism, variations in the prevalence of, p. 355.
Deaf-mutism, variations in, since 1881, p. 347.
Death and birth-rates, calculated from age statistics, p. 190.

Death and birth-rates in N.-W. F. P., compared with other provinces, p. 54.
Decade (1901—1911), conditions during, p. 50.
Decrease in females, causes of, pp. 194, 195.
Decrease in literacy, p. 308.
Definitions, difficulties of, p. 34.
Dehgani, pp. 309, 326.
Dehgans, p. 326.
De ingor mor plar, p. 242.
Deities, veneration of, p. 133.
De mera khor, p. 241.
Density and crops, p. 10.
Density and cultivated area, p. 10.
Density and education, p. 281.
Density and irrigation, pp. 10, 11.
Density and rainfall, pp. 10, 11.
Density per square mile in Abbottabad tahsil, p. 11.
Density per square mile in Baluchistan, p. 9.
Density per square mile in Bannu tahsil, p. 11.
Density per square mile in British territory, pp. 9, 281.
Density per square mile in Burma, p. 9.
Density per square mile in Central Provinces, p. 9.
Density per square mile in Charsadda tahsil, p. 11.
Density per square mile in N.-W. F. P., comparison with other provinces, p 9.
Density per square mile in D. I. Khan tahsil, p. 11.
Density, effects of, on health, p. 13.
Density per square mile in Feudal Tanawal, p. 11.
Density per square mile in Hangu tahsil, p. 11.
Density per square mile in Haripur tahsil, p. 11.
Density per square mile in Hazara tahsil, p 9.
Density per square mile in Hyderabad, p. 9
Density per square mile in Kohat tahsil, p. 11.
Density per square mile in Kulachi tahsil, p. 11
Density per square mile in Madras, p. 9.
Density per square mile in Mansehra tahsil, p. 11.
Density per square mile in Mardan tahsil, p. 11.
Density per square mile in Marwat tahsil, p. 11.
Density per square mile in N.-W. F. P., p. 9.
Density per square mile in Nowshera tahsil, p. 11.
Density per square mile in Peshawar tahsil, p. 11.
Density per square mile in the Punjab, p. 9.
Density per square mile in Rajputana, p. 9.
Density per square mile in Sindh, p. 9.
Density per square mile in Swabi tahsil, p. 11.
Density per square mile in Tank tahsil, p. 11.
Density per square mile in Teri tahsil, p. 11.
Density per square mile in trans-border area, p. 9.
Density per square mile in trans-Indus districts, p. 9.
Density per square mile in United Provinces in, p 9.
Density per square mile, variations in, p. 10.
Density per square mile, variations in, by tahsils, p. 11.
Deohri, p. 35.
Deor, pp. 241, 243.
Dependants and workers, distinction between, pp. 420, 423.
Dependants, entry of, p. 423.
Dependants, percentage of, p. 424.
Dependants, percentage of, in India, p. 424.
Dependants, percentage of, in N.-W. F. P., p. 424.
Der, p. 241.
Dera Ismail Khan, blindness in, pp. 358, 360.
Dera Ismail Khan City, as centre of trade, p. 23.
Dera Ismail Khan, culturable area in, p. 10.
Dera Ismail Khan, description of, p. 2.
Dera Ismail Khan, growth of population in, p. 62.
Dera Ismail Khan, houses in, p. 32.
Dera Ismail Khan, immigrants to, p. 79.
Dera Ismail Khan, Lahnda speakers in, p. 335.
Dera Ismail Khan, literacy in, pp. 280, 287, 295.
Dera Ismail Khan, literates in English in, p 294.
Dera Ismail Khan, literates per 1,000 in, pp. 281, 282, 295.
Dera Ismail Khan, municipal area, insane per 1,000 in, p. 343.
Dera Ismail Khan, Punjabi speakers in, p. 329
Dera Ismail Khan, Pashto speakers in, p. 322.
Dera Ismail Khan, rainfall in, p. 3.
Dera Ismail Khan, religious distribution of population of, p. 107.
Dera Ismail Khan, riverain, conditions of life in, p. 29.
Dera Ismail Khan, rural area, insane per 1,000 in, p. 343.
Dera Ismail Khan tahsil, density in, p. 9.
Dera Ismail Khan tahsil, growth of population in, p. 62.
Dera Ismail Khan, variations among Bhatias in, p. 398.
Dera Ismail Khan, villages in, p 29.
Dera Ismail Khan, variations of temperature in, p. 3.
Derajat, Powindahs of, p. 371.
Derawal, pp 312, 327.
Dev Acharaj, p. 143.
Dev Dharam, p. 150.
Devi, p. 142.
Devi ke mannewale, p. 142.
Devi ke pujari, p. 142.
Devi panthi, p. 142.
Devi parat, p. 142.
Devi pum, p. 142.
Devi Sanatan, p. 142.
Devna pujari, p. 142.
Dev Shastra, p. 150.
Dhaigar, pp. 233, 234.
Dhanial, p. 369.
Dharamsalas, p. 172.
Dharam Samaj, p. 150.
Dhoba, p. 407.
Dhobi, pp. 93, 132, 231, 292, 374, 375, 379, 386, 391.
Dhobis, literacy among, p. 292.
Dhobis, Mohammadan, p 93.
Dhobis, variations in numbers of, since 1901, p 396.
Dhobis, variations in numbers of, since 1881, p. 398.
Dhotra, p. 242.
Dhund, pp. 4, 292, 371, 377.
Dhunds, variations in numbers of, since 1901, p. 393.
Dhunds, variations in numbers of, since 1881, p. 399.
Diagnosis, accuracy of, p. 348.
Diagnosis of infirmities, errors in, p. 342.
Digar jogi, p. 144.
Dirrani, p. 242.
Disproportion of sexes, causes of, p. 201.
Distribution of population by age, p. 182.
Districts, literacy in, p. 280.
Districts, population of, p. 47.
Districts, trans-Indus, p 2.
Divisions, natural, boundaries of, p. 2.
Divisions, natural, distribution of population by occupation in, p. 427.
Divisions, natural, of Province, p. 2.
Divorce, grounds for, p. 224.
Diwan Daulat Rai, p. 109.
Dogra, p. 132.
Dogri, p. 330.
Domestic service, persons employed in, p. 437
Dud pita baccha, p. 175.
Dum, p. 229.
Dums, as intermediaries, p. 229.
Durand line, p. 1.
Durranis, pp. 40, 41.

E.

Ear piercing, p. 249.
Earthquake, causes of, p. 171.
Eastern Bengal and Assam, sex proportions in, p 191.
Education among Christians, p. 288.
Education among females by religion, p. 291.
Education among males by religion, p 289.
Education by age, sex and locality, p. 275.
Education by caste, pp. 275, 292.
Education by religion, p. 289
Education by age, sex and locality, p. 275.
Education, facilities in, p. 282.
Education, progress of, since 1881, p. 275.
Edwardesabad, p. 23.
Edwardesabad, growth of population in, p. 61.
Edwardes, Sir, Herbert, on Bannuchis, pp. 42, 163.
Edwardes, Sir, Herbert, on Hindu marriages, p. 232.
Effects of health on density, p. 13.
Egypt, sex proportions in, p. 191.
Elementary schools, number of scholars in, p. 307.
Emigration from the N.-W. F. P., p. 97.
Emigration, variations in, p. 100.
Emigrants, areas to which they go, p. 98.
Emigrants from N.-W. F. P., p. 97.
Emigrants, occupations of, p. 99
Emigrants, proportion of the sexes among, p 99.
Employment of labouring classes, p. 53.
England and Wales, area of, compared with that of N.-W. F. P., p. 8.
England, civil condition in, pp. 254, 271.
England, sex proportions in, pp. 191, 215.
English language, p. 338.
English, literacy in, p. 293.
English, literacy in, among Hindus, p. 293.
English, literacy in, among Mohammadans, p. 293.
English, literacy in, among Sikhs, p. 293.
English literacy in Bannu, p. 294.
English literacy in Dera Ismail Khan, p. 294.
English literacy in Hazara, p 294.
English literacy in Kohat, p. 294.
English literacy in Peshawar, p. 294.
English speakers, pp. 316, 388.
Enumerated population, literacy among, p. 279.
Enumerated population, religious distribution of, p. 101.
Enumeration, accuracy of, p. 49.
Enumerators, instructions given to, as to record of subsidiary occupations, p. 420.
Enumerators, instructions given to, regarding record of occupations, pp 413, 414.
Epthalites, p. 38.
Errors as to the record of occupation, p. 417.
Errors in diagnosis regarding infirmities, p. 342.
Errors in tabulation of occupations, p. 418.
Estimated population, religious distribution of, 102.
European languages other than English, p. 338.
Europeans, literate among, pp. 285, 288.
Europeans, wrong record of means of subsistence of dependants by, p. 422.
Evil-eye, belief in, p. 165.
Evil-eye, specifics against, p. 166.
Evil spirits, belief in, p. 169.
Excess of males, possible causes of, p. 218.

F.

Facilities in education, p. 282.
Fa-Hien, p. 30.
Famine, prevalence of, p. 14.
Faqir, pp. 140, 170, 381.
Faqirs, variations in numbers of, since 1901, p. 397.
Faqirs, variations in numbers of, since 1881, p. 398.
Farsi, p. 324.
Fasting, duty of, in Ramzan, pp. 160, 390.
Farz, p. 157.
Female births, defective registration of, p. 216
Female births, omission of, pp 216, 219.
Females by religion, education among, p. 291.
Females, circumcision among, p. 250.
Females, defect of, at age period '10—15', p 203
Females, defect of, causes of, pp. 194, 195.
Females, defect of, influence of migration on, p. 209.
Females, deficiency of, pp. 191, 219.
Females, Hindu, literacy among, p. 303.
Female infanticide, p. 195.
Females, marriage of, aged '15 and over,' pp. 261, 263.
Females, Mohammadan, literacy among, p. 301.
Female occupation of, p. 430.
Females, omissions of, from record, pp. 199, 206.
Females per 1,000 males, in Baluchistan, p. 191.

Females per 1,000 males, in Bengal, pp. 191, 215.
Females per 1,000 males, in Burma, p. 191.
Females per 1,000 males, in Caucasus, p 191.
Females per 1,000 males, in Central Provinces and Berar, p. 191.
Females per 1,000 males, in Coorg, p. 191.
Females per 1,000 males, in Eastern Bengal and Assam, p. 191.
Females per 1,000 males, in Egypt, p. 191.
Females per 1,000 males, in Engand and Wales, pp. 191, 215.
Females per 1,000 males, in Germany, p. 191.
Females per 1,000 males, in India, pp. 191, 204, 215.
Females per 1,000 males, in Ireland, pp. 191, 215.
Females per 1,000 males, in Kashmir, p. 191.
Females per 1,000 males, in Madras, pp. 191, 215.
Females per 1,000 males, in N.-W. F. P., pp. 191, 204, 215.
Females per 1,000 males, in Punjab, pp. 191, 215.
Females per 1,000 males, in Servia, p. 191.
Females per 1,000 males, in Siberia, p. 191.
Females per 1,000 males, in Sindh, p. 191.
Females per 1,000 males, in United Provinces, pp. 191, 215.
Females per 1,000 males, variations in, p. 200.
Females, Sikh, increase in, p. 112.
Females, universality of marriage among, p 256.
Feudal Tanawal, p. 2.
Feudal Tanawal, inaccuracy of enumeration in, p. 58.
Feudal Tanawal, density in, p. 11.
Feudal Tanawal, vital statistics not recorded in, p. 54.
Field Kanungos, classification of, p. 412.
Figures of occupations, compared with 1901, p. 431.
Food grains, prices of, p. 53.
Force public, persons employed in, p. 436.
Foreign castes, p. 386.
Friday, estimation in which held, p. 168.

G.

Gada govind ke, p. 146.
Gadha, p. 369
Gait, Mr, on accuracy of age returns, p. 123.
Gait, Mr, on diagnosis of leprosy, p. 348.
Gait, Mr., on record of school boys as illiterate, p. 283.
Gait, Mr., 'on standard of literacy among, pp. 283, 286.
Gakkhar, pp. 292, 377.
Gakkhars, literacy among, p. 292.
Gakkhars, variations in the numbers of, since 1901, p. 393.
Gakkhars, variations in the numbers of, since 1881, p. 398.
Gazar, p. 408 (footnote).
German Empire, sex proportions in, pp. 191, 215.
Ghair 'ilaqa, p. 85.
Ghalchah, p 319.
Ghar, as compared with house, p. 35.
Ghara, p. 404.
Gharbasi, p. 140.
Ghazni, p. 76.
Ghee, p. 12.
Ghilzais, pp. 125, 371.
Ghorids, p. 40.
Ghulam Ahmad, Mirza, p. 129.
Gilkar, p. 369.
Gita, Bhagwat, pp. 128, 129.
Glechari, p. 165.
Goai, p. 339.
Goanese servants, Christians as, p. 288.
Golra, pp. 367, 369.
Gopal, p. 138.
Gorakhnath, p. 144.
Gorakh panthi, p. 144.
Gorkha, pp. 81, 85, 132, 211, 338.
Gorkhatri, p. 144.
Gorkhi, pp. 309, 338.
Gorawara, p. 234.
Gosain, p. 140.
Gosain khandwala, p. 140.
Gotra, p. 233.
Government, caste, system of, p. 387.
Government, caste, system of, among Hindus, p. 387.
Government, caste, system of, among Mohammadans, p. 388.
Granthi, p. 146.
Granth Sahib. p. 105.
Graziers, as immigrants, pp. 77, 90.
Grierson, Dr., pp. 134, 135, 310, 311, 333, 337.
Grierson, Dr., on classified scheme of languages, p. 310.
Groups, Mohammadan caste, p. 381.
Groups, occupational, p. 378.
Groups, occupational, Arain as, p. 378.
Groups, occupational, Baghban as, p. 378.
Groups, occupational, Bhatiara as, p. 378
Groups, occupational. Chamar as, p. 378.
Groups, occupational, Darzi as, p. 378.
Groups, occupational, Dhobi as, p 378.
Groups, occupational, Jhinwar as, p. 378.
Groups. occupational, Jolaha as, p. 378.
Groups, occupational, Kumhar as, p. 378.
Groups, occupational, Lohar as, p. 378.
Groups, occupational, Machhi as, p. 378.
Groups, occupational, Maliar as, p. 378.
Groups, occupational, Mallah as, p. 378.
Groups, occupational, Mochi as, p. 378.
Groups, occupational, Nai as, p. 378.
Groups, occupational, Qassab as, p. 378.
Groups, occupational, Rangrez as, p. 378.
Groups, occupational, Sonar as, p. 378.
Groups, occupational, Tarkhan as, p. 378.
Groups, occupational. Teli as, p. 378.
Groups, occupational, caste, government in, p. 391.
Groups, occupational, how preserved, p. 384.
Groups, tribal and occupational, distinction between, p. 380.
Groups, tribal no authority among, in British territory, p. 390.
Gujar, pp. 4, 222, 236, 292, 337, 375, 377, 391.
Gujari, pp. 313, 317, 318, 337.
Gujari, accuracy of return of, p. 313.
Gujars, variation in numbers of, since 1901, p. 395.
Gujars, variations in numbers of, since 1881, p. 399.
Gujerati, pp. 310, 327, 339.
Gumal, the, p. 76.
Gurkha battalions, p. 428.
Gurkhas, variations in numbers of since 1901, p. 395.
Gurkhas, variations in numbers of since 1881, p. 399.
Gurmukhi, p. 321.
Gurmukh Singhi, p. 155.
Guru Arjan, pp. 146, 155.
Guru Gobind Singhi, p 152.
Guru Gobind Singhi, distribution of, by districts, p. 153.
Guru Gosain, p. 140.
Guru Govindji, p. 146.
Guru Govind Singh, pp. 104, 111, 112, 131, 146, 152, 291.
Guru Jogi, p. 144.
Guru Kabir Singhi, p. 147.
Guru Nanak, pp. 146, 155.
Guru Saniasi, p. 143
Gwalior, area of, compared with that of N.-W. F. P., p. 8.
Gwaliori, p. 336.

H

Habbiasi, p. 146.
Hajjam, p. 132.
Hamsaya, pp 172, 290, 376, 400—402, 407, 408.
Hamsaya group, Arora as, p. 401.
Hamsaya group, Bhatia as, p. 401.
Hamsaya group, Bhatiara as, p. 401.
Hamsaya group, Chamar as, p. 401.
Hamsaya group, Dhobi as, p. 401.
Hamsaya group, Jolaha as, p. 401.
Hamsaya group, Khatri as, p. 401.
Hamsaya group, Kumhar as, p. 401.
Hamsaya group, Lohar as, 401.
Hamsaya group, Mirasi (with Dum) as, p. 401.
Hamsaya group, Musalli (with Kutana) as p. 401.
Hamsaya group, Nai as, p. 401.
Hamsaya group, Paracha as, p. 401.
Hamsaya group, Qassab as, p. 401.
Hamsaya group, Rangrez as, p. 401.
Hamsaya group, Sonar as, p. 401.
Hamsaya group, Tarkhan as, p. 401.
Hamsaya group, Teli as, p. 401.
Hanblis, p. 129.
Hangu tahsil, density in, p. 11.
Hangu tahsil, growth of population in, p. 60.
Hangu tahsil, immigration from, p. 60.
Hangu tahsil, troops in, pp. 11, 17.
Hanifis, p. 129.
Haripur tahsil, density in, 11.
Haripur tahsil, description of, p. 2.
Haripur tahsil, growth of population in, p 58.
Haripur town, p. 17.
Harnakas, p. 138.
Har sok de khpal kor badshah de, p. 391.
Hashtnagar, p. 14.
Hassan, p 123.
Hassan Khel, p. 368.
Hazara, blindness in, p. 358.
Hazara, causes of greater prevalence of deaf-mutism in, p. 355.
Hazara, climate of, pp. 3, 211.
Hazara, culturable area in, p. 10.
Hazara, deaf-mutism in, p. 355.
Hazara, density in, p 9.
Hazara, growth of population in, p. 58.
Hazara, Gujari mainly spoken in, p. 313.
Hazara, higher female birth-rate in, p. 211.
Hazara, houses in, p. 32.
Hazara, immigration to, p. 73.
Hazara, Lahnda speakers in, p. 335.
Hazara, leprosy in, pp. 361, 362, 364.
Hazara, literacy in, pp. 280, 295
Hazara, literates in English in, p. 294.
Hazara, literates per 1,000 in, pp. 281, 282, 295.
Hazara, Pashto speakers in, pp. 322, 323.
Hazara, Punjabi speakers in, p. 329.
Hazara, religious distribution of population of, p. 107.
Hazara, rainfall in, p. 3.
Hazara, sex proportions in, p. 211.
Hazara, village unit in, p. 28.
Hazara, Wahabis in. 127.
Hazaras, p. 371.
Hazarkhani, pp. 59, 68.
Health, effects of, on density, p. 13.
Health, public, in last decade, p. 50.
Heavenly bodies, veneration of, p. 133.
Hindi, pp. 311, 321, 336.
Hindi, Western, p. 310.
Hindki, pp. 312, 327, 331.
Hindki as a non-Pathan, p. 369.
Hindko, pp 309, 312, 318, 327.
Hindu castes, p. 385.
Hindu castes, commensality among, p. 385.
Hindu *cum* Sikh population decrease in, pp. 116, 117.
Hindu females, literacy among, p. 303.
Hindu males, figures for, p. 115.
Hindu males, literacy among, p. 302.
Hindu Mehtar, p. 151.
Hindu Singh, p. 146.
Hindu widows, proportion to total females, p. 268.
Hindus, age distribution among, p. 184.
Hindus and Sikhs by tahsils, p. 108.
Hindus and Sikhs definition of, p. 104.
Hindus and Sikhs distinction between, p. 104
Hindus and Sikhs occupations of, p. 289.
Hindus, caste government among, p. 387.
Hindus, dependence of, under Mohammadan rule, p. 232.
Hindus, distribution of, by civil condition, p. 274.
Hindus, doubtful entries of, p 103.
Hindus, education among, p. 289.
Hindus, immigrants among, p. 287.
Hindus, immigrants, marriage customs of, p. 230.
Hindu immigrants, proportion of the sexes among, p. 83.
Hindus, immigration among, p. 211.
Hindus, incentives to marriage among, pp. 255, 256, 262.
Hindus, intermarriage among, p. 233.
Hindus, intermarriage among, influenced by Mohammadan environments, p. 233.
Hindus, intermarriage among, restrictions on, p. 234.
Hindus in the North-West Frontier Province, p. 172.
Hindus, literacy in English among, p. 293.
Hindus, marriage customs among, pp. 230 231.

Hindus, proportion of. in urban areas, p. 26.
Hindus, native born, marriage customs of, p 230
Hindus, sects of, p. 132.
Hindustani, pp. 318, 336.
Hindustani, as a local name, p. 132.
Hindustani, increase in speakers of, since 1901, p. 336.
Hindus, variations in numbers of, by sex, pp. 114, 115.
Hiranaya kasipa, p. 138.
Hiuen Tsang, p. 39.
Holi, a Hindu festival, pp. 23, 94.
House, definition of, p 33.
House, description of, p. 32.
House, new, occupation of, p. 170.
House, number of persons per, p 37.
Households, average size of, p. 36
Households, average size of, in rural areas, p. 37.
Households, average size of, in urban areas, p. 37.
Households, variations in size of, p. 36.
Houses, as compared with 'makan', 'ahata' and 'ghar', p. 35.
Houses, occupied, p. 35.
Houses, variety in, p. 31.
Hujra, pp 29, 37, 246, 402, 404, 406.
Huns, pp 38, 39.
Huqqa, p 406.
Hussain, p. 123.
Hyderabad, density in, p. 9.

I

Ibbetson, Sir Denzil, on circumcision among women, p. 250.
Ibbetson, Sir Denzil, on concealment of females, p. 200.
Ibbetson, Sir Denzil, on growth of population, 1855—1881, p. 49.
Ibbetson, Sir Denzil, on Jats, p. 374.
Ibbetson, Sir Denzil, on the community of caste, 373.
Ibbetson, Sir Denzil, on the Province at annexation, pp 41, 42, 43.
Ibbetson, Sir Denzil, on tribal type of caste, p. 372.
Ibbetson, Sir Denzil, on urban and rural areas, p. 16.
Ibtidai nikah, p. 223.
Ijab qabul, pp. 223, 226
Illiterate and literate, difference between, pp. 284, 285, 298.
Imamia school, p. 123.
Immigrants from the districts of the Punjab, p. 330.
Immigrants from Punjabi-speaking districts, p. 332.
Immigrants, graziers as, p. 77.
Immigrants, literate, p. 305.
Immigrants, literate, age of, p. 305.
Immigrants, occupations of, pp. 75, 76, 77, 90,
Immigrants, sex proportions among, p. 72.
Immigrants, the Powindahs as, p. 76.
Immigrants, winter labourers as, p. 75.
Immigration, by religion, p. 83.
Immigration, decrease in, p. 93.
Immigration, directions of, p. 74.
Immigration from Afghanistan, pp. 78—91.
Immigration from Afghanistan, decline in, pp. 88, 89.
Immigration from Afghanistan, variations in, 87.
Immigration from Nepal, p. 81.
Immigration from other provinces and states, pp. 82, 92.
Immigration from the Punjab, pp. 92—94.
Immigration from trans-frontier area, pp. 80, 85, 86, 91.
Immigration from United Kingdom, p. 82.
Immigration from United Provinces, p. 95.
Immigration from the West, pp. 75—91, 92.
Immigration, increase in, pp. 65, 84.
Immigration within the Province, p. 96.
Immigration, (1901), effects of on literacy figures, p 297.
Index, vernacular, of occupations, p. 418.
India, civil condition in, pp. 254, 262, 263, 265, 271.
India, leprosy in, p. 361.
India, literate Hindus in, p. 289.
Indian non-Sanscritic branch, (languages) p. 326.
Indian Sanscritic branch, (languages), p. 327.
India, percentage of actual workers in, p. 424.
India, percentage of dependants in, p. 424
India, sex proportions in, pp. 191, 204, 215.
India, vernaculars of, not dealt with, p. 339
Individual districts, variations in population of, p. 56.
Indo-Aryan branch (languages), p. 326.
Indo-European family (languages), p 326.
Indror, p. 241.
Industrial, special schedule, p. 409.
Industry population supported by, p. 426.
Industry, variation in the figures for, p. 433.
Infanticide, female, p. 195.
Infant marriage, p. 196.
Infirm, difficulty of accurate diagnosis of, p. 341.
Infirm, distribution of, p. 340.
Infirmities, instructions re: record of, p. 341.
Infirmities, temptation to omit to return, p. 343.
Infirmities, variation in figures for, p. 34.
Infirmities, not found in trans-frontier area, p. 340.
Infirmities, variation in figures for, pp. 347, 348.
Ingor, p. 242.
Insane, none among, Chuhras, p. 354.
Insane, none among, Musallis, p. 354.
Insane, none among, Sararas, p. 354.
Insane per 1,000 among Aroras, p. 354.
Insane per 1,000 among Brahmans, p. 354.
Insane per 1,000 among Macchis, p. 354.
Insane per 1,000 among Mallahs, p. 354.
Insane per 1,000 among Moghals, p. 354.
Insane per 1,000 among Parachas, p. 354.
Insane per 1,000 among Qoreshis, p. 354.
Insane per 1,000 among Sonars, p. 354.
Insane per 1,000 in Abbottabad, p. 343.
Insane per 1,000 in Bannu, p. 343.
Insane per 1,000 in Dera Ismail Khan, p. 343.
Insane per 1,000 in Kohat, p. 343.
Insane per 1,000 in Peshawar, p. 343.
Insane, proportionate figures for, p 351.
Insane, proportion of the sexes among, p. 352.
Insane, variations in numbers of, pp. 94, 350
Insanity, p. 342.
Insanity by age, p. 353.
Insanity by caste, p. 354.
Insanity, increase in, p. 349.
Insanity, increase in, causes of, p. 350.
Institutions, number of, p. 307.
Institutions, private, p. 307.
Institutions, public, p. 307.
Instructions as to record of infirmities, p. 341.
Instructions as to the record of subsidiary occupation, to enumerators, p. 411.
Instructions as to the record of subsidiary occupation to superior Census staff, p. 421.
Instructions regarding record of literacy, interpretation of, pp. 298, 300.
Instructions regarding record of occupations, p. 411.
Instructions regarding record of occupations, to enumerators, pp. 413, 414.
Instructions regarding record of occupations, to superior Census staff, p. 415.
Insufficiently described occupations, p. 437.
Intermarriage among Hindus, pp. 233, 234.
Intermarriage among Mohammadans, pp. 225, 382—384.
Intermarriage among Pathans, p. 383.
Intermediaries, employment of, p. 229.
Ireland, sex proportions in, pp. 191, 215.
Irrigation and density, p. 10.
Irrigation, extension of, p. 51.
Irrigation in tahsils, p. 11.
Islam, the dominant religion, p. 101.
Ismail, p. 129.
Itwar, p. 133.
Itwar Upashak, p. 133.

J

Jafir-us-Sadiq, p. 129.
Jafri, p. 129.
Jagirdar, p. 414.
Jai Kishni, p. 138.
Jaini, p. 132.
Jains, number of, p. 101.
Jaiswara, pp. 231, 374.
Jamai, p. 242.
Jamrud, p. 22.
Janj, pp. 226, 227.
Janjua, pp. 132, 367, 369.
Jaswal, p. 369.
Jat, pp. 125, 132, 236, 280, 292, 369, 371, 375, 377, 386
Jatki, p. 333.
Jats, literacy among, p. 292.
Jats, Sikh, p 377.
Jats, variations among, since 1901, p. 395.
Jats, variations among, since 1881, p. 399.
Jehangir, p. 126.
Jeo Narainpanthi, p. 138.
Jeth, p. 243.
Jews, p. 101.
Jhanda Mela, p. 161.
Jhano, p. 234.
Jhinwar, pp. 292, 374, 379, 386.
Jhinwars, literacy among, p. 292.
Jhinwars, variations in numbers of, p. 397.
Jinda kaliana, p. 141.
Jins, belief in, pp. 169, 171.
Jirga, pp. 228, 388, 389, 390.
Jirga in trans-frontier area, p. 389.
Jog, p. 144.
Jogi, pp. 142, 144.
Jogi Gorakhnath, p. 144.
Jogi Gorakhnathi, p. 144.
Jogi Panthi, p. 144.
Jograni, p. 144.
Jolahas, pp. 375, 379, 404.
Jolahas, variations in numbers of, since 1901, p. 396.
Jolahas, variations in numbers of, since 1881, p. 398.
Jowar, p 10.
Jumaat, p. 158.

K

Kabir panthi, p. 147.
Kabul River Canal, pp. 59, 68.
Kais, p. 376.
Kafilas between Peshawar and Kabul, p. 75.
Kafir Shiah, p. 125.
Kafshdoz, p. 416.
Kaghan, vital statistics not recorded in, p. 54.
Kaka, pp. 238, 244.
Kaka Sahib, Ziarat of, p. 161.
Kalabagh-Bannu Railway, employment on, p. 53.
Kalidevi, p. 142.
Kalima, p. 123.
Kalka, p. 142.
Kalka mai, p. 142.
Kam'aqal, p. 342.
Kamin, pp. 379, 404.
Kana, p. 345.
Kandis, p. 29.
Kannaujia, p. 375.
Kapur, pp. 132, 234.
Karal, pp. 127, 292, 377.
Karals, variations in numbers of, pp. 393, 399
Karam Kand, p. 145.
Karbla, p. 143.
Karma, pp. 135, 137.
Karm Kand, p. 145,
Kasbi, pp. 379, 407.
Kashina, p. 241.
Kashkari, 326.
Kashmir, area of, compared with that of N.-W. F. P., p. 8.
Kashmir, emigrants to, pp. 98, 99.
Kashmir, immigration from, pp. 74, 82, 95.
Kashmir, lepers per 100,000 in, p. 361.
Kashmir, literacy in 1901, p. 277.
Kashmir, Musalman literates in, p. 289.
Kashmir, sex proportions in, p. 191.
Kashmiri, (caste), pp. 4, 292, 325.
Kashmiri, (language), pp. 310, 315, 316, 425, 334, 377.
Kashmiris, deaf-mutism among, p. 357.
Kashmiris, literacy among, p. 292.
Kashmiris, variations in numbers of, since 1901, p. 394.
Kashmiris, variations in numbers of, since 1881, p. 393.
Katawaz, p. 76.
Kes, p. 105.
Kesdhari Sikhs, pp. 105, 146, 152.
Khairat, p. 159.
Khakrob, p. 151.
Khalsa, pp. 104, 105, 110, 111, 112, 118, 146.

Khalsa Panthi, p. 146.
Khalsa Sikhs, pp. 110, 152.
Khalsa Sodhibans, p. 155.
Khande-ke-pahul, p. 111.
Khandeshi, p. 327.
Khan Khel, p 368.
Khanna, p. 234.
Khans, p. 35.
Khatris, pp. 140, 155, 172, 231, 234, 291, 292, 294, 375, 385.
Khatris, literacy among, p. 292.
Khatris, variations in numbers of, since 1901, p. 395.
Khatris, variations in numbers of, since 1881, p. 398.
Khattak, pp. 12, 109.
Khels, p. 368.
Khemdas, p. 140.
Khemdasi, p. 140.
Khina, p. 241.
Khoja, p. 381.
Khokhar, pp. 358, 377.
Khokhar, variations in numbers of, p. 397.
Khorasan, immigration from, p. 89.
Khoshai, p. 242.
Khukhrain, pp. 233, 234.
Khushalgarh-Thall Railway, employment on, pp. 21, 23, 52, 60, 66, 92, 113, 296, 300.
Khwaja Khizar, p. 133.
Khwakhe, p. 242.
Khwakhe Skhar, p. 242.
Khyber Agency, literates in, p. 296.
Khyber Pass, p. 2.
Kin, rights and obligations of, 245.
Kingdom, United, immigration from, p. 82.
Kirars, p. 140, 155.
Kirchaff, on age of marriage, p. 264.
Kirchaff, on sex proportions in India, p. 191.
Kirris, p. 32.
Kishar, p. 237.
Kohat, blindness in, p. 358.
Kohat Cantonment, population of, in 1901, pp. 21, 23.
Kohat, culturable area in, p. 10.
Kohat, description of, p. 2.
Kohat, growth of population in, p. 60.
Kohat, houses in, p. 32.
Kohati, p. 312.
Kohat, Lahnda speakers in, p. 335.
Kohat, literacy in, pp. 280, 287, 295, 297.
Kohat, literates in English in, p. 294.
Kohat, literates per 1,000 in, pp. 281, 282, 295, 297.
Kohat, Municipal area, insane per 1,000 in, p. 343.
Kohat, Punjabi speakers in, p. 329.
Kohat, Pashto speakers in, pp. 322, 323.
Kohat, religious distribution of population in, p. 107.
Kohat, rural area, insane per 1,000 in, p. 343.
Kohat, Shias of, p. 126.
Kohat tahsil, density in, p. 11.
Kohat tahsil, growth of population in, p. 60.
Kohat, typical village in, p. 29.
Kohistani, pp. 310, 317, 326.
Kohli, p. 234.
Konkani, p. 339.
Konsh Valley, vital statistics not recorded in, p. 54.
Kori, p. 374.
Kothi, p. 35.
Koza (Khoja), p. 160.
Krishn, p. 138.
Kuchis, pp. 88, 425.
Kuka, p. 146.
Kulachi tahsil, density in, p. 11.
Kulachi tahsil, growth of population in, p. 62.
Kulachi town p. 17.
Kulachi town, proportion of the sexes in, p. 25.
Kulal, p. 404.
Kumhar, pp. 379, 404.
Kumhars, caste organisation among, p. 391.
Kumhars, variation in numbers of, since 1901, p. 394.
Kumhars, variation in numbers of, since 1881, p. 398.
Kunar River, p. 326.
Kurram Agency, literacy in, p. 277.
Kurram Agency, religious distribution of, in 1901, p. 102.
Kushans, pp. 38, 39.
Kutana, pp. 151, 292, 371.

L

Labourers, winter, as immigrants, p. 75.
Labouring classes, employment of, p. 53.
Labour, unspecified, p. 417.
Laghmani, p. 326.
Lahnda, pp. 209, 310, 312, 315, 317, 331, 333—335.
Lahnda and Punjabi, distinction between, p. 335.
Lahnda, boundaries within which spoken, p. 333.
Lahnda speakers in Bannu, p. 335.
Lahnda speakers in D. I. Khan, p. 335.
Lahnda speakers in Hazara, p. 335.
Lahnda speakers in Kohat, p. 335.
Lahnda speakers in Peshawar, p. 335.
Lahnda, terms of relationship in, pp. 237, 244.
Lahnde-de-boli, p. 333.
Lala, pp 237, 244.
Lala Jasrai, p. 141.
Lalbegi, p. 151.
Lalji, pp. 140, 155.
Lalji-panthi, p. 140.
Lambagai, p. 326.
Language returns, difficulties in preparation of, p. 311.
Languages, classification of, by areas in which spoken, p. 314.
Languages, classification of, by linguistic survey families, p. 31.
Languages, distribution of people by, p. 314.
Languages, local distribution of, p. 317.
Lashkar, p. 389.
Lasniwai, p. 223.
Lasportakawal, p. 223.
Learners, omission of, p. 284.
Learners, record of, in 1881 and 1891, p. 306.
Lepers, errors of diagnosis in the case of, pp. 346, 363.
Lepers, proportion of the sexes among, p. 365.
Lepers, variations in figures for, p. 347.
Leprosy, pp 346, 361.
Leprosy, variation in figures for, since 1901, p. 363.
Leprosy, variation in figures for, since 1881, p. 347.
Leprosy, white, p. 363.
Leprosy, wilful concealment of, p. 346.
Lewanai, p. 350.
Lewar, pp. 241, 243.
Liberal arts and professions, persons dependent on, p. 437.
Literacy, among Aroras, p. 293.
Literacy, among Awans, p. 292.
Literacy, among Baluchs, p. 292.
Literacy, among Brahmans, p. 292.
Literacy, among Chuhras, p. 292.
Literacy, among Dhobis, p. 292.
Literacy, among Gakkhars, p. 292.
Literacy, among Hindu females, p. 303.
Literacy, among Hindu males, p. 302.
Literacy, among Jats, p. 292.
Literacy, among Jhinwars, p. 292.
Literacy, among Kashmiris, p. 292.
Literacy, among Khatris, p. 292.
Literacy, among Moghals, p. 292.
Literacy, among Mohammadan females, p. 301.
Literacy, among Mohammadan males, p. 300.
Literacy, among Mohammadans, p. 280.
Literacy, among Parachas, p. 292.
Literacy, among Pathans, p. 292.
Literacy, among Qoreshis, p. 292.
Literacy, among Rajputs, p. 292.
Literacy, among Saiads, p. 292.
Literacy, among Shekhs, p. 292.
Literacy, among Sikh males, p. 304.
Literacy, among Sonars, p. 292.
Literacy, among Swathis, p. 292.
Literacy at age periods '10—15,' '15—20,' p. 286.
Literacy by age, p. 283.
Literacy by caste, p 292.
Literacy by religion, pp. 288, 289.
Literacy by religion, among females, p. 291.
Literacy by religion, among males, p. 289.
Literacy, comparison of figures for, p. 295.
Literacy, decrease in, p. 308.
Literacy, effects on, of immigration, in 1901, p. 297.
Literacy figures compared with those of 1901, p. 295.
Literacy in Bannu, p. 280.
Literacy in Dera Ismail Khan, p. 280.
Literacy in districts of Province, p. 280.
Literacy in English, p. 293.
Literacy in Hazara, p. 280.
Literacy in Kohat, p. 280.
Literacy in N.-W. F. Province, p. 277
Literacy in Peshawar, p. 292.
Literacy, instructions regarding record of, p. 298.
Literacy, standard of, pp. 276, 283, 284, 285, 298.
Literate and illiterate, difference between, pp. 284, 285, 298.
Literate immigrants, age of, p. 305.
Literate per mille in Bannu, p. 281.
Literate per mille in Dera Ismail Khan, p. 281.
Literate per mille in Hazara, p. 281.
Literate per mille in Kohat, p. 281.
Literate per mille in Natural Divisions, p. 281.
Literate per mille in Peshawar, p. 281.
Literate per mille in Sikh males, p. 304.
Literate per mille, variations in, p. 304.
Literates, ages of, pp. 295, 305.
Literates among different religions, p. 285.
Literates in Bannu, p. 295
Literates in Dera Ismail Khan, p 295.
Literates in Hazara, p. 295.
Literates in Kohat, pp 295—297.
Literates in Kurram Agency, p. 295.
Literates in Khyber Agency, p. 295.
Literates in Malakand Agency, p. 295.
Literates in Peshawar, p. 295.
Literates in trans-frontier area, p. 295.
Literates in Wana Agency, p. 295.
Literates, mostly educated outside the Province, p. 287
Literates, proportion of, p. 285.
Literates, total, in 1901 and 1911, p. 295.
Literates, variations in, by religion, p. 299.
Lohar, pp. 379, 405.
Lohars, variations in numbers of, since 1901 p. 395.
Lorimer, Mr., on Customary Law in Peshawar, p. 233.
Lucky and unlucky days, belief in, p. 168.

M.

Macauliffe on Sikh religion, p. 105.
Macedonian Satrapy, p. 38.
Machhi, p. 379.
Machhis, insane per 100,000 among, p. 354.
Machhis, variations in numbers of, since 1901, p. 396.
Machhis, variations in numbers of, since 1881, p. 398.
Maclagan, on figures for Hindus, p. 103.
Maclagan, on the translation of the word 'house', p. 35.
Madda Khel, p. 379.
Madras, civil condition in, pp. 254, 260, 261.
Madras, density in, p. 9.
Madras, sex proportions in, pp. 191, 215.
Madrasi, p. 339.
Mahadev, p. 142.
Mahajan, p. 132
Mahajan Singh, p. 146.
Mahdi, p. 128.
Mahmud of Ghazni, pp. 26, 40.
Mahsud Blockade, pp 62, 65, 91, 92, 113, 296.
Main religions, proportion between, p. 26.
Makan, as compared with 'house', p. 55.
Malakand Agency, decrease of troops in, since, 1901, p 295.
Malakand Agency, literates in, p. 295.
Males, education among, by religion, p. 289.
Males Hindu, literacy among, p. 289.
Males 'over 20' marriage of, p. 260, 262.
Males, Sikh, literacy among, p. 304.
Males, Sikh, literate per mille among, p. 304
Males, universality of marriage among, p. 255.
Maliar, pp. 292, 379.
Maliars, variations in numbers of, since 1901, p. 397.
Maliars, variations in numbers of, since 1881, p. 398.
Mali-ka-parbat, p. 2.
Maliks, pp. 42, 129, 389.
Mallah, pp. 132, 379.
Mallahs, insane per 100,000 in, p. 354.
Mallahs, variations in numbers of, p. 369.

Mama, p. 238.
Mama-nasakka, p. 239.
Mama-zoe, p. 240.
Mandar, p. 172.
Mangal, p. 368.
Manjhi, p. 333.
Mansehra tahsil, density in, p. 11.
Mansehra tahsil, description of, p 2.
Mansehra tahsil, growth of population in, p. 58.
Mansehra tahsil, wrong record of Urdu in, p. 309
Manu, p 143.
Manufactures in N.-W. F. P., p 22.
Map showing density by tahsils, p. 11.
Map showing percentage of increase of population, p. 56.
Map showing variation of population by tahsils. p 57.
Marathi, p. 339
Mardan notified area, p. 20.
Mardan notified area, proportion of the sexes in, p. 25.
Mardan tahsil, density in, p. 11.
Mardan tahsil, growth of population in, p. 59.
Marriage, age of, pp. 235, 264.
Marriage, among females '20 over,' pp. 261, 263.
Marriage, among Pathans, p. 383.
Marriage by capture, pp. 199, 227.
Marriage ceremonies, Mohammandan, description of, p. 226.
Marriage, child, p. 264.
Marriage customs of Mohammadans influenced by Hinduism, p. 221.
Marriage customs of Hindus. pp. 230, 231.
Marriage customs of Hindu immigrants, p. 230.
Marriage customs of Hindus, native born, p. 230.
Marriage customs of Mohammadans, p. 222.
Marriage in different religions, p. 258.
Marriage, infant, p. 196, 385.
Marriage, infant, in natural divisions, p. 257.
Marriage, inter, among Hindus, p. 233.
Marriage of adults, p. 259.
Marriage of males 'over 20', p. 260.
Marriage, universality of, p. 254.
Marriage, universality of, among females, p. 256.
Marriage, universality of, among males, p. 255.
Marriage. universality of, at all age, 254.
Marwari, p. 339.
Marwat tahsil, density in. p. 11.
Marwat tahsil, growth of population in, p. 61.
Marwat tahsil, villages in, p. 29.
Masat, p. 240.
Mashar, p. 237.
Masi, p. 238.
Mata. p. 234.
Maulvi Mohammad Qasim, p. 127.
Maulvi Shekh Abdullah, p. 129.
Maya, pp. 134, 135, 137.
Mazdigar, p. 157.
Mazhabi p. 155.
Mazkham, p. 157.
Mazkhotan, p. 157.
Mazpakhin, p. 157.
Mazri, p. 12.
Mean age, p. 188.
Mean age, variation in, p. 189.
Mehra, p 234.
Mehtar, pp. 103, 151, 381.
Menial and professional groups, position of the, p. 400.
Mera-tror, p. 239.
Mercury, planet, worship of, p. 133
Meo, p. 132.
Merk, Mr. on early civilization of the Province, pp. 39, 40.
Messiah, p. 128.
Midwifery unskilful, p. 197.
Migration, casual, p. 71.
Migration, extent of, p. 73.
Migration, five types of, p. 71.
Migration, influence of, on deficiency in females. p. 209.
Migration, influence of, on statistics of literacy, pp. 285, 287, 305.
Migration, influence of, on statistics of religion, pp. 115, 119, 302.
Migration, inter-district, p. 96.
Migration, periodic, p. 71.
Migration, permanent, p. 71.
Migration, semi-permanent, p. 71.
Migration, temporary, p. 71.
Migration, variation in, p. 96.
Mirasi, p. 381.
Mirasis, variations in numbers of, p 395.
Mirza Ghulam Ahmad, p. 128.
Mirzais, p. 128.
Mishwanis, p. 377.
Mishwanis, variations in numbers of, pp. 394, 399.
Mochi, pp. 386, 412.
Mochi and Chamars, occupation of, p. 416.
Mochis, variations in numbers of, pp. 395, 398
Moghal, pp. 292, 377.
Moghals, insane per 100,000 among, p. 354
Moghals, literacy among, p 292.
Moghals, variations in numbers of, pp. 395, 399
Mohammadan Dhobi, p. 93.
Mohammadan population, increase in preponderance of, p. 119.
Mohammadan rule, dependence of Hindus under, p. 232.
Mohammadans, age distribution among, p. 184.
Mohammadans, as rulers, p. 109.
Mohammadan females, literacy among, p. 301.
Mohammadans, inter-marriage among, pp. 225. 282, 382, 384.
Mohammadans, literacy among, pp. 280, 289, 290. 300
Mohammadans, literacy in English among, p. 293.
Mohammadan males, literacy among, p. 300.
Mohammadans, proportion of, in urban areas, p. 26.
Mohammadans, system of caste Government among, p. 388.
Mohammadans, variations in numbers of, p. 110.
Mohammadan widows, proportion to total population, p. 268.
Mohammadi, p. 127.
Mohammad-ibn-Abdul Wahab, p. 127.
Mohammadzai, p. 368.
Moharram, p. 123.
Mohmand, pp. 25, 75, 228, 368.
Movement of population in individual districts, pp. 52, 56.
Muafidar. p. 414.
Muhial, pp. 132, 233.
Mukti, pp. 135, 137.
Mukhlawa, p. 235.
Mulapanthi, p. 146.
Mulazimat, p. 436.
Mulk-i-ghair, p. 85.
Mullagori, p. 368.
Mullas, p. 389.
Multani, p. 309.
Musa Nika, shrine of, p. 161.
Mussaks, p. 172.
Mussallis, pp. 292, 371, 381, 406.
Mussallis, none insane among, p. 354.
Mussalman sects, p. 121.

N.

Nadir Shah. p. 324.
Nagarpanthi, p. 138.
Nai, pp. 132, 229. 368, 379, 386, 407.
Nai, as intermediary, p. 229.
Nain, circumcision performed by. on women, p 250.
Naipali, pp. 309, 315, 338.
Nais, variations in numbers of, p. 395.
Namdharis, p. 146.
Name giving, p. 248.
Nana, p. 242.
Nanak, p. 140.
Nanak Nirankar, p. 146.
Nanak-panthis, pp. 104, 105, 131, 136, 140, 146, 152, 154.
Nanak Sanatani, p. 146.
Nanak Shahis, p. 155.
Nanbais, p. 435.
Nandrer, p. 241.
Nani, p 242.
Naqshbandis, p. 129.
Narain, p. 138.
Narain Panthi, p. 138.
Narsingh, p. 138.
Nasakka Baba, ziarat of, p. 161.
Nasakka-mama, p. 239.
Native Christians, sect of, p. 120.
Natural divisions, blindness in. pp. 358, 360.
Natural divisions, climatic conditions in, p 3.
Natural divisions, contrasted ethnologically, p. 4.
Natural divisions, density in, p. 9.
Natural divisions, distribution of population in, by occupations, p 427.
Natural divisions, literacy in, p. 281.
Natural divisions, marriage in, p. 257.
Natural divisions of the N -W. F. P., pp. 2, 3.
Natural divisions, population of, p 406.
Natural divisions, variations in population of, p. 63.
Natural population, growth of population in, since 1901, pp. 63, 64.
Natural population, proportion of the sexes in, pp 192, 213.
Natural population, proportion of the sexes in, in different religions, p. 193.
Natural population, variations in, pp. 63, 64.
Naukari, returned as occupation, p. 417.
Nawabs, Saddozai, p. 109.
Nawasai, p. 242.
Nazir, p. 242.
Nepal, immigration from, pp. 81, 85, 211.
Nia, p. 242.
Nika, p. 242.
Nikah, p. 226.
Nikah-pilar, p. 226.
Nikah-wror, p. 226.
Nirankari, p. 146.
Nirmla, p. 146.
Nooh, p. 242
North-West Frontier Province, administrative divisions of, p. 1.
North-West Frontier Province, archæological remains in, p. 39.
North-West Frontier Province, area of, pp. 1, 8.
North-West Frontier Province, areas included in, p. 1.
North-West Frontier Provnice, boundaries of, pp. 1, 8
North-West Frontier Province, civil condition in, pp. 254, 260, 261.
North-West Frontier Province, climate of, p. 264.
North-West Frontier Province, date of constitution of, p. 1.
North-West Frontier Province, education in, p. 277.
North-West Frontier Province, emigration from, p. 97.
North-West Frontier Province, existence of caste in, p. 370.
North-West Frontier Province, Hinduism in, p. 172.
North-West Frontier Province, history of, pp. 38, 41.
North-West Frontier Province, lepers per 100,000 in, p. 361.
North-West Frontier Province, main religions in, p. 101.
North-West Frontier Province, percentage of actual workers in, p. 424.
North-West Frontier Province, percentage of dependants in, p. 424
North-West Frontier Province, religious distribution of population in, p. 101.
North-West Frontier Province, separation of, from the Punjab. p. 119.
North-West Frontier Province, sex proportions in, pp. 191, 204, 215.
North-West Frontier Province, state of before Mohammadan rule, pp. 40, 41.
North-West Frontier Province under Sikh rule, p. 41.
Nowshera Cantonment, p. 17.
Nowshera Cantonment, proportion of the sexes in, p. 25.
Nowshera, notified area, p. 20.
Nowshera tahsil, density in, p. 11.
Nowshera tahsil, growth of population in, p. 59.
Nowshera tahsil, proportion of the sexes in, p. 25.
Nuhn, p. 242.

O

Occupational groups, pp. 378, 379.
Occupational groups, caste Government in, p. 391.

Occupational groups, existence of, p. 384.
Occupation, community of, p. 373.
Occupation, community of, not necessary, p. 371.
Occupation, distribution of population by, p. 426.
Occupations, effect on returns of, of Census season, p. 425.
Occupations, errors in record of, p. 417.
Occupations, figures for, compared with those of 1901, p. 431.
Occupations, instructions regarding record of, p. 411.
Occupations, instructions regarding record of, to enumerators, pp. 413, 414.
Occupation, instruction regarding record of, to superior Census staff, p. 415.
Occupations, insufficiently described, p. 437.
Occupations of females, p. 430.
Occupations of Mochi and Chamar, p. 416.
Occupations, principal, p. 419.
Occupations, scheme of classification of, pp. 410, 412.
Occupation statistics, accuracy of, p. 416.
Occupations, subsidiary, pp. 419, 420.
Occupations, subsidiary, instructions regarding record of, p. 420.
Occupations, three columns provided for in general schedule, p. 419.
Occupations, traditional and actual, confusion between, p. 417.
Occupations, vague terms returned for, p. 417.
Occupations, vernacular index of, p. 418.
Odki, p. 339.
Ogai, p. 241.
Ogina, p. 241.
Ogina mera, p. 242.
Oliver on the Powindahs, p. 76.
Orakzai, pp. 2, 126, 368.
Oriya, p. 339.
Ormuri, p. 319.
Other Pathans, p. 368.

P

Pagal, p. 342.
Pahari, pp. 327, 337.
Paharpur Canal, pp. 53, 62.
Pahul, pp. 146, 155.
Pak, p. 157.
Pakhral, p. 369.
Palit, p. 157.
Pamirs, p. 319.
Pamnarganga, p. 133.
Panchayat, pp. 385, 387, 390, 391.
Pandit Sanatan, p. 145.
Paracha, pp. 292, 381.
Parachas, insane per 100,000 among, p. 354.
Parachas, variations in numbers of, p. 393.
Parachas, literacy among, p. 292.
Parasram, p. 138.
Parasrami, p. 138.
Pardah, non-observance of, in rural areas, p. 256.
Parian, p. 169.
Parsi (language and race), p. 339.
Pashai, p. 309, 326.
Pashto, pp. 309, 310, 312, 317, 322.
Pashto and Lahnda, p. 236.
Pashto, increase in its speakers, p. 321.
Pashto speakers per 1,000 of population in Hazara, p. 323.
Pashto speakers per 1,000 of population in Kohat, p. 323.
Pashto speakers per 1,000 of population in Peshawar, in p. 323.
Pashto speakers, proportional numbers in, 1901 and 1911, p. 322.
Pashto, terms of relationship in, pp. 237, 244.
Pasture and agriculture, persons dependent on, p. 432.
Patanjli, p. 144.
Pathan, pp. 4, 292, 368, 371, 373, 375, 376.
Pathans and Pashto speakers, p. 320.
Pathans, education among, pp. 280, 290, 292.
Pathans, jeaously of women among, p. 199.
Pathans, literacy among, p. 292.
Pathans, pride of race among, p. 383.
Pathans, Sir Denzil Ibbetson on, p. 376.
Pathan tribes, classification of, p. 368.
Patwari, classification of, p. 412.
Peiwar Kotal Pass, pp. 2, 75.
Percentage of agricultural population in Dera Ismail Khan, p. 426.
Percentage of agricultural population in Hazara, p. 426.
Percentage of agricultural population in Peshawar, p. 426.
Periodic migration, p. 71.
Permanent migration, p. 71.
Persia, immigration from, p. 89.
Persian, pp. 315, 318, 324.
Persons, aged, increase of, p. 183.
Persons living on their income, p. 437.
Persons, number of, per house, p. 37.
Peshawar, blindness in, p. 358.
Peshawar City, movement of population in, p. 23.
Peshawar City, Persian speakers in, p. 324.
Peshawar, climate of, p. 3.
Peshawar, culturable area in, p. 10.
Peshawar, density in, p. 9.
Peshawar, description of, p. 2.
Peshawar, description of village in, p. 29.
Peshawar, exodus from, in March 1911, pp. 23, 94, 115, 302.
Peshawar, growth of population in, p. 59.
Peshawar, houses in, p. 32.
Peshawar, Lahnda speakers in, p. 335.
Peshawar, literacy in, pp. 280, 282, 295.
Peshawar, literate in English in, p. 294.
Peshawar, municipal area insane per 100,000 in, p. 343.
Peshawar, Pashto speakers in, pp. 322, 323.
Peshawar, proportionate number of speakers of Lahnda and Punjabi in, p. 329.
Peshawar, religious distribution of population in, p. 107.
Peshawar, rural area, insane per 100,000, in, p. 343.
Peshawar, Sikhs most numerous in, p. 108.
Peshawar, state of, before annexation, p. 43.
Peshawar tahsil, density in, p. 11.
Peshawar tahsil, growth of population in, p. 59.
Peshawar, variations of temperature in, p. 3.
Peshawari, p. 312.
Petrer, p. 240.
Phupher, p. 240.
Phuphi, p. 238.
Pilgrimages, p. 161.
Pir Baba, shrine of, p. 161.
Pirghal, p. 2.
Pirmir Agha Khan, p. 129.
Pir Ratan Nath, p. 144.
Pir Ratan, Nathi, p. 144.
Pir, Roshan, p. 126.
Pioneer regiments, employment of, in 1901, pp. 113, 297.
Population, actual, proportion of the sexes in, 1901, p. 192.
Population, actual, proportion of the sexes in, in different religions, p. 193.
Population by religion, variation in, p. 110.
Population, distribution of, p. 19.
Population, distribution of, by language, pp. 314, 316.
Population, distribution of, by occupation, p. 426.
Population, distribution of religion, pp. 107, 109.
Population, enumerated, literacy in, p. 279.
Population, estimated, religion of, p. 102.
Population, growth of, pp. 50, 56.
Population, growth of, in Bannu, p. 66.
Population, growth of, in Dera Ismail Khan, p. 67.
Population, growth of, in Hazara, p. 66.
Population, growth of, in Kohat, p. 67.
Population, growth of, in Peshawar, p. 68.
Population, movement of, pp. 38—68.
Population, movement of in towns, pp. 20—24.
Population, natural, proportion of the sexes in, pp. 192, 193.
Population, natural, variations in, p. 63.
Population of districts, growth of, pp. 66, 68.
Population of N.-W. F. P., comparison of, with figures for other Provinces, pp. 7, 9.
Population of towns, p. 19.
Population, Sikh, variations in, p. 63.
Population, supported by agriculture, p. 426.
Population, supported by commerce, p. 426.
Population, supported by industry, p. 426.
Population, urban, increase in, pp. 18, 20, 23.
Polyandry, p. 272.
Polygamy, pp. 255, 272.
Ponchi, p. 309.
Portuguese, p. 338.
Pothwari, p. 369.
Potra, p. 242.
Powindahs, pp. 25, 52, 75, 76, 77, 79, 86, 87, 202, 287, 371, 425.
Powindahs as immigrants, p. 76.
Powindahs as travelling traders, pp. 22, 425.
Prahlad, p. 138.
Prang, p. 17.
Prayer, importance of, pp. 157, 158.
Prediction of sex, p. 246.
Primary schools, numbers of pupils in, p. 307.
Principal occupation, p. 419.
Private institutions, number of scholars in, p. 307.
Professional and liberal arts, p. 437.
Professional and menial groups, position of the, p. 400.
Proportions living at different age periods, variation in, p. 179.
Proportion of the sexes among insane p. 352.
Proportion of the sexes among lepers, p. 365.
Proportion of the sexes among the blind, p. 345.
Proportion of the sexes at birth, p. 215.
Proportion of the sexes in N.-W. F. P., comparison with other provinces, p. 191.
Proportion of the sexes in actual population, p. 192.
Proportion of the sexes in British territory, p. 192.
Proportion of the sexes in natural population, p. 192.
Proportion of the sexes in urban areas, p. 25.
Proportion of the sexes, variations in, p. 200.
Prostitutes, record of civil condition of, p. 252.
Province (N.-W. F. P.) early references to, p. 39.
Province (N.-W. F. P.) early rulers of, p. 38.
Province (N.-W. F. P.) natural divisions of, pp. 2—5.
Province (N.-W. F. P.) tribes living in, p. 4.
Public administration, persons employed in, 436.
Public force, persons employed in, p. 436.
Public health, state of, during last decade, p. 50.
Public institutions, number of scholars in, p. 307.
Pujari Jogi, p. 144.
Punjab, Alienation of Land Act, pp. 96, 428.
Punjab, Canal Colonies, effect of, on immigration from the Punjab, p. 92.
Punjab civil condition, in, pp. 254, 260, 261.
Punjab, density in, p. 9.
Punjab, emigrants to, pp. 98, 99.
Punjab, literate Sikhs in, p. 289.
Punjab, Pre-emption Act, pp. 96, 428.
Punjab, sex proportions in, pp. 191, 215.
Punjabi and Lahnda, p. 315.
Punjabi and Lahnda, difference between, p. 335.
Punjabi and Urdu, p. 315.
Punjabi by whom spoken, p. 328.
Punjabi, proportional number of speakers of, in Bannu, p. 329.
Punjabi, proportional number of speakers of, in Dera Ismail Khan, p. 329.
Punjabi, proportional number of speakers of, in Hazara, p. 329.
Punjabi, proportional number of speakers of, in Kohat, p. 329.
Punjabi, proportional number of speakers of, in Peshawar, p. 329.
Punjabi, speakers of true, p. 330.
Punjabi speakers, variations in numbers of, pp. 331, 332.
Punjabi, true (proper), p. 330.
Punjabi, Western, pp. 309, 310—312, 315, 317, 327, 330, 331.
Punjabi, wrong record of, pp. 311, 312, 314, 317.
Puranic Vaishnu, p. 138.
Purbi, pp. 132, 339.
Purbia, pp. 93, 103.
Purbia Dhobis, p. 375.

Q

Qabul, p. 223.
Qadian, p. 128.

Qadianis, p. 128.
Qadiris, p. 129.
Qasai, p. 391.
Qasais, caste organisation among, p. 391.
Qassab, pp. 379, 407.
Qassabs, variations in numbers of, p. 393.
Qaum, pp. 378, 396.
Qazzilbash, p. 324.
Qoran khwanda, p. 301.
Qoresh, p. 324.
Qoreshi, pp. 294, 320, 377.
Qoreshis, insane per 100,000 among, p. 354.
Qoreshis, literacy among, p. 292.
Qoreshis, variations in numbers of, pp. 393, 399.
Qutbshahi, p. 369.

R

Rabbani, p. 129.
Race, pride of, among Pathans, p. 383.
Radhaswami, p. 139.
Rafizia, p. 125.
Railway effects of, on growth of population, pp. 52, 87.
Railways, extension of, since 1901, pp. 22, 52.
Railway, Kalabagh-Bannu, p. 53.
Railway, Khushalgarh-Thall, p. 11.
Rainfall, p. 10.
Rainfall and density, p. 10.
Rainfall in Dera Ismail Khan, p. 3.
Rainfall in Hazara, p 3.
Rainfall in Tahsils, p. 11.
Rainfall in trans-Indus districts, p. 3.
Raja Gopi Chand, p. 144.
Rajasthani, pp. 310, 327.
Rajput, pp. 292, 367, 369, 377, 386.
Rajputana, density in, p. 9.
Rajputana, Hindu females in, literates among, in, p. 291.
Rajputs, literacy among, p. 292.
Rajputs, variations in numbers of, p. 397.
Ram Chand, p. 138.
Ram Chandji, p. 138.
Ram Chandrji, p. 138.
Ramdaji, p. 138.
Ramzan, month of, p. 160.
Rangrez, pp. 125, 379, 407.
Rangrez, variation in numbers of, p 394.
Ratan Panthi, p. 144.
Ratan Nath, p. 144.
Ratan Nathi, p. 144.
Record of occupations, errors in, p. 417.
Record of occupations instructions regarding, p. 411.
Record of occupations instruction regarding to enumerators, pp. 413, 414.
Record of occupations, instructions regarding, to superior Census staff, p. 415.
Regiments, Pioneer, employment of, in 1901, pp. 113, 297.
Regular Census, scope of, p. 1.
Relationship, terms of, pp. 236, 244.
Religion, age distribution by, pp. 184, 185.
Religion, different, marriage in, p. 258.
Religion, distribution of population by, p. 109.
Religion, education by, p. 289.
Religion, immigration by, p. 83.
Religion, main, in N.-W. F. P., p. 101.
Religion of estimated population, p. 102.
Religion, popular, p. 156.
Religion, population by, p. 107.
Religion, population by, variations in, p. 110.
Remarriage of widows, pp. 266, 271.
Remarriage of widows, among Hindus, p. 268.
Remarriage of widows, among Mohammadans, p. 268
Remarriage of widows, among Sikhs, p. 269.
Risalpur Cantonment, creation of, pp. 20, 21.
Rivers, veneration of, p. 133.
Roman Catholic, p. 120.
Roza, p. 160.
Rulers, Mohammadan, p. 109.
Rulers, Sikh, p. 109.
Rural areas, population of the sexes in, p. 25.

S

Sabuktagin, p. 40.
Saddozai, Nawabs, p. 109.
Sadhu Bairagi, p. 140.
Safed Koh, p. 2.
Sahajdhari Sikhs, pp. 105, 146.
Saharwardis, p. 129.
Sahni, p. 234.
Saiad, pp. 4, 125, 225, 292, 320, 376, 377.
Saiads, literacy among, p. 292.
Saiads, variations in numbers of pp. 395, 399.
Sainr, p. 242.
Saises, p. 386.
Saivas, pp. 134, 140, 142.
Sakas, p. 38.
Sakhi Sarwar, p. 161.
Sakhi Sarwar, Mela at, p. 161.
Sala, p. 242.
Saligram, p. 139.
Sam Hindu, p. 145.
Sanatan Darya, p. 133.
Sanatan Dharam, p. 145.
Sanatan Nanak Panthi, p. 146.
Sandhu, p. 242.
Sankaras, p. 134.
Sanniasi, pp. 140, 142, 143.
Sanwal Shah, p. 155.
Sanwal Shah Potras, p. 155.
Sapal, p. 367.
Sararas, pp. 371, 377.
Sararas, insane among, p. 354.
Sararas, variations in numbers of, pp. 394, 399.
Sarban, p. 369.
Sarsut, p. 132.
Sarwan, p. 369.
Satyanand Pandit Agnihotri, p 150.
Saudagar as an occupation, p. 425.
Saudagri as an occupation, p. 425.
Scarcity, p. 14.
Scheme of classification of occupations, p. 410.
Scholars, numbers of, according to departmental returns, p. 307.
School boys, employment of, as enumerators, p. 300.
School going age, p. 307.
Schools, advanced, number of pupils in, p. 307.
Schools, elementary, number of pupils in, p. 307.
Schools, other, number of pupils in, p. 307.
Schools, primary, number of pupils in, p. 307.
Schools, secondary, number of pupils in, p. 307.
Season of Census, effect of, on returns of occupations, p. 425.
Sect, record of, p. 135.
Sects, Hindu, p. 132.
Sects, Musalman, p. 121.
Semi-permanent migration, p, 71.
Serais, pp. 35, 37.
Servia, sex proportions in, p. 191.
Service, domestic, persons employed in, p. 437.
Service, unspecified, p. 417.
Seth, p. 234.
Sethi, p. 234.
Sewak Baba Ratan Nath, p. 144.
Sewak Devi, p. 142.
Sewak Gopal, p. 138.
Sewak Gopi Chand, p. 144.
Sewak Gosain, p. 140.
Sewak Jogi, 144.
Sewak Jogiani, p. 144.
Sewak Lalji, p. 140.
Sewak Mahajan, p. 140.
Sewak Panthi, p. 140.
Sewak Pir Ratan Nath, p. 144.
Sewak Sanatan, p. 145.
Sewak Sanatan Dharam, p. 145.
Sexes, disproportion of, 201.
Sexes, proportion of, among insane, p. 352.
Sex proportions, pp. 25, 191.
Sex proportions, among Hindus and Sikhs, p. 208,
Sex proportions, among Mohammadans, p. pp. 202, 203, 205.
Sex proportions, at birth, pp. 215, 218.
Sex proportions, influence of migration on, p. 202.
Sex proportions, in natural divisions, p. 211.
Sex proportions, in natural divisions, variations in, pp. 211, 213, 214.
Sex proportions, in towns, p. 25.
Sex proportions, in villages, p 25.
Sex proportions, variations in, pp. 200, 219.
Shadwal, p. 369.
Shafis, p. 129.
Shamji, pp. 140, 155.
Shamji Panthi, p. 140.
Shamsis, pp. 129, 147.
Shams Tabrez, p. 129.
Shankar Acharaj, p. 143.
Sharajawab, p. 223.
Shariat, pp. 225, 272.
Sharmana, pp. 197, 228.
Shaivas and Vaishnavas, p. 136.
Shawal, p. 2.
Shekhs, pp. 294, 381.
Shekhs, literacy among, p. 292.
Shekhs, variation in, numbers of, p. 396.
Sheonarain, p. 142.
Sherani, p. 368.
Shias, pp. 121, 122.
Shias and Sunnis, pp. 123, 225.
Shias and Sunnis, difference between, p. 123.
Shias in Tirah and Kohat, p. 126.
Shias, percentage of, p. 124.
Shias, tribes of, p. 125.
Shias, variations in number of, p. 124.
Sherkhwar Baccha, p. 175.
Shivji, p 142.
Shiv Narain, p. 142.
Shiv Panthi, p. 142.
Shiv Ramdass, p. 142.
Shiv Ramji, p. 142.
Shop-keeper otherwise unspecified, p. 417.
Shri Dev Guru Bhagwan, p. 150.
Siberia, sex proportions in, p. 191.
Sikaram, p. 2.
Sikh, Bramchari, p. 145.
Sikh, not defined at present Census, p. 106.
Sikhs, pp. 41, 104, 146, 152.
Sikhs, age distribution among, p. 184.
Sikhs and Hindus, confusion between, p. 105.
Sikhs and Hindus, distinction between, p. 104.
Sikhs by sex, p. 111.
Sikhs by tahsils, p. 108.
Sikhs, castes of, p. 385.
Sikhs, distribution of, by civil condition, p. 274.
Sikhs, education among, pp. 289, 304.
Sikh females, increase in, p. 112.
Sikhs, first appearance of, pp. 40, 41.
Sikhs, immigration among, pp. 211, 287, 304.
Sikh Jats, p 377.
Sikhs, literacy in English among, p. 293.
Sikhs males, literate per mille, among, p. 304.
Sikhs, males population of, variations in, p. 113.
Sikhs, Nanak Panthis, pp. 105, 146.
Sikhs, proportion of, in urban areas, p. 26.
Sikhs, proportion of the sexes among, p. 83.
Sikhs, rule of, in the Province, p 43.
Sikh Sabha, p. 146.
Sikhs, variations in numbers of, pp. 110, 113.
Sikhs, variations in numbers of, by sex, p. 111.
Sikhs, widow remarriage among, p. 269.
Sindh, density in, p 9.
Sindhi, pp. 312, 327, 334, 339.
Sindh, sex proportions in, p. 191.
Singh, p. 152.
Singh Sabha, pp 105, 110, 152.
Singh Sabha, circulars issued by, p. 110.
Sirkari mulazimat, p. 436.
Size of town, p. 18.
Skhar, p. 242.
Snakes, worship of, p 133.
Social units in, N.-W. F. P. how preserved, p. 382.
Sodhbans, p. 155.
Sodhbans, Khalsa, p. 155.
Sodhi, p. 146.
Sodhi, Bans, p. 155.
Sohra, p. 242.
Soil classification, p. 10.
Some Shah, p. 155.
Sonar, pp. 231, 292, 379, 385, 408.
Sonars, insane among, p. 354.
Sonars, literacy among, p. 292.
Special Industrial Schedule, p. 409.

Spells and charms, p. 167.
Spingire, p. 178.
Spinsters, number of, p. 263.
Splenai, p. 170.
Sri Ram Chand, p. 138.
Statistics, age, accurancy of. p. 175.
Statistics, caste, accuracy of. p. 369.
Statistics, civil condition, accuracy of, p. 252.
Statistics, education accuracy of, p. 298.
Statistics, infirmities, accuracy of, p. 341.
Statistics, language, accuracy of, p. 311.
Statistics, movement of population, accuracy of, p. 54.
Statistics, occupation, accuracy of, p. 416.
Statistics, sex, accuracy of, p. 206.
Subsidiary occupations, pp. 419, 420.
Subsidiary occupations, agriculture as, p. 428.
Subsidiary occupations, instructions to enumerators regarding record of, p. 420.
Subsidiary occupations, instructions to superior Census staff regarding record of, p. 421.
Subsidiary occupations of agriculturists, p. 429.
Sufi, p. 129.
Sunday, worshipper, p. 133.
Sammat, p. 157.
Sunni, pp. 121, 122.
Sunni and Shia, difference between, p. 123.
Superstitions, p. 162.
Superstitions, dying out, p. 164.
Suraj Bunsi, p. 133.
Swabi tahsil, density in, p. 11.
Swabi tahsil, growth of population in, p. 59.
Swami, p. 148.
Swat, close marriages in, p. 225.
Swat, remarriage of Hindu widows in, p. 268.
Swat River Canal, p. 53.
Swathis, pp. 292, 375, 377.
Swathis, deaf-mutism among, p. 357.
Swathis, literacy among, p. 292.
Swathis, variations in numbers of, p. 394, 399
Sweeper sects, pp. 130, 151.
System of caste government, p. 387.
System of caste government among Hindus, p. 387.
System of caste government among Mohammadans, p. 388.

T.

Tabar, p. 233 (footnote).
Tabulation of occupations, errors during, p. 418.
Tahsildar, classification of, p. 413.
Tahsils, density in, p. 11.
Tahsils, figures for, pp. 57—62.
Tahsils, figures for, in Bannu, p. 61.
Tahsils, figures for, in D. I. Khan, p. 62.
Tahsils, figures for, in Hazara, p. 58
Tahsils, figures for, in Kohat, p. 60.
Tahsils, figures for, in Peshawar, p. 59.
Tahsils, Hindus and Sikhs by, p. 108.
Tahsils, irrigation in, p. 11.
Tahsils, rainfall in, p. 11.
Tahsils, variation in population of, p. 11.
Taiamum, p. 157.
Tajaks, p. 371.
Talib-ul-ilm, pp. 306, 389.
Tamil, pp. 316, 339.
Tanaoli, pp. 4, 292, 320, 371, 376, 377.
Tanaolis. variations in numbers of, pp. 395, 399.
Taneja, p. 234.
Tangi, p. 17.
Tank tahsil, density in, p. 11.
Tank tahsil, growth of population in, p. 62.
Taqdir ka muamla, pp. 225, 374.
Tara, p. 238.
Tarazoi, p. 240.
Tarburs, p. 240.
Tarkhan, pp. 379, 384, 405.
Tarkhans, variations in numbers of, p. 295.
Tat Khalsa, pp. 105, 152.
Tawiz, pp. 166, 167.
Tazias, p. 123.
Teghbandi, p. 167.
Teli, pp. 379, 408.
Telis, caste organisation among, pp. 391.
Telis, variation in numbers of, pp. 397, 398.
Temple, Golden, p. 155.
Temporary migration, p. 71.
Teri tahsil, density in, p. 11.
Teri tahsil, growth of population in, p. 60.
Terms of relationship, pp. 236—244.
Terms, vague, returned for occupations, p. 417.
Textiles, variations in the figures for, p. 433.
Thakur, p. 138.
Thakurji, p. 138.
Thakurpujari, p. 138.
Thakurs, p. 172.
Thall, p. 17.
Thorburn, Mr., on the Province before annexation, pp. 41, 42.
Tirah, pp. 2, 39. 389.
Tirah, description of, p. 2.
Tirah, Shias of, p. 126.
Tirah, Sikhs of, pp. 102, 277.
Tirah, tribal government in, p. 389.
Tirathnath, p. 144.
Tirich Mir, fairies in, p. 169.
Tirni, p. 90.
Tochi Agency, literacy in, p. 277.
Town, areas included in, p. 15.
Town, as trade centre, p. 22.
Town, average size of, p. 18.
Town, definition of, p. 15.
Town, description of, p. 16.
Towns, larger, slow growth of population in, p. 24.
Towns, places treated as, p. 17.
Towns, size of, p. 18.
Tra, p. 238.
Trade, facilities in, p. 52.
Trade, persons dependent on, p. 435.
Trades guild type of caste, p. 374.
Trading castes, p. 402.
Traditional and actual occupation, confusion between, pp. 417, 424.
Trah, p. 238.
Training schools, pupils in, p. 307.
Trans-frontier area, administration of, pp. 1, 4
Trans-frontier area, climate of, p. 3.
Trans frontier area, density in, p. 9.
Trans frontier area, description of, p. 2.
Trans-frontier area, infirm, not to be found in, p. 340.
Trans-frontier area, Jirgas in, p. 389.
Trans-frontier area, literacy in, p. 278.
Trans-frontier area, migration from, p. 80.
Trans-frontier area, migration to, p. 70.
Trans-frontier posts, literacy in, pp. 278, 296, 297.
Trans-Indus districts, blindness in, p. 358.
Trans-Indus districts, climate of, p. 3.
Trans-Indus districts, deaf-mutism in, p. 355.
Trans-Indus districts, density in, p. 9.
Trans-Indus districts, description of, p. 2.
Trans-Indus districts, immigration to, p. 73.
Trans-Indus districts, leprosy in, pp. 361, 364.
Trans-Indus districts, rainfall in, p. 3.
Trans-Indus districts, sex proportions in, p. 211.
Transport, persons employed in, p. 434.
Travancore, literate Hindus in, p. 289.
Travelling traders, p. 22.
Trazoi, p. 240.
Tre, p. 238.
Tribal groups, no authority exists among, in British territory, p. 390.
Tribes, Pathan, classification of, p. 368.
Tribes, Shia, p. 125.
Tribes, various, variations in, p. 392.
Tror, p. 238
Tror mera, p. 239.
Tror zoi, p. 240.
Turis, pp. 225, 368.
Turk, pp. 376, 377.
Turki, p. 316.
Turks, variations in numbers of, pp. 393, 399.

U.

Udasi, p. 146.
Udhodas, p. 147.
Umar, p. 123.
Umar Laban, p. 319.
Umeyid Caliphs, p. 123.
United Kingdom, immigration from, p. 82.
United Provinces, civil condition in, pp. 254, 260, 261.
United Provinces, density in, p. 9.
United Provinces, emigrants to, p. 98.
United Provinces, immigration from, p. 95.
United Provinces, literacy in. p. 279.
United Provinces, sex proportions in, p. 191, 213.
Units. social, how preserved, p. 382.
Universality of marriage, p. 254.
Universality of marriage, among females, p. 256
Universality of marriage, among males, p. 255.
Universality of marriage, at all ages, p. 254.
Unlucky days, belief in, p. 168.
Unproductive occupations, p. 437.
Unskilful midwifery, p. 197.
Upashak Devi, p. 142.
Urban and rural areas, distinction between, p. 16.
Urban areas, proportion of the sexes in, p. 25.
Urban population, percentage of, p, 19,
Urdu, pp. 313, 321, 336.
Urdu and Gujari, p. 317.
Urdu speakers, p. 336.
Urdu, wrong record of, p. 309.
Usman, p. 123
Usuary among Mohammadans, p. 389.
Utradhi, pp. 132, 234, 367.

V

Vaccination and small-pox, p. 359.
Vague terms, returned as occupation, p. 417.
Vaishnavas and Saivas, pp. 134, 140.
Vaishnavas and Saivas, Kohistani, p. 138.
Vakil, p. 226.
Variations among agricultural tribes, p. 399.
Variations among Arains, p. 395.
Variations among Aroras, p. 395.
Variations among Awans, p. 394.
Variations among Baghbans, pp. 393, 398.
Variations among Baluchs, p. 395.
Variations among Bhatias, pp. 393, 398.
Variatians among Bhatiaras, p. 396.
Variations among Brahmans, p. 398.
Variations among Chamars, p. 395.
Variations among Chuhras, p. 397.
Variations among Darzis, pp. 397, 398.
Variations among Dhobis, pp. 396, 398.
Variations among Dhunds, pp. 393, 398.
Variations among Faqirs, pp. 397, 398.
Variations among Gakhhars, pp. 393, 398.
Variations among Gujars, p. 395.
Variations among Gurkhas, p. 393.
Variations among Hindus, p. 114.
Variations among Jats, p. 395.
Variations among Jhinwars, p. 397.
Variations among Jolahas, pp. 396, 398.
Variations among Karals, p. 393.
Variations among Kashmiris, pp. 394, 398.
Variations among Khatris, p. 395.
Variations among Khokhars, p. 397.
Variations among Kumhars, pp. 394, 398.
Variations among Lohars, p. 395.
Variations among Machhis, p. 396.
Variations among Maliars, pp. 397, 398.
Variations among Mallahs, p. 396.
Variations among Mirasis, p. 395.
Variations among Mishwanis, p. 394.
Variations among Mochis, pp. 395, 398.
Variations among Moghals, p. 395.
Variations among Mohammadans, p. 110.
Variations among Nais, p. 395.
Variations among Parachas, p. 393.
Variations among Pathans, p. 395.
Variations among Qassabs, p. 393.
Variations among Qoreshis, p. 393.
Variations among Rajputs, p 397.
Variations among Rangrezs, p. 394.
Variations among Saiads, p. 395.
Variations among Sararas, p. 394.
Variations among Shekhs, p. 396.
Variations among Sikhs, p. 110.
Variations among Sonars, p. 398.
Variations among Swathis, p. 394.
Variations among Tanaolis, p. 395.
Variations among Tarkhans, p. 395.
Variations among Telis, pp. 397, 398.
Variations among Turks, pp. 393, 398.
Variations in age distribution of population, p. 179.

Variations in age, distribution of population by religion, p. 186.
Variations in castes and tribes, pp. 392, 398.
Variations in density, p. 10.
Variations in emigration, p. 100.
Variations in figures for blindness, pp. 347, 359.
Variations in figures for deaf-mutism, pp. 347, 355.
Variations in figures for insanity, pp. 347, 349.
Variations in figures for leprosy, pp. 347, 363.
Variations in figures for literacy, p. 306.
Variations in figures for industry, p 433.
Variations in figures for textiles, p. 433.
Variations in Hindus by sex, p. 114.
Variations in immigration, p. 84.
Variations in immigration from Afghanistan, p. 87.
Variations in literacy figures by religion, p. 299.
Variations in mean age, p. 189.
Variations of population by tahsils, p. 11.
Variations among Punjabi speakers, p. 331.
Variations in sex proportions, p. 200.
Vedak, p. 148.
Vedak Sanatan, p. 148.
Vedas, p. 148.
Ved Dharam, p. 148.
Vernaculars, extra-Provincial, persons speaking, p 315.
Vernaculars of India, not dealt with, p. 339.
Vikramaditya, King, p. 144.
Village, Census and residential, pp. 28, 30.
Village definition of, p. 27.
Village, description of, in different areas, p. 29.
Villages in N.-W. F. Province, p. 16.
Village, size of, p. 30.
Villages, variations in numbers of, since 1901, p, 27.
Vital statistics, accuracy of, pp. 54, 55, 213, 216.
Vital statistics and sex proportions, pp. 213, 216.
Vital statistics, how recorded, pp. 54, 216.
von Mayr, on sex proportions in India, p. 199.

W

Wahabis, pp. 127, 247.
Wahabis as identical to Ahli Hadis, p. 127.
Wana Agency, literacy in, p. 296.
Wandiar, p. 241.
Warro, p. 227.
Water, scarcity of, p. 113.
Waziris, p. 42.
Waziris, pp. 32, 61, 75, 360.
Waziristan, description of, p. 2.
Western Hindi, p. 310.
Western Punjabi, pp. 309, 312, 315, 317, 327, 331.
West, immigration from, p. 92.
White Huns, p. 38.
White leprosy, p. 363.
Widow remarriage, pp. 266, 271.
Widows, proportion to total females, p. 267.
Widows, proportion to total females, among Hindus, p. 268.
Widows, proportion to total females, among Mohammadans, p. 268.
Widows, proportion to total females, among Sikhs, p. 269.
Woksha, p. 241.
Women, circumcision, among, p. 250.
Woman, hard life of, p. 198.
Workers (actual) and dependants, distinction between, pp. 420, 423.
Wrandrar, p. 241,

Y

Ya ba dre shu ya pa hujre shu, p. 246.
Yaghistan, pp. 4, 11, 22, 75.
Yaghistan, graziers from, pp. 77, 90.
Yaghistan, immigration from, pp. 80, 85, 86, 89, 90, 91.
Yaghistan, immigration to, p. 12.
Yazid, p. 123.
Yer, pp. 242, 243.
Yogi, p. 144.
Yor, p. 242.
Yore, p. 242.
Yorkshire, area of, compared with that of, N.-W. F. Province, p. 8.
Youre, p. 242.
Yueh chi, p. 38.
Yusafzais. pp 126, 157, 379.
Yusafzais, description of, p. 157.

Z

Zais, p. 368.
Zakat, p. 159.
Zamindar, pp. 12, 369, 412, 417.
Zamindar, as occupation, pp. 417, 427.
Zamindari, as occupation, pp. 417, 427.
Zamindars, livelihood of, p. 12.
Zams, p. 13.
Zeem, p. 242.
Zermut, p. 76.
Ziarat, Haji Bahadur Sahib, p. 161.
Ziarat, Kaka Sahib, p. 161.
Ziarat, Mianji Sahib, p. 161.
Ziarat, Nasakka Baba, p. 161.
Ziarat, pilgrimages to, p 161.
Ziarat, Pir Baba, p. 161.
Ziarat, Pir Fateh Shah, p. 161.
Ziarat, Shekh Nikai Sahib, p. 161.
Zinda Pir, p. 133.
Zoroastrians, number of, p. 101.
Zum, p. 242.